The Irish Voice
in America

The Irish Voice in America

250 Years of Irish-American Fiction

SECOND EDITION

Charles Fanning

THE UNIVERSITY PRESS OF KENTUCKY

Publication of the first edition of this volume was made possible
in part by a gift from the Irish American Cultural Institute,
a nonprofit membership foundation with headquarters
in St. Paul, Minnesota, and a grant from
the National Endowment for the Humanities.

Copyright © 1990, 2000 by The University Press of Kentucky
Scholarly publisher for the Commonwealth,
serving Bellarmine College, Berea College, Centre
College of Kentucky, Eastern Kentucky University,
The Filson Club Historical Society, Georgetown College,
Kentucky Historical Society, Kentucky State University,
Morehead State University, Murray State University,
Northern Kentucky University, Transylvania University,
University of Kentucky, University of Louisville,
and Western Kentucky University.

Editorial and Sales Offices: The University Press of Kentucky
663 South Limestone Street, Lexington, Kentucky 40508-4008

04 03 02 01 00   1 2 3 4 5

Library of Congress Cataloging-in-Publication Data

Fanning, Charles.
    The Irish voice in America : 250 years of Irish-American fiction /
Charles Fanning. — 2nd ed.
        p.   cm.
    Includes bibliographical references (p.   ) and index.
    ISBN 0-8131-0970-1 (paper : alk. paper)
    1. American fiction—Irish-American authors—History and criticism.
2. Irish Americans—Intellectual life.   3. Irish Americans in literature.
4. Ireland—In literature.   I. Title.
PS153.I78F36   1999
813.009'89162—DC21   99-12648

TO FRAN,
STEPHEN, AND ELLEN

And here is love
like a tinsmith's scoop
sunk past its gleam
in the meal-bin.

—*Seamus Heaney, "Sunlight"*

Contents

Acknowledgments

Over the eleven years of my work on this book I have been blessed with personal and institutional encouragement of many kinds. For their generous support in the form of fellowships and grants, I thank the American Council of Learned Societies, the Rockefeller Foundation, the National Endowment for the Humanities, the American Irish Foundation, the Newberry Library, the American Antiquarian Society, the Cushwa Center for the Study of American Catholicism at Notre Dame, the American Philosophical Society, and the Professional Development Committee of the Bridgewater Chapter, Massachusetts State College Association. Special thanks are due to the Irish American Cultural Institute, based in St. Paul, Minnesota, for a subvention in direct aid of the publication of this volume. My thanks also to Cleo Paturis and Edgar M. Branch for their kind permission to quote from the published and unpublished writings of James T. Farrell.

Thomas N. Brown guided my beginning research in Irish-American studies, and his friendship and wise counsel over more than twenty years have shaped my work and I hope my life as well. I thank him for having read most of this manuscript and for once again helping me to discover what I was trying to say. It is with a sense of great loss that I recall the many kindnesses that I received from the late William V. Shannon. This most generous of men helped me especially to appreciate the work of his friend James T. Farrell.

I am grateful to Shaun O'Connell, whose helpful reading of early chapters heartened me at a crucial point in this project. And for their freely given assistance of many sorts during these years, my heartfelt thanks go to Andrew Greeley, Dan Hoffman, Emmet Larkin, and Larry McCaffrey. Others to whom I am much obliged for shared insights, encouragement, hospitality, and friendship are Jim Blake, Bob Butler, Dan Casey, Jay Dolan, Dennis Flynn, Joyce Flynn, Maureen Murphy, Phil O'Leary, Bob Rhodes, Jim Rogers, and Ellen Skerrett.

For their invaluable aid in finding the books for this study I am indebted to the excellent staff of the Maxwell Library at Bridgewater State College. My thanks also to my very able research assistant, Ruth McGlynn, and to Sally Stewart for having typed this long manuscript so accurately and with such equanimity.

My friends in and out of academe have kept me going in more ways than they know. Thanks especially to Charlie Angell, Dan Callahan, Steve Callahan, Maureen Connelly, Don Johnson, Mike Kryzanek, Bill Levin, and Lorin Maloney.

This book is a kind of family history of literary generations, and writing it has helped me to appreciate the support of my sister Patti, my brother Geoffrey, my late father Charles Frederick Fanning, and my mother, Frances Patricia Balduf Fanning, who first encouraged me to be a teacher. Finally, I have dedicated this work with much love to my wife Frances Purcell Fanning and our children Stephen Charles and Ellen Frances. Whatever its failings, this is a better book for having been written during the years of our children's early development, and it would not have been written at all without Fran's encouragement and understanding.

INTRODUCTION

The Two Cycles of
Irish-American Fiction

For over two hundred years American writers of Irish birth or background have been exploring what it means to be an immigrant or ethnic
in America. Their work has much more to do with America than with
Ireland, for it is the product not of a single culture but of a collision of
disparate cultures. The result has been a uniquely American literature,
one largely concerned with minority alienation and assimilation into a
primarily urban New World environment. Such concerns remain compelling and relevant in these years of intensified worldwide immigration.
As John Berger has said, "never before our time have so many people
been uprooted. Emigration, forced or chosen, across national frontiers or
from village to metropolis, is the quintessential experience of our time"
(55). Rooted in the eighteenth century, proliferating in the nineteenth,
and flourishing in the twentieth, Irish-American literature is one of the
oldest and largest bodies of ethnic writing produced by members and
descendants of a single American immigrant group. This book is a study
of Irish-American prose fiction, which has had an extended and complex
history, in keeping with the long experience of the Irish in America, their
facility with the English language, and their extraordinary native literary
tradition in the old country. In hundreds of stories and novels writers
have chronicled the experience and changing self-image of the American
Irish. These texts establish the existence and endurance of an Irish-American literary tradition. The purpose of this book is to plot a preliminary
geography of this previously uncharted territory.

There have been two separate cycles of Irish-American fiction, one in
the nineteenth century and one in the twentieth. The first cycle has been
largely unexplored until now and the second has received insufficient
critical attention. In the nineteenth century there were three distinct
literary generations: Irish immigrant writers who came before the catastrophe of the Great Hunger of the late 1840s; writers of the Famine
generation, who came between 1850 and 1875, the period of greatest
immigration and upheaval; and writers who described the emergence of
an Irish-American middle class during the last third of the century. Their
voices were in turn confidently satiric, cautiously didactic, and anxiously
ambivalent.

A useful way to introduce the three nineteenth-century generations
is to consider the intended audience for literature in each. The pre-Famine

Irish-American community contained a large number of educated profes-
sionals, and its writers produced fiction in which satire and parody dominate. The targets of this cluster of satiric writings included various kinds
of literary propaganda: political campaign biographies, anti-Catholic "convent revelations," anti-Irish character stereotyping, and the simplistic
moralizing plots of sentimental fiction. The authors of such works had
already in place an expansive sense of audience. They wrote for a well-
read general public, appreciative of sophisticated literary effects. If the
reader were Irish, it was assumed that he was sure enough of his identity
and position to be able to laugh at himself. If a member of the host
American culture, it was assumed that he could laugh at his own stereotyping and misconceptions of the Irish.

With the coming of the Great Hunger, all of this changed. Nothing
could be further from the playful sophistication of the pre-Famine satirists
than the grimly serious, didactic fiction produced by Irish Americans of
the Famine generation. There is so dramatic a reversal because the writers
who emerged after the Famine were not a second generation, not the
children of immigrants, but a new first generation. Most of these new
novelists were themselves immigrants who had come to the United States
as adults in the 1840s. One of the great weaknesses of their fiction was
the constriction of the assumed audience. As Famine immigrants themselves, these new writers wrote only for their own kind, the audience of
traumatized refugees with whom their own experiences allowed them to
identify. Perceiving that audience to be desperately in need of guidance,
the writers produced conservative, practical novels, unambiguously dedicated to helping troubled people survive in the New World. So it was that
in a matter of a few years the fictional norm flipped over: from satiric
critique of propaganda to propaganda itself, from parody of fictional
conventions that have been manipulated for extra-literary purposes to
humorless embrace of those same conventions—sentimental rhetoric,
stereotyped characters, simplistic conflicts, and moralizing themes.

Irish-American literary accomplishment proliferated toward the end
of the nineteenth century. As on the wider American literary scene after
1875, the new, third generation of Irish-American writers joined the enthusiastic debate between advocates of genteel romantic fiction and those
of the "new realism," and the result was a reoccurence of both earlier
conceptions of intended audience. The weaker writers, the genteel romancers, created a second wave of didactic propaganda fiction aimed
exclusively at the developing Irish middle class. In place of the Famine
generation's manuals for survival in America, the next generation aimed
to instruct the new bourgeoisie in the importance and practice of being
respectable. The stronger writers were sometime realists whose sense of
audience opened out once again to include the general reading public,
though with mitigating qualifications. Their fiction was flawed with lapses
into old habits of sentimentality and romantic plot resolution, and the

resulting ambivalence kept them from sustaining a consistently realistic literary perspective. Yet these writers made pioneering efforts to count the costs and assess the damages of the previous generation's experience. And they did so from an impressive range of settings, from New York to Chicago to San Francisco, from urban ghettoes to prairie farms.

There was to be no immediate fourth literary generation, however. A number of circumstances—historical, cultural, and political, including the politics of literature—combined to end the first cycle of Irish-American fiction just after the turn-of-the-century period of heightened literary activity. The hiatus between the two cycles lasted for thirty years and constituted a form of wholesale cultural amnesia. The second cycle began in 1932 with the publication of *Young Lonigan: A Boyhood in Chicago Streets* by James T. Farrell, who followed this watershed work with fifty years of fierce dedication to the writer's trade. Farrell abjured rhetorical excess and shattered familiar sentimental conventions of plot and character, while reinventing Irish-American fiction entirely from his own experience and insight. The problem of audience did not have to be solved over again, however, for Farrell wrote for the general American reading public right from the start. What defines the new cycle's turns is changing attitudes toward the conventions of realism that are consistent with the development of American literature in the twentieth century. Farrell's use of a plain style and critical realism to examine ordinary Irish-American experience was the clear model for the next generation, some dozen writers from all over the country—regional realists who wrote first novels of Irish ethnic life in the late 1930s and the 1940s. These were followed by a chorus of voices in a range of styles that make up Irish-American fiction since 1950.

Another goal of this book is to connect the two cycles of Irish-American fiction into a single tradition. The value of this endeavor lies in the continuity from one cycle to the other of subjects, themes, and styles, plot lines and character types. The twentieth-century fiction echoes the nineteenth in a number of ways: the dominant mother in her fortress house; the first son marching off to the priesthood; the convent-educated daughter playing the piano in the parlor; parochial schoolmates turning into leaders of the Young Men's Sodality or incorrigible criminals; lives affected by extremes of dissipation, abstinence, profligacy, and piety; lives organized around ideas of religion, family, nationhood for Ireland, hard work, homeownership, the rise to respectability; tableaus of ritual gathering at deathbeds and christenings, weddings and wakes; the gift of humor and invective in public speech joined to an inability to express love and compassion in private; a penchant stylistically for formal experimentation, linguistic exuberance, and satiric modes. In these matters and others, earlier voices—Charles Cannon, Mary Anne Sadlier, Finley Peter Dunne—clarify the concerns of later voices—Farrell, Edwin O'Connor, Elizabeth Cullinan, William Kennedy.

Irish-American poetry and drama have been excluded from consideration here because of the simplicity of the former and the complexity of the latter. Over the years many Irish Americans have published poems, and by the 1880s critic E.C. Stedman was referring to an "Irish-American School" of poets. This poetry has often been popular, and the legions of green-covered volumes of verse stretching back to the 1810s and 1820s have had their effect on Irish-American literary self-consciousness. And yet, there have been few memorable Irish-American poems, especially before very recent times. The problem has been an endemic blight of programmatic melancholy or bravado that emerged from the experience and perception of forced exile. The stock-in-trade of Irish-American poetry has been the immigrant's lament for a lost, idealized homeland and the patriot's plea for Irish freedom from British oppression. Such materials make good songs but bad verse that exhibits simplistic strains of nostalgia or righteous indignation.

The situation in drama has been different. Here there has been a similar static element, to be sure, in the character of the "stage Irishman" who walks the boards early and late, speaking a brogue-laden blarney, humorous, hot-tempered, boisterous, and often the worse for drink. But the Irish have given much more to American drama than a parade of repeating stereotypes. For example, Irish-American drama evolved after the Civil War into a vehicle capable of treating ethnic life with some realism, at the same time that the more stereotypical characterizations were moving into the minstrel shows and vaudeville. And then there is the towering figure of America's greatest dramatist Eugene O'Neill, among whose achievements was the breaking of the stage-Irish mold in plays such as *A Moon for the Misbegotten* and *Long Day's Journey into Night* which contain genuinely tragic renderings of Irish-American experience. All of this constitutes a rich history that demands its own telling.[1] Still and all, these two extreme, opposing portraits—the melancholy poetic figure of the suffering exile and the comic theatrical figure of the stage Irishman—have contributed to Irish-American imaginative self-regard from the earliest to the most recent migrations. The Irish-American tradition in fiction has from its inception referred to, drawn upon, and sometimes been crippled by both portraits. "Those masterful images because complete" (W.B. Yeats's phrase) have cast their monolithic shadows over all the fiction discussed in the following pages. They do not dominate the narrative, but they cannot be ignored.

There are two other sorts of literature excluded from this book as well. As the focus will be the fictional self-image of the American Irish, writers of Irish background who have chosen not to consider Irish ethnic themes—Flannery O'Connor, for example—will not appear. Also, the history of images of the Irish created by American writers not themselves of Irish background will not be treated in any detail. However, these will be mentioned from time to time when they contribute to the understanding of a period. And one final qualification. Because there has been so much Irish-American fiction, this book is both large and narrowly focused. It contains little in the way of comparison between Irish-American and other ethnic and minority literatures. Such juxtapositions are invariably illuminating, but there isn't room for them here. Further comparative study and synthesis of cross-cultural themes and variations is important work that needs to be done. The challenge of such work will be to incorporate the proliferating insights of recent literary study of individual ethnic groups.[2]

The design of the present book is a chronological narrative from the appearance of the first piece of Irish-American writing in 1752 to fiction published in 1998. In alternate chapters I describe the general climate of the various literary generations (chapters 1, 3, 5, 7, 9) and discuss one or two important and representative writers (chapters 2, 4, 6, 8). Chapter 10 combines these methods in a survey of fiction from 1950 to 1989 that also focuses on four individuals. I have written a new final chapter for this second edition. Chapter 11 explores the persistence and nature of Irish-American fiction in the 1990s.

ONE

Backgrounds and
a Habit of Satire

An Irish-American voice first sounds clearly in a broadside that appeared on the streets of New York in 1769: "The Irishmen's Petition, To the Honourable Commissioners of Excise, &c."

> The humble petition of Patrick O'Conner, Blany O'Bryan, and Carney Macguire, to be appointed Inspectors and Over-lookers for the port of ———
> And whereas we your aforesaid petitioners will both by night and by day, and all night, and all day, and we will come and go, and walk, and ride, and take, and bring, and send, and fetch, and carry, and see all, and more than all, and every thing, and nothing at all, such goods, and commodities as may be, and cannot be liable to pay duty; and whereas we your aforesaid petitioners will at all times and at every time, and no time and times, we will be present and be absent, and be backward and forward, and behind, and before, and no where, and everywhere, and here, and there, and no where at all; and whereas your aforesaid petitioners will come and inform, and give information and notice duly and truly to the matter, as we know, and do not know, and by the knowledge of every one and no one; and we will not rob or cheat the king any more than is now lawfully practised; and whereas we your petitioners are gentlemen, and value him, and we will fight for him, and run for him, and from him, to serve him or any of his acquaintances, as far, and much farther than lies in our power, dead or alive, as long as we live. Witness our several and separate hands, one and all three of us both together.

And the piece is signed with four names: "Patrick O'Conner, Blany O'Bryan, Carney Macguire, Lawrence Sweeney." This broadside is a rollicking parody of bureaucratic jargon which satirizes the toadying of Tory office-seekers. It also heads the American branch of a noble Irish tradition—the use of the English language for the purpose of linguistic subversion. Traceable to the early collision of English and Irish noted in Elizabethan travelers' accounts, the "Irish Bull" is a linguistic self-contradiction, often embedded in digressive, circumlocutory anecdote, and aimed at confusing the issue at hand. A bull constitutes an act of violence perpetrated against English, for in it the invader's language is used against itself, with the goal of destroying meaningful discourse: not to communicate, but to obscure.

The author of "The Irishmen's Petition" was Lawrence Sweeney, a popular figure in New York City journalism in the 1760s. Sweeney was known variously as "The Penny Post Boy," because he charged a penny for delivering mail, and as "Bloody Sweeney," for his habit of calling out gory headlines of the fighting during the French and Indian Wars. He also stirred up trouble by secretly distributing the seditious newspaper, the *Constitutional Courant*, during the Stamp Act agitation of 1765. A native of Ireland, he was married in New York's Trinity Church in 1756, and his obituary in the New York *Gazette* of April 16, 1770, states that he was "as well known in this City as any Man in it, and will be perhaps as much missed." The week following his death a broadside elegy appeared, asking:

> Is Sweeny dead? Enquired the sorrowing Throng,
> Who cry'd News, News, in Accents loud and strong.
> He who was wont to raise the gen'ral Smile,
> And for whole Days a World of Cares beguile,
> Is now no more.[1]

Three other Sweeney broadsides have survived, all of them in verse: a 1766 "Ode" against the Stamp Act, "Being actually dictated by LAWRENCE SWINNEY, Carrier of News, Enemy to Stamps, a Friend to the Constitution, and an Englishman every Inch," and New Year's greetings for 1767 and 1769. The first greeting contains analysis of the French national character:

> For breaking Faith, and eating Frogs,
> No Nation so renown'd as France;
> But that in which they most excel
> The rest of Europe, is in Dance.

In the second greeting, from "Mr. Lawrence Sweeny, Esq., Vehicle General of News, and Grand Spouter of Politics," Sweeney claims birth "in the dear Irish Nation," and complains of empty pockets and illness:

> But pity poor Sweeney's delicious Conditions,
> Doom'd to torture his Guts with the Drugs of Physicians;
> Unless from their Clutches my Carcase you save,
> I Shall ne'er be in Health 'till I rot in my Grave.
>   Sing, Balinamona ora, your best Usquabaugh then for me.

Would that more of Lawrence Sweeney's work had survived. Still, the clear satiric note of this first identifiable Irish-American voice sets the tone for the first Irish-American literary generation, which emerged in the early years of the nineteenth century.

In 1790, nearly one sixth of the three million citizens of the new United States were of Irish birth or descent. Easily the largest non-English ethnic group in America, the Irish had been arriving in numbers for a hundred years. In July 1690 at the Battle of the Boyne, the Protestant forces of

William of Orange defeated the Catholic forces of James II and decisively set the direction of Irish history for the next two hundred years. In 1703 the British Parliament passed "an Act to prevent the further growth of Popery" in Ireland—the first of the ferocious Penal Laws, aimed at the systematic destruction of religious, civil, and cultural life for Irish Catholics and the maintenance of the Protestant Ascendancy in Ireland. In 1717, when Scottish settlers in Ulster began to lose their leases as a result of poor harvests and rackrenting by landlords, the first wave of three thousand emigrants left for America, thus setting in motion the most significant pattern of Irish migration before the Great Famine of the 1840s. For the entire eighteenth century, Ulster Protestants, mostly of Scotch Presbyterian background, came to America at the rate of three thousand to five thousand each year. Emigration from all of Ireland's provinces intensified after the potato famine of 1740-41 in which two hundred thousand people died. Others fled the agrarian violence carried out by peasant secret societies (the "Whiteboys," "Oakboys," and "Hearts of Steel") in the 1760s and 1770s. In addition to those who paid their own way over, the immigrants included indentured servants, redemptioners (who came hoping to find "redeemers" to pay the balance of their fares), and convict transportees (perhaps as many as twenty thousand before the American Revolution).[2]

Given the number of potentially interested readers, and recent computations suggest that there were over four hundred thousand Irish Americans by 1790, it is not surprising that Irish materials appeared early and often in American publications. Most of the eighteenth-century books were reprinted from Irish or British sources, and significant literary engagement with the experience of being Irish in America came relatively late. But the early published indications of American interest in Ireland formed an impressive context on which the first original Irish-American writers were able to build.

The first books were histories of Ireland and collections of Irish folklore, mythology, and poetry. Two substantial, multi-volume histories had American editions immediately following their publication in Dublin and London. Both Thomas Leland's *History of Ireland* (1774) and Francis Plowden's *Historical Review of the State of Ireland* (1805-06) were strongly biassed in favor of the British connection, thus appealing to the large number of Irish Americans with Ulster Protestant roots. These were countered by the first examples of what soon became a familiar Irish-American genre—Irish history written from the nationalist, anti-British perspective by fugitive rebels. Begun by the Society of United Irishmen in Belfast, agitation through the decade of the 1790s culminated in the Rebellion of 1798, which was crushed after fierce fighting in Counties Antrim, Wexford, and Mayo. A number of dynamic Irish intellectuals then fled to America, where they produced their own versions of history. John Daly Burk, who came to Boston in 1796 after expulsion from Trinity College, Dublin, for republicanism and deism, published a *History of the Late War in Ireland* in 1799. (Burk also authored the famous play, *Bunker Hill, or The Death of General Warren*, of 1797.) Exiled United Irishmen William James MacNeven and Thomas Addis Emmet published in 1807 a detailed apologia for their cause, *Pieces of Irish History, Illustrative of the Condition of the Catholics of Ireland, or the Origin and Progress of the Political System of the United Irishmen; and of their Other Transactions with the Anglo-Irish Government*. Several other such revisionist histories appeared in the years before the Famine immigration, and many more after.[3] There were also many American editions of the speeches of the patriot-orators of that generation in Ireland, John Philpot Curran, Henry Grattan, and Robert Emmet.[4]

The rich intellectual legacy of the '98 Rebellion also included James Reynolds, the creator of America's first utopian communitarian tract, Thomas Branagan, the author of an epic poem condemning slavery, and Thomas O'Connor, the editor of the first Irish nationalist newspaper in the United States. Reynolds, said to be the brother-in-law of patriot Wolfe Tone, wrote *Equality: A Political Romance* (1802), which describes the Island of Lithconia, where a communal society shares property, labor, and the raising of children equally, and marriage and money have disappeared, as have priests, doctors, soldiers, and lawyers. The adventurous Branagan had observed the slave trade in Africa and the Caribbean before writing *Avenia; or, A Tragical Poem on the Oppression of the Human Species* (1805). Started in New York City in 1810, *The Shamrock, or Hibernian Chronicle* was edited for most of its sporadic fourteen-year life by United Irishman Thomas O'Connor, who had come to America in 1801. The paper published Irish news with a nationalist slant, immigrant arrival information, literary essays, and a "Poets' Corner."[5]

Significant amounts of Irish folklore and mythology found their way quite early into print in America. These tended to exemplify what has persisted as the most marketable manifestation of Ireland and the Irish in American publishing: picturesque swatches of local color and legendry—turf-fires and fairs and fairies. In this category is perhaps the earliest Irish-American document, an eight-page pamphlet that was published in Boston and Newport, Rhode Island, in 1752, *Old Ireland's Misery at an End; or, The English Empire in the Brazils Restored*. The piece is remarkable as an early American version of a familiar Irish imaginative genre—millenial prophecy of Ireland's deliverance from her sufferings. In it, a mermaid predicts that the appearance from the sea off Donegal of an enchanted island will usher in a lasting peace, "and old Ireland will be reliev'd from all Taxes and Duties; and all those People that have of late gone to America, will return and live in this famous and plentiful Country."

A factor in the development of American interest in Irish myths and folklore was the transfer to America of the enthusiasm in the British Isles for James Macpherson's spurious "translations" (in 1760-63) of the poems of the ancient Gaelic bard "Ossian." Nostalgic, sentimentalized, melancholy (and mostly fabricated) versions of Celtic myths about Oisin and Finn, Macpherson's poems rode the late-eighteenth-century wave of antiquarian interest and anticipated the coming deluge of romanticism. In the 1770s Thomas Jefferson praised the poems highly and John Trumbull used them as the model for his satire *M'Fingal* (1775), and from there to the turn of the century and beyond, *Ossian* was widely read, discussed, and imitated in America.[6]

All manner of antiquarian/picturesque "Celtic" flotsam and jetsam surfaced in late-eighteenth and early-nineteenth century American publications. Macpherson's *Ossian* had its first American edition in 1790. A prose version of a love sonnet, "translated from the original Irish as now spoken in that part of Ireland called the Deasey's country" appeared in the *Massachusetts Magazine* in December, 1789, and was followed by a version in couplets in the next issue. The same periodical also published in four parts "A Fragment of Irish History," the description of a voyage to Ireland from Iceland in the tenth century. Mostly reprints from British or Irish journals, Irish folk tales, legends, and bits of local color also appeared frequently in the magazines of the 1820s and 1830s. Three such accounts, rife with fairies and their "good-humoured" superstitious observers, were in the Boston *Atheneum* in 1824. Philadelphia's *The Ariel: A Literary Gazette* published "Ancient Irish Bridal Customs" in 1822, "A Real Irish Direction" (a parodic circumlocution) in 1828, and "A Humorous Anecdote of Peasant Life" in 1830. Fair day in the Irish county town was a popular subject, as in *Atkinson's Casket* in 1830, where a Waterford fair turns into a faction fight. Such materials also appeared in the American Catholic press. In Boston, the *Literary and Catholic Sentinel* and its successor, the *Pilot*, published a serial version of the legend of "Naisi and Deirdre" on the *Sentinel's* front page for three months in 1835, and a fourteenth-century Ulster folk tale, "O'Cahan of Dungiven" in 1836.[7]

The demand for Irish myth, folklore, and local color also justified the early publication of several books. Cosgrave's *A Genuine History of the Lives and Actions of the Most Notorious Irish Highwaymen, Tories, and Rapparies* appeared in Wilmington, Delaware in 1799, with the avowed aim of warning people from a life of crime, such as was being led by great numbers of Irishmen. Mary Leadbeater's *Cottage Dialogues Among the Irish Peasantry* had an American edition in 1811. These vignettes in dialogue form covered farming, house chores, stirabout, the wake, whiskey, and courtship, and the preface claimed that the book captured accurately "the lower Irish."

More substantial indicators of American interest in such materials were original collections, those appearing first in the United States. *Beauties of the Shamrock, Containing Biography, Eloquence, Essays, and Poetry*, was published in 1812 by William D. Conway of Philadelphia, who admits in his introduction that "complaints against unjust proceedings constitute the chief subject of the following pages," which should come as no surprise, as he is an Irish Catholic victim of "the robbers of my native country." Included are short biographies of the harper Carolan and Jonathan Swift, recent patriotic speeches by Grattan, William Sampson, and John Philpot Curran, and a passel of poems about Irish freedom and America as refuge and example for Irish nationalists. There is also a piece of mythology, "Nathos and Minona," in which the beautiful Muirne drowns in "Lake Neagh" and her lover Orrar is killed by Blanaid because he is blind to her advances.

A curious collection of early fiction based on Irish folklore is *Tales of the Emerald Isle; or, Legends of Ireland*, by "A Lady of Boston," published in 1828. Four of these stories have their origin in folk materials. "Tradition, or Saint Kevin's Bed" is the story of a girl who falls in love with the saint, follows him around, and, in a lovesick swoon, plummets to her death from a precipice. In "Carol More O'Daly, or the Constant Lover," set in County Roscommon in 1561, the hero fights off his legacy as the son of a brigand chief to marry the daughter of his father's mortal enemy. "Bran, the Bloodhound, or the Heir of de Burgo" details the adventures of the de Burgo family of Boyle Abbey on the Bay of Carlingford in the early years of the eighteenth century. In this "extremely grand and wildly romantic" spot, the widowed heiress to the de Burgo fortune raises her son, Edmond Montressor, after her husband's death at the Battle of the Boyne. This is a Gothic production, with the looming ruins of the Cistercian Abbey near which the de Burgo Castle stands, a surrounding "forest of dark evergreens," and a great bloodhound, Bran, who becomes young Edmond's protector. The fourth folk tale, "Humble Life, or the Sycamore Tree," describes the Alanson family of "a remote corner of the County of Galway," whose patiently suffered trials are relieved by a dream which sends Philip Alanson to Lough Corrib, where he finds that a fortune is buried under his own sycamore tree at home. Thereafter, the Alansons thrive, and an elegant street "in the town of Galway" is built by their descendants. In this story the Lady of Boston reveals an informed view of the abuses of the landlord system, because the Alansons are tenants at the mercy of an agent, "who like all the agents of Irish absentees, showed no more compassion to their tenantry than negro drivers on a plantation in the West Indies do to their slaves" (39).

The remaining stories are set closer to the present, but are more Gothic and tangled in their plots. In one, a hideous murder is perpetrated by Hugh Fitzgerald, a depraved Catholic. Though "some of the best and most amiable of the human race" are Catholics, the author declares, it is because Hugh is "a Jesuit from nature and from education" that "he knew well how to dissemble" (80, 83). In the same story, however, the author is sympathetic in describing a humble innkeeper: "He was poor, he was oppressed; to sum up all, he was an Irishman. This includes all the suffering that the human race are subject to" (55). Overall, the Lady of Boston is ambivalent about the Irish, although her judgments follow conventional class lines: peasants are slovenly traitors, but poor and oppressed, while the landlord class is sometimes heroic, sometimes exploitative, and always cultured. Furthermore, if not herself from Ireland, the Lady demonstrates that Bostonians in 1828 knew something about the place. In the preface she claims "an intuitive feeling of respect for the Irish," and goes on to defend the mixture of fact and fiction in her book as a reflection of Irish attitudes: "the history of Ireland and its legends have, for centuries, been associated with its poesy and song," and "I have found romance and fable so closely blended with historical fact, that it would be a most difficult task to separate truth from fiction."[8]

A last example of the American demand for Irish local color is "Lights and Shadows of Irish Life, The Priest, The Ghost, and the Sexton," an early story by immigrant Thomas D'Arcy McGee, who became a famous, fire-breathing nationalist editor and apologetic historian during the Famine generation. Published in 1843 when McGee was eighteen and in his first full year in America, this is the only Irish story in the first volume of *Sargent's New Monthly Magazine*, a high-toned Boston literary journal whose contributors included Hawthorne and Oliver Wendell Holmes. It describes a sleepy village in McGee's native Leinster, with its "priceless trout stream, a douce landlady, a jolly old priest, and the most notable of all notable characters, the Clerk, 'Dominie,' and Sexton of the village," all clustered near "the gray ruins of an ancient friary." In the romantic plot, a triangle is resolved when these colorful characters conspire to allow a young woman to marry the man she loves, the son of a small farmer, rather than being sold off to the steward of the local "Earl of Elmwood, of Dare-Devil Hall." McGee returned to Ireland in 1845 to become a member of the literary/nationalistic Young Ireland movement. A contributor to Thomas Davis's influential journal the *Nation*, McGee also helped plan the abortive rising of 1848, after which he was forced to flee once again to America. It is hard to imagine him producing so gently picturesque a piece of writing. But it must have been the light touch and local color that carried the day with editor Epes Sargent, thereby providing the young immigrant with a few dollars.[9]

Also contributing to the extensive context of American publications of Irish materials were poems and plays. Poems, Irish and Irish-American, appeared in virtually every newspaper and periodical with Irish, Catholic, or nationalist leanings from the *Shamrock* of 1810 right on through the century. After its initial American publication in 1815 by immigrant Mathew Carey, Thomas Moore's *Irish Melodies* appeared in over thirty separate editions by 1900. Similarly, the stage Irishman was a popular figure from the moment he first walked into an American play as Trushoop, the bibulous, excitable, singing-and-dancing immigrant cooper in *The Disappointment, or the Force of Credulity*, a comic opera of 1767. He became the braggart soldier of plays during the revolutionary period such as *The Battle of Brooklyn* of 1776, and the repatriated conquering adventurer in

William Dunlap's *Darby's Return* of 1789, one of the first American works to engage the theme of returning to Ireland. One count shows no fewer than twenty-two American plays before 1828 with Irish characters, and subsequently each decade had its own dominant stage-Irish figure: Irish actor-manager Tyrone Power in the 1830s, Dublin-born actor-playwright John Brougham in the 1840s, rough and ready "Mose, the Bowery B'hoy," the intrepid volunteer fireman of music-hall farce in the 1850s, and on through Dion Boucicault and Edward Harrigan to the end of the century. Also relevant as reinforcing the stage-Irish context is one of the earliest fictional examples of an Irish-American character in a work by a non-Irishman—the servant Teague O'Regan in Hugh Henry Brackenridge's picaresque novel *Modern Chivalry*, published in four volumes between 1792 and 1815. Drinking, whistling, blarneying, and brandishing a shillelagh, Teague heads a long parade of stereotypical Irish figures in mainstream American fiction.

Especially important to the emergence of Irish-American fiction was the ready availability of American editions of fiction from the old country. The first generations of more affluent and educated immigrants probably brought Irish books with them. However, American editions of Irish novels often appeared immediately after their initial publication in Dublin or London. Maria Edgeworth's *Castle Rackrent* of 1800 marks the beginning of serious Irish fiction. A tour-de-force monologue spoken by Thady Quirk, an intelligent steward to the Rackrent family, this novel describes the bungling of Ascendancy Protestant landlords and sympathizes with the plight of the Catholic peasantry. Edgeworth's works were in print throughout the nineteenth century in America, beginning with *An Essay on Irish Bulls*, co-authored with her father Richard, published in New York in 1803 and *Popular Tales*, published in 1804. A thirteen-volume *Collected Works* appeared in Boston in 1824, and a deluxe, eighteen-volume set of *Tales and Novels* was published by the prestigious New York firm of Harper in 1832-35, and reissued the following year. *Castle Rackrent* had American editions as a separate book as far apart as 1814 and 1904.

Also very popular in America were the flamboyantly romantic "national tales" of Sydney Owenson, Lady Morgan, another Protestant in sympathy with the Catholics. Several early Irish-American writers mention her runaway London and Dublin bestseller of 1806, *The Wild Irish Girl*, which was published the following year in New York and Philadelphia in five separate editions. The American audience was probably attracted not only by Lady Morgan's nationalism, but also by her lavish use of picturesque descriptions of various sections of Ireland.

John Banim and his brother Michael, the first accomplished Catholic novelists in Ireland, wrote fiction detailing peasant life and historical events from a Catholic and nationalist perspective using the pseudonym "The O'Hara Family." Their first work, *Tales of the O'Hara Family* (1825), was published in Philadelphia in 1827 (and again in 1838) by Carey and

Lea, who continued to bring out their novels, including their most popular historical fictions, *The Boyne Water* (1826) and *The Croppy: A Tale of 1798* (1828). New York's Harper also published three Banim novels in the 1830s, which suggests that they were being read by a good many people.

One of the best known of all Irish novels is Gerald Griffin's masterpiece, *The Collegians*, a kidnap and murder tale that rises above the genre of sentimental romance by means of its plausible, compelling analysis of character and motive. *The Collegians* was available from both D. and J. Sadlier and Harper in 1829, the same year as its European publication, and the following year saw the American publication of two other current Griffin novels bound together, *The Rivals* and *Tracy's Ambition*. Griffin's stories of the life and customs of his native Munster, collected as *Tales of the Munster Festivals*, was also in American print immediately. Subsequently in the century, Griffin was popular enough for the Sadliers to publish his ten-volume *Works* three times, in 1857, 1868, and 1885.

Also very much available in America was the work of William Carleton, the nineteenth century's greatest Irish novelist and the first major writer to emerge from the Catholic peasantry. In America, Philadelphia's Carey and Hart took the lead, publishing an edition of the masterful *Traits and Stories of the Irish Peasantry* (1830) in 1833. Individual Carleton novels also appeared in American editions, including *The Black Prophet; A Tale of the Irish Famine*, published abroad and in the United States in the same terrible Famine year of 1847. An American favorite was Carleton's most sentimental novel, *Willy Reilly* of 1855. The collected works of William Carleton had five American editions between 1856 and 1885.

Also to be reckoned with are the works of the two most successful nineteenth-century perpetrators of Irish caricature, Samuel Lover and Charles Lever, whose novels were perennially popular, at least among non-Irish readers. Lover was best known for his novel of 1842, *Handy Andy*, which was published by Appleton in New York and Philadelphia in 1843. The servant of Squire Egan, "Handy Andy" Rooney is the apotheosis of the blundering, comical Irish retainer, and his revealed identity as the Irish nobleman, "Lord Scatterbrain" hardly atones for the stage-Irish stereotype. Lever was the most popular Irish novelist in nineteenth-century England, largely because of his broad-brush caricatures of Ascendancy Irish gentry and soldiers. Lever's parade of drinking, duelling fox-hunters extended from *Harry Lorrequer* (1837) to *Lord Kilgobbin* (1872). Both Lever and Lover received the blessing of the late-nineteenth-century American literary establishment in the form of gorgeously printed, multivolume collected editions from Boston's Little, Brown and Company, Lever in 1894 and Lover in 1902.[10]

Throughout the nineteenth century, the Irish writers were also published in a wide range of American periodicals, from Catholic and Irish nationalist weeklies to mainstream magazines. New York's early Catholic journal the *Truth-Teller* was publishing Gerald Griffin's stories in 1827, and the Boston *Pilot* carried fiction on its front page beginning in the late 1830s, including stories by Griffin and John Banim. As the number of immigrants increased and dispersed, the Irish-oriented press nationwide began to publish Irish fiction. From the 1860s to the turn of the century, Irish writers appeared in archdiocesan newspapers as far afield as St. Paul, Louisville, St. Louis, New Orleans, and San Francisco, and in Irish nationalist journals in Boston, Buffalo, and New York.[11] Irish fiction was also available to the general reading public. The Banims' O'Hara family stories appeared in New York mainstream periodicals in the late 1820s, and William Carleton's fiction was published in the early 1840s in the New York *Dollar Magazine* and its successor, *Brother Jonathan*, edited by Nathaniel Parker Willis and H. Hastings Weld.[12]

By the early years of the nineteenth century, there was, then, a large body of Irish history, mythology, folklore, poetry, and fiction available to those Irish Americans who were considering trying their hands at literature. The main direction taken by the first recognizable Irish-American literary generation, the writers who emerged in the three decades before the Great Famine, was toward a habit of satire. This was in itself a plausible turn of events. Pre-Famine Irish-American satire was both a natural response to American conditions and the translation to the New World of a profoundly Irish habit of mind. Vivian Mercier has made a convincing case for the centrality of a comic tradition in Irish literature in both Gaelic and English, and for the prevalence of satire within that tradition, from the early bards whose poetic ridicule was feared for its magical power to the last great satire in Gaelic, Brian Merriman's *The Midnight Court* of 1781, and from Jonathan Swift to James Joyce and Flann O'Brien. In his study of Irish comic drama from Dion Boucicault to Samuel Beckett, David Krause further extends our sense of the centrality of the Irish comic and satiric tradition, which he sees as a natural response to Irish history: "a subject people, unified by repression or humiliation, must resort to comic strategies rather than physical violence to compensate for their personal and national frustrations" (19). Krause also traces "the barbarous sympathies of antic Irish comedy" back to the Gaelic bards, asserting that "no one knew better than the antic Irish comedians that profane or devilish laughter is our emotional protection against deadly solemnity and the cruel arrows of reality. In the oral and written Irish tradition, language itself, the power of words, is a great offensive weapon, a potent and public act of comic aggression that fortifies one against one's enemies" (34).[13]

This chapter began with the broadsides of Lawrence Sweeney from the 1760s, the earliest Irish-American examples of this habit of satire. Subsequently, the Irish satiric voice continued to be raised on both sides of the conflict between England and the colonies. In the Boston *Censor* in February, 1772, the familiar stage-Irish propensities for dishonesty and belligerence were used to criticize the American revolutionaries. One "Patrick McAdam O'Flagharty, Esq.," a native of "my sweet *West* of *Ire-*

land," addresses "the sweet Electors of the Town of Boston," and offers his expertise at tarring and feathering, robbing ("I was one of the foremost of our gang, and would rob my own Father to serve the *common cause"*), and the breaking of heads ("I have got a sweet *shillaly* for all sorts of *Tories,* faith!"). Patrick is in America because his Cousin O'Connolly, "a sweet Son of Liberty," told him "that this was the country for an honest, industrious-like Gentleman to get his bread in, and rise in the world." On the other hand, in a doggerel poem, "The IRISHMAN'S EPISTLE to the Officers and Troops at Boston," "Paddy" ridicules British conduct at Concord in April of 1775: "And is it not, honies, a comical farce, / To be proud in the face, and be shot in the a-se."[14]

Other anonymous examples of an emerging climate of Irish-American satire include a "Curious Letter" that was printed in the *Gazette of the United States* in 1793. Using an atrocious brogue, Patrick O'Flaherty of Tipperary ridicules both the French Revolution and the lately formed Society of United Irishmen, and advises his countrymen to "content ourselves with volunteering, and singing treason, and drinking rebellion, just to show that we are brave Irish boys, but not carry the joak any farther." Also, when British travel-book author Sir John Carr published an American edition of his boring and fatuous *The Stranger in Ireland: or, a Tour* (1806), it was swiftly parodied by *My Pocket Book; or Hints for "A Ryghte Merrie and Conceited" Tour, in Quarto; to be Called, "The Stranger in Ireland"* (1807). The author, "A Knight Errant," deflates Carr's generalizations, ridicules his nearsighted observations of the Irish, and claims that he only took the trip in order to write the book. Even if they were not written by Irishmen, these pieces demonstrate a significant early reliance on the Irish voice for purposes of American satire.[15]

After Lawrence Sweeney, the second identifiable Irish contributor to the early vein of satire was Mathew Carey, one of the most talented of the emigrants of the revolutionary era in Ireland and America. Born in Dublin in 1760 and trained there as a printer, Carey came to Philadelphia in 1784 to avoid prosecution for publishing an attack on the British government in Ireland. He became one of the most successful publishers and booksellers of his time, with Dickens, Scott, Irving, and Cooper on his list, as well as the Douay Bible and Moore's *Irish Melodies.* A skilled propagandist, he wrote pamphlets galore in support of such causes as Catholic Emancipation in Ireland, American tolerance for Irish immigrants, tariffs to protect infant American industries, and national unity during the War of 1812. Carey also produced in 1819 a large, diffuse, but impassioned contribution to the genre of historical apologetics, *Vindiciae Hibernicae; or, Ireland Vindicated,* in which he refuted British claims of "pretended conspiracy and massacre" by Irishmen during the 1641 rising in Ireland.[16]

Three times in his career Carey replied to attacks by enemies in American journalism with self-printed satiric pamphlets. The first, published in 1786, his second year in America, was *The Plagi-Scurriliad: A Hudibrastic Poem*, a rejoinder in the manner of Samuel Butler's burlesque-heroic poem, *Hudibras*, to aspersions cast on Carey's character by Philadelphia editor Eleazer Oswald. The "two grand subjects" of the poem are "plagiarism and scurrility," Oswald's great gifts to Philadelphia journalism. Carey also includes detailed footnotes proving Oswald's plagiarism and a ready-to-use epitaph for his foe, which starts, "INHUMED beneath this stone, lies . . . A man distinguished by a malignance and rancor, Whereof (great as is human depravity) the instances are rare." For his trouble here, Carey was challenged to a duel by Oswald, and a postscript to the poem explains that Carey "received a ball in his Thigh, upon which, the Seconds interfering, a Reconciliation took place."

Carey's second work in this vein was *A Plum Pudding for Humane, Chaste, Valiant, Enlightened Peter Porcupine* (1799), a prose parody of slanders against him perpetrated by the notoriously choleric British-born journalist William Cobbett, whose American career as "Peter Porcupine" featured a vicious campaign against the Democrats. Carey's sketch of Cobbett uses the same terms that Cobbett had applied to him, beginning with "Since this viperous wretch. . . . " As an example of satirical defense of the Irish character through parody, the *Plum Pudding* sets a precedent for much writing by the pre-Famine generation of Irish Americans.

Carey's third satire was another "Hudibrastic Poem," *The Porcupiniad* (1799), also addressed to Cobbett, who is presented as the editor of *Porcupine's Gazette*, a journal devoted to calumny, Billingsgate, and buffoonery, and guided by orders from the British government, including specific instructions to generate anti-Irish propaganda:

> The Irish "outcasts" vilify,
> Paint all their deeds of blackest dye.
> In Ireland, swear, so mild's our sway,
> That none our orders disobey,
> Save lawless villains, wretched herd!
> Unworthy of the least regard;
> Wild, vicious, discontented, rude,
> A turbulent and factious brood. [Canto I][17]

Although Mathew Carey does add something to the early stream of Irish-American satire, his work is more closely related to another tradition that flourished in his time. This was the American mainstream literary phenomenon of Federalist satire against Jeffersonian Democracy, as practiced by Washington Irving, James Kirke Paulding, the Hartford Wits, and the contributors to Joseph Dennie's *Port Folio*. Modeled on the British Augustans from Butler to Pope, this controlled, reason-based, often mock-heroic vein was very different from the aggressive, antic barbarism and linguistic subversion of the Irish satiric tradition. Whereas Carey's "Hudibrastic" poems are Augustan/Federalist performances in tone and style,

Lawrence Sweeney's flights of mordant fancy are just as clearly Irish. In fact, "The Irishmen's Petition" is very like the "sesquipedalian and stilted nonsense" of William Carleton's pretentious schoolmasters and blarney- ing pedlars who deliver some inspired "humble petitions" of their own. And it is Sweeney's voice that sets the tone for the remarkable cluster of Irish-American satirists who emerged in the 1830s and early 1840s.[18]

Throughout the 1820s and 1830s in Ireland, several partial potato crop failures along with news of canal, road, and railway building booms in America made emigration increasingly attractive. More and more people left Ireland, and the new immigrants were more often Catholic and South- ern Irish, less solvent economically, and less likely to be literate than the previous generation of Irish Americans. Recent estimates of those who went directly to the United States (certainly lower than the real numbers, as many traveled first to Canada and then south) demonstrate a significant new Irish presence in America: 1815-1825, 28,600; 1826-1835, 118,400; 1836-1845, 289,700. From this mixture of established, educated Irish Americans and recent, less-educated immigrants came the audience for pre-Famine satire, the salient product of this first Irish-American literary generation. Three curious books come first, all of them containing parody and satire. Though all were published anonymously, internal evidence suggests that their authors were Irish.

The earliest, published in 1820, is *The Life and Travels of Father Quipes, Otherwise Dominick O'Blarney, Written by Himself,* a short, picaresque tale that takes its hero from the West of Ireland to Carlisle, Pennsylvania, with stops along the way in Galway, Sligo, and (courtesy of a British press gang) Ceylon. Quipes contrives to be both a political journalist and a politician and his book parodies the genre of campaign biography. In the preface, he apologizes that "the work was hastily compiled, and written amid the bustle of an electioneering campaign; at a time when all eyes are fixed upon me, and expecting to see something great and decisive from my illustrious pen." And he later attributes his journalistic success to "using a great many tropes and figures, such as the 'mysterious dagger,' 'horrible insinuation,' 'infamous wretch,' 'reptile,' 'villain,' 'scoundrel,' &c. &c."[19]

The opening pages of *Father Quipes* strike an important satiric target of the Irish voice in America. The author ridicules anti-Irish stereotypes by exaggerating them to absurdity. "Born on one of the most remote mountains of *Finnevarrah*, in the *west* of *Ireland*," Quipes is "unable to give any accurate account of my parentage, owing to the wild and savage state of that unsettled country." He is captured by bandits, thanks to a trick usually associated with monkeys: reaching into a barrel, he is unable to extricate both his hand and the "fine large potato" that he finds there. No one heeds his "hideous outcry," which is copied from "the old women who are usually hired to *keen* at our country wakes," and Quipes is taken to Galway, where "I first saw houses and barns, and women and children, with clothes on their backs," and where the natives fail to understand his language—presumably Irish. Sold into virtual slavery at the Oranmore fair, Quipes is then made to cut turf while tethered to a stake, with a daily food allowance of one potato, the tail of a herring, and "a noggin of dirty buttermilk." After a year of this, he escapes to Sligo town, where he is arrested for vagrancy, put in the stocks, and apprenticed against his will to a wheelwright. There he also contracts "an intimacy" with "the *genteel* Miss Biddy O'Rafferty," who "used to employ her leisure hours in combing my head and catching numerous swarms of those troublesome *'travellers'* [lice] who had accompanied me from the wilds of Finnevarrah, and who had established a regular form of government and administered justice on all parts of my skull." When Biddy becomes pregnant, they marry, "to save her from the evil consequences of our mutual embraces." Thus, in a few pages, the author of *Father Quipes* summarizes the full range of anti-Irish prejudices: savagery, stupidity, duplicity, squalor, and promiscuity.[20]

Throughout the book, Quipes is candid about country matters. He seduces Miss Polly Gaullagher, "a buxom young wench, whose silly ideas of honor and virtue were more easily tampered with than her fellows, and who became a prey to my lust, before she had time to attend a wedding ceremony or ask the prayers of the parson in her behalf." And he also composes a scurrilous poem about the sexual encounter of "Miss Sally" with "A colonel all covered with lace and with gold." After several more adventures, including impressment to Ceylon where he sees his first elephant ("a correct picture of which is here subjoined; for the satisfaction of the reader"), Quipes ends up in Philadelphia, where he picks up the American fascination with politics, and concludes that "the speediest way to arrive at distinction in Pennsylvania, would be to make a noise in the newspapers, and bellow and brawl at elections." A natural at polemical writing, Quipes is "courted by all the great men of the day," and lands a job as speech-writer for a Congressman. His reward for writing every word that his employer speaks on the floor of the House is "the office of Marshall of Cumberland county, from which distinguished situation I have since been kicked for incapability and laziness." Thus, the author completes the cycle of venality and deception which constitutes his assessment of American political life.

A second satire is *The Life of Paddy O'Flarrity, Who, from a Shoeblack, Has by Perseverence and Good Conduct Arrived to a Member of Congress, Interspersed with many curious anecdotes, calculated to improve as well as divert the Youths of America, Written by Himself*. As the title suggests, this short novel of 1834 parodies American rags-to-riches, moralizing fiction, and its further subtitle, "A spur to Youth, or Davy Crockett Beaten," indicates a specific target—the popular Crockett biography published in the same year.[21] An even more relevant target was President Andrew Jackson, then in his second term, the Tennessee-bred son of Scotch Presbyterian immigrants from Ulster. Published, appropriately, in Washington, D.C., *Paddy O'Flarrity* is the story of a wily, amoral, immigrant Irish boy's rise in the world of American politics. It is written with deliberately outlandish grammar—the sentences are full of tense, person, and number shifts and end in ways unpredictable from their beginnings—which contributes to the cynical message that traditional education and abilities count for nothing in the race for political advancement in America. The preface sets the tone:

> In laying before the public this short history of my life, I hope it will meet with the success for which it is intended, viz. the improvement of the Youth of America. . . . Look at many of your countrymen, at the leading men of learning and education, who are at the head of government, and look at me, who during our infantine state, were pronounced as fools by our school companions, and now called men of genius, learning, &c. Look at your Henry Clay, your Wirt, modern Demostheneses, who, like him of old, sprang from humble life, but by Perseverence acquired the pinnacle of glory they now possess. But, above all, I must not forget Patrick Henry, who, even to the age of 23 or 4 years, was considered a dunce—see what Perseverence did for him; behold how he was rejected, disappointed and laughed at for his presumption, as it was termed by the envious, and then see, notwithstanding many impediments, to what immortal fame he arrived to. And lastly, behold myself, Paddy O'Flarrity, who, from a poor Irish boy, on the wide world, without a friend, from a Shoe Black, has arisen, by Perseverence and good conduct, to a Member of Congress. Reader! go thou and do likewise.

As in the case of *Father Quipes*, the opening sketch of Paddy O'Flarrity's Irish background satirizes American stereotypes rather than the realities of life in Ireland. The child of "Raw Irish" parents, Paddy was born forty-six years ago "in the land of milk and potatoes, . . . the youngest of thirty-two children, . . . all boys in the bargain, who were as thumping paddies as ever you saw and all ambitious, striving, and enterprising, as the most of my countrymen are." Planted every year in potatoes, their farm also contained three cows, a horse, and "an old sow, which if not dead, must certainly be living yet. Ah, you old bitch, well do I recollect how often you used to slit up the back part of my leather breeches, with your old snout, and then such scorching as mammy would sure to give my back." The combination of children, potatoes, pigs, and digression is telling. Claiming a hedge school education, obtained "under a large tree, the general place of resort for the poorer class, for that purpose," Paddy explains that at age eighteen, "the oppression of my country forced me to leave the home that gave me birth and take refuge in a land where LIBERTY exists and VIRTUE is rewarded."

Landing at Baltimore penniless, Paddy takes a job as a shoe black for three months, then becomes a printer's devil and a reader of the newspapers, "thereby acquiring a knowledge of modern history which gave me a relish for that of ancient." A strange midnight scuffle in his bedroom involving Paddy, his roommate, and a "colored girl," results in eviction, and he takes off for Washington, advising that "every young man" ought to leave town, "so soon as he becomes notorious for any crime or bad conduct." There he finds employment "keeping bar for an Irishman by the name of Pat Duffy, who kept a grog shop near one of the Departments, and who was tolerably well patronised by a number of the wild young clerks of that office."

While in Washington, Paddy has an experience that provides evidence of the author's Irishness. Having arrived at his boarding-house late one night, he climbs into bed beside a sleeping man whom he takes for a fellow lodger. Soon, the landlord's wife and another lodger enter and begin courting. When the willing wife says "a'nt you afraid to do so and a dead man in the room too," Paddy feels the ice-cold face beside him and springs out of bed. "Supposing it was the dead man come to life," the two lovers run from the room, and the landlord's wife is "snatched from eternal infamy." This vignette comes from the Irish folk tradition, where it appears in many forms. Having collected it in the Aran Islands, John M. Synge used the tale in his play of 1903, *The Shadow of the Glen*, in which an old man plays dead and catches his young wife flirting with a local farmer.[22]

Paddy stays in Washington two years—until he is thrown in jail for fighting and decides "in compliance with my old adage" to go west. Stopping in Missouri, he promptly gets rid of "that dialect which is so peculiar to my countrymen," buys a new suit of clothes, assumes "a modest air," and lands a job as private tutor to the children of "Judge D——." He advises all young men to pay similar attention to dress and demeanor, "particularly where they have nothing else to recommend them." The job works out splendidly, allowing Paddy time to "improve" himself with the judge's law books, and to pick up enough Latin "to throw a superficial gloss over my learning." In addition, "my insinuating manners, which I advise every fortune hunter to assume, if he does not naturally possess them, secured me the good will of the neighbors round, and especially the Judge's family."

All runs smoothly from here. The judge is elected governor of Missouri, and Paddy falls in love with his beautiful daughter, Maria. To make himself appear worthy of her, Paddy runs for the state legislature. Because of his assistance in the judge's gubernatorial campaign, he wins a seat. A fortuitous Indian attack now assures his success. He saves Maria from being scalped, and is given her hand by the governor, with the provision that he change his name from O'Flarrity to that of the governor, "the name of one of the first families of Virginia." Paddy agrees immediately, but refuses to reveal his new name in his biography, "lest when you see me, you may say, 'there goes the Irish Paddy, the *shoe black*; the dirty villain who came to our country to cut our noses out of joint—I guess you had better staid in your own country and eat your fish and potatoes.' "

Paddy's career advances even more when he becomes an 1830s media hero: a wax reenactment of his exploit against the Indians goes on display in St. Louis. Soon enough, he is elected Speaker of the Missouri House of Representatives. After six years there, "during which time I devoted the greatest attention to electioneering more extensively," he is elected to Congress.

At this point, having traced Paddy from the display in the St. Louis wax museum, one of his thirty-one brothers appears. His story is a parody of the sentimental romance, complete with a duel, a lost inheritance, a trip to the West Indies (where, like Paddy, he marries the daughter of the governor), and a shipwreck in which his wife is drowned. The brother also reports the death at ninety-two of their father, and his burial "in the center of the potato patch."

Paddy O'Flarrity is popular in Congress from his first speech, which takes a week to prepare but is praised for its extemporaneity, and at the close of the session his constituents give him a silver cup, engraved "FAITHFULNESS REWARDED." He then concludes his narrative with predictable ambition for "a higher office still," and a challenge to the reader to "guess who I am." Thus ends this entertaining satire at the expense of the American dream of success, especially political success, which is seen as based wholly on superficial image-making and deception. Paddy O'Flarrity succeeds by denying his Irishness, assuming a veneer of culture, and letting blind ambition be his guide.

The third noteworthy anonymous satire was the immediate response to one of the earliest examples of anti-Catholic and anti-Irish violence in America, the burning of the Ursuline convent in Charlestown, Massachusetts, on August 11, 1834. That night, a mob drove the nuns and students from their beds, looted and tore up the rooms, desecrated the chapel, set fire to the convent buildings, and overturned gravestones in the nuns' burial ground. These thugs had been incited in part by Rebecca Reed, a recanting Catholic convert who claimed to have "escaped" in January, 1832, after six months as a student at the convent. Reed's misguided ramblings found their way into the Boston newspapers and were believed by many, such was the anti-Catholic climate in the city. To capitalize on the publicity after the convent burning, a ghost-written book in the tradition of "awful disclosures" of clerical life appeared in March, 1835, and became a best-seller overnight. This was *Six Months in a Convent; or, the Narrative of Rebecca Theresa Reed, Who Was Under the Influence of the Roman Catholics about Two Years, and an Inmate of the Ursuline Convent on Mount Benedict, Charlestown, Mass., Nearly Six Months, in the Years 1831-2.* This trumped-up tale of abusive treatment of unwilling novices (in which one nun dies from harsh penances) had as its declared aim, "warning others of the errors of Romanism, and preventing them from falling into its snares, and from being shrouded in its delusions" (186). Shortly thereafter, an anonymous rejoinder was published, with an equally imposing title: *Six Months in a House of Correction; or, the Narrative of Dorah Mahony, Who Was Under the Influence of the Protestants about a Year, and an Inmate of the House of Correction in Leverett St., Boston, Massachusetts, Nearly Six Months, in the Years 18—.*[23]

Like the Reed book, Dorah Mahony's effort contains several pages of endorsements of its veracity, a lengthy historical introduction labeled "Preliminary Suggestions for Candid Readers," and a closing "Letter to Irish Catholics." One endorser claims of Dorah Mahony that "I have always regarded her as a devout person, and, excepting a little staggering, exemplary in her Christian walk and conversation." Another reference to her truthfulness, morals, and modest deportment "will be signed by the whole Catholic population of Lowell and Boston, and endorsed by the Boston Post and Transcript." The "publisher" of the parody then counters the Protestant perspective of Rebecca Reed's "preliminary" history of the Reformation with his own Catholic introduction, which begins, "It is related in the history of the world that in the year 1520, there lived a big blackguard named Martin Luther." Blaming Reed's lying gossip for the convent burning, the "publisher" hopes that his book will incite Boston's Catholics to "burn down the House of Correction." And he concludes by predicting the election of a Catholic president (as soon as the Irish are able to "keep the heretics from the ballot-boxes with our shillelahs"), to be followed by the inevitable take-over by the Pope, to whom "America lawfully belongs."

Dorah Mahony's first-person narrative then begins with her recollections of Ireland. Once again, the depiction satirizes negative stereotypes of the Irish peasantry. Dorah recalls growing up in a turf house with six siblings, living on potatoes and buttermilk, and gazing at a piece of meat "hanging up in the center of the mud edifice, . . . saved for Christmas." Her father is asleep in the corner with a bound head, "for he had tarried late at the fair, and had had his head broken with a blackthorn cudgel. The pig, the darlint, was nosing him." "By living in this way," Dorah declares, "the finest peasantry in the world acquired a noble spirit of independence, and a proper hatred to the aristocracy" (23-24). Dorah's father, "an illustrious bog-trotter," has raised his family "in the fear of the Lord—the Priest, I mean." When her mother dies and her father is "transported for swearing an alibi," Dorah goes to live with an aunt. Her plans to marry Paddy Murphy change quickly when he is implicated by an informer as "a repealer and a white-boy" and a participant in the sacking and burning of "a gentleman's house." Dorah agrees "to accompany him into exile, and his share of the plunder of Squire Malone's house was enough to bring us over." On the boat to America, called on deck to observe "a flock of porpesses," Paddy falls overboard and drowns, having lost his balance because he "had not yet slept off last night's bottle." As in the earlier satires, the number of negative traits collected in a few pages here suggests ridicule, not of the Irish, but of American prejudiced perception of them.

After landing in New York alone in the world, Dorah gets temporary work as a seamstress in Newport, Rhode Island, then moves on to Lowell, Massachusetts, where she is hired by an old neighbor from Tipperary, "known to our family as a poor scholar in Clonmel," who has started a school "to tache the poor ignorint savages of this counthry larning and vartue." Not knowing how to read and write, Dorah is put in charge of the babies and instructed to "reform your pronounceation altogether," because "not the laste bit of the brogue is tolerated in my academy."

Her real trouble begins when she accepts the marriage proposal of Mr. McShane, an immigrant from Londonderry, a Boston saloonkeeper, and a Protestant member of the congregation of "Dr. Beecher, who was constantly preaching against my faith" (34). (Dorah here refers to Reverend Lyman Beecher, the noted revivalist of Congregationalism, whose anti-Catholic sermons in Boston were alleged to have been partly responsible for the burning of the Charlestown convent.) Through McShane, Dorah meets another famous minister, "Mr. Burchard, whose religious labors have made so much noise in twenty-six-day meetings." (This was Reverend Jedediah Burchard, an itinerant evangelist who was notorious in the early 1830s for theatrical ranting and suspect moral character.) Something of an Elmer Gantry, Burchard leeringly reads Dorah's mind and chides her for "thinking of Mr. McShane, and enjoying connubial felicity with him, in anticipation." Scandalized, Dorah leaves, but not before Burchard prescribes "a cubic yard of tracts, and 'Maffit's Efficacy of Camp Meeting,' which works I refused to accept, like a true daughter of the true church" (44-45).

Next, Dorah moves into Boston "among the heretics and Anti-Masons," despite warnings from her Irish friends that merely speaking with a brogue is enough to get one arrested there. "Given up to the buffetings of Satan," she agrees to marry McShane in a Protestant church after he promises not to let her "become a burthen on society by going to South Boston, as too many of my countrymen and women did" (62). At the party celebrating their engagement, McShane gets drunk and a fight breaks out. Tipsy herself, Dorah runs away, sprains her ankle, offers to claw the faces of bystanders who accuse her of being drunk, and ends up in Police Court. Framed by the arresting officers, who swear that they know her as habitually "drunken, lewd, and lascivious," Dorah is sentenced to pay $3.33 and costs or to serve "SIX MONTHS" at hard labor in the House of Correction. As she has no money, she is sent to the Leverett Street jail.

At this point, the parody of *Six Months in a Convent* begins in earnest. Rebecca Reed had described the Charlestown convent as a prison with "inmates." Dorah Mahony simply reverses the metaphor, and describes the Leverett Street jail as if it were a convent—complete with punishing "penances," homilies from the jailers, and the sheriff's exhortations that his charges embrace their true vocation as prisoners. Dorah relates the unreasonably harsh rules for the incarcerated "postulants," including "to work hard all day long and get nothing for it," and "to sleep upon sack-cloth and pipestems, in imitation of certain saints." A particularly savage "penance" is to "sweep the kitchen floor with a long-handled brush, and to eat yesterday's dinner cold," and Dorah hopes that her enumeration of such enormities will "make the blood curdle of all who read it," and "sell at least twenty thousand copies of my book" (84-85, 99).

Rebecca Reed's clumsy attempts to make ordinary convent activities seem exotic, sinister, and subversive are echoed in Dorah's lavishly tedious and redundant descriptions of life in jail. For example: "The sheriff's coffee is usually presented to him in a china cup, with a saucer and spoon to it. The servant who presents it remains standing behind his chair till he has swallowed it" (103). As Dorah's duties are mostly in the kitchen, her book contains many pages of anticlimactic description of meal prepara-tions and clean-ups. As is the case with the Reed material, the reader is constantly waiting for something interesting to happen—and it never does. Ultimately, and none too soon, Dorah Mahony makes her escape from prison by feeding beef to the yard dogs and walking out the back door and over a low picket fence. (It was reported that, although she was free to leave at any time, Rebecca Reed dramatized her departure from the Charlestown convent by climbing over the back fence.) Dorah goes straight to the Irish neighborhood of Broad Street, where the sound of a fiddle leads her to a safe house, and she is taken in, fed, and sheltered. She finds that her betrothed McShane has left town, and that a climate of prejudice against the Irish still exists in Boston, as evidenced by the mutilation on board the frigate Constitution of an effigy of "our beloved, wise, patriotic, virtuous Irish President Jackson," and by the sale of "many thousand copies" of Rebecca Reed's book (191, 198). Spirited back to Low-ell, Dorah gets back her old job with the schoolmaster, and closes her narrative with a last redundant vow "to warn others of the dangers of consorting with heretics," and to prevent fellow Catholics from "falling into prison, and from being inclosed within its gloomy walls" (200).

Evidence for Irish-American authorship of this book includes the ex-tensive knowledge and mockery of anti-Irish stereotypes, the use of Irish terms such as "white-boy" and "ribbonmen" for peasant agitators and "poor scholar" for the Clonmel schoolmaster, and the consistent, sus-tained parody of the Reed book. Moreover, the author is familiar with traditional Irish music. In prison, Dorah gets "sore lungs" from forced psalmody, which "generally consists of a long, discordant drawl, very hurtful to the nostrils." She much prefers "music of another kind," and her "favorite airs" are "Planxty Kelly" and "The Kinnegad Slashers," which have been pronounced by "several fiddlers" as "in no way injurious to the lungs." At the behest of her jailers, Dorah sings the airs, "O! in Ireland so frisky" and the "Tune the Old Cow Died Of," although she is made to stop after one stanza due to "the strength of the brogue" (116, 152-53, 187).

The book's final word, in an exact parody of *Six Months in a Convent*, is the "editor's" "Letter to Irish Catholics, Condensed from an Irish Paper," which warns of the dangers of literacy and concludes as follows:

> If people had not known how to read, do you think they would ever have burned down our Convent? (for which they will roast forever and ever and a day after.) Would they have basely stolen the gold and silver ornaments, and pulled the dead out of their graves? Would they have driven women and children from their beds into the fields at midnight? They could read the newspapers, and their brains were turned. "A little learning is a dangerous thing," as one of the fathers iligantly observes. But especially I warn you to avoid the company of heretics. Think of Dorah Mahony, who was in danger of losing her immortal soul by reason of frequenting the company of heretics. Then coming to Boston to be married to one, she ran full speed into the House of Correction. I have now said all I had to say, and more, and am satisfied with myself entirely.

Thus, the book ends with a serious, pointed reference to the desecration of the Charlestown convent. Throughout, the full range of anti-Irish prejudices is presented for ridicule: ignorance, drunkenness, clannishness, belligerence, the eagerness of colleens to marry any American who will have them, and even complicity in the papal plot to take over the United States. Furthermore, the more zealous of Boston's nativist Protestant clergymen, Lyman Beecher and Jedediah Burchard, are characterized by name as ranting fanatics, and the Antimasonic movement, then in the ascendant, is criticized as even more anti-Catholic than the Masons.[24] In the face of the trauma of the convent burning, *Six Months in a House of Correction* is an impressive response. By means of sophisticated parody and satire, the Boston Irish community retaliates here with real style.

The most intriguing of the forgotten pre-Famine writers is John McDermott Moore, an immigrant to New York City early in the century who became a versatile and widely published writer, editing two short-lived, Irish-oriented newspapers in the 1830s (the *Irishman and Foreigner's Advocate* and the *European*), writing for mainstream literary periodicals (notably *Brother Jonathan* and the *Dollar Magazine*) in the 1840s, and publishing poetry, drama, and fiction. Moore may have been forced to leave Ireland because of revolutionary activities. One of his poems suggests as much, and the evil of British rule is a constant theme in his work. In his grim tale of the 1798 Rebellion, "The Three Avengers," a troop of Welsh volunteers led by an Irish traitor perpetrates "the most dreadful atrocities" in Wexford and Wicklow, murdering women and children and firing the homes of supposed nationalists. Ambushed by "three avengers" of one such attack, the troop of one hundred is slaughtered at the "Bloody Bridge" in Wicklow, and the avengers escape to America. The story leaves no doubt as to Moore's feelings about the British.[25]

John McDermott Moore published two books, and both mark significant developments of the Irish voice in America. The first, *Lord Nial, A Romance in Four Cantos*, appeared in New York in 1834 and contains several short poems, the long title poem, and an introductory story, also called "Lord Nial," which prepares the reader for the poem, but also stands alone as an accomplished piece of fiction. The story is set in a village near the lakes of Killarney in County Kerry "in the latter end of April, in the year 18—." A mysterious wandering poet named McDermott arrives at the village inn of hospitable Tom Murphy. As it is the last day of April and the night is stormy, Murphy predicts "close fists and sour faces among the farmers by the morrow," and tells a neighborhood legend by way of explanation. Thirteen hundred years earlier, the mighty and benevolent ruler of the Killarney area, the prince O'Donohoe, bid his friends farewell on the first of May and rode straight into Mucross Lake. Arriving at the center, he bowed three times, and disappeared into the water. Thereafter, he was often seen by his subjects "riding over the lake, followed by ten thousand beings all as bright as angels." In more recent times, he has appeared only on the first of May, and if it is a fine day this is taken as a sign of "a sunny summer and plentiful harvest."

McDermott is much excited by this tale, for it seems to relate to his own situation. He has been writing a poem about the achievements of Lord Nial, a patriot chief and supposed "martyr to the cause of freedom," who has just appeared to him in a vision, and commanded him to go to Mucross Lake on May 1 to receive a revelation. McDermott then goes off to the lake, the storm abates before midnight, and he returns the next afternoon with a wild tale. He claims to have seen at daybreak standing on the water, "ten thousand forms" of warrior knights and ladies, their leader, Lord Nial himself, and a minstrel with a lyre who handed him a book and said, "Nial redeems his pledge." (Evidently, Nial is a later incarnation of the legendary O'Donohoe.) McDermott then shows the book, "a small black bound volume of Celtic poetry," to Murphy, and explains that "it is in Irish, and my task is to translate it."

Remaining in Killarney, McDermott buckles down to the job, which takes exactly a year, and on the next April 30, he gives over his work to Murphy. That night McDermott disappears, and, hearing a piercing cry in the street, Murphy sees "an exceedingly tall woman, clad in a snowy raiment, running in the direction of the lake to which she was pointing with her long, meagre arm." Murphy follows this figure to the lake, arriving at dawn on May 1, in time to watch McDermott wave goodbye and walk into the water. The poet seems not to drown in the shallows, but to "instantly . . . become nothing." The lake is subsequently dragged every day for three weeks, but no body is recovered. Presumably, McDermott's translation is the four-canto "Lord Nial" which follows the story in Moore's volume.

That poem is remarkable only for its ambition: 130 pages of text and thirty-five pages of detailed explanatory notes. Conventionally and clumsily rhymed, it is a narration of one day's battle, in which the Kerry troops rounded up by Lord Nial are all killed after killing ten times their number of British followers of Henry II. It is May 1, and O'Donohoe rises with his host to welcome the dying Lord Nial and Mary, his true love, into the lake, which becomes a figure for Heaven.

Both the poem and the story are early examples of the use of Irish legendary and folk materials in an original American book. Moore thus takes the efforts of such pioneer collectors as William D. Conway and the "Lady of Boston" one step further. His extensive notes convey his appreciation for the legends, and Moore has effectively revivified them by creating the three-part progression from O'Donohue, identified in the notes as a semi-mythic figure from the Irish pre-Christian era, to Lord Nial, glossed as the "Red Branch Knight," Lord Fin Nial of Kerry who battled the troops of Henry II on the plain beside Mucross Lake late in the twelfth century, to McDermott, the nineteenth-century poet-mediator between Gaelic and English versions of the earlier tales. All three figures are united by their miraculous disappearance in the lake on the first of May. The suggestion that they will rise again to exhort the Irish people to freedom from British rule places them in the millenial tradition that came over to America as early as "Old Ireland's Misery at an End" of 1752. Moreover, a second progression, from Lord Nial's minstrel to the poet McDermott to John McDermott Moore, is a metaphor for the continuity of the Irish literary tradition, and for its translation into the New World.

An important, related theme in the story "Lord Nial" is the destruction of the old Gaelic culture. The poet McDermott views his task of making an English version of the Irish text with bitterness: "but what can I do?—have we not substituted the mixed jargon of fifty tongues for our own beautiful and poetic language? and so, if I give the Celtic version of my poem, it cannot find readers even in Irishmen; for alas! the few who yet dare to speak the language of their country, are in general confined to those to whom poverty, or oppression, has denied the privilege of education." After completing his translation, McDermott declares that "after all I fear it is little better than a parody on the original," and he conveys a sense that such labor is really an admission of defeat, an act of complicity in the relinquishment of Irish cultural identity.

The story "Lord Nial" has other strengths as well. Moore's prose is fairly straightforward, with few of the ruffles and flourishes of Gothic fiction on similar subjects. In fact, this is more than simply a ghost story. Moore strongly hints that the black book may have contained not a Gaelic text, but only McDermott's English poem: "at times [Murphy the inn-keeper] fancied he could trace a similitude between the English and the Celtic manuscript," which reinforced his sense that McDermott was "under the influence of some strange delusion." After the poet's death, Murphy searches in vain for the magical Gaelic black bound volume. In addition, a possible suicide motive is established when McDermott is seen kissing "a small hair locket, which he ever wore suspended by a ribbon round his neck.—Haply he was the victim of love!" And the story concludes, "McDermott, if dead, is at rest." Thus, we are not really sure where the truth lies, and the result is a touch of enriching ambiguity— something of the combination of psychological realism and otherworldly mystery found in the tales of Moore's contemporary Nathaniel Hawthorne, whose first collection appeared three years after Lord Nial.

Eight years later in 1842, Moore published a second book, The Adventures of Tom Stapleton, in the opening issues of a New York mainstream literary magazine, Brother Jonathan. "Very popular" as a serial (according to the advertising), this novel was then published as a book by the Brother Jonathan Press in May, 1843. Three more editions followed, including one in London, where its title was Life in America.[26] In this worthy successor to the ambitious Irish themes of Lord Nial, Moore commits himself wholly to the American scene, specifically New York City in "183-," and to satire. Tom Stapleton is a good-humored presentation of several aspects of Irish New York in the 1830s: the frivolity of bachelor boarding-house life at "202 Broadway," the summer social whirl among "the fashionable set" at Rockaway Beach, the city's grimy underside in a "dock-loafers' den," and the lively political scene at Tammany Hall. Also included are a business trip to the dull hinterlands of Troy and a holiday party in a determinedly Dutch village on the upper Hudson. Seemingly well acclimated by now, Moore celebrates New York as "a very mine of marvels" for the novelist, a place "so ripe and teeming that if it was only fairly explored, its rare gems and precious metals would furnish capital sufficient for a goodly catalogue of comedies, tragedies, tales, romances, and extravaganzas." And as for characters, "dear delightful New York is the El Dorado of heroes, visionaries, fortune hunters, loafers, Jeremy Diddlers, disconsolate authors, and all other interesting characters, ad infinitum." Residing in "cheapness and gentility" at 202 Broadway is "as suspicious a fraternity of young, middle aged, and antique gentlemen about town, as ever lived by their wits in a large city." These include "several lawyers without briefs; one or two poets without muses; not a few speculative ministers about to agitate new systems of religion, . . . a fair ratio of quack doctors, quack dentists, quack playactors, and quack portrait painters; the whole being sprinkled here and there with a few tolerably honest fellows."

The presiding "universal genius" of the boarding house is an Irishman, Philip O'Hara from "Donnaraile" (Doneraile in County Cork), a man of myriad abilities,

> who wrote pamphlets and newspapers; brought out a new patent vegetable pill, manufactured chiefly from pulverized potato skins, and strongly recommended by a list of certificates as long as a liberty pole, for the cure of consumption, sore eyes, and the king's evil; kept a land office as much for the sale of property in the moon as anywhere else; invented a navigable steam balloon, and organized a company to put it in operation; performed, when hard up, as supernumerary at all the theatres; lectured on phrenology; cut corns; gave private instructions in the mysteries of the Thimble Rig—and would, I am persuaded, have undertaken to have produced the perpetual motion, for a couple of tumblers of whiskey punch, and under forfeiture of his head in case of a failure. [5]

O'Hara is not a mere stage-Irish stereotype, however. He is a rounded character, an intelligent, likeable hustler, only mildly crooked, and trying to survive with grace and humor by finding a wealthy wife. Although he dearly loves to talk blarney, drink whiskey punch, and sing (the novel contains several airs—words and music both), there is more to him than that. O'Hara is a good and faithful friend to Tom Stapleton, his fellow-boarder and the novel's narrator. He reveals a serious side when he and Tom discover a starving man, and O'Hara remembers his suffering countrymen in Ireland: "the sound is familiar to me. . . . I have heard it before. It is the bloodless voice of a human being dying for the want of food." And when O'Hara helps a beggar, Tom contends that he has "one of the most gentle, and generous hearts . . . when excited by the claims of woe or wretchedness."

A quieter and less idiosyncratic character, the narrator Tom Stapleton displays the sensitivity to language and consciousness of its abuses for social and political ends that Moore showed in the lament for the loss of Gaelic in "Lord Nial." Tom has a good ear for dialects, and his ramblings around New York are enlivened by comic renderings, in the service of undercutting pretension and hypocrisy, of many voices: a pseudo-aristocratic Frenchman, a Cockney pretender to British nobility, phlegmatic Hudson River Dutch villagers, and the shady and jaded dock loafers.[27] There are also several examples of Irish brogue, the relative thickness of which indicates social and occupational distinctions. (Phil O'Hara has few such mannerisms, while the Tammany politicians are full of them.) There is even one trenchant reference to Gaelic. Dead broke, O'Hara swindles a crowd of sensation-seeking New Yorkers by posing as "the renowned Chinese Juglar and Wizard, Boo Loo Chu," in whose "Magic Mirror" the spirits of the departed are said to appear to their surviving friends. At the crucial moment, the wizard shouts "at the very highest pitch of his voice a few wildly sounding words," then exits by the stage door. The stunned silence is broken by one patron's exclaiming, "By the mortial, it wasn't Chinese at all he spoke, but good night, ladies and gentlemin, in pure Irish." Thus, the only use for the Irish language in Moore's novel is to help deceive an English-speaking audience: not to communicate, but to obscure.

The strength of the novel is its detailed description of New York Irish life. Moore satirizes the *nouveau riche* when Tom and Phil O'Hara go out to Rockaway Beach in search of rich women to marry. The young men gain entry into "society" by passing themselves off as a "scion of the noble house of Pembroke" and the nephew of the Irish "Earl of Mount-Cashel." Phil proceeds to annoy their new acquaintances with constant references to the origin of their wealth in trade, while Tom assesses this pretentious "set of exclusives" acutely: "this society had no charm for me. It had all the assumptions of a privileged aristocracy, without any of its ease or confidence. Its members, conscious of the smell of the shop, and wishing to disguise it, were mostly mounted on stilts, from which they rarely descended" (17). Tom's visit to a Hudson River village is also marked by close observation of the natives, countrymen of Rip Van Winkle who harbor "a sort of vague impression that America is the Netherlands under a new name," wherein they "have been lords of the soil from the days of Adam." Tom describes vividly his attempt at getting directions from a tavern full of stolid Dutchmen grunting behind their meerschaums, and his exposure to a rollicking dance and "bundling" party at a local farm.

The bulk of the novel, and especially its analysis of the Irish, is given over to the campaign for New York City alderman of the Yankee aristocrat Anthony Livingston, the father of Tom Stapleton's great love, Lucy. When Livingston calls on an Irish political ally, Barney Murphy, to manage his campaign, the race is on. The first step is the entertainment at the Livingston mansion of four delegates to the nominating convention at Tammany Hall. Barney instructs the members of the family in their proper roles: "Well, I see you're all perfect; but I have just wan word more to say to you. I know every throb of an Irishman's heart just as well as if it was baitin' on my hand before me. Now it's mad; now it's merry; and fifty other ways; but it's never so happy as whin it's frettin' about poor *Granu Wale*. Thrait an Irishman well, an' he'll love you; but show him that you love an' pity Green Erin, an' he'll fight an' die for you!"(26). The reception is a great success. Livingston declares his heartfelt support for Irish freedom, his wife dances a creditable jig with Mickey Dooley, and Lucy sings an Irish song to significant effect: "the conclusion found them subdued almost to weeping. So potent are the effects of his national music on the heart of the poor Irish exile." As Moore's words here indicate, the satire throughout the development of this plot line is gentle. He presents the Irish delegates and voters as not stupid, but rather connected with authentic emotion to their homeland and their own kind. Free from reformist zeal or mortification at the actions of his compatriots, Moore is only poking good-natured fun at the undeniable political influence of the mere fact of being Irish.

The election boils down to a heated debate between incumbent Alderman Stubbs and Mr. Livingston about their relative sympathy for the Irish. (Obviously neither has a drop of Irish blood.) Stubbs seems to have carried the day when he produces his infant son—newly christened "by the honored name of Patrick" as "an offering on the shrine of my pure Irish feelings." But Lucy Livingston rescues her father by appearing on the bed of a horse-drawn wagon, dressed entirely in green and playing "The Harp that Once through Tara's Halls" on an Irish harp. When Barney Murphy exhorts the crowd to take "the true [election] tickets out of Hibarnia's own beautiful fingers," the tide turns and Livingston wins his seat. Moore ends this chapter by assuring his audience that "all the particulars so far as they relate to the baby and the lady" actually happened in a New York election.

Such an avowal of verisimilitude is necessary because *Tom Stapleton* also contains a strain of parody of the conventions of popular sentimental romance. Running counter to the realistic/satiric main plot of Irish-American politicking is a romantic/burlesque subplot of intrigue, kidnapping, disguised identity, and attempted murder. Falling afoul of New York harbor pirates, Tom Stapleton is nearly killed and thrown overboard. At the peak of danger, Moore blithely changes the subject until the next installment. Moreover, in counterpoint to the realistic central dialogue between Tom Stapleton and Phil O'Hara is a series of tongue-in-cheek sentimental soliloquies by Tom on the subject of his uncertain love life. Introducing Tom as a failing suitor for the hand of Lucy Livingston, whose "blue eyes have somewhat discomposed the serene of thy philosophy," the novel's opening paragraphs parody the rhetoric of sentimental fiction: "Well, here thou art, O Tom Stapleton! Quite a model in a small way of comfort and elegance, and one of the happiest rascals under the sun. . . . So, gentle reader, soliloquized your obedient servant, Tom Stapleton, as he sat one bleak winter's night, several years ago, in his snug little *sanctum*, which looked out into Broadway in the goodly city of Gotham." That this is parody is clear immediately, when Tom's flowery, self-pitying invocation of the lovely Lucy is cut short by two squalid and violent incidents: a mugging outside the window in which a ruffian lets his victim go free because she's "shriveled up with brandy or as ugly as sin," and a police-court vignette in which a destitute girl is jailed for drunkenness when she is really only weak from hunger and exposure.

Demonstrating Moore's sensitivity to language and his hero's ability to laugh at himself, these soliloquies occur periodically through the novel; for example, on the morning after a brawl, instigated by Phil O'Hara, between an Irish road gang and some New York Dutchmen: "No. 202 Broadway—Time, 10 o'clock—Tom, *solus*. 'O, Tom Stapleton, thou art a bright youth—an incontinently nice young man for a small tea party; and ought, by all means, to make a pilgrimage to some romantic peak that overhangs the sea, and throw an immortal somerset into eternity. Spirit of vexation, here's an invitation to tea at Livingston's, and my face tatooed all over like a New Zealander's, to say nothing of an eye fancifully mosaiced in red, and deeply imbedded in a frame of ebony' "(33).

Moore's final parodic concession to the sentimental tradition is the novel's conclusion. Tom Stapleton marries Lucy Livingston, Phil O'Hara marries a young woman of wealth, and, in a brisk, implausible reckoning, all the other main characters are given their just deserts. Moore makes this "brief disposition," he states, "in respect to a time-honored custom, . . . which readers would not willingly see treated with disrespect."

The four editions in book form of *Tom Stapleton* suggest the existence of an audience sophisticated enough to enjoy such rhetorical play as the disparity between realistic satire and sentimental melodrama. Moreover, the novel identifies Moore as a significant Irish-American satirist. His aim here is clearly the exposure of human foibles—from Rockaway Beach to the city docks. And the New York Irish are one of his prime targets, notably Phil O'Hara's blarneying style and the view of Tammany political power based on home ties rather than issues. The criticism here is gentle, though, and mitigated by Moore's sympathetic references to the terrible conditions back in Ireland. It is, in effect, early enough in the game for an Irish-American writer to be able to risk laughing at his own pretensions as a novelist and at his fellow Irishmen.

This looseness about the Irish self-image is even more pronounced in Moore's short play, *Patrick O'Flynn; or, The Man in the Moon*, published in *Brother Jonathan* in June, 1842. Subtitled "An Extravaganza," the play is a wild entertainment entirely in rhyme, featuring nonsense dialogue, songs, and dances. Far from defensive, Moore here confronts, uses, even celebrates the stage-Irish traits of drunkenness and belligerence. The climactic final number of the play features O'Flynn enthroned on a hogshead as Bacchus, singing a song in praise of "mountain dew," the chorus of which is in Gaelic!

To summarize his contribution, the several surviving works of John McDermott Moore exemplify the best in Irish-American literary self-consciousness before the Great Famine. The defining characteristics are interest in traditional Irish materials, a pronounced sensitivity to language and dialects, the sophisticated manipulation of literary forms, and a sense of identity secure enough to allow satiric self-scrutiny and even burlesque appropriation of negative Irish stereotypes.

The last example is one of the best of the early satires, *The Priest's Turf-Cutting Day, A Historical Romance*, published in 1841 by its author, Thomas C. Mack. Unknown except for this book, Mack has in it produced the most sustained example of the pre-Famine consciousness of linguistic subversion. Set in the dismal little village of Ballywhooloquin in County

Kerry, this short novel satirizes many aspects of Irish life, mainly by deft parody of familiar rhetorical conventions of the time. Nearly all of the main events are speeches, in which transparently hypocritical orators reveal their selfishness and corruption. An overall satiric frame is provided by the narrator's voice, which parodies the tone and jargon of travel books by collectors of folklore from England or America.

The novel opens with the narrator's observant eye trained on Bally-whooloquin, a village of one thousand souls on the banks of the River Shannon: "When approaching this town from any of its three entrances, you will see a line of thatched cabins on each side of the road, the walls of which are invariably built of mud. The next object that will attract the eye is a row of manure heaps, one collected exactly in front of each cabin; to a stranger's first view it would present the appearance of a line of fortifications rudely thrown up in defence." The narrator then runs a gauntlet of "cur-dogs" and beggars, including the redoubtable "Bill of the Bowl," a veteran of "twenty years at the fairs and markets, sitting in a bowl, he having no legs," but capable of leaping up and running away after receiving his dole. Thus is the theme of avaricious hypocrisy struck at the outset. It is, however, the occasion of the death of the village piper that brings out the narrator's professionalism as a collector, and the result is an extended parody of the erstwhile folklorist:

> As I had yet a few days to wait for the turf-cutting, I embraced this opportunity to see an Irish wake. I went early in the evening, and beheld the unfortunate defunct laid on an old door, in the middle of the floor, on his back. His bagpipes were at his head; the fragments of the fatal quart bottle carefully collected together, and broke up in small pieces, as they were to be distributed to the mourning friends of Thyge as a lasting relic of the well-beloved piper. There was twelve candles, six at each side; these were to represent the twelve tribes of Israel, and also as typical of the twelve shining stones on Aaron's breastplate. But above all, they were to show the deceased light across the bridge which separates purgatory from Abraham's bosom; and the bridge, having received some injury from the ravages of time, required repairing. Therefore there was a plate put on the feet of the corpse to receive the half-pennies, to be placed at the disposal of the Purgatorian Society for this purpose. [53-54]

The significant strain of anti-clericalism in Irish satire, which figures mightily in Brian Merriman's *The Midnight Court*, also appears in pre-Famine Irish America in Thomas C. Mack, whose most important satiric target is the lazy, avaricious parish priest, Father Mick Murphy. "The greatest orator in all Munster," Father Mick deigns to preach in Bally-whooloquin only once a year, on the Sunday preceding his "turf-cutting day," when the villagers are expected to show him their gratitude. His rousing sermon deplores the sinfulness of his flock and urges atonement in the form of money, food, drink, and turf—all to be delivered on his day: "All of yees what hasn't mate, send men; and all of yees what hasn't men, must send mate; and all of yees women that hasn't eggs, send butther; and all yees that hasn't butther, send eggs—and when you are done, walk in order to Conehure's till ye get your whiskey. And I now pronounce that the first of yee's a vagabone what raises a Botha—I will curse you, bell, book, and candle light"(10). Terrified by their priest's eloquent threats, the parishioners silently acquiesce to his demands. As a parting shot, Father Mick orders Paddy Brian to marry Moll Murtoch because they walked home together after his last turf-cutting day. His interest in local customs piqued, the narrator decides to stay for the wedding and the turf-cutting.

The second rhetorical posturer is the schoolmaster, Mr. Whiggy, a garrulous old bore who takes every opportunity to mouth the platitudes of Irish nationalism. At Moll Murtoch's wedding, he tells a rambling tale of "Brian Borhome," who "put one foot on Drogheda, and the other foot on Sugar Loaf Hill, and slashed away at the Hill of Howth with his battle-axe," until "he kilt all the Danes with the rocks he knocked about." He goes on to deliver an inflammatory speech, exhorting the villagers to "look back at the fiery zeal of our fathers in defence of their native soil," and to "be preparing" to rise again by training in arms, clandestine meetings, and the occasional burning of a landlord's house. It is clear that Mr. Whiggy is all talk and no action, but Mack also registers impatience with the Parliamentary agitation of Daniel O'Connell, Ireland's first great modern politician. Under his organizing leadership the Catholic Association had pressured Parliament in 1829 into conceding Catholic Emancipation, which restored some of the freedoms lost under the Penal Laws, including the right to hold public office. Subsequently, O'Connell committed himself to the campaign for repeal of the Act of Union of Great Britain and Ireland which reached its climax in a series of huge rallies in 1843, but when he canceled what was to have been the largest of these meetings at Clontarf, that campaign and his efficacy as "the Liberator" ended. At another wedding celebration in *The Priest's Turf-Cutting Day*, one of the villagers sings a song in which O'Connell appears as an ineffectual, swaggering rhetorician:

> Mister O'Connel, the pride of our isle,
>   In the parliament house his great talents did soar;
> He finished 'em off in his own happy style;
>   And swaggered his head like the tail of a boar.
> By St. Patrick, he gave 'em fine speeches galore;
> By St. Patrick, he gave 'em fine speeches galore. [20]

It is yet another speech that ultimately disrupts the wedding. The "gauger" (tax collector) has been invited to the festivities by Father Mick. His presence bespeaks Mack's sense of collusion between the Catholic Church and the Protestant Ascendancy. "Considerably corned, and fast asleep, dreaming of policemen and whiskey stills," the gauger is abruptly awakened and asked to propose a toast. "Fancying that he was in very different company," he raises his glass "for the glorious, pious, and immortal memory of the great and good King William, who freed us from pope and popery, brass money and wooden shoes." The result is "a general rush, . . . to see who would have the honour of tearing out the gauger's windpipe." News of this trouble reaches the estate of Captain Robert Saxonboor, Ascendancy landlord and commander of the Loyal Tierbread Infantry. Himself laid up with the gout, the Captain sends his son Robert, Jr., off with the troops to put down what he thinks is a general uprising. Needless to say, the occasion provides the opportunity for the Captain's speech, which begins as follows: "My son, the long wished-for time has at length arrived, when the escutcheons of the Saxonboor family will be augmented and emblazoned by marks and trophies of distinguished acts of valour and fame, which has never been known since the landing of our brave ancestors." When his son manages to break up the wedding party and jail the bride and groom, Captain Saxonboor is convinced that he has gained a peerage, and he celebrates by drinking himself into a stupor. Summoned from Limerick with reinforcements, a regular-army general, "foaming with rage at being thus duped," releases the prisoners, chastises the Saxonboors as "not fit to carry any commission of any rank," and strips them of command of the yeomanry.

The Ascendancy legal system also comes under Mack's satiric scrutiny in the depiction of the rigged trial of an innocent man. When Parson Eagerfund's house and Captain Saxonboor's town mansion are "burnt down by the white-boys," Murty Dhun, the hapless village drunk and an obvious scapegoat, is arrested. Murty is tried before Lord Norberry, who dozes through the proceedings, waking up only to help sway the jury and to pass the sentence of hanging with a barrage of high-toned moral pronouncements. To sustain his humorous tone, Mack here mitigates the tragedy of this mockery of justice by contriving Murty's escape to America.

The turf-cutting day itself turns out to be an occasion not only for labor, but also for dancing and sports—wrestling, leaping, vaulting, and kicking the football. The highlight is the public reading of an American letter from New Orleans, which provides Mack with a last satirical target, the immigrant's epistolary optimism about life in the New World. Really a form of propaganda for emigration, the letter is equal parts cheery digression and naive misunderstanding of America. Written by the semiliterate friend of the correspondent, it features his discovery of Creoles ("cry ouls"), misinterpretation of the derogatory term "Greek," and a description of work as a canal laborer that omits mention of the backbreaking toil and everpresent threat of canal fever. Here is a sample from this interesting example of dialect writing:

Illeen ma cushlamachree, this is a grate place intirely; there is pepel here as yaller as the mud of the cabin, wat in ireland we cals yaller molats, but they cals um here cry ouls; fath, it's a quare name, but that's wat they cals um. But the pepel is very civel to us, an' cals us greeks, an' you know that's a grate name. Mister wiggy, the schoolmasther, wus always boastin' about that name; an' there grate magishuns, here, intirely; fhat do yu think i saw um do wid me own ise? fait, then, my hand an' word for you, i saw um move a hole hous, to mile of ground, an' it wus cows they puld wid; the cows was al in a ro, like the way the wild gees fli to the logh, and fhat made me wundher more, was, me jewel, to se the riges of praties walkin' afther it; for fhat good wud be to muve the hous, you se, widout the praties. [63–64]

The correspondent goes on to suggest that if Daniel O'Connell could be coaxed to America, "i believe we cud have him prisidint."

The Priest's Turf-Cutting Day is a consistent satire in which demogoguery is exposed and parodied on all sides. The only group largely exempt from Mack's critical eye is the peasantry, who suffer from the self-serving verbiage of everyone else. The ingenuousness of the peasants is pointedly illustrated in the American letter, which, in a further irony, may also delude them into emigrating. Mack's novel contains an inclusive diagnosis of a society riddled with rhetorical exploitation. From the pulpit to the Ascendancy bureaucracy to Parliament, in the name of religion, nationalism, keeping the peace, and dispensing justice, those in power twist the English language to their own ends, and an uneducated, gullible peasantry pays the bills. Small wonder that the alternative of escape to America is presented in such a rosy light. At one point in the narrative Mack abandons the frame of parody and the truth of the Irish situation breaks through, as the folklorist/narrator observes "materials before my eyes of a fine race of men, who are naked and hungry through the oppression of their task-masters. I must say that their piratical oppressors, when blustering about freedom in the wilds of Africa, much resemble the hollow roaring of the ocean when bellowing through the caverns of Ballyheigh, searching its crevices for victims to swallow up in the common gulf"(59).

To conclude, there emerged in the Irish America of the 1820s and 1830s a literary habit of satire, with roots in the eighteenth century, that constituted the first recognizable pattern of Irish response to American immigration. Struck at the outset with Lawrence Sweeney's broadside "Petition," the theme of linguistic subversion dominates. These early writers demonstrate an impressive sensitivity to language that takes the form of satiric exposure of the abuses of speech for ignominious ends, and for this purpose, parody is the natural method. *Father Quipes* and *Paddy O'Flarrity* satirize the immigrant's dream of success and the venality of political aspiration by parodying American campaign biographies. *Six Months in a House of Correction* satirizes anti-Irish-Catholicism in Boston by parodying the popular fiction of convent revelations. The overall structure of *Tom Stapleton* is a parody of sentimental romance, and that of *The Priest's Turf-Cutting Day* is a parody of folklorist travel books. In Moore's book, many aspects of American life, social, political, and literary, are satirized through parody of speech and dialects, and in Mack's book, Irish life is similarly treated through parody of the various rhetorical ploys of that society's leaders.

All of these books also satirize native American stereotypes of the Irish by reproducing them in exaggerated comic versions. In addition, the nature of this material dictates a further dimension of comic self-satire, an acknowledgement that the Irish do, in fact, drink, fight, blarney, and backbite, perhaps to excess. Taken together, this cluster of primarily entertaining treatments of sensitive issues of group identity suggests that this first Irish-American literary generation and its audience were sophisticated, highly literate, confident, and unthreatened by the strange, new American culture in which they found themselves. This was an immigrant generation that could laugh at itself, at its foreign background, and at native American prejudices against it. With the coming of the Famine immigrants, all such laughter stopped.

TWO

The Profession of Novelist:
James McHenry and Charles Cannon

The first Irish-American novel, *The Irish Emigrant, An Historical Tale Founded on Fact*, was written by "An Hibernian," and published in Winchester, Virginia, in 1817. The author may have been one Adam Douglass, who filed the book with the Virginia state clerk, and the location, at the head of the Shenandoah Valley, was a focal point for immigrants from Ulster. As early as 1760, a visiting Scottish nobleman found Winchester inhabited by "a spurious race of mortals known by the appellation of Scotch-Irish" (Jones 895). *The Irish Emigrant* is ambitious (filling two volumes of 200 pages each), intensely nationalistic (dedicated to the cause of Irish freedom), and emphatically unsatirical. In fact, the novel is crippled by its stuffy tone of high moral seriousness. His preface declares the author's aim: "to perpetuate in the memory of the writer . . . the country that gave him birth. . . . An Irishman, he glories in the idea of being so" (I, iii).

As the novel opens, the protagonist Owen M'Dermott, a fugitive from the failed Rebellion of 1798, reclines "on the bank of the Majestic Potowmac," hails Columbia as the "land of the free" and the home of the "Brave Emigrant," and ruefully compares the "degradation" of Irish "bondage" to the "sweets of freedom" in America. In large part an extension of this comparison, the novel that follows traces Owen's progress from his family's large estate near Randalstown on Lough Neagh in County Antrim, through his participation in the rebellion (major battles in Antrim and Wexford are described in detail), to his flight to Philadelphia and settlement on a Virginia plantation. The M'Dermotts are aristocratic Catholics, an unexpected touch given the large Ulster Presbyterian element in the emigration to Virginia. However, this fact helps to complicate Owen M'Dermott's love interest, a requisite in the genre of melodramatic romance to which this novel belongs. Owen loves his Antrim neighbor Emma Oniall, whose Catholic grandfather had quarrelled with James II and joined the armies of William of Orange at the Battle of the Boyne. The result for the Onialls was a place in the ruling Protestant Ascendancy, and ever since, their family has been "tuned to Irish degradation." A French connection is established through Owen's friend, William Fitzgerald, who had taken part in the French Revolution and subsequently helped persuade the ruling French directory to support a rising in Ireland. Having helped storm the Bastille, Fitzgerald "had discovered what savage acts man could be guilty of when supreme authority was vested in him," and he has returned to Ireland to coordinate the French contribution to the rebellion.

The brutality of British rule in Ireland is another major theme, illustrated first when Owen returns from his meeting with Fitzgerald to find that British troops have plundered and burned his estate to the ground, and "cruelly butchered" his father and sister. These "deamons with minds blacker than hell" have acted in response to mere rumors that the M'Dermotts have seditious tendencies. Owen's response is to commit himself wholly to the 1798 rebellion. He gathers his tenants into an armed force of 200 men and quarters them in a fort built on the still smoking site of the M'Dermott estate. In succeeding months, this army follows him through several bloody engagements against the British.

The Irish Emigrant also establishs a connection between the American Revolution and the movement to free Ireland, as did the apologetic histories of 1798 fugitives Burk, MacNeven, and Emmet. Here the American analogy is established by Emma Oniall, who flees her father's castle after learning that he has put himself at the head of a troop of Orangemen, committed to quelling the rising. It is Emma, a secret nationalist and a student of history, who proposes "the example of a Washington," whose "unwearied perseverance in the cause of his country" provides a lesson of "exalted patriotism" to the Irish (I, 127). The idea is reinforced when Emma meets a young Virginian, Mr. Warren, who declares: "Would to God this once sainted Island would copy after our example and become unanimous; disunion I perceive is the bane of Ireland, and a woeful tergiversation pervades the minds of her inhabitants" (II, 62).[1]

After the collapse of the rebellion and the dispersal of his troops, Owen M'Dermott marries Emma and they accept Warren's offer to accompany him to settle in America. The author next provides a list of reasons justifying their decision, and that of the "vast" number of their fellow Irish who have "flocked in thousands from the interior to the seaports, willing almost rather to sell themselves as slaves for life, than to remain in a country where nothing but endless miseries awaited them." The reasons include "a constitution altogether equitable, and equitably administered," the previous emigration of so many fellow Irishmen, some of whom "actually sold themselves for their passage" (as indentured servants), and the offer of "asylum to all emigrants who might wish to free themselves from the persecutions of despotism" (II, 177).

What follows may be the earliest rendering of an archetypal pattern in Irish-American fiction: the reluctant departure from Ireland, a transitional sea-change from grief to hope, and the dazed and wondering arrival in the New World. Owen and Emma M'Dermott stand "with their arms folded across on the quarter deck until the green isle of Erin appeared like a speck in the ocean; and when they could no longer perceive it, they burst into tears" (II, 183). Still, as monied aristocrats the M'Dermotts experience a comfortable, cabin-class crossing, insulated from the sufferings of so many of their fellow fugitives, and when they land, Mr. Warren gives them a Potomac River plantation as a wedding gift. Thus, their first impression of Philadelphia and its citizens is understandably positive: "the regularity of the streets, the order of the inhabitants, the neatness that was observed in every department, the public buildings standing in simple elegance," and the "cheerful serenity, as if completely contented with their fate" of everyone on the street: "Farmer, Merchant, Mechanic, Lawyer, and Legislator, all mingled in the same mass, as candidates for the same immortality" (II, 184-85).

As a novel *The Irish Emigrant* is no great shakes. It is a typical early nineteenth-century popular romance, replete with melodramatic plotting and stereotypical characterizations. Alas, form follows content as well. Discursive and windy, the book is syntactically tortuous, stuffed with high-flying rhetorical flourishes, and seeded with digressions on the natural beauty of the Antrim coast and the antiquity of the Oniall family. Nor are there any chapter divisions to break up the rolling tide of each 200-page volume. The book is nonetheless valuable for its inaugural position and early presentation of a number of issues, incidents, and character types. The author follows the conventions of the day, as in the novels of Maria Edgeworth, by creating heroic aristocrats and bumbling, humorous, or treacherous peasants, but *The Irish Emigrant* is atypical in that the hero Owen M'Dermott is a Catholic aristocrat, and one whose view of religion, labeled as "liberal in the extreme," is remarkable for its tolerance of the "different denominations of Christianity." Arguing against treating Catholicism as a "monopoly," Owen vows to "permit every man to worship the God who made him as he pleases," and praises the belief of Americans "that there was no monopolizer of religion, except their own consciences" (I, 8-9; II, 177). Such relativism will have no place in the fiercely didactic Catholic-tract novels of the Famine generation.

The "Hibernian" author also makes an interesting distinction between the national character of Irishmen and Americans. Admiring American equanimity at the expense of what he now sees as excessive and mercurial Irish passion, Owen M'Dermott declares that the American knack of keeping "within the due bounds of reason" is a "counterbalance," preferable to "that brilliancy of genius for which his own countrymen were so eminently distinguished." He even observes that his own "warmer passions had now become moderated." This admission of their own excessive wildness occurs in several other early Irish-American sources, including travelers' accounts and the novels of James McHenry.[2] There is certainly an unresolved contradiction in the treatment of these matters in *The Irish Emigrant*. The "Hibernian" author supports the movement to free Ireland from British oppression, as represented here by Owen M'Dermott's heroic participation in the 1798 rising. And yet, that rebellion was the product of the very passion that the Americanized Owen comes to suspect, and happily replaces with the "counterbalance" of reason. Already, assimilation brings a confusion of values.

So it is that Emma Oniall M'Dermott counsels her husband to "strive to forget the scenes thro' which we have been obliged to pass," to "bury in oblivion" the memories of having "seen our country become a colony, her inhabitants disgraced, her green fields stained with blood, and her patriots doomed to exile" (II, 185-86). The novel closes with Owen and Emma settled on their beautiful Potomac estate, content to be in a country where "all things had now come to a proper level, and man was found as he ought to be." However, one last honest observation mitigates the romantic complacency of this ending. The final round of praise for America concludes as follows: "in Columbia alone there was true liberty, except in one instance, which it is true was a disgraceful one—that a part of the human species are held in bondage, and that of the most ignominious description, merely in consequence of their differing in color from their own fellow creatures" (II, 199). In Virginia in 1817 this may even have been a courageous qualification. At any rate, the abhorrence of slavery echoes the consciousness of injustice and desire for freedom in Ireland apparent in the novel's opening chapters.

This first Irish-American novel is also the first Irish-American historical novel, and its presentation of Irish nationalism, the dominant concern of such fiction, echoes resoundingly through the subsequent literature. Indeed, one of the best latter-day examples, Thomas Flanagan's *The Year of the French* (1979) also deals with the rebellion of 1798. Nationalism is a created and creative concept, and literature has often had much to do with its generation and growth. In Irish-American nationalistic fiction, there have been from the outset two somewhat contradictory perspectives and goals: the Irish presented as suffering victims in order to elicit sympathy, and as vigorous heroes, in order to encourage action. In *The Irish Emigrant*, as often in later novels, both perspectives appear and remain unresolved. Owen M'Dermott responds heroically to the persecution of his family, and yet, when the rising fails, he himself suffers the sorrows of forced emigration. Moreover, the country to which he flees also appears as a contradictory example—at once a free society achieved through violent revolution and an asylum for oppressed, defeated revolutionaries. Like most of the books of this type that follow it, this first Irish-American historical novel delivers a number of ambiguous and contradictory moralizing messages.

There have been a great many such novels, in part because of strongly held convictions about Irish nationalism, but also because they are perennially popular and relatively easy to write. First of all, the plots are never a problem. The facts of Ireland's turbulent history provide a convenient and intrinsically interesting underlying structure. Emerging naturally from this context are Catholic/Protestant and tenant/landlord conflicts which often explode into violence. It is also easy to mix historical personages, often in the background, with invented protagonists who experience the common round of injuries, illnesses, recoveries, and triumphs. Also predictable are problematic love affairs involving people on either side of the basic conflict. All such goings on can be fleshed out with set-piece descriptions of Irish customs, the topography of the area, including picturesque castles and cabins, mountains and bogs, and the marks of the changing seasons. The whole is then liberally salted with Irish place names and snatches of Gaelic. Given a formula with so many stock elements, the author has only to insert the details of whichever set of events have been chosen—the names, dates, places, and battles. Following *The Irish Emigrant*, the next use of these formulaic historical materials came only a few years later in the 1820s, when Irish-American fiction was well and truly launched.

Two men, one a Protestant immigrant from Ulster, the other the son of Catholic immigrants to New York, were the first Irish Americans to attempt full-scale careers as American novelists. The elder by fifteen years, James McHenry published his last novel in 1831, two years before Charles James Cannon published his first. Neither was very successful and both died at the age of sixty, McHenry in 1845 and Cannon in 1860. Stretching from McHenry's first novel, *The Wilderness* of 1823, to Cannon's last, *Tighe Lyfford* of 1859, the persistence and variety of their fictional grapplings with their own backgrounds make them pioneers in the definition of Irishness for an American audience.

Utterly conventional and often heavy-handedly serious, McHenry and Cannon lacked the healthy, sophisticated perspective of the pre-Famine satirists. However, they did have one important thing in common with the other Irish-American writers of their generation. Like "Paddy O'Flarrity" and John McDermott Moore, they saw themselves not as displaced provincials, but as American writers with legitimate claims on an American audience. Primarily a propagandist for his own Ulster Presbyterian world view, McHenry aimed to educate the American public about his people. He also casually appropriated American historical settings and characters, including the French and Indian War and George Washington. And among his many ambitious literary projects was the *American Monthly Magazine* in Philadelphia, of which he was the founding editor. Never quite sure of his literary identity, Cannon was more of a thwarted, suffering artist, and yet he too saw himself as primarily an American writer, for he moved in New York literary circles, championed the poetry of "our own Poe," and dedicated his first novel to James Fenimore Cooper. Both McHenry and Cannon also had their plays produced on the American stage.

Through poems and plays, essays, editorships, and novels, James McHenry was the first Irish immigrant to make a strong bid toward earning his American living in belles lettres. Born in 1785 to an Ulster Presbyterian family in the sea-coast town of Larne, County Antrim, he trained for medicine and set up as a doctor. Interested from his youth in literature, he published two books of poetry on Irish themes and edited a Belfast literary journal before coming to America for economic reasons in 1816 or 1817.[3] The McHenrys lived first in Baltimore, then in Western Pennsylvania's Butler County, then in Pittsburgh. In 1823, his literary *annus mirabilis*, McHenry published *Waltham*, a long narrative poem about the American Revolution, and two novels, and also moved to Philadelphia to start up the *American Monthly Magazine*. Inspired by Walter Scott's Waverly novels and James Fenimore Cooper's *The Spy*, McHenry set out to write popular romantic novels with historical settings. His second novel, *The Spectre of the Forest*, dealt with witchcraft persecutions in seventeenth-century Connecticut and has no connection with the Irish. However, the other three of his first four, one set in America and two in Ireland, constitute the first significant body of Irish-American fiction by an individual.

Appearing in the spring of 1823, McHenry's first novel was *The Wilderness; or, Braddock's Times, A Tale of the West*.[4] It opens with a description of the Fraziers of County Derry, the first Ulster Protestant immigrant family in American fiction. Gilbert Frazier is born about 1700, "somewhere between Colerain and Londonderry." At twenty-one he marries Nelly M'Clean, "a pretty rosy-cheeked, fair-skinned Irish girl," and they settle on the townland of Maughrygowan. His ambition to make her "a lady" prompts a plan to make his fortune in America and then to return to Ireland. Gilbert estimates that this will take him seven years, for his is the immigrant's dream of easy wealth, and America is "the bright Eldorado of his imagination, where everything he did was to be so richly remunerated, that his very scratching of the ground would cause it to teem with wealth, and spreading his hands to heaven would bring down a shower of gold." Gilbert and Nelly sail from Londonderry in April of 1723, and their passage follows the familiar rhythm. Tearful when the promontory of Inishowen fades from sight, they experience a "boisterous" and sickness-ridden voyage of three months, and land in Philadelphia with "twenty gold guineas." When these have been reduced to ten, Gilbert perceives with some dismay that he will have to go to work: "Work! an' was it for that, after a', that I left the snug toonlan' o' Maughrygowan, an' cam' owre the ocean, whan I thoucht I wad become a gentleman on my very landin!" (I, 7-8).

McHenry attributes the Fraziers' Ulster burr, along with their ambition and frugality, to their "mixture of Scotch Blood." Gilbert is a Presbyterian and a devout supporter of his "kirk," and when his first-born son is christened Patrick, "in honor of his native tutelary saint," McHenry is quick to point out that Gilbert is "no Catholic." Although "the warmth of his Irish blood" is responsible for occasional "levities and indiscretions," these are few in number (I, 10-11). Moreover, McHenry soon introduces a lower-class Irish Catholic character for contrast and comic relief. This is Peter M'Fall, a Dublin "body servant," who speaks with a pronounced, uneducated brogue, and delivers an exasperating prattle of bullish circumlocutions and colorful metaphors. His expressions brand him as a superstitious Catholic ("Holy Bridget!," "By my sowl, sir!," "By the holy Derg!"), and he can be counted on to sing and dance at the drop of a hat, even in the threatening wilderness, for, as McHenry explains, "the Irish" are noted for "a fervency of feeling, by which they are enabled to suppress the suggestions of care." Congenitally merry, superstitious, and incapable of giving a straight answer, Peter M'Fall is, in short, a stage Irishman.

Peter is the servant of the novel's real hero, Charles Adderly, an idealized paragon of virtue and the son of another Ulster Protestant immigrant who has become a wealthy merchant in Philadelphia. It was as a student at Trinity College, Dublin, that Charles met and hired Peter. They enter the novel in 1752, with Charles leading an expedition to the Ohio River to take possession of a tract of land for the "Ohio Company," of which his father is a director. Near this tract, Gilbert Frazier and his family are now farming with great success. McHenry gets them there through a series of wildly implausible events, including capture and transportation to the West by Indians. Along the way, the Fraziers have had several children and adopted one daughter, Maria.

Charles Adderly meets the Fraziers when he stumbles upon their farm after surviving a battle along the river with French and Indian forces bent on keeping the Ohio Company out of their territory. Coincidentally, Adderly's father Thomas is revealed as an old friend of Gilbert Frazier's from the same area of Ulster, and when the beautiful Maria sings a song about their shared home, "The Haunts of Larne," Charles promptly falls in love with her. This is almost certainly a poem by Larne-native James McHenry, who wrote much verse lamenting his exile from Ireland. A delicate, decorous piece ("Ah! Lovely Larne! must I ne'er see, ne'er see thee more?" I, 107), it contrasts strongly with "Peter M'Fall's song," which registers feelings of loss to very different effect ("In Ireland so frisky, / with girls and with whiskey, / How happy was I when a strapping young lad," I, 80). Thus, McHenry further distinguishes Protestant from Catholic Irish.

The plot of *The Wilderness* soon thickens to the consistency of pea soup with the introduction of the young Colonel George Washington, who comes to the West in November, 1753, as a special envoy from Virginia Governor Dinwiddie to attempt a settlement with the French at Fort Le Boeuf, near the Frazier farm. His mission fails, the French and Indian War begins in earnest, and Washington returns to Virginia, but not before he also falls in love with Maria Frazier. Two years later he is back in the wilderness with General Braddock's army, which suffers a disastrous defeat and the death of its commander at the Battle of Braddock's Field. At this point, McHenry claims to give "more circumstantial details" of Braddock's "celebrated but unfortunate expedition" than are available in "any public history at present extant." This bid for a wide readership was successful enough for the book to have a London edition, also published in 1823, with the sub-title, *The Youthful Days of Washington.*

After the battle, the Fraziers and Charles Adderly decide to move back East to Philadelphia, because of the increased danger from French and Indian dominance of the Ohio River area. Charles marries Maria, and though Colonel Washington takes this personal defeat gracefully, we are left with the implication (however unkind to his wife Martha) that his subsequent devotion to his country is a direct result of his rejection by Maria. The novel contains many additional twists of plot, and one last wrinkle solidifies McHenry's first effort as a conventional romantic novelist. All through the 500 pages, a noble and dignified Indian prophet named Tonnaleuka has been getting Charles Adderly, the Fraziers, and even Washington, out of trouble on a regular basis. At the end, he reveals himself to be Maria Frazier's real father, an aristocratic Scotch Highlander who fled to America after support for the Stuarts collapsed following the death of Queen Anne. Thus, no Indian is presented as being too virtuous, and Maria ends up being enough of a blue blood to marry the hero without scandalizing the fiction-buying public.

An early (August, 1823) reviewer saw the "hand of genius" in *The Wilderness*, but also found the dialogue "heavy" and the story "needlessly amplified." Nine years later in 1832, in a piece satirically titled "Irish-American Literature," the *New England Magazine* displayed a fully developed prejudice in describing Gilbert Frazier as "an Irish bog-trotter" and declaring that the "verbal style" of the novel could not be judged, "seeing that it is not written in English."[5] *The Wilderness* is certainly a much flawed piece of work, saddled by the conventions of popular romance—static, stereotyped characters and the sort of preposterous, convoluted plotting that John M. Moore sends up in *Tom Stapleton.* The novel is notable chiefly for its pioneering presentation of two contrasting Irish immigrant types: sober, industrious, persevering Ulster Protestant farmers and gentry, and the flighty, loquacious Dublin Catholic body-servant. *The Irish Emigrant* of 1817 had countered these stereotypes somewhat in its portrayal of a Catholic aristocratic hero. With *The Wilderness*, on the other hand, James McHenry brings back the social and religious stereotypes established by most English and Anglo-Irish novelists and playwrights who had dealt with Ireland up to the 1820s. To American readers of the Edgeworths and the Sheridans, Charles Adderly and Peter M'Fall were familiar faces indeed.

A year after *The Wilderness*, in 1824, McHenry published his first novel with a wholly Irish setting, *O'Halloran; or, The Insurgent Chief, An Irish Historical Tale of 1798.* In the preface, McHenry claims to give a strictly impartial rendering of major events of "the conspiracy and insurrection of the United Irishmen," whom he nonetheless praises for their "talents, courage, and disinterested patriotism." He further claims to include "numerous facts that have never yet appeared in print" about the rising in his native Antrim, portions of which, "it was our lot, although then in our childhood, personally to witness." (McHenry had been a boy of thirteen in Larne in 1798, and his early poem "Patrick" had also dealt with aspects of the rising.) He goes on to explain that writing this book fulfills a promise made to his Aunt Nancy, who wanted him to publish a narrative of the rising, "interweaving therewith . . . an account of the views and feelings, manners and customs of the people of Ulster, at the conclusion of the last century." A student of Irish history and politics, Aunt Nancy had marked the absence of "anything like an accurate account of the people among whom she had spent her whole existence." She had particularly deplored "the invidious and unfair comparison" drawn by "the authoress of the 'Wild Irish Girl' . . . between the Southern and Northern inhabitants of the Island." The best-selling Irish novel of Sydney Owenson, Lady Morgan had had six American editions in 1807 and 1808. It features a love affair between a profligate Protestant Ascendancy figure and the mysterious daughter of a dispossessed Catholic chieftain and protector of the old Gaelic culture. This contrast rankled McHenry, who goes on to defend his Ulster Protestant compatriots by declaring that Lady Morgan "ought, especially, to have spared her attacks upon that portion, to whose activity and intelligence the nation is chiefly indebted for whatever it possesseth of either prosperity or importance." Such sentiments thus prepare the reader for a continuation of the contrast between Northern Protestants and Southern Catholics in *The Wilderness*.

No improvement over his previous novels, the plot of *O'Halloran* is another popular-romance stew of calamities, coincidence, disguised identities, and a tangled story of love, unrequited, requited, villainous, and pure. The novel's importance is in its successful fulfillment of McHenry's two aims, as his preface concludes, of presenting in American fiction the first "fair statement of the manners of the people of Ulster, and of the part they had taken in the late rebellion." This time around, McHenry's hero is twenty-two-year-old Edward Barrymore, a Dublin-bred member of a wealthy, titled family of Irish Protestants, supporters of "every high-handed measure of the government" in Ireland, and "rigid sticklers for the protestant ascendancy" (27). The time is May 1797, and Edward, having just graduated from Trinity College, is vacationing on the Antrim coast. He slips on the rocks and is rescued from drowning by O'Halloran of O'Halloran Castle, the area's Protestant landlord and a leader of the United Irishmen, who plan an armed rising against British rule. Falling in love with O'Halloran's beautiful granddaughter, Ellen Hamilton, Edward soon learns of the coming rebellion. In contrast to the author of *The Irish Emigrant*, who fully supported the "Year of Liberty," McHenry, through his spokesman Edward Barrymore, believes in the Union of Great Britain and Ireland. He agrees with the "just and constitutional demands" that caused the United Irishmen to be founded: "a reform in the representation of the commons, emancipation of the catholics, and a melioration of the tythe system," whereby Catholics had to pay to support the Protestant clergy (48). McHenry attributes most of the worsening trouble to the appointment as Viceroy of Lord Camden, whose harsh policies increased oppression and drove the Irish toward the radical alternative of armed revolution to break the tie with England. This, McHenry (and Barrymore) abhor. The novel describes in detail the reaction in Antrim to the imprisonment and execution for treason of the popular farmer, William Orr, "a respectable man of this county," and McHenry declares that Ulster would not have risen if, instead of the innocent Orr, the government had picked "some profligate disseminator of the newfangled French doctrines of deism and equality . . . as the victim of its vengeful policy" (164).

In *O'Halloran*, these views are shared by two additional spokesmen for moderation, both of whom serve as alter egos for McHenry. "The Recluse," Saunders, a mysterious hermit of the coastal caves, urges Edward Barrymore to help him dissuade O'Halloran from taking up arms as a United Irish leader. (He is later revealed to be Ellen Hamilton's father, in hiding because he killed a man in an honorable duel.) Edward's other judicious friend is M'Nelvin, a young poet and Ellen's unrequited lover. At several points in the novel, drawing-room entertainments at O'Halloran Castle feature poems by M'Nelvin and the Recluse, and these turn out to be actual poems by McHenry. The familiar themes include a patriotic lament for Ireland's past culture and the song of an American exile. Like the poet M'Nelvin, James McHenry had a hunched back. In addition, Ellen was the name given to McHenry's lost love in several poems and a story. In what is surely something of a self-portrait, McHenry describes M'Nelvin as warm-hearted, but "prey to a melancholy disposition," because of his great "susceptibility of feeling" (113). And the poet is speaking for the author when he speaks passionately of "the natural rights of man," the "iniquity of arbitrary rule," the "maintenance of security and order" through enforced laws, and "the accumulating miseries of his country," due to "mismanagement" by Lord Camden (120). There is no question of dissolving the British connection here. M'Nelvin and Barrymore feel that changes in the law and its administrators will solve Ireland's political problems.

This Unionist position is confirmed in Edward Barrymore's actions following the failure of the rising in Antrim. McHenry describes the fighting that took place in June 1798, including the skirmish at Larne that he may have observed as a boy. As leader of the Antrim United Irishmen, O'Halloran here takes the position held in reality by Henry Joy McCracken, the dashing young Presbyterian cotton manufacturer who was later executed for his participation in the rising. O'Halloran fares better. Tried and sentenced to hang, he is freed when Edward Barrymore pays a 3000-pound fine. Edward's true political feelings come out, however, when the French land a small force at Killala, County Mayo, in August to support the rebellion. Both he and his father enlist in the army of Lord Cornwallis, which defeats the French and ends the threat to British rule.[6] Naturally, as his reward for service, Edward wins the hand of Ellen Hamilton, and her grandfather O'Halloran lives long enough to see several great-grandchildren.

McHenry mends Lady Morgan's slanders by making all of his admirable characters good Irish Protestants: the hero Edward Barrymore, O'Halloran and his granddaughter, her father Saunders and the poet M'Nelvin. Moreover, as in *The Wilderness*, the only Catholic who figures at all in this novel is the hero's comical servant. Edward's "man" Tom Mullins is a "wild Irishman" from "up the country" with a penchant for drink and a pretty face. McHenry's own anti-Catholic feelings surface when Tom explains that he went into service because "priest O'Bletherem" refused to give him a dispensation to marry his second cousin without a twenty-pound bribe, and "swore he would never let our souls, that is after they are dead, out of purgatory, if we got married and didn't pay him" (96-97).

A significant attempt to describe the "manners of Ulster" is McHenry's introduction of blind Arthur O'Neil, the last of the great Irish harpers, to give Ellen Hamilton lessons. Fully appreciative of the Irish musical tradition, Edward Barrymore looks at O'Neil as "a remnant of antiquity," and "yield[s] him all that veneration and homage which was once yielded to the bards of Tara." Moved by the old air, the "Blackbird," Edward rues O'Neil's position as the last of his kind, but the harper replies that "I shall no more be the last of Irish harpers, than M'Nelvin shall be the last of Irish poets. Yes; gloomy as our present prospects now are, a day shall yet dawn in which the bard and the harp shall flourish together, and be cherished in the hearts of Irishmen" (41-42). This exchange seems a direct reply to *The Wild Irish Girl*, in which the Catholic heroine's harp is a symbol of the decline of the old Gaelic culture and its neglect by the Protestant leadership.[7]

McHenry's other attempts at evocation of the local color of his home place help relieve the tedium of his plot. These include descriptions of the Antrim countryside and wild coast and the homes and dialect of the area's Presbyterian farmers. One vivid picture is the monthly yarn market at Larne, where Edward Barrymore finds a bustling scene of clothes and cutlery hawkers, "travelling hucksters called ginger-bread women," a man atop a table "selling waistcoat patterns and shawls by auction," and "an old female balladeer" who sings a new rebel song, the ballad of "Blarris Moor." McHenry comments that such songs "did more to increase the numbers of the conspirators than all the efforts of the French emissaries, or the writings and harangues of all the political philosophers, and age-of-reason men of the times" (62-63).

Despite many limitations, thus, *O'Halloran; or, The Insurgent Chief* has some merit. McHenry does bring news of the North of Ireland into American fiction, with his moderate Unionist picture of the 1798 rebellion in Counties Antrim and Mayo, and his sketches of Ulster geography, society, and musical culture, from the harp to street balladry. In addition, he provides a fictional self-portrait in M'Nelvin, the idealistic, melancholy poet. The failure of such meliorist measures as he advocates in the novel to alleviate distress in Ireland may have been one reason for the young author's emigration twenty years after the rebellion.

Even if he had a backlog of manuscripts to draw upon, McHenry was publishing fiction at a furious pace in the early 1820s. His fourth novel in three years, *The Hearts of Steel: An Irish Historical Tale of the Last Century*, appeared in 1825. In a valuable preface, McHenry speaks directly of his own goals and of issues central to the pre-Famine Irish-American community. He begins by announcing an ambitious project of historical fiction using Irish materials. Coming hard on the heels of *O'Halloran*, with its treatment of the "Ninety-eighters," this new novel is the second of a planned series of "national narratives" which will delineate "the character, objects, and proceedings of each of the principal insurrectionary confederacies that have, for the last two hundred and fifty years, afflicted Ireland." Toward this end, McHenry claims to have collected "both from traditional and written sources, much information not to be met with in regular history," because "for many years" he "possessed the very best opportunities of collecting these traditions." (He was over thirty when he left Antrim for America.) He goes on to explain that the Hearts of Steel was a secret society formed "thirty years anterior" to the events of 1798 in *O'Halloran*, and that the projected third volume will go back further still, to 1690 and the Battle of the Boyne, and will describe the achievements of Ulster's "celebrated 'Enniskilleners'" in "that critical period of Irish history." This volume never appeared, but the breadth of the project outlined here is impressive.

McHenry further declares that his second concern is linguistic. Once again, he will reproduce the language of Ulster's "lower and middle classes," who speak "a dialect very similar to that spoken by the Scotch Lowlanders, from whom they are mostly descended. The more perceptible shades of difference between these dialects consist in the tone and turn of the expression, and the structure of the sentences, rather than in the pronunciation of the words, although in this there is also a frequent dissimilarity." Also apparent in *The Wilderness* and *O'Halloran*, McHenry's scrupulous attention to dialect is explained in this preface as a part of his largest ambition—to enlighten the American audience about Ulster, and, in so doing, to refute an already well-established character stereotype:

> It would seem as if no other idea could be entertained of an Irishman than that of a rash, superstitious, although sometime shrewd ignoramus, who can neither speak without making a bull, nor act without making a blunder. It is

imagined that the Irish are all Papists and bog-trotters. It is forgot, or rather in most instances it is not known, that in the province of Ulster alone, nearly two millions of people, at least one-fourth of the population of the whole Island, are neither the one or the other.

It would also seem that McHenry has forgot his own contributions to the stage-Irish tradition—the Catholic body-servants in his earlier works. When he continues in this vein, however, his own prejudice emerges: "The world is scarcely ever informed that an industrious, prosperous, and intelligent race of men, equal in number to the whole population of Scotland, inhabit the Northern province of Ireland, who possess scarcely a single trait of character resembling that compound of turbulence, rudeness, ignorance, superstition, servility, and awkwardness, which, in the conception of foreigners, constitutes the half-civilized being called an Irishman." For this "false notion of the Irish character," Mc-Henry blames "the Teagues, the Pats, the Larrys, and the Dennises of a tribe of romance-writers who have endeavored to amuse their readers with pictures of Irish buffoonery." He recognizes these as "mere copies of copies," traceable in literature from "the days of the Tudors" to "Miss Edgeworth herself." Contrary to the stereotypes, McHenry claims for the Irish remarkable diversity of character, and finds only one trait "common to them all; namely warmth of temperament," which, however, also "varies extremely, not only in degree, but in mode of operation, in different districts, and among different classes." (Remarked in *The Irish Emigrant* as well, this "warmth" seems to be the universal Irish characteristic, found in Catholics, Protestants, lowborn and highborn.) Finally, McHenry warns "the reader of the following history" not to expect to be "diverted by the blundering of bull-makers, or the clownishness of bog-trotters. . . . for the simple reason that none such are indigenous to the country that witnessed the exploits of the Hearts of Steel," although "some such characters may be found in certain districts of Ireland," and "in former times, they may have been numerous enough to have formed a prominent feature in the character of the country."

As this preface suggests, *The Hearts of Steel* contains a full fictional treatment of a central controversy of nineteenth-century Irish-American life: the "Scotch-Irish" question. Here, as in *The Wilderness*, McHenry creates characters that embody the Ulster Presbyterian's desire to disassociate himself from the unwashed hordes of Irish Catholic immigrants. The tone is set in the opening pages by McHenry's distorted perspective on the plantation of Ulster by his lowland-Scots forebears in the seventeenth century. He sees the wholesale confiscation of Catholic property as a "plausible" reaction to "native Irish" lack of hospitality, "the intolerance, harshness, and cruelty with which, whenever they had the power, they treated the professors of the British religion who lived amongst them" (I, 3-4). The specific vehicle for this rationalization of the British national policy of plunder is McHenry's presentation of the only fully rendered Catholic family in his fiction, the M'Manuses. Dispossessed of his ancestral lands in County Meath after the Battle of the Boyne, Brian M'Manus flees with his clan followers to the glens of Antrim, where he dies, bequeathing to his son Dermid "a bigotted and useless hatred towards England and Protestantism." Brought up to "ignorance and sloth," Dermid spends his time harassing fair-minded Protestant magistrates who are only doing their duty by prosecuting "any Catholic culprit." He is encouraged by "a fanatical priest," Father O'Dogherty, who preaches that "the duty and glory of every true Catholic" is "to cherish eternal hatred, and to inflict on every fair opportunity an unrelenting revenge" upon Ulster Protestants. "To rob a Protestant was, in his estimation, meritorious and honorable; and to murder one, a passport to Heaven." McHenry is careful not to generalize to all Catholics, and he points out that the priest who replaces O'Dogherty is "a man of mild temper and more liberal views." However, there are no admirable Catholic major characters in this novel, and McHenry's sympathies are clear throughout. Dermid M'Manus passes on his hatred of Protestants and the "family distemper" of "audacious turbulence" to Edmund, or "Munn," his first son, who grows up to support, passionately and irrationally, what McHenry calls "the Catholic, or aboriginal Irish side" of all questions. On the other hand, second son Bernard is influenced by the "well known principles of peace and toleration" of his mother, the daughter of a Protestant. Developing "a distaste for the superstitious religion of his fathers," Bernard ultimately turns Protestant (after McHenry has led us through refutations of papal infallibility, the pope's claim of succession from St. Peter, and transubstantiation), and solidifies his conversion by marrying the daughter of a Presbyterian minister, Reverend McCulloch.

Naturally, the contrast between the adult lives of these two M'Manus sons supports McHenry's distinction between Catholics and Protestants. Bernard becomes a faithful husband and father. After his wife dies suddenly, he leaves his infant daughter Isabella with her grandfather (instructing Reverend McCulloch to keep her safe from the Catholics), and sets off to make his fortune. Heartbroken at not being able to support his family at home, Bernard here conveys the sense of loss at leaving Antrim that appears in all three relevant McHenry novels. On the other hand, Munn becomes a full-time troublemaker. First a free-lance night-raider against the Protestants, then a smuggler of illegal whiskey, he graduates to serious political intrigue in 1745, by leading 150 men over to Scotland in support of Charles-Edward, the Pretender. After the defeat of the insurgent Highlanders at Culloden, Munn returns to Ireland in hopes of instigating a rising there. He becomes a founder of the Hearts of Steel, a new secret society which begins by maiming cattle and burning barns, but moves on to torture and murder of a Protestant estate agent. The

"Steel-Men" are ultimately suppressed and the novel ends with a reconciling marriage in the younger generation.

The Hearts of Steel is a clumsy, long-winded novel of 750 pages with a tortuous plot that has only been touched on here. McHenry does, however, succeed in filling out further his picture of Ulster. For example, his descriptions of dwelling-places provide a microcosm of eighteenth-century Irish society previously unavailable to an American audience. These range from a decorous Ascendancy castle, to Reverend M'Culloch's frugal, spotless cottage, to the thatched, dirt-floored, two-room cabin of a Presbyterian small farmer, with oaten cakes "hardening" over a turf-fire. Of particular interest is the sagging but still impressive mansion of the exiled M'Manuses, old Catholic aristocrats running to seed on a promontory in County Antrim. Surrounded by a stable, coach-house, barn, and garden, their two-story, slate-roofed stone house remains "the most dignified-looking" in the area. It boasts a library of priceless Gaelic manuscripts, "the compositions of native Irish bards, philosophers, and divines, whose labours have never yet appeared in public, to the great loss of the literary world," and a harper's room, complete with the family harp, rescued from "the trying days of 1690," and "a multifarious assortment of musical books, both printed and in manuscript, principally of Irish and Gaelic origin." Lest these Catholics seem too sophisticated, McHenry undercuts the description to illustrate the corruption of the old Gaelic culture from within. The library is "hung round with crucifixes and images of saints and angels," and the family confessor, Father O'Dogherty, has supplemented the collection with "a dozen of quires filled with declamations and denunciations against England and heresy." The family harp sits unstrung, gathering dust, and Dennis M'Clurkin, harper to the M'Manuses, is something of a charlatan. Having been the only candidate for the position, he knows few of the old harp tunes and those imperfectly, and much prefers the fiddle, which he plies for his livelihood at neighborhood balls and christenings. A thoroughly "modern" musician, Dennis "neglected the more honourable for the more profitable employment" (I, 38-43). However slanted his presentation, McHenry's depiction of the M'Manuses contributes to the long tradition of aristocratic "big houses" in Irish fiction begun in Maria Edgeworth's Castle Rackrent of 1800. Like the house of the M'Dermotts in The Irish Emigrant, McHenry provides an early example of the Catholic big house.

As in all of McHenry's novels, social distinctions are here indicated by dialect or lack of it. As aristocrats, albeit Catholic and corrupted, the M'Manuses speak entirely without dialect inflections. They share with the Anglo-Irish upper classes a stilted conversational pattern that is one of the least attractive aspects of McHenry's craft as a novelist. On the other hand, the several minor characters from the Presbyterian tenantry do speak in dialect—the same near-Scots burr that McHenry remarks in the preface and uses in his earlier novels. After the high-toned flights of the major figures, the Scotch-Irish dialect is refreshingly earthy and direct. The twenty-page deathbed narrative of one old farmer's life story is an impressive tour de force.

About the doings of the Hearts of Steel McHenry is substantially correct. The agitation actually began in 1770, as a response by hard-pressed tenants to rackrenting and evictions on the Antrim estates of Lord Donegall. Cattle-maiming and destruction of barns and houses did lead to the calling of military reinforcements from Dublin, and the movement was suppressed by 1775. Many of the most active Steel-Men fled to America, where they started new "Hearts" organizations and went on to fight in numbers against the British in the American Revolution. Certainly, most Americans in 1825 were much less familiar with the Hearts of Steel than with, say, the rebellion of 1798, chronicled in *O'Halloran*. And so, McHenry's second Irish novel can be said to have provided significant historical background about the North of Ireland. Once again, his elucidation of the history and manners of his native place excuses, to an extent, a creaking, romantic plot and cardboard characterizations.

McHenry's other literary ventures can be quickly summarized. His *American Monthly Magazine* lasted only one year (1824), during which time it provided a forum for his very definite opinions about literature and politics. Although an Ulster Protestant, he blames the troubles in Ireland on abuses of the system by rapacious landlords, and he also advocates Catholic Emancipation, which Daniel O'Connell's political force was to win in a limited way in 1829. In literary matters, he frequently lambasts the "Lake School of Poets," and urges a return to the classical style of Pope. Produced in Philadelphia in December 1827, McHenry's first play, *The Usurper*, made use of Celtic legendary materials. A blank-verse drama of murderous, over-reaching ambition set in the Druidic past, the play's only distinction is its position as the first tragedy based on Irish myth to be performed on an American stage. Other plays and novels followed, none of them using Irish materials, and McHenry's unfortunate final bid for literary immortality was an unreadable epic poem in ten books based on the Old Testament account of the Flood, *The Antediluvians; or, The World Destroyed*, published in 1839 and 1840.[8]

In an essay in his *American Monthly* in 1824, McHenry remarked a cultural change in his lifetime from a general attitude that novel-reading was a frivolous waste of time to a respect for fiction as a source of information. Contending that historical novels were superior to ordinary fiction, he thus justified his own attempts in the genre, as providing the materials of history in a more palatable form. (He also tested his potential audience by printing excerpts from his two Irish novels in his magazine.) The audience was apparently not forthcoming, for neither *O'Halloran* nor *The Hearts of Steel* had a second edition in McHenry's lifetime, while at least two of his American historical novels were reprinted. This lack of popular success is probably the reason why McHenry abandoned his idea to chronicle 250 years of Irish rebellions in fiction. He suggests as much in the introduction to his novel of 1831, *Meredith; or, The Mystery of the Meschianza, A Tale of the American Revolution*. In an invented dialogue, the publisher tells the author that his previous novel, *The Betrothed of Wyoming* (a tale of Indian massacre in Western Pennsylvania in 1776), did well enough, and that he should go on to produce another "short but sweet" novel; "And hark ye, Mr. Novelist, let it be truly American, and historical, and descriptive, if you please, of the spirit-stirring times of our glorious Revolution" (6). Never able to support his family by writing alone, McHenry continued to practice medicine sporadically, and even kept a draper's shop near his home on Second Street in Philadelphia. A familiar figure in the city's literary and journalistic circles, he became a close friend of one of the best known Irish Americans of his day, publisher, journalist, and occasional Hudibrastic poet, Mathew Carey. Through the good luck of a political connection, McHenry was appointed United States Consul at Londonderry in October, 1842, and he died at the age of sixty in 1845, while on consular duty in his old hometown of Larne.

The three novels discussed here contain James McHenry's best work. Though hobbled by the conventions of popular romance, all make pioneering contributions to the Irish voice in America. Scattered earlier pieces exist (notably *The Irish Emigrant* of 1817), but McHenry's is the first examination sustained over several works of important themes. He introduces Irish Protestant characters, the Ulster setting, and the Scotch-Irish dialect. He presents the attitudes of Ulster Presbyterian immigrants toward Irish Catholics and Irish nationalism. In this regard, his novels and prefaces demonstrate that even before the Famine, the Scotch-Irish saw themselves, and wanted Americans to see them, as emphatically better prospective citizens than the Catholics from the South. Furthermore, although he acknowledges that Irish peasants have real grievances, McHenry never condones the struggle for separation from Great Britain. He may be a citizen of recently separated America, but he remains an Ulster Unionist, and his series of novels was to have been a history of "insurrectionary confederacies that have . . . afflicted Ireland." Needless to say, these views were not often shared by the Catholic novelists of the succeeding, Famine generation. In addition, McHenry's two Irish novels and his ambitious though unfulfilled plan for more constitute early concrete embodiments of the transfer to American soil of the Irish historical imagination. Fed by the immigrant's nostalgia for home, the backward look becomes a prime impetus for Irish-American novelists. Finally, that plan to use in fiction 250 years of Irish revolutionary history exemplifies what remains James McHenry's most attractive trait—his whole-hearted, energetic commitment to a writing career through those hard, early days on the American literary scene when only Washington Irving and James Fenimore Cooper were truly successful. There is apparent in McHenry's string of novels, plays, essays, lyric poems, and, yes, even his antediluvian epic, a confident enthusiasm that still comes through as admirable.

The son of Irish Catholic immigrants, Charles James Cannon was born in New York City on November 4, 1800. With no advantages of wealth or education, he grew up and earned his living as a clerk in the New York Customs House and a part-time advisor to Catholic publisher Edward Dunigan, for whose company he compiled school readers and a spelling book. Devoted to literature, Cannon belonged to a circle of New York Catholic intellectuals, including priest-novelist Reverend Dr. Charles Constantine Pise and historian of American Catholicism John Gilmary Shea. Cannon seems always to have been frustrated at the small amount of writing time available to him, and yet he managed, like James McHenry, to turn his hand to all manner of literary ventures. In the course of a doggedly tenacious career, he produced four volumes of verse, several plays, and nine works of fiction. The poems and plays, unvaryingly sentimental and conventional, are far from memorable, although one of the latter, *The Oath of Office*, was performed at New York's Bowery Theater in March, 1850. Set in fifteenth-century Ireland, it dramatizes the familiar, tragic story of Mayor Lynch of Galway City, who hanged his own son (thereby coining a term for vigilante execution by the rope) to observe the letter of the law and his "oath of office."[9]

Following his first collection of poems by two years, Cannon's first novel, *Oran, The Outcast; or, A Season in New York*, appeared in 1833. Published anonymously, as were all but one of his nine novels, it was dedicated to James Fenimore Cooper, "not more as a mark of admiration for his genius, than respect for the pure republicanism of his principles," and it contains a conversation in which Cooper is praised by a main character, Margaret Hosmer, as "the most purely American of any writer amongst us." The first hint of Cannon's connection with Ireland comes when her other favorite novelists are listed as including (along with Scott, Irving, and Miss Sedgewick), three Irish writers—Banim, "Lady Morgan, with all her flippancy," and "Miss Edgeworth." Not that things Irish or Irish-American have much to do with *Oran, the Outcast*. In his dedication, Cannon states that his aim is "delineating the manners of that portion of NEW YORK SOCIETY, which arrogates to itself the title of "GOOD," and to this end he spins a conventional romantic yarn of love, mystery, and identity concealed and revealed, involving genteel New Yorkers with names like Tenniswood and Moneyflush. In among the thrills and coincidences is a mild attempt at satiric exposure of the pretensions to superiority of New York's upper class. And here the Irish come in—as objects of unwarranted scorn. For example, a servant described as "a short, stout, sandy-haired, freckle-faced daughter of the 'ould sod,' in a short, thin, pink muslin frock, long black woolen petticoat, high leather shoes, and blue stockings," is criticized by the socialite Miss Tenniswood for speaking too freely: "The ideas of independence and equality with which the creatures' heads are filled, render them almost useless." Miss Hosmer responds by calling her friend "a sad little aristocrat" (I, 36-37).

Early in the novel, to refute his friend's opinion that "the poor of this city may be divided into two classes—the dissipated and the depraved," the enlightened protagonist Chillingworth takes him on an errand of mercy "to an Irish family, living at the farther extremity of a wretched alley." They come into a room "neither spacious nor comfortable," but "perfectly clean." What follows is the first description of an Irish tenement room in an American city by a writer who could have been raised in such a place:

> The well-scrubbed floor had been lately sanded; the few chairs were arranged so as to give all possible room; the table, on which were three lighted candles, was covered with a coarse white cloth, and, on a broad unplaned board, laid upon the naked cords of a bedstead, lay the corpse of a child. At the fire sat a couple of old women smoking, and talking in a low tone, in a language not understood by the young men, and on the floor stood a short, stout, middle-aged woman, wringing her hands in all the violence of a mother's grief, who exclaimed, on beholding Chillingworth, "Och, but this is the sorrowful house for you to come to this morning, sir!" [I, 104-05]

Cannon is not ready to develop such characters, however. When Chillingworth offers to pay the burial expenses, he is told they have been paid by "Mr. Oran, the Outcast," and we are returned to the central mystery of the novel. The tangled plot hinges on Oran Lorton, the mixed-blood son of a former slave and her master, General Olmsted, who has been disowned and rendered an outcast by his father. Somehow, he becomes a secret force for good in New York, providing funds and sympathy for the poor, and, ultimately, solving the problem of a misplaced murder indictment, thus allowing Miss Hosmer to marry. Although the themes of slavery and miscegenation are potentially explosive, Cannon makes little of them here, and the novel ends with a cloying love poem on the happiness of the newly married couple.

Oran, the Outcast, is most interesting for what it omits. The Irish characters are few, inconsequential, and patronizingly presented as capable of speaking freely, testifying to the truth, keeping a clean house, and feeling real grief. Even more significant, given Cannon's subsequent religious fiction, is the total absence of reference to the Catholic Church. In this, his first attempt to follow his idol, Cooper, to literary fame, Cannon has minimized his own background to produce a thoroughly conventional romance, whose main characters are all upper-class New York Protestants.

Cannon's second work of fiction, *Facts, Feelings and Fancies* (1835) consists of a motley group of stories and poems, for which the author apologizes in a preface, stating that "most of the pieces . . . were written years ago, in the intervals of labour or disease, by one who has never known the advantages of education," and others "were hastily concluded while his work was going through the press."[10] "Remorse" is a florid tale of love and intrigue in a Hudson River village among aristocratic New York Dutchmen. "Estelle" is a love story set in medieval France, "Cousin Sue" describes New York and New Jersey "squires" about town, and "Amy Dayton" tells of love and treason during the American Revolution. These are the disparate attempts of a young author in search of his proper subject matter. The book is notable only for the inclusion of Cannon's first Catholic and Irish stories. The former is a stock, melodramatic endeavor, "The Cross," the deathbed narrative of an American "Indian nun," a Catholic convert who is martyred with a rosary around her neck.

Far and away the best work in the collection is Cannon's first Irish story, "The Beal Fire" (101-19), which takes place in County Donegal around the time of the rebellion of 1798. This curiously elliptical tale suggests Cannon's difficulty in getting time to write, for it seems more like notes for a novel than a finished story. Far too much happens in its nineteen pages, and yet it is more sparely written than the other fiction in the collection. Cannon introduces a set of conflicts familiar in the literature of Irish nationalism: Catholics vs. Protestants, the peasantry vs. the aristocracy, and love for a woman vs. devotion to the cause. The story is set on the Donegal coast near Bloody Foreland Point, where a rising is being planned by the priest Father Egan (inspired by the American Revolution, which he observed while a missionary), and the Mother-Ireland figure of old Norah Keenan, who declares that "peace can never come within my dwelling . . . until the freedom of my country is restored." Cannon makes use of a setting familiar in much Irish fiction. The eastern aisle of the ruined Abbey of St. Killian is the trysting place of a pair of lovers, and a vault under the abbey, reached through a coastal cave, is where the rebels meet. It is St. John's Eve, and the traditional Beal Fire lighted on a nearby hill will be an important signal. In the story's truncated climax, the rebels are captured by government troops thanks to an informer, and their leader, old Norah Keenan's son, is hanged. Cannon's only piece of Irish historical fiction, "The Beal Fire" represents one of many rejected directions in his search for suitable themes. It survives as an early (1835) appearance in American fiction of a strong voice of Irish Catholic nationalism, which is clearly presented in the character of Father Egan. As such, the story is a foil to the Presbyterian Unionist perspective in James McHenry's novels.

Typical of Cannon's verse, the poetry in this collection contains more feelings and fancies than facts. There are love sonnets, melancholy apostrophes, and pseudo-Byronic rhyming tales of dark-browed, brooding heroes. Again, though, there is interesting Irish material, including a nationalistic song of "Regenerate Erin—Erin asthore!" and a long poem,

"The Proscribed," the tragic story of two Irish patriots of the heroic age, Fergus and Nial, one more early example of the translation into Irish-American writing of Irish legendary themes.

Because Cannon was a writer of limited abilities, it is possible to trace easily his pioneering struggles with a central issue for nineteenth-century Irish-American novelists—whether and how to write identifiably religious or ethnic fiction. Following the unfocused collection of *Facts, Feelings, and Fancies*, Cannon wrestled with this issue, for the most part unsuccessfully, in his four novels of the 1840s, and his prefaces to these novels explicitly register his vacillation throughout the decade. In the first of these books, *Harry Layden: A Tale* (1842), Cannon attempts to produce a popular sentimental romance that also incorporates Catholic doctrine.[11] In the preface, he reveals his ambiguous feelings about the venture, declaring that the novel was not written primarily as a defense of his faith, but "for the purpose of saying something in favour of that portion of the Christian family which every dabbler in literature feels himself at liberty to abuse." The limping plot is stock romantic claptrap, and features the rags-to-riches progress of an orphaned hero, Harry Layden, whose unflinching Catholicism is his only unique characteristic. The Irish figure briefly at the beginning of the novel, where North-of-Ireland native Con Dorion and his large family pick up the lost, wandering Harry and take him along to Con's new job cutting a road through the back woods. (Cannon praises the Irish as the "pioneers of internal improvement" in America.) Con speaks with a bit of a brogue, and Cannon allows that he drinks to excess on his occasional trips back to New York City, where he visits the "Boys" of the "Irishtown" section. Nonetheless, the family is a happy one. However, after two years together in a log cabin, the senior Dorions both fall ill, and their children, Harry included, are given up to the Protestant Overseers of the Poor. Having survived this first test of his faith, Harry goes on to become "that worst of slaves—a Factory Boy!" in the new mill town of Rapid Run.

Cannon emphasizes the religious issue in his subplot, which traces the rocky romance between the Catholic Hugh Redmond and the New York aristocrat Agneta De Ruyter, whose violently anti-Catholic father disinherits her when she marries Hugh. Cannon also includes a description of an evangelical Protestant camp meeting, a shameful, "frenzied" three-day affair, at which a local girl is victimized by a lusting preacher. This is much worse, he assures the reader, than anything that happens at "patterns" in Ireland or Scottish "Holy Fairs." Meanwhile, after many predictable trials, Harry Layden, his Catholicism intact, emerges as a wealthy man, the inheritor of the fortune of a woman who befriended him, and marries Agneta Redmond's daughter. As she has also regained her fortune, there is plenty of money around to make comfortable the declining years of the Dorions, who return near the end of the novel. By no stretch is *Harry Layden* a good book. Its interest lies in Cannon's introduction of some Irish-American and more Catholic materials, a direction that continues in his next two novels.

With *Mora Carmody; or, Woman's Influence* (1844), Cannon began his association with the New York Catholic publishing house of Edward Dunigan, and the result was his most explicitly didactic and Catholic novel so far. A short, disclaiming preface indicates Cannon's desire to avoid being labeled as Irish. Taking exception with the reviewer of his previous work who called him "an Irish Roman Catholic," Cannon says that, although proud of his descent from people "who have suffered more for conscience' sake, during the last 300 years than all the other nations of the earth," he is not an *Irish* Catholic. Instead, "he is, what many of the maligners of the Faith which he professes are *not*, in the best sense of the word, a NATIVE AMERICAN." *Mora Carmody* is a stock conversion narrative, the aim of which, as Cannon says in a postscript, is to explain what Catholicism really is in these anti-Catholic times. (This was the year of serious anti-Irish and anti-Catholic rioting in Philadelphia, and sporadic nativist outbursts had been taking place over the preceding decade.) The only indications of Irishness are the names of the protagonists, Hugh Carmody and his saintly sister Mora, and a single mention of "the cruelties practiced, almost within our own day, by tolerant England upon poor, down-trodden Ireland, for her unshaken adherence to 'the faith once delivered to the saints' " (61).

In the book, the narrator Marbury escapes his frenetic city existence to rest in a small New England village. Lodging with the Carmody family, he discovers that they are Catholics when their nightly rosary keeps him awake. Furthermore, rather than attend the public school, young Hugh Carmody is being taught at home by his sister Mora, with whom Marbury falls in love. Of Puritan descent, he has many misgivings about Catholicism, and his heated debates with Mora are the vehicle for Cannon's elucidation of church doctrines. In their first exchange, Mora assures Marbury that some non-Catholics can get to heaven, and they are off, covering before they are finished the Spanish Inquisition, the Pope as anti-Christ, purgatory, idolatry, the Virgin Mary, and the existence of saints. During Marbury's stay, a nativist mob burns down the half-built Catholic church in the village, causing much pain to the Carmodys and giving their lodger something else to think about. All of this does, indeed, bring about Marbury's conversion, but not before he manages to lose track of the Carmodys. Five years later, Marbury contracts yellow fever in the South and is nursed in a Catholic Hospital by a Sister Anasthasia, who dies of the disease before he comes out of his fever. Shortly thereafter, Marbury meets Hugh Carmody, about to attend Georgetown University, who tells him that the nun who gave up her life for him was none other than the beloved Mora.

The influential Catholic reviewer Orestes Brownson complained that the Catholic material in *Mora Carmody* lacked the "fulness and degree of evidence which must command intellectual assent on the part of the Protestant reader," and he further advised all Catholic novelists to "invent some method of disposing of their heroines without sending them to a convent" (134-36). Perhaps in response, Cannon's next novel, *Father Felix: A Tale* (1845), contains even more instruction in church doctrine and two conversions instead of one. In his preface, Cannon declares that his ideal reader would be a Protestant who will examine "the old religion" and "become a Catholic." Farther than ever from Cannon's own experience, the protagonists are all aristocrats. Sarah and Paul Fenwick are the descendants of old-line Catholics who came to America with Lord Baltimore, and their prospective marriage partners, Anne and Adrian, both of whom convert to Catholicism to make the way smooth, are similarly well born. Again, Cannon embraces the Catholic and avoids the Irish connection. Much of the novel is a patchwork compendium of the instruction in Catholicism of Anne and Adrian by the priest Father Felix, Anne's cousin and the son of Huguenot and Puritan parents who disowned him when he converted many years earlier. Cannon even footnotes a catechism, *The Faith of Catholics*, "a book to which the author has been indebted for most of the explanations put into the mouth of Father Felix." The only reference to the Irish comes when Father Felix brings first communion to blind Johnny Dowd, who is dying of scarlet fever. The last living child of a long-suffering, poverty-stricken widow, Johnny dies the perfect, heroic death, with a prayer on his lips. The narrator declares that Mrs. Dowd's reaction is typical: "with that eloquence peculiar to the Irish in their sorrow, she bewailed the desolation of her situation" (141). Thus Cannon echoes a similar description of the deathbed eloquence of the Irish poor in his first novel, *Oran, the Outcast*.

Two years later, *Scenes and Characters from the Comedy of Life* (1847) embodies yet another shift of focus. The opening "Advertisement" heralds Cannon's abrupt departure from the ranks of Catholic-tract novelists, by claiming that "the following is a story—and nothing else;—with as few pretensions to originality of design or execution as the humblest of its class, and whether it have a moral or not the reader will determine." The novel constitutes an abrupt turnabout. Not only does it contain no lessons in Catholic doctrine, but it is also Cannon's first novel to deal in any depth with Irish-American life. However, his attitude toward both Catholicism and Irishness remains equivocal, and he has not determined the proper literary uses of either aspect of his own background. *Scenes and Characters* is an odd, incoherent novel, part satire of anti-Catholic extremism, part sentimental biography of an Irish immigrant's son. As the title suggests, it is a poorly integrated collection of vignettes embedded in a clumsy narrative that jerks along in three-year bounds. The protagonist is Jack Toland, the son of an honest Irish farmer in Maple Grove, thirty miles from Ilium in upstate New York. The family prospers because of Jack's father's industry and sobriety and his wife's talents as a spinner, but her death and his unfortunate remarriage to an idle, termagant Scottish woman lead to disaster. Mr. Toland takes to drink, and eventually dies of a fever, leaving Jack on his own, intelligent, educated, but penniless. He goes down to New York City to make his fortune, and does so, becoming a journalist and part-time poet, and marrying his childhood sweetheart. (Jack's avocation allows Cannon, like James McHenry, to recycle some of his own poems.)

Throughout the novel, Cannon's uneasiness about both Irishness and Catholicism are evident. Being Irish is equated with the propensity to drink, and little else. The narrator comments that Mr. Toland's early sobriety is "a little strange for an Irishman," and he later becomes an alcoholic. Although his faith is seen as admirable (the first Mass in Maple Grove is said in the Tolands' house), it does not save Mr. Toland from eventual dissipation and a "poor and despised" death. Nor does the church play much of a part in the life of his son Jack, who remains a Catholic and converts his fiancee, but succeeds in New York with very little spiritual inspiration. In addition, the novel's portraits of an Irish Catholic priest and his flock are ambiguous and condescending. "A fair specimen of the priests of his church, who were to be found in the Northern and Middle States" in the recent past, the "coarse-featured and uncouth" Reverend Mr. Quigley, the first priest in Maple Grove, exudes a rough-hewn piety. "With little of the gentleman in his appearance, and less in his manner, . . . with no knowledge of the literature or politics of the day to render his conversation pleasing to a chance acquaintance," Father Quigley is nonetheless a good priest, because of his devotion, zeal, and "the quiet unobtrusiveness of his demeanor," and because his parishioners "were not likely to rub off the rust which he had brought with him from home, being at that time, with few exceptions, both very poor and very illiterate."

There is detectable here a more realistic rendering of Irish-American Catholicism than Cannon had previously attempted, and its harsh terms suggest that he is trying hard to abjure the "Catholic novelist" label. Somewhat in his old vein, though, is the novel's satire of Upstate New York anti-Catholicism in the portraits of several bigoted Protestants, notably Brother Dawdling, who is convinced that "the priests in Cuba are in the habit of daily putting to death numbers of little niggers, of whose flesh they make a sort of haricot, of which they are very fond," and Brother Hoover, who gives up his general store in Ilium for a more profitable career as a temperance lecturer, and who proves himself a hypocrite by committing bigamy while in a drunken stupor. Though mildly amusing, these caricatures do not save the novel, but, rather, add discordant notes to what remains at best a mixed bag.

Scenes and Characters from the Comedy of Life appeared in 1847, one of the terrible years of the Great Hunger in Ireland. From what follows in his career, it seems that the Famine and its American consequences were catalysts for Cannon's finally finding his most appropriate fictional materials. After the four failed novels of the 1840s, all of which suffer from his inability to get perspective on his own background, Cannon published a collection of stories and two last novels that contain by far his best work, because of the more realistic and fuller engagement with the life that was his own as an Irish Catholic American in turbulent times.

In 1855, Cannon published two works of fiction, one of his worst, and one of his best. *Ravellings from the Web of Life* is a group of tales told by a circle of friends and collected by "Grandfather Greenway," Cannon's only use of an explicit pseudonym. All but one of these stories are potboilers full of the mysterious orphans and identity revelations that riddle Cannon's weakest fiction. Only one, the best of a bad lot, has anything to do with the Irish. In "The Devil's Chimney," fifteen-year-old Ellen O'Donnell comes to New York City from the North of Ireland with her father. Left an orphan, she becomes a dressmaker and works herself into a case of consumption, which is cured when she leaves the city for a job upstate in "Stoney Bottom" as nurse to the children of Mickey Muckridge, the town's political boss. The son of an Irish immigrant, a liquor dealer, and a lapsed Catholic, the boisterous "Boss Mick" is everything Cannon abhors in his fellow second-generation Irish Americans. A positive foil to Mick is his clerk, the sensitive young poet Florence Nagle, "doomed to toil, day after day, under the humiliating exactions of a cold-hearted taskmaster, . . . while the energies with which heaven has endowed [him] are . . . hourly withering away, and must soon become extinct" (303). The suffering clerk/poet is a figure for Cannon, himself, and he appears again more fully formed in Cannon's last novel, *Tighe Lyfford*. When Ellen O'Donnell meets him, Nagle is reading "Miss Owenson's 'Wild Irish Girl'," which has rekindled his sympathies for the "bitter wrongs of poor, downtrodden Erin" (276). Acting upon Ellen's advice, Nagle leaves Stoney Bottom for New York and an apprenticeship in a law office. Twelve years later, he is a successful lawyer and part-time literary man about town. The opposition of Nagle's respectable achievements and Muckridge's disreputable scramble to affluence is the story's main theme. At one other point, Cannon makes a sympathetic reference to the trials of the Famine immigrants, described as "mostly of that class, who are called by the natives, the *Low Irish*—a people who have escaped from poverty and degradation at home, to meet with labor and contempt in the land of the stranger" (316). In the novel published that same year, Cannon finally becomes explicit in an extended way about these matters of pressing contemporary concern.

Bickerton: or, The Immigrant's Daughter, is Cannon's only novel to be grounded in current events.[12] It was published in 1855, and the eight years (his longest gap) since his previous novel had seen the worst of the Famine, the beginning of the floodtide of immigration to America, and the institutionalizing of nativist reaction in the Order of United Americans, or "Know-Nothing" Party, in sixteen states. By making plausible fictional use of this urgent historical context, Cannon was able to write his most coherent and realistic novel, in which he confronts the collision of immigration and nativism that was disrupting American life in the early 1850s.

Once again, Cannon's preface is ambivalent and self-deprecating. He insists on the truth of his novel's portrait of intolerance, but explains that he has declined to draw a complete portrait of American bigotry so as not "to frighten the timid, or to hold up to the hatred or scorn of other nations the land of his birth." He then apologizes for introducing theological extracts "into a work of light literature," but declares that these express his own convictions authoritatively. But he goes on to undercut himself by "granting, to those who do not like that kind of reading, his full permission to pass them unread." Cannon has thus apologized in advance for criticizing American bigotry toward the Irish and including Catholic doctrinal materials. So compromised a man could never have been a first-rate artist, and yet, the very tensions that defeated him make his work a clarifying embodiment of Irish-American identity in the eventful twenty-five years from the early 1830s to the later 1850s.

Bickerton is the only Cannon novel to follow the archetypal pattern of the immigrant narrative: a backward look at the old country, the crossing as transition and trial, the traumatic landing in an alien land, and the hard road to respectability. It opens on the deck of a crowded immigrant ship from which Manus O'Hanlon, driven from home "by the scourge of the oppressor," sees Ireland for the last time, "a mere speck between sky and sea." A sailor roughly pushes him below ("there's no room for such as you here"), and O'Hanlon muses wryly, "Heaven help us! . . . there seems no place for such as me any where." In steerage, the O'Hanlons commiserate in Gaelic, which Cannon praises fo containing so many "beautiful terms of endearment," but Mrs. O'Hanlon is inconsolable at the loss of "home and country." She reaches America in a weakened condition, believing that she has come here "only to die." The Irish passengers are dumped on a sand spit in New Jersey, through the scheming collusion of "bloodsuckers" (the agents at Derry and the shipowners), who thus avoid having to pay a New York City tax on immigrants. Rain falls steadily, O'Hanlon's money is stolen, and his wife dies and is buried in the sand, "in a grave unmarked by cross or stone, dug by the hands of her husband." Cannon has made this the most harsh of beginnings.

With his young daughter to support, the grieving O'Hanlon takes the first job offered, canal digging in the Midwest, and is thrust in with a gang of his "greenhorn" countrymen, whom Cannon is quick to criticize with some passion as unrestrained, savage, and "ignorant as the iniquitous laws under which they were born could make them" (26-27). Drunkenness, nightly brawling, and "faction fights" on Sundays "have left a stain upon the Irish name in that part of the country which will not soon, if ever, be effaced." Cannon somewhat mitigates this indictment by declaring that "the labours of the missionary priest, and of the true disciples of Father Mathew" (the famous Irish temperance priest) in the years since the O'Hanlons emigrated in the previous generation have brought a "vast moral improvement of our canal laborers." Manus O'Hanlon remains aloof from his rowdy fellow workers, and spends his scanty leisure time with his daughter, educating her, taking long walks in the country, and planning for their future. Although he has acquaintances in New York City, he wants to save enough money on his own to appear before them respectably. He works until winter, only to find that the job's contractor, Dougherty, has fled in the night with all of his laborers' earnings. Bitterly disappointed at such treatment by one of his own, weakened to near exhaustion by his labor, O'Hanlon heads east with his daughter, resigned to appearing before his New York friends "in the garb of the common laborer." On the way, he dies of exposure to the cold, and his daughter is found and sent to a county poor house. In his portrait of this quiet, sober, intelligent man, Cannon creates an alternative to the stereotypical Famine-generation immigrant. However, at the same time, his rendering of O'Hanlon's belligerent, bibulous, and treacherous compatriots corroborates prevalent notions about the Irish in the 1850s. These conflicting attitudes reflect Cannon's position as a member of the transitional generation of relatively established Irish Americans who watched the Famine influx with mixed feelings.

The scene now shifts to Bickerton, a large Eastern port-city with great extremes of poverty and wealth and many antagonistic "Christian" sects. There Cannon traces the career of the town's leading citizen, Pelatiah Hubbard, from about 1812 to the present, the early 1850s. Brought up to hate foreigners and popery, this self-made business leader has become a reasonable man and friend to the poor, regardless of their religion. He thus supports the campaign of the town's Catholic priest against the teaching of the Bible in public schools, and when a nativist, anti-Catholic secret society, the Thugs of Hindostan, are formed in Bickerton, Hubbard opposes them, declaring that popery ought to be combatted openly. (The Thugs are Cannon's version of the Know-Nothing Party, which posed a very real threat to immigrants of the 1850s, including the Irish.) Hubbard's son, Fred, attends a meeting of the Thugs, who offer to run him for the state senate, owing to his family's name in town, but he soon repudiates them by quoting long passages from the two works for which Cannon apologizes in his preface: a pastoral letter from the Bishop of Cincinnati and a speech by the Hon. R.M.T. Hunter of Virginia, in both of which Catholics are defended as loyal Americans who should be allowed to practice their religion unmolested.

Meanwhile, Fred Hubbard also seems to be falling in love with Debby Scroggs, the adopted daughter of the Reverend "Fire-and-Brimstone"

Scroggs, pastor of Rock Church in Plymouth Place, who supports the
Thugs and lives next door to the Hubbards on Bickerton's best street.
(Cannon describes his church as "a gray granite structure of the New-
England-Barn order, upon whose cruet-shaped turret was perched a glittering Shanghai, that was forever turning its tail to the wind—to show
the controlling influence of the popular breath even in religion.") Scroggs's
Catholic counterpart is Father Eldridge, the learned, tolerant priest of St.
Mary's, the son of a Yankee father and an Irish mother. Berated constantly
by her stepfather, Debby Scroggs goes to Father Eldridge, and the revelation comes that she is really Manus O'Hanlon's daughter, Aileen, and
that she has kept the seeds of her Catholic faith through a devotion book,
her father's only legacy. Cannon stretches even farther, making Father
Eldridge Aileen's nearest relation. His mother and Manus O'Hanlon were
brother and sister! Aileen soon turns twenty-one and leaves the Scroggses,
taking shelter, with Father Eldridge's help, in St. Mary's Convent. Nativist
agitation in Bickerton comes to a head shortly thereafter, in two violent
events. Lured out on a false sick call, Father Eldridge is given a mock trial
by the Thugs (disguised in black-face), then tarred and feathered. In a
footnote, Cannon here cites "the brutal treatment of Fr. Bapst by certain
of the people of Ellsworth, Maine." This real tar-and-feathering of the
priest who later became the first president of Boston College took place
in October, 1854, less than a year before *Bickerton* was published.[13]

The second event is a large nativist demonstration in Bickerton, by
which "popish-foreignism was to be frightened out of the land." The
noisy parade, with banners, placards, and a huge Bible float, marches
into "Little Dublin," the city's Irish section, with a brass band playing
"Boyne Water," the anthem of Ulster Protestantism. Unfortunately, and
probably by plan, the demonstration coincides with All Saints' Eve, or
"Holi-eve," which Cannon rightly traces back to the pre-Christian harvest
festivals of ancient Ireland. As this is Little Dublin's major neighborhood
holiday, the streets are filled with people. Here the Thugs' parade turns
savage, guns are discharged, and several innocent Irish, including women
and children, are killed and wounded. When the enraged Little Dubliners
retaliate with shovels and sticks, the nativist mob heads for St. Mary's
Church, burning houses along the way. Bickerton's mayor, himself a
Thug, refuses to send in the police, and much damage is done to the
church before the state militia finally responds and stops the riot. Meanwhile, Fred Hubbard has rescued Aileen O'Hanlon from the mob at the
church in the nick of time. The historical precedents for this scene include
the extensive anti-Catholic Philadelphia riots of 1844, during which thirty
people were killed and three churches destroyed.

Cannon's description of Little Dublin and the rioting is the most interesting part of the novel. For once, he becomes a realistic writer, exposing the climate of hatred at the height of Know-Nothing agitation in
the 1850s, and taking the time to describe in some detail urban Irish

working-class life. A port city, Bickerton suggests Boston, for Little Dublin looks like the old North End during the Famine immigration, "being narrow and ill-paved, with walks that would hardly admit two abreast, and houses, mostly of wood, of two stories in height, with small windows, and doors formed of an upper and lower part, and broad wooden stoops with comfortable seats" (169). The noisy and swarming streets, "where there was plenty of fun and no little fighting," Cannon attributes to the natural gregariousness and gaiety of the Irish, which "whole ages of suffering have been unable to crush out of the national heart." Admiring these traits, he nonetheless sees them as excessive, especially when combined with intemperance, and he preaches greater decorum by praising the largely successful efforts of Father Eldridge in improving manners and eradicating abuse of drink. At the same time, Eldridge recognizes the wisdom of allowing this immigrant generation to retain Old-World customs such as the Holi-eve celebration:

> "Let them enjoy themselves in their own way," said the priest of St. Mary's, "since they will not enjoy themselves in ours. Let them have their set days and seasons, and their social gatherings, where the aged meet to smoke and talk over old times, and the young for 'a bit of innocent divarsion,' when it matters not how much they 'welt the flure,' as long as they do not welt one another. There is no more sin in a jig or a song than there is religion in a long face." So they still adhered to many of the customs of their native land, and enjoyed, without fear of the priest, their frequent gatherings. [173]

Cannon's meliorist position on this issue is particularly enlightened for a member of his transitional generation of established Irish Americans in a time of nativist upheaval, when many were stampeded into wholesale relinquishment of the old ways.

At the end of *Bickerton*, Fred Hubbard marries Aileen O'Hanlon and turns Catholic, but a final realistic touch is Cannon's refusal to generalize from one happy union of Yankee and Irish. Instead, he makes clear that the trouble is far from over. The Thugs win a majority of governmental positions in the next election, and the Bickerton newspaper's report of Fred's marriage and conversion ends with a warning: "Let your young men take heed how they marry lovely Catholic wives, and come to spend their honeymoon in Rome. There is more danger to their protestantism in the experiment than they are aware of." So ends Cannon's most direct treatment of the problems of being Irish and Catholic in America. *Bickerton* is no masterpiece, but Cannon's penchant for sentimental digression and romantic plot entanglement is at least held in check by the authenticity and relevance of his chosen themes.[14]

Published four years after *Bickerton* in 1859, *Tighe Lyfford, A Novel*, opens with yet another apologetic preface. Cannon declares that it "has been called a novel; and it is nothing more," that it has no ulterior purposes ("The author has no spleen to gratify, no enemies he would openly

confront"), and that the story is "a fiction, and as a fiction let it be judged."
In fact, *Tighe Lyfford* is more advanced in terms of stylistic clarity, balanced
plotting, and characterization than *Bickerton*, and it contains what looks
to be a confessional self-portrait of Cannon himself which is painful
enough to have prompted his disclaimers. Cannon comes full circle in
beginning what will be his last novel with a description of the same type
of poor, Irish, New York City tenement accommodation that appeared in
passing in his first novel, *Oran, The Outcast*. He is still fighting the stereotype of Irish slovenliness, lately resurrected in public opinion of the Famine immigrants, for he insists that the "small room" exemplifies "poverty without its usual attendants, squalor and untidiness. . . . The walls
had been lately white-washed, the uncarpeted floor was clean as scrub-
bing could make it, and the hearth, where a poor fire was burning under
a well-scoured tea-kettle, was in the most perfect order" (6). The time is
the present, and the fifty-year-old woman sitting "despondingly" at the
window is Mrs. Condon, an Irish immigrant, "celebrated in her youth as
the 'Rose of Inver,' " and still beautiful, though careworn. Her life has
been extremely hard: her husband and ten of their thirteen children are
dead, and a recent robbery and fire have rendered her all but destitute.
"Widowed, poor, and no longer young," she has no "hope of a brighter
earthly future." Still, her Catholic faith and "the almost perpetual sun-
shine within her breast" keep her cheerful most of the time. The family
lives hand-to-mouth, and Mrs. Condon and her eight-year-old son are
waiting for her two daughters to bring home food for supper. These are
Nelly, twenty-five, plain, humble, and in domestic service, and Lizzie,
nineteen, lovely, and too proud to be a servant.

The plot involves a classic opposition between the impoverished,
kindly, religious Condons and their fellow immigrants and former friends,
the Lyffords, who have waxed wealthy, pretentious, and agnostic. Before
his death, Mr. Lyfford made money in the liquor trade, and the two
families have drifted apart because of Mrs. Lyfford's desire to separate
her son, Tighe, from his childhood sweetheart, Lizzie Condon. "Purse-
proud, vulgar," and condescending to the Condons, Mrs. Lyfford wants
her boy to marry well. Cannon shows that although she has money, Mrs.
Lyfford has remained coarse by giving her the only pronounced brogue
in the novel and describing her avocations as beer-drinking and gossip.
Influenced by his mother, young Tighe has "quite forgotten himself, and
wouldn't believe now that he's the same Tighe Lyfford who once lived in
a kind of shanty in Stagg Town, where his father's first money was made
by selling distilled abomination at two cents a glass, or three cents a half-
pint." A student/apprentice in a law office, the young man consorts with
a foppish crowd, attending Fifth Avenue salons and late-night rowdy
parties, and dabbles in agnosticism, "the fashionable indifferentism of
the day." A foil to Tighe is Nelly Condon's beau, the likeable, down-to-
earth Mark Hurley, whose love song "My Dark Irish Girl" illustrates the

acknowledgement of ethnicity that Cannon now advocates: "I love all that's lovely, as other men do, / But more than the lovely I love what is true; / And brighter than diamonds—purer than pearl / Is the truth that enhaloes my Dark Irish Girl." Throughout the novel, Cannon draws his didactic contrast between the Condons and Lyffords obviously, and the conclusion comes as no surprise. The crisis here, not for the first time in a Cannon novel, is a false accusation of murder. Lizzie Condon disappears mysteriously and Tighe Lyfford is charged with her death. When she reappears just as mysteriously, Tighe comes to his senses; he discards his bad companions, returns to the church, and marries Lizzie.

An interesting digression here is the address at New York's "Stuyvesant Institute" of Maurice de St. Remy, a young Catholic intellectual, who speaks for Cannon in dissecting current nativist ideas of Anglo-Saxon supremacy and anti-Catholicism. Branding as "simply ridiculous" the claim that American prosperity is traceable to "Anglo-Saxon energy diffused among us through Puritan blood," St. Remy cites the impossibility of tracing American blood lines back to the Anglo-Saxons, and declares that "some little credit is certainly due to the other races of which we are composed for their readiness in adopting that enterprise, and the unflagging industry with which they have carried it on" (135-36). On the religious issue, he refutes the "outcries of ignorance and fanaticism, mendacity and malice" lately abroad in the land by declaring that "he who could receive for truths the absurdities with which the creed of Catholics is charged, must be, unquestionably, a fool; while the man who would deny to his brother all liberty of thought is a tyrant." In this way, Cannon works in a last rejoinder to the Know-Nothing climate of the 1850s.

A fascinating aspect of *Tighe Lyfford* is its depiction of Charles Cannon's personal struggle. In the characterization of Aleyn Woodnorth, like Cannon a customs-house clerk and disappointed writer, we find the closest look in any of this literature at the frustrations that so many of these forgotten early writers must have felt. Our first view of Woodnorth comes when he helps Tighe Lyfford escape from a street fight, then invites him home to his threadbare rooms in a "respectable brick tenement." Though under fifty, Woodnorth is "the remnant only of a once handsome man," now "bent and wasted." While a promising but penniless youth, he had made a disastrous career decision, giving up a promising legal apprenticeship and literary pursuits for the apparent security of a municipal clerkship in the New York Customs House. The cost of this decision has been his one true love, his freedom, and his peace of mind. His fiancee's father forbade marriage to a political appointee, the spoils system has rendered him "the slave of another's will" for life, and he has since found himself performing "duties of a most laborious and engrossing nature" that have "an unfavorable effect upon the mind," and leave him unable to fulfill his literary ambitions. (Cannon had previously used the exact phrase "duties of a laborious and engrossing nature" to excuse the faults of the poetry in his 1851 collection, which had been dedicated to "my fellow clerks.") Having worn down his health trying to write at night after clerking days, Woodnorth ultimately gives up literature to become "that most miserable thing—a mere office holder, a creature in whose ambition there is nothing ennobling, and in whose heart the fire of manly pride is dead" (95-96). He is a thoroughly broken man, condemned to "drudge for a miserable pittance" while "bound to a public desk," and remorseful at having "frittered away his gift of genius." Withall, we are told that Catholicism has brought him peace, for he nightly lays "the burden of his miseries at the foot of the Cross."

At a salon gathering where Tighe encounters him again, Woodnorth provides insight into the aesthetics of Cannon's Irish and Catholic literary generation. Proclaiming the necessity in poetry of "purest sentiment and delicate fancy," he quotes one of his own poems (another recycled Cannon poem) as illustration, and goes on to assure his audience that true religion, rather than "mere religious sentiment," would have improved the verse of Chatterton, Burns, Byron, Keats, and "our own Poe, scarcely inferior in genius to the greatest of these, whose career was marked by such extremes of folly as to lead the charitable to suppose them the effect of insanity." Woodnorth then discusses the writer he most admires—the Irish novelist, Gerald Griffin. He declares that "patience, perseverance, and faith" brought this "poor, unknown, unfriended Irish boy" to lasting literary fame "at the early age of twenty-seven." But far more impressive to Woodnorth is Griffin's decision to give up the literary life at the height of his fame and withdraw from the world as a Christian Brother. "The mind that could conceive, and the hand that could execute the admirable portraits of Hardress Cregan, Danny Mann, Lowry Looby, and Eily O'Connor were not those of a visionary," and yet Griffin "had learned the hollowness and utter worthlessness of every worldly pursuit, and how little the gratification of our most earnest desires for fame can satisfy the cravings of an immortal spirit" (71). Woodnorth admits that thinking about Griffin is painful, because the Irish writer's "unshaken purpose," first literary and then religious, is so different from what his own muddled life has been. These sentiments seem close to the bone for Charles Cannon as well. The apologetic, contradictory prefaces and the fits and starts and failed experiments of his own part-time writing career come into sad relief as measured against the worldly and spiritual successes of Gerald Griffin, three years his junior, who had died a Christian Brother in 1840.

Woodnorth's end is bleak. After twenty years of dedicated service, he is dismissed from his job by a customs-house political plot, fomented while he is sick at home. Nursed by his old flame, he makes her promise never to allow his son to take a political appointment: "Let him be a mechanic, a day labourer, any thing that will leave him his manhood, rather than that miserable slave—a dependent upon office for his daily bread" (205). Though consoled by his religion, Woodnorth dies at the conclusion of the novel a troubled, thwarted man. *Tighe Lyfford* was Charles Cannon's last novel; a year after its publication, he died on November 9, 1860, at the age of sixty. Six years later, another disappointed novelist took a job in the New York Customs House. Herman Melville's tenure of nineteen years (until 1885) was shorter than Cannon's but no less bitter.

Toward the end of Cannon's career, Catholic journalist Orestes Brownson began to notice his books again. Brownson was the most influential Catholic literary critic of his time, and his views will be explored further in the next chapter. In an 1857 review of Cannon's poems and plays, Brownson recognizes that Cannon's basic problem has been an inability to establish a consistent literary identity. A man of "deep religious sensibility," Cannon often gets "his moral lessons" wrong. "He writes as a man who has earnest Catholic faith combined with the moral notions of philanthropists, sentimentalists, and Transcendentalists. His tone is too Catholic for non-Catholics, and not Catholic enough for Catholics, and in this fact, we suspect, lies the secret of his not having met with that brilliant success to which he aspires" (503-07). In reviewing *Tighe Lyfford* two years later, Brownson also finds Cannon's fiction to be insufficiently Irish to be popular. He says that a writer such as Cannon, trying to write with a Catholic element for a Catholic audience, "can succeed only by pressing in a national sentiment of some sort to his aid." Moreover, the appeal must be to "a foreign nationality," because "comparatively few of our Catholic population have any American sentiments or traditions. He or she who can write a good Irish story may succeed; but he or she who has the misfortune to have no nationality but the English or the American, will find few readers for a purely literary work among Catholics" (410-11). Presumably, Cannon has also failed to play the ethnic card with sufficient strength.

Brownson has indeed identified Charles Cannon's dilemma. His novels are too Catholic for the general (and possibly anti-Catholic) audience, and neither Catholic nor Irish enough to appeal to America's largely ethnic Catholic readership. The problem corroborates Cannon's position as a transitional figure whose works bridge the first two literary generations of the Irish voice in America. His nine novels, from *Oran, The Outcast* of 1833 to *Tighe Lyfford* of 1859, document the difficulties of establishing a fictional identity on both sides of the watershed of the Great Hunger. Certainly, this particular problem was not shared by the younger generation of Irish-American writers who came of age immediately after the Famine, few of whom could be accused of insufficient Catholicity. But Charles Cannon blazed trails for the others to follow. Despite a hard road of personal hardships and professional ambivalence and misdirection, he was the first Irish-American Catholic novelist to hammer out a body of fiction that somehow deals with the characters, environments, and problems of his own people.

THREE

The Famine Generation:
Practical Fiction for Immigrants

A typical novel of the Famine immigration and a good illustration of the difference between the first two Irish-American literary generations is Peter McCorry's *Mount Benedict, or The Violated Tomb. A Tale of the Charlestown Convent* (1871), a fictional version of the burning of the Ursuline convent in 1834. McCorry's preface declares his aim and sets the hyperbolic tone. Because "outrageous outbursts of popular passion" against Catholics continue, and "places dedicated to the worship of God . . . are oftentimes despoiled for the gratification of a wild fanaticism," McCorry has here "put on record the committal of a deed of shame and horror, in order that its exposure may in the future deter men from the performance of such crimes" (v). The novel describes the growth of friendship between two girls: Boston Protestant Cecilia Morton and Irish Catholic immigrant Kate Crolly, a servant in the home of Mr. and Mrs. Alvah Morton, Cecilia's guardians. The Mortons, whose son is a Methodist minister, are vociferously anti-Catholic, but Kate is spared much suffering when she and Cecilia become close friends. Because of the encouragement of the Ursuline sisters at Mount Benedict, Cecilia ultimately converts to Catholicism and Kate joins the order as a nun. While this plot is developing, McCorry gives his version of the real events leading up to the convent burning in alternate chapters. The conspirators meet at an old school house to hash over the wild stories of " 'Becca Reed—who was kept in a dungeon in that Nunnery, on bread and water, till she made her escape." Denouncing "that blarsted Nunnery, where poor girls were entrapped against the constitootion of Massachusetts," the men vow drunkenly to "uproot all Nunneries out of America" and to send "the Papishes and Roman Babylons" back where they came from (180-81).

The climax is McCorry's highly emotional rendering of the events of August 11, 1834. The nuns and their pupils are driven from the convent in the dead of night by the Boston mob and the buildings are burned: "What a sight! The splendid Convent in smouldering ruins, tainting the morning air with a charred smell. Its inmates scattered over the country far and wide, like a flock of poor defenceless lambs, who had fled from the approach of a herd of ravenous wolves. That pale and trembling daughter of the community searching for her lost treasure, and doomed to discover instead, NOTHING BUT A VIOLATED TOMB! The coffins had been burst open, and the mortal remains left exposed. O! What a scene to witness!" (221). At this point, the two plots come together. "When the flames were at their highest," Cecilia Morton's aunt and guardian comes on the scene and declares "that HER EYES HAD NEVER BEHELD SUCH A GLORIOUS SIGHT! The unfortunate woman was instantly struck blind, and remained so till the end of her life" (216). To conclude, McCorry denounces bitterly the botched trial and unjust acquittal of the chief instigators of these crimes and the refusal of all concerned to pay an indemnity to the Ursuline order. He blames the "Puritan State" of Massachusetts, which has yet to "redeem itself from the foul stain incurred by its apathy," and the novel ends on a high rhetorical pitch: "The Ruins of the Convent of Mount Benedict and its Violated Tombs remain as they were left by the hands of the desecrators, save in so far as they are covered with the mouldering ivy that would conceal the lawlessness of nearly forty years ago" (233, 236).

It is a very long way from the controlled, sophisticated satire and parody of "Dorah Mahony's" *Six Months in a House of Correction*, which was published less than a year after the convent was burned, to the blatant propaganda of McCorry's book, which is narrated in a shrill voice of outrage and indignation more appropriate had the atrocity occurred not thirty-seven years earlier, but the previous day. What fell between 1835 and 1871, the dates of publication of these two fictional responses to the Charlestown tragedy, was the shadow of the Great Hunger in Ireland.

This greatest of Irish national tragedies began with the failure of the potato crop over one third of Ireland in the autumn of 1845. The second failure, in July and August, 1846, was general throughout the country, and spurred the first significant winter emigration in Irish history. In 1847, famine and disease spread like wildfire, and although it was much less blighted, the potato crop was too small to stem the rising tide of hysterical flight. But 1848 was the killer year. That harvest-time, the blight was again universal, and virtually the entire potato crop was destroyed. This was the death blow to the Irish rural culture that had existed for centuries. From this time on, for the bulk of the Irish people, emigration was a viable, often unavoidable, alternative to life on the land at home. Another aspect of the tragedy was the inadequacy of relief efforts by the British government, and the additional damning evidence that grain and livestock from Anglo-Irish estates continued to be exported to England throughout the Famine years. Contemporary observers reported that the most immediately noticeable difference about post-Famine rural Ireland was a new silence. Before the Famine, there had been music at every teeming crossroads, much of it provided by beggars singing for their supper. Afterward, the land was quiet.

When the worst was over, the figures told a grim tale. During the years of the actual blight, one million people died of starvation and related diseases, and nearly one million and a quarter emigrated. The population of Ireland had dropped from nearly nine million to six and a half million people. As Oliver MacDonagh declares, "relatively speaking, no other population movement of the nineteenth century was on so great a scale" (417). The ten-year estimates for Irish emigration to the United States during this period are dramatic: 1846-1855, 1,442,000; 1856-1865, 582,400; 1866-1875, 645,700. The actual numbers are certainly higher. Some immigrants entered illegally, and between 1846 and 1855, over 300,000 Irish people came to Canada. As many of these ultimately headed south, the total number of Irish immigrants to the United States in the crucial first ten years was at least 1.6 million. The blood-draining habit of emigration thus established continued for the rest of the century and beyond, with half a million people leaving Ireland every ten years up to World War I. The result was a continuing net decrease in population, unique among European countries, that would not be reversed until the late 1960s.[1]

Those who left Ireland for America in those hard, early years endured the pain of leaving home, the perils of the voyage by sea, and the problems of settlement in the New World. For a total cost of five to seven pounds, an Irishman could get to America, usually by way of Liverpool, the nearest main-line port of the trans-Atlantic trade. Living conditions in Liverpool lodging houses and then in the "coffin ships" themselves were often nearly intolerable—unconscionably overcrowded, filthy, and disease-ridden, with no proper provisions for good water, cooking, sanitation, or privacy. Many people died in these crossings and many more were scarred in various ways. In addition, to the surprise of many, getting to America was only the beginning of their troubles. The new arrivals faced in the "sweet land of liberty" of their dreams a significant negative reaction from their hosts. An established culture still overwhelmingly Anglo-Saxon in origin and Protestant in religion was not about to welcome with open arms a heavy influx of Irish Catholic immigrants, most of whom were impoverished country people, unprepared for urban industrial life or employment. Prejudice, discrimination, and explosive collisions were the order of the day beginning in the late 1840s, and the turbulence culminated politically in the Know-Nothing movement of the early 1850s, when nativists swept to victory in a number of state and local elections. The immigrants also faced a harsh work life as a vulnerable urban proletariat, "a huge fund of poor, unskilled, cheap, almost infinitely exploitable labor," as John Kelleher has said, a "labor force [that] was expended, with a callousness now hard to comprehend, in building the railroads and dams and mills, in digging the canals, in any crude, backbreaking job" ("Irishness" 38). For most men, this meant pick and shovel labor, for women, domestic service or factory work. Also present were the corollaries of life as an underclass—wretched housing, pauperism, alcoholism, and disproportionately high mortality rates from accidents, violence, and disease. In addition, this generation was mostly stuck in their impoverished situations. Occupational and social mobility became possible only for their children.[2]

The Famine generation's fiction reflects and clarifies this complex of experiences and emotions. Life in Ireland during and following the Famine, the horrors of the crossing, the traumas of resettlement for an agrarian people suddenly thrust into modernity in an unfriendly country with an alien world view—in all of these areas the fiction produced by Irish-American witnesses contributes valuable detail and pattern. It is no wonder that these circumstances generated a conservative, practical fiction, unambiguously didactic and dedicated to helping troubled people get along. Nothing could be further from the playful sophistication of the pre-Famine satirists. In a matter of a few years, the fictional norm had been overturned: from satiric critique of propaganda to propaganda itself; from lively, even experimental, engagement in aesthetic and stylistic matters to frequent avowals (in prefaces, mostly) of suspicion of fiction other than the baldly didactic as a subversive medium threatening to morality; from parody of fictional conventions that have been manipulated for extraliterary purposes to humorless embrace of those same conventions—flowery, sentimental rhetoric, stereotyped characters devoid of complexity, simplistically Manichaean and melodramatic conflicts, and forced, predictable moralizing themes.

This reversal is so dramatic, in the first place, because the writers who emerged after the Famine of the late 1840s were not a second generation, not the children of immigrants, but a new first generation. Between 1845 and 1875, seven people wrote at least three novels each, in which being Irish in America is of central concern. All seven were themselves immigrants, all seven came to America as adults (the youngest was twenty-one), and the five for whom accurate dates exist all came between 1844 and 1850. Two of these novelists were priests, Fathers John Boyce and Hugh Quigley, three were primarily journalists, Peter McCorry, Charles G. Halpine, and Dillon O'Brien, one, David Power Conyngham, was a veteran of both the 1848 Irish rebellion and the American Civil War, and one, Mary Anne (Madden) Sadlier, was the first important woman in Irish-American publishing. Father Quigley and Mrs. Sadlier are the subjects of chapter 4; the others appear in this chapter. In addition, most of the authors who wrote only one or two novels were also immigrants.

A great weakness of this generation's fiction was the constriction of the assumed audience. As Famine immigrants, these new writers wrote only for their own kind, the traumatized refugees with whom their own experiences allowed them to identify. Perceiving that audience to be desperately in need of guidance, the writers produced didactic, utilitarian novels with three major purposes: Catholic-tract fiction to exhort the immigrants to keep the faith on alien soil, immigrant-guidebook fiction to instruct the newly arrived on how to get along in America, and nationalistic-political fiction to aid the cause of freedom from British rule back in Ireland. Often the three aims were addressed by a single author, and occasionally within a single novel. The plots and themes of Famine-generation fiction exhibit variations on a fairly predictable pattern:

1. A hard life of great suffering in Ireland is presented, marked by landlord exploitation, famine, painful eviction from the old home, and the reluctant decision to emigrate. At the same time, the country of Ireland is often seen as an ideal pastoral home, only temporarily despoiled by the British invaders.

2. The crossing to America is seen as a wrenching rite of passage, the violence of which is often symbolized by a fierce storm at sea.

3. The disorientation of the immigrant's first months in the New World is evoked, with swindles, humiliation, and the most dangerous threats to morality and the faith.

4. Right and wrong ways of meeting these challenges are exemplified in the contrasting careers of Irish Catholics who keep the faith and those who lose it. Failure most often means succumbing to drink, dissipation, and early death. Success means working hard, holding a job, and keeping one's family together and Catholic. There are very few spectacular achievements, economic or otherwise, in this cautious body of fiction. The reality of life for this generation was too harsh to support what would have been cruel fantasy.

5. The moral of the story is pointed with directness and emphasis, often four or five times in the last few pages.

This pattern is recognizable as the Irish-American version of a venerable American type, the rags-to-riches moralizing tale, which loomed large in the imaginations of this generation and its writers. Reference to the model and telling qualification of its promises appear in Thomas D'Arcy McGee's advice to his fellow immigrants in his New York *Nation* for February 10, 1849:

> You may buy in Cork, in Dublin, or in Liverpool, or wherever you sail from, a little shilling book, which I earnestly recommend to you as the best preliminary study for an Emigrant. It is called *The Life of Franklin*, and therein you will read how, by industry, system, and self-denial, a Boston printer's boy rose to be one of the most prosperous, honorable, and important citizens of the Republic. It will teach you that in America no beginning, however humble, can prevent a man from reaching any rank, however exalted; that, though the land does not grow gold, neither does it smother any energy by which fortune is created; that, above all, the genius of the people, and the State, is entirely and radically, *practical*. These are lessons you should have by heart.

One convention recurs in novel after novel as a means of illustrating the points being made: the deathbed scene. The good die peacefully, surrounded by loving family, and not without occasional angelic music and lighting; the bad die horribly, weeping, gnashing their teeth, and calling—too late—for a priest. An important crux of feelings for Irish and Irish-American cultures, this convention remains strong through the rest of the nineteenth century. Indeed, it is not fully exorcised until the final page of James T. Farrell's third *Studs Lonigan* novel, *Judgment Day*, published in 1935.

Because of the demands of the greatly expanded audience, there was much more American publication of Irish literature in the Famine generation than previously. Although most were industrially unskilled, as many as seventy-five percent of the Irish immigrants to America in 1850 were probably literate in English, and by 1910 the number exceeded ninety percent. Important in the dissemination of literature from the old country, and crucial for the development of a new Irish-American literature, was the establishment of a number of Catholic publishing houses by 1850— all, as it happens, by Irish Americans. These were as follows: in New York, Edward Dunigan and Brother, P. O'Shea, and P.J. Kenedy & Sons; in Boston, Patrick Donahoe, whose weekly newspaper the *Pilot* became the most influential Irish Catholic journal in America at this time; D. and J. Sadlier of New York, Boston, and Montreal; and in Baltimore, John Murphy and Hedian & O'Brien. In the late 1840s and early 1850s, these houses began to publish Irish and Irish-American fiction in addition to their stock-in-trade, devotional literature, prayerbooks, and Catholic school readers. Also in response to their new audience, they began publishing collections of Irish music. Patrick Donahoe brought out three such collections very early, including editions of Moore's *Irish Melodies* and *Songs of Our Land* (divided into "sentimental" and "patriotic" songs) in the 1850s.[3]

There were also more Irish-American periodicals to fill the needs of the new immigrants, and many of these also published fiction. In the already established newspapers, discussed in chapter 1, a shift occurs, and there begins to be less Irish fiction (by the likes of William Carleton and Gerald Griffin), and more Irish-American fiction. Patrick Donahoe's *Pilot*, which had pioneered in the printing of Irish fiction in the 1830s and early forties, made the shift by publishing Mary Anne Sadlier's first two novels in 1850. The *Pilot* was edited from 1848 to 1858 by Father John Roddan, himself a novelist. The first issue of the New York *Irish World* (August 12, 1849) carried a front-page serial novel written by its editor, Patrick Lynch. A didactic tale of the rise to success of the son of a fugitive from the Irish Rebellion of 1798, "Enterprise, A Tale of the Hour" inaugurated a regular fictional feature. Begun in 1857, the Sadlier Company's New York *Tablet* also published much fiction, including the first, serial versions of many of the novels of the publisher's wife, Mary Anne Sadlier. Irish-American fiction also ran in several other New York City newspapers, and in Buffalo, Louisville, Kentucky, St. Louis, St. Paul, Minnesota, and New Orleans.[4]

Of course, Irish-American poetry and drama continued to be published and performed in the Famine generation, and their respective dominating stereotypes, the suffering exile and the comic Irishman, continued to proliferate. In the poetry, though, there is a noticeable shift of mood. Pre-Famine Irish-American poetry contained an optimistic strain, often in ambitious epic forms, marked by celebration of Ireland and predictions of Irish freedom. But after the Famine, the backward look, wistful, nostalgic, and lamenting, comes to the fore and dominates through the rest of the century.

A survey of fictional treatments of Irishness by non-Irish writers of this period reveals a number of disparate efforts. Given the magnitude of the diaspora, there are relatively few mentions of the Irish in what has come to be considered the American literary mainstream. In my reading, only a few passages stand out. Edgar Allan Poe, whose father was thought to be of Irish descent, tries his hand at the brogue spoken by a native of Connaught in one short sketch. Nathaniel Hawthorne's *American Notebooks* contain descriptions of Irish shanty towns near Portland, Maine, and Concord, Massachusetts. Charles Farrar Browne takes an entertaining look at Irish-American nationalism in "Artemus Ward among the Fenians." Henry David Thoreau meets three Irishmen near Walden Pond, one of whom prompts his observation that "the culture of an Irishman is an enterprise to be undertaken with a sort of moral bog hoe." And in his novel *Redburn: His First Voyage* (1849) Herman Melville describes vividly the terrible living conditions of Irish immigrants stranded in Liverpool waiting for passage, and then in steerage on the way to America, where near-starvation and an outbreak of cholera take their toll.[5]

There are also a number of justly forgotten anti-Catholic and anti-Irish novels of poor quality, in which the squalid living conditions and general moral turpitude extant in the new urban ghettoes are "exposed." These tend to contain sensational portraits of drunken, violent Irish who wreak havoc on their own families and American society at large. They include *Caroline Tracy, The Spring Street Milliner's Apprentice, or Life in New York in 1847-8* (1849, the story of a prostitute), Robert F. Greeley's *Violet, The Child of the City: A Story of New York Life* (1854, the focus is a tenement called "The Old Brewery"), and Lucius M. Sargent's *An Irish Heart* (1836), a typical temperance tale which traces the downfall of an Irish immigrant who ruins his own and his family's lives and points the twin morals of total abstinence and immigration restriction.[6] One interesting example is *The Tenant-House; or, Embers from Poverty's Hearthstone* (1857) by A.J.H. Duganne, which evokes in great detail "Foley's Barracks," a frightful tenement groaning with Irish Catholic depravity. Duganne, whose initials stand for Augustine Joseph Hickey, was probably Irish himself, and, if so, he also exemplifies the shift in sentiment about claiming and supporting Irishness at the time of the Famine immigration. His pre-Famine works include patriotic poems about Irish freedom, a charming "Irish ghost story" told with respect for folk tradition, and a romantic novel,

The Two Clerks; or, The Orphan's Gratitude (1843), which traces a poor boy from Boston's North End to valiant soldiering with Irish wild geese under Bolivar in South America. And yet, Duganne went on to be elected as a Know-Nothing to the New York State Assembly in 1855, and to publish *The Tenant-House* two years later.[7]

Anti-Catholic fiction had been a staple of American publishing since the heyday of Rebecca Reed and Maria Monk in the mid-1830s, but the Famine immigration, the consequent growth of the Catholic church, and the rise of the Know-Nothings resulted in a surge of such books in the 1850s. Titles such as *Sister Agnes; or, The Captive Nun, By a Clergyman's Widow* (1854) were typical, and there was even a new turn on the burning of the Charlestown convent. Published in 1854, Charles W. Frothingham's *The Convent's Doom: A Tale of Charlestown in 1834* features a wily Jesuit and a treacherous Irish servant girl. By describing the Ursuline convent as a prison for Protestants and a Playboy mansion for priests, Frothingham argues that its destruction was justified. On the other side of the coin, there were also a number of pro-Catholic novels by non-Irish writers, for, as Willard Thorp puts it, at some point "nearly every Catholic novelist . . . makes a bow to the Irish Catholics in America." Typical here was the prolific sentimental novelist Mrs. Anna H. M. Dorsey, who dedicated a pair of novels in 1869 "To the Irish People, brave and unconquered." *Mona the Vestal* features a druidess who is converted to Catholicism in the fifth century by Saint Patrick himself, and *Nora Brady's Vow* traces the fortunes of a recent immigrant to Boston who is befriended by publisher Patrick Donahoe.[8]

In returning to fiction by Irish Americans, Peter McCorry is a useful, organizing figure because his novels fulfill so clearly the didactic purposes that dominated his literary generation. An Ulster Catholic immigrant journalist and ardent Irish nationalist, he spent time in Boston, perhaps working for Patrick Donahoe, and went on to New York City, where he edited the *Irish People* in the early 1870s. This "Weekly Journal of News, Politics, and Literature" was the official organ of the New York branch of the Fenian Brotherhood, the nationalist organization that had been founded in America in 1858 by John O'Mahony. Named for the Fianna, warrior heroes of Irish legend, the Fenians gained strength and training in arms during the Civil War, when Fenian "circles" operated openly in the Union Army. Using the pseudonym "Con O'Leary," McCorry also wrote three novels, all of which were published by Patrick Donahoe in Boston.[9]

Already discussed, *Mount Benedict, or The Violated Tomb* (1871) is very much a Catholic-tract novel. As a servant in an anti-Catholic household, Kate Crolly has her faith severely tested, and she emerges triumphant into her vocation as a nun. At the same time, her friend Cecilia Morton is led toward her conversion to Catholicism by the kind of extended catechetical instruction familiar to the genre. McCorry's second novel, *The Irish Widow's Son, or The Pikemen of '98* (1869) is a nationalist propaganda piece, written, according to its preface, "to foster among [the author's] countrymen, a continued love of those who dared everything for their dear country," and "a hope that must never be extinguished but in death" that Ireland will be "freed from the unholy alliance of English connection" (vi). The novel focuses on British atrocities against Ulster Catholics during the rebellion of 1798, including the burning of Catholic houses, fields, and churches and the murder of innocent women and children by a drunken soldiery. The climactic event is the burning of the cabin of the Widow Rogan because her son Cormac, the novel's hero, is a rebel leader. During the attack, the widow dies of heart failure, and McCorry declares her to be "another sacrifice in the cause of Ireland; another name added to the list of martyrs; another soul escaped from its earthly tenement to bear witness before the Throne of the Most High to the persecutions of the Irish race" (97). He then gives his "Historical Account" of the two major battles of the rising in Ulster at Antrim and Ballynahinch, at which Cormac Rogan distinguishes himself with great courage. Ultimately, Cormac escapes to America where he marries his Irish sweetheart and raises a large family, and the novel ends with a broad hint that Cormac's descendents are Fenians: "No truer hearts beat for Ireland today than theirs; and whether they are members of a certain Irish organization is left to the reader to imagine" (224). *The Irish Widow's Son* provides a Catholic, nationalist answer to the view of rebellious Ulster presented fifty years earlier in the historical novels of Presbyterian Unionist James McHenry.

There were many such answers in the fiction of the Famine generation, probably because the rebellion of 1798 had been the most recent praiseworthy attempt at Irish freedom, with a large pantheon of heroes (Edward Fitzgerald, Wolfe Tone, Henry Joy McCracken, and, in the tragic coda of his 1803 rising, Robert Emmet). Major David Power Conyngham, who participated in the Young Ireland rising of 1848 and in the American Civil War, wrote two such novels. Aiming (in a preface) "to lay the naked truth before the liberty loving people of America," in *The O'Mahony, Chief of the Comeraghs: A Tale of the Rebellion of '98* (1879), Conyngham sets the last Gaelic chieftain of the Comeragh Mountains against the fiendish Earl of Kingston, known as "the wolf of the Galtees," who terrorizes the peasantry from his Mitchelstown castle. The rising in Wexford is the novel's climax. And in *Rose Parnell: The Flower of Avondale: A Tale of the Rebellion of '98* (1883), he presents the fighting heroine as "simply the embodiment of all the noble and patriotic qualities which have characterized the Parnell family down to the present day." Here the preface claims that his purpose is "to infuse a patriotic spirit into the hearts of my readers," and "educate them in the duties they owe to their native country."[10] In addition, immigrant journalist Charles G. Halpine churned out three pot-boiling novels about the '98 rebellion in a single year, 1856, and two new histories of the period were published in America in 1851 and 1856.[11]

There are also a number of nationalist propaganda novels that deal with the recent past of the Great Hunger, evictions, and forced emigration. To this group, David Power Conyngham contributed *The O'Donnells of Glen Cottage: A Tale of the Famine Years in Ireland* (1874), in which a Tipperary family suffers starvation, then eviction into a snow storm, after which the mother dies of exposure. Forced to emigrate, young Frank O'Donnell lives out a prevalent dream of his generation's fiction: he succeeds, makes money, returns to Ireland, and buys back his old home. Mary L. Meany's *The Confessors of Connaught; or, The Tenants of a Lord Bishop* (1865) is the fictional account of the real eviction by the Protestant bishop of Tuam in 1860 of Catholic tenants who had refused to send their children to his school. It contains dramatic scenes of families driven into the November cold, with clusters of small children huddled around piles of furniture in the rain. Alice Nolan's *The Byrnes of Glengoulah: A True Tale* (1870) details evictions and a rigged murder trial in Wicklow, based on a real case in Westmeath in 1846, the upshot of which is the unjust execution of an innocent man. And Patrick Sarsfield Cassidy's *Glenveigh; or, The Victims of Vengeance, A Tale of Irish Peasant Life in the Present* (1870) is also based on a real set of evictions, in Donegal in 1863.[12] Here, a young girl is clubbed to death by a "crowbar brigade" of ruffians imported from the Glasgow docks to enforce the court orders, and the dissolute landlord rents out his reclaimed farms to Scottish shepherds and takes off for a life of sinful self-indulgence in Venice.

The astonishing fiasco of the June 1866 Fenian invasion of Canada in which Irish-American military units crossed the border in a symbolic protest against British colonialism also spurred immediate literary efforts. These range from the doggerel poems of Chicago Fenian Michael Scanlan, *Love and Land* (1866), to William Kelly's "Irish Historical Drama," *The Harp without the Crown; or, Mountcashel's Fair Daughter* (1867), to a novel by "Scian Dubh," *Ridgeway: An Historical Romance of the Fenian Invasion of Canada* (1868). This extremely sanguine novel, describes the Fenian "nation within a nation" as large, organized, and sure to effect Irish freedom eventually. Indeed, had General John O'Neill had 2000 men instead of 600, he would certainly have "liberated" Canada from British oppression! As this very mixed bag of novels attests, both of the contradictory characterizations of earlier nationalist fiction persist in the Famine generation. Suffering victims like the Widow Rogan and the evicted tenants of Glenveigh and active heroes like the Widow's son Cormac and Rose Parnell continue to appear.[13]

Peter McCorry's third novel is an explicit instruction manual in the pitfalls of America for immigrant women. *The Lost Rosary; or, Our Irish Girls, Their Trials, Temptations, and Triumphs* (1870) is dedicated to "the ever faithful Irish girls in America."[14] In the preface, McCorry says that the need for such a novel was suggested to him by Patrick Donahoe, "the eminent Irish and Catholic publisher of America," and he hopes that "our IRISH GIRLS will profit by every line of what is written especially for their benefit" (v-vii). Certainly, he and Donahoe were right about the prospective audience in the Famine generation. Nearly half of the over two-and-one-half million Irish immigrants to America between 1846 and 1875 were women. McCorry's plot traces two pairs of emigrants from County Donegal, Barney McAuley and Tim Heggarty, and the girls who love them, the cousins Mary and Ailey O'Donnell. The men sail first, in June 1845, and the narrative of their voyage features a classic rendering of the storm at sea symbolizing the painful immigrant transition. McCorry is fully aware of the metaphorical value ("How like to the voyage of life was that passage of the 'St. Patrick'!"), and he focuses the figure to encompass the experience of Irish Catholic women emigrating to alien lands: "Storms and trials you will meet, brave hearts,—but remember your night of storms upon the sea. Temptations will surround you; sin will encompass you; aye, as the dark waters surround you now. Then remember your only hope. Call back the Faith that saved you when Hope was trembling at your hearts. That will be your anchor, brave Irish girls, when alone and battling against every storm" (63). Specific admonitions follow about the "quicksands and shoals that will beset thee," which include "soft words and honeyed speech" and "foul words and practices," and the height of the persistent moralizing is a capitalized list of virtues that McCorry asks the "pure daughters of Erin" to cultivate: self-abnegation, chastity, "a flower that out-rivals all glories of earth," modesty, "sweetest of virtues," honesty, success, "always best when moderate and unaccompanied with too strong a desire, lest its companions in virtue should suffer by its exaltation," and suffering, "the lot of all and not without its finer advantages" (113-14). The last two virtues in particular indicate a disjunction between Irish immigrant and mainstream American thinking in this generation. The concepts of immoderate success and advantageous suffering both rub against the grain of hustling, optimistic mid-nineteenth-century America.

Prevalent in much Famine-generation fiction, these ideas corroborate Kerby Miller's conclusion, based on analysis of thousands of letters and other personal testaments, that "many Catholic Irish were more communal, dependent, fatalistic and prone to accept conditions passively than were the Protestants they encountered in either Ireland or America; and less individualistic, independent, optimistic and given to initiative than were these Protestants. In short, they were more sensitive to the weight of tradition than to innovative possibilities for the future." Theirs was "a world-view which valued conservatism, collective behaviour, and dependence, and limited responsibility in broad areas."[15] Still and all, Hasia Diner has documented the many ways in which Peter McCorry's audience of Irish immigrant women were "thrust into positions of power and authority" (69), and responded aggressively, resourcefully, and with considerable success, at first as domestic servants and factory operatives and later as teachers, nurses, clerical workers, and salespeople.

Furthermore, the evangelical piety exuded by many novels such as McCorry's places them in the Catholic mainstream, supporting Jay Dolan's assertion that "by the 1860s" an emotional, pietistic "devotional Catholicism . . . had become the dominant trait of American Catholicism" (212).[16] For the Irish, this suggests a transfer to America of the "devotional revolution" that Emmet Larkin has charted in post-Famine Ireland, where Mass attendance, reception of the sacraments, and performance of devotions all increased dramatically, as did the number of priests and nuns. Larkin sees the psychological shock of the Famine as only partly responsible. He suggests that the underlying cause of the change was that the Irish "had been gradually losing their language, their culture, and their way of life for nearly a hundred years before the famine," and that devotional Catholicism "provided the Irish with a substitute symbolic language and offered them a new cultural heritage with which they could identify and be identified and through which they could identify with one another" (649).

Of course, Peter McCorry's heroines are more than equal to the challenges of immigrant life. Mary O'Donnell's father dies, after having been rackrented out of his family's ancestral land holding in Donegal, and Ailey O'Donnell comes down with famine fever and ends up in a squalid, overcrowded fever ward in the nearby town. Mary heroically nurses her cousin back to health, and the two girls take ship for America in 1848, one of the worst Famine years. Following a hard, ten-week crossing, they land in New York and begin to make their way as servants. As effortless practitioners of McCorry's virtues, they naturally avoid the temptations of life in the New World. A predictable contrast is provided by their fellow immigrants, the Clarkson girls, who fall into a slack and sinful round of drinking, dancing, and dangerous flirting. One of them even marries a Protestant minister who specializes in luring Catholics away from the fold. McCorry provides advice about how to find decent housing and steady work, while avoiding the confidence men who "have become such adepts in deception, that they are able to recognize, by the sound of the emigrant's voice, which particular county in Ireland he belongs to, and who use the same dialect, when addressing the new-comer" (130). Throughout the novel, the lost rosary of the subtitle functions as a symbol of Catholic faith in America, and it becomes the implausible means of the O'Donnell girls' deliverance to permanent safety. A parting gift from Barney McAuley to Mary, the rosary is lost in the shuffle of eviction and emigration, and it miraculously turns up again hanging on a Celtic cross in a New York cemetery. Luckily, the cross marks the grave of a child of Mr. and Mrs. O'Meara, who meet the girls there and befriend them. An immigrant twenty years earlier, Mr. O'Meara has become a successful merchant "who owed his position to his industry, perseverance, and integrity in business" (166). The O'Mearas provide encouragement for the girls and good jobs for Tim and Barney, and a joyous double wedding concludes the action.

Of the other immigrant-guide novels, John McElgun's *Annie Reilly; or, The Fortunes of an Irish Girl in New York* (1873) provides the fullest description available of the Queenstown (Cork) to Liverpool to New York journey of the Famine generation.[17] In the 1850s, Annie Reilly's family is evicted from their small Munster holding through the machinations of a despicable middleman, Ryan, the local pork butcher. At the same time, Annie's beau, James O'Rourke, is accused of conspiring to steal arms from a police barracks. Both young people flee to America, where they hope to be reunited, but they travel on different ships and lose track of each other. McElgun describes the squalor of the lodging houses and the danger of Liverpool "man-catchers," the "motley crowd of ship-runners and lodging house keepers" who meet the boats from Ireland "like a pack of hungry wolves," and "carry off their spoils in the shape of innocent men, women, and children who had probably never seen a city before" (93-94). He also knows well the similar gauntlet of hustlers faced by the immigrants when they land at Castle Garden. James O'Rourke is immediately swindled by an "intelligence agent," who sets him up with a fictitious job in a non-existent dry-goods store. After finding a crowded boarding-house (fifty people in fifteen rooms over a saloon) and a job as a longshoreman, James ultimately heads west to the Pennsylvania oil fields. Although she is harassed by a loutish Scotsman, Annie's crossing is easier, and she finds in New York the exhorting example of her relatives, the Sweeneys, who, through sobriety, piety, "industry and good habits," have achieved middle-class respectability, complete with a brass plate on their front door. Needless to say, James and Annie find each other again (at Sunday Mass) and marry near the end of the novel.

There were many more such novels and there is little to distinguish among them. Charles Halpine turned out two for the New York *Irish American*, one of which, *Us Here; or, A Glimpse Behind Know-Nothingism in One of the Rural Districts* (1857), is interesting for its description of the battle between an Irish immigrant journalist and a group of Know-Nothings who are publishing a nativist newspaper, *The True American's True Flag*. Sometimes the setting of these fictional guidebooks was elsewhere than the United States, perhaps to instruct by comparison. Mary L. Meany's *Elinor Johnston* (1868) deals with the struggles of Irish immigrants in London, her *Maurice and Genevieve* (1868) takes place in France, and a missionary priest, Father John McDermott, wrote a novel about the Scottish missions, *Father Jonathan; or, The Scottish Converts: A Catholic Tale* (1853).[18]

Two odd, unusual Famine-generation literary figures are the humorist Charles Graham Halpine and the Gothic fantasist Fitz-James O'Brien.

Halpine demonstrates that Irish-American satire was still alive in those trying years, and the unlikely catalyst for his contribution was the Civil War. Nearly 150,000 Irish-born soldiers and many sons of immigrants fought in the Union Army, some in exclusively Irish regiments. Famous Union generals of Irish background included Philip Sheridan, Michael Corcoran, and exiled 1848 rebel Thomas F. Meagher. Irish Confederates also mustered into such recognizably ethnic units as the Emmet Guards of Virginia and the Emerald Guards of Alabama.[19] The war generated a new sub-genre of Irish-American propagandizing fiction: romantic stories of Irish participation in the war effort, one aim of which was to encourage Irish acceptance into mainstream American society. Irish-American newspapers featured many such stories. Typical is "Edward Tracy, A Story of Irish American Patriotism," published in the New York *Irish World* in 1874. The hero is an immigrant who achieves success in banking despite being accused of divided loyalties by his colleagues. When the war comes, he joins Meagher's Irish Brigade, is first made a lieutenant for heroism, and then killed leading a courageous charge at Fredericksburg. Nor does the author stop here. Edward Tracy's mother comes over from Ireland, arriving in time to cradle her dying son in her arms. Then she promptly enlists in the cause as a nurse. Thus the moral of "Irish-American patriotism" gets stated twice.[20] This sort of story continued to appear through the end of the century and beyond. (As late as 1938, there was a new one in *The Old Parish*, a collection of stories about the Irish in Fall River, Massachusetts, by Doran Hurley.) The theme of personal courage proving devotion to America is uppermost, and often in this fiction, the Irish-American hero, if he is still alive, has his virtue rewarded by getting to meet President Lincoln. An antidote to such solemnities appears in the irreverent writings of Charles G. Halpine.[21]

Born in 1829, the son of a Church of Ireland minister in County Meath, Halpine had a typical Protestant Ascendancy upbringing. He dabbled at Trinity College, Dublin, read for the law in London, and came to America in 1850 to make his fortune. His career in journalism and light verse began in Boston, where he contributed to B.P. Shillaber's *Carpet-Bag*, the short-lived (1851-1853) but influential humorous periodical in which Mark Twain's first published story appeared. After moving on to New York City, Halpine worked as a journalist on several different newspapers, incidentally turning out the serial novels mentioned earlier in this chapter. When the Civil War began, he joined New York's Irish 69th Regiment.[22]

While stationed at Morris Island, South Carolina, in August, 1863, Halpine drew up the first "dispatches" featuring Private Miles O'Reilly, an Irish-American Union soldier, "a brawny, large-boned, rather good-looking young Milesian, with curly reddish hair, grey eyes, one of which has a blemish upon it, high cheek bones, a cocked nose, square lower jaws, and the usual strong type of Irish forehead" (*Life* 155). Immediately popular and widely reprinted, these pieces were collected early in 1864 into a wartime best-seller, *The Life and Adventures, Songs, Services and Speeches of Private Miles O'Reilly*.[23] Even President Lincoln is said to have been amused, and the book may have helped to counter the bad publicity about Irish Americans that had followed the violent draft riots in New York in July, 1863, during which mostly Irish mobs wreaked havoc for three days in protest against an unfair conscription act that allowed anyone with $300 to buy his way out of the army.

The character of Miles is mostly stage-Irish: he is excitable, voluble, bibulous, witty, and a trickster. But Halpine also uses him to address in a satiric vein important issues of the war years. As assembled in the book, the plot line of the "dispatches" is as follows. Miles is arrested and interned at Morris Island for song writing. (His satirical songs, written in a mild brogue to familiar Irish airs, were the basis of his popularity.) Lincoln pardons him, he is lionized at an author's reception in New York, and he ends up invited to the White House, where he meets the president and scandalizes the diplomatic corps with an irreverent song about eighty-year-old British Lord Palmerston's affair with the much younger "Mrs. O'Kane." Miles's most famous song, "Sambo's Right to Be Kilt," satirizes cold-bloodedly those who opposed Negro enlistment in the Union Army. Professing to be a "liberal" on the issue, Miles says "I'll let Sambo be murthered instead of myself, / On every day in the year" (55). Upon reaching New York, Miles's satiric base widens to include the spoils system in urban politics:

> Och, the coalition,
> For a fair divishin
> Of the city spoils, that was lately made;
> It now proves a shwindle,
> Which but sarves to kindle
> Into fiercer fury min of every shade. [63]

In the prose narratives that frame the songs, Halpine occasionally manages serious observations, as when General Meagher of the Irish Brigade declares at Miles's White House reception that "the communion of bloody grave-trenches on every field, from Bull Run to where the Chickamauga rolls down its waters of death" has transformed the American Irish from a race of exiles to "proud peers of the proudest and brave brothers of the best" (159-60).

Halpine also published a sequel, *Baked Meats of the Funeral* (1866), a mixed bag of newspaper stories with very little to do with Private Miles. After the Civil War, Charles Halpine had only a frenetic three years of life remaining. He worked as a journalist, edited his own anti-corruption newspaper, supported the Fenian movement, and was elected to the lucrative position of New York City Register of Deeds in 1867. In August of the following year at age thirty-eight, he died of an accidental overdose of chloroform, taken to combat chronic insomnia. The figure of Miles

O'Reilly never really comes alive. He is no more than a hook upon which to hang his creator's songs. Halpine does keep barely alive the tradition of Irish-American satire, but his books are pale beside the more substantial works of pre-Famine writers such as John M. Moore and Thomas C. Mack, who created much more sustained and convincing satiric renderings of Irish-American experience. Still, in his combination of humor and seriousness partially rendered in brogue, Halpine's Miles paves the way for Finley Peter Dunne's Mr. Dooley in the 1890s.

A second odd, fascinating figure is Fitz-James O'Brien, a clever writer who was born in 1828 in County Cork, where his father was a lawyer. O'Brien was raised comfortably on family estates in West Cork, and he observed the effects of the Great Hunger first-hand as a sensitive adolescent. Skibbereen, one of the hardest hit areas, was only a few miles from his home. The experience prompted O'Brien to write a poem, "The Famine," calling for relief to the suffering peasantry, which was published in the *Nation* in Dublin in 1846 when he was eighteen. In 1849 he came into a considerable inheritance, which he took to London and squandered in a little over two years. He also published more poems and his first story, "The Phantom Light," which featured West Cork tales of fairies, miracles, and omens. When the money ran out, O'Brien came over to New York City in 1852, and quickly established himself as a leader of the "Bohemian" literary group (which included Walt Whitman) that gathered at Pfaff's rathskeller on Broadway. O'Brien contributed essays, stories, and poems to magazines such as *Harper's*, and he also wrote six plays. When the Civil War began, he joined the Union Army's Seventh Regiment, and he was killed in action at Cumberland, Virginia, in 1862, at the age of thirty-four.[24]

Despite his background, O'Brien has not been seen very often as an explorer of Irish-American themes. But several of his poems convey the exile's nostalgia for Ireland; he wrote at least three short reminiscences of Irish life; and his play, *A Gentleman from Ireland*, describes the unhappy visit to England of a member of the Irish gentry. Published in 1858, this "Comedy in Two Acts" was performed on the New York stage. Most interesting, though, are O'Brien's Gothic stories of the supernatural, on which what is left of his reputation rests. Critics have seen him primarily as an imitator of Edgar Allan Poe, but "The Phantom Light" demonstrates that he also knew his own Irish folk tradition of ghosts and the occult. A more direct influence may have been the transformations of such materials into memorable fiction by his Irish contemporary Joseph Sheridan Le Fanu.[25]

Furthermore, two of O'Brien's most famous stories contribute subtly to the Famine-generation Irish voice in America. In "The Lost Room" the narrator lives in two rooms on the second floor of a huge old house in New York City. While walking in the garden one dark night, he is accosted by a mysterious old man who warns him that his fellow tenants are "enchanters, ghouls, and cannibals." Returning hastily to his rooms, the narrator finds them transformed into the meeting place of six masked figures who invite him to join them at a luxurious feast. Recoiling in horror from what he sees as an offer to eat human flesh, the narrator agrees only to gamble for his rooms with a throw of the dice. He loses and is driven into the hallway, and the door to his room disappears. "Since that awful hour," the story ends, "I have never found my room." In this story published in 1855 by an Irishman who had seen the effects of the Famine firsthand, the choice of cannibalism or dispossession must have carried special meaning. Moreover, O'Brien establishes a specifically Irish context here, for the narrator recalls an ancestor who left his lands on the County Cork coast to defend himself before Queen Elizabeth against accusations of piracy. Returning after a lengthy stay in London, he found that his property had been appropriated by an Englishman, and he subsequently spent "the best portion of his life in unsuccessful attempts to reclaim his vast estates" (310-31).

In "What Was It?" a muscular, ape-like creature drops on the narrator's chest from the ceiling in his darkened bedroom and nearly chokes him to death. A switched-on light reveals that the attacker is invisible, but a plaster cast taken after the beast has been chloroformed reveals that it is shaped like a man, four feet in height, with a flattened nose and a ghoulish face that "looked as if it was capable of feeding on human flesh" (392-407). Because its captors cannot feed it properly, the creature eventually starves to death. Again, the motifs of starvation and cannibalism recur. And, indeed, there were reports from places such as Skibbereen of people reduced to this horrible exigency during the Famine. In addition, the alien beast is close enough to the prevalent nineteenth-century cartoon stereotype of Irishmen as apes to constitute an Irish-American "invisible man," a forerunner of Ralph Ellison's powerful metaphor for African-Americans.

The more imaginative, complex, and influential novelists of the Famine generation are the subject of the rest of this chapter and chapter 4. Three writers remain to be discussed here: Dillon O'Brien, John Roddan, and this generation's most sophisticated novelist, John Boyce. The first was versatile and adventurous enough to produce an archetypal emigration-and-return novel, two American "western tales," and a mystery set in Ireland. Dillon O'Brien was born at Kilmore, County Roscommon, in 1818, the son of a prosperous Catholic landowner with estates in Roscommon and Galway. Educated by the Jesuits at Clongowes Wood College, he married Elizabeth Kelly, the daughter of a respected Galway magistrate and huntsman, and began married life as a country squire on one of his family's holdings. The Great Hunger ruined the O'Brien family, for their generosity toward Catholic tenants during the Famine years rendered them landless by 1850. Shortly thereafter, Dillon O'Brien with his wife and four children sailed for America. After two or three years in

Detroit, O'Brien took a job running the Indian school at La Pointe, Madeline Island, Wisconsin, an isolated fishing and trading post on Lake Superior. There, he wrote his first novel, *The Dalys of Dalystown*, which opens with an autobiographical framing chapter in which the narrator places himself at La Pointe in "the winter of 185—" in "a cold, windy, miserable shanty," overlooking a lake shore "that appeared desolation itself, not grand or awe-inspiring, but bleak, blank, and dreary." Here, subject to fits of intense longing "for the blazing, cheerful, laughing fire in the big old family grate at home" in Ireland, the narrator wrote his book while "frozen in" over several winters. Deliverance came in 1863, when the O'Brien family, which now included six children, moved to St. Paul, Minnesota, where Dillon O'Brien soon became editor of the Catholic weekly newspaper, the *Northwestern Chronicle*. *The Dalys of Dalystown* was published in St. Paul in 1866.[26]

Perhaps through the combination of extreme isolation and nostalgia for home, O'Brien produced a competent novel, overlong at 500 pages, but full of plausible incident and observation of Irish life in the early nineteenth century. In the opening chapter, the narrator is visited by an Irishman who relates the story of the Dalys of Dalystown. At their first meeting, the narrator confesses that although he loves America for having provided a home to his children and "millions of my countrymen," the New World cannot be home to him because his roots are "too deep in my native land to allow of their taking hold with the vigor of new shoots in another soil." He has set down this story for his own benefit, "for while dwelling on the past, I have been won into forgetfulness of the present" (9-10). Typical of the Famine generation, the narrator's sense of permanent dislocation is reflected in the novel's happy ending—a return to Ireland for the hero and his family.

The story opens in the early 1820s on the troubled estate of kindly Catholic landlord Godfrey Daly in the northeast corner of County Galway near its border with Mayo and Roscommon. (This was O'Brien's own homeplace, and the novel is probably based on his family's experiences.) A compassionate landlord who "let his lands cheap, and was never known to dispossess a poor man," Godfrey Daly has come under the power of the evil middleman O'Roarke, who holds the mortgages on the Dalystown estate. After *The Irish Emigrant* (1817) and James McHenry's *O'Halloran* (1824), this is the third Irish-American novel to describe a Catholic "big house." As such it strikes a significant variation on the theme initiated in Maria Edgeworth's *Castle Rackrent* (1800), where conniving middleman Jason Quirk takes over the estates of genial, profligate Sir Condy Rackrent. In *The Dalys of Dalystown* the dispossessed family regains the big house through the agency of success in the New World. This American solution to an Irish problem appears elsewhere in the Famine generation, notably in the novels of Mary Anne Sadlier discussed in chapter 4. In O'Brien's novel, young Henry Daly, the protagonist and rightful heir, falls in love with a penniless orphan governess, Rose O'Donnell, and is thus prevented from saving his home by marrying well. Perceiving the difficulty, Rose sacrifices her love by emigrating to America, leaving Henry much saddened.

The activities of a peasant secret society of "Ribbonmen" form a second strand of the plot. Vowing vengeance on middleman O'Roarke for having driven scores of tenants from their homes, the Ribbonmen plot his death. Maddened by the memory of his own dead wife and child, driven from their home into a killing rain by O'Roarke, one of the peasants agrees to murder him, and does so on a deserted road, formerly the site of a large village whose inhabitants had been hounded from their homes by O'Roarke. Because this Ribbon lodge has been established by a spy for the British, whose job it is to foment trouble and then inform on the group, O'Roarke's murder leads only to the exposure and breakup of the secret society. According to the narrator and the Dalys, this is as it should be. Although he describes peasant grievances vividly, O'Brien here declares that lawlessness will not solve the problems of the tenantry. He does not condone the murder.

When his mortgages come due, the heart-broken Godfrey Daly falls ill and dies, knowing that his estate is forfeit. After a wrenching farewell to his old home, the dispossessed Henry Daly sets off for America in search of fortune and Rose O'Donnell. The year is 1825. He obtains both with relative ease, finding Rose in a backwoods Canadian cabin and a substantial living as a farmer in Michigan. Along Henry's way, O'Brien provides several apostrophes of praise for American self-government and freedom. And he even borrows a Hudson River School and Cooperesque refutation of the complaint that the New World lacks a sense of the past. True, there are no ancient man-made monuments, he admits, but "the giant pine has fallen over the mound which marks the Indian's grave," and the naturally decaying tree is a more "fitting emblem of mortality" than the "tinseled lie" of a European cemetery's mausoleum (457).

Twenty years pass quickly: boom years in America, terrible years back in Ireland. As spoken by Henry Daly, O'Brien's judgment of the causes of the tragedy of the Famine is clear and angry. Accusing "most" landlords of having been "tyrants to the poor [and] toadies to the English government," he marks the irony of that government's now having kicked the landlords "into the poor house, . . . the famine being a far quicker and more effectual agent . . . to uproot the Celtic race from Ireland. Then we are to have the millennium there, in the shape of English landlords, Durham cattle, and Scotch agriculturalists!" This soliloquy concludes with a warning delivered from the immigrant's perspective: "But bide-a-wee, gentlemen, the Irish Celtic blood is prolific, and while your Saxon and Norman blood is growing stagnant, it is running in wild waves over the earth" (491).

In 1848, the now wealthy Henry Daly hears that "those few brave spirits, scorning life, whilst gaunt famine slays their countrymen by tens of thousands, have taken the field." He knows that this latest rebellion will fail, for "who could put men's hearts into those famished skeletons, who lie down to die, while the cars laden with grain on its way to a foreign market, pass their doors, whose hunger is mocked by the sleek skins of the beasts that graze beside them in undisturbed security" (489-90). There is, however, one piece of good news from Ireland. The Dalystown estate is about to be sold by middleman O'Roarke's simpering fool of a son. Thus, Henry Daly sails for Ireland to buy back his family's old home.

The conclusion of this novel is effective. Henry Daly rides out alone on horseback to Dalystown, "and there, in the calm light of evening, lay the old place, stretched out before him; the crows wheeling round, and the gray turrets and gables peeping through the trees." He passes "the rusty gate, broken off its hinges, the empty gate-house, the grass-grown avenue," and, peering through a window of the house itself, he finds "that the ample grate had been torn from its setting and carried away, leaving a dark, cave-like opening, while the top slab of the marble mantle piece lay broken in two across the hearth" (505-06). This powerful image of the old order's decline leaves Henry momentarily discouraged. But hope returns when some of the still faithful Dalystown tenants appear to welcome him home. Over the next few days, "a cavalcade of friends" solidifies that welcome, and the novel ends with Henry standing on the steps of Dalystown, declaring: "My friends, here on the threshold of my old home, standing in the presence of my God, I promise you that I shall wall round my property with the smiling cottages of a tenantry whose interests and mine shall be as one" (518). In this way, O'Brien allows a measure of fulfillment to the persistent Irish-American dream of the exile's return. However, his conservative solution to Ireland's tragic problems is more sympathetic landlords, not the return of the land to the peasantry. The book's quiet ending certainly mitigates the admonitory power of those "wild waves" of immigrant Irish blood.

Throughout this novel O'Brien has scattered vivid memories of life in the West of Ireland. In addition to a detailed rendering of the Dalystown house and demesne, these include descriptions of horse racing at the Galway Hunt, an old-time peasant fair, and a faction fight between the Murphys and the Joyces. O'Brien's presentation of the hardships suffered by the tenantry is reasonable and sympathetic, and the novel is blessedly free of the convention of making the peasants speak in a demeaning brogue. It is also clear that O'Brien was not writing to make a narrowly sectarian point. The Dalys are Catholics, to be sure, but religious differences play no part in the story, for the villainous middleman is also ostensibly a Catholic. Still, these realistic elements are undermined by a few implausible turns of plot and the stereotypical, black or white major characters, the evil O'Roarke, the saintly Godfrey Daly, and the resourceful, heroic, Henry. However, *The Dalys of Dalystown* is better than most of the novels of its type for two reasons. First, as reinforced by the framing device of the narrator frozen in at Lake Superior, the romantic theme of the vindicated exile's return to Ireland has resonance for O'Brien's generation of reluctant immigrants. Second, O'Brien is not the unconscious victim of the conventions of didactic fiction. He knew that he was writing a romantic novel with an idealized hero. In an aside after one of the realistic passages, he imagines a reader's impatience with him for interrupting the tale. To the demand, "Let me hear something of Henry," the narrator replies that his hero is asleep, and "should I bring him before you now, it would destroy the romantic feeling with which, I am rejoiced to think, you are beginning to regard him—for his nightcap is slightly pulled down over one eye, and his mouth is wide open. Ah! There goes my poor book into the fire, while the 'Mysterious Elopement' occupies its place. So much for being natural" (381). This literary self-consciousness breeds a narrative restraint which saves the book from the worst excesses of sentimental/romantic fiction.

After moving to St. Paul, O'Brien wrote three more novels, all less successful than *The Dalys of Dalystown*. *Dead Broke, A Western Tale* (1873) is the story of a Scottish immigrant to the Michigan Territory whose son wanders the West and ultimately returns to his home. Throughout, the characters are flat and vapid, and O'Brien's attempt to write a popular novel of Western local color is a failure. Ironically, this was the one O'Brien novel to be published in Ireland—as a serial in the *Irish Monthly* of 1882. In *Frank Blake* (1876), O'Brien returns to an Irish setting, the village of "Renville," a sea-side resort town in Connemara early in the nineteenth century, to tell a story of love and intrigue. The romance between Royal Navy Lieutenant and Catholic Frank Blake, in charge of the coast guard detachment at Renville, and Susan Howard, the daughter of the village's Church of Ireland rector, culminates in Susan's conversion to Catholicism. The mystery develops when Frank Blake is arrested for the murder of Robert Eyre, the dissolute, fox-hunting son of the district's big landlord, Lord Eyrecourt. A surprise witness saves Frank, the returned immigrant Willie Joyce, who found the real murderer in New York and extracted a signed confession before his death in a Mulberry Street tenement. In the end, Frank and Susan marry, and Willie Joyce remains in Ireland as head gamekeeper for Lord Eyrecourt. As in *The Dalys of Dalystown*, O'Brien drew upon his family memories to describe the hunts and balls of the County Galway gentry, and again, his use of Irish materials to which he was nostalgically attached makes the book readable. O'Brien's last novel, *Widow Melville's Boarding House* (1881) takes place in Fairoaks, an "orderly town" of three thousand in one of the Western states, in which the Widow Melville supports herself and her son Harry by feeding and housing a pleasant group of boarders. The boy grows up and wanders off to make his fortune, returning to settle in his hometown after having struck it rich in the California gold fields.

The solace and product of O'Brien's hard, early years of exile on Lake Superior, *The Dalys of Dalystown* is far and away his best novel. The other three seem to have been casual enterprises, written as they were after his fortuitous settlement in St. Paul, where he made a busy and comfortable life. As editor of the Catholic weekly the *Northwestern Chronicle*, O'Brien became a close friend of Archbishop John Ireland and a committed prose-lytizer for temperance and the Catholic colonization movement. Like Ireland and the other colonizers, he believed that the answer to most Irish-American problems lay in a second migration—from the pernicious urban environment to healthful, Midwestern farms. After 1869, O'Brien lived on his own farm until his death in 1882, and he spent years working toward the founding of the Irish Catholic Colonization Association in 1879. What links all four of his novels is the persistence of the theme of the exile's return. Both Henry Daly and Willie Joyce end up back in Ireland with comfortable livings, and in the American "Western" tales, the wan-derers in *Dead Broke* return to Michigan and Harry Melville comes back to Fairoaks.

Father John T. Roddan was the author of a refreshingly intelligent and witty contribution to the genre of Catholic immigrant novels of in-struction. Born in Boston of Irish immigrant parents in 1819, John Roddan entered the priesthood in his twenties and, because of his brilliance, was sent to Rome to study at the College of Propaganda by Bishop John Fitz-patrick. Returning home after his ordination in 1848, he became a mis-sionary priest over a wide area south of Boston, including the towns of Hingham, Quincy, Randolph, and Bridgewater. He also began contrib-uting to the *Pilot*, which was at that time the official organ of the diocese of Boston, and he was soon appointed editor, a post which he held until his untimely death at age thirty-nine in 1858. Father Roddan kept the *Pilot* to a high literary standard, while contributing a good deal of sound editorial advice to Irish immigrants over the course of those turbulent years.[27] He seems more a figure from the pre-Famine period than his own time, and, indeed, his life and his novel of 1850, *John O'Brien; or, The Orphan of Boston*, form a kind of bridge to that happier time for Irish Americans and their fiction.

During the years of his *Pilot* editorship, Roddan was a prominent member of a respected coterie of Catholic intellectuals in the Boston dio-cese, including Bishop Fitzpatrick, Father John J. Williams (who became the next bishop), Father John Boyce (the Famine generation's most tal-ented novelist), and the controversial journalist Orestes Brownson. Hav-ing passed through Congregationalism, Presbyterianism, Universalism, and Unitarianism, with a stint at the Brook Farm utopian community thrown in, Brownson had become an enthusiastic Catholic in 1844. He brought the convert's zeal to the pages of his magazine, *Brownson's Quarterly Review*, in which he advocated a conservative Catholicism that stressed militant defense of the faith and discouraged accommodation with Protestants. It was less than fortuitous that Brownson was the most influential reviewer in his time of Irish-American fiction, which he treated consistently as a sub-genre of Catholic fiction. Although some of his criticism was sensible, his theological rigidity blinded him to the worth of some writers, and his equally uncompromising advocacy of immigrant assimilation made him an uncongenial reviewer of any literature with a pronounced ethnic flavor. Brownson didn't much like the Irish, and his reviews of Irish-American novels are full of complaints about the overemphasis of Irishness at the expense of Catholicism. Contending that writers who "defend themselves on national instead of Catholic grounds" are creating damaging divisions within the Church, Brownson says that "the Irish themselves in this country need no special defense, and are best defended, not as Irish, but as Catholics, in common with the whole Catholic population of the country" ("Irish" 542). Wholly without sympathy for the crisis of cultural identity that the Famine generation was facing, Brownson insists that to succeed in America, the Irish immigrant should forget the past and become a respectable citizen of the United States as quickly as possible. For taking this position so strongly, he was attacked in the Irish-American and Catholic press, and New York's Irish-born Archbishop Hughes rebuked him publicly at the Fordham University commencement in 1856.[28] Still, in Catholic literary circles, Brownson was much heeded in the 1850s, especially in Boston, where, as Donna Merwick states, "he was the eye of the needle through which a priest had to pass to 'get published.' For he controlled Patrick Donahoe, whose publishing house was long the most influential in Boston Catholicism; he dominated *The Catholic Observer*, . . . he published *Brownson's Quarterly Review*," and "[his] ideas also came to dominate the *Pilot*" (15-16).

As his preface declares, Father John Roddan wrote his one novel, *John O'Brien; or, The Orphan of Boston*, for "God's poor," from "the middle and lower ranks of society," especially "Catholic parents who neglect their children," and "those children who are running wild in the streets . . . in danger of losing their faith" (vi). He means the Famine immigrants, whose inundation of Boston was in full flood in 1850. Like his protagonist John O'Brien, Roddan was eight or nine when his father died, and as he lived through the same years as a poor Irish boy in Boston, the novel is probably partly autobiographical. John's trials among the hostile Yankees of Boston and Hartford are warnings that locate his story firmly in the tradition of moralizing fiction for immigrants, and there are also a number of extensive doctrinal disquisitions that retard the flow of the narrative. And yet, Roddan's sharp wit and sense of humor and his presentation of John as a healthily mischievous boy with a talent for finding trouble make much of the book pleasurable reading. In addition, it contains a wealth of detail about the problematic relations between Catholics and Protestants in New England before 1850, and about the daily lives of young clerks and apprentices on their own in American cities.[29]

Orphaned at eight, John O'Brien encounters numbers of Yankee Protestants at his various jobs, in lodging houses, and just walking around in the streets. As in the grimly serious books written to defend the faith, most of these Yankees are nefariously committed to separating Catholics from their religion. However, Roddan spares us the grimness. More amused than truculent, he provides a colorful parade of proselytizing Methodists, Baptists, Episcopalians, Unitarians, and revivalists, with noticeable wit and an eye for the humorous tics of fanatical behavior. These include descriptions of a French Methodist farmer in Newton, who rails that "Ze Papiss are ze hogs, ze goats, ze brutes. Zey worship one image; zey hang, burn, and kill all good Christians"; a revivalist "camp meeting" where the doors are locked and pictures of hellfire drive the young women into anxious fits ("It is quite a coincidence, that the sinners who need consolation most are precisely those to whom it is very pleasant to administer comfort"); and a fine parody of the sort of trash that, according to Willard Thorp (47-8), was actually being published in the 1830s in Samuel Smith's anti-Catholic journal, *The Downfall of Babylon*: "It seems that sausages are made of Protestant meat in some of the West India Islands. The way it is done is this: The churches and convents have dungeons under them, for the punishment of heretics. One of these is a sausage factory. The Protestant is tumbled into a kind of hopper, that soon makes mince-meat of him. He goes in, buttons and all, at one end, and comes out at the other, half a mile of sausages. These are reserved for the eating of priests and nuns" (201).

Roddan's satiric gift is only half the story here, however. He was also coming under the influence of Orestes Brownson at this time, and on occasion he seems to be shaking himself into the solemnity of a theological treatise. There is, for example, a long discussion of the possibility of salvation outside the Catholic Church. (Unlike his inflexible mentor, Roddan leaves the door open for all but lapsed Catholics, whom he reluctantly agrees to damn.) The Brownson touch is also apparent in the lack of reference to Ireland and Irish customs in the novel. It is not surprising that Irish-American characters in a novel by a priest should define themselves primarily as Catholics, but it must surely have been a conscious decision to keep all news of the Famine out of a novel about the Irish in America published in 1850. Brownson liked *John O'Brien* very much, praising its "dashing, bold, and simple" style, and declaring that "the author is master of the subjects on which he touches, and he gives us lessons from experience that we shall do well to heed" (124). Roddan remains genuinely angry about the burning of the Charlestown convent and the acquittal by a Massachusetts court of the accused conspirators sixteen years earlier. Although Massachusetts, Boston, and Charlestown have forgotten the event, Roddan declares that God remembers: "The story of the black ruins is written in His book; and beneath the picture of a holy retreat, made a wilderness by the rage of man, there is a sentence—I AM THE LORD: I WILL REPAY!" (196-97). Perhaps because he witnessed the events of August, 1834, as a boy of fifteen, Roddan's anger in 1850 seems more real and less rhetorical than Peter McCorry's, twenty years further along in 1871.

John O'Brien tells us a lot about what life was like for such a boy growing up in Boston in the 1820s and 1830s. There are gang fights on Boston Common between boys from the North and South End, details of the working world for apprentice shoemakers and law clerks, errand boys, and farm laborers, and even a description of the wholly ineffective boys' "House of Reformation," where beginning thieves share their expertise and come out worse than they went in. Roddan also describes the "temptations" of the idle hours for young Catholics, which include bad books, the theater, fire and militia companies (both are only excuses for group drinking and rowdiness), and tea-parties. In 1834, John joins the Mechanic Apprentices Library Association in Cornhill, which provides him with "opportunities for mental improvement" in the form of a library of a thousand volumes, a well-stocked newspaper collection, a winter season of lectures, and classes in elocution. And yet, after pronouncing the Association "a very good school for us all," Roddan goes on to say that "still, mixed societies *always* hurt a Catholic soul," because they create "the very worst sort; that is, l-i-b-e-r-a-l Catholics." There is, he declares, "but one remedy, and that is, to make such a society exclusively Catholic" (240-41). Again, the shadow of Brownson falls.

The novel's conclusion comes full circle, as John O'Brien, now an enlightened adult, secure in his faith and on his way to economic success as well, finds Gallagher, an Irish errand boy, about to repeat all of John's youthful errors. After setting the boy straight, John goes on to marry his childhood sweetheart, the servant-girl Mary Riley, who bears him a son. Roddan thus avoids the most obvious autobiographical and moralizing resolution. John O'Brien does not become a priest. Written during a crucial watershed time for Irish-American culture, Father Roddan's novel is a fascinating document because it looks both ways at once. It mixes the pre-Famine habits of satire, parody, and playfulness with the humorless didacticism and defensiveness of the Famine generation.

In his January, 1849, review of a first novel by an Irish immigrant, Orestes Brownson made an early diagnosis of the ills of Famine-generation fiction and hopefully predicted a change for the better:

Unhappily for Ireland, it has long been her fate to find her worst enemies in her own children, and to suffer more from those who would defend than from those who would traduce her. She has rarely, if ever, spoken for herself. Her best and soundest men have remained silent. Her character has been left to the mercy of her Protestant enemies, or, what is even worse, to her own conceited and moonstruck patriots. The work before us leads us to hope that a new era in her history is about to dawn; that the time has come when we may hear the genuine Irish voice,—not the melodious wail of Moore, exciting compassion, but killing respect,—not the voice of bombastic orators and ignorant editors, turning even Irish virtue and nobility into ridicule,—but the voice of enlightened patriotism, of manly feeling, sound sense, and practical judgment. [60]

The novel in question was *Shandy McGuire; or, Tricks upon Travellers. Being a Story of the North of Ireland*, and its author was a priest in Worcester, Massachusetts, Father John Boyce.

The best educated and most intellectual of the Famine-generation immigrant novelists, Boyce had been born in Donegal town in 1810, the son of a respected hotel owner and magistrate. He was educated for the priesthood at St. Finian's Catholic Academy in Navan, County Meath, where he received highest honors in rhetoric and philosophy, and at the national seminary at Maynooth, where he was ordained in 1837. Boyce served in Irish parishes for eight years, during which time he also became involved in the Young Ireland movement of nationalistic writers and intellectuals. Some of his earliest published writings were contributions to the movement's newspaper, the *Nation*. In 1845, at the age of thirty-four, Boyce came to America and assumed an isolated pastorate at Eastport, Maine. Two years later, he moved to the increasingly Irish parish of St. John's in Worcester, which became the home base for his busy life as a missionary priest to several central Massachusetts towns. Boyce soon became a contributing member of the intellectual circle of Boston-area priests, most of them Irish and Irish-American, who included Bishop Fitzpatrick, Fathers Williams and Roddan, and the Jesuit faculty at Holy Cross College. He began to publish his fictionalized reminiscences of Ireland serially in the *Pilot*, and Fitzpatrick suggested that he make a novel of his work. The result was *Shandy McGuire*, which was published in New York by Edward Dunigan in 1848. This was followed by two other novels, *The Spaewife; or, The Queen's Secret* and *Mary Lee, or the Yankee in Ireland*. In all three, Boyce used the pseudonym "Paul Peppergrass."[30]

Boyce also talked and wrote a fair amount about the nature of religious experience for Catholics. Donna Merwick says that "as early as 1851, Boyce's lectures and writings had but one emphasis: Catholicity is a psychological phenomenon which uniquely recognizes the varieties of religious appetites and satisfies each. . . . he intended to combine epistemology and psychology. For this purpose he assumed implicitly the developmentist position of Newman regarding religious knowledge as well as a proto-Jamesian position on the importance of feeling" (52). Also appearing in his novels, Boyce's emphasis on the emotions in religion supported the general movement toward devotional, evangelical Catholicism in his time. Similar tendencies had also swept through American

Protestantism, of course, even reaching the rational heights of Unitarian Cambridge, where a chair to study the "religion of the heart" had been established at Harvard. Because of these progressive ideas, Boyce ran afoul of the redoubtable Brownson, who continued to preach his intellectual, exclusive, and non-ethnic brand of Catholicism. The debate between these two in Boyce's novels and Brownson's reviews dramatizes significant issues and tensions in their Irish-American and Catholic cultures. Father Boyce was a highly intelligent and sensitive man, a painter as well as a novelist, and he is also remembered as a strong defender of his immigrant parish during the nativist agitations of the 1850s. Not particularly healthy or happy, Boyce was known to have a drinking problem. He died in Worcester at the age of fifty-four in 1864, and was buried in a mass grave for the priests of St. John's parish.

Set in Boyce's native Donegal in the 1820s, *Shandy McGuire* describes in solid detail the multi-leveled, troubled Ulster society in which he was raised, a culture on the verge of dissolution. There is no more thorough presentation in his generation's fiction of Irish peasants, gentry, and clergy, both Protestant and Catholic. In addition, although it is clear that Boyce's sympathies lie with his fellow Ulster Catholics, he avoids the simplistic stereotyped characterizations in the novels of his contemporaries, and makes a genuine attempt to create believable, rounded characters on both sides. *Shandy McGuire* appeared in 1848, in the midst of the Great Hunger, and Boyce alludes to the ongoing tragedy in his homeland by setting this novel in the aftermath of a previous famine, that of 1816-22. Drawing on his own childhood memories, Boyce "remembers well to have seen the long, white, downy hair of hunger covering the cheeks of boys and girls of tender age, as they came, in the dusk of the evening, to seek relief" (101). He goes on to lay the blame for Irish pauperism on British policies: the Act of Union, the abolition of primogeniture, the encouraging and penal enforcement of emigration, systematic rackrenting by absentee landlords, and, particularly in Ulster, the formation and militarization of the Society of Orangemen, bound "by solemn oath and covenant of blood in a common bond of hatred to every thing even approaching to Catholicity." "Thus," Boyce concludes, by the time of this story of the mid-1820s, "the Catholics were completely in the power of their enemies, without leaders, arms, money, or other means to maintain an opposition. They found themselves destitute of every succor—a beggared race, a starving people" (94-103). Boyce explains all this for "the American reader," who is perhaps uninformed about the real causes of the current (1848) Famine in Ireland, and he enforces the message with detailed, emotional descriptions of the squalor and suffering of daily life among the peasants. He also uses these terrible conditions to explain why membership in the secret revolutionary society of Ribbonmen is on the rise in Donegal during these years. Furthermore, as this novel opens, there has just been an additional grave provocation. After having had her character impugned by a vicious Protestant estate agent whose advances she had discouraged, a young Catholic peasant girl, Mary Curran, has died of a broken heart.

Like many in his generation of educated immigrants, those who produced the novels of this chapter and the next, Boyce held an Old-World, conservative view of the proper ordering of society. Himself a member of the gentry, he believed that the future of Ireland depended on its leadership continuing to be drawn from his class, and on the continuance of a hierarchical social structure. Thus, Boyce's peasant characters are conventionally goodhearted, passionate, long-suffering, and religious, and they also tend to be comic figures, excitable, bibulous, wily tricksters who operate comfortably just outside the law. (The illegal distilling of poteen "since time immemorial" is mentioned on the opening page.) In this group, the main figure is Shandy McGuire, a Ribbon society leader who is famous throughout the district for his "tricks upon travellers." The all around popular man, Shandy presides at wakes and weddings as a noted singer and teller of tales, and he relishes his position as "scripturian of the parish." Significantly, however, Boyce presents Protestant peasants in the same way. The members of the local Orange lodge are not black-hearted villains, but also to some degree comic figures given to excitability, drink, and subversive behavior. On both sides, thus, the peasants are the poorly equipped, at times childlike, victims of an unjust system foisted upon them from above. They are not to be blamed for the mutual hatred and violence between them. Boyce remembers this society vividly, and the novel contains a number of effective local color scenes, including a fair in Donegal town that features livestock displays, sugar candy sellers, and a ballad singer whose lament of a murder by Orangemen brings the police to break up the crowd.

It is clear early in this novel that, in Boyce's socially conservative view, both the intolerable status quo and any hopes for the future are the responsibility of the upper classes, from which he takes all of his really significant characters. Though unmistakeably the villains of the piece, Boyce's Protestant gentry and clergy are presented as humorous and human. The result is deft, gentle satire, a far cry from the simplistic propagandizing of most such characterizations in Irish-American fiction at this time. Donegal's Church of Ireland rector is the Reverend Baxter Cantwell, a stiff-necked graduate of Trinity College and the son of an English immigrant to Ireland. Nicknamed "Baxter Trueblue" for his "intolerant, persecuting spirit" towards Catholics, he is also seen sympathetically, like the Reverend Mr. Prouty in Trollope's *Barchester Towers*, as the long-suffering husband of a dour, demanding Englishwoman.

Cantwell's son Archy, on the other hand, is a more conventionally black-hearted villain. It is he who bears responsibility for the death of Mary Curran, and he remains unconcerned for "a peasant girl's reputation." As organizer of the Orange Lodge and estate agent for Colonel

Templeton, the area's big landlord, Archy is ruthless in his dealings with a peasantry whom he perceives to be "savage," and he performs with relish his standing order to evict as many Catholics as possible. He counters his father's ineffectual religious recruiting efforts with his own heartless policy: "When you cannot reform them, exterminate them, and by every means in your power. Leave no means untried; degrade them, impoverish them, persecute them. Misery and beggary and destitution *may* convert them, but the Bible *never*" (61).

Boyce draws Colonel Templeton as a typical Ascendancy landlord of his time: "a high Conservative in politics, a Transcendentalist in religion (we borrow the word from the dictionary of religions for the year 1847), an Orangeman by public profession, a member of the Carleton Club, a whipper-in of the Tories, a retailer of Irish murders and riots in the House of Commons, and an avowed and declared enemy of the Catholics of Ireland" (188). Still, even this list of traits has an edge of wit, and there is humor rather than hatred in Boyce's picture of the earnest landlord trudging solemnly to his tenants' cabins to dispense "the hated tracts: 'Anti-Christ Exposed; Romanism Defeated; The Man of Sin Cloven Down by Five Blows of the Holy Bible; Papist Idolatry; Daisies of Piety; Primroses of Devotion; Dahlias of Faith,' etc., etc." (192). Although Templeton cites American slavery to corroborate his proprietary feeling toward his tenants ("Was not the soil his own—and did he not propagate them on it?"), Boyce also declares that "he was nevertheless possessed of not a few redeeming qualities," notably that "on the bench he was an honest and upright magistrate," who never permitted religion to influence a decision. Colonel Templeton fears the influence of "this French and American republicanism, creeping in day by day through the press," and of emigrants' reports of "this free exercise of their religion which Congress has guaranteed to the Irish in America." His remedy for the threat against Ascendancy rule is to try to keep the Irish peasantry ignorant of the "parallel between its own social condition and that of the United States" (200).

While the Ascendancy Episcopalians attempt to convert the Catholic peasantry with a genteel high seriousness in keeping with their station, a rough and ready proselytism is being practiced further down the social ladder by the Methodists. Boyce condemns the underhanded techniques of urging conversion with bribes of soup and the kidnapping of Catholic orphans, but, again, he sees the comic possibilities in the familiar character of the Methodist Bible Reader, represented by the clumsy evangelist Ebenezer Goodsoul, a passionate but gloomy man given to flights of rhetoric that his reluctant listeners find more humorous than offensive. He refers to Donegal as "Babylon" and the Catholic peasants as "Amorites," and scandalizes a potential convert by asking her to testify in church about how her heart feels. "I'll have none av his dhirty insiniashins," declares the woman, who was lured there in the first place only by Goodsoul's offer of clothes for her family.

The many and varied attempts of Reverend Cantwell, Colonel Templeton, and Mr. Goodsoul to convert the Catholic peasantry fill up a good deal of the plot of *Shandy McGuire*. The other area of great activity involves the schemes and counter-schemes of Shandy's Ribbonmen and Archy Cantwell's Orange Lodge. In the end, Archy gets his just deserts; he is found murdered on the grave of the peasant girl whose death he caused. Of course, the Catholic faith of the peasants is never in doubt. To make this clear, Boyce speaks through Archy Cantwell, whose obvious intelligence makes him that much more depraved: "They never can be converted by ordinary means. Do you think a Catholic, who from his infancy saw himself surrounded by the sacraments of his church, and from which he received, or at least thought he received so much consolation amid all his trials and disappointments of life, will be content with a bare book which he cannot understand?" (59). In continuing this discussion within the Cantwell family, Boyce puts his own belief in the importance of felt experience in religion into Archy's speech: "The word of God to [Catholics] is but a book—it is a thing without eyes, ears, tongue, or understanding. . . . It is but a dead monitor, the priest is a living one. The Bible may convince the intellect, but the heart, the seat of the sensibilities, requires a far different action to impel it."

Naturally, the Catholic gentry and clergy are the moral exemplars in *Shandy McGuire*. A clear role model for Boyce's audience is intelligent, cultured, aristocratic Ellen O'Donnell, who feels "as every Irish woman ought to feel." Educated "in the convents of Italy," Ellen is the daughter of an Irish emigré painter, the last in the line of O'Donnell kings of Donegal, who now lives in Florence. Passionately devoted to both Catholicism and Irish nationalism, Ellen introduces the central moral dilemma of this novel—a central dilemma, indeed, for all of Irish history. The issue is further clouded by her problematic love affair with Captain O'Brien, the Irish Protestant commander of the British garrison in Donegal. O'Brien is sympathetic to the peasants' grievances, however, and more than tolerant of Catholics. In fact, he is seriously contemplating conversion and marriage to Ellen, and the burning of the Catholic chapel by an Orange mob is the last straw. The Captain converts to Catholicism, marries Ellen, throws his British commission into the fire, and exhorts Shandy McGuire and his Ribbonmen to "prepare for the day of retribution, . . . and scourge the Saxon oppressors from the soil that bore ye." The mob's action also brings Ellen around to overt support for violent revolution; she declares that "I would rather see a revolution tomorrow, with equal chances of victory and defeat, than see day after day this beggared nation whining and supplicating for mercy at the feet of a foreign despot" (336, 341).

These strong words from the female protagonist anticipate the position ultimately taken by the character who stands at the moral center of this troubled society—Father Domnick, the parish priest of Donegal town. Extremely intelligent, educated in Spain, most at home surrounded by books in his library, Father Domnick is seen as providing necessary guidance to his parish of good-hearted, but unsophisticated peasants.[31] Undoubtedly mirroring Boyce's own ideas, the progression of Father Domnick's thinking about Catholicism and Irish nationalism is the most interesting aspect of *Shandy McGuire*. In the course of the novel, the priest experiences a remarkable conversion to the advocacy of violent revolution. At the beginning, he supports the decision of the Catholic bishops of Ireland to condemn members of secret societies by cutting them off from the sacraments. In the middle of the novel, he still condemns as "treason" a patriotic friend's assertion that all Irishmen ought to reaffirm their opposition to English tyranny.

The crucial, climactic event for Father Domnick's thinking, and for the novel, is the firing of his chapel, house, and beloved library by a mob of Orange Lodge members led by Archy Cantwell. Heartsick, Father Domnick decides to emigrate to Spain, where he will die away from home. Amid the ruins of the O'Donnell castle, the priest dramatically declares to Colonel Templeton his conversion to violent revolution: "when the time arrives—and it will soon come—that this nation, in the spirit and strength it shall have husbanded for the struggle, shall meet her enemies in the field, to die martyrs or live freemen, then beware of the priest; for when that hour comes, peace will be a crime and resistance a duty." To the colonel's shocked response, "Peace a crime! and this from you!" Father Domnick replies even more strongly: "Yes, from *me*, . . . and if the Irish people were prepared for a revolution tomorrow, I would, old as I am— and this head is white with the snows of eighty winters—I would be found amongst the foremost in the fray, . . . to encourage my brave countrymen while speech was left me, to drive you and all your Saxon breed from their native soil" (349).

That Father Domnick speaks also for Father Boyce is clear from an earlier apostrophe to the reader, in which the author speaks with passionate directness from the perspective of the present—1848 and the Great Hunger. Boyce condemns "the selfish demagogue and the pious ecclesiastic [who] have so long wailed their 'patience chant' over desolate shrines and beggared worshippers, that even now, when the worshippers are rotting, and the shrines are plague-pits, they cannot stop the tune, but cry on, till men are forced to put their fingers in their ears to keep out the sickening drone." Such politicians and priests, declares Boyce, are traitors to humanity: "They come with the voices of angels to soothe down the indignant heart,—to teach men to die of famine for the love of God and the interests of their country,—to hush them into silence and resignation to their fate, when they appeal to them in the name of a merciful God, for succor and counsel in their hour of distress" (254-55).

There is no more stirring refutation in this generation's literature of the prevalent fatalistic counsel that the Irish should accept their role as suffering Christian martyrs. And what makes Boyce's election of violent action over Christian pacificism so powerful is that it emerges in a novel written by an Irish priest and marked throughout by intelligence and a fair-minded rendering of characters on both sides of the conflict as human beings rather than caricatures. Surely it was his espousal of this position, untenable to the Catholic hierarchy, that made continuance as a priest in Ireland after 1845 impossible for Boyce. A similar politics was preached by Father Hugh Quigley, another immigrant priest who left Ireland under a cloud, and whose three novels will be discussed in chapter 4. A categorical propagandist, Quigley was more typical of this literary generation. His unambiguous heroes and villains reflected his own Manichaean view of the Irish Catholic world, and his patriotic priest-characters exhibit none of the realistic subtlety of Father Domnick's rational progression to acquiescence in armed revolt.

Shandy McGuire was popular enough to have three editions in relatively short order (1848, 1850, 1853), and a dramatized version was staged in 1851 as Shandy Maguire; or, The Bould Boy of the Mountains. Also, the book received a number of favorable reviews, demonstrating that Boyce's combination, virtually unique in his Irish-American generation, of intelligence, realism, and the refusal of simplistic propagandizing was appreciated. In the literary mainstream, Godey's Lady's Book mentioned Shandy McGuire twice—as "a very good story" and "a fine Irish novel." In his New York Nation, Thomas D'Arcy McGee called the novel "an able and truthful sketch of life and manners in the North of Ireland." Deploring the "heart-sickening libels" of the caricatured Irish types "on the stage of a petty theater" and in the fiction of Mrs. Hall and Charles Lever, McGee asserts that Shandy McGuire could only have been written by an Irishman who had seen of what he speaks. McGee ends his review by praising Father Domnick's climactic speech and recommending it "to the notice of our own Irish clerical readers."[32]

Very different, and revealing the conservative Catholic opposition to Boyce's ideas about religion and Irish nationality, is the review of his primary intellectual adversary, Orestes Brownson. After beginning with the hope that Boyce may someday speak with "the genuine Irish voice," Brownson goes on to convey his opposition to Irish and Irish-American chauvinism, to what he sees as the wrongheaded setting of the Celt above the Saxon. He uses most of this long review to explain his own solution to the Irish question, one that ignores Boyce's vision of Ireland. Condemning the previous year's Young Ireland rising as the product of "intolerant nationality," he urges compromise instead of violence. In the midst of the Great Hunger, which he fails to mention, Brownson is able to say that "it will be hard to prove that [England's] policy has not been in the main just and necessary," and he calls for the Irish to acknowledge their allegiance to the crown, and to elect to Parliament intelligent, pragmatic spokesmen who can work through proper channels to redress the abuses of landlordism. These Irish M.P.s should be "men who, while they love their country, love also the empire" (58-88).

When he gets around to *Shandy McGuire*, Brownson never even mentions the crucial character of Father Domnick, much less his climactic conversion to violent revolution. Instead, he complains that the Protestant characters are "worse than the average of the class they are intended to represent," and that Ellen O'Donnell lacks the "repose of manner" and "quiet dignity" necessary for a proper exemplary heroine. He concludes by restating the very theme of Famine-generation propaganda fiction that Boyce's stirring apostrophe to the reader refutes—the contention that suffering and emigration have been good for the Irish. Brownson declares that "they have so prospered spiritually under their temporal adversity, that we almost dread to see them exposed to the temptations of temporal prosperity. They are now fulfilling an important mission in evangelizing the world, . . . and great will be their reward in heaven" (89-90).

Such a destructive misreading of his major themes may explain the pains that Boyce took to get even with Brownson in his second novel. This was *The Spaewife; or, The Queen's Secret. A Story of the Reign of Elizabeth* (1853), a clumsy, 750-page historical novel, the ostensible subject of which is Queen Elizabeth's defection from youthful sympathy for Catholicism in order to gain power, and her subsequent persecution of Catholics, especially in Ireland. The "secret" is her illegitimate child, who is saved from execution and raised by a "spaewife," or fortune-teller. But the real villain of this novel is Orestes Brownson, who is satirized at length in the portrait of Sir Geoffrey Wentworth, the Earl of Brockton, "an old man of great learning and eccentric habits" and "an inveterate enemy of the Anglican Church." Wentworth exhibits the Brownsonian characteristics of elitist intellectualism, refusal to acknowledge the importance of the heart in religious experience, and intolerance of non-Catholics. To debate Wentworth, Boyce creates the character of Father Peter, a combination of himself and his friend Bishop Fitzpatrick, who leads Wentworth's daughter Alice to the light of religious tolerance and appreciation of the emotional aspects of Catholicism. In his wholly negative review of *The Spaewife*, Brownson ignores both the theological debate and the satire at his expense, and only remarks of Wentworth that he "is represented at one stage as too imbecile for the spirit and energy he betrays at another." Though the novel has "high pretensions" and has been "generally commended by the Catholic press," Brownson declares, "it strikes us as too grave for fiction, and too light for history" (279-80).

It is not clear whether his audience knew that he was an Irish immigrant and a priest, but as "Paul Peppergrass," Father John Boyce was a respected novelist in the 1850s. *Shandy McGuire* had had three editions and *The Spaewife* had been published in London (by Charles Dolman) as well as America in 1853. Boyce's third and last novel, *Mary Lee; or, The*

Yankee in Ireland, was serialized in the Baltimore Catholic monthly, the *Metropolitan*, and then appeared in book form simultaneously in Baltimore and Boston in 1860. After his death in 1864, Boyce continued to be read; all three of his novels were republished in the late 1860s and 1870s. In *Mary Lee*, his best novel, Boyce addresses directly the situation of being Irish in America in his time.[33] He explains in an introductory chapter that one motive for writing the book was to refute American "national prejudices" against the Irish, citing "such pictures, for instance, as the 'Priest and the Bottle,' the 'Fiddler and the Beggars,' the 'Confessor and the Nun.' " Boyce appeals to a hypothetical fair-minded reader: "if you be man enough to think for yourself, [then] instead of viewing Ireland in printshop and pantomime, look at her face to face with your own honest eyes" (19).

Like *Shandy McGuire*, *Mary Lee* is set in Boyce's home county of Donegal, but on its wild and beautiful northern coast of rocky peninsulas and fiords. The time is the very recent, post-Famine past—"June, 185-." The most important character is "the Yankee in Ireland," Mr. Ephraim C.B. Weeks, a swaggering, garrulous, underhanded native of Ducksville, Connecticut. Having arrived in Ireland "to speculate in matrimony," Weeks is plotting to marry Mary Lee, another of Boyce's models of pure, Irish womanhood. Mary is ostensibly the daughter of Mr. Lee, the lighthouse keeper at Inishowen Head, but Weeks knows that she is really the orphaned child of wealthy Irish aristocrats, the Talbots, whose fortune he hopes to gain by marrying her. Weeks is being aided in his scheme by his cousin and host, Mr. Robert Hardwrinkle of Crohan, a grim Presbyterian landlord and magistrate, who professes Christianity loudly while tyrannizing his Catholic tenants. Having observed the Irish in New England "dramatized on the stage, tried at the bar, and dissected at the pulpit," and judged them to be "no better than South Sea Islanders," Weeks is confident of the success of his suit: "how could he possibly fail in a land of such ignorance and beggary as Ireland?" (124).

Weeks is a type of the arrogant American abroad. Fighting fire with fire, Boyce has created a satirical portrait of a Yankee in Ireland to counter Yankee caricatures of the Irish in America. Upon his arrival in Donegal, Weeks suggests to the first Irishmen he sees that they ought to import Yankee lecturers to "wake up" the natives "to a sense of [their] capabilities." His complacent chauvinism is immediately apparent, as he declares that "it's the duty of every free-born American, wherever he goes, to enlighten mankind as to the character, enterprise, social advancement, and universal intelligence of his countrymen" (54). Weeks's dedication to his patriotic "duty" in no way prevents him from being personally unscrupulous. Nor can he see any moral contradiction here. He is an unconscious hypocrite, and Boyce astutely presents the Yankee's peculiarly innocent amalgam of generalized altruism and individual dishonesty. In short, Weeks is a confidence man, created from the mold pioneered by

New England's "Down East" humorists of the 1830s and given its darkest definition in Herman Melville's bleak 1857 allegory of American huckstering duplicity, *The Confidence Man*. Like Melville's chameleon figure, Weeks is revealed late in the novel to be masquerading. Though born and raised a Connecticut Yankee, he has lived in many places and used several names. Lately, he has become a Virginia plantation owner, and he is really only a cousin of the man he is pretending to be.

And yet, despite his glaring faults, Ephraim Weeks is closer to the earlier, warmly humorous Yankees, such as Seba Smith's Major Jack Downing, than to the biting cynicism of Melville's protagonist.[34] Once again, Boyce demonstrates his ability to create rounded characters. Weeks is a comic, not a sinister, figure, "bred and born in the midst of speculators," and encouraged from infancy "to speculate in marbles and hobby horses" (124). The Irish enjoy tricking him, and there is little real malice on either side. Though occasionally exasperated, his hosts mostly just laugh at his unthinking, automatic self-confidence, and his naive, narrow-minded complacency. Boyce even credits Weeks with surprisingly generous economic inclinations. Quick to lend money to his neighbors, "he was by no means a mercenary man. Nor was he, like most lovers of money, envious of his neighbor's prosperity." These mitigating touches lend credence to Boyce's formidable negative criticisms of the American type that Weeks represents.

Weeks's most important function in this novel is his embodiment of the Yankee (and, by implication, American) value system. "Mr. Weeks represented a large class of his countrymen of New England," says Boyce, and he is explicit about the traits of the type: "*Smartness* to him was every thing. It was the embodiment of all the virtues, moral and intellectual— the only quality for which man deserved admiration or respect. . . . Learning was nothing in his estimation, if it failed to realize money; nay, the highest mental accomplishment was not only valueless, but contemptible without money." Boyce again demonstrates his social conservatism in laying the blame for Weeksian/Yankee corruption partly on the "universal scramble" of American social mobility, which he contrasts with the old order of Europe: "Whilst in other countries each grade in the community had its own legitimate trades and occupations," in the United States, "every body snatched at what came handiest. The tailor dropped his needle and mounted the stump; the lawyer burned his briefs to trade in molasses; the shoemaker stuck his awl in the bench and ascended the pulpit; and the shopboy flung his yardstick on the counter and went off to edit a Sunday newspaper" (124-25). To underscore his own preference for a hierarchical society ruled from the top, Boyce goes on to assure his readers that Weeks "was not an American gentleman, by any means, either in habits or education. . . . and those of his fellow-citizens who could rightfully claim that distinction would never have recognized him as one of their number. He was, in short, a Yankee." As Ireland herself generated an indigenous mercantile middle class later in the nineteenth century, this sort of feeling came more to the fore there. Contempt for the hustling shopkeeper, the "gombeen man," also became a dominant theme in Irish literature when the collision of values that Boyce registers here began to hit home.

Boyce also indicts the subordination of religion to business in America by means of clever satire. His tongue loosened with whiskey (he arrived in Ireland a teetotaler, but was soon converted), Weeks delivers a revealing explanation of the "liberal" view of religion espoused by "the merchants and traders of New England." Stating his own creed to be "a first cause and the perfectability of man," Weeks turns the Protestant ethic into a transparent rationale for rapacity:

> Yes, ladies and gents, whatever tends to cripple trade or impede the progress of social advancement, whether it be a new theory or an old theory, a new creed or an old creed, we strangle it. We *strangle* it as the heathens in old times used to strangle deformed children. Business men in our country ain't so very particular as to difference in religious denomination. They don't care much whether the creed be Orthodox, Universalist, Episcopalian, or Baptist, if it only gives free scope to intellect, and a clear track for human progress. [267-68]

"I'm a Yankee," Weeks declares, "and them sentiments are true blue Yankee sentiments. We ain't a-goin' to be fettered by any form of religion under the sun; if it don't encourage trade and commerce, it don't suit us—that's the hull amount of it."

As Weeks explains, there is only one creed that Yankees object to—Roman Catholicism. The reason is that "the laws and rules of the Catholic church hain't got no joints in 'em; you can't bend 'em no shape or form." Weeks credits his generation for having "shaken ourselves free from the trammels both of pilgrim and priestly rules," and arrived at a modern, practical religion. American ministers "seldom preach about sin, or hell, or the ten commandments, or that kinder subjects, because such themes are calculated to disturb and perplex business men, to the injury of trade. And we have long made up our minds that trade must be cared for, whatever else suffers." Weeks's peroration is pure manifest destiny: "I can never believe . . . that the Founder of Christianity intended a nation so intelligent, so intellectual, and so civilized as ours should be bound down hand and foot by the strict rules of the gospel." Having adapted the rules "to the interests of the state and the requirements of society," America "must go ahead—we can't help it—prosperity forces itself upon us. . . . Nothing can bar our progress, for our destiny is universal empire" (268-70).

Also important in this novel is Boyce's presentation of the corollary of Weeks's attitude toward the Irish in Ireland; that is, the Yankee, American treatment of the Irish immigrants in the United States. At one point some of the local peasants get Weeks arrested as "a notorious cow thief." When he casts about for someone to vouch for his good name and innocence, Boyce says that "he felt precisely as an unfortunate Irish Catholic feels in New England, when arrested for robbery, and happens to reflect he is the only stranger in the township, and without a friend to say a word in his favor" (150). One concerned peasant woman questions Weeks about conditions in America: "they tell us the poor Irish there isn't trated much better than slaves. . . . Why, I have a letther in my pocket here, from a niece of mine, that's livin in a place called Boston, and she tells me it's tarrible to think of what they suffer" (234). Weeks replies that "only the lower orders of our people" treat their servants so poorly; for the most part, "Why, golly, we love them like brothers." Weeks soon desists from this line, however, for he comes to understand that "such barefaced humbug as he was then attempting would only make matters worse," because his Irish questioners "knew as much about the persecution their countrymen suffered in New England as he did himself." One of Boyce's accomplishments in this novel is the contrast he establishes between the "faith" and values of Ephraim Weeks and those of his Irish hosts: on the one hand, Unitarian vagueness, the Protestant work ethic, mercantile individualism, and celebration of a secular, materialist, mobile society; on the other, Catholic doctrinal certainties, agrarian community, and belief in spirituality and a stable, hierarchic social order. Boyce thus provides the clearest fictional diagnosis in his generation of the cultural and philosophical barriers to assimilation that were being faced by the Famine immigrants. The conflict in world views accentuated in the scholarship of Kerby Miller and others is here corroborated in fiction.

As in *Shandy McGuire*, a number of characters fill out Boyce's inclusive picture of rural Donegal society. And again, their traits reveal his class bias. The peasants are typically good-hearted, mischievous, comic figures, while the gentry and clergy are the educated, serious-minded citizens, on whose shoulders the future of Ireland rests. This novel also has its famous local prankster—Lanty Hanlon. Like Shandy McGuire, Lanty has a jest and a trick for everyone, and he is also a committed patriot who risks his neck to work for Irish freedom. His most dangerous mission here involves the kidnapping of landlord Hardwrinkle's daughter, an exploit that makes him an instant folk hero in the district. Moreover, Boyce draws his thoroughly admirable characters from the gentry and clergy. Mary Lee, of course, turns out to be the daughter of an aristocrat. In addition, the novel's hero is the well-born Randall Barry, a university man, Catholic, and patriot. The leader of Donegal's secret nationalist force, he has a price on his head. When captured, thanks to underhanded work by Hardwrinkle, Barry chooses the gallows rather than the option of asking the Queen's pardon. A third role model from the gentry is Kate Petersham, the daughter of a wealthy and respected Protestant magistrate and the lord of Castle Gregory. Kate's family are Church of Ireland Episcopalians, not Presbyterians, and much is made of the cultural gap between them and the coarse Hardwrinkles. Kate is religiously tolerant, a well-read admirer of Jonathan Swift and Thomas Moore, and a supporter of Irish freedom. In fact, it is on her champion steeplechaser that her friend Randall Barry ultimately makes his escape. To be sure, Kate eventually becomes a Catholic, thanks mostly to the example of Mary Lee, but even before her conversion, the local parish priest praises her as "an Irish girl in every sense of the term . . . with a heart full of true piety" (328).

Another of Boyce's semi-autobiographical, learned priests appears in *Mary Lee* as well. The parish priest is the Oxford educated Father John Brennan, who is Kate Petersham's spiritual advisor, a close friend of Mary Lee, and a supporter of Randall Barry's rebel cause. (Presumably, the revolutionary conversion experience undergone by Father Domnick in *Shandy McGuire* is no longer necessary after the Famine.) Father Brennan is also Boyce's spokesman in his continuing debate with Orestes Brownson, who appears in *Mary Lee* thinly disguised as Dr. David Henshaw, a Scottish barrister and recent Catholic convert, and an Oxford classmate of Father Brennan's. Boyce is summarizing his quarrel with Brownson in his sketch of Henshaw's "ultra" views of religion. "Yet but a novice in the church," Henshaw "only saw her doctrine under its severest aspect. Her dogmas and anathemas were the only signs of her divine power he could discover, whilst the more gentle and delicate operations of her spirit on the hearts of men were entirely hidden from his view." Boyce cites Henshaw's consignment of all non-Catholics to hell as an example of his religious despotism: "His head was Catholic, but his heart was that of a pagan philosopher—as cold and unfeeling as a stone" (117).

When Henshaw visits Ireland, which he immediately dislikes, the two old friends clash again, and throughout the novel, Henshaw/Brownson's rigid, intellectual, exclusive Catholicism collides with Brennan/Boyce's emphasis on their religion as flexible, charitable, and consoling. This is in keeping with Boyce's belief in the primacy of the heart in religious experience, and with his own ministry among poorly educated Famine immigrants in Worcester. Moreover, the Henshaw figure represents another aspect of the negative reception of the Famine immigrants in America. Even within their own church, they could be given the cold shoulder by arrogant co-religionists who had been in America longer or who saw Catholicism less emotionally. Father Brennan is similarly tolerant in his views about literature. Like Kate Petersham, he appreciates Swift and Thomas Moore, and he joins her in asking Henshaw, "Can't we admire a man's writings without inquiring into his faith?" In reply, Henshaw dismisses Moore as "a very respectable songster in his way, but an immoral man, a bad Catholic," and a corrupter of youth, "because in losing his faith he lost his morality also" (165-67). Boyce was the only Irish-American novelist of his generation to actually suggest in print that books have value separable from the purely didactic. Connected here is his sophisticated sense of humor, reflected in the balanced satiric portraits, unmarred by blinding bitterness, of his people's adversaries in Ireland and America.

The conventions of plotting were not Boyce's strong point, and he brings the action of *Mary Lee* to an implausibly neat conclusion. Thanks to Lanty Hanlon and Kate Petersham's horse, Randall Barry escapes hanging and ends up marrying Mary Lee, whose real father, the Catholic aristocrat Mr. Talbot, returns to bestow a livelihood upon the newlyweds. The villainous Hardwrinkle is killed in a riot, and Ephraim Weeks leaves Ireland in a huff on the New York packet from Derry, swearing that "you couldn't find such a tarnation set of varmints in all almighty creation" as the Irish. Scandalized by Father Brennan's theological and literary liberality and his complicity in revolutionary activities, Dr. Henshaw also departs with a sour judgment of Ireland: "Here's abduction, robbery, forgery, riot, and murder, all in a single week. Good heavens! Sir, there is not such another country on the face of the globe" (387).

As reviewer, Orestes Brownson once again had the last word, and his January 1860 assessment of *Mary Lee* is another example of willful misinterpretation. He begins by suggesting that it is "bad taste" for an immigrant to criticize his adopted country (so poorly represented in this novel by the Yankee, Weeks), but his ingenious main tack is to accuse Boyce of slandering his own, Irish people: "His book strikes us, as far as we have known them, to be a caricature, we had almost said, libel of the Irish national character." Quoting at length Dr. Henshaw's parting criticism of Ireland, Brownson declares that if Boyce's novel portrays the Irish accurately, then "the words he puts into the mouth of Dr. Henshaw near the close of the book are none too severe." Moreover, Boyce's performance in *Mary Lee* is typical of Irish literary self-scrutiny: "Indeed, none of the Irish writers of fiction seem to us to do full justice to the Irish character, not even Gerald Griffin. The best of them fail to catch the heroic element of the Irish nature, or to bring out its poetry." Instead, Irish writers such as Banim, Carleton, Lever, and Lover present their own people as "a mixture of the ascetic and the rowdy, the saint and the rapparee, great in a row, intractable and treacherous in the cause of liberty and nationality." Thus, Brownson sets himself up as defender of the Irish character against the slanders of such as Father Boyce: "we have entirely mistaken their character, if they do not act far more from principle and less from mere impulse, and if they are not a far more sedate and self-sustained people than our author represents them."

As for Ephraim Weeks, Brownson sees "no great necessity for introducing a Yankee at all. An Irish adventurer might have played the part assigned to him just as well." Asserting that Boyce's "only motive" in creating Weeks was the unmannerly desire "to show up a live Yankee and the universal Yankee nation," Brownson never addresses the major points of Boyce's characterization: the glaring gap between Irish and

American cultural values that the Yankee articulates, and the related picture of Yankee prejudice against the Irish immigrant. Similarly, Brownson
ignores the very real issue for the immigrant church of emotional vs.
intellectual Catholicism in declaring that the character of Dr. Henshaw
"serves no purpose" in the novel. Recognizing the satirical portrait of
himself here, Brownson claims not to be offended by Boyce's attempt to
"pay him off somewhat as Byron did his 'English Bards and Scotch Reviewers.' " He goes on to reply to two of the points raised by Henshaw.
About the doctrine that outside the Catholic Church there is no salvation,
Brownson is perfectly clear: "never should we hesitate to impress, as far
as in our power, on any one we converse with on the subject, that salvation
is attainable in our Church, and not elsewhere."

Extremely important to the Irish-American publishing world in this
generation is the second point that Brownson addresses here—the judgment of literary works on Catholic moral grounds. He declares that "a
Catholic reviewer has the right, if he sees fit, to review any book under
the point of view of Catholic faith and morals, and no other." The author
of such a review is not necessarily ignorant of "the literary and purely
artistic merits of a book." It is only that he is performing the higher duty
of moral watchdog for the faithful: "We do not ask the writer of fiction
to teach dogma or moral theology, but we do ask him to avoid doing
anything to offend either." Using Boyce's example of Jonathan Swift,
Brownson draws the distinction that helps explain the conformity to conservative Catholic literary standards of most Famine-generation novelists:
"We are willing to give nature fair play, but we are not willing to commend
nature when it opposes faith or morals. We admire Swift, but we would
not commend his *Tale of a Tub*, or recommend writers to copy his smut,
although his genius was great, his patriotism praiseworthy, and he, for
the most part, one of the most elegant writers in the language." In a
masterly damnation with faint praise, Brownson ultimately judges Boyce's
novel to be a piece of trivial nostalgia: "As a work of art, *Mary Lee* has
grave defects; as a picture of life and character, we do not think it just,
or trustworthy; but as a work intended to amuse, and to recall to the
author's countrymen in their exile, the memory of scenes and incidents
in their own native land, to brighten the face with a smile, or to moisten
the eye with a tear; . . . it deserves high praise" (118-30).

This dismissal of *Mary Lee* as unrealistic is the final irony, for Boyce's
novels are as close as this generation ever got to sustained realism. Boyce
considers crucial, volatile issues for Ireland and Irish America, he makes
a significant attempt to create rounded characters, and, in the service of
both aims, he uses a humorous mode reminiscent of the pre-Famine satirists. He avoids the sentimentality of rhetoric and situation, the simplistic
stereotyping, the insistent, propagandizing didacticism of his contemporaries, and through it all, he blessedly abjures the deathbed convention:
no one of consequence dies, on stage or off, in his novels. Only one other

Irish-American novel of this time, his friend Father Roddan's *John O'Brien* of 1850, approaches the sophistication of Boyce's work. Brownson misses all this, perhaps because, as a Yankee and a conservative Catholic, he is doubly criticized in this body of fiction. Boyce's was a pluralistic, tolerant view of society and religion, which could have led to the kind of accommodation with the dominant American culture that his generation desperately needed. But Brownson's was the louder voice, as Merwick suggests in placing Boyce as "the first of a line of Catholic writers in the Boston area to strive for a personal kind of self-expression that had wider aims than institutional religion and its polemics. Eventually these writers were rendered all but inaudible and driven into virtual hiding by the preeminence of Brownson and the spate of small-minded, untalented apologists who followed him" (40-1).

Although he would not have admitted it, Brownson was right in predicting that Father John Boyce would eventually speak with "the genuine Irish voice" for his time. A last example of this is a passage of outspoken eloquence in the middle of *Mary Lee*. As in his repudiation of passive suffering during the Famine in *Shandy McGuire*, Boyce again drops his narrative stance and speaks directly to the reader—this time of the situation of the Irish in America. In this passage, Boyce manipulates the conventions that enslaved his contemporaries, for it begins as a sentimental description of a Donegal graveyard into which Ephraim Weeks has wandered, which the immigrant reader is asked to remember through the familiar nostalgic appeal that characterizes the "exile's lament" in song, poem, and story throughout the nineteenth century: "Dear Irish reader. . . . do you remember the shady little corner where the dear ones lie buried—the grassy mound where you knelt to drop the last tear on bidding farewell to the land you will never see again?" But then something extraordinary in Famine-generation fiction occurs. The rhetoric of nostalgic recollection crumbles under the pressure of authentic anger, and the passage becomes a passionate statement of the disillusionment experienced by Boyce's generation of immigrants. He deplores the wholesale rejection of Old World identity that seems the price of assimilation on exclusively American terms: "But they tell you here. . . . you must forget the past; you must renounce your love for the country that gave you birth; you must sever every tie that knits you to her bosom; you must abjure and repudiate her forevermore." Finally, Boyce builds with the force of unmediated feeling to a peroration that is, in effect, a curse aimed at those immigrants who would too easily deny their heritage in order to be accepted in America. The burning of the Charlestown convent in 1834, the Philadelphia anti-Irish riots ten years later, and the mass xenophobia of the just-ended decade of the 1850s are behind these hard words:

And behold the return they make you for these sacrifices! They give you freedom! What! freedom to live like helots in the land they promised to make your own—freedom to worship your Creator under a roof which a godless mob may, at any moment, fire with impunity—freedom to shed your blood in defence of a flag that would gladly wave in triumph over the extinction of your race. Speak, exile! are you willing to renounce your fatherland for such recompense as this? O, if you be, may no ray of sunlight ever visit your grave— no friend or relation, wife or child, ever shed a tear to hallow it. If you've fallen so low as to kiss the foot that spurns you, and grown so mean as to fawn upon a nation that flings you from her with disgust, then go and live the degraded, soulless thing thou art, fit only to batten on garbage and rot in a potter's field. Go! quit this place, for the sight of an old Irish churchyard has no charms for you. [222-25]

FOUR

Mrs. Sadlier
and Father Quigley

This chapter considers two novelists of unequal significance. Mary Anne Sadlier was the most prolific and influential writer of the Famine generation, and also the first important Irish-American female voice. In all, she published some sixty volumes in a variety of literary modes, many of which were in print for the entire second half of the nineteenth century. In explaining the difficulty of dating first editions of her books, Willard Thorp has said that "her early novels were evidently read to pieces" (99). Sadlier's eighteen novels of Irish history and American immigrant life thus demand close attention. These works, all of them published between 1850 and 1870, are the essential body of fiction for understanding the experience of the Famine immigrants and the conservative Catholic ideology by which many of them lived. On the other hand, Father Hugh Quigley was no more prolific or influential than his contemporaries discussed in chapter 3. However, his three novels, published between 1853 and 1873, recapitulate perfectly the three major didactic purposes of this generation's practical fiction for immigrants: instruction in keeping the faith in *The Cross and the Shamrock*, support for Irish freedom in *The Prophet of the Ruined Abbey*, and advice about how to succeed in *Profit and Loss: A Story of the Life of a Genteel Irish-American*. Thus, Quigley's novels serve as a coda for his generation's fictional concerns. In addition, with its critique of gentility, his third novel introduces an important concern of the following generation's fiction, and thus forms a bridge to chapter 5.

After her mother's early death, Mary Anne Madden was raised by her father Francis, a wealthy merchant, at Cootehill, County Cavan, in the Irish midlands, where she had been born on the last day of 1820. Encouraged by her father, she published poetry at the age of eighteen in a genteel London magazine, *La Belle Assemblée*. Orphaned by Francis Madden's death, which followed serious financial setbacks, Mary Anne left Ireland in 1844 and came to Montreal. There, in November 1846, she married James Sadlier, who was managing the Canadian branch of the Catholic publishing company which he and his brother Denis had founded in New York City in 1837. The Sadliers had come from County Tipperary in 1830 with their widowed mother, and their first publishing venture had been a successful monthly serial edition of Butler's *Lives of the Saints*. In 1853, when the firm bought out the list of pioneering Irish-American publisher John Doyle, the D. & J. Sadlier Company became the largest

Catholic publishing house in America. The James Sadlier family lived in Montreal for fourteen years, during which time Mary Anne bore six children and also managed to begin what was to be an amazingly prolific career as a novelist, essayist, and translator from the French. Being married to a publisher helped her get started, and the Sadlier Company acquisition in 1857 of a Catholic newspaper, the New York *Tablet*, guaranteed that most of Mary Anne's novels would appear at least twice—as weekly *Tablet* serials and as books. (The *Tablet* succeeded Thomas D'Arcy McGee's *American Celt*, which had been bought by the Sadliers.) By 1860, when the family returned to New York City to live, Mary Anne Sadlier was established as the best known Irish Catholic voice in American letters.

As the center of New York's Catholic intellectual community, Sadlier held frequent social gatherings at her home on East Broadway and her summer place at Far Rockaway on Long Island. Her friends included journalist Orestes Brownson, novelist J.V. Huntington, New York's powerful Archbishop John Hughes, and Irish revolutionary and writer Thomas D'Arcy McGee. Following her husband's death in 1869, Sadlier turned more to strictly religious subjects, fiction and non-fiction, and in the 1880s she went back to Montreal to live with her married children there. In later years, Sadlier collaborated on several books with her daughter, Anna Theresa, who went on to become a successful and prolific Catholic author in her own right. In 1903, at the age of eighty-three, Mary Anne Sadlier died in Montreal and was buried beside her husband James in Calvary Cemetery, Woodside, Long Island.[1]

On December 29, 1849, Patrick Donahoe's Boston *Pilot*, the most popular Irish-American newspaper in America, contained a call for subscribers that promised the appearance in January of "an Irish Prize Tale of thrilling interest, written expressly for the *Pilot*." This was Mary Anne Sadlier's *The Red Hand of Ulster; or, The Fortunes of Hugh O'Neill*, which ran on the *Pilot*'s front page from January 5 through March 9, 1850, and then appeared as her first novel published in book form. The novel was a fictional rendering of the Irish rebellion under O'Neill's leadership which ended with the Irish defeat at Kinsale in 1601 and the Flight of the Earls in 1607. It was followed by nine more novels set at various crucial junctures of Irish history, most of which appeared first as serials in the *Pilot* or the New York *Tablet*. In one preface Sadlier explains her ambition as a historical novelist in terms recalling the rhetoric and hopes for the effect of the arts on events of her Irish contemporary Thomas Davis. She will present the "great and noble" deeds of the Irish past in order to exhort her countrymen "to enoble our country and give her that place amongst the nations to which the glory of her sons entitles her" (*Confederate* 3).

Sadlier's ten historical novels follow the stock formulas of plot, characterization, and setting of the genre. A brief survey arranged by internal chronology will convey their range and lead to the most important of these books, in which she deals with the Great Hunger experienced by her own generation. In *The Heiress of Kilorgan; or, Evenings with the Old Geraldines* (1867), descendants of the aristocratic Fitzgeralds tell stories of their illustrious ancestors around the fire in their run-down mansion house at Kilorgan in Limerick. The first tale traces the family to Gerald FitzWalter of Wales, and subsequent stories deal with the fifteenth and sixteenth century exploits of the most famous Fitzgeralds, the rebellious Earls of Desmond and Kildare. *MacCarthy More; or, the Fortunes of an Irish Chief in the Reign of Queen Elizabeth* (1868) describes the life and adventures of Florence MacCarthy Mór, the "Munster Machiavelli," who jousted with British forces for control of the Killarney district in the late sixteenth century. *The Red Hand of Ulster* (1850) deals with the Ulster Rebellion of 1595-1601. *The Daughter of Tyrconnell: A Tale of the Reign of James I* (1863), set after the 1607 Flight of the Earls, details the suffering of Mary O'Donnell, the daughter of the exiled Earl of Tyrone, at the hands of James I, who adopted her. *The Confederate Chieftains: A Tale of the Irish Rebellion of 1641* (1860) is a fictionalized history of this rising, from the meeting of conspirators in September 1641 to the death of Owen Roe O'Neill, "the greatest, and bravest, and wisest" of the leaders, during Cromwell's successful campaign against the rebels in 1649. Set in Tipperary in 1766, *The Fate of Father Sheehy* (1863) tells of the heroic priest and patriot who went underground as a beggar, only to be betrayed by informers. In *The Hermit of the Rock: A Tale of Cashel* (1863), which takes place in the 1820s, a mysterious old hermit who tends the graves and ruins on the Rock of Cashel holds the key to an unsolved murder. *The Old House by the Boyne; or, Recollections of an Irish Borough* (1865) is a romantic tale of love and intrigue in an old mansion near Drogheda around 1840. That Sadlier wrote her serial novels to weekly deadlines in the manner of Charles Dickens is clear from a note in the *Tablet* of April 1, 1865, temporarily suspending publication of this one, due to the "dangerous and protracted illness of one of the author's children." Also set "just before the awful period of the Famine" is *Maureen Dhu, the Admiral's Daughter: A Tale of the Claddagh* (1870), a love story in which the beautiful daughter of a fisherman is wooed by a Galway merchant.

Most of these home-based novels were very popular with Sadlier's nostalgic immigrant audience, and they tended to have more editions than her "American" books. (There were at least five nineteenth-century editions of *The Confederate Chieftains, The Fate of Father Sheehy,* and *The Hermit of the Rock,* and six of *The Heiress of Kilorgan* and *The Old House by the Boyne.*) But the most popular of Sadlier's Irish historical novels was the only one in which she confronted her generation's great shared disaster. First appearing in 1853, with at least eight editions published by the end of the century, *New Lights; or, Life in Galway,* takes place in a Connemara village near Lough Corrib just after the worst years of the Famine. The novel alludes to the horrors of the late 1840s without describing them in detail, however. Its main object is to expose "the nefarious system of proselyting going on from day to day, and from year to year, in the remote and famine-stricken districts of Ireland."[2] To this end, Sadlier describes the attempted recruitment of "new lights" by "Bible-readers" or "Jumpers," who prowl Connemara with armloads of tracts, promising soup to starving Catholics in exchange for conversion to Protestantism. All such activities are encouraged and rewarded by the area's largest landlord, the boorish and violently anti-Catholic Mr. Harrington Ousely.

The main plot involves the family of Bernard O'Daly, a strong farmer fallen on bad times because of the Famine. In the mainstream Famine-generation literary tradition are the novel's two emotional peaks—the death of Bernard's wife Honora and the family's subsequent eviction from their cottage. (Both events are illustrated in line drawings at the front of the book.) Both tragedies are laid at the landlord's doorstep, as his violent rebuff of Honora O'Daly's plea for an extension on the rent hastens her decline, and the evicting bailiff is acting under Ousely's orders to evict Bernard unless he converts on the spot to Protestantism. These scenes are classics of their type. On her deathbed, Honora forgives Ousely, encourages his daughter Eleanor to become a Catholic, and offers her last, sympathetic prayers for the family she is leaving behind. And at the eviction, Bernard O'Daly is forced from the home of his father and grandfather, bereft even of his old overcoat, which the heartless bailiff orders him to leave on its peg. Emigration is a minor theme in *New Lights*. To help their family survive, two of the O'Daly sons go out to Philadelphia, where they get jobs as steward on a steamboat and clerk in a store. They send back money that arrives too late to prevent the eviction, but in time to ease their father's last years.

The novel is most valuable for its early (1853) presentation of two attitudes that help define Sadlier's world view and that of a significant portion of her generation of immigrant Irish Catholics. First of all, both plots and several digressive examples support what Sadlier sees as an unshakeable identification of Ireland and Catholicism that is rooted in "the almost innumerable multitude of saints and heroes, poets and sages," and the "monasteries, and cathedrals, and churches, and stone-crosses" (283-84). Second, Sadlier reveals her political conservatism in opposing peasant retaliation against the persecutions of Ascendancy landlords and the government. Despite the encomiastic treatment of the great figures of the violent nationalist past in her historical novels, when the incensed neighbors of Bernard O'Daly threaten to drive off the eviction party with upraised spades, Father O'Driscoll disperses them, declaring "If the man has done wrong, leave him to God—He is the Avenger—not you!" The repudiation of violent redress here is a part of Sadlier's more general acceptance of suffering, including that experienced during the Famine, as God's plan for His chosen people. Thus, Honora O'Daly's death is presented as a prized opportunity to illustrate the workings of true faith. This expression of fatalism and piety corroborates the world view in nineteenth-century Ireland and Irish America elucidated in the work of Emmet Larkin and Kerby Miller, discussed briefly in chapter 3. These attitudes were crucial to the Famine-generation writers. The identification of Irishness with both Catholicism and suffering helped them make sense of their world and its central tragedy. In Sadlier's eight American-set novels this perspective persists.

In the January, 1850, number of his *Quarterly Review*, Orestes Brownson had suggested that someone ought to "write a tale entitled the Orphan of New York or the Orphan of Boston—the Irish Orphan or the Catholic Orphan—which should be adapted to the condition of the poor orphan *boys* among ourselves." This tale should take such a boy "from very childhood through the actual difficulties, dangers, and temptations which beset boys of this class, up to virtuous manhood." Patrick Donahoe responded to this challenge by offering a fifty-dollar prize and serialization in the *Pilot* for the best novel written to these specifications. Brownson himself judged the contest, and the winner was *Willy Burke; or, The Irish Orphan in America*, by Mary Anne Sadlier. Following serialization, Donahoe published *Willy Burke* as a book, and Brownson promptly praised it in his *Review* as indicating "that a new literature, equally popular, but far more Catholic and healthy, is beginning to make its appearance among us" (538). And so Sadlier's career as a novelist of the Irish in America was auspiciously launched.

Sadlier's preface to *Willy Burke* establishes the constant didactic aim of all her American-set fiction, "written for the express purpose of being useful to the young sons of my native land, in their arduous struggle with the tempter, whose nefarious design of bearing them from the faith of their fathers, is so artfully concealed under every possible disguise." She goes on to identify the focus here as the business world and its goal of wealth, and to provide a rationale for the Famine migration as having "a noble part to play over all the earth, that of spreading the true faith" (3-4).

Though very much a commissioned performance in which no character or situation is more than stereotypical, *Willy Burke* nonetheless inaugurates the most familiar pattern of Famine-generation fiction. It opens in about 1830, as the family of Andy Burke, rackrented out of their Tipperary farm, set off for the "Eldorado" of America. Theirs is the archetypal trauma of emigration. At an "American wake" in their cabin, "the friendship of years was rent asunder, as though by death." Travelling first to Liverpool, the family takes ship for New York, and during the "rough and tedious" crossing, Andy Burke comes down with fever and dies, admonishing his children to love their mother and their religion in the "strange country" to which they are bound. The survivors who land in New York are Mrs. Biddy Burke, "more dead than alive" from affliction and grief, and her four children, including two boys, Peter, thirteen, and

Willy, eleven. Twelve months later, two of these children have died of cholera, but Mrs. Burke has begun to make a bit of money taking in washing. Also, Peter Burke has his first job as an errand boy and Willy is attending the local public school. The opposition of their divergent careers is the first example of the obvious but effective Sadlier technique of presenting contrasting characters to point her moral.

His mother is shocked when Willy reads a passage from his geography book to the effect that the Irish people "were kept in a state of gross ignorance by the Romish clergy, and were sunk in the grossest superstition" (38). When she also learns that the pupils read the Protestant Bible daily and receive instruction on the evils of popery from a minister, Mrs. Burke removes Willy from the school. Going there had been the idea of Mrs. Watkins, a wealthy New Yorker and washing customer of Mrs. Burke's, and a woman of pronounced anti-Catholic feelings. She comes under attack here both for her avowed aim of "snaring" Catholic youths for Protestantism and for her "luxurious" and leisured life-style. Overly proud and headstrong from his success as an errand boy, Peter Burke takes his brother's place at school and as Mrs. Watkins's protege, casually dismissing the possibility of losing his faith in the bargain. He goes on to repudiate his family and religion, thereby breaking his mother's heart. Unable to overcome the weariness resulting from her many trials, Mrs. Burke lapses into a fever and dies. The boys then begin working for a Catholic hardware dealer, who finds them a boarding-house run by Scots Catholics. Within a few days, however, Peter has returned to the Watkinses, who have offered him one dollar more per week than the hardware store. On his own from this point, Willy undergoes several trials. Naturally, his faith is never threatened, and he even manages to make a convert of a fellow clerk while rising in the company through hard, honest labor.

Meanwhile, Peter drifts further and further from his family and the church. Having embraced the secular values of the New York business world, he asks Willy, "You that's such a good Catholic all out—what good is it doing you?" This is the question that in her preface Sadlier has said this book was written to answer. However, the connection between Willy Burke's faith and his eventual good fortune is indirect at best. His supervisor, a crusty old German Protestant, converts to Catholicism on his deathbed and leaves Willy $5,000, which solves both the Burkes' money problems and Peter's apostasy. Willy's generous offer to split the money with his brother "touched his heart, and opened it to better feelings," and Peter returns to the church. In her conclusion, Sadlier claims to have depicted "the part which a Catholic boy is called upon to act in society," and to have shown "the beneficial results which may accrue from the fulfillment of his duty." But it is the bald contrivance of the deathbed legacy, rather than the combination of Catholicism and honest labor, that provides the happy ending. Sadlier is a long way in *Willy Burke* from solving the contradiction between the American dream of success in this world and the fatalistic Catholic tendency to give primary attention to the afterlife. In fact, she never came any closer.

With the strong backing of Donahoe and Brownson, Sadlier was off to a flying start as fictional advisor to the Famine immigrants. Seven thousand copies of *Willy Burke* were sold in the first few weeks, and three editions were published by the end of the second year, 1851. Sadlier went on to write seven more Irish-American novels which constitute an illuminating progression in thinking about Irishness in America. Beginning with the pitfalls of the business world for Irish boys in *Willy Burke*, she tended to examine one pressing challenge to Irish-American life per novel. These include issues of education, the slum environment, domestic service, and the rise to respectability.

Elinor Preston; or, Scenes at Home and Abroad (serialized in 1857 and published as a book in 1866), contains what seem to be Sadlier's personal reminiscences of Ireland and her own emigration to Montreal. The Prestons are a well-to-do, middle-class Catholic family who spend holidays at the Killarney lakes and send their sons to Clongowes Wood College. Orphaned by her father's death in 1843, as was Sadlier, Elinor Preston sails for America on a fast packet of the Black Ball Line out of Liverpool. During the pleasant voyage she meets friendly people, dines at the captain's table, and dances the nights away. In New York City, she is taken in hand by a former Dublin friend, who shows her the sights, then brings her up the Hudson River, through Vermont to Lake Champlain, and finally to Montreal, praised as "the chosen city of Mary," where Elinor plans to settle. Ultimately, she ends up in a small village on the St. Lawrence River, teaching French and English and instructing the parish priest on Irish history. The value of this uneventful little book lies in its description of a middle-class emigration such as Sadlier's must have been, an experience closer to that of Owen M'Dermott, the eighteenth-century "Irish Emigrant" of the first Irish-American novel than to that of the majority of immigrants in the coffin ships of the Famine years.

Aunt Honor's Keepsake, A Chapter from Life (1866) opens with a preface containing Sadlier's most spirited defense of fiction: "I have found moral and didactic stories doing more good, and exercising a more marked influence on the minds of ordinary people, than works of either instruction or devotion." She hopes "to reach those who will not read pious or devotional books in what way we can, and to foil the spirit of the age with his own weapons." The particular aim of the present work is to convince the reading public "that the great want of our day in these American cities is Catholic institutions for the protection of destitute Catholic children" (vii-viii). Here Sadlier also departs from her more typical third-person, omniscient stance to create a first-person narrative in which her protagonist, Charlie O'Grady, tells his own story. He begins with hazy recollections of early childhood in a poor peasant family in Ireland. His first vivid memory is of his own emigration with Aunt Honor in 1841, which Sadlier presents as a powerful, initiatory event, complete with raging storms at sea. Their arrival in New York City prompts a brief excursion into literary realism. The two O'Gradys get living space in a fourth-floor room over a grog shop where two families already live. Babies cry, older children play nearly naked on the dirty floor, and "the steam of the washing, the smell of the soap suds, mingling with that of the cooking, such as it was, made it scarcely possible to breathe, especially for those coming in from the fresh air" (18). The adults, men and women both, reveal themselves as gin drinkers given to violent, screaming fights, leading a squalid "cat-and-dog life," with "neither comfort, rest, nor peace amongst the ten or twelve individuals inhabiting that room." Sadlier describes one terrible night when a drunk man knocks out his wife with a poker and is taken away by the police.

The only work Aunt Honor can get is sporadic washing and ironing, and she and her nephew go hungry much of the time. On Christmas Eve, Charlie and another hungry boy are caught stealing a loaf of bread. Brought before a magistrate, they are sentenced to the House of Refuge of the Society for the Reformation of Juvenile Delinquents. Sadlier now warms to her main theme—the exposure of the House as a snare for Irish Catholic children. Superintendent Watchem and his brutish staff expend their energies beating and cajoling Catholic boys into renouncing their "Romish idolatry." Priests are never allowed in, and Aunt Honor is barred after one visit because she tells Charlie to keep saying his prayers. The telling scene is the death of little Kevin O'Byrne, a staunch Catholic who refuses to knuckle under to Watchem's propaganda. A delicate boy, Kevin falls ill, but continues to quote his catechism and infuriate the staff. His dying request for a priest is refused, and his last words are "I'm a Catholic anyhow—thanks be to God! Jesus! Mary! Joseph! Help me!" Charlie O'Grady declares that "his dying scene was a sermon for us!" What began with a realistic rendering of tenement life ends in sentimental melodrama. Charlie is "reformed" into Methodism and sent off to Illinois, where he narrowly avoids marrying his own long-lost sister. "Aunt Honor's Keepsake," the old prayerbook of their youth, reveals the kinship, and the experience jolts Charlie back to the Catholic Church. The novel concludes with a solicitation of funds for the New York Protectorate for Destitute Roman Catholic Children.

Five Sadlier novels stand out as her most ambitious and significant treatments of major themes for her generation of immigrants. The earliest of these is The Blakes and Flanagans, which was serialized in McGee's American Celt, and then published in 1855 as a book.[3] In her preface, Sadlier declares the motive and locus for her entire fictional enterprise: "It is needless to say that all my writings are dedicated to the one grand object; the illustration of our holy faith, by means of tales or stories. The drama of these in general, and of this one in particular, is taken from every day life." She goes on to distinguish between her "practical stories" and popular romantic fiction. Instead of writing "a more attractive story" full of "hairbreadth scapes from flood and field," Sadlier has tried "to make the whole as natural and as familiar as possible. I do not profess to write novels—I cannot afford to waste time pandering merely to the imagination, or fostering that maudlin sentimentality, which is the ruin of our youth both male and female. . . . One who has Eternity ever in view, cannot write mere love-tales; but simple, practical stories embodying grave truths, will be read by many, who would not read *pious books*. Such, then, is the *Blakes and Flanagans"* (v-vi).

This long novel represents a significant advance for Sadlier in complexity of plot and number of characters. Again, her main structural device is contrast between right and wrong ways of being Irish and Catholic in America. She traces the fortunes of two New York immigrant families, the Blakes and the Flanagans, through three generations and twenty-five years, from the period "before Nativism had developed itself into Know Nothingism," to the present of the early 1850s. A leather-dresser by trade, Tim Flanagan is "a real homespun Tipperary man, hot-blooded, blustering, and loud-spoken, yet kind and generous and true-hearted" (10). He and his wife are "good, old-fashioned Catholics," whose "chief ambition" is "to bring up their children in the same faith." In this they are eminently successful, raising five "cheerful, docile, and obedient" children—Ned (who is twelve when the novel opens), Thomas, John, Ellen, and Susan. Tim Flanagan's older sister is married to Miles Blake, a Galway man and "provision store" keeper on the next block. Having lost several children through illness, the Blakes are left with only two, Henry and Eliza. A marked divergence in values is immediately clear, for the Blakes "were more anxious for making money than anything else," and "religion was, with them, only a secondary object—all very well in its place, so that it did not engross too much time or attention" (11-12). The story that now unfolds corroborates in every detail this contrast between the old-fashioned Flanagans and the progressive Blakes.

The main issue here is the "School Question," which had been a burning controversy in New York in the late 1830s and early forties. During these years, the increasing Catholic population had demanded state aid for parochial education and complained bitterly about Protestant proselytizing in New York's public schools. The agitation had come to a head in 1842, when the state legislature officially secularized the public schools by replacing the Protestant-dominated administration of the Public School Society with a less prejudicial Common School system.[4] Starting in about 1830, the education of Blake and Flanagan children exemplifies the Catholic historical perspective. Mostly because it is cheaper, Miles Blake sends his children to the public Ward School, where his son Harry soon learns to be "ashamed of having Irish blood" and to joke about how long it takes his sister to say her prayers. The "slick," sophistical teacher preaches religious relativism, sneers that "the Roman Church" is "corrupt and far behind the age," and sets the class working so hard at their geometry that Harry "soon forgot his honest indignation in the all-important struggle to *keep* his place, and get a higher one, if possible." This over-emphasis on intellectual achievement worries Harry's mother, who declares that "I'd rather have them taught more of religion and less of them foolish *ometries*, or whatever they are" (25). Of course, things are ordered very differently at St. Peter's School, where the young Flanagans are being taught by "their old-fashioned Catholic teacher," Mr. Lanigan, who wants his pupils to be "as thoroughly Irish as himself," and "as Catholic as your heart could wish." Mr. Lanigan believes "that if the parents took pains to keep the traditions of our race constantly before their children, we should have little reason to complain of the demoralization of our youth, and their backslidings from the faith" (31). The obvious contrast continues as the Flanagan girls receive the *Lives of the Saints* in an "old Dublin edition" from their teaching nun, while Eliza Blake gets an anti-Catholic book about the Reformation as a reward for "punctuality, correct deportment, and diligent attention to her studies." Sadlier's position in the debate between faith and intellect is clear. She abhors the glorification of learning for its own sake in the public school, and praises the concentration on the catechism at St. Peter's. Father Power, the pastor of the parish, declares that because not many can be both, it is better to be a Christian than a learned man. Influenced by his Protestant, public school teachers and fellow pupils, Harry Blake begins to read novels (the frivolous kind, as defined in Sadlier's preface), and to attend the theater, where he learns "to confuse right and wrong."

Predictably, the children grow up with very different ambitions. While Harry Blake considers college, politics, and the law, Ned Flanagan gets a job as a clerk in the company where his father is a leather-dresser. John Flanagan joins his brother in the leather trade, which Sadlier describes as "honest work," and the boys ultimately take over their father's business. Their brother Thomas responds to his education by entering the priesthood. Meanwhile, Harry Blake attends Columbia College and becomes a cynic and a "Broadway swell," thanks, in Sadlier's view, to the atheistic teachings of the "Columbia bigwigs." He goes on to become a lawyer and a politician, and his repudiation of his religion is complete when he joins the Freemasons and marries a rabidly anti-Catholic Protestant woman. Ironically, Harry continues to make good use of his "Irish blood" to get elected and reelected to public office. A thoroughgoing hypocrite, he joins the Tammany Hall Democrats only because they have the power, and supports Daniel O'Connell's movement to repeal the Union of Great Britain and Ireland only to get votes.

On the other hand, through the Flanagans, Sadlier advocates sincere expressions of Irishness and the keeping of Irish customs. These include marching with the Hibernians in the St. Patrick's Day parade, throwing "family parties" with Irish music and dancing and recitations of Thomas Moore's poems, and full participation in the "old Celtic practice" of large funerals. Fully aware of what the currently flourishing Know-Nothings would make of such sentiments, Sadlier sets up a debate between Miles Blake and his nephew, Ned Flanagan. When Miles warns that "men can't be Irishmen and Americans at the same time; they must be either one or the other," Ned answers that "I myself am a living proof that your position is a false one. I was brought up, as you well know, under Catholic—nay, more, under Irish training; I am Irish in heart—Catholic, I hope, in faith and practice, and yet I am fully prepared to stand by this great Republic, the land of my birth, even to shedding the last drop of my blood, were that necessary. I love America; it is, as it were, the land of my adoption, as well as of my birth, but I cannot, or will not, forget Ireland" (164).

In the contrasting lives, and especially the deaths, of the Blake and Flanagan daughters, Sadlier sustains her contrast. When the sickly Susan Flanagan dies of consumption, "her last glance" falls on the crucifix and "her last moments were of the most exquisite happiness." On the other hand, after finishing the public primary school, Eliza Blake compounds her danger by going on to a "fashionable academy," then marrying a Protestant and losing her faith. She dies suddenly in childbirth, unshriven and shrieking for a priest. Eliza's mother dies "of a broken heart" soon after her daughter, and Sadlier comments that "God was not cruel; he was only just," and that it might have been better had Eliza followed "her brothers and sisters to an early grave." Similarly merciless is Sadlier's rendering of the death of Henry Blake's firstborn son. Named Ebenezer at the insistence of Henry's Protestant wife, who also forbids Catholic baptism, the child dies of a sudden fit, just after his grandmother Blake has warned Henry that "if anything happens before [baptism], your child's blood will fall on your own head. . . . Remember, the loss of a soul is no trifling matter" (278).

Of further importance in the delineation of a system of values for Irish Americans in this novel are sub-plots involving two other contrasting families, the Dillons and the Reillys. A year's illness causes John Dillon to lose his business, and he has to move his family to a dirty alley apartment, where he ultimately dies. His son Hugh, a public school classmate of Harry Blake's, has turned into a drunkard and a thief, and his daughter Celia becomes a prostitute. Appearing at his father's funeral, "a cigar in his mouth, and his white hat drawn down over his eyes," Hugh Dillon shocks the mourners by sneering, "I'll be hanged if I go with him to that there Popish burying-ground." Shortly thereafter, he and his gang of "b'hoys" embark on a New Year's Eve spree, glutting themselves at several Bowery taverns and threatening to break the head of anyone demanding payment. Along the way they smash up the fruit stall of a "poor old Irishwoman" in their path. Hugh Dillon pockets her "handful of coppers" and curses her as "a damned Irish beggar" (262-63). Later that same evening, with the old woman's pennies in his pocket, Hugh is shot dead outside a German tavern by patrons who refuse to submit to his bullying. Having lived and died outside the church, he is buried in Potter's Field. This vivid scene echoes through subsequent Irish-American fiction. Forty years after Sadlier's novel, Finley Peter Dunne's Mr. Dooley shakes his head at the similar tragedy of an Irish boy turned violently against his own kind, and forty years after that, another New Year's Eve ends in drunken violence in James T. Farrell's *Studs Lonigan*.

The other subplot provides an opposing model of "filial piety" in the person of Tom Reilly, a Catholic-school friend of the Flanagan boys. When his widowed mother hears that he's been keeping company with Alice Byrne, she criticizes his infidelity—to her! Greatly distressed, Tom explains that although he had been fond of Alice, he has long since seen the error of his ways and introduced her to his friend Mike Sheridan, who now plans to marry her. Much moved, Mrs. Reilly asks if Tom thinks she has been selfish to keep him from marrying, and he promptly answers, "Why, no, mother,. . . . I have been, and I'm sure am still, all the world to you, and it was only natural that you should wish to have no rival in my affection." The scene ends with mother and son beaming at each other, "the light from one face . . . reflected on the other," and with Sadlier driving home the moral of this fierce lesson in the necessary self-immolation of children on behalf of their parents: "Tom made the required sacrifice, and it made his good mother happy, and drew down the blessing of God, for God loves, and promises to reward self-denial" (349). Later in the novel, Sadlier reports on "the quiet happy home" of the Reillys. Tom saves his money, avoids theaters and frivolous sprees, gives liberally to Catholic charities, keeps his mother "as well dressed as any woman of her age needs to be," and sends her to Staten Island or Rockaway Beach every summer. In a last, unintentional irony, Sadlier says that the Reillys, mother and son, "had a god-child in every family amongst their friends," including that of Mike Sheridan and Tom's old flame Alice Byrne. The negative impact of all-encompassing devotion to family becomes a major theme of Irish-American fiction in the twentieth century. But Sadlier has here shown that the expectation of personal sacrifice in the name of filial duty was firmly established in this culture in 1855.

The conclusion of *The Blakes and Flanagans* is a last reiteration of its major theme of contrast. In the third generation, the Flanagans continue to produce "good, obedient" children, "well liked by God and man," while Harry Blake sends his children to Columbia, "where his own faith had been shipwrecked." They emerge into "the front ranks of the Know-Nothings, urging on the godless fanaticism of the age, in a crusade against the religion of their fathers and the children of their own race" (378). The novel ends with the reiterated choice between Blakes and Flanagans, Dillons and Reillys ("I would beg all Catholic parents to look on this picture and on this"), and a chilling indictment of parents who abdicate responsibility for the religious education of their children as "more inhuman than the heathens of China and of Madagascar who destroy their helpless infants. They throw them to be eaten by dogs or swine, or expose them to savage denizens of the forest, but what is the destruction of the body in comparison to that of the soul?" (390).

Extremely popular in its time, *The Blakes and Flanagans* had five American editions between 1855 and 1863, as well as two German editions (1857 and 1866) as *Alt-Irland und Amerika* (Koln: J.P. Bachem). Orestes Brownson thought the novel put too much stress on the Irish. Believing that Sadlier ought to have dealt more broadly with "Catholic Americans," he declared that it was too narrowly "national" a tale and played into Know-Nothing hands by presenting Irish Catholics as an alien group (195-96). Brownson was right to feel uncomfortable, for *The Blakes and Flanagans* cannot, in the end, be read as an argument in favor of assimilation into American life. Instead, the novel is significant for its presentation of Sadlier's Irish and Catholic conservative views, which emerge as very much at odds with the secular values of American society. Although Ned Flanagan claims to be both Irish and American at once, the novel by no means resolves this opposition. Instead, Harry and Eliza Blake thoroughly assimilate American social, economic, and occupational ambitions, thereby losing their own and their children's souls. The Flanagans know how little the world means and when to stop aspiring, and by remaining Irish, Catholic, and in the leather business, their family is literally saved from damnation. Sadlier advocates taking the pious, unambitious peasant out of Ireland, and making him a pious, unambitious, working-class American. Filial piety and family duty are also central to Sadlier's system of values. The older Blakes are ignored by their wayward children, while the Flanagans remain central and respected in their family circle. Throughout, Sadlier presents Catholic family life as the cement that can hold her beleaguered culture of Famine immigrants together. The subplots make this point most graphically, as Hugh Dillon denies his family and dies a violent, hell-bent death, while Tom Reilly denies his own life for his mother and emerges a hero.

The Blakes and Flanagans also illustrates Sadlier's deep-seated misgivings about intellectual curiosity and the pursuit of learning for its own sake. Crucial here is her opposition of the permissive public school and the orderly parochial school, where traditional lessons are learned in traditional ways. Also reflecting this attitude is her suspicion of all but the most didactic fiction, both in her prefaces and in details such as the pernicious effects of novel reading on Henry and Eliza Blake. Nothing could be further from the practice of the pre-Famine satirists, and Sadlier would certainly have deplored their sophisticated, playful attitudes toward the craft of fiction and the problems of being Irish in America. Ironically, Sadlier probably valued least the element of this novel, and of her other fiction, that makes her books worth reading today. Despite its preachiness and melodrama, *The Blakes and Flanagans* is, page by page, through most of its length, a story of the daily, domestic lives of ordinary people who are praised for living ordinary lives.

In her preface, Sadlier explains that her next important American-set novel, *Con O'Regan; or, Emigrant Life in the New World* (1864) "was written in connection with a movement which it is pleasant even to remember—the Buffalo Convention." The reference is to the Irish Emigrant Aid Convention, the brainchild of Sadlier's friend and fellow immigrant Thomas D'Arcy McGee, which met in Buffalo in February of 1856. The plan, which never got off the ground, was to form joint-stock companies which would purchase large tracts of farm land in the Midwest and sell them back to Irish immigrants on the installment plan. Although she refers to her novel as "a plain unvarnished tale," it is clear from the preface that *Con O'Regan* is a piece of propaganda in the interest of the Buffalo scheme. Sadlier says that it first appeared serially in McGee's *American Celt*, and because of the connection with the Buffalo Convention, the novel was probably written in 1856. Serialized again in the Sadliers' *Tablet* in 1863, Con O'Regan appeared as a book the following year.[5]

Having left his young wife and two children back in "Ballymullen," Con O'Regan arrives in "a New England city" (probably Boston) in the fall of 1844, and finds his sister Winny, ill-clad, shivering, and employed doing "housework" for very little pay. The first friends from home that Winny takes her brother to see are Paul and Nora Bergen, who are living with their four children in a damp, cold cellar, "some eight or ten feet underground." Already an experienced hanger-out on corners, six-year-old Patsy Bergen talks back to his parents and refers to new immigrants as "Irish Paddies." Having invited Con to share a meal with his family, Paul Bergen goes on to admit that "things are not so plentiful here as we all remember them in the farmers' houses about Ballymullen; we haven't the big fat pots of bacon and cabbage,—or broth that a spoon would stand in; no, nor the fine baskets of laughing potatoes that would do a man's heart good to look at them; but what there is, you're welcome to, and so, if you don't want to insult me, you'll just sit over at onst an' fall to." Sadlier explains this vestigial hospitality as an example of "those old home-virtues which make the peasant's cot in Ireland a palace of content" (22-23). Considering the proximity of the Famine to this narrative, Sadlier's romanticizing of peasant life is an extraordinary exaggeration in the service of her stated aim of convincing the Irish to leave the cities for western farms.

More evidence accrues as Con finds "thousands of our poor country people" worse off than the Bergens, packed into tenements at the rate of "ten or twelve Irish families in a house," and treated "like dogs" by native Americans who vilify them as "ignorant Irish Papists." Upon observing the urban Irish "living by hundreds in squalid poverty," Con muses to himself: "Isn't it a queer thing all out that so many shut themselves up in towns this way, where most of them never rise higher that day-labourers, and them all—one might say—used to a country life at home" (93-94). The chief problem, as Con sees it, is initial financing. Before solving this problem (for the O'Regans, at any rate), Sadlier provides several more examples of the ill effects on the Irish of the pernicious urban environment. The evil of drink is a prime target. A teetotaler, the serious-minded Con refuses to attend a dance at Phil McDermot's saloon, for he knows "very well that night dances in taverns or public houses were everywhere and always condemned by the Church as inimical to Christian morality." The publican McDermot is himself presented as a traitor to his own kind, because he lures Irish Americans to drunkenness and corruption for personal profit. The most vivid example of the curse of the bottle is poor Paul Bergen. Despondent about being out of work, Paul starts drinking and playing cards at home. When his feverish child asks for water, the inebriated Paul gives him gin by mistake, and the boy dies. The heartbroken father solemnly vows permanent sobriety. Also affected adversely by life "amongst a worldly and irreligious people" is Con O'Regan's co-worker, Tom Houlahan, who exemplifies the denial of Irishness and Catholicism by the children of immigrants. Con is shocked by Tom's contempt for his parents, Ireland, and religion, and their heated exchanges enforce Sadlier's warning about "the fearful gulf which passing years will create between [Irish parents] and their offspring—a gulf which *may* be eternal" (258).

Sadlier sees all of these as primarily urban problems, and her solution is that of the Buffalo Convention—resettlement on farms in the West. Unfortunately, she makes no realistic attempt to answer the economic question. Instead, the O'Regans get to Iowa through another *deus ex machina* device. At the risk of his life, Con saves his employer's money in a fire, and his reward is financial backing to begin life as a farmer in Iowa. Paul Bergen and his family also go West, thanks to a letter from his brother offering to stake Paul to a farm. The Iowa that these immigrants find is Edenic, an Irish-American version of the pastoral myth of the virgin land: "When Con and Paul were taken in succession to survey their new possessions, they could hardly believe their eyes that it was wild land on which they looked. The undulating surface of the prairie was covered with the delicate herbage of Spring, green and soft as that which carpets the valleys of the Emerald Isle. The fairest and brightest-tinted flowers were scattered around in rich profusion, and altogether the scene had that pastoral character which belongs to a high state of cultivation" (333).

Bringing the Emerald Isle into the comparison prepares Sadlier's audience for the description of the Irish-American community that follows. This is no less than Ireland in miniature on the American prairie. Even better than the old country because the land is easier to work and the farmers work for themselves instead of the landlord, Iowa is otherwise indistinguishable from Ballymullen. Everyone in the place is Irish, and they sing the old songs, and keep up the old customs of dancing parties and large home wakes. In contrast to the selfish scramble for individual advancement in the American cities, these Irish farmers help raise one another's cabins and crops. Their children are taught by Andy Dwyer, a strict but kindly schoolmaster from "home," whose classroom features "a nice picture of the Blessed Virgin over the master's seat, with a smaller one of St. Patrick for a *vis-a-vis* on the opposite side of the room." And the parish priest, Father Doran, who visits the school "almost every day," is the undisputed leader, temporal as well as spiritual, of the community.

Clear proof of the positive effect of the move from city to country is the transformation of little Patsy Bergen, who arrives from the East a disrespectful street urchin, already denying his heritage in the manner of Tom Houlahan: "I a'nt an Irish boy, I was born in B——." After three years on the prairie, Con O'Regan can look at Patsy and praise the "healthy influences that had changed the little Yankee rowdy into a genuine Irish boy, full of the traditional virtues of his people, and susceptible of every noble and generous feeling" (373). "I wish to God," says Paul Bergen's brother, "that we had more of our own people out here. This is the place for them, and not the smoky, dirty suburbs of the cities, where they're smothered for the want of pure air, and, worse than all, where they get into all sorts of ugly scrapes by reason of the bad company they fall in with, and the bad example they see wherever they turn" (335).

Sadlier's Iowa is not, of course, a place that ever existed. As far from reality as the island that appears off the Donegal coast every seven years, this is a daydream of escape from both the Irish Famine and the American slum. Sadlier leaves the Bergens and O'Regans after three years in Iowa, basking in the May sunshine of this visionary landscape, surrounded by bountiful crops, hogs and horses, neat, pretty cabins, respectful, quiet, "genuine Irish" children and even "rale Irish Shamrock growin' in the garden." No more than *The Blakes and Flanagans* does *Con O'Regan* argue that the Irish should adjust to the conditions and values of life in America. Through the escape to an idealized Ireland-in-Iowa, Sadlier avoids confronting the real problems of the Famine immigrants, even though she presents these with some force in the first two-thirds of the novel.

Here, as in her other novels, a selective realism operates. Her descriptions of slum conditions, poor pay for backbreaking labor, and nativist discrimination and insult are accurate enough, but her unshakeable conviction of her mission as a moralizing novelist demands a solution— and one that rewards characters who remain faithful to Irishness and Catholicism. Thus, to solve what were essentially unsolvable problems, Sadlier is forced to drop realism in favor of her familiar old ploy (used first in *Willy Burke*) of economic relief as reward for a chance act of heroism. Still and all, as her prefaces continue to declare, Sadlier believes herself to be a realist, writing in opposition to popular romance, which she sees as morally reprehensible. And, in fact, *Con O'Regan* is one of her better novels. She grounds her sense of the evils of city life for Irish immigrants in authentic detail, and the characters here are among her most fully developed and complex. She obviously worked hard on this novel of nearly 400 pages. If she was finally unable to refrain from providing idealized answers, at least she asked honest questions.

The third of Sadlier's more important novels is *Confessions of an Apostate; or, Leaves from a Troubled Life* (1864), which was first serialized in the *Tablet* in 1858. The novel opens with the sudden appearance of Simon Kerrigan, a reclusive old man who takes a cottage near Glendalough in County Wicklow. After two years he dies, leaving with a priest the manuscript of his autobiography, written "to deter others from treading that path which he had found so fatal." That manuscript constitutes the remainder of the novel, a sustained dramatic monologue that expresses convincingly the lifelong remorse of conscience resulting from one man's apostasy. This is Sadlier's least cluttered narrative, for the first-person voice of the suffering protagonist saves her from the propensity toward preaching and flowery digression. For once, Sadlier has created a believable character from the inside and sustained his tone of voice over the course of a novel.

Simon Kerrigan was born near Glendalough and the famous ruins of St. Kevin's monastery, the son of a small farmer whose death releases the boy to dream of "success" in the great world beyond the valley of his happy childhood. Simon's is an American dream, and he sets off in about 1810 for Boston, explaining that "a voyage to America was then far different from what it is now, and was considered a sort of neck-or-nothing enterprise, that was either to terminate in an ocean-grave or a fabulous amount of wealth" (35). Upon landing in "the stately old Puritan city," Simon gets a job in a hardware store and a room in a boarding house, and soon discovers the prevalent local opinion of his kind: "to be a Catholic was bad enough, but to be an Irishman and a Catholic reduced a man to the very lowest social grade." A kindly fellow-boarder advises him that to "go ahead fast," he need only "keep your Popish notions to yourself, and don't let anyone know what persuasion you belong to." A fellow Irishman further explains to Simon that the roots of Boston's anti-Catholicism are in the "nonsensical" tall tales of the Protestant clergy, who are compared, in a rare humorous aside, to Ireland's traditional storytellers: "they earn their living, the creatures! by making stories and telling them. The only difference is, Simon, that the *seanachies* used to tell about ghosts and fairies and the like, and the ministers' stories are all about Popery!" (50).

At first, Simon seems to be on the right track. Enrolling for night school courses in "grammar, arithmetic, and bookkeeping," he comes under the tutelage of Philippus O'Sullivan, a sympathetic Kerryman out of the hedge-school tradition. But Simon makes the same mistake as Henry Blake by drinking too "copious drafts" of "that profane learning which, compared with the spiritual, and wanting *it*, is worse than use-less." Promoted to a clerkship, he makes advances in the business world and simultaneously drifts into religious indifference. In four years, he has cast off what he now considers the "superstition" of Catholicism and gone over entirely to "hideous skepticism." A sign of his new depravity is Simon's relief at the death of his old teacher, who had nagged him about religion: "I reveled in my sense of freedom like a bird escaped from a cage" (100). Next, Simon jumps at the chance of a better job in New Haven, although he knows full well that Connecticut is the state in the Union "most opposed" to Catholicism. To avoid being connected with Irish Catholics, he changes his name to Kerr and begins to consort entirely with "Protestants of the evangelical school," most of whom think he is of lowland Scots background. These include his new employer, Deacon Samuels, and his vivacious daughter Eve, with whom Simon falls in love. Their Protestant wedding is the watershed event for Simon. No sooner is the ceremony over, than "conscience took up the lash and commenced the work of castigation which has hardly yet ceased, after years of remorse and sincere repentance."

Predictably, worldly success follows spiritual ruin. Simon gets a third of his father-in-law's business as a sort of dowry and eventually takes over the firm, but his wife, sensing his inability to embrace Protestantism, condemns him as a hypocrite, and their four children grow up to be virulent anti-Catholics. Simon's suffering increases considerably as he realizes that "my apostasy affected not myself alone but every child I had, or might yet have, ah! and their children after them." About this time, having heard from other immigrants about Simon's conduct, his family back in Ireland disowns him. In a last, bitter letter, his brother reports that the news of his apostasy is about to kill their mother. His pride stung, Simon replies that he "felt all the better" for his defection from Catholicism. Shortly, he learns of his mother's death and is all but overcome by a flood of remorse and grief.

From this point, Simon Kerrigan/Kerr's life is a living hell of continuous self-torture. His children, "the pride of my heart, and the solace of my wretchedness," fall ill and die, all except Joel, the first-born son, upon whom "all our hopes were centered." However, because of his "foundation of Puritanical ice," the boy grows up a "cold and heartless" atheist. Having discovered his father's background from his mother, Joel contemptuously accuses Simon of being an alien and a hypocrite. Infuriated, Simon knocks his son down, nearly killing him. This horrific scene is followed immediately by the death of Simon's wife, and a nightmare vision of his dead mother at Glendalough warning him to repent. Together, these events break the "evil spell," and true "Christian repentance" for his sins enters Simon's heart. He returns openly to the Catholic Church, causing general "horror and indignation" in New Haven, and moves back to Boston alone. There, for twenty years Simon leads "an obscure and peaceful life," until he has a last disturbing encounter with his son. While visiting a priest in Philadelphia at the time of the nativist riots of 1844, Simon sees Joel at the head of the mob attacking St. Augustine's Church: "Never shall I forget the demoniacal expression of his once handsome features as he waved his arm and called on the others to burn down the 'Mass-house' and clear the city of the rascally Irish. The sight has never since left my eyes" (250).

For Simon, this is the last straw. No longer able to abide in "a country where such guilt and misery had been my lot," he returns "to the dear old land which in an evil hour I quitted." At the end, Simon Kerrigan concludes that Ireland is still the best place to be a Catholic. Comforted by "the monuments of ages of faith around, and the same faith ever living and acting amongst the people," he has found a measure of peace: "Here, amid the solitude of the desert city, I meditate on the years I passed in a foreign land, and rejoice that the feverish dream is over" (251-52).

The three novels just discussed embody a progression in Sadlier's thinking that reflects a central dilemma of the Famine immigrants. Their understandable reaction to the threat to identity posed by the alien, inimical American society was to cling tenaciously to their old ways and values, and the enforced living in urban ghettoes made this consolidation easier. In *The Blakes and Flanagans* (written before 1855), Sadlier still believes the implied moral of her first novel, *Willy Burke* (1850)—that the immigrant can remain Irish and Catholic by keeping the culture and practicing the values of the old country and ignoring those of the new. In *Con O'Regan* (c. 1856), the escape to the pastoral West seems to keep the American possibility alive, but this is really an illusion; Iowa is a proper home for Irish immigrants only because Sadlier has turned it into an idealized Ireland. Now, in *Confessions of an Apostate* (serialized in 1858), Sadlier has given up the ghost. The "feverish dream" from which Simon Kerrigan awakes on the final page is the American dream, and the novel ends with an emphatic rejection of the New World.[6]

Sadlier's next American-set novel reiterates that rejection so strongly as to leave no doubt about the issue. *Bessy Conway; or, The Irish Girl in America* (1861) is an instruction manual for working girls similar to that for boys in *Willy Burke*. In its preface Sadlier declares her aim of indicating to Irish servant girls "the true and never-failing path to success in this world, and happiness in the next." Her subsequent description of the American environment suggests a deepening pessimism about the possibilities of American life for the Irish: "Perhaps in the vast extent of the civilized world, there is no class more exposed to evil influences than the Irish Catholic girls who earn a precarious living at service in America." In fact, such are "the awful depth of corruption weltering below the surface, and the utter forgetfulness of things spiritual" in American cities, that "it is a matter of surprise that so many of the simple-hearted peasant girls of Ireland retain their home-virtues and follow the teachings of religion in these great Babylons of the west" (iii-iv). The novel opens on the comfortable, fifty-acre farm of Denis Conway, near Ardfinnan on the River Suir in County Tipperary. The year is 1838 and Denis's daughter Bessy is about to leave for America. Far from being a destitute fugitive, the girl has been tempted to "see the world" by the offer of domestic service from the American wife of a sea captain on the Liverpool-New York run. She travels to New York in the captain's suite, with certain employment ahead and several friends from home making the same voyage. Despite the relative comforts of her crossing, however, the archetypal pattern of trauma persists. Bessy gets very seasick on the first leg from Waterford to Liverpool, there is a dangerous storm as the New York-bound ship passes Ireland and nearly runs onto the rocks, and Sadlier describes steerage passengers gazing "through the mist of tears on that fast-fading dream of beauty," thinking "that nothing could ever repay them for the sacrifice they were making." Also along for the ride (to thicken the plot) is Henry Herbert, the son of the Conways' landlord at Ardfinnan, who confesses to Bessy that he is following her out of love. She discourages him in no uncertain terms, explaining that her parents would never sanction her marriage to a Protestant.

As soon as the ship docks in New York, Sadlier begins to use the technique of contrasting characters. Paul Brannigan, an honest, devout fellow-immigrant and Bessy's protector, eschews drink and takes up the trade of shoemaker. On the other hand, Ned Finnigan, one of Bessy's friends from home, uses his savings to start a saloon, and is soon drinking too much himself. Additional bad examples for Bessy are provided by two fellow servants, Bridget, who stops going to Mass and soon loses her faith, and Mary Murphy, who puts on airs and silk dresses when only a week off the boat. None of this deters Bessy, however, and her model conduct soon gets her promoted to house maid.

Early in the novel a discussion of the much higher proportion of priests to laity in Ireland prompts Sadlier to reiterate the preference in her preface for the old country over the new. The immigrant priest Father Daly articulates the basic contrast between poor but spiritual Ireland with the "calm repose" and "contentment which springs from true religion," and the "feverish whirl" of hustling, secular America, driven by "honor-seeking!—money-seeking!—office-seeking!" (125). In typical Sadlier fashion, the priest goes on to rationalize the increased Irish emigration as God's way of "fertiliz[ing] His infant Church" in America.

Curiously, Sadlier avoids illustrating her pessimism about America with hair-raising tales of Irish Americans fallen into horrible sin. In letters home, Bessy Conway explains immigrant problems in the abstract, and no one in her circle of Ardfinnan emigrants gets into serious trouble. The worst that happens is Mary Murphy's elopement with a fast-talking "swell" without her parents' permission, and even she is married by a priest. Bessy, herself, does so well that she is able to start a savings account. (Sadlier advises servant girls to go and do likewise, to avoid the pawnshops, and not to spend all their earnings on clothes.) Of the perils of domestic service suggested in the preface, Bessy faces only one. When her employer returns to Europe, Bessy is hired by a woman in the throes of a conversion from Episcopalianism to evangelical Methodism who orders her servants to nightly prayers. Bessy refuses and is fired, but she gets another good situation immediately, working in the home of a doctor.

Meanwhile, as Bessy and her friends are making their way in New York, the Famine has come to Ireland. Ultimately, even a strong farmer like Denis Conway cannot pay his rent. The family is left with only "the grace of God and his holy peace," and the bailiffs come to evict them. As the furniture piles up outside the Conways' door, Sadlier executes one of her least plausible plot resolutions. Bessy herself walks up the road, having returned to her home for good. She pays the bailiffs and the furniture goes back inside. Subsequently, Henry Herbert also returns to Ireland, a changed man and a Catholic convert. Taking over the family estate, he becomes a model landlord, "an example to the surrounding gentry," and, at last, the successful suitor for Bessy Conway's hand. To conclude, Sadlier reiterates her rejection of America when Bessy, now an experienced emigrant, warns her Tipperary neighbors that "thousands of Irish girls in New York" have lost their Catholic faith as a direct result "of their going out alone to America, without any one to advise or direct them, and them falling into bad places at the very first." Her parting advice is to "Keep your girls at home—if *you* can live here, so can they, and you'll find it better in the long run."

This unrealistic resolution involves a double distortion. Bessy Conway did so well in America, and the Famine years were so terrible in Ireland, that her return to the old country is implausible on both counts. Bessy's return is motivated more by Sadlier's pessimism about American city life for Irish Catholics than by the demands of realistic fiction. Moreover, the picture of a successful immigrant girl returning to Ireland to rescue her family in "the terrible year of the Famine" is formidable wishful thinking. This is the tenant-farmer's equivalent of the return to the big house in Dillon O'Brien's *The Dalys of Dalystown* (1866). Sadlier's audience certainly responded, for *Bessy Conway* had six American editions in the nineteenth century, more than any other Sadlier novel with an American setting.

Sadlier's last ambitious novel and one of her most revealing, is *Old and New; or, Taste Versus Fashion* (1862). In it, she warns her Irish-American audience about the mixed blessings of making it into the middle class. Again, she works by contrast—of old versus new money and accompanying displays of good taste and frivolous fashion. Atypically in the Sadlier canon, this is entirely a novel of observation and instruction on social issues. Catholicism is a given to all concerned, and no one loses his faith. Here the sins are all against propriety, and the repudiations are of Irishness only. *Old and New* presents three families afflicted with severe cases of the bourgeois bends. Sadlier introduces the Hacketts, Gallaghers, and Fogartys through their houses, for she knew well that home ownership was the badge of middle-class respectability in America, and that for an immigrant family it loomed even larger, representing a potential ticket to acceptance into the adopted society, proof that the stranger had made his own "American" way. The house as central symbol recurs frequently in Irish-American fiction, as would be expected given its importance in the culture.

So it is that *Old and New* opens with a description of a row of three houses on "one of the 'up-town' streets crossing the avenues" of New York "some five or six years ago" (about 1856). First is the home of Henry Hackett, a widower and modestly successful grocer with three daughters, "who could play the piano, and read French (at least they said so), and paint, oh! such nice flowers, and work most beautifully in Berlin wool," and who refuse "to turn their attention to such vulgar practices as the making of beds, cooking of victuals, knitting or darning stockings." The Hackett girls have only disdain for their modest house, "such an old rookery of a place, old faded bricks, and common white shutters! and only *two stories high*! . . . And us finished and home from school!" Their contempt is sharpened by the fact that "two brown-stone houses, one of three, and the other of no less than four stories, had provokingly reared themselves on either side," the outer manifestations of the worldly success of Tom Gallagher, a butcher, and William H. Fogarty, a baker. Worst of all, the six Gallagher daughters and one Fogarty child had been school companions of the Hackett girls, who get no sympathy from their father, a practical man whom his daughters see as having "no more spirit than a coal-heaver." The other two families are more indulgent to their daughters, all of whom exhibit the pretensions and slavish attention to current fashions that Sadlier attributes to their finishing-school experience. In addition, all the girls are ashamed of their Irish background and take pains to avoid acknowledging it.

The great figures of contrast enter the novel through Sadlier's description of their house, "an old-fashioned residence some two miles farther up town, but much nearer the East River." As she warms to her subject, Sadlier speaks reverently of "dwellings that remind us of the good old times when *New Amsterdam* was a staid and sober city," and she praises the "antique gables and high-pitched roofs" of "these ancient dwellings of the real 'New York aristocracy' " (73-74). Such is "Rheinfeldt House," with "its pointed gable towards the river, and its antique front overlooking its own sloping lawn," its "double tier of covered verandahs," "successive rows of old casement-windows," and "balustrade of light, open tracery running along the base of the roof."

In this exemplary mansion, where good taste is a moral force, live Bertha Von Wiegel and her mother, the widow of an aristocratic German Catholic whose family home this is. This family's Irish connection is revealed when Bertha quotes for her mother's enjoyment "The Bells of Shandon" and "The Groves of Blarney." It seems that Madam Von Wiegel is an Ascendancy Protestant, raised in an Irish castle where she was wooed, won, and converted to Catholicism by her husband, who had stopped there on his grand tour. Bertha Von Wiegel was brought up mostly "at the old castle in Ireland" with her grandmother, also a Catholic convert. There, she picked up habits that scandalize the Hackett-Gallagher-Fogarty ladies. She wears plain, serviceable clothes, takes a hand in the cooking and chores at Rheinfeldt House, and uses phrases that "any common Irish person would say." In sharp contrast to the bourgeois ladies' obsessions with clothes, parties, and social climbing, is Bertha Von Wiegel's intelligent interest in things Irish. She quotes from Ossian and the Irish poets, sings the songs of Tom Moore and Carolan, and speaks knowledgeably about the folklore of her mother's home area, having collected tales on her own at peasant firesides. She even keeps up on the latest developments in Irish archeology, asking, in a letter to her Irish relatives, whether a recently discovered hoard of Celtic jewelry "corresponds with any of the *fibulae* described by Walker in his Treatise on the Dress of the Ancient Irish."

Also running counter to Bertha Von Weigel's decorous, retiring ways is the blatant concern for the marriage market of the Hacketts, Gallaghers, and Fogartys. This reaches an early peak in the novel with the wedding of the eldest children of two of the families—Sam Fogarty and Eliza Gallagher. The wedding is as "fashionable" as possible, even to a "thousand dollar" honeymoon tour of Niagara Falls and Lake Champlain, and it prompts the reasonable Henry Hackett to make an unflattering comparison with weddings back in Ireland, where "there were no silks, or satins or jewelry, or frizzled locks—no receptions or wedding-towers, but there was peace, plenty and contentment" (98).

Once the social contrasts are established, the bulk of the novel details the eventful romantic entanglements of the various young women—notably the Gallagher girls and Bertha Von Wiegel. Mrs. Gallagher and her three eldest daughters flee to Saratoga for a summer husband-hunting tour, traveling in an extravagant new carriage bursting with dresses for dining, walking, dancing, and sleeping, along with "all the other costly trifles that go to make up the toilet of a New York Fashionable Lady." Once there, in another example of Sadlier's harsh treatment of the wayward, the girls get what they deserve—in the form of disastrous infatuation with Messers Winter and Frost, spurious Southern gentlemen and the reputed owners of huge plantations in South Carolina. To their father's great grief, Ellie and Mag promptly marry the two charlatans, who soon get a chance to show their true colors. Tom Gallagher loses his money in a bank failure, and Frost and Winter take the first train South, never to be heard from again. The symbol of their fallen fortunes is the Gallagher family's move from their mansion to "a two-story cottage not far from the

line of the Third Avenue Railroad," sparsely furnished with "cane-bot-
tomed chairs, and all such vulgar appurtenances."

Meanwhile, a mysterious former lover has re-entered Bertha Von Wiegel's life. This is Major Edgar Montague, an Irish officer in the British
army, who comes calling to Rheinfeldt House with his companion, Captain Bellew. Naturally, Montague is an Ascendancy aristocrat, the second
son of Lord Dunmore, whose Irish estate is in the neighborhood of Castle
Mahon, where Bertha Von Wiegel was raised. During her adolescence
there, Bertha had fallen in love with Montague, as "the nearest approach
I had ever seen" to Samuel Richardson's hero Sir Charles Grandison.
Although he was a Protestant, it also appeared to Bertha that "his lofty
intellect had caught glimpses of Catholic truth." Now, Montague declares
both his undying love for Bertha and his recent conversion to Catholicism,
and they marry immediately. He then goes off with the British Army to
India, and Bertha moves back to Ireland to take up permanent residence
at Castle Mahon. Because one of the younger Gallagher girls goes with
the new Mrs. Montague as seamstress and maid, Sadlier is able to point
the contrast between the two families and her novel's main moral in Annie
Gallagher's letter home to her sister: "I can now see the difference that
exists between Taste and Fashion—the Old and the New, in other words
the quiet, easy, natural life of those to whom wealth and position are not
new, when compared with the empty, artificial, make-believe life of people who are, as we were ourselves, wholly devoted to show" (453).

As for the other two middle-class families, the Fogartys continue to
prosper, though afflicted by occasional attacks of poor taste (their first
grandchild is given four names, "Herbert-William-Thomas-Samuel Fogarty," and "some would have had George-Washington superadded"),
while the Hacketts come back strongly after a fire destroys their home
and grocery stock. Amazingly, Sadlier uses this trouble to enforce her
view of the dangers of romantic fiction. Sarah Hackett falls asleep while
reading *The Fatal Secret*, which the girls have been hiding from their father,
and upsets an oil lamp, causing the blaze. The contrite Sarah emerges as
her father's sober, industrious helpmate, and "one salutary change ef-
fected in her by that night's disaster," declares Sadlier, "was a horror of
bad books, and nothing would ever after induce her to read or even to
open one."

In her conclusion, Sadlier restates this novel's sustained criticism of
a "prevailing folly of Irish-American society, . . . the scarcely concealed,
and too often openly-paraded, contempt of everything *Irish*. . . . Not that
I would have them love America less as the great and free and noble
country of their birth, but I would have them respect Ireland more than
they do." Alluding to the stage-Irish conventions, Sadlier warns the
younger generation "not to laugh at Ireland through the exaggerated and
unnatural caricatures drawn by her enemies for stage effect," but rather
"to study what Ireland was, and is, to see what Ireland and the Irish race

have done, and so to judge of her claims to a share of the world's respect" (484).

Sadlier is here advising the permanently settled American children of the Famine immigrants, and yet, what she advocates is a corrective backward look at Irish history and culture. Indeed, *Old and New* is her third American-set novel in a row in which the protagonist returns to Ireland to live at the end: the apostate Simon Kerrigan, Bessy Conway, and now Bertha Von Wiegel. In addition, the moral spokesman and exemplar in this novel is the most un-American of its characters, Bertha's mother, Madam Von Wiegel. There is evidence in the final pages of negative reader response to the guidance offered here. Sadlier seems to be answering criticisms of the *Tablet* serialization of *Old and New* in the months (February through August of 1862) prior to its appearance as a book, when she denies the complaint "that I have dealt too hardly with persons who rise by their own industry from an inferior position in society." Citing the success of Tom Gallagher, Henry Hackett, and "the Fogartys generally," she explains that "it is not the ascent of our people in the social scale which I have satirized, but the follies and extravagant pretensions of some amongst them when they do succeed in gaining a position." She then reiterates the moral of her tale: "Taste, as opposed to Fashion, I have endeavored to illustrate in the quiet, natural, unpretending life of the really elegant and refined Von Wiegels," who have been "purposely connected . . . with high aristocratic circles in the Old World in order to show the difference between vulgar show and refined taste" (480). Early in the novel, Madame Von Wiegel strikes the same note in explaining the tasteless abuse of wealth by American parvenues as natural "in new countries like this where the lines of distinction between the different classes of society are not so clearly defined" (91). This is an early critique of newly bourgeois Irish America—and from a surprising perspective. Sadlier looks down from above with European snobbishness rather than up from below with New World levelling sentiments. In this, as in so much else, she goes against the American grain.

On the issue of Irish freedom from British rule, Sadlier steers a similarly conservative course. She registers disapproval of visiting physical-force nationalists by describing one "Roland McFustian," who "was out with Smith O'Brien and the rest of them at Slievenamon, and knocked down a policeman with a blow of his fist," during the abortive rising of 1848, and who is coming to New York "to seek his fortune like every one else." Although even his supporters admit that "Roland hasn't done much, that's a fact," McFustian will be honored with a mayoral reception, a dinner at Tammany Hall, and a torchlight parade, all because "they say he's a wonderful great hand at making a speech" (323).

The treatment in *Old and New* of the movement for women's rights completes Sadlier's full rendering of her conservative social views. Two women "attired in a fashion half masculine, half feminine, but rather inclining to the former" visit Rheinfeldt House, introducing themselves as the Reverend Julietta Fireproof, B.A., Bachelor of Arts, and Dorothea Mary Wolstoncroft Brown, the famous lecturer on "Woman's Rights, Spiritualism, and Negro Slavery." In refusing to sign their petition claiming "the right to plead the cause of oppressed womanhood at the bar of the Senate, yea, and at the bar of justice," Madam Von Wiegel again speaks for Sadlier: "I belong to a Church that teaches unlimited submission to the Divine Word, and holds with St. Paul that women should obey their husbands, and, moreover, keep silent in public assemblies." As for "the custom which consigns us women to the shades of domestic life," she sees in it "a merciful dispensation for us, and a wise provision of the Divine Ruler for the wants of the human family" (129-30). Sadlier's position is hardly surprising. In the first place, as a formulation of what Nancy Cott has called "the canon of domesticity," this idealized view of woman's role in family life was widely held in mainstream, middle-class, nineteenth-century America. Second, that view was equally popular in Sadlier's own immigrant subculture. The Famine-generation's religious, journalistic, and literary spokesmen also counseled reliance on family life to bring their community through the continuing crisis of these years. As will be seen in the next chapter, belief in the traditional role of woman and mother as the cornerstone of Irish-American culture solidified into dogma in the following generation.

With *Old and New*, Mary Anne Sadlier's career as the self-appointed moral and practical guide for the Famine generation of immigrants from Ireland came to an end. Her subsequent fiction—the cursory *Aunt Honor's Keepsake* and four Irish historical novels—adds nothing to the philosophy whose presentation was her motivating goal as a novelist. Easily the most prolific and widely read of the Famine-generation writers, Sadlier was the first formidable literary force in Irish-American culture. Her ten novels set in Ireland established the genre of Irish historical fiction firmly on the American literary scene, thereby fulfilling the promise of James McHenry's novels of the 1820s and also serving as examples for the several other contributors to that genre in her generation—Alice Nolan, Mary L. Meany, Patrick Sarsfield Cassidy, Charles G. Halpine, and David Power Conyngham. Her eight novels set in America are similarly validating for the genre of Irish immigrant fiction that was pioneered by Charles Cannon and carried on in the novels of John Roddan, John Boyce, Peter McCorry, Dillon O'Brien, and John McElgun. It is in this second area that Sadlier made her two greatest contributions—as a chronicler and as a guide. To her credit, she avoids the temptation (to which Cannon and others succumbed) to lace her novels with turgid theological disquisitions. She sticks throughout to the goal and method stated in her preface to *The Blakes and Flanagans*: "the illustration of our holy faith by means of tales and stories." And while her plots and characterizations suffer from their enforced subservience to her moralizing aim, her novels contain a wealth of detail about the daily, domestic and working lives of mid-nineteenth-century Irish Americans. This is selective realism, but realism nonetheless. From a tenement room housing twenty people to the new bourgeoisie at Saratoga Springs, from the day's events at a parochial school to the jigs, reels, and verse recitations of an evening's entertainment, there is more of the social experience and circumstances of the Famine immigrants in Sadlier's fiction than anywhere else. Describing both squalor and success, she has a secure place near the beginning of the tradition of Irish-American delineation and critique of ethnic city life that culminates in the novels of James T. Farrell.

Sadlier's second contribution is her clear fictional embodiment of a functional ideology for her generation, that of conservative Irish Catholicism. On the very positive side, this was a system of values that worked. Religion, family, community, and a measure of ethnocentric pride were the elements that held this beleagured generation of immigrants together. And Sadlier's novels contributed by giving that system a fictional voice. On the other hand, there were the less attractive aspects: fatalistic acceptance of suffering; opposition to American intellectuality, democracy, progress, and ambition to succeed; advocacy of the old order of traditional customs, the patriarchal family, and a hierarchical society. Moreover, the rejection of America in Sadlier's later novels is also a logical extension of her view of the world. This was far from being a paranoid view. Nativist prejudice against this immigrant generation was a real and threatening context which helps to explain Sadlier's advising the immigrant to hold tenaciously to his Irishness and Catholicism, and (ultimately) to go back home if he can. The Sadlier American-set novels are the most graphic fictional examples available of the jarring collision in the 1850s and 1860s of the profoundly dissimilar Irish Catholic and American Protestant cultures.

Still and all, despite her real contributions in troubled times, Mary Anne Sadlier remains an unsympathetic writer. In contrast to the all-too-human ambivalence of a Charles Cannon, the iron-clad certainties of Sadlier are disturbing. She is the most persistent of propagandists and her armor never cracks. Her manipulation of plots, characters, and literary conventions is single-minded, self-assured, and sometimes merciless. Sadlier praises young men who sacrifice their own lives for their mothers, sentences hapless, improvidently married girls to lives of lonely remorse, and blames drunks and sinners for the deaths of their parents and children. In a similar vein are her profound distrust of pleasure (be it in saloons, dance halls, or romance novels), and her invariable treatment of suffering and sacrifice as opportunities to be embraced, of which the most prized is the happy death. In Sadlier's eighteen Irish and Irish-American novels the consistent authorial presence is the chilling voice, neither vulnerable nor humanly implicated in her decisions, of a dispensing judge who adheres to the letter of the law and enjoys her work too much.

A much-traveled immigrant priest, Father Hugh Quigley was born near Tulla in County Clare in December, 1819. He was educated at hedge-schools and worked for a time on the famous "trigonometrical survey" of Ireland in the early 1830s before deciding to become a priest. Quigley refused to take the oath of allegiance to the British government required of students at the national Catholic seminary at Maynooth, and instead went off to Rome where he was ordained after five years of study. A contemporary biographer declares that Quigley was "ever since he could think, a REBEL, as were all his ancestors in Donegal and Clare." First appointed curate in his home parish of Tulla, he went on to Killaloe, where his advocacy of his parishioners' stealing food from their landlords during the Famine got him in trouble with the authorities. Threatened with transportation, he went on the English and Scottish missions for some time, and returned to Ireland to join the Young Ireland movement. Shortly after the failed rising of 1848, in which he is thought to have participated, Quigley emigrated to New York, having written Archbishop Hughes and received a missionary appointment. For his first ten years in America, he served on a mission circuit based at Troy, New York. Subsequently, he was a missionary priest in upstate New York, Milwaukee and LaCrosse, Wisconsin (among the Chippewa Indians), and Eureka, California (among miners). For a time, he was Rector of the University of St. Mary in Chicago. Over these eventful years, he published three novels and an idiosyncratic history of *The Irish Race in California and on the Pacific Coast* (1878) which begins in ancient Ireland, covers the Irish discovery of America by St. Brendan (about which Quigley has no doubts), and concludes with celebratory biographical sketches of prominent Irish Californians, classified as "Statesmen, Capitalists, Military Men, Clergymen, Journalists, and Doctors," with a chapter for each. He died while on a visit to his first American station in Troy, New York, in 1883.[7] Quigley's three novels embody the didactic purposes of Famine-generation fiction so emphatically as to render those purposes memorable.

Published in Boston by Patrick Donahoe in 1853, *The Cross and the Shamrock; or, How to Defend the Faith* was extremely successful, selling some 250,000 copies by 1878, most of them presumably to Famine-generation immigrants. The flavor of this novel is conveyed in its impressive trail of subtitles: "An Irish-American Catholic Tale of Real Life. Descriptive of the Temptations, Sufferings, Trials and Triumphs of the Children of St. Patrick, in the Great Republic of Washington. A Book for the Entertainment and Special Instruction of the Catholic Male and Female Servants of the United States. Written by a Missionary Priest."[8] This is a quintessential Catholic-tract novel, and in his preface, Quigley gives four standard reasons for having written it: first, to alleviate the dangerous condition of his "poor, neglected, and uninstructed brethren," the Famine immigrants, and "to remove prejudice from the public mind"; second, to provide "some antidote, some remedy" to "the corruption of the cheap, trashy literature that is now ordinarily supplied for the amusement and instruction of the American people . . . in every rail-car, omnibus, stage-coach, steamboat, or canal-packet"; third, to supply Irish Catholics with "cheap and amusing literature, to entertain them during the few hours they are disengaged from work," literature "having for its end the exal-tation and defence of his glorious old faith, and the vindication of his native land"; and fourth, by recording certain "manly defences" of Ca-tholicism, to enable his audience "to refute, in a simple, practical manner, for the edification of their opponents, the many objections proposed to them about the faith." Finally, Quigley asserts that his novel "has been written in great haste, and by one who, in five years, has not had a single entire day for recreation, or unoccupied by severe missionary duty. Let not the critics forget this" (v-x).

The Cross and the Shamrock owes its setting to Quigley's own mission station, the New York and Vermont farming communities northeast of Troy, and the novel describes in detail the life of a typical missionary priest in rural America in the 1840s and 1850s. Here, Father O'Shane's extensive pastorate spreads out from "the city of T——" through the surrounding countryside, and in the opening chapters he administers the last rites to a woman in the city and sets out immediately in a raging snowstorm to convert a dying Yankee "forty miles out in Vermont." The description of "Mass in a Shanty" in rural Vermont for Irish railroad workers, servants, and farm laborers is surely based on Quigley's own experience:

> The largest shanty in the "patch" was cleared of all sorts of lumber. Forms, chairs, tables, pots, flour and beef barrels, molasses casks, and other nec-essary stores were all put outside doors. The walls, if so we can call them, of the shanty, were then hung round with newspapers, white linen table-cloths, and other choice tapestry, while a good large shawl, spread in front of the altar, served as a carpet on which his reverence was to kneel and stand while officiating. Green boughs were cut in a neighboring wood lot and planted around the entrance by the men, while around the altar and over it were wreaths of wild flowers and blossoms, gathered by the little girls of the "patch" in the adjacent meadows, in order to prepare a decent place for the holy Mass. [121-22]

So many "women and rough-fisted men" are "gathered around the door of the temporary confessional," that it is "near noon" before the Mass begins. Reminiscent of Sadlier's belief that Irish emigration provides a valuable opportunity to proselytize, the priest encourages his flock to "regard themselves as missionaries engaged in God's service to spread the knowledge of the true religion in this virgin soil," and he exhorts the railroad workers by observing that "if they were not here employed on these public works, probably the holy sacrifice would not be, for years and years to come, offered up in such places as this." Quigley reports that "the effects of this one visit even were felt by the overseers and employers of these men for months to come," and one Yankee farmer grudgingly admits that "those much-abused priests are far ahead of our dominies in knowledge of religion and human nature. It is impossible otherwise to account for the influence they exercise over the ungovernable Irish race."

Quigley does not, however, romanticize the conditions of the Famine immigrant work force. The novel contains an extended, indignant protest against "the trials, tears, labors, sufferings, and injustice which our indifference or avarice has inflicted on those thousands of our fellow-creatures whose hands have built [the railroads]." To blame for the fact that "of all the men living, the railroad and day laborer of this 'free country' is the most ill-treated and oppressed," is the refusal of the United States government "to protect the laborer by law." To illustrate, Quigley describes the heartless swindles of speculators who lure Irish immigrants into the woods, promising them nonexistent housing and food. These laborers work long hours for little pay, buy necessities dearly at company stores, and are often short-changed and abandoned at the end of a job. A favorite self-serving trick of the speculators is the encouragement of faction fights, as when a Connachtman is paid by the company to lead his countrymen against workers from Munster and Ulster, so that "by driving off their *far-up* and *far-down* enemies, they could have a year's job, and a dollar a day." Quigley's outspoken attack against immigrant exploitation in the name of progress also contains the suggestion that such opinions got him in trouble: "There is no man daring enough to speak a word in favor of the cruelly-oppressed railroad man, except an odd priest here and there; and even he has often to do so at the risk of having a revolver presented to him, or having his character maligned by the slanders of the moneyed ruffians whose crimes and excesses he may feel it his duty to reprimand" (114-15).

In the mainstream of Catholic-tract fiction, however, is the novel's primary plot involving the trials and ultimate triumph of the O'Clery family, who are driven from their County Clare farm "when landlords began to root out the people from their homes." Having taken the cholera "within sight of land," O'Clery dies after a few days in America, leaving his wife and four children to fend for themselves. Indeed, the novel's opening chapter is "A Death-Bed Scene," in which Mrs. O'Clery dies in a tenement room in "T——" on a pallet of straw. Hers is a stereotypical happy death, and the scene embodies the first of the novel's many lessons: "Let the most obstinate unbeliever attend but a few times by the bedside of a dying Catholic, and observe the piety and faith of the priest and people around the bed of the true believer," and "it is impossible for him not to perceive the superiority of the Catholic religion to all other forms of worship that ever existed" (19).

Called to Vermont, Father O'Shane is unable to prevent the chief villain of the novel, the town poor-master, Van Stingey by name, from spiriting the O'Clery orphans away—first to the poor-house and then to the farm of the anti-Catholic Prying family on the New York-Vermont border. Fortunately, the oldest child, fifteen-year-old Paul O'Clery, is devout and intelligent enough to keep himself and his siblings Catholic in this inimical environment, and it is he who provides most of Quigley's "manly defences" of the faith—in a series of debates with the Presbyterian minister, Mr. Gulmore. These range from a refusal to eat turkey on Friday to involved refutations of Protestant misinformation about Catholicism. These continue and increase when Paul leaves the farm to work for Mr. Clarke, an Episcopalian lawyer in the Vermont state capital. Not only does Clarke become a Catholic, but he is followed into the fold by the entire membership of the "Literary and Religious Society of Vermont" to which he belongs. This troop of fifty converts contributes money to send Paul O'Clery off to college, where, not surprisingly, he decides to become a priest. Paul becomes a big-city pastor, then a bishop, and Quigley leaves him "a pillar of God's Church, and an ornament in his sanctuary, as archbishop in one of the great cities of British India, in Asia."

The weakest part of *The Cross and the Shamrock* is Quigley's clumsy working out of the fates of the other O'Clery children through conventional romantic plotting. Rescued and inspired by Paul, one girl becomes a nun. The second is lost for years and discovered as the adopted daughter of the fabulously wealthy Mr. Goldrich. After joining her sister in the convent, she dies of a fever contracted "in caring for the poor negro slaves of New Orleans. She preferred to die a saint than live a princess." But Quigley reserves for the youngest O'Clery child, Eugene, a sentimental martyrdom of surpassing bathos. Having been farmed out to a much stricter, even sadistic proselytizing Protestant family, Eugene is beaten, starved, and locked in a cold shed, where he expires on the morning of All Saints' Day, "sacrificed, like his divine Master, to the demon of cruel sectarianism" (209). Quigley further glosses the event in the familiar terms of his Irish generation's self-image as fated for persecution: "and thus is Erin, even in America, still true to her Heaven-appointed destiny,—which is, that of being a missionary and a martyr in the new world as well as in the old."

The Cross and the Shamrock also contains frontal attacks against "Know-nothingism" of a ferocity that helps explain Quigley's inability to find a permanent home in Ireland, England, Scotland, or America. Lumping together "followers of Mormon Smith, Joe Miller, Theodore Parker, and spiritual raps" as nativist enemies of the Catholic Irish, he explains their bigotry in simple terms, guaranteed to alienate many: "With the word *liberty* ever on their lips, like the lion's skin on the ass, to deceive, the sects, great and small, from the Church of England down, down, down to the Mormons or Transcendentalists, through the grades of Presbyterian, Methodist, Baptist, all play the tyrant in their own way. All act the despot, and would exercise spiritual tyranny if in their power. . . . modern, as well as by-gone records show, that, wherever Protestantism had the power, *there* the few were oppressed by the many" (116-17). Given this attitude, it is no wonder that Quigley moved so often and had an occasional revolver pointed at him.

Orestes Brownson criticized *The Cross and the Shamrock* on two counts, consistent with his position as an "Anglo-American" Catholic supporter of immigrant assimilation. Declaring that the novel "could have been written by nobody but an Irish missionary priest, and one in whom nearly all contradictions meet," Brownson decries Quigley's immoderate, Manichaean characterizations: "For ourselves, we wish he had mingled his lights and shades with a little more care. His Irish characters are saints, and his Yankee characters natural-born devils. This is carrying the matter a little beyond the limits of romance." Second, Brownson criticizes Quigley's persistent linking of Catholicism with Irishness: "We think it a poor policy to attempt to make nationality our principle reliance, especially in a country like ours, for the preservation of Catholicity." Quigley ought to have "spoken of the characters . . . simply as Catholics and non-Catholics, not as Irish Catholics and Yankees. This constant appeal to a foreign nationality is one of the causes that gave rise to the Native-American party." Besides, "Irish nationality cannot be preserved for any great length of time on American ground. It is greatly enfeebled in the second generation, and counts for nothing in the third. . . . The children of Irish parents very naturally fall into the American habits of thought and action, and soon learn to look with a sort of aversion on what, without offense, we may call *Irishism*, or to wish to get rid of it, as a supposed obstacle to their success in life" (269-70). Brownson here refutes not only the obvious exaggerations of Father Quigley, but also the conclusions of his friend Mrs. Sadlier. Failing to recognize that connecting Irishness and Catholicism was the understandable defense of an immigrant group whose very identity was being threatened, Brownson provides the simplistic solution of the secure native American—forget the past and start over—without acknowledging the potential psychological damage of jettisoning one's entire cultural heritage. As has been seen in chapter 3, Brownson much preferred the moderate position of his friend Father John Roddan. However, in articulating the confused anger of the reluctant immigrant, Quigley is closer to the bone, and more of a spokesman for his generation.

The preface to Quigley's second novel, *The Prophet of the Ruined Abbey* of 1855, answers Brownson directly. The two purposes stated are determinedly ethnocentric. First, "to save from oblivion and decay the legends and popular traditions on which [the story] is principally founded, and which are here, as the author believes, for the first time committed to print." And second, "to keep alive and kindle in the bosoms of the Irish Catholic people of this republic genuine sentiments of patriotism and religion, both of which are threatened with danger, on the one hand, from the treachery of a few bad Irishmen themselves, and on the other, from the arrogant assurance of a few fickle-minded spirits, who would persuade the Irish race of this great continent to forget their country, their origin, their descent, their history, their traditions and bygone glories, which are nicknamed 'Irishism,' and as the inevitable consequence, though this may not be intended, to forget their Religion!" (5-6). Quigley refuses to follow the advice of "a few individuals" (surely including Brownson) who have asked the Irish, "the best Catholics in America, or the world, to obliterate all the venerable monuments of the pedigree of saints and kings from which we have sprung, and to amalgamate with the *parvenu* nondescript breeds of the New World." On the contrary, because they are a missionary race "chosen by God to be his agents in the regeneration of the modern-world," the Catholic Irish ought to "remain separate from the people which they are ordained to regenerate or reform" so as to avoid adopting "their prejudices and vices." In thus turning the "racial purity" argument of the nativists against itself, Quigley tars himself with the same brush as his enemies. He takes Mrs. Sadlier's advocacy of Irish cultural pride one step closer to fanaticism.

Orestes Brownson certainly got the message, for his review of *The Prophet of the Ruined Abbey* quotes from Quigley's preface and claims that his "morbid jealousy" has caused Quigley to misunderstand Brownson's position, which "says not one word against the study of Irish history, Irish antiquities and traditions; it does not tell the Irish that they should forget or neglect them; it does not depreciate their value in themselves considered; it only says, that it is of no use urging them as an argument to remove the prejudices which it is alleged the American people have against the Irish, for the world judges a people by what it is and can do here and now, not by what it once was or once did." Brownson also criticizes Quigley's advocacy of violence, complaining that "the author professes to be an O'Connellite, but he writes with the spirit of a Young Irelander." Granting England's wrong against the Irish, Brownson still can see "no good likely to result from efforts to influence the Irish in this country with hatred to the Anglo-Saxon race. It will not better their condition here, or render them more able to serve their countrymen at home. It seems to us very possible to love and esteem the Irish without hating everybody else" (143-44).

The Prophet of the Ruined Abbey opens "a year or two before the close of the war of American Independence" in Cloughmore, County Waterford, where Father Senan O'Donnell is about to be hanged by the government for the crime of marrying a Protestant to a Catholic. Extremely unlikely for eighteenth-century Ireland, this brutal sentence sets the novel's propagandistic tone. His brother, Captain Charles O'Donnell of the French cavalry, effects Father O'Donnell's escape with the aid of Terry O'Mara, the local rebel leader of five hundred Irishmen. At first, the priest is reluctant to give up his martyr's crown, but he agrees to change clothes and places with Charles upon learning that a rebellion is being planned. Father O'Donnell walks out over the hills to Cork City, where a small French yacht arranged for by his brother picks him up and sets off for America. But the yacht founders in a fierce storm off the coast of County Clare, and all hands apparently drown. Meanwhile (the action is fast and furious in the early chapters), Terry O'Mara also engineers Charles O'Donnell's escape as he is being transferred to Dublin Castle.

At this point, Quigley's decidedly unpriestly ferocity manifests itself again. For his complicity in the escapes, O'Mara is punished hideously by "the cruel soldiery of England." Quigley describes the rebel's return to his burned-out cabin, where he finds the "hacked, naked, and mangled" body of his wife hanging from a tree, "with two of her children poniarded, and suspended by the flaxen hair of their mother down by her sides!" The heartsick O'Mara swears vengeance on "a portion of the clotted blood of his wife and children," gathered "in cold livid lumps into his handkerchief."

Now the scene shifts again—to the seven-hundred-foot Cliffs of Moher on the Clare coast, where Father O'Donnell has landed, the only survivor of the storm that wrecked his America-bound yacht. Unable to scale the rocks, he finds a cave which turns out to connect by a man-made passage to a vaulted room back under the cliffs. Able to subsist on seaweed and mussels, and seeing God's will in his situation, Father O'Donnell decides to remain a hermit on that spot, praying for the conversion of the heathen and the freedom of Ireland.

Here Quigley's purpose of preserving "legends and popular traditions" becomes central to his plot. Earlier examples in the novel include the translation into couplets of a keen prepared by local peasants for the hanging of Father O'Donnell, and folk tales of St. Patrick and St. Colman told in a gathering of rebels in the hills near Slieve-na-mon. But now Quigley takes an entire chapter to relate the legend of "The Laveragh Lynchagh, or The Long-Haired Prince." In "the days of Pagan Ireland, some time before the reign of Dathi," this warrior prince ruled "a great portion of the country beyond the Shannon" from his castle in the limestone of western County Clare. The tale hinges on a curious custom. The Long-Haired Prince allowed himself to be shaved but once a year, on May 1, by one of his nobles chosen by lot, and after the shaving, that noble was put to death. After twenty years of this, the prince relented, and spared the life of the barber, one of his best young supporters. Soon, the secret was out. Quigley gives it in Gaelic first, then in English: "The savage prince whose yoke you've borne for years, / Instead of human, hath a horse's ears." Refusing to serve a monstrous master, the prince's subjects revolt and put him to death. Remarking this legend's "striking affinity to the fabled Midas of Ovid," Quigley suggests that many tales of "the classical Greek and Roman poets . . . were modelled on, if not copies of the more ancient Irish and Etruscan legends." A proud son of the County

Clare, Quigley declares that this story "was often related to us at the old fireside, by grave and venerable men, not far from the splendid ruins of this selfsame castle of the old horse-eared tyrant aforesaid" (189-90). This folk tale is relevant in the novel because Father O'Donnell discovers that his cave is actually the subterranean "dark road" over which the Long-Haired Prince led his barber-victims to fling them into the ocean. Further exploration reveals that the cave-passage leads up into a churchyard near a ruined abbey, the symbol to the priest of "ruin and devastation" caused by "the civilization of England." (This idea of a coastal cave leading to a ruined abbey also appears in Charles Cannon's first Irish story, "The Beal Fire" of 1835.)

The stage is now set for Quigley's major use of legend in *The Prophet of the Ruined Abbey*, as advertised in the full subtitle, which promises "A Glance of the Future of Ireland: A Narrative Founded on the Ancient 'Prophecies of Culmkill,' and on Other Predictions and Popular Traditions Among the Irish." Quigley is here promising an Irish-American version of a long-established Irish prophecy (supposedly traceable to Columcille, the sixth-century saint) in which Ireland overcomes her enemies in a cataclysmic final battle preceded by supernatural signs like those in the Book of Revelation.[9] While scavenging in among the rocks, Father O'Donnell finds a baby in an eagle's nest. Around the child's neck is a relic of the true cross that Father O'Donnell had given (just a year and a day before this visitation) to the Catholic woman whose marriage to a Protestant man got him in so much trouble. The priest thus recognizes the child as the offspring of that woman, a descendant of "the noble House of Ossory, princes of Leinster" and that man, a Scottish chief and member of "the royal House of Stuart." Father O'Donnell recognizes the boy, whom he christens "Brefni," as "the DELIVERER of my holy country from foreign oppression," and the incarnation of "Culmkill's Prophecy," which he remembers as predicting the deliverance of Ireland by "a man of PEACE" (229-30). As the priest well knows, fulfillment of the prophecy is not yet at hand. At the age of fifteen, in about 1795, the boy escapes on a passing galleon to Spain, where he will begin working toward the freedom of his people.

Subsequently, the rebel leader Terry O'Mara reenters the novel. Discovering Father O'Donnell's hermitage on Christmas Day, 1798, Terry relates the history of the failed Rebellion of that year, in which he and Charles O'Donnell fought side-by-side. Quigley conveys his own position when Terry attributes the several rebel victories to "the courage infused into the troops of the insurgent forces by the burning words and noble example of your friends, Rev. John Murphy and Rev. Mr. Roche, and several other priests who joined our ranks."[10] Quigley thus counters the prevalent denunciation of violent revolution by the Irish and Irish-American clergy of this and succeeding generations. Father O'Donnell now becomes "the Prophet of the Ruined Abbey," predicting that the worst is yet to come: "After the sword shall come the plague and the famine. . . . A million graves shall open their devouring mouths in a day, and the glutted earth, surfeited with human carcasses, shall refuse further interments! And famished dogs shall feed upon human flesh!" Only after this, "the darkest hour of Erin's night," will Ireland be saved by the return of Brefni, "the joint-heir of the Scotch and Irish noble houses." That same evening, Father O'Donnell is shot by a British soldier on guard at the ruined abbey, and he dies his martyr's death on the morning of St. Stephen's Day. Terry O'Mara buries him in the mouth of his hermit's cave in the cliff and the novel ends.

The Prophet of the Ruined Abbey is Quigley's best novel. Though flawed by the blood-curdling propaganda of his anti-British position, it succeeds as an unabashed prophesying romance, an exercise in dramatized traditional dreaming untrammeled by the need for a realistic base. Also, the novel seems motivated not only by nationalism, but by the immigrant's genuine fear of losing his culture. With his inclusion of the legends of Clare and Columcille, integrated well into this romantic context, Quigley has done something concrete to preserve the traditions of his native place. In addition, he contributes to the genre of millenial prediction of Irish deliverance found first in America in "Old Ireland's Misery at an End" of 1752.

A product of his sojourn on the Minnesota mission, Quigley's last novel was published in 1873. Profit and Loss: A Story of the Life of a Genteel Irish-American, Illustrative of Godless Education, has as its purpose "the guarding of youth against the dangers that beset their paths in the practice of the precepts of the Catholic Religion." The possibility of achieving "gentility," combined with the wholly negative connotation which the condition carries in this book, mark it as indicative of the transition between the Famine generation, of which Quigley was a member, and the new middle class, represented by many of his younger parishioners in the 1870s.

The novel traces the material rise and moral fall of the son of a rack-rented emigrant from County Kildare who settles a 300-acre farm on the St. Croix River near Brighton, Minnesota. With success in the New World as a farmer, Michael Mulroony becomes socially ambitious, and he sends his son Patrick to the Protestant "Brighton Academy," hoping that the boy will pick up "the real refined Yankee nasal accent." At first, Patrick is ridiculed by his fellow students for being Irish: "Some would ask him how near related he was to St. Patrick, and how many potatoes it took to make the Saint's beads." But he is defended by the teacher, Miss Polly Spoones, who sees in his ambitious streak a foothold for conversion to Methodism, which Quigley defines as "the religion, the nursery, the paradise of the animal passions, where the lowest instincts of our fallen nature find congenial nourishment and support" (82). Evidently, the eighteen years between his second and third novels had left Quigley unmellowed.

In a sequence recalling Sadlier's ill-fated Blakes, young Patrick Mulroony soon begins to put on Protestant airs, attending Methodist "sociables," winning prizes at school spelling bees, and calling himself "Paran M. Ronay." His dangerous waywardness is opposed by his mother, and throughout the novel, Quigley's major critique of the pitfalls of gentility takes the form of a running debate between these two, the Irish immigrant and her American child. Suspicious from the start of the Brighton Academy and the friends her son makes there, Mrs. Mulroony predicts that "When you change your name, the change of your religion and principles are sure to come about soon." Sure enough, Patrick confesses that he has stopped going to the sacraments and begun to rise in the Protestant-dominated town. In fact, he declares that "I never had finer prospects, mother. Don't you notice the many nice premiums I brought home to adorn your parlor from the academy, and I have a fair chance to become County Superintendent of Schools in a year or two." Mrs. Mulroony's answer echoes the novel's title and main theme: "I don't speak of your profit as an office-holder, but of a *profit* far more desirable, that is, to gain a crown of immortal glory in heaven. And if you neglect your religious duties you surely forfeit these honors, and lose your soul."

Ultimately, Patrick confirms his mother's worst fears by marrying his old schoolmistress, Polly Spoones, who has emerged as a husband-hungry spinster. She names their baby boy "Younglove Butler Spoones Ronay," fills their home with Methodist ministers and elders, and soon begins an affair with Elder Redtop. At this, Patrick finally comes to his senses. His patience exhausted, he assaults Redtop, and is sent to the State Prison for attempted murder. There, he repents of the "Godless education" at the root of his apostasy, reckons up his material "profit" and spiritual "loss," and returns to the Church. In his final chapter, Quigley resolves his tale with lightning speed and a touch of callousness. Polly Spoones divorces Patrick, wins his house and property "by a fiction of law," and marries Elder Redtop. However, she and her child almost immediately die of smallpox, and Redtop goes mad and is sent to the Lunatic Asylum. On the other hand, Patrick takes back his name ("once more I am free—I am Patrick Mulroony"), is released from prison three years early for good behavior, and moves to the East, where he becomes a wealthy contractor.

In addition to the clear message of its main plot line, *Profit and Loss* contains three exemplary minor characters who embody Quigley's values. The foil to Patrick Mulroony/Ronay in his own generation is Mickey Bocagh, a rough-tempered Irish river man who is both a teetotaler and a militant Catholic. Quigley wholeheartedly approves when Mickey defends the faith by knocking down his employer, a Methodist farmer who "placed a large slice of fat pork on the top of Mickey's mashed potatoes" on a Friday. This occasion also prompts Quigley to criticize the prejudiced coverage of Irish-American news:

In the village of Brighton the slight injury he received was exaggerated into a severe fracture of his skull. In the county town, the report had it that the farmer was killed. In the large cities of the Northwest, the telegraph told of his having been shot by an Irishman, who burned his house over his carcass, to escape detection. In Chicago it was posted in large capital letters that a respectable American family were murdered by an Irish laborer, and their residence, after having been plundered, was burned. Farther East, in Boston and New York, the telegrams had it that several respectable American families were murdered by a party of Irishmen. Finally, in Harper's Nasty Pictorials, there was a hideous picture of a party of drunken Irish Catholics, murdering a family of innocent American Methodist Protestants. [263-64]

The last reference here is to the offensive anti-Irish caricatures of Thomas Nast, which were popular in *Harper's Weekly* in the 1870s.[11]

Perhaps representing Quigley himself, the Brighton parish priest, Father John, is an immigrant missionary who has relinquished "his prospects of advancement in the ranks of the clergy of his native diocese" of Cashel, Tipperary, to serve "the exiled children of Saint Patrick." His sacrifice gives Quigley the opportunity to repeat the familiar idea that the Famine migration has a proselytizing precedent and rationale that make the catastrophe understandable as part of God's plan for the Irish: "Today, it is in the United States, Canadas, South America, the Australian continent and islands, as well as the East and West Indies, that we can find the Irish missionaries engaged in the same holy work as their fellow countrymen, during twelve hundred years and more" (200).

Quigley does not, however, follow the Sadlier conservative line, which calls for passive acceptance of inevitable Irish suffering. Instead, he continues to support violent revolution in Ireland. His spokesman on this issue is the quick-witted, erudite Irish schoolmaster, Mr. Haley, who demolishes the Methodists in debates about Christianity and the Irish intellectual tradition. An active member of the Fenian Brotherhood, Haley recites a clearly political poem, "written by himself on a late visit of his to Ireland, two years ago, on an unfortunate Fenian mission." This "Exile's Farewell to His Native Land" blames the Great Hunger squarely on the Ascendancy and the Catholic clergy and refutes Sadlier's advocacy of return to Ireland in no uncertain terms:

> Thy smiling vales, and crystal streams,
>   And fields of emerald green,
> No longer thrill thy exile's heart,
>   Since to the British Queen,
> Thy dastard sons, by tyrant lords,
>   And slavish priests bow'd down,
> Profanely pay that homage due,
>   To no foreign throne or crown. [284-85]

Quigley remains the complex figure "in whom nearly all contradictions meet" of Brownson's early review. His novels (and his life as well) contain an unresolved, though recognizably Irish, mixture of Catholic Christianity and violent nationalism, and he both exposes prejudice against Irish Catholics and practices literary bigotry toward Anglo-Saxon Protestants. Certainly, the hyperbole, extremist passion, and philosophical confusion in Quigley's novels contrast sharply with the controlled rhetoric and consistent, conservative ideology of Mary Anne Sadlier's books. Indeed, their lives were very different: the troubled and troubling itinerant priest, wending his irascible, solitary way across America, and the established novelist/publisher, the respectable doyenne of New York Catholic literary society. And yet, they share a fierceness, a truculence, which supports Kerby Miller's evidence that this was a profoundly alienated generation of immigrants. Their novels seem so different primarily because they focused their anger in opposite directions. Quigley attacks those whom he sees, with fanatical plainness, as his generation's mortal enemies—the Protestant Ascendancy in Ireland and the Anglo-Saxon hegemony in the United States. Sadlier reserves her wrath for her own kind—those immigrants who have failed to meet the American challenge to their Catholicism and Irishness. However, whether directed outward or inward, the always raised voice remains a constant for both writers. In the end, anger seems the fitting response of their Famine generation to the experience of reluctant flight from a blighted homeland to a strange and inhospitable New World.

FIVE

Respectability and Realism: Ambivalent Fictions

Katherine E. Conway's *Lalor's Maples* of 1901 is a representative novel for its time in a number of ways. Born in Rochester, New York, in 1853, Conway began a career in journalism there, then moved on to Buffalo and finally Boston, where in 1883 she became an assistant editor of the *Pilot* under John Boyle O'Reilly. She went on to write several Catholic moral guidebooks, some genteel/sentimental verse, a collection of stories, and two novels.[1] Conway's fiction contains a mixture of realism and sentimental romance that is prototypically defining for her Irish-American literary generation. *Lalor's Maples* is her most realistic book, probably because it is based in part on her own early life. Rochester becomes Baychester, and the protagonist is the convent-educated, journalist daughter of a newly rich Irish-American contractor.

The best chapter in Conway's novel is the first. Before stereotypes begin to accumulate, before the plot starts to tangle, Conway creates a perfect set-piece description of the rise to middle-class respectability of an Irish immigrant family. John Lalor is an intelligent builder with the instincts of an architect. After a hard Irish childhood marked by many uprootings between Ireland, England, and Scotland, he settles in England himself, but has to leave because of trouble growing out of his association with Irish nationalists. He arrives in America with his wife and daughter and only enough money to get to Baychester, where he has been told there is canal work and a related building boom. Sixteen years from his first job as a construction worker, he has his own contracting business employing 300 men and is thinking of running for mayor. The time is the late 1860s and he is thirty-nine years old. To validate and celebrate his success, Lalor builds a new house on Baychester's best street, River Avenue, which has lately been undergoing a population shift from old-line Yankees to newly wealthy Irish. Through the chapter, Lalor's immigrant narrative runs parallel to a detailed description of the building of his house: from the pouring of a foundation so large that one critical onlooker compares it to the town hall, to an inventory of the rooms and furnishings, which include patterned carpets, mahogany and horsehair chairs, and a mantelpiece Madonna "won at a church fair" (11). All of this rings true, as does the culminating scene, in which, on his first evening in the new house, John Lalor softly touches the keys of his new piano, and thinks of his penniless landing at New York sixteen years before. The completed house is a valid symbolic embodiment of the Lalor family's social and economic rise. Unfortunately, the novel soon bogs down in a mire of genteel-romantic stylistic flights and wild turns of plot, but the house, named "Lalor's Maples," remains its saving grace. As a central symbol it anchors the book and provides the one sustained realistic focus.

In this conception, Conway may have been influenced by Mary Anne Sadlier's *Old and New* (1862), but a more likely model, especially for a writer in Boston, is William Dean Howells's *The Rise of Silas Lapham* (1885). As the sharpest literary chronicler of American middle-class life in the Gilded Age, Howells recognized the private home as the most powerful measure of social position. So it is that the building of his new house on the fashionable "water side of Beacon Street" proclaims Silas Lapham's progress from poor Vermont beginnings to success as a paint manufacturer in Boston. Of course, Howells is critical of the Lapham family's embrace of materialism, and Silas's moral rise at the end of the book is made to follow from his self-ordained economic ruin. Refusing to cheat to save his fortune, he loses his new house and most of his business, and returns greatly chastened to Vermont.

Conway was not capable of sustaining this much realism, and although the Lalor family also suffers a great calamity, her novel ends with a dramatic resurrection of first-order sentimental romanticism. Still and all, she does begin well, and the characters are presented plausibly at first. John Lalor is a likeable, hard-working man, on his way to becoming a power in Baychester politics. We are told that his three hundred workers vote "as one man the ticket of his choice." His wife bullies him at home, and once they are settled in the new house, she takes it over so completely that he begins to look like a boarder. The most memorable character in the novel, Mrs. Mary Lalor holds over her husband the familiar club of having married beneath her station. This is first apparent when she undercuts a neighbor's admiration for The Maples by asking, "what is it to the house that he took me from?" Even more indicative is the exchange that follows the family's first dinner in the new house. Lalor presents his wife with the deed, declaring that "I took you from a good house, Mary, and I've always planned to give you back as good for it." Conway then tells us what Mrs. Lalor thinks but does not say aloud: "Her maiden home, long magnified by the enchantment of distance, suddenly shrank to its true proportions before Mary Lalor's eyes, which glowed gently under a happy mist, as she pressed her husband's hand" (14-15). Although the question comes up again, Mrs. Lalor never admits that The Maples is by far the finest house in which she has ever lived. Thus, the source of her power over her husband is seen to be a conscious lie of past domestic grandeur. From here on, she rules the house and her family with a cold, controlling arrogance, all the more rigid because it is hypocritical.

As the novel progresses, verisimilitude declines, and Conway creates a Catholic-tract rendition of Cinderella, with Mrs. Lalor as the wicked stepmother, love-lorn first daughter Margaret as her willing accomplice, and delicate, sensitive, second daughter Mildred as the long-suffering protagonist. Timid, intensely religious, and devoted to the family, Mildred (who also writes poetry) is an easy mark for the other women, who torment her without mercy. The plot turns on the house. Business reverses for John Lalor and high-handed spending by his wife and Margaret threaten their ownership of The Maples. The mortgage ends up in the hands of Palmer Ellis, Baychester's unscrupulous Protestant newspaper editor for whom Mildred is working as a reporter. Though older than her father, Ellis is drawn to Mildred. Ultimately he demands that she choose: marriage to him outside the Catholic Church or the eviction of her family. Because owning The Maples corroborates her self-deluded sense of her proper position, Mrs. Lalor cannot bear the thought of leaving. Such a move would destroy the fabric of her fairy-tale version of her life as having followed an inexorable curve from respectability to immigrant laborer's wife and back. Thus, when the crisis comes, Mrs. Lalor puts tremendous pressure on Mildred to marry Ellis, even to the point of declaring that "it will kill your father" to leave the house. Given Conway's orthodox Catholicism, Mrs. Lalor is here willing to sacrifice her daughter's soul to save The Maples. John Lalor deplores his wife's obsession, but he is powerless against her. Instead of defending Mildred, he turns to drink. Mildred is nearly torn apart by the strain of all this, but her faith proves stronger than her mother. She runs away from home and The Maples is lost.

On the morning of the family's departure from the house, Mrs. Lalor kneels on the threshold and shouts a frightening "malediction" at the absent Mildred: "May the Lord strike with His just vengeance and most bitter curse my undutiful child, and all others who have had a hand in our ruin, and the first that crosses this threshold into the home from which I am driven today" (267). This tableau of the arrogant mother brought bitterly to her knees and cursing her own daughter is the novel's most powerful image. As such, it completes the characterization of Mrs. Lalor that was begun in the opening chapter. She is an early and powerful negative mother figure in Irish-American literature. The novel, though, does not end here, and the denouement seethes with pot-boiling calamity and coincidence. Palmer Ellis is shot by his estranged first wife, who then kills herself. On his deathbed, he calls for the Bishop of Baychester and confesses to a string of seductions and murders stretching back to his youth. He further confesses that he is both a Catholic and an Irish immigrant. Finally, he deeds The Maples back to Mildred, and dies. Sufficient to the novel's ending is the diction thereof. Conway's style becomes at its worst just the sort of confection that was parodied so well in Stephen Crane's *Maggie: A Girl of the Streets* (1893). Mildred's reward is marriage to her childhood sweetheart, Raymond Fitzgerald, "a knightly hero to [his] mother and sister, and worthy to be the light of the purest and sweetest maiden's dreams" (160). Thus, didacticism and sentimentality rise up in the later stages of *Lalor's Maples* to overcome the promising realism of the opening.

It is this vacillation that makes Conway's novel a defining prototype. Her generation produced a literature of ambivalence, the poles of which were the two opposed concepts that were at war in the American literary mainstream of the day: genteel romance and the "new realism." Basically a New-World version of British Victorianism, the "genteel tradition" in American letters called for the inculcation through literature of Christian morality, piety, and respectability. Its supporters argued that art ought to provide ideal models for conduct, and that certain themes, character types, and situations were potentially corrupting and thus improper subjects. To a large extent, popular taste echoed these values. Toward the end of the century, adult best-sellers included a number of moralizing historical romances (*Ben Hur, Quo Vadis, The Prisoner of Zenda*) and books now considered children's classics (*Heidi, Treasure Island, Black Beauty*). On the other hand, the realists argued, in the words of their champion Howells, for "the simple, the natural, and the honest" as literary criteria. They indicted the Victorian values of the genteel tradition as distorted, hypocritical, constricting, and tyrannical, merely the expression of a worn-out romanticism and wholly unresponsive to the realities of American life— especially urban life. Furthermore, the supporters of realism saw as undemocratic (and hence un-American) the preference for and deference to characters of wealth and high social standing in much genteel fiction, and they called for fiction about common people leading ordinary lives.

Irish-American writers of the generation that came of age between 1876 and World War I joined this debate by internalizing it, thereby creating ambivalent fictions such as *Lalor's Maples*, in which romance and realism coexist uneasily. Such literature mirrors the uneasy, transitional, ambivalent culture that produced it. With memorable clarity, John V. Kelleher has traced the emergence of an Irish-American middle class to the evening of September 7, 1892, when "Gentleman Jim" Corbett defeated John L. Sullivan, "The Boston Strong Boy," for the world heavyweight boxing championship. Kelleher sees both men as archetypes. Sullivan, boisterous, hard-drinking, and having dominated the sport by sheer brawn, "was still the meaningful symbol of what the Irish here had perforce to be proud of: native strength, the physical endurance that made possible the 'Irish contribution to America' that orators and writers have since sentimentalized so much." As for Jim Corbett, he was "equally representative. . . . a prophetic figure: slim, deft, witty, looking like a proto-Ivy Leaguer with his pompadour, his fresh intelligent face, his well-cut young man's clothes. He was, as it were, the paradigm of all those young Irish-Americans about to make the grade. . . . These were the children of what you might call the 'hidden Irish,' who, by 1890, were the vast majority of the Irish in America: the men and women who, though denied opportunity for themselves, confidently counted on it for their children, and, like millions of later immigrants, scraped and saved to give their children a fair start" ("Irishness" 38-39).

Of course, this transformation had been in process for years. The inevitable separation of immigrant parents and their American children, wrought by changes in environment, education, opportunity, and aspiration, had begun as soon as the Famine Irish began to marry and raise families in the New World. William Shannon has remarked on the "ambiguous, indeterminate state" of the American Irish at the turn of the century. There were still thousands of new immigrants turning up every year as well as many long-settled immigrants stuck in the laboring classes. Between 1845 and 1870, about 2.5 million Irish people had come to America. But between 1871 and 1921, when the first of the immigration restriction laws began to close the golden door, 2.1 million more joined them. To complete the ten-year, mid-decade population summaries through the onset of World War I, the numbers are as follows: 1876-1885, 490,400; 1886-1895, 541,400; 1896-1905, 394,300; 1906-1915, 346,600. The 1890 U.S. Census registered the largest number of Irish-born American citizens ever—1,870,000, and it also counted 4,140,000 native-born Americans whose parents had both come from Ireland.

As for those who had "made it," they were the "lace-curtain Irish," a term in use by the 1890s which, in Shannon's definition, "while denoting a certain level of financial achievement, . . . connotes a self-conscious, anxious attempt to create and maintain a certain level and mode of gentility." As Shannon describes this confused culture, "the desire to join the 'ins' conflicted with the desire to lead the 'outs.' The wish to climb socially ran counter to the impulse to champion the rebellious, restless poor. The options for individual Irishmen were numerous: conventional success or frustrated insurgency, individual assimilation or the chauvinism of the Irish community, bleached-out respectability or labor radicalism, adherence to the political machine or acceptance of good government ('goo goo') values" (142-45).[2]

Similarly, the inability of Irish-American writers to decide between respectable romance and rebellious realism constitutes the most pervasive and revealing characteristic of the fiction of this, the third nineteenth-century Irish-American literary generation. This ambivalence took every possible form. Some individual novels and stories begin realistically and end romantically. Or vice versa. Some writers produced first novels of considerable realistic power, only to turn in subsequent fiction to the bland formulas of popular romance. Or vice versa. Not that there were no consistently respectable Irish-American writers. The creators of sentimental romance we have always had with us. It is just that no promisingly realistic Irish-American novelist was able wholly to abjure genteel literary values in favor of hard-nosed cultural self-assessment. This was a great loss. Of the literary cultures available to Irish Americans of this generation, only the realistic tradition would have allowed them to focus on their own kind in a healthy way, to provide truly useful criticisms of life. Some writers came closer than others, though, and these proto-realists will be discussed in the second half of this chapter.

Lalor's Maples is thus typically flawed, and yet, although they prove too hot for Conway to handle, serious questions about Irish-American life do get asked in this novel for the first time. Mrs. Lalor's dominance creates a crippling imbalance in the family power structure, and her acquisitive obsession with the house results in a perversion of values to the extent that if her daughter Mildred had remained "dutiful" she would have been destroyed. These questions appear often enough in subsequent fiction to be considered archetypal. Houses and mothers have been important in Irish-American novels from the beginning, and a powerful recurrent conjunction of characterization and symbolism in such fiction since the Famine has been the dominant mother who controls a house that also functions as a novel's central organizing symbol. The persistence of these themes conveys their importance in American ethnic life.

A number of causes suggest themselves for the emergence of an Irish-American domestic matriarchy. As one of her traditional duties was to provide religious instruction, the Irish mother's role in the old country was probably strengthened by the increased emphasis on religion in post-Famine Ireland that Emmet Larkin has called a "devotional revolution." Further, the growth of devotional Catholicism in late-nineteenth-century America would have been similarly reinforcing. In addition, the experience of immigration probably encouraged matriarchal dominance. As most Irish immigrants came from agrarian backgrounds and ended up in American cities, they had to find new ways of making a living. Often women were able to get steadier, year-round employment more easily than men; for example, in the mills, doing piecework sewing at home, or as domestic servants. Moreover, after having held jobs, immigrant women could then marry and move into their traditional homemaking and mothering roles, while their husbands kept walking out into the hostile world every day. The result could easily have been a subtle transfer of power and family control from the struggling male provider to the grounded, less threatened "woman of the house."[3]

Reinforcement of such attitudes and of the connections among home, motherhood, and status appears in the Catholic moral guidebooks of the day. Representative here is *The Mirror of True Womanhood, A Book of Instruction for Women of the World* (1877) by an Irish immigrant priest, Father Bernard J. O'Reilly, whose aim it was to "preserve the Home" by instructing women to live "a life of faith, loving above all things self-denial and self-sacrifice" (3). To this end, he provides examples from the life of Christ, the saints, and especially the Virgin Mary, and applies them to women in various situations, including governesses and schoolteachers (in a chapter on "Maidenhood"), "Toilers of the Shop and the Loom," domestic servants, and, most important, wives and mothers. O'Reilly begins by defining the home as "the sacred sphere within which God has appointed that true women should exercise their sway, that most blessed kingdom which it is in their power to create." He exhorts Catholic women to "make of their abode a paradise" by imitating Christ and His mother in the practice of "lively faith, a piety full of sweetness and modesty, a generous hospitality, holiness of life, serenity, and innocence of conversation." By this example, husband and children alike will profit, for "all have to learn from you how to love, how to labor lovingly, how to be forgetful of self, and mindful only of the welfare of others." All of this the woman accomplishes "within that world which is your home and kingdom" (6-17). This book's great popularity (fifteen editions in the first five years) suggests that it expressed the values of its audience of middle-class Catholics—notably, the central position of the mother as spiritual guide, custodian of the family's emotional life, and ruler of the home as kingdom and microcosm.[4] In this climate, which is the Irish-American version of the general nineteenth-century "cult of domesticity" (Nancy Cott's phrase, previously seen in the novels of Mary Anne Sadlier), the development of a tendency toward matriarchy is even more plausible.

As to the importance of the private home and its connections with the dominant mother, the house is also a powerful symbol in Irish-American life. Nineteenth-century immigrants brought with them from Ireland strong emotions about houses. For one thing, there was the "big house" of the landed, mostly Protestant aristocracy, a place of gardens and grandeur representing unattainable wealth and status. For another, there were the myths and realities of eviction, the experience of being driven from one's cabin and then bearing witness to its destruction by battering ram. Certainly, these associations made the possibility of owning a home in the New World keenly appealing to the Irish. Also there was the uniquely American equation of middle-class respectability with the private dwelling on its plot of land. And for the immigrant outsider, the house was also a place of refuge from the new society's strangeness and dangers. It kept the alienated family from the American cold, likely full of unfriendly natives. It both supported and helped to define the family. And so as the one unthreatened bastion, the home became the central institution of immigrant life. This situation further reinforced the mother's dominance in the family, because, as Bernard O'Reilly declares, the home was exclusively her "kingdom." Thus, her house became the immigrant mother's refuge and her strength.

An additional clarifying gloss to the conjunction of mother and house in Irish-American fiction is Gaston Bachelard's conception in *The Poetics of Space* of the importance to the imagination of both the reality and the idea of "our house [which] is our corner of the world. . . . our first universe, a real cosmos in every sense of the word" (4). The house is a part of the imaginative baggage that all humans carry around, and this universal house of the imagination, says Bachelard, is invested with maternal traits that spring naturally from its function as protector from the elements and elemental fear. Citing literary evidence, he shows that the house as mother is a compelling, even unavoidable metaphor in which "faced with the bestial hostility of the storm and hurricane, the house's virtues of protection and resistance are transposed into human virtues" (46).

These are impressive associations: Bachelard's connection of house and mother in the imagination, the particular significance for Irish immigrants of the house, and the Irish-American matriarchal tendency, itself reinforced in the home. Thus, the conjunction of house and mother is a formidable joining of Marx and Freud that reveals central concerns of Irish-American culture. The uses in ethnic fiction of this powerful complex of themes dates back at least to Mrs. Sadlier's novels, and it becomes increasingly prevalent through the rest of the century and beyond. These themes continue to appear in twentieth-century Irish-American fiction by James T. Farrell, Brendan Gill, Elizabeth Cullinan, William Kennedy, and others.

As a corollary to the rise of a Catholic middle class in America, there began to be a significant Catholic intellectual culture in this generation, a complex of respected secondary schools and universities, urban intellectual coteries, and publishing outlets. Just as the crucial factor for the dissemination of Famine-generation fiction had been the establishment of an active network of Catholic publishing houses, in the following generation, a similar role was played by magazines. This was the great age of magazine publishing, and much late-nineteenth-century Irish-American fiction first appeared in the burgeoning periodical press. Many of these were Catholic organs, and they included two influential journals founded in 1865, the *Catholic World*, edited by Orestes Brownson's friend and fellow convert, Paulist Father Isaac Hecker, and *Ave Maria*, edited after 1874 by Father Daniel Hudson at Notre Dame. New York had a number of these journals, including the Sadlier family's *Tablet* and P.V. Hickey's *Catholic Review* and *Illustrated Catholic American*. Boston had a notable secular Irish journal, *Donahoe's Magazine*, started in January 1879 by the indefatigable publishing pioneer Patrick Donahoe, and advertised as "the cheapest Irish Catholic magazine in the world," dedicated "to the Irish Race, at Home and Abroad," with the aim of providing "reading that will elevate and instruct the present and rising generations." (It was merged into the *Catholic World* in 1908.) Also published in Boston (and carrying fiction regularly) was the *Sacred Heart Review*, which started as a parish periodical in East Cambridge and by the nineties had the highest circulation (40,000) of any American Catholic weekly.[5] In addition, the Irish and Catholic weekly newspapers continued to print a good deal of fiction right through the turn of the century. Notable among these were the *Western Watchman* of St. Louis, the *Northwestern Chronicle* of St. Paul, the New Orleans *Morning Star*, New York City's *Irish American* and *Free-*

man's Journal, and the Boston *Pilot*. Thus, Catholic journalism nurtured Irish-American fiction, as hundreds of short stories and serial novels appeared in these various outlets. The built-in audience and opportunity for publication was particularly important for Irish-American women, most of whom got started in the Catholic press, which welcomed their efforts. There were also, however, negative aspects. The more astute writers came to recognize that the uncritical praise of their work by Catholic literati (as long as that work supported "Catholic" ideology), actually retarded their artistic growth. Even more unhealthy in the long run was the blanket Catholic opposition to literary realism, which resulted in the publication of fiction in the Catholic organs most of which was thoroughly didactic in aim and romantic in character.

Unique in its character and coherence, the Boston Irish literary scene in the latter decades of the century needs to be examined in some detail. By about 1880, the Boston Irish community had produced a significant literary coterie, a cluster of twenty or so publishing poets, novelists, essayists, and translators. The focus of this effort was the Boston *Pilot* and its dynamic editor John Boyle O'Reilly. This was in fact the second Boston Irish literary circle, the first having been the Famine-generation group that included Bishop Fitzpatrick, Father (later Archbishop) Williams, and the priest-novelists Fathers Roddan and Boyce.

The life to age twenty-five of John Boyle O'Reilly reads like an Irish-American romantic novel from the Famine generation. Born in 1844 in County Meath, he joined the Fenian movement in his teens while serving a printing apprenticeship in England, then returned in 1863 to Ireland where he joined the British Army with the aim of organizing Irish recruits to overthrow the government from within. Discovered, tried, and convicted as a Fenian conspirator, O'Reilly was incarcerated in a number of British prisons, including the notorious Dartmoor, and then transported to the British penal colony at Bunbury, Western Australia, where he arrived in February 1868. After nine months, he made a spectacular escape to a New Bedford whaling ship which brought him to Philadelphia in November 1869. The following year he settled in Boston, where he landed an editorial job on Patrick Donahoe's *Pilot*, Irish America's leading weekly newspaper. Thus launched, O'Reilly began a twenty-year career, cut short by his sudden death in 1890, which made him the most respected literary Irishman in America. The *Pilot* had 100,000 subscribers when O'Reilly got a job there in the summer of 1870. Founder Patrick Donahoe soon recognized his abilities by making him editor. After a series of fires nearly ruined Donahoe's publishing ventures, O'Reilly and Boston's Archbishop Williams bought the *Pilot* in 1876. Despite the official archdiocesan affiliation, O'Reilly remained editor-in-chief with full editorial control. In this position, he exerted moral pressure in the form of liberal editorials, essays, and speeches on the pressing social problems of his time. His reasonable, moderate voice was raised consistently in support of the rights of the disadvantaged, including the laboring classes, Blacks, and American Indians. He spoke for unions and strikes but against violence, and for equitable distribution of wealth but against socialism.[6]

On Irish matters, O'Reilly also walked a tightrope. He was an enthusiastic advocate of Irish "race pride," especially its literary and cultural manifestations. However, on the issue of Irish nationalism, he repudiated his youthful Fenianism and became the leading Irish-American spokesman for home rule through parliamentary "moral force." In this he supported the policies of Charles Stewart Parnell, whose rise and fall dominated Irish history in the last quarter of the century. As Parliamentary Party leader and "uncrowned king," the charismatic Parnell brought Ireland to the brink of legislated home rule in the 1880s, only to have all hope dashed at the end of the decade. The adultery and divorce scandal involving Mrs. Catherine O'Shea cost Parnell his leadership and his life in 1891 and left Irish nationalism in shambles. These were also the years of Michael Davitt's Irish National Land League, an organized resistance against rackrenting and evictions during which the term "boycott" was coined. O'Reilly also supported the "Land War," which resulted in significant victories in tenant/landlord relations.

Thomas N. Brown has called O'Reilly his generation's "compassionate middleman." He was, in fact, the living embodiment of ambivalence, and the strain of holding it all together may have hastened his death at forty-six from an overdose of sleeping medication. His forceful personality inspired fierce loyalties, and his passing brought forth a flood of heartfelt eulogies in praise of his personal qualities and genius for mediation between Boston's Irish and Yankees. Indeed, O'Reilly's position and literary accomplishment won him more honors than any other Irishman had ever received from Boston's Brahmin establishment, in the palpable form of invitations to join their clubs and requests to compose occasional verse for the dedication of memorials to Wendell Phillips in 1884, Crispus Attucks in 1886, and, a culminating coup, the re-dedication of Plymouth Rock in 1889.

As his generation's leading cultural figure, O'Reilly exerted tremendous influence on late-nineteenth-century Irish-American literature. The decade of his greatest national visibility—the 1880s—was crucial, for the debate between romance and realism was raging and an increasing number of young Irish-American writers were cutting their teeth and deciding which way to go. Twice as many Irish-American novels appeared in the 1890s as in the 1880s.[7] Unfortunately, O'Reilly's greatest influence on this body of writing was negative. It came through his leadership of the Catholic literary campaign against realism and naturalism. Opposition to Emile Zola, the other continental realists, and their American followers was an article of faith in Catholic cultural circles, and even the most talented writers enlisted in the ranks against what one of them, John Talbot Smith, called "the literature of dirt, doubt, and despair" produced by "the school of style-and-stench." The anti-realists included the two most promising novelists of this generation, Smith and William McDermott, (both discussed later in this chapter), as well as Maurice Francis Egan (discussed in chapter 6), the heir to O'Reilly's leadership of Catholic letters.[8]

O'Reilly exerted his influence most directly in his own *Pilot* circle, which appears to have taken his critical dicta as gospel. The most important writers here were his assistant editors James Jeffrey Roche and Katherine E. Conway and contributing poet Louise Imogen Guiney. In his criticism, much of it in *Pilot* editorials, O'Reilly was a determined opponent of the "new realism." Deploring "the abnormal, the corrupt, the wantonly repulsive," he argues that "all art deals with nature and truth, but not with all nature and all truth." Claiming that style and "cleanliness" are more important than realism, and that "French realism is nearly always unclean," he lambasts "foreign purveyors of nastiness and the native analysts of sawdust" while praising "real" storytellers such as Dickens, Thackeray, and Scott, whom he calls "romantic Realists." Ridiculing the "apostles of dullness" of the Howells-led "realistic school," O'Reilly inverts the usual critical terms to call for a new sort of novelist: "The true realist will not make mud pies and tell the world to behold that they are real mud; but he will mould beautiful images from the clay, and then his real will become ideal, which is ART. The world is waiting for him to come."[9]

Although his criticism consistently supported respectable/romantic "morality in fiction," O'Reilly's own literary productions embody the ambivalence of his Irish-American generation. Written for syndication in the *Pilot*, his first novel *Moondyne* (1879) is an unassimilated mix of sentimental plot and serious social criticism. The latter is effective when O'Reilly sticks to the specifics of the flawed prison system in England and Australia. In these sections, based on his own experience as a transported Fenian, the novel contains powerful realistic detail. Especially effective are his descriptions of a convict ship and of the daily round of life in the Western Australia penal colony. The novel is dedicated "To all who are in prison, for whatever cause," and its protagonist is a British convict who has been transported for stealing to avoid starvation. "Moondyne" (his nickname in the bush) escapes, makes his fortune in Australia, and ends up reforming the penal systems in Australia and India in order to rehabilitate rather than embitter those convicted of crimes. On the other hand, O'Reilly's generalizing passages of social philosophy are flatly didactic and grafted awkwardly onto the novel. In these, he advocates a radical redistribution of land in England in order to eradicate poverty by producing a nation of small farmers. The plot also falters, for it features a typically romantic love story that advances by fairly preposterous leaps and bounds. The characters conform to type as well. Moondyne is described as "god-like, beautiful," the love of his life is as pure as the driven snow, and their adversaries are blackly villainous.

O'Reilly's second novel is a strange but appropriate work for this natural mediator. *The King's Men: A Tale of Tomorrow* (1884) is literally an Irish-Yankee collaboration. The book was written by O'Reilly and three of his Boston literary friends, Robert Grant, John T. Wheelwright, and Frederick J. Stimpson, who divided up the chapters and met on Saturday nights to put them together. It was something of a success in the Boston *Globe*, where it first appeared serially. A futuristic novel set in the late 1960s, *The King's Men* must have owed something to O'Reilly in its conception, for it describes the end of the British monarchy. Deposed by a republican revolution twenty years before the novel opens, King George V has set up a court in exile in Boston. The fledgling British republic, which includes England and Ireland, has had a difficult beginning. Its first president had been a genial Irishman, O'Donovan Rourke. (The name is close enough to O'Reilly's friend Jeremiah O'Donovan Rossa, the diehard Fenian, to be an inside joke.) But after Rourke's untimely death the second president is Bagshaw, a cigar-chomping demagogue in the mold of Boss Tweed and Tammany Hall. Most of the novel describes a royalist conspiracy against the British republic led by the protagonist Geoffrey Ripon, a disinherited earl. O'Reilly's hand seems evident in the passages in which Ripon reasons to the conclusion that representative government must replace monarchy, even if the temporary price is Bagshavian demagoguery.

In addition, two other chapters of *The King's Men* seem to be O'Reilly's work. The first is a humorous description of King George's Boston exile. When his money runs low, George has to move from the city's best hotel to a less exclusive place in the South End which takes him in only after he agrees to let them use his name in advertising. Initially, there is much excitement over the establishment of George's "court" and the Anglophile Boston "swells" compete fiercely for his attention, but when the king brings his mistress onto the scene, the proper Bostonians soon lose interest in him. The satire of both the vain monarch and the toadying, fickle crowd of Boston socialites is mild but effective. The second O'Reilly chapter is the description of Geoffrey Ripon's incarceration as a traitor in Dartmoor Prison, which looms "in the centre of its wide waste of barren hills, huge granite outcroppings and swampy valleys" (193). Ripon and his fellows discover and repair a rough monument to dead French and American prisoners from the Napoleonic War and the War of 1812 that had been built a hundred years earlier in 1867 by a group of jailed Irish rebels. While reading the inscription, Ripon feels "akin with those who slept below," and imagines "the Celtic patriots raising the cairn and cutting the sweet old Roman words [*Dulce et decorum est pro patria mori*] on the monolith" (212). Shortly after, Ripon makes his escape. In this vignette O'Reilly is recalling in fiction his own experience as a young Fenian prisoner in Dartmoor.

When added to the convict and Australian scenes in *Moondyne*, this completes O'Reilly's fictional use of his own youth as a Fenian patriot. Given the extraordinary nature of that experience and O'Reilly's obvious literary ambition, this record is meagre enough to suggest conscious self-censorship. And if he did so little with such rich materials (one thinks of Melville mining so thoroughly his own few years of shipboard experience), it is no wonder that O'Reilly never got around to dealing in fiction with Boston Irish life. Certainly his duties as *Pilot* editor, public-spirited citizen, and family man (with a wife and four daughters) were heavy. And yet the literary denial of exciting Irish materials is still striking. It must have been rooted in his sense of himself as cultural mediator between Boston's Irish and Yankees. Too much about Fenians and "the cause" would not have furthered rapprochement. Indeed, *The King's Men* is itself the embodiment of that mediation, the bridging of the gap between two so disparate cultures. A noble attempt, this literary alliance of three Yankees and an Irishman was necessarily flawed and fragmented.

It was, however, his poetry that made O'Reilly's reputation in literary Boston, a recently dominant subculture that was now sliding toward moribund gentility in the form of the canonized complacency of its "Good Gray" poets, Longfellow, Lowell, Whittier, and Holmes. O'Reilly's best-loved poems were undeniably genteel and sentimental. These include "The Cry of the Dreamer" (for escape from the world) and "The Rainbow's Treasure" (sought by a wandering poet). O'Reilly's most anthologized poem remains "A White Rose," which begins "The red rose whispers of passion / And the white rose breathes of love." Thomas Beer has located this side of O'Reilly mordantly: "He had met the American definition of a poet fully; ladies recited the vaguely radical stanzas of 'In Bohemia' where recitation was encouraged and the pretty lyric of the roses was a legend on Christmas calendars, dusted with snowy mica and edged with shamrocks" (108). But there was ambivalence here as well, for O'Reilly did write several poems that are openly critical of the social fabric. The famous "In Bohemia" does in fact contain some pointed barbs. Bohemia has "No gilded dullard native born / To stare at his fellow with leaden scorn," and the critique of "The organized charity, scrimped and iced, / In the name of a cautious, statistical Christ," is echoed in Finley Peter Dunne's harsh renderings (discussed in chapter 6) of the damage done by relief agencies to the pride and spirit of the Irish poor. Also, in "The City Streets" O'Reilly makes the contrast starkly between opulent mansions and squalid tenements, and in "From the Earth, A Cry" the speaker envisions the earth itself crying out for exploited millworkers and their haggard families, exhorting the "starving and dangerous myriads" to "own the earth in their lifetime and hand it down to their children."[10]

Thomas N. Brown has said that O'Reilly's greatest achievement was "the Boston *Pilot* in the years of his editorship. In its pages week after week, year after year, he labored to build a bridge between the American and the Irish-American communities." Brown goes on to summarize

O'Reilly's ambivalence by describing him as "in a classic way the marginal man, pulled in one direction by genteel Boston and in another by his immigrant constituency and by conservative authorities within the Church." Brown reckons the loss to Irish-American letters succinctly: "A novel that would have explored the realities of the immigrant community and that other community to which the Irish wanted entrance would not have been pleasing to either. . . . It would not be many years before others, far less qualified than O'Reilly, would undertake the exploration. But O'Reilly remained silent about that which he knew best. Had it been otherwise, he might today have a place in the body of American literature" ("Layman" 84, 90).[11]

Of the other Irish-American writers in the *Pilot* circle, Katherine Conway has already been discussed as the author of the classic ambivalent novel, *Lalor's Maples*. Similarly, her other novel, *The Way of the World and Other Ways: A Story of Our Set* (1900), combines effective satire at the expense of a snobbish Catholic literary society, "The Daughters of St. Paula," and a climactic deathbed scene of which Mary Anne Sadlier would have been proud. Conway's collection *The Woman Who Never Did Wrong and Other Stories* (1909) is uniformly sentimental. James Jeffrey Roche was born in Queens County, Ireland, and came to Boston in 1866 by way of earlier immigration to Prince Edward Island. He became assistant editor of the *Pilot* in 1883 and assumed the editorship upon O'Reilly's death in 1890. Katherine Conway then took over from Roche in 1905. As his encomiastic biography of his mentor illustrates, Roche idolized O'Reilly, and he continued O'Reilly's *Pilot* editorial policies. His own literary production was palely imitative of his master. A genteel poet, Roche also ventured into popular fiction, but wrote nothing directly about his own times or Irish-American life. *The Story of the Filibusters* (1891) is an adventure novel about Central America and *Her Majesty the King: A Romance of the Harem* (1899) mildly satirizes the Spanish-American War's Board of Strategy from the oblique perspective of a pseudo-Oriental romance.[12]

After O'Reilly himself, the most talented of the *Pilot* writers was Louise Imogen Guiney. Her father Patrick Guiney was an immigrant from County Tipperary who became one of the most famous Irishmen in Boston through his heroism in the Civil War. Having enlisted as a private in the Massachusetts Volunteers, he distinguished himself in over thirty battles, lost an eye at The Wilderness, and was mustered out a general. His health in ruins, General Guiney was kept alive (in his daughter's words) "by nursing and by force of will" until his death in 1877. The only child to survive infancy, Louise was educated at the Sacred Heart convent school in Providence. O'Reilly accepted her first poems for publication in the *Pilot* in 1880 when she was nineteen, and her first volume, *Songs at the Start* (dedicated to O'Reilly) appeared in 1884. Guiney also began to be recognized in Yankee literary circles, and she dedicated her first collection of essays, *Goose-Quill Papers* (1885) to her Brahmin mentor, Oliver Wendell

Holmes. A trip to Ireland while on the grand tour from 1889 to 1891 provided first-hand exposure to the Irish literary renaissance which was just then gathering steam with the poetic and proselytizing efforts of young William Butler Yeats and the revival of Gaelic culture through the linguistic, folklore, and organizational work of Douglas Hyde. Caught up in the excitement, Guiney met the principals in this burgeoning movement and became good friends with two, Katherine Tynan and Dora Sigerson.

Returning to Boston, Guiney faced the problem of supporting herself and her mother on her father's small and diminishing inheritance. Working diligently at writing, she sold poems and essays to leading periodicals, *Harper's* and the *Atlantic* as well as the *Catholic World* and the *Pilot*. The proceeds were nowhere near enough, however, and in 1894 Guiney was forced to take a political appointment arranged by a friend of her father's as postmistress at Auburndale, Massachusetts. Here, as she puts it in a letter, "I had some rather rough sailing, thanks purely to my being a Catholic; i.e., one likely at any moment to give over the government mail, and the safe keys, to the Pope!" What she faced was opposition to her appointment in the form of a boycott of the Auburndale Post Office by the American Protective Association, an anti-Catholic, anti-immigrant group that was the most vocal of the contributors to the new surge of nativism in the 1890s. Fond of disseminating "Popish plot" propaganda, the A.P.A. reacted strongly against the flood of "new immigrants" from Southern and Eastern Europe in these years. Guiney was rescued by friends who flocked in from Boston to buy great numbers of stamps, the sale of which provided most of the job's income. Later in the 1890s, Guiney got another job doing cataloging at the Boston Public Library, but it was always rough going, and finances were a factor in her decision to move permanently to England in 1901. She lived frugally in Oxford and London, continued to write and do literary research on seventeenth-century British poetry, and died in Oxford in 1920 at age fifty-nine.[13]

Louise Guiney is important because she provides the purest example of a set of ideas that were pervasive in her Irish-American literary generation—American Celticism. There was extensive American interest in and contribution to the Irish and Gaelic literary and cultural revivals in the last third of the nineteenth century. As was discussed in chapter 1, American interest in Celtic antiquarian matters goes back to the eighteenth century. In the Famine generation, where there was otherwise an understandable decline in such things, at least one novelist, Father Hugh Quigley, argued forcibly for the preservation of Irish folk materials, which he incorporated into his own novel of 1854, *The Prophet of the Ruined Abbey*. Published in that same year was another immigrant's book that helped keep Irish traditional culture alive in those dark years, *Bits of Blarney*, "a series of Irish stories and legends collected from the peasantry," by Robert Shelton MacKenzie. Its reissue in 1884 also indicates increased interest in the next generation. Also quite early was P.M. Haverty's *Legends and Fairy*

Tales of Ireland, published in 1872 with a preface proclaiming it as the first "general collection of the fairy tales and legends" of Ireland to appear in America. Haverty's aim was ethnic self-awareness. Complaining of the "innumerable republications of Mother Goose rhymes and English nursery rhymes," he declared that "the recollection of the beautiful and wildly romantic stories of fairy and banshee, leprechaun and phooka are almost unknown to the children of even the first generation of Irish in this country."[14]

Throughout the revival period, there were a number of significant Irish-American contributions, both linguistic and literary. The brother of the noted Irish historian and linguist Patrick Weston Joyce, Robert Dwyer Joyce, a medical doctor, had emigrated in 1866 to Boston where he made some of the earliest contributions on either side of the Atlantic to the popularization of Gaelic literature and culture. In 1868 he published *Legends of the Wars in Ireland*, a compilation of folktales and legends from the thirteenth through the eighteenth century. He supplemented this with two books published in Boston by Patrick Donahoe, *Irish Fireside Tales* (1871) and *Ballads of Irish Chivalry* (1872), and with his own verse translations of *Deirdre* (1876) and *Blanid* (1879), based on popular tales from the Ulster (Red Branch) Cycle of Irish legends. A bestseller, *Deirdre* sold 10,000 copies in its first month. Even the Brahmins took notice, as James Russell Lowell called it "the best epic poem of the century." Wisconsin native Jeremiah Curtin was the first collector of Irish folklore with real field experience, gained while working for the U.S. Bureau of Ethnology among American Indians. He made several trips to Ireland in the 1880s and published three respected anthologies of Irish myths and folktales, beginning with *Myths and Folklore of Ireland* (1890). Their popularity was demonstrated when some appeared serially in Sunday supplements of the New York *Sun* in 1892-93.[15]

W.B. Yeats had several connections with American Celticism. He wrote one of his first Irish essays (in 1886) about Robert Dwyer Joyce's poems and he drew upon Curtin's collections for some of his earlier reworkings of Irish folk materials. Also, between 1887 and 1892 Yeats published a number of original essays in the Boston *Pilot* and the Providence (Rhode Island) *Journal* on individual Irish writers (Lady Wilde, William Allingham, Ellen O'Leary) and larger concerns of the budding cultural movement ("Ireland's Heroic Age," "The Irish National Literary Society," "A Poetic Drama"). An early, enthusiastic promoter of the Irish revival, *Journal* editor Alfred Williams also wrote essays on Irish literature in the *Catholic World* and published a valuable anthology of *The Poets and Poetry of Ireland* in 1881. The Gaelic language movement also had early American support. The first American "Philo-Celtic Society" for the revival of Gaelic was founded in Boston in 1873, four years before a similar group in Dublin. By 1880, the New York Society for the Preservation of the Irish Language was sponsoring Gaelic concerts and language study, and in 1881 the *Gael*, a bilingual English/Gaelic literary periodical, began publication in Brooklyn. Moreover, the Gaelic League began to sprout American branches immediately after its foundation in Ireland by Douglas Hyde in 1893.[16]

Also indicating public interest were immediate American editions of the seminal works of the Irish revival, Yeats's poems and plays, John M. Synge's plays, and Hyde's translations of tales (*Beside the Fire*, 1890) and poems (*Love Songs of Connacht*, 1893). David Greene has remarked on the importance of Yeats's first trip to America in publicizing contemporary Irish letters. From November 1903 to March 1904, Yeats spoke to large and receptive audiences from Carnegie Hall to California, from Harvard and Yale to the Catholic University in Washington and Notre Dame. Greene also notes the watershed American publication in 1904 of an inclusive ten-volume anthology of *Irish Literature* edited by Justin McCarthy, Douglas Hyde, Lady Augusta Gregory, and others. Impressively printed in both DeLuxe and reader's editions, this four thousand-page work included selections from 344 authors, fairy and folk tales, ballads, Gaelic literature (in the original with cross-page translations), and critical essays by McCarthy, Yeats, Hyde, and others. "Obviously intended to dramatise the respectability of Irish literature," says Greene, "its impact as propaganda, and as something more than propaganda was considerable," for "Americans could now comprehend, in one huge work, the entire and impressive sweep of Irish literature" (xii).

There were significant contributions here, and Irish-American support of these various projects was often sincere and useful. However, the phenomenon of American Celticism also had unhealthy effects, especially on Irish-American literature in this generation. Late-nineteenth-century Irish America found two propaganda uses for Celticism. The first was an actively political use. Thrown on the defensive by nativist-encouraged "Anglo-Saxon myth-making" on the part of Anglophile historians such as James Anthony Froude and Goldwyn Smith, "the Irish," says Thomas N. Brown, "emboldened by their increasing economic and political status, elaborated a Celtic interpretation of history." American Celts found in ancient Irish history examples of military heroism, political leadership, and "typically American virtues," including "representative government, trial by jury, and popular education." Brown declares that in this form "the Celtic myth served as a useful defensive weapon at a time when prevailing American opinion had it that America in its people and institutions was essentially Anglo-Saxon" ("Origins" 343-45).

The second use of Celticism was literary. John Kelleher has traced the Celtic literary convention back to Matthew Arnold's *On the Study of Celtic Literature* of 1867. He lists Arnold's "Celtic touchstones" as "piercing regret and passion, . . . magic and piercing melancholy and doomed bravery and ineffectualness and verbal sensuality and splendid dream-haunted failure and the exquisite spiritual sensitivity of the Celt." He points out that major writers such as Yeats and Synge were "too big to be contained" by such a formula, but that it appears in pure form in the works of minor figures. In fact, says Kelleher, the clearest embodiment of the convention is in a poem published in 1911 by an Irish American, Shaemus O'Sheel. The title says it all: "They Went Forth to Battle But They Always Fell." Kelleher explains that what made this poem and the whole Celtic formula attractive was its embodiment of a "new view of Irish history which explains defeat and removes its sting. It suggests that the Irish were beaten . . . because they were distracted by more important, if less pressing, matters: matters indeed so profound that only a Celt could understand them or even be aware of them, and then only when he was not attending to business. They were beaten because, in other words, they were *fey*, doomed by their own spiritual sensitivity" ("Arnold" 216). As O'Sheel declaims, "It was a secret music that they heard. . . . Ah these / By an unwarlike troubling doubt were stirred, / And died for hearing what no foeman heard." Another dimension of literary Celticism is conveyed by Yeats's title for his 1893 collection of folk tales—*The Celtic Twilight*—which became a catch-phrase for the early phase of the literary revival. The haziness of twilight goes along with supposed Celtic spirituality. Both suggest distance from the harsh realities of mundane modern life. This escapist attitude was much in the air in the 1880s and 1890s. And its popularity in Irish-American literary circles was another cultural defense against literary Anglo-Saxonism, which was at least as rampant as the political brand.[17]

The Irish-American embrace of Celticism had several meanings, one of which certainly involved respectability. The Irish had "made it" to the extent that this was their first American generation to be able to afford the luxury of a purely literary self-definition. A combination of the Irish cultural reality of the Celtic revival and the American social reality of the rise of a middle class, American Celticism was as far removed from the realities of most Irish-American lives (Irish too, for that matter) as the Famine generation's didactic romanticism had been. The movement certainly had some positive effects; for example, its encouragement of pride in the Gaelic past, a sense of the uniqueness of a shared historical tradition, and appreciation of the picturesque aspects of contemporary life back in Ireland. Certainly, Celticism sold—and continues to sell—a lot of books.

But the negative impact was more significant. A distorted sense of one's heritage, extending even to the recent past, is not in the long run good for anybody. As "Emerald Isle" sentimentality and nostalgia became rampant, they led to unhealthy romanticizing of even the least attractive aspects of Irish life. By 1923, for example, an Irish-American writer was capable of personifying destitution as "the beloved companion [of the Irish peasant], the Lady Poverty of St. Francis's vision, walking barefooted and starry-eyed on the Irish hills."[18] Celticism allowed Irish Americans in the literary life to be both Irish and respectably romantic at once, and also to ignore unpleasant aspects of the contemporary world. Most damaging of all to the literature was the fact that encouragement of the misty, romantic "Celtic twilight" vision of Irishness constituted discouragement of a realistic approach to Irish-American letters. Why write or read about the often painful and embarrassing situations of urban Irish Americans next door when one could dwell on picturesque tales of fairy folk, mythic heroes, and the contented peasantry of the old country, three thousand miles away?

A pure strain of American Celticism appeared in Boston, where the pressures of anti-Irish nativism and the weight of an Anglo-Saxon literary establishment were particularly strong. And Louise Imogen Guiney provides the clearest case in point. Given her respectable upbringing and convent education, her connections with younger writers in Ireland, the influence of John Boyle O'Reilly, and her brush with the A.P.A., it is no wonder that Guiney's literary efforts embody the Celtic conventions and assumptions virtually to the letter. Her expatriation to Oxford was the logical extension of the imaginative escape that she had already made in her writing.

Guiney wrote four impressionistic biographical sketches of people whose "romantic" lives fascinated her. To a man, her subjects are heroic failures, courageous but doomed because they are too unworldly and spiritual to succeed. ("They went forth to battle but they always fell.") In *Blessed Edmund Campion* (1908), Guiney describes the Catholic martyr as out of touch with and scorning the political realities of Elizabethan England. In *"Monsieur Henri": A Footnote to French History* (1892), she renders the heroic death at twenty-three of Count Henry de La Rochejaquelin, the idealistic leader of a doomed provincial rebellion in France in 1795. The other two biographies are of Irishmen. In *Robert Emmet, A Survey of His Rebellion and of His Romance* (1904), Guiney stresses two things about the leader of the hopeless 1803 rising in Dublin: his "beautifully gay" embrace of martyrdom for a lost cause, and his utter unworldliness—"he lived not so much in the scene around him as in the society of the illustrious and sainted dead" (14). Last, she produced a biography with selected poems of Irish poet James Clarence Mangan (1897), who had died destitute in Dublin in 1849. Presenting a litany of Mangan's misfortunes ("he was poor, infirm, homeless, loveless"), Guiney declares that "it may be unjust to lend him the epitaph of defeat, for he never strove at all," and she attributes his death at forty-six to the same conditions "which have visited poets from the earth's beginning, those which the comfortable world, well-clad, well-dined, with its feet on the fender, finds it hard to believe in at all" (5, 18). Mangan was, in short, the archetypal failed Celt, a sensitive, unrecognized, lost soul.

How completely Guiney has accepted the assumptions of Celticism is clear from the one essay in which she examines Irishness directly. Written just after her 1889 visit to Ireland, the essay, titled "Irish," begins:

"They say the Celt is passing away. . . . For he represents yesterday, and its ideals: legendry, ritual, the heroic and indignant joy of life, belong to him; and he can establish no manner of connection with modern science and the subjugating of the material universe; with the spirit of to-day and to-morrow." One almost expects her to be setting up these ideas to knock them down. Instead, she goes on to argue that "venerable Ireland has failed, as the world reckons failure," because "she has fallen back into the sullen interior life, into the deep night of reverie" (153, 157). In other words, Ireland has failed to become "modern" because the Irish are listening to Shaemus O'Sheel's "secret music." Furthermore, this retreat into the "brooding dark" is seen as more noble than giving in to the practical modern scramble for success. Again, defeat is rationalized, justified, praised. Guiney's own literary flights toward the ideal are further reflected in her detestation of the realistic movement. She deplored the fiction of Ireland's first realist, George Moore, and in her essay on "Willful Sadness in Literature," she argues against the same tendencies that so disturbed O'Reilly and other Catholic critics: "The play which leaves us miserable and bewildered, the harrowing social lesson leading nowhere, the transcript from commonplace life in which nothing is admirable but the faithful skill of the author—these are bad morals because they are bad art" (234) Guiney wanted her own literary reputation to rest on her poetry, and she called her collected poems of 1909 *Happy Ending*. These fall into predictable categories: poems with medieval settings, replete with knights errant striving toward ideal, unrealizable goals, poems full of vague, sentimental abstractions with titles such as "The Search," "To an Ideal," "Fact and the Mystic," and poems (her best) conveying her love of the real world of trees, flowers, and changing seasons.

Guiney also published one collection of stories. *Lovers' St. Ruth's and Three Other Tales* (1895) is full of martyrdoms and lost causes, in settings as various as England in 1620 and Civil War America. She published the stories reluctantly, and wrote a friend that she could only tolerate "the Irish one, . . . even that I can stomach with difficulty." In fact, this story, "The Provider" (93-123), is her best. In it, a ten-year-old boy sacrifices his life to save his family from starvation in the Dublin slums. The time is the present, and before the heroic sacrifice there is solid description of actual slum conditions. But this was as close as Guiney ever came to addressing the pressing problems facing the real Irish in Ireland and America in her time. Her grudging preference for it may suggest her sense of the possibilities of the stories that she couldn't quite bring herself to tell. Her letters also suggest another side, for they are spontaneous, bright, and genuinely funny in ways she never allowed herself to be in print. She wrote her Irish friend Dora Sigerson as follows about placing a poem: "Your 'Banagher Rue' got taken at once by the *Catholic World*, the first magazine to which I sent it; and you will infer that I went on a hunt for some correct Gaelic spelling with which to embellish your refrain, and fished it at last from the deep sea, in the person of a funny ancient bartender in Boston who is of culture compact."[19] It is one of the blows to Irish-American letters inflicted by Celticism that Louise Guiney could not have told us more about that bartender and about her own experiences being Irish in Boston. She could, for example, have described what it felt like to be a sensitive young woman standing behind the grill at the Auburndale Post Office listening to nativist catcalls. That would have been an Irish-American story worth telling—no Celtic twilight or secret, dreamy music, but the clear, cold light of a nineteenth-century New England day.

By century's end, the trickle of "Celtic" texts had become a stream. The fairy and folk dimension had by then already become established as a money-making publishing area, and it has been a major piece of the respectable/romantic Irish-American literary market ever since. One of the many successful folktale collections, published in 1888 and favorably reviewed by Yeats in the Providence *Journal*, has a title that indicates the genre well: D.R. McAnally's *Irish Wonders: The Ghosts, Giants, Pookas, Demons, Leprechawns, Banshees, Fairies, Witches, Widows, Old Maids, and Other Marvels of the Emerald Isle, Popular Tales as Told by the People*. One writer who switched gears into the new, perhaps more lucrative mode, was Patrick Sarsfield Cassidy. His first novel, *Glenveigh, or the Victims of Vengeance. A Tale of Irish Peasant Life in the Present* (1870, discussed in chapter 3) had been a fictional version of the true story of evictions on a Donegal estate in 1863. But his second, published in 1892, was *The Borrowed Bride: A Fairy Love Legend of Donegal*, a book-length poem containing a love story set in ancient Donegal about a beautiful woman abducted by fairies and rescued by a young Gaelic chieftain. The book has extensive notes on Gaelic words and ancient Irish customs, and in its preface Cassidy praises "ancient Ireland—golden Ireland—richer in antiquities and Pelasgic remains, in heroic traditions and spiritual creations than almost any country of Europe." Another fascinating example of Irish-American use of the Celtic/Gaelic past is *Dervorgilla; or, The Downfall of Ireland* (1895) by Anna C. Scanlan, a fictional version in purplest prose of the life and times of the woman over whose hand the fighting began that ended with the invasion of Ireland by the troops of England's Henry II in 1170. Scanlan hopes to shift the blame for the start of the British occupation from "a hapless, helpless woman" to the "quarrels and wars" of the men in her life, O'Rourke and Dermot McMurrough. At the same time, she describes in great detail the customs, poetry, and music of Gaelic Ireland before the invasion, to establish the sophistication of that culture.[20]

There was also a fearsome amount of green-tinted poetry generated in these years. Many of the writers whose fiction is discussed in this chapter also wrote verse, most of it in the romantic/genteel vein to which the nostalgic and picturesque vision of Ireland lends itself all too readily. Among these are the entire *Pilot* circle of O'Reilly, Conway, Roche, and

Guiney, and there were many, many others. The genre can best be sampled by looking into a huge green-covered tome, *The Household Library of Ireland's Poets, with Full and Choice Selections from the Irish-American Poets*, edited and published in 1887 by Daniel Connolly, and organized thematically to includes poems of "The Affections, Home and Childhood, Sentiment and Retrospection, Patriotism, Loss and Sorrow, Morality and Religion."[21]

The writers of this, the third Irish-American literary generation, were actually second-generation Irish, because they were, in fact, the children of the Famine immigrants. Many of these writers never wavered for a minute or a paragraph from the dictates of the genteel tradition. After all, this new literary generation coincided with the emergence of an Irish-American middle class. Themselves charter members, many novelists consciously wrote for this audience of new bourgeoisie and promulgated through their fiction the bourgeois values of genteel respectability. In addition, as we have seen, Irish-American fiction of the previous, Famine generation had been predominantly romantic, didactic, and sentimental, thereby providing precedents and models. Furthermore, Thomas Davis and the Young Irelanders of the 1840s had created something of a genteel literary tradition in Ireland as well, one to which many immigrants felt nostalgically tied. Thus, the new "respectable" writers were the true heirs of Mary Anne Sadlier, Hugh Quigley, and Peter McCorry, and the result of their labors was a new wave of didactic propaganda fiction. Like their Famine-generation predecessors, these writers used fiction to defend the Catholic faith, to proselytize for Irish freedom, and to instruct their readers in how to live in the New World. The main difference is a raising of the tone and level of expectation of what constitutes a proper, successful life. The Famine generation had written survival manuals; the following generation wrote etiquette books.

This seems a turgid and dreary vein, but it is important not to ridicule the efforts, including literary, of this culture to become respectable. Although the effort led many writers away from the more promising path of the realistic movement, it was part of a much larger, thoroughly understandable, and even laudable effort. The virtues of respectability were necessary for any sort of advancement in America for oneself or one's children. Caught in the throes of the transformation from a pre-industrial society in Ireland to an urban, industrial American world, Irish immigrants needed to develop new habits of reliability at work and in the home. With such steadiness came new opportunities and aspirations. For all of this, the blanket term "respectability" applies, and in a wholly positive way. On the other hand, respectability in literature meant a number of things detrimental to the development of the kind of honest self-assessment of one's culture that informs any generation's most valuable art.

There were many such novels, but the concerns of the pure strain of late-nineteenth-century, genteel/sentimental Irish-American fiction can be summarized briefly with a few examples. First, there were the Catholic-tract novels. In her preface to *The Joint Venture: A Tale in Two Lands* (1878), E.A. Fitzsimon states her aims of countering "the humorous travesties of Lever and Lover" with pictures of "intelligent and refined" Irish characters, and of presenting "the sacrifice of inclination to duty [as] an everyday occurrence in the Catholic home." To these ends, she tells the tangled tale of a family of Irish and Irish-American scholar/aristocrats who are obvious role models for her audience. The novel is replete with death-bed scenes, treatises against divorce, vocations, and examples of romantic love sacrificed to filial or religious duty.[22] The stock-in-trade of Famine-generation novelists such as Mary Anne Sadlier, these conventional materials were popular enough to be anthologized themselves in the following generation, when Augustine O'Reilly published a compendium of *Strange Memories: Death Bed Scenes, Extraordinary Conversions, Incidents of Travel, etc.* in 1880. The chapter headings include "Angels Bring the Priest," "Why Little Girls Die Young," and "Death in a Ball Dress" (a cautionary anecdote).

Second, there were the Irish-nationalist propaganda novels. Particularly ambitious was John Brennan's *Erin Mor: The Story of Irish Republicanism* (1892), which takes a group of Irish freedom fighters from Famine-ravaged Limerick to San Diego, by way of the American Civil War, the Fenian movement, Know-Nothing and A.P.A. agitations, and the formation of the Irish National League in Chicago. Throughout, the dream of "Erin Mor" (Great Ireland) drives the protagonists and keeps them from succumbing to the American temptations of whiskey and politics, "the graveyard of the Irish race." An attractive image of the Irish nationalist appeared in the popular play *Peg O' My Heart* by J. Hartley Manners, in which the daughter of an Irish agitator has an eventful life in Ireland, England, and America. Manners published a fictional version in 1913, and by 1918 the play had been performed over 10,000 times.[23]

Third, were the novels dedicated to the inculcation of genteel, middle-class values. The most accomplished and popular writer of these was Maurice Francis Egan, who is discussed at length in chapter 6. A handy anthology of such works is the collection edited in 1897 by Eleanor Donnelly, *A Round Table of the Representative American Catholic Novelists, at Which Is Served a Feast of Excellent Stories*. Here leading Irish Catholic writers illustrate genteel standards of behavior in settings as various as Colonial Maryland, Italy, the Adirondacks, and Hawaii.[24] In many of the respectable/romantic novels the categories tend to run together. For example, in *The Lovers, or Cupid in Ireland* (1891) by J.L. Meany, love blossoms among aristocratic Catholics vacationing in County Clare, but the romance is complicated by the fact that the suitor is an English Protestant lord who also opposes political liberty for Ireland. He gets the girl only after converting to both Catholicism and home rule. And so it went, through a large number of Irish-American books, representative of a good deal of energy and aspiration toward literary and cultural gentility.

The rest of this chapter will be concerned with the Irish-American realists, writers who, while crippled to varying degrees by ambivalence about what fiction ought to accomplish, still achieved a measure of realism. The following chapter will present in more depth this generation's two most important contrasting figures: the very respectable Maurice Francis Egan and his opposite number, Finley Peter Dunne, the one writer of his time to sustain a realistic perspective through a significant body of work, and thus Irish-American literature's first genius.

A measure of support for Irish-American realism came from popular culture. Despite the prevalence of slapstick and stereotyping, the musical comedies of Edward Harrigan contained recognizable situations from Irish urban life, as did the plays of second-generation-Irish dramatists Augustin Daly and James A. Herne. Most important here were the eight plays about the rise to respectability of the Mulligan family of New York City that Harrigan and his partner Tony Hart produced in the 1870s and 1880s. Harrigan was praised as a realist by William Dean Howells, who found him "a true dramatist, who loves the life he observes." Harrigan continued to write plays into the 1890s, and his novel, *The Mulligans* (1901), was a collection of incidents from the Mulligan plays in which the satiric target is Cordelia Mulligan's campaign for lace-curtain status, featuring the acquisition of a piano for the parlor, an ill-fated move from Mulligan's Alley to a Madison Avenue mansion, and a triumphal return visit to Ireland.[25] By 1910, a national campaign by the Ancient Order of Hibernians had driven the stage Irishman, even in Harrigan's mild form, from the American theater. Indeed, Dublin's Abbey Theatre players felt the wrath of the A.O.H. and United Irish-American Societies when John M. Synge's *Playboy of the Western World* was met with protests and legal injunctions during the Irish group's first American tour in 1911-12. Irish-American drama broke through into the cultural mainstream when Eugene O'Neill's *Beyond the Horizon* won a Pulitzer Prize in 1920.

Additional reinforcing models for Irish-American realists came from the appearance in the 1890s of realistic works about Irish-American life by writers from the American literary mainstream. Much of this fiction by non-Irish Americans was urban local color or "slum fiction," and it emerged from the milieu of journalism which was the seedbed for many pioneering realistic writers, including Stephen Crane, Theodore Dreiser, and Frank Norris. A number of writers explored the urban Irish scene. Richard Harding Davis wrote *Gallegher and Other Stories* (1891) about a street-wise newspaper office boy. Brander Matthews's *Vignettes of Manhattan* (1894) include glimpses of Irish saloon life in Hell's Kitchen. Edward W. Townsend wrote stories of Bowery boy "Chimmie Fadden" (*Chimmie Fadden, Major Max and Other Stories*, 1895) and of an Irish girl from Mulberry Street (*A Daughter of the Tenements*, 1896). Probably the most famous example is Stephen Crane's use of the Bowery Irish in *Maggie: A Girl of the Streets* (1893).[26] The mainstream writers who dealt most successfully with the American Irish were Sarah Orne Jewett and Harold Frederic. Jewett wrote a number of stories in the late eighties and the nineties about Irish immigrants to her own coastal Maine which describe the difficulties of assimilation sympathetically. Frederic dealt with Irish materials in two novels. *The Return of the O'Mahony* (1892), about the sojourn in Ireland of a Yankee from New York, graphically depicts agrarian poverty and British governmental unresponsiveness. And *The Damnation of Theron Ware* (1896) presents an intellectual Irish priest and his immigrant flock in upstate New York with solidity and understanding.[27]

Finally, as in the Famine generation, many non-Irish but Catholic writers toward the end of the century wrote idealizing fiction about the Irish in the service of Catholic-tract didacticism.[28] On the other hand, there were also non-Irish writers who contributed to the upsurge of nativism in the 1880s and nineties by continuing to turn out anti-Catholic and anti-Irish fiction of the type prevalent during the Famine generation. The new generation's spate of nativist fiction included the *Shantytown Sketches* (1897) of Philadelphian Drexel Biddle, divided into three sections, Irish, Jewish, and Black, all offensively caricatured, Alvan F. Sanborn's *Meg McIntyre's Raffle, and Other Stories* (1896), which features ignorant brogue-laden characterizations of the corpulent widow, crooked politician, and drunken reprobate, and Rufus Shavley's *Solid for Mulhooly: A Sketch of Municipal Politics, Under the Leaders, the Ring, and the Boss* (1881), the story of the progress of a corrupt Irish immigrant from bar-boy to ward boss to Congressman, narrated in a tone of scathing contempt. A classic of this type is Harriete Keyser's violently anti-Catholic novel, *Thorns in Your Sides* (1884), published by the respectable New York house of Putnam, in which are contrasted the "ignorant Irish romanists" and the "indomitable" Ulster Protestants of an earlier migration.

Thus, with the encouragement of Irish-American dramatists and non-Irish realistic novelists, and perhaps in retaliation against the stereotyping and prejudice of nativist writers, a significant number of Irish-American writers of fiction did embrace the tenets of the realistic movement to some degree. These pioneers began to count the costs of having "made it," to assess the damages of the nineteenth-century Irish immigrant and ethnic experience in America. In their best work there is once again, as in pre-Famine fiction, an expansion of possibilities: a sense of literature as critical self-assessment beyond didactic moralizing or escapism, and a sense of a wider audience of literate Americans beyond one's own kind.

At this point, more needs to be said about Kerby Miller's thesis that the American Irish saw themselves as "involuntary exiles," even when they were succeeding quite well in the New World. Miller attributes this pervasive negative self-concept to "a traditional Irish Catholic world-view—with its emphases on communalism as opposed to individualism, custom versus innovation, conformity versus initiative, fatalism versus optimism, passivity versus action, dependence versus independence, nonresponsibility versus responsibility" (*Emigrants* 428). As was discussed in chapter 3, a fair amount of Famine-generation fiction corroborates Miller's view, which is consistent with the traumas suffered by the Famine immigrants. However, late-nineteenth-century fiction, both respectable and realistic, is marked by a confidence and energy inconsistent with Miller's sense that the "image of the self-pitying, Anglophobic Irish 'exile' " continued to dominate from beginning to end (1921) of the great Irish diaspora. Nor does that image emerge in pre-Famine fiction with its aesthetic sophistication and confidence. Miller's thesis is based on exhaustive analysis of Irish-American newspapers, oratory, songs and ballads, letters and memoirs, and folklore—just about everything, in fact, except fiction. But fiction must be counted as providing a strong, positive Irish voice through the course of the American nineteenth century. Irish Americans who fashioned their experience into fiction did not limit themselves to the gray monotone of the exile's lament.

By 1880 over a third of America's Irish-born citizens were living outside the East coast, and that significant dispersal is reflected in this generation's fiction. In addition to Katherine Conway's Rochester and John Boyle O'Reilly's Boston, notable realistic writers and their fictional locales include the following: the Rochester of Henry Keenan, the Manhattan of James W. Sullivan, Myra Kelly, Harvey J. O'Higgins, and Eugene Clancy, the upstate New York of William A. McDermott, John Talbot Smith's Connecticut, Toronto, and Adirondack Mountains, the Pennsylvania coal fields of Patrick Justin McMahon, the Wisconsin and Michigan lumber camps of John W. Fitzmaurice, John T. McIntyre's Philadelphia, the Chicago of Clara Laughlin and Finley Peter Dunne's Mr. Dooley, Kate Cleary's Nebraska prairies, and George Jessop's San Francisco.

The writers who produced this generation's most consistently realistic fiction wrote novels and stories containing a familiar ambivalent pattern consisting of realistic settings, characterizations, and incidents marred by concessions to sentimental romance in the form of implausible resolutions of plot. Most important, though, was the fact that these writers began to write genuinely critical fiction. They began to analyze their own culture and its "rise" by asking for the first time a number of questions: what had been the price of achieving respectability, of having had to work so hard and long at backbreaking jobs, of having used politics as a way out, of having grown up in insulated and isolating ghetto communities and families? They also joined other late-nineteenth-century American writers to explore the effects on the human spirit of urban "slum" life. And they began to criticize their culture's literary heritage as well, by including in their own fiction alternatives to such conventions as the triumphant Irish Catholic hero and the climactic, sentimental deathbed scene. However tentative their accomplishments, what Ezra Pound said of Walt Whitman is true of these writers: "It was you that broke the new wood, / Now is a time for carving."

One of the pioneering fictional criticisms of American ethnic life was *Tenement Tales of New York* (1895) by James W. Sullivan, a New York journalist and union organizer who wrote several books about labor and the urban poor. The most powerful "tenement tale" is that of "Slob Murphy," an eight-year-old street urchin whose life and death are narrated in four stark movements: "His Manner of Life, His Death, The Wake, His Funeral."[29] Already bound for trouble, "his mother dead, his father a drunkard, the house filled with rough workingmen, and his only companions those of the street in a miserable neighborhood," Pat Murphy dies after having been trampled by horses. Sullivan's realistic description of the little boy's wake and funeral sharply undercuts the traditional Irish Catholic deathbed scene perfected by the Famine-generation writers. Upon hearing of his playmate's death, another boy asks promptly, "Wot's dey a-goin to do wit' his old cloze?" It is only a step from here to the grimly anticlimactic death of Studs Lonigan at the end of James T. Farrell's trilogy. The "cold pantomime" of grief at the wake by Pat's drunken father is even more chilling, and the sordid funeral, where all the participants—undertaker, gravediggers, priest—cut corners and rush mechanically through, completes the disturbing critique. Indicting the "poisonous moral atmosphere" that has produced this minor-key tragedy, the narrator, a steamboat worker, recognizes that "dirty, ragged, bad Slob had had goodness in him which ought to have had a chance." Engaged in the lives of the people described, this narrative voice conveys compassion that is a far cry from the ironic distance in, for example, Stephen Crane's *Maggie*. In this and in his use of underclass slang to serious, noncomic effect, Sullivan brings a new dimension into Irish-American literature, one available elsewhere at this time only in the dialect voice of Finley Peter Dunne's Mr. Dooley.

In "Minnie Kelsey's Wedding" (45-65) Sullivan describes another impoverished young life, that of an eighteen-year-old girl who works a backbreaking six-day week of ten-hour days in a factory where "the heavy, discordant buzz of the machinery grinds into her very brain" and "the vitiated air dries up the blood in her veins." Minnie's dream of escape through a boyfriend and marriage leads her to a dangerous flirtation with a racetrack gambler, during which she considers the plausible alternatives of prostitution and suicide. Sullivan also satirizes the lace-curtain Irish in "Threw Himself Away" (91-113), in which the genteel Irish members of the "East Side Chaucer Literary Society" deplore the marriage of one of their own to "a common Jew Sheeny." They ignore the rejoinder by one rational member that "for a long time we Irish were ostracised" as well, until the narrator, a club officer, discovers that his friend is an unemployed shiftless wastrel, supported by his wife's hard work as a milliner. It is the

Jewish wife, not the Irish husband, who has "thrown herself away." In another story, "A Young Desperado," Sullivan presents an orphan newsboy, Skinny Maguire, who lives by his wits on the streets of New York, and whose litany of ethnic and family memories is an eloquent commentary on the disparity between illusion and reality in some parts of late-nineteenth-century Irish America. Skinny's version of the Celtic twilight runs as follows: "I kin 'member my fader. His fader was a king in Ireland an' wore a crown o' glitterin' gold, like in de t'eayter. Dey had soldiers in de courtyard an' fairies in de woods. And everybody fought like fun, an' dey downed de landlords. But—I'm hungry" (212). In other stories, Sullivan creates realistic portraits of Italian and Russian immigrants—particularly as exploited urban laborers. Though a sideline from his active life in the labor movement, Sullivan's *Tenement Tales* constitute a landmark literary accomplishment.

Two women contributors to the end-of-the-century fictional depiction of Irish-American life mixed promising realism with genteel/sentimental tendencies. Both Kate Cleary and Myra Kelly died young without fulfilling their considerable potential. The daughter of Irish immigrants, Kate McPhelim Cleary grew up in Chicago in a family of journalists. Married in 1884, she went off with her new husband to a small Nebraska prairie town to set up in the lumber business. There she had six children, became a legendary cook (contributing to *Good Housekeeping*), and published fiction and poetry. In 1898 the family returned to Chicago where business reverses forced her to turn out pot-boilers at the rate of a story a day. Cleary's better fiction was published in respected journals such as the *Century*, *Harper's*, and *McClure's*, and she was about to publish a collection of her stories at the time of her death in 1905 at age forty-two. Reflecting her own odyssey, Cleary's best fiction deals with Irish life in Chicago and rural Nebraska. A typical Chicago story, "The Mission of Kitty Malone," describes a destitute couple from Tipperary, forty-nine years married, who are struggling to survive in a rented room on Blue Island Avenue. With her husband sick with pneumonia, Kitty Malone is forced to go up to city hall to get a relief ticket to purchase a side of bacon for Thanksgiving dinner. The Malones are saved by the return of their son from the Philippine War, but while the ending is romantic, the story is still notable for its moving description of the devoted immigrant couple faced with the shame of going on relief.

Cleary's Nebraska stories are an effective antidote to the anti-urban romantic pastoralism of Mary Anne Sadlier's *Con O'Regan* and the propagandists for rural colonization who believed that moving to the country would solve all Irish-American ills. Cleary's pictures of the Middle-Western rural alternative have the powerful bleakness of Hamlin Garland's collection of fictional revisions of the agrarian myth, *Main-Traveled Roads* (1891). "The Stepmother" evokes the grinding, repetitive labor, the loneliness, and the spiritual poverty that ultimately defeat the second wife of a luckless, inconsiderate Irish farmer who fills his days with drinking steady enough to mitigate his sense of failure. The absence of communicated feeling in this unhappy family strikes an important theme that is emphasized in later Irish-American fiction, notably the novels of James T. Farrell.[30] In a lighter vein are Cleary's treatments of the familiar second-generation theme of the perils of respectability. These include stories of a man whose snobbish children are scandalized by his old clothes and rough ways, a suddenly wealthy woman who arrays her family in inappropriate Kansas City finery and hosts "ice-cream socials" in the boiling Nebraska summer, and a widower who tries unsuccessfully to turn his reluctant daughter into "an ornament to sassiety."

In her brief, active, and assiduous life Kate Cleary published hundreds of stories, poems, and essays. She even had time for a novel, *Like a Gallant Lady* (1897), in which a romantic adventure plot is laid against a realistic background of desolate prairie life. "The only people who associate solitude, romance and all that sort of thing with the plains," declares one character, "are those who write about them without having had any personal experience." Cleary's best work establishes her as an Irish-American realist of great promise—unfulfilled because of family commitments, the economic troubles that drove her to write formula fiction, and her early death. She deserves to be remembered as a good writer and a courageous woman.[31]

Born in Dublin, Myra Kelly came to New York with her physician-father, who set up a medical practice on the Lower East Side. She became an elementary-school teacher there and chronicled her experiences in three collections of stories, beginning with *Little Citizens, The Humors of School Life* (1904), that describe the collision of old and new customs in the "First Reader" classroom of Constance Bailey, the sympathetic teacher of Jewish and Irish immigrant children. Most of the stories involve Miss Bailey's adventures with street-wise but essentially innocent Jewish children who challenge the unworldly abstractions of her teacher-training, but a minor theme, one that appears often in this generation's fiction, is the shifting character of the neighborhood, which leaves the residual Irish families feeling displaced. In one story Associate School Superintendent Timothy O'Shea is the resentful observer of "the happy hunting grounds of his youth grown ragged and foreign." Most of her stories are light in tone, and Kelly's is a sympathetic presentation of the problems of assimilation as seen through the microcosm of a classroom full of children. Her best stories prefigure the cultural collisions in such latter-day classics as Grace Paley's "The Loudest Voice" (1959), about New York Jewish children with Catholic teachers. Before her untimely death at age thirty-five, Myra Kelly was moving in the direction of popular romance. Her latest works of fiction include two novels, *The Golden Season* (1909), a sentimental tale of the college years of two upper-middle-class New York girls, and *Rosnah* (1908), a love and mystery story set in a big house in Ireland during the Land War of the 1880s.[32]

A few other short-story and single-novel writers deserve mention, though none is as accomplished as Sullivan, Cleary, or Kelly. One strange book is *The Shanty Boy: Or, Life in a Lumber Camp* (1889) in which Michigan journalist John W. Fitzmaurice uses a mixture of documentary observation, anecdote, and song "to tell the story of the lumber woods . . . taken directly from shanty life as I beheld it." The result is another Irish-American country heard from—that inhabited by immigrants to the Michigan and Wisconsin lumber camps. As a tonic for ill health, the narrator leaves civilization (at Roscommon, Michigan) to observe his fellow Irish lumbermen. He finds several examples of recognizable Irish culture in the big woods, including an Irish folk tale freshly placed in the American wilderness in which Ned Madigan plays cards with the devil and nearly loses his soul. Fitzmaurice also describes a Saturday night in camp featuring a performance of Edward Harrigan's "The Mulligan Guards," an exhibition of jigs and reels, and heartfelt renderings of the emigrant ballads "The Flower of Kildare" and "The Hat My Father Wore." The novel also contains recollections of the Civil War exploits of Irish lumbermen, including an original poem about a shanty-boy hero at Fredericksburg.

Southeastern Massachusetts and Cape Cod is the setting for James Riley's *Christy of Rathglin* (1907), a mixture of romantic incident and realistic local color, which traces the rags-to-riches career of an evicted tenant from County Longford who ends up in Provincetown, Massachusetts, by way of an archetypal stormy crossing of the Atlantic and an adventurous stint in the Carver Regiment during the Civil War. There is realistic description of life among the crusty Yankees, including attendance at Bridgewater Normal School, but the novel ends with a thoroughly implausible return to the old country, where Christy's son enters parliament to fight for home rule.

The secret society of labor agitators, the Molly Maguires, is the subject of *Philip; or, The Mollie's Secret. A Tale of the Coal Regions* (1891) by Patrick Justin McMahon. Set in the 1870s in central Pennsylvania, the novel mixes realistic description of the dangerous job of the miners and their infrequent relaxation at Irish dancing parties with a tangled romantic plot involving the discovery of a lost son and the thrilling rescue of a group of miners from a flash fire. Real people have walk-on roles, including James McParlan, the Pinkerton man whose infiltration broke up the Mollies. McMahon believes that the Mollies were "originally instituted for a good purpose" and had "many respectable and influential citizens" as members. However, having "lately degenerated into a reckless party," they deserved eradication.[33]

In this great age of magazines, a number of short fiction writers also contributed to the mosaic of Irish-American literary realism. One of the most prolific was Harvey J. O'Higgins, an Ontario native who became an urban journalist in Toronto and then in New York, and who began to place his stories in *Scribner's*, *Collier's*, and *McClure's* magazines around 1900. O'Higgins was an early chronicler of the newly middle-class urban Irish, the "clerks and bookkeepers, shopgirls and working women" of New York, as he describes them in one story. Often flawed with the touch of easy sentimentality, his stories nonetheless provide valuable detail about the daily lives of these transitional Irish Americans. The kinds of jobs and lives which were just becoming theirs constituted something brand new in American society. O'Higgins was also a pioneer creator of American detective characters.[34] Other proficient short stories and their locales include Anne O'Hagan Shinn's stories of New York City and Nova Scotia, Owen Frawley Kildare's stories of the Irish and Italians on the Lower East Side, Patrick Casey's stories of San Francisco hoboes, and Amanda Matthews's stories of emigrants leaving Donegal. Uncollected early Irish-American stories are a rich hoard, yet to be fully examined.[35]

The four writers who remain to be discussed, George Jessop, Henry Keenan, William McDermott, and John Talbot Smith, were this generation's most accomplished realistic novelists. George H. Jessop brings valuable ideological and geographical perspectives to late nineteenth-century Irish-American literature. Born into the Protestant Ascendancy at Dury Hall, County Longford, Jessop studied law and letters at Trinity College, Dublin, and began a literary career by contributing to the London magazines. In 1872 he went out to San Francisco, where he soon got work writing for the *Overland Monthly*, which had been founded four years earlier by Bret Harte. Jessop eventually made his way to New York City, where in the mid-1880s he began contributing to the humorous (and often anti-immigrant) periodicals *Puck* and *Judge*. In New York, Jessop contributed fiction to Richard Watson Gilder's *Century Magazine* and began writing plays in collaboration with Brander Matthews and libretti for stage-Irish musical comedies. His works of fiction include three novels and a collection of stories, all of which exhibit his generation's ambivalence. His work in all areas of the literary life reflects his sympathies with his social class and with British rule in Ireland.[36]

Published in the *Century* in 1888 and 1889 and collected as *Gerald Ffrench's Friends* (1889), Jessop's first stories are his best work, perhaps because they are the largely autobiographical record of his own hand-to-mouth journalistic apprenticeship in Northern California between 1873 and 1878. The book's preface explains that "the purpose of these chapters is to depict a few of the most characteristic types of the native Celt of the original stock, as yet unmixed in blood, but modified by new surroundings and a different civilization." These stories provide a detailed rendering of the California Irish, as seen through the eyes of Gerald Ffrench, a young Protestant Irish graduate of Trinity College, newly arrived in San Francisco "to try his fortune." Typical is "The Rise and Fall of the 'Irish

Aigle,' " set in San Francisco in 1874.[37] Fresh off the boat and down to his last dollar, young Gerald Ffrench agrees to edit the *Irish Eagle*, a nationalist newspaper founded by a group of garrulous immigrant "patriots." (The story is based on Jessop's experience editing such a paper, the *National*.) He presents the founders of the "Irish Aigle" as ignorant, bibulous, blarneying rhetoricians whose self-important deliberations are delivered in a broad brogue: "Fri'nds and fellow-countrymen, the death knell of Saxon opprission has nearly sthruck. . . . We're agreed, I belave, that the pin is mightier nor the sword," and so on. Jessop further uses the five founders of the newspaper to satirize what he judges as Irish nationalist obsession with the past and facile support of violence—as long as it takes place six thousand miles away. Dunne's Mr. Dooley takes a similar view in his sketches of Irish-American nationalist activities in Chicago. But Jessop goes further—to a brand of satire rooted in snobbery, in describing the *Eagle* editorial page: "There breathed the fiery utterances of Cummiskey, the butter-seller; there sparkled the neat epigram of O'Rourke, the truckman; there were set forth the lucid arguments of Foley, the tanner; there the reader might trace the sportive fancies of Brady, the bookbinder; and the whole bore witness to the massive genius of Martin Doyle, the shoemaker." Gerald is appalled to find that the *Eagle*'s founders denounce the Fenians as cowardly "advocates of half-measures." These "advanced Nationalists" want to burn London and Liverpool and "put to the sword the Houses of Parleymint." And yet, he agrees to turn out three editorials per week for the *Eagle*: "one on organization, one on the manifest duty of Irishmen, and one on the theory and practice of dynamite." Inevitably, the paper fails, and Gerald is released without receiving his back pay. He goes on to work on "more business-like journals," having "imbibed a hearty hatred for Irish nationalists and all their ways."

Jessop's prejudices recur in several more stories in *Gerald Ffrench's Friends*. In "An Old Man from the Old Country," Old Luke Quinn is an illiterate heavy-drinker who is reduced to forelock-tugging subservience before Gerald when it becomes known that the Ffrenches were Quinn's family's landlords back in Ireland. Declaring that Gerald should not have to work, Quinn, who has made a fortune in real estate, offers fawningly to set him up as a gentleman. "Under the Redwood Tree" contains the portrait of another immigrant success, lumber baron Mike Kearney, about whom Gerald is reporting for a magazine. He comes to admire Kearney's strength, but when his son dies of scarlet fever, the powerful man is reduced to "wild and purposeless lamentation," which comes, explains his doctor, from "the depths of his nature come to the surface—the nature of a barbarian, almost of an animal." In "Extracts from the Correspondence of Mr. Miles Grogan" Jessop creates a stereotypical Irish-American politician. A thoroughly unscrupulous New York saloonkeeper who runs for alderman by exchanging free drinks for votes, Miles Grogan opens shop for wholesale bribe-taking on the principle that public office ought to be "worked . . . fer the best good of the people an' fer his own." To a friend's criticism of his "arrested moral development," Grogan replies "I niver was arristed." The story is a series of semi-literate letters between Grogan and a lawyer-friend in Boston delivered in an exaggerated brogue. The Boston *Pilot* strongly criticized Jessop's "shallow caricature" of Irish America. Comparing "The Irish Aigle" to a story by Sara Orne Jewett, "a true artist, informed with the spirit of humanity," John Boyle O'Reilly makes Jessop an object lesson in the inadequacies of "the school of realistic fiction who cannot touch the popular heart, let their pictures of life be ever so photographically accurate, simply because they do not write from their own hearts, and have not the heavenly gift of human sympathy."[38]

Jessop's next book, *Judge Lynch. A Romance of the California Vineyards* (1889), indicates the beginning of his shift away from realism. A flabby potboiler of a mystery, the novel, which began as a play by Jessop and Brander Matthews, lacks the concrete detail of the earlier stories. "Judge Lynch" is not a character, but the vigilante-imposed lynch law in effect in the wild Northern California of the novel's setting. The one Irish character is Pat Byrne, an immigrant hustler who has fought his way to a position of political and economic power in the vineyard region. The owner of a newspaper, a saloon, and a thriving vineyard, Byrne is yet another stereotypical blarneying political boss, transplanted to the West coast. Jessop went on to write two more novels wholly in the vein of popular romance, which, like so many others, he found in the green-tinted twilight of his native land. *Where the Shamrock Grows; The Fortunes and Misfortunes of an Irish Family* (1911) is a story of high life and horse racing in the squireen class in Ireland, based, in Jessop's words, on "conceptions derived from Lever." In his last novel, *Desmond O'Connor* (1914), he moved even further afield to produce a historical romance of the Irish Brigade in Flanders, described as "a love story that moves through camps and courts, siege, battle, adventure, misunderstanding, to a happy ending." Jessop thus followed a typical pattern for his generation—moving from promising (albeit slanted) realism to popular romance, and never looking back.

Henry Francis Keenan was born into a poor Irish family in Rochester, New York, in 1849. He went off to the Civil War as a private and returned to become a journalist on the Rochester *Chronicle*. Around 1870 he moved to New York City to pursue his career on the New York *Tribune*. Between 1883 and 1888, Keenan worked full-time as a novelist, producing four books, none of which made money. Subsequently, he returned to newspaper work and his surviving letters reveal him to have been bitterly disappointed in his failure to succeed as a writer.[39]

Based on the experience of the generations of Rochester Irish that included his parents and grandparents, Keenan's best novel, *The Aliens* (1886), tells the story of the Boyne family, who arrive in "Warchester" from Belfast sometime in the 1830s. At the outset, Hugh Boyne distinguishes himself before the dockside crowd by rescuing his son Denny and the son of Mayor Warchester from drowning. At the mayor's home that evening, a discussion of the immigration "problem" ensues. Irish and German stereotypes emerge and most of the guests favor immigration restriction, although Governor Darcy, himself of Irish descent, refutes them: "If our ancestors had been of your mind, I should have been toiling in the bogs of Kerry today." Some of the talk in the predominantly Anglo-Saxon Protestant gathering is vicious: "I never realized the humorous inspiration of Swift's plan for the utilization of babies until I remarked the rabbit-like fecundity of the Irish mother," declares the mayor's wife, and one of her guests replies: "No wonder Ireland has a famine every few years when the baby crop beats the potato crop!" (14-17).

Keenan himself is guilty of stereotyping in his presentation of the opposing fates of the German Ritters and the Irish Boynes. Blessed with "a servility born in the bone and bred in the long life of emphasized class distinction," the Ritters settle stolidly into the American scene. On the other hand, because he is a Celt ("None so faithful when trust is given them; none so rancorous when doubt is instilled"), Hugh Boyne drinks up his stake and disappears. His wife Kate ruins her health under the strain of trying to keep the family together, and Northern Irish discord also plays a part in the tragedy. A true-blue Ulster Protestant, Hugh Boyne's brother James is "a man of strong prejudices, holding the Irish in the loathing and hatred he had learned in his childhood in London-derry, where once a year the alien English celebrate the conquest of the hated Celts" (62). Because Kate has brought the contamination of Catholicism into his family, James Boyne, comfortably settled in Warchester, heartlessly evicts his sister-in-law and her children. They end up in the almshouse, described vividly by Keenan, where Kate goes mad and dies at the age of thirty.

The novel now switches to the first-person narrative of the orphaned Denny Boyne, through whom Keenan presents the trials of growing up as a "Paddy boy" in the public schools: "I couldn't understand the reproach," Denny recalls, "or why Irish was so repulsive or intolerable, but it became my horror by day and my torture by night" (75). Mitigated somewhat by the friendship of Dilly Dane, the fair-minded daughter of a rich Yankee farmer, Denny's sufferings nonetheless result in his acceptance of "alien" status at an end-of-term party in the schoolhouse. Ignored in their classmates' games, Denny and his sister Norah "did not feel at all neglected, for they had come to regard themselves very much as the colored aliens of the South. They were set apart by the crime of their birth, and were quite content to be permitted to see the gayeties of their betters, without being part of them" (164). There is no dearth of additional incident in this tangled narrative. Denny Boyne enlists for the Mexican War and goes through the Vera Cruz campaign with General Scott. Then, in an implausible denouement, Hugh Boyne returns to

Warchester as a wealthy adventurer, thus clearing the way for his penniless son to marry Dilly Dane. The novel is flawed by these melodramatic
turns of plot, and by uneven narrative pacing, as one night can fill a
chapter, while years fly by in a single sentence, all without a controlling
sense of proportion.

The strongest part of this novel is Keenan's probably autobiographical
presentation of the varieties and psychological effects of anti-Irish prejudice in upstate New York in the mid-nineteenth century. In a *Pilot* editorial
John Boyle O'Reilly praised the accuracy of Keenan's picture of "ostracism
and persecution," which, "as thousands of our readers can verify," was
"too terrible not to be true." O'Reilly went on to indicate what was for
him a typical lesson: "unhappily, there is much to be learned from it, not
only by those who once despised and oppressed those aliens, but by men
and women of every race who still permit themselves to draw a distinction
against any of God's children, because of color, creed, or race."[40] Two
other Keenan novels are of interest. *The Money-Makers: A Social Parable*
(1884) was written as a reply to John Hay's novel *The Breadwinners*. One
of the first nineteenth-century American novels to support the labor
movement explicitly, Keenan's book contains a description of the violent
Orange-Green riots in New York City on July 12, 1871, during which
hundreds of Irish Protestants and Catholics fought over the issue of British
rule. Based on Keenan's own experiences in the Civil War, *The Iron Game:
A Tale of the War* (1891) contains graphic scenes at Washington and Bull
Run from the perspective of a foot soldier.

The most accomplished all around man of letters of this Irish-American literary generation was William A. McDermott, who wrote using the
pseudonym "Walter Lecky." Born in Ireland in 1863, McDermott came to
America as a child and grew up in Lawrence, Massachusetts. As a young
man he traveled widely. Beginning at age seventeen, he was a journalist
in the tenement districts of New York and Chicago for five years, and he
also visited New Orleans, Mexico, and Europe, where he met Cardinal
Newman and Pope Leo XIII. He taught at Villanova University, studied
for the priesthood later in life, and spent his last years as pastor of a parish
in the Adirondack Mountains. There he wrote most of his books, which
include the two most perceptive contemporary studies of American Catholic literature, *Down at Caxton's* (1895) and *Impressions and Opinions* (1898),
several short stories, and three novels set in New York City and the
Adirondacks. McDermott writes sympathetically and without sentimentality about ordinary working-class and rural people in a clear prose style
free of clutter and genteel adornment.[41]

Mr. Billy Buttons. A Novel (1896) provides a compassionate picture of
the mostly French-Canadian inhabitants of a small Adirondack community told from the perspective of the town's doctor, a thoughtful, understanding man. Billy Buttons is an Adirondack guide and homespun
philosopher. Some of the tales in this anecdotal novel are his, while others

are gleaned by the doctor on his rounds. McDermott has a strong instinct for exposing hypocrisy and cant, and in one chapter, a smooth-talking itinerant Methodist minister insinuates himself into the trusting little Adirondack community of Squidville. His projects include starting up a savings bank and marrying the daughter of the town's hotelier. He departs like a thief in the night with the townspeople's savings, leaving his pregnant wife to raise their child alone. This novel also has a strangely violent conclusion. After a lovely appreciation of the four Adirondack seasons, the book ends abruptly with the murder of the aging Billy Buttons by an intruder who steals his money and makes off into the big woods. The murderer's mangled body is found in the river logjam the following spring. Although there are many examples of man's inhumanity scattered through its pages, there is something darkly pessimistic about ending the book this way.

Of greater direct relevance to the Irish voice is McDermott's second novel, *Père Monnier's Ward* (1898). Here there are two plot threads, again reflecting this generation's ambivalence about the requirements of fiction. These are an Adirondack romance and a realistic story of New York politics. The romance involves an orphan girl who becomes the ward of Père Monnier, the parish priest in an Adirondack village. Upon reaching adulthood, the girl drifts off to New York City, where her life and hard times include a "mock wedding" to an unscrupulous married man who then abandons her. She returns to Père Monnier in the Adirondacks where she dies young and repentant, declaring on her deathbed that "I know the wages of sin is death."

The realistic plot line strikes this generation's common theme of the moral danger of politics. This section of the novel is an archetypal depiction with satiric bite of the political rise and moral fall of an Irish immigrant.[42] James Fortune is a Catholic orphan who has been raised as a servant by a Protestant Poor Law Guardian in Stranorlar, County Donegal. The boy flees his harsh life as "poorhouse trash" on the immigrant ship *Blackbird* bound for America with Allingham's air "Adieu to Ballyshannon" on his lips. Narrowly escaping death from shipboard fever, young James is befriended in New York by a generous fellow Donegalman, Jamie McDade, a tavern keeper and ward boss. Bright and opportunistic, James Fortune begins his political career by praising Ireland and exhorting his fellow immigrants to "admit that [they are] Irish, and Irish to the backbone." He founds the Shamrock Club, "which met weekly at McDade's to discuss the best means of freeing Ireland—and at the same time of holding a grip on New York." Fortune then marries McDade's pretentious, social-climbing daughter and vaults up the New York political ladder, from alderman to congressman to a mansion on Fifth Avenue. Upon reaching this pinnacle, Fortune resigns all of his Irish memberships, declares himself against the "spirit of [foreign] nationality in free America," and has his child baptised "Chichester Hartley Fortune" in the

Episcopal Church. In a final stroke of hypocrisy, Fortune joins the St. Andrew's Society and affirms his "Scotch-Irishness" at their annual dinner: "he boasted of his ancestors, strong of limb and sparing of speech, who had come to Ireland from that land of lands, the home of Walter Scott and Bobby Burns. He was proud of being Scotch-Irish, and with pride he referred to what those of that race had done in the upbuilding of the great American people. Some of them, he continued, had like himself been born in Ireland—a mere accident; but their love of Scotland was, if he might say so, strengthened instead of weakened by that accident."

In these years, Ulster Presbyterian immigrants and ethnics were in fact expending a good deal of energy in the form of pamphlets, books, and new organizations to establish the "Scotch-Irish" as a separate ethnic group. A classic of its type is *The Scotch-Irish in America* (Princeton: Princeton University Press, 1915) by Henry Jones Ford, a six hundred-page tome which seeks to distinguish the Protestant Scotch-Irish from the Catholic "wild Irish." Of course, such efforts go back at least to James McHenry's novels in the 1820s.[43] For the clarity and wit of his treatment of issues such as this, William A. McDermott has a secure place in Irish-American fiction. That he chose to deal so rarely with these materials was a great loss to his generation. He died at the age of fifty in 1913.

The strongest novelist of this ambivalent generation was John Talbot Smith, who also rounds out the nineteenth-century tradition of Irish-American priests who wrote fiction. More than any other Irish-American novelist of the late nineteenth century, Smith avoided the pitfalls of the preceding Famine generation—the complacent, creaking didacticism of Mary Anne Sadlier, the bitterness of Hugh Quigley, the pained anger of John Boyce—to produce a body of fiction with impressive thematic and geographical range and a predominantly realistic vision. The son of Bernard Smith, a railroad worker, and Brigid (O'Donnell) Smith, John Talbot Smith was born in Saratoga, New York, in 1855. He attended the Christian Brothers school in Albany, went into a seminary in Toronto, and was ordained a priest into the diocese of Ogdensburg in 1881. He worked at a small mission on Lake Champlain until 1889, when his superiors recognized his literary potential by releasing him from his mission duties and allowing him to pursue a writing career in New York City. Smith lived in New York for twenty years—editing the weekly literary periodical the *Catholic Review* from 1889 to 1892, founding the Catholic Summer School of America and the Catholic Writers and Actors Guilds, serving as chaplain to several organizations, and writing history and fiction. Like Father Hugh Quigley before him, Smith made use of his pastoral mission experiences in the writing of many stories and four novels set in Canada, the Adirondacks, New England, and New York. He also wrote a story for children, *The Prairie Boy*, and some Catholic history, including a history of the Ogdensburg diocese, a biography of Catholic writer Brother Azarias, and a book on education for the priesthood. He died in Dobbs Ferry, New York, in 1923.[44]

In Smith's first novel, *A Woman of Culture. A Canadian Romance* (1880), Toronto is the setting for a depiction of the opposition of New World materialism and Irish spirituality. John McDonell is a wealthy widower, an Irish immigrant, and a lapsed but conscience-ridden Catholic, who has given up his religion in order to pursue money and power through unscrupulous means. He is brought to his senses at the novel's opening when he learns that his daughter Nano has become an atheist. McDonell blames his own bad example and Nano's education at a secular boarding school where the teachers "were of the transcendental school. . . . great admirers of Margaret Fuller and Emerson." After a considerable plot tangle the climax of the novel takes place within the context of a thoroughly Irish event—an Orange/Green riot on the Toronto streets on March 17, prompted when "the Williamite mob had sworn vengeance on the 'croppy' who should deck himself that day in the green." In an act of heroism, McDonell acknowledges that he is a "Papist" to the mob of Orange-draped ruffians, who then give him a fatal beating. We are told that "the courage of his lately awakened faith" has rendered McDonell "a martyr. . . . He might have escaped uninjured, but he would not deny his religion" (313). On his deathbed, McDonell pleads that his daughter return to the Church. However, in a realistic turn of events, she refuses. Destined to die young, her constitution broken down by the events of these years, Nano looks "into the dreaded rottenness and oblivion of [her conception of] the grave." And yet, her death contains a glimmer of hope: "She suffered much, and. . . . We know that the mercy of God reaches far out towards the suffering" (353). At the least, Father Smith has come a long way from the iron-clad system of retributive justice in Mary Anne Sadlier's novels.[45]

Smith's second novel, *Solitary Island* (1888), takes its protagonist Florian Wallace from the Thousand Islands of the Saint Lawrence River to New York City where he embarks on a career in politics. This largely romantic novel is closest to realism in its version of the theme of the moral danger of Irish-American political life. Florian makes his way by his insincerely eloquent speech-making on behalf of Daniel O'Connell and Irish freedom, for which he cares not a whit. Here Smith criticizes the easily swayed "Irish Demos," and his spokesman is the novel's moral exemplar, Scott, the mysterious hermit of Solitary Island. Implausible romantic tangles soon take over, however, and Florian progresses from a seat in Congress at age thirty-one, to the revelation that he has noble Russian blood, to a dramatic reversal of fortune, after which he heads back for Solitary Island in rags toward a hermit's penitent life. Smith's message is clear. The renewal of Florian's Catholicism saves him from a life of sin in urban politics.

Smith next published *His Honor, the Mayor, and Other Tales* (1891), stories that contain analyses of immigrant/ethnic cultural tensions in Ontario, New York, and New England. The third (1897) edition of this popular book carried the subtitle, "Tales of the Puritan and His Neighbors." Smith's most consistently realistic piece of fiction, the title story "His Honor, the Mayor" is a successful rendering of the ill effects of combined social and political ambition in late-nineteenth-century Irish-American life. Michael Delaney has risen from Kerry immigrant day laborer to wealthy American grocer, a solid, middle-class figure in the small city of Kinderkin near the Connecticut/New York border. A coalition masterminded by Democratic Judge Coogan and Republican businessman DeWitt Van Houven convinces Delaney to run for mayor. Once elected, the Irishman disappoints their expectation that he will be the tool of their special interests, deciding instead to become a reformer by applying the sound principles of his grocery business to city government. Here he has some success, although most of the townspeople refuse to take "Mayor Mick" seriously, and continue to see Kinderkin's first Irish Catholic mayor as merely a curiosity.

Throughout the story, Smith satirizes the social pretensions that accompany the rise of the Delaneys to "first family" status. Their "promenade" at Sunday Mass becomes an event in the Irish neighborhood. Despite the warning of the parish priest, eldest son Jack goes off to Yale to spend a year "in idleness and mischief." (The danger, both moral and intellectual, of non-Catholic higher education is a theme in several of Smith's stories.) Mrs. Delaney and daughter Joanna demand a more active social life, packed with luncheons and parties. And the mayor himself changes his hairstyle and dress to the extent that his old friends fail to recognize him.

Clothes are in fact Smith's major, effective metaphor for this archetypal transformation of an immigrant family. At the presumed height of his success, Mayor Delaney sums up his accomplishments as follows: "The best people in Kinderkin sat at his table, his wife and daughter moved in society, his son was in Yale with the sons of Senators and millionaires, and he himself could wear a dress suit with ease and was the leader of a party" (206-07). The Mayor's disillusioning fall is hastened by the inevitable political crunch against those who put him in power, a visit to his son among the frivolities and dissipations of New Haven college life, and his wife's new taste for ostentatious jewelry. His daughter's scandalously low-cut dress at her coming-out party is the last straw, prompting Delaney to realize just how far he has come and in what direction: "I'm mayor no longer. Coogan can take his leadership, an' fill the offices wid broomsticks if he likes. I'll stay at home an' run a grocery an' try to bring up a family that won't shame me bones when I'm dead an' gone. Go to bed the whole of yees" (216).

Smith could also be tolerant of political bossism. In "The Baron of Cherubusco" (122-48) the reforming Irish priest in an Adirondack town comes to see that the "Baron" has a heart, and that, despite its dependence on vote-buying, his machine can deliver social services to the poor. Smith thought enough of this story to select it for inclusion in the *Round Table of the Representative Catholic Novelists*, and it shows him to be skeptical of easy stereotypes of his fellow Irish Americans, even in the political arena. Of the other stories in *His Honor, the Mayor*, several strike themes of immigrant collision with nativist feeling. The best of these, "The Deacon of Lynn" (1-31), describes the campaign of Deacon Lounsbury to rid his Connecticut town of the influx of Irish ("Such ignorance, such filth, such degradation no country in the world can show") who have come to work in the cotton mills. The scenes of tenement life and factory work in terrible conditions for small pay are effective: "At five in the morning [an Irish child] was standing at the spinning frame, and with the exception of three quarters of an hour for meals, she stood till seven at night. The close air of the spinning-room was foul with flying oil and cotton, and being Irish there were other and more painful hardships in store for her." The story traces the successful battle of the Irish community to buy land for a grave-yard and church.

In Smith's next novel, *Saranac. A Story of Lake Champlain* (1892), the strongest element is the presentation of friction between two immigrant cultures in the Adirondack region of upstate New York, the Irish and the French Canadians. The observation of the tensions resulting from "all sorts of customs and traditions and sentiments in Saranac" centers in the household of a formidable Irish matriarch, Mrs. Sullivan, a Limerick native whose widowed daughter had married a "Frinchman" and borne him two children, Remi and Elise. All are now living with Mrs. Sullivan, who declares that "afther fightin' the Frinch for thirty years, here I have a houseful o' thim" (2). The novel opens on New Year's Day, and the French Canadian custom of seeking the blessing of one's elders causes Mrs. Sullivan to renew a long-standing complaint about the "Frinch notions" of her grandchildren, notably their emotional expressiveness, which offends her more austere sense of propriety. Her Francophobia is tempered only when a neighbor reminds her of the French support for Ireland in the 1798 rising.

Smith draws on his own diocesan experience to describe vividly the daily life of Saranac's Catholic communities. Father McManus presides over a monthly parish dance attended by the whole town, at which "the last figure was made up of Irish airs." The year's high point is the annual church fair, which begins with the unleashing on the town of "twenty persuasive maidens" as advertising canvassers, and concludes with the twelve-night-long event itself, with contests for a doll and a gold watch, a restaurant, shooting-gallery, side-shows and booths, and a full-scale production of a melodrama. Unfortunately, the plot becomes another tangled web of intrigue through which Smith points his moral of the distinction between God and Mammon. But the novel's final image comes back to its strength. The solitary Father McManus is "left alone saying his office" as he walks the road between church and graveyard, "now facing the living, now facing the dead, mindful of both, feeling more keenly than usual the little distance between them, and sad that death must be the end of everything. Then the sun disappeared, and the darkness came on, and the priest went away to his tea and his books" (279-80). In such scenes we are privy for a moment to the life of nineteenth-century mission priests in isolated pastorates.

Smith's last, most ambitious, and most accomplished novel was *The Art of Disappearing* (1899). Set in New England, New York, and Ireland, the novel describes a number of touchstone events for late-nineteenth-century Irish America—from the failed Fenian Rising in Ireland in 1867 to the dedication of St. Patrick's Cathedral in New York in 1879. In 1866, a naive young New England "aristocrat" Horace Endicott meets charming and sophisticated Monsignor O'Donnell of New York City, "prelate of the Pope's household, doctor in theology, and vicar-general of the New York diocese" on a train between New York and Boston. The train derails, killing a fireman to whom the Monsignor administers the last rites. The touching event and the impressive priest (with whom he shares stimulating conversation that evening at an inn) cause Horace to rethink his inherited prejudice against Catholics: "some years ago, I would have studied his person for indications of hoofs and horns—so strangely was I brought up." Their conversation touches upon what Monsignor O'Donnell calls the "art of disappearing." He contends that a person could in fact disappear by assuming the identity of another person to whom he bears some resemblance, a person probably dead but expected back after a long absence. Upon returning to his home, Horace comes upon his adored bride of ten months in adultery. He leaves without her seeing him, and, vowing to disappear, seeks out the Monsignor, who arranges his assumption of the identity of a New York Irish American from the Cherry Hill section of the East Side, young Arthur Dillon, who had run away to California ten years earlier and most probably died there. Dillon's mother Anne agrees to the identity change in return for "a handsome income," as a favor to the Monsignor, who has presented Horace as "a respectable young man of wealth, whom misfortune has driven into hiding."

Although the premise is unrealistic, it allows Smith to present the New York Irish of the 1860s and 1870s from the perspective of an observant outsider who is accepted as an insider. The Dillons are respected community members, and Horace/Arthur is thrown among "the high Irish," a group which he recognizes "by its airs, its superciliousness, and several other bad qualities. It was a budding aristocracy at the ugliest moment of its development; city officials and their families, lawyers, merchants, physicians, journalists, clever and green and bibulous." Amidst the parvenues, however, Horace also discerns the community's real leaders, "the pillars of Irish society, solid men and dignified women," who include "the dashing General Sheridan," Monsignor O'Donnell, and the head of Tammany Hall, John Sullivan. Horace/Arthur learns about politics by observing a mayoral campaign pitting anti-Irish incumbent Mayor Quincy Livingstone (a distant relative of Horace's, ironically) against an Irish Catholic financier. It is important to note that Smith presents Tammany chieftain Sullivan as a thoroughly admirable leader, "truly a hero on the battle-ground of social forces." It's the next generation of political and social climbers that bothers him. The Irish candidate wins despite a dirty-tricks campaign by Livingstone in the description of which Smith makes use of historically accurate incidents. The anti-Irish forces first bring in Professor Fritters, "an Oxford historian with a new recipe for cooking history." Sponsored by "the Columbia College crowd," Fritters embarks on a series of lectures illustrating "how English government worked among the Irish, and how impossible is the Anglo-Saxon idea among peoples in whom barbarism does not die with the appearance and advance of civilization." The model here was British historian James Anthony Froude, whose American lecture tour in 1870 featured contrasting pictures of Anglo-Saxons as natural rulers and Celts as natural slaves.

Second, "the star of the combination" masterminded by Mayor Livingstone is "Sister Claire, the Escaped Nun," whose lectures and sensational book, *Confessions of an Escaped Nun,* become the talk of the town. "Dime novels are prayer books beside it," declares Horace/Arthur, who enlists in the struggle to preserve the reputation of his assumed community. He succeeds in pricking the anti-Irish bubble by exposing Sister Claire as an unemployed actress/dancer of shady repute and forcing her to withdraw her book from circulation with a public apology. The historical models for the escaped nun go all the way back to Maria Monk and Rebecca Reed in the 1830s. Smith also includes a journalist/poet based on John Boyle O'Reilly. Doyle Grahame, an Irish nationalist and confidante of Arthur Dillon, is invited (as was O'Reilly in 1889) to read a poem at the rededication of Plymouth Rock. "Think of it," says Grahame, "a wild Irishman, an exile, a conspirator against the British Crown, a subject of the Pope, reading or singing the praises of the pilgrims, the grim pilgrims. Turn in your grave, Cotton Mather, as my melodious verses harrow your ears."

Another strand in the plot involves Irish-American nationalism. Horace/Arthur is much impressed by dedicated Fenian Owen Ledwith, whose eloquent presentation of England's wrongs against Ireland wins from Horace a gift of $5,000 to finance a secret voyage to Ireland to test Ledwith's idea to invade the mother country from America with one hundred ships. (Arms were in fact shipped from New York to Sligo during the Fenian Rising in May 1867.) Smith presents Ledwith as a thoughtful man whose arguments against British rule in Ireland have a measured clarity. So moved is Horace/Arthur, that he joins Ledwith and his lovely daughter Honora on the test-voyage to Ireland. Landing at a Donegal fishing village during the 1867 Rising, they witness a skirmish during which two young Fenians are killed.

Meanwhile, a social-history plot strand focuses on Anne Dillon, who has begun to assume airs on the basis of her new-found subsidy from Horace. Motivated by the desire to enter "the charmed circle of New York society," Anne takes French lessons, tries to eradicate her brogue, and rents a box at the opera, a front pew at the Cathedral, and a summer "villa" at Coney Island. Her greatest triumph is a visit to Ireland, where she is the guest of a new-found friend from the New York social whirl, the Dowager Countess of Skibbereen. Smith understands the mixed feelings of the native Irish toward a returning successful immigrant, and he presents the ironies of the situation effectively. Around this time, critical and satiric portraits of the returned "Yank" began to appear in the literature of Ireland as well, in fiction by George Moore, Shan Bullock, and Seumas O'Kelly.[46] Anne Dillon's visit coincides with her "son's" Fenian excursion, so the plot thickens considerably from this point on.

Toward the end of the novel, Smith makes an extraordinary attempt to heal the rift between Irish nationalism and Catholicism. On his deathbed, the despairing nationalist Owen Ledwith is persuaded back to the faith and a salutary perspective by the arguments of Monsignor O'Donnell. Their exchange is one of the high points of the novel. In this context, the violent family division at Christmas dinner over religion and nationalism after Parnell's fall in Joyce's *A Portrait of the Artist as a Young Man* (1916) comes to mind. What Smith attempts in his Irish-American setting is a powerful reconciling vision. The Monsignor's speech is remarkable for its inclusion of the Fenians and other nationalists as part of the worldwide struggle for freedom in which he sees the Catholic Church as the central force. In addition, St. Patrick's Cathedral becomes the symbol of Irish-American accomplishment. O'Donnell sees St. Patrick's as a compelling refutation of the Anglo-Saxon Protestant leadership of New York and America, those who have "described [the Irish] race as sunk in papistical stupidity, debased, unenterprising." He goes on to explain the "message" of the Cathedral as powerful symbol: "I am the child of the Catholic faith and the Irish; the broad shoulders of America waited for a simple, poor, cast-out people, to dig me from the earth and shape me into a thing of beauty, a glory of the new continent. . . . I am a new bond between the old continent and the new, between the old order and the new." And this, he continues, "is the glory of the Irish. This is the fact which fills me with pride, American as I am, in the race whose blood I own; they have preserved the faith for the great English-speaking world" (241-43). The priest's eloquence and the cathedral's symbolism work upon the dying Ledwith, who comes to acquiescent revelation: "Of course, he could see it all, blind as he had been before. The Irish revolution worked fitfully, and exploded in a night, its achievement measured by the period of a month; but this temple and its thousand sisters lived on doing their

good work in silence, fighting for the truth without noise or conspiracy."
Ledwith dies at peace, his eyes upon "the golden spires, and the shining
roof, that spoke to him so wonderfully of the triumph of his race in a new
land, the triumph which had been built up in the night, unseen, uncared
for, unnoticed" (246).

In the end, the melodramatic premises of the plot come back to haunt
Smith, but even here there are some interesting touches. Horace Endicott's
wife still has a detective on his trail. The detective happens to be married
to "Sister Claire," the "Escaped Nun," whose hatred of Arthur Dillon
forces her to a kind of instinctive enlightenment. She senses that Dillon
is really Horace, and hounds her husband to prove the deception. The
defeated Mayor Livingstone comes in again too—as Sonia Endicott's lawyer. Although this is implausible, to say the least, the reactions of all
concerned to the possibility of the identity switch do advance the major
theme of Smith's novel. Citing the detestation of her husband and their
class for the Irish, Sonia exclaims: "My Horace live among the Irish! That's
not the man. He could live anywhere, among the Chinese, the Indians,
the niggers, but with that low class of people, never!" And Livingstone
concurs: "What course of thought, what set of circumstances, could turn
the Puritan mind in the Celtic direction? . . . he knew no Endicott could
ever be converted" (287, 334). Thus Smith returns us to the novel's opening
conversation between Horace Endicott and Monsignor O'Donnell and
reinforces his main point. Of course such a transformation is possible.
Puritan can turn Celt because both are human; they have been separated
in America only by the artificial walls of prejudice and discrimination.

And this idea leads to the novel's resolution. After beating back the
challenges of the detective, his former wife, and her lawyer, Horace/
Arthur admits to his betrothed, Honora Ledwith, that he was but is no
longer Horace Endicott: "I hated Horace Endicott as a weak fool. He had
fallen lowest of all his honest, able, stern race. I beat him first into hiding,
then into slavery, and at last into annihilation. I studied to annihilate him,
and I did it by raising Arthur Dillon in his place. I am now Arthur Dillon.
I think, feel, act, speak, dream like that Arthur Dillon which I first imagined. When you first knew me, Honora, I was playing a part. I am no
longer acting" (356-57). That Arthur Dillon is actually able to marry Honora Ledwith is evidence of Father Smith's liberal theological ideas. In
sanctioning the marriage, Monsignor O'Donnell cites the "Pauline Privilege" that allows a Catholic convert to marry another Catholic if the wife
of his first, unreconcilable marriage remains an infidel and secures a civil
divorce. The way thus cleared, Arthur marries Honora in St. Patrick's
Cathedral to end the novel on a joyous note.

The final scene recapitulates Smith's symbolic connection of St. Patrick's Cathedral and Irish attainment of respectability in America. "In the
building that day," muses the new Arthur Dillon, "gathered a multitude
representing every form of human activity and success. They stood for

the triumph of a whole race, which, starved out of its native seat, had clung desperately to the land of Columbia in spite of persecution." This assemblage of soldiers, business leaders, educators, artists, journalists, politicians, and clerics "bore witness to the native power of a people, who had been written down in the books of the hour as idle, inferior, incapable by their very nature." And as for the cathedral itself, "What a witness, an eternal witness, to the energy and faith of a poor, despised people, would be this temple! Looking upon its majestic beauty, who could doubt their powers, though the books printed English slanders in letters of gold? . . . Thereafter the temple became for him a symbol, as for the faithful priest; the symbol of his own life as that of his people" (365-66).

Certainly Smith's is an idealized vision. He tries to have it both ways in presenting the Catholic Church as having brought the Irish into the promised land of American mainstream respectability, while simultaneously claiming that the spread of Catholicism is the ultimate, vindicating achievement of the Irish in America. And yet, there is also real power in this peroration and authority in Smith's delineation of what was, after all, a legitimate success story. The Irish had achieved a great deal by the end of the nineteenth century, and the Church had significantly aided the achievement. Respectability and religion did go hand in hand. At the same time, Smith does not blindly celebrate newly bourgeois Irish America. Instead, he pointedly satirizes the less attractive aspects of New York Irish society. Like most of his novels, *The Art of Disappearing* contains romantic plotting and a dash of idealization, making it one more piece of ambivalent fiction. But it also has historical verisimilitude, accurate cultural observation, plausible characterizations, and a clear style free of moralizing cant. More effectively than any other novelist of his generation, John Talbot Smith uses the techniques of literary realism to examine and criticize Irish-American middle-class life.

SIX

Mr. Egan and Mr. Dooley

Maurice Francis Egan and Finley Peter Dunne are representative figures of the third nineteenth-century Irish-American literary generation. Both were sons of immigrants who had made it into the burgeoning Irish middle class, the emergence of which defined the period. Maurice Egan's father had come to Philadelphia from County Tipperary early in the second quarter of the century. A genial Democratic ward politician, he became a successful businessman (director of a foundry) and married a high-toned Christian Philadelphia woman. Peter Dunne's father had come with his parents from Queens County to New Brunswick at the age of six. As a young man, Dunne moved on to Chicago, where he built a successful business in carpentry and lumber. Seemingly a typical Chicago Irishman with no significant intellectual inclinations, he was a lifelong Democrat and supporter of Irish nationalism. His wife, born Ellen Finley in County Kilkenny, was a lover of Dickens, Scott, Thackeray, and Irish literature who encouraged her children in reading and the life of the mind.

Both Egan and Dunne came of literary age in the last quarter of the nineteenth century—but in very different ways. Born in 1852, Egan received his secondary education at the hands of the Irish Christian Brothers at Philadelphia's newly opened LaSalle College. He went on to do graduate work in English literature at Georgetown College in Washington, D.C. In 1877 he embarked on a long, distinguished career in Catholic journalism and university teaching that was to take him from New York's Catholic literary coterie to the halls of Notre Dame and the Catholic University of America. Born in 1867, Dunne graduated last in his class at Chicago's West Division High School and immediately took a job as a cub reporter for a daily newspaper, the *Telegram*, in June, 1884. He subsequently worked on six different Chicago papers before moving to New York in 1900. By the 1890s, the most productive writing decade for each, Egan and Dunne were established figures in their chosen literary arenas: Egan as a respected Catholic man of letters and Dunne as a street-wise urban journalist. They were also firmly established as polar opposites on the literary spectrum: Egan as the quintessential romantic writer whose dozen works of fiction mirror perfectly the genteel Irish-American mind in its nascent state, and Dunne as the pioneering realist whose chronicles of the common life of working-class immigrants constitute the coming of age of Irish-American fiction. Their differences dramatize the two opposing strains of the Irish voice in American literature at the end of the nineteenth century.[1]

Maurice Francis Egan was the child of parents whose lives exemplified the characteristic division of their generation between Irishness and Catholicism as components of identity. A pre-Famine immigrant and self-made successful industrialist, the elder Egan had been proud of his Irish heritage, having boasted, according to his son, that in his life, "he had done everything that any honest Irishman could do." He had, for example, helped to defend his parish church during the anti-Catholic riots of 1844 in Philadelphia. A student of Irish history and culture, he devoured accounts of the Irish Brigade in France, and passed on to his son tales of the ancient Irish kings, the poetry of Thomas Moore, and the novels of William Carleton. Egan also recalls his father's delighted reading of Charles G. Halpine's Civil War sketches of Private Miles O'Reilly. On the other hand, he remembers his properly Philadelphian mother as "the opposite of my father in every way." Of English, Irish, and Scottish ancestry, she had, in her son's view, but "little trace of the Celtic," and was "a cultivated and beautiful person, religious, almost ascetic, who looked on the Irish as a strange race capable of violating all Philadelphia conventions." Egan recalls his mother's sudden conversion to "devout" Catholicism: "On one unhappy Sunday afternoon, 'Monte Christo' was rudely snatched from my entranced hands. Dumas was on the list of the 'improper'. . . . Now the wagon of the circulating library ceased to come as in the old days." Significantly, Dumas was replaced by Butler's *Lives of the Saints* and Mary Anne Sadlier's *The Blakes and Flanagans*, which the boy enjoyed as "a delightful satire." Moreover, as his mother began to perceive the Egans' neighborhood deteriorating—a tell-tale sign was the opening of an oyster bar—she let her son play with fewer and fewer children. These various tensions have a lot to do with Maurice Egan's literary career. As a writer, he was very much his mother's son.[2]

After literary study at Georgetown College, Egan returned to Philadelphia in 1877. His practical father urged a career in the law, but Egan began to contribute to the *Saturday Evening Post* instead. He wrote his first novel, *That Girl of Mine* (1877), in two weeks for a pulp romance series. Filled with improbable romantic action and set in the post–Civil War Washington society from which Egan had just come, the book was successful enough for him to write a sequel, *That Lover of Mine*, for the same series. A year later, Egan entered the New York literary life with a letter of introduction to Richard Watson Gilder of the *Century*, a few published sonnets, the two romantic novels, and an adequate supporting income from his father. He took full advantage of the established network of Catholic publishing outlets and opportunities, beginning by accepting an editorship at the Catholic journal *Magee's Weekly*. He moved on to the *Illustrated Catholic American*, then to P.V. Hickey's *Catholic Review*, and finally to the *Freeman's Journal* as an associate editor in 1881. Throughout the eighties in New York, Egan wrote essays, reviews, poems, and short fiction, and was a part of the literary scene that included Gilder, Brander

Matthews, William Dean Howells, and Henry James. Egan remained a New York Catholic journalist until his appointment in 1888 to the chair of English literature at the University of Notre Dame, which he called his "Sabine farm," a place where he hoped to write "something fine." He moved on to a similar post at the Catholic University of America in Washington in 1896. One of the few things Egan had in common with Finley Peter Dunne was friendship with Theodore Roosevelt, who appointed him American Minister to Denmark in 1907, a post which he held until 1918. Notre Dame awarded him the Laetare Medal for distinguished service as a Catholic in 1911, and he died in 1924.

When he arrived in New York in 1878, Egan recalls noting "the beginning of a great Catholic movement," and "a chance to take a step forward in the evolution of Catholic literature, of which Mrs. Sadlier, author of *The Blakes and Flanagans* and Dr. J.V. Huntington, author of *Rosemary*, were the principle interpreters." Clearly, Egan knew the previous generation's work—in its Irish as well as its Catholic dimensions—and he strove consciously to improve upon it. He says that by the middle 1880s "my ambition . . . was not to elevate the tone of the American literature written for Catholics, but to create a taste for a broader kind of literature." Dismissing as "anaemic" most of the fiction then being printed by Catholic publishers, he goes on to describe the Irish-American literary situation in the generation previous to his own:

> Many of the books were written for the Irish immigrant of the first generation who had but recently arrived. The taste of the older persons who had come from Ireland early in the forties or before that was much more cultivated than that of the newcomers. In fact, the newcomers were unwilling to read anything except what concerned itself with the history of Ireland or with the history of the Church. It was a time when a publisher with an Irish name could announce a series of the lives of deceased bishops—sell eighteen parts with profit, and then retire in opulence, forgetting to finish the nineteenth or twentieth. Lives of St. Patrick and St. Brigid, provided they were profusely illustrated and gilded, might be stretched to any number of parts.[3]

In the event, Maurice Egan fell well short of his ambition to write fiction of lasting literary value. He is not without accomplishments, however, in his chosen sphere as a Catholic literary figure. Paul Messbarger has placed Egan centrally and sympathetically as "the foremost arbiter of Catholic taste for two generations," a man who "as teacher, scholar, polemicist, novelist, poet, and journalist, . . . defined the Catholic man of letters for his time." Messbarger sees Egan as the writer who "redeemed the domestic and contemporary scene for his fellow Catholics" by creating "a native American Catholic fiction with American locales, subjects, and themes," which "turned Catholic readers and writers away from the exotic fantasies of Europe and the past" and "offered a simple and basic social identity to Catholics." That identity was middle-class respectability, achievable by "hard work, sobriety, cleanliness, and propriety," and without loss of the Catholic dimension of life. While admitting that Egan's novels are as "melodramatic" and "apologetical" as anything in Mrs. Sadlier and the Famine generation, Messbarger also credits these books as containing pioneering depictions of "the varieties of life experienced by contemporary urban Catholics" (80-87).

In terms of tracing the Irish voice, the important point about Egan is that his decision to become a Catholic American writer involved a rejection of the possibility of also being an Irish-American writer. The literary consequences of that rejection make him the archetypal genteel figure of late nineteenth-century Irish-American fiction and the perfect foil to Finley Peter Dunne. Egan's novels document vividly the trade-off that was pervasive in his generation of Irish Americans. As Chicago's cantankerously unassimilated Irish journalist John Finerty put it, the new middle class had decided to be "Cawtholic, not Irish." Not surprisingly, the only contemporary Catholic critic to question Egan's eminence was a fellow novelist who also happened to be an Irish immigrant. This was Father William McDermott, a writer of considerable talent discussed in the previous chapter. His 1895 essay on Egan makes important points about the dangers for writers of this generation of the Irish/Catholic literary and cultural situation. Citing E.C. Stedman's placement of Egan in the "Irish-American School" of poetry, McDermott complains that writers such as the Norwegian-born H.H. Boyeson are labeled true Americans, "while the literary sons and daughters of Irish parents, born and striking root in American soil, are marked with a foreign brand. It is the old story of English literary prejudice reproduced by American critics." McDermott goes on to say that Egan "has been unfortunate to be a pioneer in Catholic American literature," where his "chance of corrective criticism has been slight." This is because "the class to which Mr. Egan belongs has no criticism to offer its literary food givers. If an author's book sells, his name is blazoned forth in half a hundred headless petty journals. His most glaring defects become through their glasses mystic beauty spots. He is invited to lecture on all kinds of subjects. A clique grows around him, whose duty it is to puff the master." Thus, the immigrant writer chastises his second-generation counterpart for having settled into a comfortable position within an exclusively Catholic literary world, where "the rabble shout and eulogious criticism" hold sway (*Caxton's* 55-61).

Egan's own literary criticism is marked by his genteel/romantic and didactic/Catholic predilections and also seems flawed by a deeper lack of judgment. His persistent lobbying for romance over realism leads him to several howlers, which include praise of F. Marion Crawford and Mrs. Oliphant over Howells, James, Tolstoy, and Dostoevsky, preference for the humor of Booth Tarkington over that of the "vulgar" and "detestable" Mark Twain, and an attack against Walt Whitman's poems as "excrescences." Egan also praises the "optimistic sentimentalism" of popular

fiction by Mrs. E.D.E.N. Southworth, an acquaintance from his Washington student days, for having "answered to the demand of a public that
is moral and religious, that needs to be taken into countries which savour
something of Fairyland, and yet which are framed by reality." And he
castigates the realists and naturalists for their joylessness, pessimism,
materialism, and bad example—paying special attention to Emile Zola,
who attempted "to make literature scientific" and instead "became a creature so monstrous that even curiosity became disgusted." In addition, as
an editor of the landmark ten-volume edition of *Irish Literature* of 1904,
he contributed an essay on "Irish Novels" that predictably contrasts the
merely "sociological" accuracy of Maria Edgeworth, John Banim, and
William Carleton with the preferable focus of Irish Revival writers such
as Yeats and Lady Gregory on a "literary or artistic standard. . . . In the
new movement art counts for much,—and there is the old yearning for
the mysticism of the past."[4]

Egan's uneasy grapplings with his own and his generation's Irish
dimension appear often in his fiction. They come to the surface strongly
in three novels and several stories. Egan's novels have the same fatal flaw
that mars the fiction by other limited writers of his generation, Irish and
otherwise, in that he cannot go the distance to consistent literary realism.
Although he claims to be reacting against the Sadlier/Huntington school
of Catholic fiction, Egan, as his own literary criticism makes clear, ultimately shares their sensibility and assumptions about the necessarily didactic aims of literature. Thus, like Katherine Conway and others
discussed in chapter 5, his novels are mixtures of realistic materials and
the sentimental conventions of nineteenth-century popular fiction.

In his first important novel, *The Disappearance of John Longworthy* (1890),
Egan's damaging contradictory doubleness emerges in actual references
to the fiction-reading habits of the two main women characters. He ridicules dime-novel sentimental romances in illustrating Nellie Mulligan's
lack of culture by showing her absorbed in "Wooed But Not Won; or,
Irene's Baleful Triumph," in which "Lady Geraldine Mount-Joie bids the
pale but soulful artist leave her, . . . because he is poor, though of a noble
race." And yet later on he praises Esther Galligan, the novel's heroine,
for having read "few novels, and these of the old-fashioned kind; she
knew Walter Scott and Miss Austen by heart. Love, in her eyes, was a
spiritual and sacred thing, and also a romantic thing, untouched by those
practical considerations of which the modern novel is full."

As Egan's novels go, *The Disappearance of John Longworthy* has a fairly
simple plot, although it does rely on disguised identity. The independ-
ently wealthy protagonist suddenly disappears in New York City in the
late 1880s. An eminent writer on "social issues," he has decided to disguise himself as a photographer in the Bowery in order to observe slum
life at first hand. Longworthy's slumming allows Egan to describe American city life with a fair amount of realistic detail, and there is good sense

in his presentation of contrasting ideas about the reform of urban conditions. Longworthy's naive plan to improve the Bowery by providing free concerts in a beautifully renovated hall results in brawling buffoonery in the opening-night audience. His friend Esther Galligan counters with practical suggestions: turn the concert hall into a market selling fresher, cheaper produce, get volunteer "rich Catholic women" to teach home economics, and funnel money through the Church to buy clothing for the poor.

On the other hand, Egan makes salient use in *John Longworthy* of the two dominant conventions of the previous Famine generation of Irish-American novelists: a sentimental deathbed scene and a crucial conversion to Catholicism. The death of little Rose O'Connor, a "pure lily" of the slums, is as bathetic as anything in Mary Anne Sadlier. The innocent victim of a terrible home environment, Rose dies of a blow from a flatiron thrown inaccurately by her gossipy, inattentive mother at her drunkard of a husband. Because it delivers her from this pernicious environment, Rose's death is seen as fortunate by the attending priest: "[Such children's] perfume sweetens the life around them; but when God takes them early in their youth they are blessed." Egan presents this scene wholly without mitigating irony: "the little child's soul was lifted in the arms of her Guardian Angel to the mercy-seat of God, as the dawn struck the window" (224, 228). Moreover, Rose's death is the linchpin of the novel, for it leads directly to the protagonist's climactic conversion. Hearing the "Hail Mary" at the child's deathbed, John Longworthy feels "a new peace in his heart" and becomes a Catholic, after which he goes on to marry Esther Galligan.

The heart of this novel, crucial to the definition of Egan as the essential genteel Irish-American writer, is his presentation of the contrast between working-class and middle-class Irish-American life. Here his ambivalent double vision comes to the fore. There is realistic description of both subcultures, but always in the didactic service of deploring slum life and presenting bourgeois respectability as an unequivocal goal. Egan describes the Bowery tenement house, "The Anchor," where John Longworthy centers his social observations, as the "most squalid, most hopeless, most wretched" of places. Longworthy's focus is on two Irish immigrant families. The O'Connor family history is tragic throughout. Self-indulgent and frivolous, Mrs. O'Connor blames herself for her daughter's death, and she herself dies in prison a week after Rose's funeral. Rose's father is a brutal drunkard with no redeeming spark. At one point, a social worker has to brandish a red-hot poker to keep him from stealing his ailing daughter's supper. Egan presents the O'Connors, who live with their four children in two filthy rooms at the Anchor, as typical slum dwellers, and he wonders how Rose and her older sister could have emerged "so honest, so untainted, in this beer-reeking and pestiferous air."[5] The second Irish working-class family described here is that of Nellie Mulligan, this novel's most interesting character. A counter-girl at Lacy's Emporium, Nellie is coarsely outspoken, a flamboyantly tasteless dresser, and the organizing force of the shopgirls' social club, the Lady Rosebuds. But she is also good-hearted, honest, and practical. The same traits of vitality and ambition that make her vulgar also make her a spirited example of her generation, the emerging lower middle class of young clerks and shopgirls who are beginning to rise above their immigrant parents' lot as servants and laborers.

Egan presents Nellie Mulligan as a foil for the moral and social exemplars of his novel, the cultured and respectable Galligan sisters, Esther and Mary. When their brother Miles wants to marry Nellie, the sisters recoil from the "vulgar and frivolous" girl "that goes to all the picnics." And yet, although Egan may not have intended it, there is something to Nellie's angry rejoinder that the Galligans are "codfish aristocracy—people who would if they could, but they can't, you know," and to her reminder to Esther that "we are not savages here, if we *do* live in a tenement-house. It's not long since your father and mother lived in one" (193, 211). Esther's answer to Nellie conveys Egan's underlying didacticism. Her parents got out of the slums because they were not guilty of the "carelessness and heartlessness" that pervade the Anchor. Living in the substantial house left to them by those industrious parents, the Galligans are Egan's model genteel Irish Americans. Their neighborhood, "one of the most comfortable precincts of the East Side," embodies their steadfast, satisfied middleness. Recalling the judgments of taste in architectural terms of Sadlier's *Old and New*, "it is too near Canal Street to be fashionable, or even liked by nice people who do not pretend to fashion. There the houses are roomy, substantial, solid-looking. . . . they are as respectable in appearance as a Hollandish burgher." Both young women are teachers in a nearby convent school, and they supplement their small incomes by renting rooms to "various respectable people."

Their brother, Miles Galligan, is another story entirely. His character is Egan's first contribution to his generation's familiar fictional denunciation of Irish-American politicians. Miles's principle function is to provide a warning example of the evils of unethical political ambition. A lazy, weak-willed loafer with a propensity for drink, he is a Tammany Hall hanger-on who hopes to slide into a sinecure by simple loyalty to the party. At the end of the novel, Miles's fate is unclear. Thanks to John Longworthy's money, he gets a seat in the state legislature, after promising to leave his sisters in peace and to work for "tenement-house reform," but Mary Galligan still fears "that this brother of hers may die in his sins."

After revealing his true identity and then turning Catholic, John Longworthy goes on to marry Esther Galligan at the end of the novel. It is significant that this novel's protagonist is a highly cultured and traveled man (he was raised abroad) whose independent wealth rescues the Galligans from their threadbare gentility—and who is also an old-line Anglo-Saxon Protestant by birth. Longworthy converts to Catholicism but not to Irishness. In fact, the gist of Egan's attitude here toward the Irish component of his characters' identity is the archetypal second-generation-genteel rejection of the old country. He expresses this in his description of the Galligan sisters' condescending attempt to rehabilitate the drunken John O'Connor after the deaths of his daughter and wife. They do so by plastering his apartment with magazine portraits of John Mitchel and "a miscellaneous collection of Irish patriots in all attitudes" and scenes from "Picturesque Ireland." The implication is that a lout of limited intelligence such as O'Connor may thereby be seduced back to interest in "his home." But the further implication is that respectable Irish Americans like the Galligans have gone beyond concern for such nostalgic bric-a-brac. Certainly, there is nothing left in the Galligans' house or daily life to signal their Irish background.

This attitude toward Irishness has as its corollary disapproval of the "new immigrants" from Southern and Eastern Europe. Egan is as quick to forget his own origins as any, and, through the narrator's voice in this novel, he advances a prejudicial theory of immigration in his time: "to be poor means to herd with the outcasts of old nations. The creature that has committed nameless crimes in his own country flees to this city of refuge." An innocent child being raised in a New York tenement house "passes each day on the common stairway the spawn of the worst European cities. She hears nightly shrieks and cries and oaths, such as Dante never heard in his vision of hell." (So much for the tired and poor, the huddled masses yearning to breathe free.) With unintentional irony, Egan goes on to observe ruefully that the number of Irish in this environment is "fading away before the swarm of newcomers." Of the sixty families living in the Anchor, "there were many Russian Jews, some of their Polish brethren, a large number of Italians, a few Chinese," and only six Irish families. "Where are the snows of 1850?" he asks. "How many times had 'I Dreamt I Dwelt in Marble Halls' echoed through those drawing-rooms, now fast becoming tenement-houses?" (137-39).

Certainly the Galligan sisters have left ethnicity behind. The only reference to their origins comes when Esther recalls their parents' generation as having quarrelled among themselves in prosperity, and "helped one another in adversity, after the manner of most Irish fathers and mothers." This sense of community is very much in the past now, for Egan tells us that the sisters have retained few friends from those days. Their refusal to practice the social "innovations" adopted lately by "the girls in the neighborhood" has isolated the Galligans, but, as Mary Galligan puts it, "we have never been of them, and that is the reason people call us old-fashioned." Loss of community is the clear price of respectability, and Egan's novel does not question the cost. This point is reinforced in the depiction of Miles Galligan, whose Tammany Hall brand of politics constitutes a hypocritical false community, a cynical, self-serving substitute for the real thing. Equally clear is Egan's sense of late-nineteenth-century

Irish-American ghetto life as dramatically in decline. His presentation of the horrors of the O'Connor family and the Anchor speaks for itself. Entirely absent here is any sense of the retention by the Irish working class of this generation of the community values of the Famine immigrants. The community recalled by the Galligans in their parents' generation is as much a nostalgic ghost as the strains of "I Dreamt I Dwelt in Marble Halls." As will be seen, Mr. Dooley takes an opposing view. Writing at the same time, Finley Peter Dunne both observes the persistence of Irish-American working-class community and deplores the signs of its imminent passing. Egan's equivocal admiration for Nellie Mulligan notwithstanding, he is advocating for his Irish-American readers the establishment of middle-class Catholic identity. At the same time, he repudiates the retention of Irish identity on which many Famine-generation writers such as Mary Anne Sadlier insisted. This is the crucial distinction between the two generations, and it mirrors the gap between immigrant and second-generation Irish America.

The second Egan novel to address directly issues of Irishness in America is *The Vocation of Edward Conway* (1896). Again, the discordant clash of sentimental romance and touches of realism results in artistic failure. Egan echoes Famine-generation fiction in the melodramatic excesses of plot and heavy-handed Catholic-tract didacticism of this novel. But he also manages to satirize with clear-headed realistic perspective some of the foibles of the culture in which his plot and religious apologetics have snared him. These include suspect attitudes toward the Irish and a number of distinctly laughable pseudo-religious movements.

The characters in this novel are exclusively upper-middle-class, sophisticated Irish Catholics. Major Dion Conway had emigrated from Ireland as a child. Having served with distinction in the Civil War, he became a career army officer, thereby following a familiar route to respectability for Famine-generation immigrants. A nominal Catholic, Major Conway had given in to the wishes of his Irish Protestant wife and raised their six daughters as Episcopalians. Now a widower, the major is in charge of an elite army retirement colony at "Swansmere-on-Hudson," New York. Bernice, the last Conway daughter at home, is engaged to the colony's Anglican chaplain, the Reverend Giles Carton, who is the first target of Egan's religious satire. A pretentious High Church dandy given to Anglican medievalism, Carton has built an exquisite pseudo-Gothic chapel, "St. Genevieve-of-Paris," replete with designs by Tiffany and La Farge. His "Book of Hours" for the Lenten season recommends "slight flagellations," and contains a recipe "for making hair-shirts out of old horsehair sofa-cushions." When a young parishioner falls ill with smallpox, Carton is too afraid of becoming infected to minister to him. As a last resort, the Catholic priest Father Haley is grudgingly sent for. He comes immediately, and so comforts Willie Ward that the boy converts to Catholicism, thereby infuriating his parents, who then become two more targets of Egan's satire. Willie's father is a free-thinking transcendentalist whose reading of Emerson and Thoreau has caused him to reject all formal creeds, and his mother is a hysterically emotional evangelical Christian.

Yet another target is a fuzzy Oriental mysticism in which Bernice Conway has been dabbling. Egan was a strong supporter of Catholic schools, and Bernice's miseducation at "a fashionable school" is largely to blame for her having picked up "the usual tendencies: the Browning tendency, the tendency to make 'sweetness and light' and Matthew Arnold her guiding stars, and for a while a tendency to explore theosophy." This last has been encouraged by a lecture on Madame Blavatsky, the founder of theosophy, given by the turbaned, mauve-robed, and yellow-slippered "Lal Shin Fane, supposed to be a Mahatma" (62-3). Subsequently, Bernice's gospel has become this fake mystic's book, *Nirvana and the Lotus*. On its flyleaf is the inscription, "Om mani, padme, om! The dewdrop slips / Into the shining sea." In this conjunction of details, Egan pokes fun at the aesthetic Orientalism of the nineties, and his specific target may be William Butler Yeats. Interested at this time in theosophy and Madame Blavatsky, Yeats had also written many poems with lines as dewy as these. And the mystic's name may be a reference to Yeats's own contradictory doubleness in the nineties—"Lal" for Lalla-Rookhian romanticism from Thomas Moore and "Shin Fane" as the phonetic spelling of Sinn Fein, "Ourselves" in Gaelic and a rallying cry of Irish nationalism.

Into this tangled theological scene comes the novel's hero, Edward Conway, the son of Major Conway's dead cousin Raymond, whose family had also emigrated from Ireland but settled in Virginia and remained Catholic. Quietly cultured and strongly religious, the Georgetown-educated Edward is shocked to find that his cousins are Protestants. At Swansmere on business about his father's estate, he gets Bernice thinking about Catholicism and finds a congenial friend in the intelligent Father Haley, who instructs him on the depth of Northern anti-Catholic feeling, which is described as "the pathos of mistaken conviction and unconscious blindness." The plot of *The Vocation of Edward Conway* defies summary, for it includes most of the stock elements of the sentimental/romantic bag of tricks: attempted murder, a long-buried crime, amnesia, mistaken identity, suicide, and deathbed conversion. So ludicrous are the complications that the effective satiric elements seem out of place. It is puzzling that Egan could have had perspective in fits and starts and lost it so totally in constructing his plot. Suffice it to say, after many gyrations, the novel ends in a stampede of conversions, as Major Conway, his daughter Bernice, and the cowardly rector Giles Carton all turn Catholic. The only surprise here is that Edward Conway doesn't get the girl. Bernice marries Giles while Edward acknowledges his long-simmering vocation and becomes a priest.

The novel also contains pointed satire of Protestant Ascendancy attitudes toward Irishness of the type seen in chapter 5 in George Jessop's fiction. Egan scores a palpable hit in mocking the attempt by Protestant Irish immigrants to disassociate themselves from the Catholic Irish through the character of Alicia McGoggin, a friend of the Conways and a very High Church Protestant from Ulster. Alicia describes her own private saint, Saint Garetha, "an early Briton," as "so near, so British,— not Roman or foreign at all," to which the knowing Edward Conway replies, "So Scotch-Irish!" "Exactly," agrees Alicia (131). (Chicago's John Finerty had a contribution here as well. In reply to adverse remarks by Ulstermen in 1895, he defined the Scotch-Irish as "indigestible fragments of animal matter which Ireland has failed to assimilate over three centuries.") Egan also introduces an arrogant Ascendancy aristocrat, Lady Tyrrell, Bernice Conway's maternal grandmother who is visiting America. Her explanation to Edward Conway of the Irish Land War is a classic of self-justifying snobbery: "Before America was invented, we hadn't half the trouble we have now. It is you that make the farmers too independent. In my grandfather's time, the tenant looked on his landlord as a superior being; now they'll not even take off their hats to you unless you speak to them first" (231).

That the "Scotch-Irish" Alicia McGoggin and the landlord-sympathizing Lady Tyrrell are both Irish Protestants helps to underscore Egan's urging that Irish-American Catholics accentuate the Catholic facet of their identity in America. It is, however, no part of his argument that they also stress their Irishness. Although he acknowledges the plight of the Irish peasantry and ridicules the spurious Scotch-Irish distinction, Egan includes no peasant characters in this novel, and it is a long way back to Mary Anne Sadlier's advocacy of Irish history, books, games, and music. In fact, Edward Conway even counters Father Haley's reference to Irish hospitality by laughing, "You don't claim that as an exclusively Irish virtue, do you?" Edward Conway represents the thoroughly assimilated, cultured and sophisticated, upper-middle-class Irish-American Catholic— with the accent very much on the Catholic, as is demonstrated in his climactic election of the priesthood. He neither asserts nor denies his Irishness, but it is as a Catholic that he functions as Egan's protagonist and didactic role model.

In his long, prolific career, Egan also wrote poetry, moralistic novels "for boys," and a large number of stories.[6] Published first in Catholic periodicals such as *Ave Maria*, Egan's short fiction hews even more closely than his novels to the didactic formulas of exhortation to Catholic respectability. And again, Irish identity is consistently rejected or ignored. A dominant theme is the danger of mixed marriages, and typical here is "How Perseus Became a Star," the story that Egan selected for inclusion in the 1897 anthology, *A Round Table of the Representative American Catholic Novelists*. The son of Irish Catholic immigrants, Perseus Mahaffy renounces his faith for "an assured position in the town" by marrying, in the Baptist Church, the daughter of the leading Protestant citizen. An atheistic life, during which he allows a Catholic friend to die calling in vain for a priest, leads to a bad end, at which the conscience-stricken Perseus also dies unshriven and terrified of Hell. His mother pronounces the moral: "You're too ignorant to know the miserable price for which you've sold your soul. Your grandmother starved in the famine rather than change her religion, or seem to change it even for a moment. Why was your father poor? Why were we exiles? For one reason only: we kept the faith" (132).

Egan wrote several other cautionary tales in this vein. His baldly formulaic novel *A Marriage of Reason* (1893) uses the Sadlieresque device of tracing two Irish Catholic immigrant girls, both of aristocratic background. One marries a Catholic and lives happily, while the other marries a Protestant (for his money) and goes swiftly to the dogs. Similar themes dominate in a second novel which Egan published in 1893, *The Success of Patrick Desmond*. Here the young hero from a poor Irish family is tempted by the promise of wealth to give up his religion. Resisting, he achieves spiritual "success" as leader of the town's Catholic temperance movement.[7] Egan also wrote a number of stories about spoiled priests. In "Carmel" James Delaney is the son of Famine immigrants "who had come to New York with him, a little child, in the year '50." Intended for the priesthood, "for which he had neither vocation nor inclination," the boy refuses to enter the higher seminary after "an expensive college course" that has left his parents "almost penniless in their old age." He has to leave home to escape the burden of guilt and shame imposed upon him, and Egan blames "a system of education which, unhappily, is very prevalent among Irish Americans."[8]

The division between residual, declining Irishness and ascendant Catholicism is even more pronounced in the third of Egan's direct treatments of the issue, a novel that also turned out to be his most popular work of fiction. In his autobiography, Egan remarks on the success of a group of stories about Irish immigrants that he published in the *Century Magazine* between 1902 and 1909. He credits these stories with bringing him increased "outside literary work" in the years after they began to appear. Thus, it was natural for him to combine them (with a few editorial revisions) into a novel, *The Wiles of Sexton Maginnis*, in 1909. The title indicates the prevailing tone of stage Irishry which helps to explain the project's popularity in an establishment periodical such as the *Century*. The novel illustrates the extent to which Egan's embrace of genteel cultural standards led him to denigrate his own kind—the American Irish. The time is the present—about the year 1900. The setting is the factory town of Bracton, a suburb of Baltimore made up largely of working-class and newly middle-class Irish and Italians. The center of events is the Catholic parish of St. Kevin's, the new pastor of which is the urbane, sophisticated Father Stephen Wetherill Blodgett. It is again significant for Egan's attitude toward the Irish that Father Blodgett, the novel's cultural exemplar, is neither

Irish nor Italian, but, like John Longworthy in the earlier novel, an old-line Anglo-Saxon Protestant who has converted to Catholicism. The novel's protagonist is Lewis Maginnis, a down-at-heels immigrant who appears on the convent front stoop on a cold February day looking for work. Befriended by the nuns because, like most of the Bracton Irish, he is a native of County Kerry, Maginnis ends up as the parish sexton and handyman. From this position he wins the hand of the flirtatious Mary Ann Magee, much to the chagrin of her mother, who believes Mary Ann is marrying beneath her station. A formidable parish figure, the widow Magee is a stout and opinionated matriarch referred to far and wide as "Herself."

These and other Irish characters are the most obviously stereotypical in Egan's fiction. Maginnis is that familiar stage-Irish type, the comic retainer, a step-n'-fetchit man with all the predictable traits: not too bright but clever, invariably good-hearted, possessed of a quick tongue and natural wit, given to blarneying, and unable to resist meddling in the affairs of others. His mother-in-law, Mrs. Magee, is the typical working-class aspirant to the bourgeoisie who will never arrive. A hearty purveyor of gossip, sensitive to every tremor on the social ladder of Bracton, she is the domineering head of her own and her daughter's households. When the Maginnis twins are christened Finn and Finola, "Herself" starts a battle royal by demanding that the names be changed to Alphonsus and Philomena. Their refusal costs the Maginnises their lodging—they are driven out to find their own house by Mrs. Magee's protestations. The town's leading citizen, Mayor O'Keefe, is also a predictable type, a politically astute rhetorical blusterer given to election-day dirty tricks to keep himself in power. Egan is particularly condescending in his depiction of the mayor's wife as a type of the newly bourgeois, elevated from her old neighborhood and friends into a tasteless, lace-curtain mansion and "obliged to appear in public incased in a jet-decorated black silk gown, from which her generous proportions seemed only too willing to escape." Fresh from a convent school where she learned social graces and foreign languages, their daughter Rosalia now sits at the piano in the parlor and mispronounces the words of German songs, learned "when her father had an eye on the coming Hanoverian vote" (87-88).

The plot of *The Wiles of Sexton Maginnis* is a series of events variously shaped by the well-meant but ill-fated meddling of Maginnis and Mrs. Magee. Father Blodgett begins by romanticizing his new flock: "Here there could be no social ambitions, no climbing for power, no rivalries. This spot and these honest folk would have delighted the heart of St. Francis. To guard these sheep, to guide them, to be part of the simple annals of the poor—this were happiness enough!" (35). His nephew Guy Wetherill, grandson of the American ambassador to England and holder of a German Ph.D. in chemistry, comes to town and falls in love with Rosalia O'Keefe, and when he converts to Catholicism and marries the girl, Father Blodgett is left with mixed feelings: "He felt that he ought to be happy; but, even as he blessed them, the thought crossed his mind that Rosalia might one day look like her mother" (112).

Meanwhile, Mrs. Magee plots with Maginnis to keep the Moldonovos and O'Keefes, leaders by virtue of their wealth of the town's warring Italian and Irish factions, from taking over the parish: "I'm not one for keepin' up factions, or for nationality in religion; but I'd hate to see that bold Isabella Moldonovo singin' soprany in the choir and the O'Keefe girl bossin' the Holy Angels' Sodality." To further his mother-in-law's cause, Maginnis invents an ascetic monk, Brother Gamborious, and an eccentric matron, Miss Violet Kingswood, whose opposition to Father Blodgett's association with the Moldonovos and O'Keefes Maginnis reports regularly to his employer. Bemused by his sexton's transparent falsehoods, Father Blodgett is equal to the challenge of Bracton. With his simple faith and natural diplomacy, he brings the factions together. The Moldonovos and O'Keefes each subscribe a thousand dollars for the completion of the church building, "and the societies of St. Rita and St. Patrick are to have a joint banquet on the Fourth of July" (64).

The Irish-Italian rivalry flairs up again when young John Moldonovo runs for mayor on a platform of civic virtue against the machine of incumbent O'Keefe. Scandalized by the possibility of an Italian mayor, Maginnis vows that "nary a nagur or dago shall vote, if I can prevent it." Mayor O'Keefe enlists Maginnis in an unscrupulous plan to assure his victory. The Italians and blacks are to be lured by Maginnis to a free chicken barbecue on the outskirts of town. Then O'Keefe will have the power lines cut so that the trolleys will not be able to bring them back until after the polls close. Maginnis, however, changes his mind. Stung by his wife's accusation that he is merely the tool of O'Keefe, Maginnis makes sure that the Italians and blacks vote before they head out for the picnic, and Moldonovo wins the election by twenty-six votes.

The Irish fare even less well in Maginnis's next adventure. One of Bracton's first citizens, Civil War veteran Colonel Grayson, has a daughter who scandalizes the town by deciding, after reading about women's rights, that she wants a career. Blanche Grayson announces that she will begin by delivering a public lecture in the Bracton Town Hall. The subject, drawn from a course that she's been taking at the local college, is to be "The Domination of the Celt in Literature." Blanche's aim is "to expose—with the assistance of Professor MacNiall's notes—the fallacies of the Anglo-Saxon" (259). Her friends, family, and fiancé are horrified, and the latter asks scornfully if she is "going to do 'the escaped-nun racket' " (270). The ubiquitous Maginnis promises to help Blanche by filling the hall with Kerrymen. To do so, he changes the title of the lecture before delivering the copy to the printer. The lecture is packed with men, and when Blanche begins by accusing Pope (Alexander, that is) of maliciousness and treachery, the audience erupts in catcalls and groans. When an egg hits the stage, Blanche flees into the arms of her fiancé, and promptly promises to give up her idea of a career. The reason for the disruption is not far to seek. The Kerrymen thought she was attacking the Pope in Rome, because Maginnis had rewritten the advertisement to read, "Lecture: 'The Damnation of the Celt in Literature,' by An Escaped Nun." It is hard to sort out Egan's many targets here, but he seems to be ridiculing a number of things: appreciation of the Celtic element in literature, the seriousness of nativist fiction of convent revelation, and the idea that a woman could rationally consider a career. And of course, Maginnis and his fellow Irish laborers are the dupes of the entire process. While the *Century* audience may have enjoyed this, it is hard to imagine Irish Americans laughing very hard.

The concluding chapters of the novel introduce a new character, Michael Carmody, a retired musical comedy actor who "had sung and danced in good old Harrigan and Hart times, when his brogue was inimitable," and who is still capable of a creditable version of "The Kerry Dance" (330). An unpaying guest in the Maginnis home for several months, Carmody "was never weary of retailing the incidents of his debut. He had driven the horses of the first real fire-engine seen on any stage, in one of Mr. Augustin Daly's early plays" (333). He is, in short, an authentic stage Irishman, and Egan's treatment of him is one of the most interesting parts of this novel. Through typical meddling, Maginnis engineers Carmody's marriage to the pretentious but good-hearted widow, Mrs. Juno Fortesque Towner (formerly Jane Turner) who "loved theatrical people and theatrical anecdotes," and the newlyweds move to New York City. They are visited there by Maginnis and his wife in the novel's final chapter. The Maginnises have been getting letters from the new Mrs. Carmody detailing her husband's success on the "legitimate" stage in a tragic drama, *Heliogabalus*, that she wrote for him. To their surprise, they discover Carmody doing a vaudeville turn as "Rafferty in the Kerry Dance."

The Maginnises are much moved by Carmody's performance. "I smell the primroses and see the fairy-ring," declares Maginnis. But Egan makes sure that the reader knows his taste is questionable by having him also say, "I was never much for poetry, except for 'Moore's Melodies' and 'Willy Reilly and His Colleen Bawn' " (373-74). Maginnis is also indignant that their friend is "ashamed of doing a good Kerry song and dance," and the experience "converts" him "to stick to the truth as far as I can." The novel ends with Maginnis's unintentionally ironic vow: "I've taken liberties with the truth myself, I admit *that*; but a *real* liar like Carmody is too much for me. . . . If a man was ever converted by a terrible example, I'm that man."

A final example of Egan's denigration of Irishness is one of his last stories, "The Necessity of Being Irish," published in *Scribner's Magazine* in 1914. The lovely, cultured daughter of a self-made man of wealth marries a serious young academic, Dion Fitzgerald. The bride's father complains of the young man's stuffiness by pointing out that his new son-in-law has "an Irish father and mother who'd turn in their graves to hear him read 'Dooley' in an eastern-shore Maryland accent! He can't see a joke." The daughter replies, "Daddy, he can't help not being Irish. . . . You're only Irish on one side, and Dion doesn't always laugh at your jokes because he's preoccupied." At first, Egan seems to be advocating ethnic consciousness here, but this turns out not to be the case. Exhorted to be more "Irish" by his new wife, Fitzgerald lands a history position at the University of Chicago by writing a humorous speech and cleverly steering his father-in-law's large donation from biology to the history department. At the end of his career in fiction, Egan is still equating Irishness with blarney, ready wit, and a dash of deviousness in the cause of self-serving careerism. Nor can he see beyond Mr. Dooley's brogue. On this score, he hasn't learned much in forty years of the literary life.

Indeed, Finley Peter Dunne's Mr. Dooley strikes many of the same chords as Egan's novels—from ethnic rivalries and political machinations to the piano in the parlor and the naming of babies—but with a considerable difference. Dunne's saloonkeeper/philosopher is a sympathetic member of the community whose customs he observes. When Mr. Dooley satirizes the pretensions of the new Irish middle class, his laughter is kindly. These are, after all, his own people. Furthermore, Mr. Dooley appreciates the value and laments the loss of the old working-class ethnic community, fast disappearing in the rush toward respectability. Dunne's is an intelligent perspective on the price of assimilation in human terms, delivered with respect and compassion for all who were affected by the turbulent social changes in late-nineteenth-century Irish America. Egan, on the other hand, laughs from the outside. He satirizes lace-curtain pretensions, but not as a way of measuring and regretting the loss of the old community. He laughs at that as well. The cultural model in *The Wiles of Sexton Maginnis* is Bracton's Anglo-Saxon convert priest, Father Blodgett. The alter ego for Egan himself, Blodgett represents a genuine, unforced sophistication that the immigrant generation of Maginnises, Magees, and O'Keefes can never hope to attain. In this novel, their attempts are always laughable, and the satire is always condescending. In a word, Egan is a snob. His fiction reveals him to be an assimilated, unembarrassed Catholic, but of a particular elitist type. The price he has willingly paid for his adjustment is a wholesale rejection of the Irish part of his background. It is his total lack of sympathy for the ethnic dimension of his characters that makes him the essential genteel novelist, blinded to the richer possibilities of his material by his appropriation of mainstream middle-class American values. Egan's fiction embodies the distance he has put between his own Irish origins and his sense of himself, while providing a special and unintended insight into the pervasive movement toward respectability that was epidemic in Irish America at the turn of the century. Maurice Francis Egan probably thought that his fiction diagnosed the disease, but his own was clearly a terminal case.

The first voice of genius in Irish-American literature is that of Finley Peter Dunne. There are flashes of greatness among the third-generation realists and the first-generation, pre-Famine satirists, to be sure. And yet, and even though his chosen form was not fiction but the usually ephemeral newspaper column, it was Peter Dunne who created the first truly memorable Irish character in American literature, the aging, immigrant bartender Martin J. Dooley, and the first fully realized ethnic neighborhood in American literature, Bridgeport on the South Side of Chicago. In addition, Dunne resurrects and impressively augments the tradition of Irish-American satire that had been in decline since the Famine generation.

For years, "Mr. Dooley" has had a secure place in the hearts of historians and journalists as the source of some of the most trenchant short speeches ever delivered on the state of the American nation. Ever since his clear-headed critique of the Spanish-American War brought Dunne's creation to the attention of a national audience, analysts of the American scene have been quoting glittering bits of his wisdom. Stretching from 1898 to the First World War, Mr. Dooley's tenure as resident American comic sage was remarkable both in its length and in the consistent high quality of the mostly occasional commentary. For all this, a grateful nation thanked Peter Dunne by making him the most popular journalist of his time. But there was much more to him than the years of center-stage national commentary and celebrity status. Before fame overtook him, Mr. Dooley had had a very productive talking life in his native Chicago. By the time the battleship Maine was sunk at Havana, 215 Dooley pieces had already appeared in the Chicago *Evening Post*, and most of them were concerned with Irish-American daily life in Bridgeport. When the popularity of his humorous perspective on the "splendid little war" in Cuba made it possible for Dunne to collect his early pieces as *Mr. Dooley in Peace and in War* (1898) and *Mr. Dooley in the Hearts of His Countrymen* (1899), he passed over much of the Bridgeport material because he believed that it would not appeal to his new national audience. However, it is precisely their specific locality that keeps these neglected pieces alive. They illustrate the validity of the creed of Patrick Kavanagh, whose own poetry is rooted in the small farms and fields of his native County Monaghan: "Parochialism is universal; it deals with the fundamentals."[9] I have previously argued that Finley Peter Dunne belongs in the first rank of American writers as a pioneering social historian and literary realist.[10] That case will be made afresh here in the larger context of the Irish-American literature that precedes and follows Dunne's accomplishment, poised as it is in the middle of the story, between the immigrant nineteenth century and the ethnic twentieth century.

Finley Peter Dunne entered the exciting world of Chicago journalism at the age of sixteen in June 1884. Over the next eight years he worked for six different newspapers and moved up fast. At nineteen he was covering the White Sox for the *Daily News*, at twenty-one he was City Editor of the *Times*, and at twenty-five in 1892 he arrived as editorial page chairman at the *Evening Post*, which soon became Mr. Dooley's first home. Dunne had previously experimented with Irish dialect in his political reporting. He often enlivened city council news with comical transcriptions of the brogues of Chicago aldermen. Now, at the suggestion of the *Post*'s managing editor, he began to write a weekly column featuring Colonel Malachi McNeery, a saloonkeeper in the tenderloin district of the city. McNeery was modeled on a friend of Dunne's, Jim McGarry, whose Dearborn Street saloon was a gathering place of newspapermen and visiting celebrities, including boxer John L. Sullivan and actor James O'Neill. The real catalyst for the column, though, was the grandiose 1893 World's Fair, and the Colonel's adventures on the exotic Midway became so popular that his prototype McGarry ordered Dunne to stop making fun of him. Dunne acquiesced by shipping Colonel McNeery back to Ireland at the end of the Fair.

Two weeks later, the *Evening Post* for Saturday, October 7, 1893, carried the first appearance of Mr. Martin Dooley, a saloonkeeper from Archer Avenue in Irish-working-class Bridgeport. The shift in location is significant. McGarry's barroom in the Loop was a worldly, exciting place, and Dunne had portrayed Colonel McNeery as a sophisticated friend of the great. On the other hand, a bar out in Bridgeport was likely to be a community institution, dispensing solace and companionship to a stable clientele of Irish millworkers, draymen, and streetcar drivers. From the outset, Dunne understood the special character of a neighborhood saloon. Mr. Dooley's brogue is thicker than Colonel McNeery's, which signals the social transition from the Loop to "Archey road." But most important, Dunne brings us into a parochial neighborhood culture where people are placed by family, geography, and reputation. The very first Dooley pieces contain the seeds of Dunne's accomplishment—the imaginative creation of Bridgeport. Mr. Dooley lived on Archer Avenue until 1900, when Peter Dunne moved to New York and the second phase of his career, as a nationally syndicated humorist. In his earlier, Chicago setting—his only real home—Mr. Dooley provides many riches unavailable elsewhere.

There is first of all the issue of the brogue, the background of American and Irish-American dialect writing that Dunne emerged from and transformed. Dialect was of course a major component in the portrayal of the stereotypical "stage Irishman" in nineteenth-century drama. In addition, fiction and journalism also contained numbers of similar broad-brush, condescending caricatures, displaying the familiar, if contradictory, traits of ignorance, wiliness, and garrulity, always in the service of provoking laughter at supposed Irishness. Writers from the American literary mainstream throughout the nineteenth century made full use of the brogue to help create derogatory pictures of the alien immigrant hordes. Teague O'Regan, the bumbling Sancho Panza figure in H.H. Brackenridge's 1792 picaresque novel *Modern Chivalry*, stands at the head of this line. And there were a number of particularly unpleasant examples published in Mr. Dooley's day as part of the new wave of nativism that swept across America in the 1890s.[11] In American journalism, the brogue goes back at least as far as it does in fiction. And again, perhaps because of the general interest in urban local color at the time, there were quite a number of Irish dialect voices in American newspapers in the 1880s and 1890s when Dunne was starting out. John Joseph Jennings's sketches about the Widow Magoogin and her cousin Officer Mike ran in the St. Louis *Post-Dispatch* and *Critic*. For the Brooklyn *Eagle*, Maurice E. McLoughlin created "the Gowanusians," Irish settlers beside the Gowanus Canal who included the social-climbing McSniffigans and saloonkeeper's wife Mrs. Mulgrew. Ernest Jarrold's "idylls" of ten-year-old Mickey Finn, the son of immigrants to Coney Island, appeared in the New York *Sun* and *Leslie's Weekly*. Mr. Dooley even had dialect rivals in his own city, where "Officer Casey on the City Hall Corner" conversed with "the Connemara cop" in the Chicago *Times-Herald*. Without exception, these dialect columns use an awkwardly insistent brogue and slapstick-comic situations to ridicule the Irish in all the old familiar ways.[12] In the context of the overwhelmingly negative tradition of Irish dialect writing, the opposition to Mr. Dooley voiced by a number of Irish-American editors in the 1890s becomes understandable. When they saw the brogue, they saw red. Chicagoan John Finerty, who as we shall see, had other reasons for disliking Dunne, editorialized in his weekly paper the *Citizen* against "the devil of dialectism" in general and Finley Peter Dunne in particular, as the perpetrator of "an atrocious brogue, such as only the very lowest of the Irish peasantry indulge in," the aim of which was "to make fools and bigots laugh" (Fanning, *Dunne* 157-59). However, had he been able to read Mr. Dooley more objectively, Finerty would have seen the brogue used in new and salutary ways.

First of all, the voice itself is a kind of miracle. Far from being a language expert, Dunne was only trying, as he explained in an 1899 interview, "to make Dooley talk as an Irishman would talk who has lived thirty or forty years in America, and whose natural pronunciation had been more or less affected by the slang of the streets" (Way 217). Dunne was also aware of the dangers of dialect writing for a general audience, and here he successfully walked a tightrope, managing to suggest the brogue without sacrificing clarity. Working simply with a few sure strokes, he made of the Dooley voice a flexible, serviceable medium. The dialect is conveyed by occasional contraction (th', gettin') and expansion (gr-rand, ta-arget), with a sprinkling of Irish pronunciations (quite [quiet], jood [dude], a cup of tay) and holdovers from the Gaelic (soggarth [priest], omadhon [lout], gossoon [little boy]). Dunne's ear for the rhythms and timing of this Irish-American urban speech is everywhere remarkable. In even the slightest Dooley piece, we hear a living voice.[13]

Even more important is the range of tasks to which Dunne set the inimitable Dooley voice. Certainly, although he is the first immigrant city-dweller in the group, Mr. Dooley belongs in the nineteenth-century American tradition of the crackerbox philosopher or wise fool, along with such unlettered dispensers of wisdom in dialect as Major Jack Downing, Petroleum V. Nasby, and Artemus Ward. In addition, Dunne had a few positive precursors in Irish-American dialect writing. He may have been aware of Charles G. Halpine's Civil War dispatches of Private Miles O'Reilly, which had their pointed satirical moments. And there was the extraordinary phenomenon of pre-Famine Irish-American satire as practiced by John M. Moore, Thomas C. Mack, and the anonymous authors of *Six Months in a House of Correction* and *The Life of Paddy O'Flarrity*. Dunne shares with these predecessors a common bag of verbal tricks: cacography, juxtaposition of incongruous predicates, nouns, and proper names, misquotation of classics and the Bible. However, Dunne-as-Dooley also significantly broadens the range of subjects and deepens the range of tones that can be sustained in the vernacular dialect voice. Even when making serious points, as in the Civil War pieces of Nasby, Ward, and Miles O'Reilly, the earlier dialect writers kept themselves wrapped in the protective cloak of humor. To be sure, Mr. Dooley provides a number of classic humorous narratives also, including sketches of family feuding and fear of marriage, rough-and-tumble politicking, and mock-heroic ceremonial occasions such as the St. Patrick's Day parade. And yet, even when he is being funny, Mr. Dooley provokes laughter not because he knows so little, but because he knows so much. He is witty, satirical, cutting. He exposes delusions rather than being victimized by them. In addition, and in contrast to his later manifestation as the purveyor of comic perspective on national issues, Mr. Dooley is funny in only half of the Chicago pieces. He is often utterly serious in theme and tone, dealing with such subjects as starvation in Ireland and Chicago, wanton murder and grim retribution, and heroism both quiet and spectacular, in an appropriate voice that achieves at times a tragic resonance. That Dunne accomplished so much without strain constitutes an expansion of the possibilities for fiction of the vernacular voice. On a smaller scale, Dunne's achievement is comparable to Mark Twain's decision to let Huck Finn tell his own story.

In sum, through Mr. Dooley, Finley Peter Dunne made a number of pioneering contributions to American literary realism. As an urban local colorist, he described the life and customs of Bridgeport in the later nineteenth century. As the creator of substantial character sketches of Irish immigrants, he affirmed that the lives of ordinary people were worthy of serious literary consideration. And finally, he brought forth the community and its people through the vernacular voice of a sixty-year-old smiling public-house man. Major figures in literary realism's first two generations acknowledged Dunne's part in their movement. Declaring that "no one but an Irish-American could have invented such an Irish-American, or have invested his sayings with such racial and personal richness," William Dean Howells called Mr. Dooley "wise and shrewd and just for the most part," and capable of "the last effect of subtle irony." And Theodore Dreiser wrote that "as early as 1900, or before," Mr. Dooley had "passed into my collection of genuine American realism."[14] Dunne's Dooley columns are cameo etchings of the archetypal Irish immigrant themes and characters with the precision and vividness of illuminated corners of the *Book of Kells*. The themes include memories of the Famine, the turbulent voyage to America, the shattered dream of gold in the streets, the hard life of manual labor, the sufferings of the poor, the pains of assimilation, the gulf between immigrants and their children, and the slow rise to respectability. And the characters include Civil War veterans, heroic firemen, stoic, exploited millworkers, rackrenting, miserly landlords, failed politicians who lose their money, successful ones who forget their friends, lace-curtain social climbers with pianos in the parlor, and compassionate, overworked parish priests.

The Dooley pieces are populated with a large cast of recurrent characters, many of them modeled after real people. John McKenna was a genial Republican politician from Chicago's Brighton Park neighborhood. During the Bryan-McKinley campaign of 1896, Dunne invented Malachi Hennessy, a working-class Bridgeport Democrat, to argue against McKenna, thereby allowing Mr. Dooley to stand comfortably in the middle, exploiting the comic potential of both sides. After the election, Hennessy took over the listening post, presumably because, as a slow-thinking millworker with a large family, he was a more typical Bridgeporter than McKenna, and a better foil for Mr. Dooley's wit. Of the other important characters, Police Sergeant John Shea, political kingmaker William Joyce, Aldermen Billy O'Brien and Johnny Powers, and the local parish priest Father Kelly were real-life Chicagoans who lent their names and some of their idiosyncracies to Dunne's cast. And of course, presiding over all is the saloonkeeper—Mr. Dooley himself: satirist, social critic, and philosopher, generally cynical but specifically kind; at the least (in his own words) "a post to hitch ye'er silences to," at the most, a provider of companionship and solace to bone-weary working people.

By accretion of the weekly Dooley columns, a whole picture emerges, and Dunne has stitched this world together with landmark references throughout the series. All movement for Mr. Dooley is defined in relation to the "red bridge" that joins Bridgeport to the rest of Chicago. Archey road is a lively main street extending from Dooley's saloon to the political capital of Bridgeport at Finucane's Hall. Social status is reckoned by the proximity of one's home to the rolling mills and the gas house. And meandering backdrops for many scenes are provided by the Chicago River and its swampy runoff, Healey's Slough. Thus firmly placed in the imagination, Bridgeport blossoms as a believable ethnic subculture with its own customs and ceremonies, a social hierarchy rooted in ancestry, family, and occupation, and a shared perspective on the world.

That subculture takes shape when Dunne's columns are arranged in thematic groups. The result is the great nineteenth-century Irish-American novel—in pieces. The rest of this chapter briefly surveys Dunne's Chicago Dooley pieces, organized as follows: memories of Ireland, emigration, and the early years in America; daily life in Bridgeport in the 1890s; Chicago Irish politics as viewed from Archey Road; the tragicomic phenomenon of Irish-American nationalism after the fall of Parnell; Mr. Dooley's pioneering presentation of the common man as hero; and his sensitive register of the seismic shocks to the Irish-American community brought on by the emergence of a middle class. This last is the great theme of this generation, and only Dunne explores it in depth. The chapter will end with consideration of some of the strangest and some of the strongest Dooley pieces. The former help to place Dunne in the Irish and Irish-American traditions of satire and linguistic subversion; the latter help to explain why Mr. Dooley left Bridgeport behind in 1900.

When he first appeared in the *Evening Post* in 1893, Martin Dooley was already over sixty. In the course of the Chicago pieces, Dunne provided him with a plausible past, stretching back to a childhood Christmas in Ireland when "th' lads that'd been away 'd come thrampin' in fr'm Gawd knows where, big lads far fr'm home in Cork an' Limerick an' th' City iv Dublin—come thrampin' home stick in hand to ate their Christmas dinner with th' ol' folks" (5). The piece in which Mr. Dooley describes his own emigration during the Famine may be quoted whole as an example of the small miracles that occur in Dunne's best columns:

"Poor la-ads, poor la-ads," said Mr. Dooley, putting aside his newspaper and rubbing his glasses. " 'Tis a hard lot theirs, thim that go down into th' say in ships, as Shakespeare says. Ye niver see a storm on th' ocean? Iv coorse ye didn't. How cud ye, ye that was born away fr'm home? But I have, Jawn. May th' saints save me fr'm another! I come over in th' bowels iv a big crazy balloon iv a propeller, like wan iv thim ye see hooked up to Dempsey's dock, loaded with lumber an' slabs an' Swedes. We watched th' little ol' island fadin' away behind us, with th' sun sthrikin' th' white house-tops iv Queenstown an' lightin' up th' chimbleys iv Martin Hogan's liquor store. Not wan iv us but had left near all we loved behind, an' sare a chance that we'd iver spoon th' stirabout out iv th' pot above th' ol' peat fire again. Yes, by dad, there was wan,—a lad fr'm th' County Roscommon. Divvle th' tear he shed. But, whin we had parted fr'm land, he turns to me, an' says, 'Well, we're on our way,' he says. 'We are that,' says I. 'No chanst f'r thim to turn around an' go back,' he says. 'Divvle th' fut,' says I. 'Thin,' he says, raisin' his voice, 'to 'ell with th' Prince iv Wales,' he says. 'To 'ell with him' he says.

"An' that was th' last we see of sky or sun f'r six days. That night come up th' divvle's own storm. Th' waves tore an' walloped th' ol' boat, an' th' wind howled, an' ye cud hear th' machinery snortin' beyant. Murther, but I was sick. Wan time th' ship 'd be settin' on its tail, another it'd be standin' on its head, thin rollin' over cowlike on th' side; an' ivry time it lurched me stummick lurched with it, an' I was tore an' rint an' racked till, if death come, it 'd found me willin'. An' th' Roscommon man,—glory be, but he was disthressed. He set on th' flure, with his hands on his belt an' his face as white as stone, an' rocked to an' fro. 'Ahoo,' he says, 'ahoo, but me insides has torn loose,' he says, 'an' are tumblin' around,' he says. 'Say a pather an' avy,' says I, I was that mad f'r th' big bosthoon f'r his blatherin' on th' flure. 'Say a pather an' avy,' I says; f'r ye're near to death's dure, avick.' 'Am I?' says he, raising up. 'Thin,' he says, 'to 'ell with the whole rile fam'ly,' he says. Oh, he was a rebel!

"Through th' storm there was a babby cryin'. 'Twas a little wan, no more thin a year ol'; an' 'twas owned be a Tipp'rary man who come fr'm near Clonmel, a poor, weak, scarey-lookin' little divvle that lost his wife, an' see th' bailiff walk off with th' cow, an' thin see him come back again with th' process servers. An' so he was comin' over with th' babby, an' bein' mother an' father to it. He'd rock it be th' hour on his knees, an' talk dam nonsense to it, an' sing it songs, 'Aha, 'twas there I met a maiden down be th' tanyard side,' an' 'Th' Wicklow Mountaineer,' an' 'Th' Rambler fr'm Clare,' an' 'O'Donnel Aboo,' croonin' thim in th' little babby's ears, an' payin' no attintion to th' poorin' thunder above his head, day an' night, day an' night, poor soul. An' th' babby cryin' out his heart, an' him settin' there with his eyes as red as his hair, an' makin' no kick, poor soul.

"But wan day th' ship settled down steady, an' ragin' stummicks with it; an' th' Roscommon man shakes himself, an' says, 'To 'ell with th' Prince iv Wales an' th' Dook iv Edinboroo,' an' goes out. An' near all th' steerage followed; f'r th' storm had done its worst, an' gone on to throuble those that come afther, an' may th' divvle go with it. 'Twill be rest f'r that little Tipp'rary man; f'r th' waves was r-runnin' low an' peaceful, an' th' babby have sthopped cryin'.

"He had been settin' on a stool, but he come over to me. 'Th' storm,' says I, 'is over.' 'Yis,' says he, ' 'tis over.' ' 'Twas wild while it lasted,' says I. 'Ye may say so,' says he. 'Well, please Gawd,' says I, 'that it left none worse off thin us.' 'It blew ill f'r some an' aise f'r others,' says he. 'Th' babby is gone.'

"An' so it was, Jawn, f'r all his rockin' an' singin'. An' in th' avnin' they burried it over th' side into th' say, an' th' little Tipp'rary man wint up an' see thim do it. He see thim do it." [10-12]

Mr. Dooley's version of the archetypal crossing-narrative includes the familiar storm-at-sea metaphor for the initial trauma of emigration, but it is unique in a number of ways. He serves notice immediately that the mood of sentimental melancholy traditionally associated with the last glimpse of Ireland will not be indulged here. Mr. Dooley's parting image of the Emerald Isle is "th' chimbleys iv Martin Hogan's liquor store." An additional balancing check on emotion is provided by the several appearances of the windy nationalist from Roscommon, whose denunciations of the royal family get louder and more inclusive as his distance from British oppression increases. And yet, the hardship of crossing in the stuffed, unsanitary "coffin ships" of the Famine years is the clear and moving center of this piece, achieved by Dunne's focus on the widower and his ailing child. The short, final sentence speaks for itself: "He see thim do it."

Mr. Dooley also recalls his generation's youthful illusions about America as the place "where all ye had to do was to hold ye'er hat an' th' goold guineas'd dhrop into it. . . . But, faith, whin I'd been here a week, I seen that there was nawthin' but mud undher th' pavement—I larned that be means iv a pick-axe at tin shillin's th' day" (12-13). And he proceeds from here to present in great detail the colors of the Bridgeport passing scene in the 1890s. Social life centers naturally around the Catholic Church, and typical in its crisp observation is Mr. Dooley's description of the annual parish fair at St. Honoria's in 1895, featuring "Roddy's Hibernyun Band playin' on th' cor-rner," a shooting gallery, booths selling everything from rosaries to oyster stew, and a raffle for a doll, a rocking chair, and "a picture iv th' pope done by Mary Ann O'Donoghue" (42-44). Other parish productions include the staging of "The Doomed Markey" by the "St. Patrick's Stock Company" with Denny Hogan in the title role, and an experimental "temperance saloon" which closes on its opening night after the patrons have "dhrunk thimsilves into chollery morbus with coold limonade." There are secular events as well, some quite lively. A genealogy lecture in the school hall erupts into a brawl over whose ancestors were kings and whose only dukes. At a benefit social for an ailing bartender, big O'Malley rolls fifty-four, then swallows the dice to ensure victory. And during a Dooley family reunion the emotional climate shifts from nostalgia to name-calling until "they wasn't two Dooleys in th' hall 'd speak whin th' meetin' broke up."

Politics was the most visible and controversial of Irish-American career opportunities in the late nineteenth century, and as an experienced political reporter, Dunne was well able to describe the Irish contribution to Chicago's government. The Dooley political pieces constitute a valuable inside narrative of the Irish pursuit of power and a vivid microcosm of ward politics and the urban machine. Here Dunne was careful to work against the prevailing stereotypes. Often labeled a reformer, perhaps because his career fits comfortably into the time frame of muckraking campaigns against municipal corruption, he is really nothing of the kind. Instead, Mr. Dooley is invariably nostalgic for the old days of rough-and-tumble politicking, he is sympathetic toward those who have used politics to escape the killing rut of manual labor, and he remains unconvinced that reformist political solutions (such as "destroy graft" and "outlaw patronage") will make life better for more people than the old ways. Rather than condemning corruption, Mr. Dooley recalls with relish his own service as precinct captain in his corner of the old Sixth Ward in the 1870s: "I mind th' time whin we r-rolled up twenty-sivin hunderd dimocratic votes in this wan precinct an' th' on'y wans that voted was th' judges iv election an' th' captains." Or again, "I mind whin McInerney was a-runnin' f'r county clark. Th' lads at th' ya-ards set up all night tuckin' tickets into th' box f'r him. They voted all iv Calvary Symmitry an' was makin' inroads on th' potther's field." Further reminiscences of rioting between rival torch-light paraders, brick-throwing at primaries, and bone-bruising nominating conventions support Mr. Dooley's judgment that "politics ain't bean-bag. 'Tis a man's game, an' women, childer, cripples an' prohybitionists 'd do well to keep out iv it" (219).

Mr. Dooley also provides several capsule biographies of politicians in which he is sympathetic to the Irish use of politics as a means of rising in the world. For example, his sketch of the career of Nineteenth-Ward alderman Johnny Powers asks the reader to consider the introduction of "this quite, innocent little groceryman" to the ways of the city council: "He didn't meet so manny men that'd steal a ham an' thin shoot a po-lisman over it. But he met a lot that'd steal th' whole West Side iv Chicago an' thin fix a gr-rand jury to get away with it" (243). In several such pieces, Mr. Dooley is much more tolerant of unabashed grafters from poor back-grounds than of hypocritical reformers whose own white-collar crime goes unnoticed. One of his memorable closing lines says it all: "Niver steal a dure-mat, . . . If ye do, ye'll be invistigated, hanged, an' maybe ray-formed. Steal a bank, me boy, steal a bank" (234).

Not that Mr. Dooley sees Chicago's Irish politicians as golden-hearted Robin Hoods. He perceives quite clearly the dark side as well, and some of his political biographies end tragically. One young tough with "th' smell iv Castle Garden on him" rises through his reputation for rough-house bullying to become boss of the ward, then commits the unpardonable sin of betraying his community. He moves up to Michigan Avenue and leads the citizen's committee formed to prosecute his old supporters. In other vignettes, political aspiration ruins the lives of decent men. One "dacint, quite little lad" parlays a successful saloon into an aldermanic seat, then sacrifices his reputation to the lure of easy money. Defeated for reelection and deserted by his customers, "all he had left was his champagne thirst." Significantly, Dunne kept Mr. Dooley in character by refusing to tell any of the tragic political tales at election time, when they might have been construed as reforming in impulse.

In keeping with his age and station, Mr. Dooley is consistently skeptical of "th' wave iv rayform" whenever it threatens to wash over Bridge-port. Ultimately, it is his sophisticated sense of the complexity of life that keeps him from seeing any clean and simple way to cut through the tangle of interests, self-serving and selfless, in urban politics. He expresses this in a kind of parable: "I butt up again a man on th' sthreet an' he falls again another man an' that man reels again you, Hinnissy, walkin' along th' curb, ca'm an' peaceful, an' out ye go into th' mud. . . . Th' crow is up in th' three, no doubt, black an' ugly, stealin' me potatoes an' makin' me life miserable with his noise, but whin I throw a club at him he's out iv th' way an' it smashes into a nest full iv eggs that some frind of mine has been hatchin' out" (249). It is this note of frustration edging toward despair about the political process that unfits Mr. Dooley for the role of reformer. Certainly, this attitude is grounded in Dunne's own first-hand experience as a political reporter, but it is also connected to his realistic conception of Mr. Dooley as an aging Famine immigrant, because no people could have had less faith in political solutions than the nineteenth-century Irish.

Mr. Dooley also provides healthy perspective on the American contribution to the movement to free Ireland from British rule. He recalls his Uncle Mike's participation in that most bizarre of events, the 1866 Fenian invasion of Canada: " 'Uncle Mike,' says I to him, 'what's war like, an-nyhow?' 'Well,' says he, 'in some rayspicts it is like missin' th' last car,' he says; 'an' in other rayspicts 'tis like gettin' gay in front iv a polis station,' he says" (262). Dooley also remembers debates in Bridgeport meetings of the secret revolutionary organization, the Clan na Gael, about how best to achieve Irish freedom. As a lapsed Clansman, a one-time believer in violent revolution who now espouses milder tactics, he takes satiric advantage of the Clan's alphabetical codes, secret handshakes, and elaborate structure of officers and "camps."

Dunne often responded to Irish nationalist events with immediate, skeptical Dooley columns, which constituted realistic assessments in the dark years after the fall of Parnell. The passage of a Third Home Rule Bill in the House of Commons in 1893, Prime Minister Gladstone's retirement from public life in 1894, and a serious British cabinet crisis in 1895 are all noted by Mr. Dooley, who refuses to be fooled into believing that Irish freedom is close at hand. About the contributions of the American Irish to the cause, Mr. Dooley has mixed emotions: sympathy for the rank-and-file nationalists and suspicion for the motives of their leaders. "Did ye iver," he asks in 1895, "see a man that wanted to free Ireland th' day afther to-morrah that didn't run f'r aldherman soon or late? Most iv th' great patriotic orators iv th' da-ay is railroad lawyers. That's a fact, I'm tellin' ye. Most iv th' rale pathriots wurruks f'r th' railroads too—tampin' th' thracks."

Mr. Dooley carefully scrutinizes the cluster of natonalist commemorations in his community, including the St. Patrick's Day parade and the annual August 15 picnic of Chicago's United Irish Societies. Invariably, he finds these events to be part harmless fun (for those attending) and part self-serving hypocrisy (for the speech-makers). Mr. Dooley's reports of such goings-on often contain effective parodies of bombastic Irish freedom oratory. One of his favorite targets was Chicago journalist John Finerty, whose nationalist weekly the *Citizen* had been vociferously in favor of the Dynamite Campaign in the early 1880s when American-financed terrorists set off bombs all over London. Mr. Dooley pointedly distinguishes rhetoric from performance when he recalls bringing a fake bomb into the office of "Th' Explosive," a Finerty-style newspaper, "when th' movement to free Ireland be freein' quantities iv dinnymite was goin' on." The terrified editor leaps through his front window and the next day changes his paper "into an organ iv th' undhertakers' association" (273-75). With these columns, Dunne made enemies among Irish nationalist editors. Finerty often lambasted him editorially, and New York's Patrick Ford refused to advertise a collection of the Dooley pieces. But to those who listened, Mr. Dooley provided perspective on the Clan na Gael and Fenian past, warnings of the ever-present threat of venal political aspiration, determined deflation of the excesses and hypocrisies of nationalist rhetoric, and a realistic assessment of the unpromising status of the movement in Ireland and America. He spoke clearly and rationally on matters that more often stirred the fanatic heart.

Dunne's greatest contribution to Chicago and American history and literature is his solid and sympathetic characterization of Mr. Dooley's working-class-immigrant clientele. In column after column, he created characters and situations corroborating the faith of the literary realists in the possibility of dignity, heroism, and tragedy in the common lives of common people. There is, for example, the story of the old widower Shaughnessy, "a quite man that come into th' road before th' fire," who "wurruked f'r Larkin, th' conthractor, f'r near twinty years without skip or break, an' seen th' fam'ly grow up be candle-light." His family history reads like an O'Neill tragedy in miniature. Driven reluctantly toward the priesthood, the oldest boy dies bitterly of consumption. The second son is a charming ne'er-do-well who burns himself out and also dies young. As for the first daughter, Mr. Dooley says only that "she didn't die; but, th' less said, th' sooner mended." Further deaths and desertions leave Shaughnessy with one child, Theresa, who "thought on'y iv th' ol' man, an' he leaned on her as if she was a crutch. She was out to meet him in th' avnin'; an' in th' mornin' he, th' simple ol' man, 'd stop to blow a kiss at her an' wave his dinner-pail, lookin' up an' down th' r-road to see that no wan was watchin' him." In time, Theresa makes a good marriage— to the "prisident iv th' sodality"—but in relieving the weight of the family's accumulated social failure, she leaves her father with a last burden. After the wedding reception, Mr. Dooley waits up for a time with the old man and ends by creating a simple, powerful image of his loneliness: "I looked back at him as I wint by; an' he was settin' be th' stove, with his elbows on his knees an' th' empty pipe between his teeth" (99-100).

Dunne had begun this piece with a reflection on the nature of heroism that reveals his purpose: "Jawn, . . . whin ye come to think iv it, th' heroes iv th' wurruld,—an' be thim I mean th' lads that've buckled on th' gloves, an' gone out to do th' best they cud,—they ain't in it with th' quite people nayether you nor me hears tell iv fr'm wan end iv th' year to another." That Dunne is consciously revising accepted notions of heroism in these pieces is also clear in the Memorial Day column of 1894, where Mr. Dooley remarks that "th' sojers has thim that'll fire salutes over their graves an' la-ads to talk about thim, but there's none but th' widdy f'r to break her hear-rt above th' poor soul that died afther his hands had tur-rned to leather fr'm handlin' a pick" (24). Other quiet heroes in the Dooley pantheon include little Tim Clancy, "the Optimist," who copes cheerfully with the problems of supporting a family of ten on "wan twenty-five a day—whin he wurruks" in the steel mill, and Pat Doherty, a legitimate Civil War hero who has returned quietly to his job at the mill, while blowhards who never left Chicago wave the bloody shirt. Infuriated by the Memorial Day mouthings of a political hack in Dooley's saloon, Doherty delivers a withering blast against war and hypocrisy:

> "Did anny man iver shoot at ye with annything but a siltzer bottle? Did ye iver have to lay on ye'er stummick with ye'er nose burrid in th' Lord knows what while things was whistlin' over ye that, if they iver stopped whistlin', 'd make ye'er backbone look like a broom? Did ye iver see a man that ye'd slept with th' night befure cough, an' go out with his hooks ahead iv his face? Did ye iver have to wipe ye'er most intimate frinds off ye'er clothes, whin ye wint home at night?" [29]

Dunne also extends the literary potential of the common life into the dimension of tragedy. Exemplary here are his stories of Chicago firemen, who risked their lives daily in their tinderbox city, "consthructed," in Mr. Dooley's words, "f'r poor people out iv nice varnished pine an' cotton waste." The most admired man in Bridgeport, Fireman Mike Clancy performs feats of great and irrational courage that smack of hubris. He drives the hose cart around corners on one wheel, dives into falling buildings, and rescues people by descending the ladder head first, because "I seen a man do it at th' Lyceem whin I was a kid." Clancy is flawed in that he doesn't know when to quit. Promising his wife that he will retire after "wan more good fire . . . a rale good ol' hot wan," the fireman goes off to his death. The piece ends with a memorable image of the common man as tragic hero, one of the few such images indigenous to the Irish-American community in the nineteenth century: "An' Clancy was wan iv th' men undher whin th' wall fell. I seen thim bringin' him home; an' th' little woman met him at th' dure, rumplin' her apron in her hands" (113-15).

Remarkable in these sketches is Dunne's ability to sympathize, through Mr. Dooley, with the situations of the Bridgeport heroes and victims. And the key to that sympathy, as to the realism of the pieces, is in Dunne's fully imagined conception of Dooley as a member of the community he describes. That conception comes through clearly in two sketches of the lives of young Bridgeport criminals. Jack Carey, "the idle apprentice," is "a thief at tin year," in the city jail at twelve, and "up to anny game" from then on. Branded a chronic troublemaker, Carey is hounded by the police, and a bitter feud develops between him and a fellow Bridgeporter, Officer Clancy, who succeeds in getting Carey sent "over th' road" to the state penitentiary. Upon his release, Carey murders Clancy in broad daylight in the middle of Archer Avenue, and is himself shot down by a squad of police. For Dooley's patron John McKenna, the moral is clear: "It served him right." But Mr. Dooley is not so sure: "Who? . . . Carey or Clancy?" is his ending question (157-59). The spectacle of two Bridgeporters turning against and destroying each other has left him too disturbed to be able to sort out causes and assign blame. A similar story is that of a child of religious parents, Petey Scanlan, who "growed up fr'm bein' a curly-haired angel f'r to be th' toughest villyun in th' r-road." His career ends after he has robbed a store, terrorized Bridgeport, and fled to his parents' home. Having berated Lt. Cassidy for making a scandal before her neighbors, Mrs. Scanlan leads Petey to the patrol wagon on her arm, and is left "settin' in a big chair with her apron in her hands an' th' picture iv th' lad th' day he made his first c'munion in her lap." Again, Mr. Dooley can only shake his head in bewilderment: "Who'll tell what makes wan man a thief an' another man a saint? I dinnaw" (160). These are not the reactions of Finley Peter Dunne, a sophisticated editor with progressive leanings, but of Martin Dooley, an aging Irish immigrant, puzzled and pained at these signs that his own community is dissolving.

A major contribution of the Chicago Dooley pieces to the literary self-consciousness of the American Irish is Dunne's presentation of the crumbling of the old ghetto communities that had been established by the Famine generation of immigrants. As in the best work of his fellow realists discussed in the previous chapter, Dunne documented the late-nineteenth-century Irish as an ethnic group in the throes of serious strains and transformations not entirely for the better. Despite its distinctive coloration, Mr. Dooley's Bridgeport was not a stable community. By the nineties the children of the Famine immigrants (those who, as Dooley remarks, had been "born away from home") were making it into the American middle class in large numbers—but not without cost to their sense of identity as individuals and as an ethnic group. The stairway of upward mobility was strewn with cases of swallowed pride and stifled traditions, and the Chicago Dooley pieces embody the peculiar mixture of fulfillment and frustration that went along with being Irish in America at that time. Pioneering, incisive, and memorable are Dunne's delineations of three important indicators of the dissolution of community in Bridgeport: the scramble for material success and respectability in the older generation, the inevitable gap between immigrant parents and their

American children, and the widening gulf between an emergent bourgeoisie and the poor who are always with us.

The American dream of success drove damaging wedges into the
immigrant community. Irish landlords rackrent and even evict their tenants in several pieces, which illustrate how land and money hunger are
breaking up Bridgeport. "Of all th' landlords on earth," Mr. Dooley gen-
eralizes, "th' Lord deliver me fr'm an Irish wan. Whether 'tis that fr'm
niver holdin' anny land in th' ol' counthry they put too high a fondness
on their places whin they get a lot or two over here, I don't know; but
they're quicker with th' constable thin anny others" (127). Related here
is Mr. Dooley's sense of the now familiar rhythm, already established in
his time, of the flight of older, successful residents to new neighborhoods
to escape an influx of poorer groups, a phenomenon which gets definitive
fictional treatment in Farrell's *Studs Lonigan* trilogy. The ethnic makeup
of Bridgeport was changing rapidly in the nineties, and Mr. Dooley contrasts the "fightin' tinth precint" in the old days, when it was the strong-
hold of "ancient Hellenic" heroes from Mayo and Tipperary, and the same
precinct in 1897, by which time "th' Hannigans an' Leonidases an' Caseys" have moved out, "havin' made their pile," and "Polish Jews an'
Swedes an' Germans an' Hollanders" have "swarmed in, settlin' down
on the sacred sites" (122). A particularly disturbing sign of "change an'
decay" is the appointment of a "Polacker" as tender of the strategic red
bridge, which takes control of the gate to Bridgeport out of Irish hands
(123). Often Dunne satirized the new nativism of old immigrants, the
American Protective Association, and Anglo-Saxon supremacists, as
when Mr. Dooley declares that "an Anglo-Saxon, Hinnissy, is a German
that's forgot who was his parents" (*Peace and War* 54).

In addition, the Dooley pieces are full of references to the disappearance of the old "rough an' tumble" in favor of the insidious scramble
for genteel status. For example, in Mr. Dooley's youth only people who
were under arrest got their names in the paper. But now, "I see hard
wurrukin' men thrampin' down to the newspaper offices with little items
about a christenin' or a wake an' havin' it read to thim in th' mornin' at
breakfuss befure they start to th' mills" (136). Another case in point, and
an example of Dunne's gift for sparkling dialogue, is the debate between
Mr. and Mrs. Hogan on the sensitive subject of naming their children.
After the births of Sarsfield, Lucy, Honoria, Veronica, and Charles Stewart
Parnell Hogan, the old man tries to name his tenth child "Michael" after
his father. "Ye'll be namin' no more children iv mine out iv dime novels,"
he declares. "An' ye'll name no more iv mine out iv th' payroll iv th'
bridge depar-rtmint," says his wife. In the end, Mr. Dooley is on hand
to watch the new baby christened—Augustus, "th' poor, poor child" (138-
39).

Signs of dissolving cultural unity naturally appeared early among
Bridgeport's young people, and Dunne created several characters who

reveal the problems of a generation gap compounded by immigration. The tragic dimension of this important theme is explored in Mr. Dooley's stories of the young criminals, Jack Carey and Petey Scanlan. More often, however, he provides lighter treatments of this typical ethnic conflict. Notable here is Molly Donahue, a lively, fad-conscious Bridgeport teenager who squares off against her immigrant father in a half-dozen Dooley pieces. She first scandalizes the neighbors by riding a bicycle down Archer Avenue in bloomers, after which she is sent off to confession to receive "a pinance th' like iv which ain't been knowed in Bridgeport since Cassidy said Char-les Stewart Parnell was a bigger man thin th' pope" (142). Mr. Dooley blames Molly's education at a stylish convent school where "she larned to pass th' butther in Frinch an' to paint all th' chiny dishes in th' cubb'rd, so that whin Donahue come home wan night an' et his supper, he ate a green paint ha-arp along with his cabbage" (140). In other appearances, Molly campaigns for the vote, for Elizabeth Cady Stanton's revised "Woman's Bible," and for the liberation of the New Woman "fr'm th' opprision iv man." Finally, the Donahues purchase the ultimate symbol of the new respectability—a piano in the parlor, and Molly's recital for the envious neighbors prompts a classic confrontation between old customs and new pretensions. Instead of the "Wicklow Mountaineer" requested by her father, Molly pleases her mother by playing "Choochooski" and Wagner, "th' music iv th' future" (144-45).

Higher education also began to be possible for the Irish in the later nineteenth century, and Bridgeport boys come trooping home from South Bend and Wisconsin with long hair, altered speech, and delusions of superiority. In one piece, the Dennehy boy comes home from Notre Dame and shames his father into wearing his shoes after supper and getting his bucket of beer from the corner saloon "in a handbag." A piece about education which brings together several important themes is the one about the parochial school graduation of "Hennessy's youngest" in 1895. After a recitation of Emmet's speech from the dock, a flute solo of "Kathleen Mavourneen," and a moralizing play reminiscent of Mary Anne Sadlier's fiction in which the devil and a good angel fight for the soul of Tommy Casey, the Hennessy boy gets up to give the valedictory address wearing "a long black coat an' a white nicktie. . . . What was needed to be done, he said, was f'r young min to take up th' battle iv life an' fight it out coorajously. He'd been very busy at school for some years, but now that he'd gradjooated he thought he'd have time to put things in ordher." This little scene dramatizes in a flash two sad gaps—one social, one cultural: the distance between immigrants and their children and the distance between realism and genteel rhetoric. The Hennessy boy has separated himself from his father by two suits of armor: the long black coat and the brashly dispensed, fuzzy rhetoric of moral uplift that he has learned at school. A stolid millworker of few words and Mr. Dooley's favorite butt, Hennessy is much disturbed by his son's speech. The occasion forces him

to grope through to a kind of enlightenment, and the result is his one
unanswerable remark in the Dooley canon:

"His father come over with me afther th' intertainment an' he looked blue.
'What's th' matther with ye?' says I. 'Does it remind ye iv ye'er own boyhood
days,' I says, 'whin ye was gradjooated be th' toe iv th' hidge schoolmasther's
boot?' I says. 'No,' says he. "Tis not that,' he says. 'I was on'y thinkin' afther
hearin' Joe's o-ration,' he says, 'that I've lived a misspent life,' he says. 'I
niver give care nor thought to th' higher jooties iv citizenship,' he says.
'Mebbe,' he says, 'I had to wurruk too hard,' he says. 'Go home,' says I. 'I'm
goin' to close up,' I says." [50-52]

A great eroding force against Irish-American community in the 1890s
was the growing tension between middle-class respectability and the constant of poverty and destitution. The national economic depression of
1893-1898 was aggravated in Chicago by an exploding immigrant population, labor unrest, and a series of bitter-cold winters. The suffering of
Bridgeport's poor is a frequent Dooley topic, and he renders it with the
mingled anger, frustration, and compassion of a member of the afflicted
culture. The result is a chunk of living social history available nowhere
else. An important theme is the difference between heartless, humiliating
organized relief programs and personal charity dispensed with consideration for the pride of the recipient. Out-of-work laborer Callaghan tells
the sanctimonious St. Vincent de Pauls to "take ye'er charity, an' shove
it down ye'er throats," even though the cost of refusal is his family's health
(166). And Mrs. Hagan, the wife of a blacklisted railroad worker, drives
the Ladies' Aid Society from her door, even though "some iv thim was
f'r foorcin' their way in an' takin' an invintory" (169).

Dunne brought a Swiftian savage indignation to his strongest pieces
on the contrast between rich and poor, many of which were written during
the winter of 1896-97, the fourth in a row of hard winters in Chicago, and
the worst. In one piece Sobieski, a laid-off immigrant millworker, is driven
by desperation and his eight freezing children to pick up bits of coal on
the railroad tracks, a "far worse" crime, says Mr. Dooley, "thin breakin'
th' intherstate commerce act." Surprised by a watchman and frightened
by his gun, Sobieski starts to run away and is shot in the back. Then he
"pitched over on his face, thried to further injure th' comp'ny be pullin'
up th' rails with his hands, an' thin passed to where—him bein' a Pole,
an' dyin' in such a horrible sin—they'se no need iv coal iv anny kind."
In scenes such as this, Dunne is doing his part to overturn the popular
literary convention of the happy death. Had he been properly "educated,"
Mr. Dooley suggests cynically, Sobieski would not have been in the railroad yard at all, but "comfortably joltin' th' watchman's boss in a dark
alley downtown. Idyacation is a gr-reat thing" (197-98).

One of the most memorable Dooley pieces is the haunting story of
Mother Clancy, a stoical immigrant from Galway who finds herself des-

titute on alien soil. For remaining aloof and independent, this woman is feared by her neighbors. For speaking Gaelic—her own language—she is branded a witch and her house is stoned. On the point of starvation, she comes asking for help to the pompous Dougherty, chairman of the "Society f'r th' Relief iv th' Desarvin' Poor," who cuts her to the quick by offering only to "sind a man to invistigate ye'er case." The piece concludes as follows:

> "I dinnaw what it was, but th' matther popped out iv Dougherty's head an' nayether that day nor th' nex' nor th' nex' afther that was annything done f'r th' Galway woman. I'll say this f'r Dougherty, that whin th' thing come back to his mind again he put on his coat an' hurried over to Main sthreet. They was a wagon in th' sthreet, but Dougherty took no notice iv it. He walked up an' rapped on th' dure, an' th' little priest stepped out, th' breast iv his overcoat bulgin'. 'Why, father,' he says, 'ar-re ye here? I jus' come f'r to see—' 'Peace,' said th' little priest, closin' th' dure behind him an' takin' Dougherty be th' ar-rm. 'We were both late.' But 'twas not till they got to th' foot iv th' stairs that Dougherty noticed that th' wagon come fr'm th' county undertaker, an' that 'twas th' chalice made th' little priest's coat to bulge." [191-92]

As Mr. Dooley recognizes, the tragedy here is that everyone in this story is Irish. Before the Famine, cottage doors in Ireland stood open at mealtimes, and anyone passing on the road felt free to come in. When the Famine came, the doors were shut out of dire necessity. There simply wasn't enough food to go around. Here in America, land of plenty, Mr. Dooley finds the doors being shut once again—but for a different reason. In some ways, the price of respectability was very high indeed. Dunne chose not to republish most of his tragic poverty pieces, for he seems to have bridled at their biting social criticism. While preparing his 1899 collection *Mr. Dooley in the Hearts of His Countrymen*, he wrote his publisher that "I have piled up my old Dooleys—enough for ten books—none of which could be read by a taxpayer" (Fanning, *Dunne* 209). Still, in spite of Dunne's own misgivings, this group of columns is a moving testament of concern for the urban poor, and a rare firsthand account of a crisis potentially as destructive to the Chicago Irish community as the Famine had been to the peasants of Ireland.

Two last groups of Dooley columns remain to be examined: first, the pieces that illustrate the aspect of Dunne's genius that makes him the rightful heir to the linguistic subversives and experimentalists of pre-Famine Irish-American fiction, and second, the powerfully dark pieces of Dunne's last Chicago year that suggest why his Bridgeport chronicle stopped dead at the end of 1897. The Chicago Dooley pieces contain satiric, parodic, and linguistic accomplishments that carry on the Irish and Irish-American tradition of linguistic subversion that was introduced in chapter 1. This idea of using the English language against itself is traceable to that obscuring, linguistic self-contradiction, the "Irish Bull," first noted in Ireland by Elizabethan travelers, and it carries through later periods on down to James Joyce's attempt in *Finnegans Wake* to turn English into his own language. The satiric flights of Jonathan Swift in *A Tale of a Tub* and *The Battle of the Books* also come to mind, as does the "sesquipedalian and stilted nonsense" of William Carleton's pompous hedge-school philomaths. Moreover, the acknowledged heir to Joyce in this regard has been Flann O'Brien, whose fiction and newspaper columns as "Myles na Gopaleen" kept the tradition of linguistic subversion alive into the 1960s.[15] There is also a dark side to this linguistic comedy. Ultimately, the act of subverting the language can become the only meaning conveyed. With its message that real communication is impossible, the act comes to a dead end in absurdity or nonsense, and is finally an expression of despair. Perhaps Samuel Beckett provides the last word here, in his decision to write in French, thus relegating English to the secondary position of translation, and in the denial of objective validity conveyed in so much of his drama and fiction.

Dunne's Irish-American predecessors in the vein of linguistic subversion include Lawrence Sweeney, whose 1769 broadside parody of humble petitioning opened this book, Mathew Carey, whose "Hudibrastic" mock-epic polemics in defense of himself and his Irish background appeared at the turn of the nineteenth century, and the remarkable group of satirists who flourished in the twenty years before the Famine immigration. In Dunne's time, there were also other books published indicating that the structural loosening up and language play of the pre-Famine satirists, lost to Irish-American literature in the Famine generation, had reappeared toward the end of the century. Set in New Orleans, James Dugan's *Doctor Dispachemquic: A Story of the Great Southern Plague of 1878* (1879) is a strange collection of slapstick sketches and anecdotes featuring the quack doctor, a graduate of a "cold water medical school" who treats all illnesses with an ice-water spray. One patient, Mike O'Grady, gets a transfusion of blood from a mongrel dog and ends up trying to tree a cat. A pair of allegorical California novels further demonstrate an adventurousness about linguistic experimentation. In *Mucca Scob, or Threads of Pre-Historic and Present History Concatenated* (1885) by Teague M. Kelly, a pre-historic Indian narrator is joined by an influx of "Fire Landers" who prospect for gold, build bridges, and cause trouble all over northern California. The novel is full of indecipherable code names for people, places, and events. James Doran's *Zanthon: A Novel* (1891) is a sustained and less obscure allegory of nineteenth-century Irish immigrant history. The protagonist is a prophecy man from "Footford" in an unnamed country, obviously Ireland. There are some vivid descriptions of the Famine, landlord-tenant relations, inadequate government efforts to relieve suffering, and emigration to the American West, and a climactic prediction of America as a just and classless society in the future.

The best of these novels is a bizarre, picaresque tale out of San An-

tonio, Texas, *Timothy Winebruiser: A Narrative in Prose and Verse* (1886) by
James Nestor Gallagher. Very like the pre-Famine political satires of *Paddy
O'Flarrity* and *Father Quipes*, this book details the life and adventures of
a brash young Irish Texan who leaves school "twelfth in a class of a dozen"
and ends up in the state legislature, after an extremely checkered career
that involves grave-robbing, alligator-wrestling, the law, teaching school,
attempted (and successful) marriages to two rich southern belles, and
constant drinking and fighting. The tone throughout is rollicking and
randy, and features disgusting enumerations of strange foods consumed,
risqué paeons to the female body, and declarations of contempt for gen-
teel/romantic literature. (The preface asserts that the book contains "no
tear-drowning love scenes nor marrow-raking exploits.") There are also
a number of parodies—of secret society initiation rites (when Timothy
joins the local grange), political oratory (when he runs for office), and
sentimental verse (which he perpetrates at the drop of a hat). A similar
vein also runs beyond Dunne into later Irish-American fiction, from the
bravura conversational performances in Edwin O'Connor's novels to the
rhetorical flights toward nihilism in J.P. Donleavy and Tom McHale. The
final chapter of this study will return once more to these matters.

At any rate, practiced by writers before the Famine, lost to the Famine
generation, and reclaimed by Finley Peter Dunne was the Irish and Irish-
American tradition of linguistic and satiric exaggeration and excess. Like
so many others in this line, Mr. Dooley's is a voice drunk on language,
capable of outrageous punning, bizarre turns of phrase, wildly surreal
juxtapositions, non-sequitorial anecdotes, and inspired flights toward
nonsense. Dunne's love of language and fascination with its potential
come through in Mr. Dooley's insistent verbal playfulness. There are
enough ingenious double-entendres and portmanteau words scattered
through the Dooley pieces to warrant at least passing comparison with
Joyce, the master wordsmith. "Jackuse," screams Emile Zola at the trial
of Captain Dreyfus, "which is a hell of a mane thing to say to anny man."
Admiral Dewey cables home from Manila that "at eight o'clock I begun
a peaceful blockade iv this town. Ye can see th' pieces ivrywhere," while
on the Cuban front "Tiddy Rosenfelt" lays single-handed siege to "San-
dago." And when the smoke clears, and President McKinley asks "What
shall we do with th' fruits iv victhry?", a voice from the audience answers
"Can thim." There is great admiration expressed for Rudyard Kipling's
occasional verse: "Ivrything fr-resh an' up to date. All lays laid this mornin'." The first Thanksgiving features a football game between the Lambs
and the Arks, and the star players are Cotton Mather, Bradbury Standish,
Preserved Fish, and Canned Salmon. Meanwhile in Chicago, a city that
rose "felix-like" from the ashes of the 1871 Fire, the river flows backward
toward its "sewerce," the German "Turnd'-ye-mind" meets in Schwartz-
meister's back room, and Lake Shore millionaires marry to the strains of

"th' Wagner Palace Weddin' March fr'm 'Long Green,' " after exchanging
vows before "Hyman, which is the Jew god iv marredge."

There are also occasional sustained linguistic and imaginative flights
into surreal absurdity. One of the best is Mr. Dooley's wild commentary
on the use of expert testimony in the trial of Chicagoan Adolph Luetgert,
who was accused in 1897 of murdering his wife and mingling her remains
with the raw materials in his sausage factory. All hell breaks loose when
the court calls in a college professor to give scientific evidence:

> "Profissor," says th' lawyer f'r the State, "I put it to ye if a wooden vat three
> hundherd an' sixty feet long, twenty-eight feet deep, an' sivinty-five feet
> wide, an' if three hundherd pounds iv caustic soda boiled, an' if the leg iv a
> guinea pig, an' ye said yestherdah about bi-carbonate iv soda, an' if it washes
> up an' washes over, an' th' slimy, slippery stuff, an' if a false tooth or a lock
> iv hair or a jawbone or a goluf ball across th' cellar eleven feet nine inches—
> that is two inches this way an' five gallons that?" "I agree with ye intirely,"
> says th' profissor." [313]

After all this, Mr. Dooley declares that "the jury'll pitch th' tistimony out
iv th' window, an' consider three questions: 'Did Lootgert look as though
he'd kill his wife? Did his wife look as though she ought to be kilt? Isn't
it time we wint to supper?' "

Dunne had a great gift for parody, and a major theme throughout his
career as Mr. Dooley is the abuse of political speech for selfish ends. In
this he recalls his pre-Famine satiric predecessors: Lawrence Sweeney and
Mathew Carey, the willfully nonsensical, self-praising campaign biographies of "Father Quipes" and "Paddy O'Flarrity," and the parodies of
political oratory in Moore's *Tom Stapleton* and Mack's *The Priest's Turf-
Cutting Day*. Of course, Dunne also has distinguished compeers in the
dissection of political posturing back in Ireland, from Jonathan Swift's "A
Modest Proposal" to James Joyce's "Cyclops" chapter of *Ulysses*, with its
definitive critique of one-eyed nationalism. For his part, Mr. Dooley is a
master at detecting propaganda. He exposes rhetorical excess and hypocrisy on every possible political level: in his own Bridgeport precinct,
in downtown Chicago municipal affairs, in the camps and journals of the
Irish nationalists, in the 1896 presidential campaign, and in the jingoist
speeches of apologists for American imperialism in Cuba and the Philippines. And everywhere, the humorous deflation of the highfalutin is
one of Dunne's favorite means of cutting through to the deeper duplicity
of character whose exposure is at the core of so much of his best work.
Thus, linguistic subversion reinforces literary realism when presented
through the clear-eyed perspective of Mr. Dooley.

By 1897, the fifth year of his editorship at the Chicago *Evening Post*,
Dunne's inside perspective on the realities of American city life had
brought about a significant darkening of his world view, which was passed

along to Mr. Dooley. Although the leaven of humor remains, there is in the Dooley pieces of that year a definite downhill slide toward cynicism and pessimism. The tone was set on December 5, 1896, with the story of the death of Mother Clancy, the Galway woman. Then came a powerful group of pieces published through the harsh winter. The piece about the starving Sobieski shot for stealing coal appeared in January, and was followed by a Dooley attack on Chicago's humiliating plan to have relief money distributed by policemen: "Why don't they get the poor up in a cage in Lincoln Park an' hand thim food on th' ind iv a window pole, if they're afraid they'll bite?" (200). Next came a chilling anecdote from the Famine years in Ireland in which a tenant maddened by his child's death murders his landlord. In March and April the slide continued with a cynical four-part series on Chicago politics in which Mr. Dooley runs for mayor as the self-proclaimed tool of street-railway robber baron, Charles T. Yerkes, promising to "deliver over a blanket morgedge on th' town to that saint on earth, th' Sthreet Car Magnum," who "searches out th' hearts iv men, an' whin he finds thim r-rings thim up" (248). This group ends with the despairing political parable of the crow in the tree.

In May 1897, Dunne began an exploration of the human propensity for self-delusion that carries through the rest of the Chicago Dooley pieces. The first is a treatment of suicide as the ultimate delusion, because "th' man that kills himsilf always has th' thought sthrong in his mind that he will be prisint at the ceremonies, lookin' on like a man in th' gallery iv th' Lyceum Theater" (302). Mr. Dooley goes on from here to mark Queen Victoria's Diamond Jubilee in June 1897 by exposing the popular faith in progress as a general delusion: "I have seen America spread out fr'm th' Atlantic to th' Pacific with a branch office iv The Standard Ile Comp'ny in ivry hamlet. I've seen th' shackles dropped fr'm th' slave, so's he cud be lynched in Ohio" (305). Next, Mr. Dooley claims that Bridgeport working men are deluding themselves on the Fourth of July: "Today they're cillybratin' th' declaration iv indepindince that they never heerd tell iv. To-morrah they'll be shovellin' sand or tampin' a thrack with a boss standin' over thim that riprisints all they know iv th' power iv providince" (308). Never does Dunne allow Mr. Dooley to express the hope that men can become less deluded. On the contrary, he begins to accept self-delusion as a necessary condition of life. In explaining why he refused to attend the dedication of a new statue downtown, he argues that "to me th' Logan monymint is a hundred miles high an' made iv goold. That's because I niver seed it. If I'd gone with you it'd be no higher than an Injun cigar sign an' built iv ol' melted down dog tags an' other joolry" (311).

This black mood continued into the fall with Mr. Dooley's assessment of a scheme for municipal ownership of the street railways and electric plants: "It's on'y a question iv who does th' robbin'. Th' diff'rence is between pickin' pockets an' usin' a lead pipe." And in November came a definitive portrait of a rackrenting Irish-American landlord who had "tinants be th' scoor that prayed at nights f'r him that he might live long an' taste sorrow" (130). At last, during the Christmas holidays of 1897, Dunne wrote a bleak yet beautiful three-part meditation on the inevitable cycle of suffering and self-delusion in which Bridgeport and the world are caught. This remarkable group of pieces marks the virtual conclusion of his Bridgeport chronicle. Shortly after the turn of the year, Dunne officially ended the series with a bitter farewell piece in which Mr. Dooley searches for concrete, positive results attributable to his talking career in Chicago and finds none: "An' what's it come to? What's all th' histhry an' pothry an' philosophy I've give ye an' th' Archey road f'r all these years come to? Nawthin. Th' la-ads I abused ar-re makin' money so fast it threatens to smother thim. Th' wans I stud up f'r is some in jail an' some out iv wurruk" (326). At the end of the piece, Mr. Dooley locks the door and turns out the lights, "perhaps for the last time." This was no casual good-bye. Halfway through his own thirtieth year, Peter Dunne had despaired of changing the world with his pen. In addition, the decision to relinquish his position as their spokesman also indicates Dunne's identification with the people of Bridgeport. To keep on creating parables of their suffering without real hope of helping them had become too painful. So Mr. Dooley left home rather than continuing to live among neighbors whose troubles he could only observe with frustrated anger.

One month later, in February 1898 the declaration of war against Spain provided a convenient vehicle for the return to conversation of the man who had confessed in his January farewell piece that " 'tis har-rd f'r me to lave off talkin'." A safe, general topic, the war lent itself to brisk, light handling, with little risk of emotional involvement for Dunne. Thus, with the sinking of the battleship *Maine* in Havana harbor, Mr. Dooley returned to the Chicago newspaper scene. The rest of his story is well known. The American people outside Chicago soon loved Mr. Dooley, as they had loved Hosea Biglow, Artemus Ward, and the folksy platform image of Mark Twain; for Dooley's lilting, skeptical voice remained blessedly lucid and rational. Moreover, a number of things happened to Dunne himself after 1898 to solidify the new Dooley role as a national figure. He moved to New York, thus cutting himself off from the Chicago genius loci, and he embraced syndication with its confining restrictions of topicality and tactfulness. This is not to deny the importance of Mr. Dooley's national commentary. Certainly, America was a better place for the twenty years of laughter and perspective that he provided in the second phase of his career. And yet, we ought also to regret what was lost. Appropriately, the only reviewer in Dunne's own time to understand the full extent of that loss was Francis Hackett, himself an Irish immigrant to Chicago and a veteran journalist and novelist there and in New York. In reviewing Dunne's last collection, *Mr. Dooley on Making a Will* (1919), Hackett pulls no punches in accusing Dunne of having rendered Mr. Dooley "stereo-

typed Irish or stage-Irish" in order "not to forfeit amused indulgence."
Hackett regrets that Dunne's great gifts have been used "to bring laughs
to hold down his job as court jester to the American people—or, more
properly, the American bourgeoisie. For it is the bourgeoisie whose limitations this American Juvenal has accepted." He has spent himself "on
the facetiae of summer resorts, cards, golf, newspaper fame, newspaper
doctors, newspaper Darwinism, newspaper Rockefellers and Carnegies.
. . . Yet it is the heart of life which really invites the genius that Peter
Dunne has squandered. Had he given his comic perception free rein,
what might he not have done for America?" Such, in Hackett's ironic
view, are "the penalties of respectability. Mr. Dunne is a true humorist
but not sufficiently disreputable" ("Mr. Dooley" 236).

In the three holiday pieces that constitute his last extended effort as
Mr. Martin Dooley of Bridgeport, Dunne's mind moves in a steadily widening arc from particular to universal, culminating in an eloquent statement of philosophy. "The approach of Christmas," the first piece begins,
"is heralded in Archey Road by many of the signs that are known to the
less civilized and more prosperous parts of the city. The people look
poorer, colder, and more hopeful than at other times." Enter Mr. Dooley—
to complain that exchanging gifts is often a painful custom, at least among
the poor of Bridgeport: "Ye can't give what ye want. Ivry little boy ixpects
a pony at Chris'mas, an' ivry little girl a chain an' locket; an' ivry man
thinks he's sure goin' to get th' goold-headed cane he's longed f'r since
he come over. But they all fin'lly land on rockin'-horses an' dolls, an'
suspindhers that r-run pink flowers into their shirts an' tattoo thim in
summer." So frustrated is Mr. Dooley by this annual disappointment,
that he goes out of his way to hurt poor Hennessy with an uncharacteristic
cutting rejoinder. Having just returned from a successful shopping expedition, Hennessy offers to get his friend whatever he wants for Christmas, "if 'tis within me means." Dooley strings him along, then asks for
the Auditorium Building, and Hennessy goes away "with the rocking
chair under his arm, the doll in his pocket, and dumb anger in his heart"
(317-19). A week later on Christmas Eve, Hennessy has regained his spirits, and enters the bar with a cheery "Merry Chris'mas." Once again, Mr.
Dooley is uncooperatively pessimistic, citing the constancy of poverty
along the road: "What can annywan do, I'd have ye tell me. If ye'd cut
up all th' money in th' sixth war-rd in akel parts ye cudden't buy a toy
dhrum apiece f'r th' fam'lies iv Bridgeport. It isn't this year or last. 'Tisn't
wan day or another. 'Tis th' same ivry year an' ivry day. It's been so iver
since I come here an' 'twill be so afther I'm put away an' me frinds have
stopped at th' r-road house on th' way back to count up what I owed
thim" (320).

Finally, on the following Saturday, Dunne and Dooley ring in the
New Year of 1898 with a meditation on the human condition in the form
of a parable of accepted suffering and necessary self-delusion. Summa-

rizing the downward sweep of the previous year's columns, the heart of this piece is a prose poem, the central metaphor of which is grounded fittingly in the common experience of the Irish-American laborer, for whom, in the end, all the Chicago Dooley pieces speak.

"All th' years is akel an' th' same," said Mr. Hennessy sententiously. "All th' years an' th' days."

"Thrue f'r ye," said Mr. Dooley, "yet 'tis sthrange how we saw our throubles into reg'lar lenths. We're all like me frind O'Brien that had a conthract on th' dhrainage canal. He thought he was biddin' on soft mud, but he sthruck nawthin' but th' dhrift. But he kept pluggin' away. ' 'Twill soften later,' he says. Th' ingineers tol' him he was a fool. 'Twas dhrift all th' way through. He rayfused to listen. He knew he'd come to th' mud th' nex' day or th' nex' an' so he wint on an' on an' fin'lly he got through an' made a good, clane job iv it. He looked back on his wurruk an' says he: 'I knowed it was dhrift all th' time, but if I'd let mesilf think that what was ahead was as har-rd as what was behind, I'd thrun up th' job an' broke me conthract,' he says. 'I niver borry throuble,' he says, 'but I've had to borry money to pay me men.' So it is with us. We've all taken a conthract to dig through th' glacial dhrift. We know its glacial dhrift to th' ind, but we make oursilves think 'twill come aisy wan iv these days. So we go on, with pick an' shovel, till th' wurruk is done an' we lay it down gladly." [323]

SEVEN

A Generation Lost

In 1926 Thomas Beer's Irish-American informant in *The Mauve Decade* wrote: "The Amerirish in X [his home city] who come back fondly to me in memory were the middling kind. They lived in a little colony of frame houses on three parallel streets back of St. Mary's. The men were superior mechanics or shopkeepers or little lawyers. The Nordics held them at arm's length and treated them in a half-humorous, half-condescending way, as the middle-class American treats the Catholic Irishman. . . . It is the weakness or the excessive sentiment of the Amerirish that no writer has spoken of that life in realistic terms" (111). This was far from true, as we have seen, but the important point is that by the 1920s it seemed to be true. In the Irish-American literary generation that came of age just after 1900, no writer built a career of consistent accomplishment based on the example of the proto-realists such as James W. Sullivan, William McDermott, John Talbot Smith, and Finley Peter Dunne. Nineteenth-century Irish-American fiction, including the period of heightened literary activity in the 1890s, had been forgotten. The second, twentieth-century cycle of Irish-American fiction began and ran on its own, independent of the nineteenth-century cycle. What happened was a form of cultural amnesia. There had been dozens of writers and hundreds of novels. There was "new wood" broken by writers in the last quarter of the old century, ready to be "carved" in the new. There certainly still continued to be an Irish-American ethnic life through the first three decades of the twentieth century. But writers emerging from that background did not use it to build careers as realistic novelists. There were in fact a number of promising writers starting out with the new century who began by exploring Irish ethnic experience. All of them either went on to other subjects or stopped writing entirely. Moreover, the two writers of Irish background who went on to the largest literary success in America after World War I, F. Scott Fitzgerald and John O'Hara, both avoided detailed exploration of the ethnic dimension. The concern of this chapter will be this new literary generation's wholesale movement away from consideration of Irishness.

The general decline of Irish-American cultural self-consciousness can be explained in part by concrete historical reasons. With the approach of World War I, Irish-American ethnic assertiveness became positively unsavory in the eyes of many non-Irish Americans. When the War began in August 1914, anti-British feeling surfaced again strongly in Irish-American nationalist circles. The Clan na Gael executive sent a secret message of support to the Kaiser, and less rabid Irish-American organizations also supported the Central Powers. Moreover, in the context of increasing support for United States entry into the War, the timing of the 1916 Easter Rising in Dublin was less than popular in mainstream America. This unsuccessful but symbolically weighty opening to the Irish Revolution of 1916-21 ended with 3,000 casualties and the British execution of the sixteen leaders of the rising as traitors in time of war. In 1914, President Woodrow Wilson made his famous "hyphenated Americans" speech at the unveiling of a monument to Commodore John Barry, whom Wilson praised as "an Irishman whose heart crossed the Atlantic with him," unlike some Americans, who "need hyphens in their names because only part of them has come over." Wilson and Theodore Roosevelt became the leading spokesmen in the hue and cry against "divided loyalties" which intensified with America's entry into the War in April 1917. This campaign, the War effort as England's ally, and the negative perception of Irish nationalism after the Easter Rising all contributed to a significant dampening of the fires of Irish-American ethnic self-assertion during these years.

Two further blows to Irish-American ethnicity, literary and otherwise, were the bitter conclusion of the Irish Revolution and the passage of immigration restriction legislation. The treaty signed in December 1921 to end the Revolution created the problematic partition of Northern Ireland and the Irish Free State, which, in turn, led to the heart-breaking "Troubles" of Civil War for two more years. This prolonged strife helped to destroy the powerful patriotic/nationalist component of Irish-American identity. The war in the old country was close enough to being over to satisfy the grandchildren, and even many of the children, of the nineteenth-century immigrants. And to many, the Troubles were an extremely painful coda, much better left unexplored. The agitation for immigration restriction eventually brought about severely restricted quotas which affected Ireland along with everyone else. A provisional measure passed by Congress in 1921 was succeeded by the Johnson-Reed Act of 1924, which established small and decreasing permanent quotas for admission to the United States. These quotas, along with increased competition for jobs from blacks and from other immigrant groups caused a dramatic shift in the destinations of Irish immigrants. On average, 22,000 Irish came to America yearly through the decade of the 1920s, but by 1930 three times as many Irish were emigrating to England as to America, and in the decade of the 1930s the average yearly number of Irish immigrants to America dropped to 1200. This pattern has persisted into the 1980s. With new blood from Ireland severely curtailed, Irish America became emphatically an ethnic rather than an immigrant subculture.

Furthermore, well on into the 1920s, Irish America remained an ambivalent culture in transition, still busy shoring up its hard-won incursions into the middle-class. Nor had that middle class, from whom presumably most aspiring writers would have come, been established long enough to be comfortable exploring its own shortcomings. Finally, on top of all this came the Great Depression, which effectively kept the Irish ethnic dimension in American literature in abeyance on into the 1930s. The Depression certainly devastated the working-class and newly-middle-class Irish, and not many Irish-American young people in these hard times would have had the temerity to embark upon careers as novelists. Fewer still would have seen their own backgrounds as fertile or lucrative soil for fiction. In fact, Irish Americans of college age had crossed the national average for college attendance rate by 1910, but they tended to choose pragmatic and respectable rather than artistic careers.

Most of the harder evidence behind the breaking off of the first Irish-American literary cycle comes after 1914. However, the crucial decade was 1900 to 1910. In these years, while the example of the preceding, ethnically active literary generation was still fresh, younger writers began to reject the communities, customs, and characters of their own ethnic backgrounds as proper materials for fiction. In this rejection, they were probably encouraged by the American literary establishment. An important chapter in the politics of literature needs to be written about the effect on immigrant and ethnic literature of the mainstream publishing-editing-reviewing network in the early 1900s. Anglo-Saxon supremacist, Anglophile, and anti-Catholic influences would have been particularly unhealthy for aspiring Irish-American writers. To determine whether such influences existed in the publishing establishment, ethnic writing needs the kind of literary history that has been applied to nineteenth-century domestic fiction written by American women.[1] A good beginning has been made here by Christopher Wilson, who notes in his study of "literary professionalism in the progressive era" that, while the proliferating magazines of the 1880s and 1890s welcomed realistic, colloquial depiction by authors "whose experience was outside the established literary gentry," the book trade was much more conservative. "Most major publishing firms," says Wilson, "remained basically colonial (regarding England) in orientation and taste, aristocratic in manner and aspiration, and regional (Eastern)" until much later (62,68). Nor does the dramatic turn-of-the-century reorientation of American book publishing with its new emphasis on the national best-seller seem to have benefited aspiring ethnic writers. Given the lack of encouragement by mainstream publishers, the Catholic press and publishing houses continued to provide outlets for Irish-American writing. However, the advocacy of "ideality" and opposition to realism that had characterized the official Catholic literary platform in John Boyle O'Reilly's time continued on into the new century. This orientation dominated the influential journals *America*, *Ave Maria*, and the *Catholic World*, and was passed on to *Commonweal* and *Thought*, the new Catholic intellectual journals founded in the 1920s.[2] So there was little help from Catholic literary circles for an Irish-American writer contemplating a career as a realistic novelist in the 1910s and 1920s.

Thus, Irish-American fiction really began over again with the publication in 1932 of *Young Lonigan: A Boyhood in Chicago Streets* by James T. Farrell. The Farrell generation had to establish anew the precedent of creating an American fictional world from Irish ethnic materials. Farrell himself spoke often of having had to invent his literary self from nothing, and he certainly stands out as singularly committed to the writer's life and to Irish-American materials by the late 1920s. Obviously, some writers could have made good use of such materials, while others did quite well without them. John O'Hara belongs in the former category and Scott Fitzgerald in the latter. At any rate, it remains extraordinary that the decline in the ethnic dimension of literature by Irish Americans after the turn of the century was so great that the next generation practically had to reinvent Irish-American fiction, so cut off had they become from its nineteenth-century roots. The final three chapters of this study assume that this twentieth-century reinvention was successful and that the forgotten nineteenth-century context clarifies the accomplishment of latter-day Irish-American writers such as Farrell, Edwin O'Connor, Elizabeth Cullinan, and William Kennedy.

To be sure, the vein of green-tinged, romantic Irishry continued to flourish in Irish-American fiction after 1900. True to the categories established in the nineteenth century, novelists were persistent in creating the full range of effects—from peasant picturesque to larger-than-life heroic. An example of the former is *Just Stories* (1914) by Gertrude M. O'Reilly, a collection of rustic local-color sketches of daily life in Galway and Cork on such topics as "The Peeler and the Goat" and "The New Inkybator." The author hopes to "bring the pleasant memory of home to those who like myself have wandered," and to "give some little glimpse of Ireland to those who have not had the joy of looking on her face." At the other end of the scale is a novel such as *Katrine* (1909) by Elinor Macartney Lane, which features a quintessential romantic hero, Dermot McDermott, a melancholy Celt and wounded veteran of the British army in India who ends up dominating the lives of a family of Carolina planters. Lane's preface indicates her stereotyping: "It is difficult to tell the story of Irish folk intimately and convincingly, the bare truths concerning their splendid recklessness, their unproductive ardor, their loyalty and creative memories, sounding to another race like a pack of lies." Some among the younger generation of popular romancers were impressively prolific. Born in South Boston to Irish immigrants in 1868, James Brendan Connolly wrote fiction about the sea and sailors. With his first collection of stories, *Out of Gloucester* (1902), he embarked on a production of ten novels and hundreds of stories. Some of his sailors are Irish, but these are no more grounded in place than any other of Connolly's crew of footloose, wandering characters. Also extremely prolific, Syracuse native Harold Mac-Grath wrote nearly forty novels of international adventure and intrigue, from *Arms and the Woman* (1899) about a German princess in London to

The Other Passport (1931). In his most Irish novel, *The Luck of the Irish: A Romance* (1917), MacGrath sends Bill Grogan, a New York plumber's helper and poetic dreamer, around the world to marriage in Singapore, thanks to a surprise inheritance.[3]

Of Irish-American writers at the turn of the century who began as ethnic realists and then abandoned the enterprise, Finley Peter Dunne is the salient example. His decision to leave his native Chicago and the Dooley neighborhood sketches for New York City and nationally syndicated opinion pieces was archetypal and may have influenced others. Four other writers who made a similar decision to stop exploring their own Irish backgrounds were Kathleen Norris, Clara Laughlin, John T. McIntyre, and Donn Byrne. Kathleen Thompson Norris was born in San Francisco in 1880 to a family with Irish on both sides. Her colorful maternal grandfather, Paul Moroney, was an itinerant Irish actor born in London who had gone West to San Francisco by wagon in 1852. Her even more colorful paternal grandmother, Maria O'Keefe Thompson, had come out from Cork in 1840 to Honolulu, where she ran a boarding house. Her son Jimmy married Paul Moroney's daughter Josephine, and Kathleen was their second child, raised as a Catholic and a member of what she called the San Francisco "Irishtocracy." About 1900, Kathleen Thompson got work editing the society column for the San Francisco *Call*. Over the next few years she was courted and won by a fellow journalist, Charles Norris, the brother of novelist Frank Norris. Married in 1909, they went East to New York to try to become professional writers. Charles got a subeditorship on the *American Magazine* and Kathleen set out to write fiction. Her career began auspiciously, with the surprising, smash success of her first book, the short novel, *Mother* (1911), a sentimental tale of a young schoolteacher's dawning appreciation of how much she loves her mother. Kathleen Norris went on to write some ninety books, most of them popular romances of domestic life among the fairly well-to-do, in which occasional thorny issues of the day are raised and dispatched with superficial ease.

Predating by several months the publication of *Mother*, Norris's earliest stories show signs of realistic promise using Irish materials. "What Happened to Alanna" and "The Friendship of Alanna" describe the newly rich Irish in San Francisco in the generation just after that in George Jessop's "Gerald Ffrench" stories discussed in chapter 5. The focus is the family of the Honorable F.X. Costello, "undertaker by profession, and mayor by an immense majority." Recently and unashamedly wealthy, the Costellos live in a "costly, comfortable, incongruous, and hideous" mansion which they believe to be "the finest in the city, or the world." The stories describe the exuberant and generous involvement of the family in the life of their parish. Eight-year-old Alanna plays a major role in a colorful church fair and a parish theatrical production to celebrate Mother Superior's golden jubilee. These stories contain a refreshingly direct and perceptive look at the development of an Irish middle class in the golden West. Thompson's unembarrassed admiration for the Costellos would have been difficult in New York or Boston. Occasionally in her long writing life, Norris returned to Irish-American materials, but there is little depth and less critical realism in her treatments of the newly rich in *Little Ships* (1925) and the lower-middle-class in *The Callahans and the Murphys* (1924).[4]

Clara E. Laughlin was the daughter of immigrants from Belfast who had come to Milwaukee and then settled in Chicago. Beginning as a journalist, Laughlin became an editor at *McClure's Magazine* in the 1890s. She became a popular sentimental/genteel writer with her first published novels, *The Evolution of a Girl's Ideal* (1902), *When Joy Begins* ("A Little Story of the Woman-Heart," 1905), and *Felicity* (1907), and she went on to write a number of successful travel books as well. Her single foray into realistic fiction was the 1910 novel, *"Just Folks"*, about the poverty-stricken Casey family who live in a back basement in Chicago's old Nineteenth Ward not far from Hull-House in a neighborhood in transition from an Irish to a Jewish ghetto. Published first as a group of stories in *McClure's* and *Ainslie's* magazines, the novel adds the unifying consciousness of a narrator, a juvenile-court probation officer for the ward. By exposure to the Casey family's many troubles, young Beth Tully learns the complexity of human relations and her limits as a solver of social problems. The mother Mary Casey is a true matriarch, holding her family together by hard work, sheer determination, and prayers to the Blessed Virgin. The cornerstone of her sustaining faith is love for her unreliable but charming husband, presented plausibly by Laughlin as a disarmingly naive believer in his own doomed schemes to rescue the family from poverty.

Also effective is Laughlin's contrast between Mary Casey's strength and faith and the "broken-spirited" weakness of her hypochondriacal, childless sister, the "ginteel" but profoundly unhappy Mrs. Foley. Laughlin presents the Caseys' teeming cellar as clearly preferable to the Foleys' moribund "swell" lakefront apartment with its "mantel-shelf shrouded in a voluminous purple drape and burdened with innumerable fancy cups and vases" (140). At the same time, Laughlin describes realistically the "starvation of many sorts" that ultimately drives the eldest Casey daughter to leave home. A factory worker since she was eleven, seventeen-year-old Angela Ann answers the advertisement of an unscrupulous dramatic agent who packs her off in a carousing "road company" to the downstate coal mining area. Several months later, the girl returns ill and contrite and unable to answer her mother's pleading question: "Tell me ye've kep' dacint, gyurl." Nevertheless, she is forgiven and taken back into the family, and Laughlin clearly presents Mary Casey's heartfelt sympathy for her daughter as preferable to Mrs. Foley's pose of scandalized respectability. Strong stuff for a woman writer at this time, Laughlin's compassionate position here has much in common with the pioneering critique of genteel values in Kate O'Flaherty Chopin's astonishing novel of 1899, *The Awakening*, in which the heroine refutes boredom and society's hypocrisy with her own suicide. Mary Casey is a strong woman whose honest, expressive emotions are to be trusted: joy at the birth of a new child, grief at her baby's death and her daughter's desertion, forgiveness at her daughter's return. Beth Tully recognizes her as irrefutably sincere: "Mary Casey lived too deeply and truly to miss any essential element of life" (223). Unfortunately, this character and the realistic depiction of life among the urban poor in *"Just Folks"* are unique in the Laughlin canon, which is otherwise populated with a parade of cardboard gentlefolk in idealized, romantic settings.[5]

The son of Patrick and Sarah (Walker) McIntyre, John T. McIntyre was born in 1871 in Philadelphia, where he went through high school and began to write sketches for the Sunday newspapers. He was encouraged toward fiction by the prestigious Chicago *Chap-Book*, which accepted a story in 1897, and his first published book was *The Ragged Edge: A Tale of Ward Life and Politics* (1902), a realistic novel of daily life in a Philadelphia Irish neighborhood. McIntyre wrote a few more stories in the vein of urban, ethnic realism, and then took his career abruptly in another direction and began writing juvenile historical fiction (*Fighting King George*, 1905) and detective novels (*In the Dead of Night*, 1908). Through the teens and twenties he produced several novels in these genres, and he also wrote a few successful melodramas for the stage. McIntyre returned to adult serious fiction toward the end of his life, and wrote *Slag* (1927), a grim story of gangsters, and two additional novels of urban life, *Steps Going Down* (1936) and *Signing Off* (1938).

The Ragged Edge was the most promising realistic Irish-American novel of the lost generation that preceded the beginning of James T. Farrell's career. "A Tale of Ward Life and Politics" in South Philadelphia, it features a detailed description of a campaign for city selectman between machine and reform candidates. There is backroom maneuvering over a streetcar contract, a candidates' parade led by the Emmet Band, election tampering, and analysis of the rise of Boss McQuirk from dump-cart driver to silk-hatted ward committeeman. Only in Dunne's Mr. Dooley columns is there so close a study of the quest for political power in urban Irish America in the 1890s. Also reminiscent of Mr. Dooley is McIntyre's solid evocation of an Irish neigborhood. A complex social life centers around Kelly's saloon and the slightly tonier Oyster Bar Club. The system of education leads from parish schools to the Academy of the Sacred Heart "where the girls of the parish are taught by the gentle-mannered sisters," to the Normal School teacher-training program that represents the height of intellectual aspiration in this community. Irish nationalism is debated hotly at the barbershop, and some of those arguing about the fall of Parnell and the rise of John Redmond are rumored to be former members of the Clan na Gael.

The Ragged Edge opens with an effective organizing event, as the attention of the entire ward turns to the death of old Larry Murphy, neighborhood patriarch, successful immigrant, and landlord of Murphy's Court. In one classic vignette, at Murphy's front-parlor wake the O'Hara sisters mutter prayers in Gaelic and sway "back and forth in unison," causing one onlooker to remark, "It's comin', . . . divil choke thim!" What comes is the keen, "a long low wail . . . that immediately filled the kitchen doorway with the grinning faces of the men." At this point, the dead man's niece approaches and orders the old women to stop, explaining that "the custom is not understood in this country" (63-4). Here the pressures of American middle-class respectability dictate the withholding of emotion in the house.[6]

McIntyre's earlier short fiction also contains realistic rendering of Irish-American experience. For example, "The Three Wise Men" (1906) evokes late-nineteenth-century parochial school life. Riley and Hopkins, two of the rougher students, set out to win the St. Augustine Day prize, awarded for writing a two-hundred-word essay on the three greatest men in the world. Their researches in the neighborhood reveal a variety of attitudes. The fruitseller Old Shamus names Brian Boru, Daniel O'Connell, and Parnell. (That the boys only recognize Brian, who "licked somebody in Ireland once: we got a picture of it being done," is a measure of their generation's distance from the old country.) Dan Callahan the bartender chooses the contemporary heroes of this subculture, "Jack Dempsey, John L., and Fitz." Finally, by astute detective work, Riley and Hopkins discover that the list of the parish priest (and contest judge) would include St. Augustine, Shakespeare, and Mozart, and by looking up these three in the library, the boys win the prize. The picture here of the parochial school and the priest as a man of real culture and erudition is vivid and convincing. The story certainly provided an antidote to the plethora of brogue-laden, caricatured Irish priests that had already begun to populate magazine fiction in this period. It is a pity that John McIntyre turned away from this material for the next three decades of his writing life.[7]

Born in 1889 to an itinerant Irish family temporarily in America, Brian Oswald Donn Byrne was raised in South Armagh. He studied in Dublin, traveled in Europe, and came back to America in 1911. Here he married an Irish girl in Brooklyn and began to write poems and stories. Published in 1914 and 1915, Byrne's first stories were followed by a novel, *The Stranger's Banquet* (1919), which deals with labor unrest in a shipyard owned by a larger-than-life Irish seafarer. Though successful enough to be sold to the silent movies, it is a very uneven book, and the New York *Times* reviewer counseled Byrne toward a promising future, "provided he is willing to leave realism to others and devote himself to the sort of mystic romance which would seem to be his proper métier." Having taken this advice to heart, Byrne had a huge success in 1921 with *Messer Marco Polo*, a love story of Marco Polo's journey to China as narrated by an Irish storyteller. Subsequently, he made his popular and lucrative way as a purveyor of romantic, Celtic-twilight Irishry, in novels set in the recent past (*The Wind Bloweth*, 1922) or the more distant past (*Blind Raftery and His Wife, Hilaria*, 1924). These novels are facile, readable, popular romances, full of colorful scenes and simplistic moral choices.

Byrne's earliest work suggests that he could have become a significant realistic writer, had fortune and fame as a romancer not attracted him. One of his first stories, "The Wake," is a restrained, moving treatment of an unhappy marriage between a young girl and an old farmer. The ill-fated solution to circumstances that drove so many Irish people to America, this familiar situation also appears in John M. Synge's first play *The Shadow of the Glen* of 1903. Set in contemporary Ireland, "The Wake" was as close to the real problems of his own fellow exiles as Donn Byrne ever came. *The Stranger's Banquet* also has some realistic materials, however, for it explores strikes and incipient unionization and contains portraits of socialists, anarchists, and I.W.W. agitators. Moreover, Byrne touches on the perils of American success in his characterization of the dissipated son of old Shane Butler Keogh, the rugged immigrant ship-building magnate. A golf champion and graduate of Groton, the boy marries a scheming social climber and becomes a desperate alcoholic.

Such themes were not to engage Byrne for long. His twelve subsequent works of fiction constitute a full-scale retreat from realism. His career is thus a fitting symbol of the literary rejection of their own immediate ethnic past by his generation of Irish-American writers. Another symbol of that rejection was Byrne's purchase of a castle in West Cork, where he died in an automobile crash in 1928, only thirty-eight years old. At least one contemporary Irish critic approved Byrne's career direction. The anti-realist Shane Leslie praised "the fine flag of romance which Donn Byrne unfurled from a castle in Cork," while deploring the "mean and meaner streets in which Gissing and Zola and George Moore delved for their muddy material." In the same piece, Leslie scolded James Joyce for having "poured forth the Liffey into the Cloaca Maxima of Letters."[8]

Ambivalence about ethnicity in the emerging Irish-American bourgeoisie appears in the later nineteenth century in the fiction of Maurice Francis Egan and others. The most famous earlier twentieth-century examples are two writers who, like their lesser known and slightly older contemporaries such as Byrne and McIntyre, also avoided concentrating on realistic ethnic materials in their own fiction. Despite his brief life of forty-four years and his relatively small corpus of fiction, F. Scott Fitzgerald has been much studied and praised. John O'Hara lived to age sixty-five, wrote many books, and has had a fluctuating critical reputation. Both chose not to write very often or very directly about their middle-class Irish backgrounds, and thus their fiction will not be discussed in detail in this study of Irish-American literary self-images. There has been significant critical work done on the Irish dimension in both writers, however, and the following brief discussion owes much to these earlier essays.[9]

The grandson of Famine immigrants on his mother's side and descended from an old-line, partly Irish Maryland family on his father's, Francis Scott Key Fitzgerald was raised in St. Paul, Minnesota, and educated in the East at the private Catholic Newman School and at Princeton. Early, perceptive acknowledgements of Fitzgerald's Irishness and his ambivalence came from his friends Edmund Wilson and Malcolm Cowley. In 1922 Wilson wrote that "in regard to the man himself, there are perhaps two things worth knowing, for the influence they have had on his work. In the first place, he comes from the Middle West. . . . The second thing one should know about him is that Fitzgerald is partly Irish and that he brings both to life and to fiction certain qualities that are not Anglo-Saxon. For, like the Irish, Fitzgerald is romantic, but also cynical about romance; he is bitter as well as ecstatic; astringent as well as lyrical. He casts himself in the role of playboy, yet at the playboy he incessantly mocks. He is vain, a little malicious, of quick intelligence and wit, and has an Irish gift for turning language into something iridescent and surprising." Wilson's observations followed Fitzgerald's first two novels, *This Side of Paradise* (1920) and *The Beautiful and Damned* (1922), when all seemed possible for the dashing young novelist. On the other hand, Cowley was sensitive to the downside of Fitzgerald's ambivalence in his 1934 review of *Tender Is the Night*: "Fitzgerald has always been the poet of the American upper bourgeoisie; he has been the only writer able to invest their lives with glamor. Yet he has never been sure that he owed his loyalty to the class about which he was writing. It is as if he had a double personality. Part of him is a guest at the ball given by the people in the big house; part of him has been a little boy peeping in through the window and being thrilled by the music and the beautifully dressed women—a romantic but hardheaded little boy who stops every once in a while to wonder how much it all cost and where the money came from. In his early books, this divided personality was wholly an advantage; it enabled him to portray American society from the inside, and yet at the same time to surround it with an atmosphere of magic and romance." Lately, "and now that the ball is ending in tragedy," Cowley continues, "he doesn't know how to describe it—whether as a guest, a participant, in which case he will be writing a purely psychological novel; or whether from the detached point of view of a social historian." In another piece, Cowley compares Fitzgerald to Finley Peter Dunne: "Like Dunne, he had been accepted into the ruling Protestant group, and unlike Dunne he wrote about that group, so that his Irishness was a little disguised, but it remained an undertone in all his stories; it gave him a sense of standing apart that sharpened his observation of social differences."[10] Herein, thus, are the positive and negative sides of ethnic ambivalence in American literary culture. With few exceptions (Charles Cannon and John Boyle O'Reilly are two), nineteenth-century Irish-American writers were spared the full force of this tension because they neither aspired to nor achieved the mainstream literary success in which Fitzgerald especially was the trailblazer. And Fitzgerald found his way in part by largely ignoring the possibilities for fiction of the ethnic dimension.

The son of a flamboyant "Celtic mother," born Beatrice O'Hara, Amory Blaine in *This Side of Paradise* is the first Irish Catholic protagonist in a novel by an Irish Catholic American writer whose *bildungsroman* ends with the rejection of his faith. Amory also comes to reject the interest in Irish ethnicity fostered by his mentor Monsignor Darcy, who taught that "Ireland was a romantic lost cause and Irish people quite charming, and that it should, by all means, be one of his principal biases" (24). By the end of the novel, like so many observers of World War I, the Irish Revolution, and the bickering in Irish-American nationalist support groups, Amory is fed up with "the rancid accusations of Edward Carson [the Ulster Unionist leader] and Justice Cohalan [leader of the New York-based Friends of Irish Freedom]." He "had grown tired of the Irish question; yet there had been a time when his own Celtic traits were pillars of his personal philosophy" (210-11).

Robert Rhodes has charted Fitzgerald's fictional uses of Irishness, beginning with Amory Blaine's collegiate embrace and post-graduate rejection of his "Celticism," a process that mirrored Fitzgerald's own experience under the influence of his teacher Monsignor Sigourney Fay and his new friend of 1917, Irish romancer Shane Leslie. Next came *The Beautiful and Damned* (1922), in which the non-Irish protagonist Anthony Patch dallies with an Irish-American shopgirl, Geraldine Burke, to whom he tells a romantic tale of an Irish aristocrat and wild goose, the Chevalier O'Keefe, an exile in France whose own temptation by a peasant girl leads to his death. Rhodes suggests that the tale is "Fitzgerald's brief gesture to his own more noble Irish past" and a "bitter and ironic private joke" about the dire consequences of association with peasants, of whom the shopgirl is a modern example. "Whatever the Patches may think of their own place in an American aristocracy, Irish Americans are beyond the pale" (40). Rhodes goes on to say that "Fitzgerald's line of development was to eliminate or to denigrate Irish connections for his protagonists. With *The Great Gatsby* (1925), . . . he seems to have brought them nearly to a vanishing point" (41). Here, however, the background of nineteenth-century Irish-American fiction can be illuminating. While it is true that the only Irish in the novel are some of the names on Gatsby's party guest list, we have seen the powerful uses to which previous Irish-American writers have put the private house as central symbol. Fitzgerald may have been emphasizing the rags-to-riches contrast in making his protagonist not an Irish American, but a young man probably of East European stock by way of North Dakota. Nevertheless, the transformation of Jimmy Gatz to Jay Gatsby that crystallizes in the mansion at West Egg is a classic immigrant/ethnic success story, in the vein of Conway's *Lalor's Maples* (1901), Dillon O'Brien's *The Dalys of Dalystown* (1866), and Mary Anne Sadlier's *Old and New; or, Taste versus Fashion* (1862).

Rhodes marks the significant change in Fitzgerald's fictional uses of Irishness after *The Great Gatsby*. In *Tender Is the Night* (1934), he returned to painful autobiographical materials in creating a protagonist, Dick Diver, with some Irish background who is married to an emotionally disturbed woman, Nicole Warren Diver. Ultimately, it is the Warren family money, represented by Nicole's sister Baby Warren, that leads to Dick Diver's corruption and collapse. In the same years of his work on this novel, Fitzgerald wrote a series of stories about a St. Paul part-Irish adolescent Basil Duke Lee in which, as Rhodes puts it, he "returned to the question of his uneasy Irishness," and "open[ed] the door to his own past . . . to reappraise it, and to find in it some understanding of his and Dick Diver's situation" (43). The results in both cases are inconclusive—in large part because of Fitzgerald's inability to achieve a consistent fictional perspective that could resolve the doubleness noted in Cowley's review of *Tender Is the Night*. Despite his considerable artistic gifts, Fitzgerald was no more able to heal his ambivalence about wealth and social status than were his nineteenth-century Irish-American literary forebears. He remained like Nick Carraway, the narrator of *The Great Gatsby*, who describes the position beautifully: "High over the city our line of yellow windows must have contributed their share of human secrecy to the casual watcher in the darkening streets, and I was him too, looking up and wondering. I was within and without, simultaneously enchanted and repelled by the inexhaustible variety of life" (36). Robert Rhodes finds a clarifying progression in Fitzgerald's fictional orientation toward Irishness and material success. The pattern runs from "adulation of wealth" in *This Side of Paradise* to "strong condemnation" in *Gatsby* and "severe criticism" in *Tender Is the Night*, with a parallel movement "from Fitzgerald's rejection of the Irish, to their moderate acceptability, to Irish Dick Diver's victimization by power and wealth." Rhodes also suggests that had Fitzgerald completed *The Last Tycoon*, he might have brought a new complexity and depth to his use of ethnic materials with Kathleen Moore, the Irish-born heroine, Pat Brady, the Irish-American villain, and the Jewish protagonist Monroe Stahr, "a figure of both power and integrity" (45-46).

William Shannon has pointed out that Fitzgerald's main psychological theme is the relationship between men of lower social background and women of high status or great wealth, and his main social theme is "the heartbreak and moral failure at the center of America's material success." Shannon declares that these themes come naturally to an Irish American of Fitzgerald's "lace-curtain" generation, "well-to-do Irish in American cities in . . . the first two decades of this century," who "stood near and yet outside the golden circle of the Protestant establishment in this country" (235-36). As we have seen, these themes were struck by many earlier

Irish-American writers. The formula of rags to riches to moral grief was brought to its first polish by Mary Anne Sadlier in the Famine generation, and it runs through Irish-American fiction, early and late. Moreover, Fitzgerald's Irish Catholic background made him as much a moralist as any of his predecessors. It is one more indication of his doubleness that despite his reputation as high-living chronicler of the Jazz Age, the wages of sin are as clearly presented in his fiction as in any nineteenth-century Irish-American novel.

A doctor's son from Pottsville, Pennsylvania, John O'Hara was a middle-class boy whose dreams of attending Yale were shattered by his father's death. He made his own way as a journalist, first in Pottsville and then in New York. His early fiction, particularly his stories, won critical praise, and his later, longer novels were damned by reviewers and devoured by a reading public that made him one of America's best-selling novelists and a very wealthy man. Seldom in his large corpus of fiction does O'Hara make significant use of Irish-American protagonists and settings, and it has been convincingly argued that this avoidance did, in fact, hurt him as a writer. For example, William Shannon declares that O'Hara "picked at his Irishness like a scab. It is one of the furious impulses that agitate his work, but he has never fully confronted his past and made peace with it. His evasiveness has impoverished his fiction." In his ambitious, very long later novels especially, "he writes about the kind of person he is not and the way of life he has not experienced"; that is, "the upper-class Protestant establishment" (244-45, 247).

The much-quoted self-description of Jimmy Malloy, the autobiographical journalist in O'Hara's second novel *BUtterfield 8* (1935) is the earliest fictional evidence of O'Hara's lifelong crippling ambivalence:

> I want to tell you something about myself that will help to explain a lot of things about me. You might as well hear it now. First of all, I am a Mick. I wear Brooks clothes and I don't eat salad with a spoon and I probably could play five-goal polo in two years, but I am a Mick. Still a Mick. Now it's taken me a little time to find this out . . . for the present purpose I only mention it to show that I'm pretty God damn American, and therefore my brothers and sisters are, and yet we're not Americans. [66-7]

Edmund Wilson's assessment of O'Hara's accomplishment in mid-career (1940) unfortunately remained valid all the rest of the way. "Primarily a social commentator," says Wilson, O'Hara "has explored for the first time from his peculiar semi-snobbish point of view a good deal of interesting territory: the relations between Catholics and Protestants, the relations between college men and non-college men, the relations between the underworld and 'legitimate' business, the ratings of cafe society." Mostly, his protagonists come to some form or other of social-class grief: "They are snubbed, they are humiliated, they fail. The cruel side of social snobbery is really Mr. O'Hara's main theme." While he analyzes "the

social surface . . . with delicacy, and usually with remarkable accuracy,"
Wilson continues, "his grasp of what lies underneath it is not, however,
so sure. His point of view toward his principal characters tends to be
rather clinical; but even where his diagnosis is clear, we do not share the
experience of the sufferer." Similarly, Thomas Flanagan suggests that "the
mold of [O'Hara's] vision was set by [his first novel] *Appointment in Samarra*, a bleak world of meaningless social ritual, incoherent passions, and
suicide. . . . That world, with its secret affirmations and rejections, its
insignia, its badges of manner and dress, had become the substance of
his fiction. But the substance had become all surface, frozen carapace-
hard, and nothing beneath the carapace, nothing at all."[11]

In O'Hara's long, later novels especially, elaborated surface detail coexists with characters whose depths and motivations either remain unexplored or are confusingly attempted. And yet, he was always a master of
shorter forms in which a gesture or a word can carry enough significance
to bring the sort of revelation or "epiphany" that came to be expected of
the short story after James Joyce's *Dubliners*. Thus, in "Price's Always
Open" the unbridgeable social gulf yawns when the New York girl from
the summer crowd asks the Cape Cod townie boy "What is Holy Cross?"
And O'Hara never wrote better than in the early story "The Doctor's Son,"
which contains solid portraits of his physician father and of himself as an
immature adolescent, thoroughly grounded in descriptions of the poor
Irish "patches" of the Pennsylvania coal fields during the great influenza
epidemic of 1918. Lacking Fitzgerald's compensating larger vision of the
death of the American dream, John O'Hara remained trapped by his own
unresolved lace-curtain anxieties. These come through in his fiction in
his endless measurements of the nuances of American, old-moneyed respectability. Such obsessive, petty concerns are a poor substitute for significant criticism of life. The eternal, calculating parvenu, O'Hara is the
Maurice Francis Egan of his generation.

An exchange of letters between Fitzgerald and O'Hara in 1933 directly
reveals each man's ambivalence about being Irish. A contributor of short
pieces to the *New Yorker* since 1928, O'Hara had not yet begun his first
novel when he wrote to praise Fitzgerald's characterization of an Irish-
American social climber in a recent story:

> And that easily we get to the second thing you've done so well: Lowrie, the
> climber; and I wonder why you do the climber so well. Is it the Irish in you?
> *Must* the Irish always have a lot of climber in them? Good God! I am the son
> of a black Irish doctor (gone to his eternal reward) and a mother who was a
> Sacred Heart girl, whose father was born Israel Delaney (Pennsylvania Quaker
> who turned Catholic to marry an immigrant girl, Liza Rourke). My old man
> was the first doctor in the U.S. to use oxygen in pneumonia, was recognized
> by Deaver as being one of the best trephiners and appendix men in the world.
> But do I have to tell you which side of the family impresses me most? I doubt
> it. You've guessed it: because Grandfather Delaney's connections included

some Haarmons from Holland and a Gray who was an a.d.c. to Washington, and I have some remote kinship with those N.Y. Pells, I go through some cheap shame when the O'Hara side gets too close for comfort. If you've had the same trouble, at least you've turned it into a gift, but I suspect that Al Smith is the only Irishman who isn't a climber at heart. Anyhow, in Lowrie you've done a sort of minor Gatsby.

About a month later, O'Hara began writing *Appointment in Samarra*, in which throwing a drink in the face of the "climber" Harry Reilly is the catalyst for the chain of events that culminates in the suicide of the novel's Anglo-Saxon protagonist Julian English. Fitzgerald was struck by O'Hara's letter, and replied three weeks later as follows:

> I am especially grateful for your letter. I am half black Irish and half old American stock with the usual exaggerated ancestral pretensions. The black Irish half of the family had the money and looked down upon the Maryland side of the family who had, and really had, that certain series of reticences and obligations that go under the poor old shattered word "breeding" (modern form "inhibitions"). So being born in that atmosphere of crack, wisecrack and countercrack I developed a two-cylinder inferiority complex. So if I were elected King of Scotland tomorrow after graduating from Eton, Magdalene, and the Guards, with an embryonic history which tied me to the Plantagenets, I would still be a parvenu. I spent my youth in alternately crawling in front of the kitchen maids and insulting the great.[12]

Such discomfort about identity and status goes a long way toward explaining what got lost in Irish-American fiction between 1900 and 1932. A similar daunting ambivalence plagued the Laughlins, McIntyres, Byrnes, and Dunnes, their late nineteenth-century forebears, and their slightly younger contemporaries, including Fitzgerald and O'Hara.

Another kind of lost generation consists of writers who begin and then abandon literary careers. A clarifying example of an abortive Irish-American writing life in these times is that of Eugene Clancy, an otherwise unknown writer who published a few promising stories between 1909 and 1915 and then dropped out of sight. His best story provides a last example of the ambivalent fictions of this uneasy ethnic subculture. Published in *Harper's Magazine* in 1915, "The Cleansing Tears" opens with promising candor: "Without any particular rhyme or reason, Ralph Madden had been fed into the down-town clerk-machine the day after he left the public school." Plausibly described are the "home atmosphere . . . charged with supreme indifference to such questions as vocation, character, ability, and choice," and a boy "allowed to set forth without guidance on a reckless adventure." Ralph Madden fills the void of dull office work and empty home life with evenings in "billiard rooms and moving-picture shows," and he quickly assumes the street-corner values of "the crowd." Referred to by Clancy as "the code," these include talking fast and "wise," hiding all emotion, and treating women only as objects of sexual pursuit. Keeping in favor with his friends becomes Ralph's only measure of how to act: "He feared nothing so much as a loss of popularity." Meeting a nice girl from the neighborhood, Ralph puts "the code" into action, and the result is a "gulf of misunderstanding between them," a painful contrast between the innocent and shyly hopeful girl and the callow Ralph, whose conversation runs to glib remarks and innuendoes designed to be retold to his pals on the corner. Their only real communication comes during an afternoon visit to Bronx Park, where Ralph forgets the code and they share "a simple, natural, and, to them, absorbing conversation" about their goals in life. Ralph soon recovers, though. Imagining himself "a hunter who has cunningly set the trap," he takes the girl to a low dance hall at Coney Island, orders drinks, and frankly proposes sexual intimacy. Epitomizing the gulf between them, his words "cut the girl's heart like a lash," and she stops seeing him. Uncontrite, Ralph goes back to the corner, where "day by day he became more perfectly representative of the mean and pitiful type which in his innocence he idealized."

In a word, Ralph Madden is the Studs Lonigan of an earlier generation. The environmental elements are the same: the emptiness of home and work alike, the assumption of street corner values to fill the void, the inability to communicate positive emotions, and even the symbolic opposition of the green park and the boozy dance hall. But here the resemblance stops. Clancy's promising realistic conception is ruined by the stereotyped characterization of Ralph Madden's saintly mother. Suffering her "lumbering, beer-swilling" husband's abuses in silence and unable to express her "hopeless" love for her son, Mrs. Madden is a shadowy figure—until she falls terminally ill. On her deathbed she reveals to Ralph what Clancy calls "the mother-heart. He understood now how she had yearned for him, how she had suffered; what a lonely, neglected life hers had been. And he had not seen! He had scarcely given her so much as an occasional careless embrace and perfunctory kiss." The realization of his mother's unselfish love changes Ralph's life: "He knew himself at last—the spark had been struck. He had found his soul." After shedding the "cleansing tears" of the title, Ralph vows to begin a "new, a decent life, in memory of her," and he is ultimately reunited with the girl from Bronx Park.[13]

Clancy has been unable to carry his convincingly bleak vision to a plausible conclusion. Instead, he lapses into a familiar set of conventions from nineteenth-century Irish-American fiction in which the mother is often an idealized figure, a paragon who holds her family together, fires her children with religious zeal, and provides selfless love, moral guidance, and a spotless kitchen. As we have seen, examples abound in the fiction of Famine-generation writers such as Mary Anne Sadlier of the climactic happy death of the saintly mother, after which those left behind resolve to live better lives, dedicated to her memory. And this is what happens in "The Cleansing Tears." So strong is the pull on his imagination of these conventions, that Clancy sacrifices his story to them. Despite the evocation and criticism of narrow, impoverished urban lives, the idealized figure of Mrs. Madden tips the balance of the story to sentimental melodrama. The result once again is unresolved tension between critical realism and respectable romance. It remained for James T. Farrell to resolve such vacillation with one smashing stroke.

There was, however, at least one Irish-American writer in the 1920s who created a body of fiction that depended primarily on his own background and early life. This was Jim Tully, a fascinating figure whose sudden appearance caused something of a stir on the American literary scene. Born in a small Ohio town in 1888 to Irish immigrant parents, Tully was raised in a Catholic orphanage after his mother's death when he was five or six. At thirteen he took to the open road for six years as a vagabond "road kid," living by his wits on the edge of the law, spending some time in jails, and working occasionally as a migrant farm laborer and factory hand, a circus roustabout, and a professional boxer. These eventful early years became the matter of Tully's autobiographical fiction. He landed eventually in Los Angeles, where he wrote his first novel, *Emmett Lawler*, which was published with some good critical notices in 1922. Its initial appeal, and that of Tully's subsequent fiction, was its seemingly authentic glimpses of life at the bottom of American society. The New York *Times* reviewer praised Tully for having chronicled an "American Inferno" of underclass life in a "brave and priceless" book. *Emmett Lawler* begins where so much nineteenth-century Irish-American fiction left off—with the sentimentalized death of the saintly mother. A lover of poetry, especially Keats, and the strong center of her family, the Irish immigrant Mrs. Lawler dies giving birth to a dead child. "A dead eagle, born for the mountains, whose clipped wings had forced her to walk the mud roads of Ohio," she "closed her eyes upon a world from which the fairies of her girlhood had long since vanished" (3). Six-year-old Emmett and his siblings are barred from their mother's funeral because they haven't decent clothes to wear, and are then given over to an orphanage, a huge, forbidding place with 500 children and scanty provisions. The boy survives on the memory of his mother and grows up to have a poetic and belligerent "Irish" temperament. His ultimate decision to write out his experiences comes from his mother's shaping influence.

At twelve Emmett is given over to an illiterate Ohio farmer who encourages him to read aloud from *Pilgrim's Progress*, the King James Bible, and *Robinson Crusoe*. Eventually, Emmett grows to young manhood and goes on the bum. Tully's descriptions of hobo life helped make his reputation. Praising the hobos, most of whom "measure higher in intellect than the average plodding laborer," he asserts that "the young tramps are often adventurers frothing over with life," especially in the United States, for "in no country in the world has tramping reached the art that it has in America. The young American hobo in sheer capacity for suffering and endurance, daring and deviltry, shows qualities every day that are worthy of a higher cause" (135-36). The book contains vivid descriptions of riding the rails cross-country and life in hobo camps. "Jungling up" around a makeshift cook stove in one camp, Emmett hears an informed debate about Civil War generalship with references to Napoleon and Hannibal. As protection from the railroad police, he carries a battered prayerbook on the advice of an experienced tramp: "A lot of these dicks are Irish, and if they search you and find this on you, they'll think you are all right" (143). Tully also describes low-life in Mississippi, the worst state in the union for hobos, in the New York Bowery district, and in Chicago's tenderloin, where hungry tramps steal scraps from the lunch counter at "Hinky Dink" Kenna's saloon. Emmett also puts in time working for a circus, and the novel ends with his bloody, brutal, and short career as a boxer. The novel is stylistically clumsy, ill-shaped, and distractingly anecdotal, and the revelations of underclass life have lost their innovative punch, but with this controversial book Jim Tully was well launched.

Over the next ten years, Tully compiled what he called his "Underworld Edition," five more novels based on his own youthful adventures. Often he retold the same crucial events, for example his mother's death, from slightly different perspectives, and each novel centers on a different aspect of the material presented first in *Emmett Lawler*. *Beggars of Life* (1924) describes vagabond life, including the dirt and danger of riding the rails, a sexual initiation from a kindly prostitute, and a harrowing deathbed scene as an old tramp coughs blood and dies in a flophouse. *Circus Parade* (1927) describes the seedy small-time con artists in a "ten-car circus" traveling through the Deep South, among them Slug Finerty, the short-changing ticket seller, and Silver Money Dugan, an accomplished swindler of innocents who want to join a circus.

The most explicitly ethnic of these books is *Shanty Irish* (1928). Here the focus is on Tully's forebears, notably his grandfather Hughie Tully, a Famine immigrant admired by his grandson because "he had at least one great quality—detachment. He did not live to please others" (117). A hard-working laborer who digs ditches from a reservoir to surrounding farms, old Hughie regales Jim with Irish songs and fairy tales told during long evenings in saloons. He also relates sobering memories of the Famine years, when "thim that lived through it didn't live. They died an' come to life agin. An' yere niver the same once ye rise from the dead—somethin' has gone out ov the heart o' ye" (3). The old man's death at the end of the novel breaks the narrator's closest tie with his own people. Dealing mostly with Tully's experiences in jail, *Shadows of Men* (1930) contains several portraits of incarcerated lost souls and ends with a graphic description of a hanging. Finally, *Blood on the Moon* (1931) again retells experiences from Tully's hobo years and contains another affectionate portrait of his grandfather Hughie, who predicts a troubled life for Jim because the boy was born "at the time of blood on the moon" (56). The increased redundancy of anecdote in this book indicates that with it Tully had pretty much written himself out on the subject of his picaresque youth. He was unable to move on successfully to other themes, and he died virtually forgotten in 1947.

Throughout the 1920s Tully's books had gotten a number of impressive reviews. George Jean Nathan called him a great American realist whose work "rings clear and true and honest," and H.L. Mencken, who became a friend, declared that Tully "has all of Gorky's capacity for making vivid the miseries of poor and helpless men." He remains noteworthy for his persistence in dealing with ethnic and social realities in a time when many writers were ignoring these areas. He is thus one of the very few writers who forge a link in the 1920s between the two cycles of Irish-American fiction. In addition, Tully's depiction of underclass life, particularly the often sordid, violent world of railroad tramps and hobos at the turn of the century, constitutes a precedent for the work of William Kennedy, the contemporary Irish-American writer whose Albany novels also describe the lives of homeless vagabonds. In fact, the example of Tully underscores Kennedy's achievement in rendering similarly intractable materials with a style, sweetness, and moral center that are far beyond his predecessor's capability.[14]

Actually, Tully's limits were recognized succinctly in a short review of *Shanty Irish* that appeared in the student newspaper of the University of Chicago in March 1929. "Tully is at best a surface realist," says this reviewer. "He can depict action with a brusque clarity, and he has a formula for building up plausible saloon and jungle dialogue. Against this must be weighed his sentimentality, his melodrama, and his anti-social attitudinization, which is masked by a savage and staccatoed crudeness of style, and a barbarity of subject." Not only has he never created a "complete, consistent and plausible character," but "Tully lacks the power, the intensity of vision, the subtlety of feeling to transform this raw, crude stuff into something on a higher artistic level." The reviewer was a part-time student at the university named James T. Farrell. Hard at work on his own first fiction, his was already a discriminating, instructive voice in the criticism of Irish-American literature.

EIGHT

James T. Farrell and
Irish-American Fiction

In February 1930 a negative review of a new, encomiastic biography of Donn Byrne appeared in the *Saturday Review of Literature*. The reviewer was the unknown but outspoken James T. Farrell, then twenty-five with one published story. As in his previous assessment of Jim Tully, he had read Donn Byrne's fiction carefully, understood its serious failings, and explained them crisply: "He was a sleepy traditionalist, weakly repeating Yeats's cry that 'Romantic Ireland's dead and gone.' His work, particularly the Irish tales, are essentially shallow. . . . Byrne's values were lodged in the uncritical and boasting Irish tradition of national glory. . . . It was false literature, as false as the portrait of 'Blind Raftery' with its hero-villain psychology." Equally wary of Byrne's facile romanticizing of the old country and Tully's sentimentalizing of the American underclass, Farrell was working away at fiction that he felt would provide what these predecessors lacked. He later declared, "I wrote the book, that is, the three novels, *Studs Lonigan*, with much concern for clarity." What he wanted to be clear about was the American, urban world in which he had grown up, and which he had never seen depicted honestly in fiction. That world was also an ethnic, an Irish-American world, a fact of his life that Farrell acknowledged both early and late. In a February 1932 letter to Ezra Pound, who had just read the galleys of *Young Lonigan*, the trilogy's first volume, Farrell declared: "As to the Irishness of it. I generally feel that I'm an Irishman rather than an American, and [*Young Lonigan*] was recommended at [its French publishing house] as being practically an Irish novel." Thirty years later he wrote: "I am a second-generation Irish-American. The effects and scars of immigration are upon my life. The past was dragging through my boyhood and adolescence. Horatio Alger, Jr., died only seven years before I was born. The 'climate of opinion' (to use a phrase of Alfred North Whitehead) was one of hope. But for an Irish boy born in Chicago in 1904, the past was a tragedy of his people, locked behind *The Silence of History*." Moreover, in two unpublished short pieces probably written near the end of his life, Farrell said: "Those who were my ancestors were Irish. They are my people. I am of them and from them. . . . I am Chicago born, and American, but I am also an Irish-man." And in an essay published four months before his death in 1979, Farrell declared, "But I am an Irish-American and even though I don't make any special claims for the group, I'm glad that I belong. Irish-

Americans are no more the salt of the earth than any other national or racial groups."[1]

What is true of other writers in this study is also, of course, true of James T. Farrell: Irish ethnicity is one of several dimensions in his work, and it needs to be seen as a part of the whole. Irishness is, however, a crucial and defining part of Farrell's literary landscape. He also found the ethnic dimension of his work problematic. As late as 1965, he wrote that "the validity of Irish-American experience, and my characters is as definite as that of Jewish characters. However, I still am engaged in the struggle to establish that validity beyond doubt." Farrell was also a pioneer in this endeavor, for he had to establish anew the precedent of creating an American fictional world from Irish ethnic materials. As was discussed in the last chapter, there were few models for the fictional uses of "Irish-American experience" in the literary generation of Farrell's youth in the teens and twenties.

Farrell's sense of the added obstacle of having been an American writer born into a working-class background in 1904 is captured in the epigraph from Chekhov that opens his novel *Bernard Carr*: "What writers belonging to the upper class have received from nature for nothing, plebeians acquire at the cost of their youth." Farrell expanded this idea in a 1945 letter containing a list of the distortions and simplifications on which he was raised. He explains that "an American writer of plebeian origin . . . is brought up on banalities, commonplaces, formal religious fanaticism, spiritual emptiness, an authoritative educational system (it is less so now than it was in my day), Horatio Algerism and so on. . . . He doesn't begin with a consciousness of the complications which are the source material of writers in a more sophisticated culture, and he doesn't absorb forms and traditions. His subject matter is his own world around him, and from that he gradually expands."[2] These same simplistic assumptions infused the genteel/sentimental strain of nineteenth-century Irish-American fiction from Mary Anne Sadlier to Maurice Francis Egan. Farrell had to break through this cultural mind set on his own to create fiction that honestly rendered and criticized urban ethnic life.

Farrell did, however, know and recognize the value of the one nineteenth-century Irish ethnic writer of genius, and he acknowledged fellow-Chicagoan Finley Peter Dunne at the opening of his own first novel, *Young Lonigan*, in the front-porch revery of Studs's father:

Nope, his family had not turned out so well. They hadn't had, none of them, the persistence that he had. . . . Well, Pat Lonigan had gone through the mill, and he had pulled himself up by his own bootstraps, and while he was not exactly sitting in the plush on Easy Street, he was a boss painter, and had his own business, and pretty soon maybe he'd even be worth a cool hundred thousand berries. But life was a funny thing, all right. It was like Mr. Dooley

said, and he had never forgotten that remark, because Dooley, that is Finley
Peter Dunne, was a real philosopher. Who'll tell what makes wan man a thief,
and another man a saint? [17][3]

So it was that with Jim Tully and Donn Byrne as negative examples
and Peter Dunne as an isolated positive example, James T. Farrell began
the second cycle of Irish-American fiction in 1932 with the publication of
Young Lonigan: A Boyhood in Chicago Streets. The son and grandson of Irish
Catholic working-class laborers, he was born and raised in a South Side
Chicago neighborhood that became the setting for much of his remarkable
body of work, which constitutes the greatest sustained production in
twentieth-century America of quality fiction in the realistic tradition. Filling to date over fifty volumes, this corpus includes hundreds of stories
and four large fictional cycles, which are further connected as progressive
explorations of their main characters' varying responses to American urban environments. These related groups are the *Studs Lonigan* trilogy, the
O'Neill-O'Flaherty pentalogy, the *Bernard Carr* trilogy, and the *Universe
of Time* sequence, of which nine volumes (of a projected thirty) were
published before Farrell's death in 1979.

The first two groups, the three Lonigan and five O'Neill novels, share
a setting (the South Side neighborhood around Washington Park where
Farrell himself grew up), a time frame (roughly 1900 to 1930), and several
characters. Farrell's own childhood in Washington Park had much more
in common with the experience of Danny O'Neill in the second series
than with that of Studs Lonigan. However, with a wisdom unusual in
young writers, Farrell knew that in order to deal objectively with his own
youthful, exaggerated feelings of hatred and rejection of his background,
he had to tell Studs's story first. Thus, in part *Studs Lonigan* is the exorcism
desired by Danny O'Neill when, in the middle of the *Lonigan* trilogy in
which he is a minor figure, he vows that "some day he would drive this
neighborhood and all his memories of it out of his consciousness with a
book" (372). Instead of the tight, almost fatalistic narrative drive of the
Lonigan trilogy, the five O'Neill-O'Flaherty novels are diffused and epi-
sodic, and in this more relaxed structure is embodied a broader but still
unsentimentalized view of urban society.

The *Bernard Carr* trilogy, published between 1946 and 1952, continues
the action of the O'Neill novels in dealing with the young manhood of a
working-class Chicago Irishman with literary ambitions who has moved
to New York in search of experience and perspective. His ambition is akin
to that of James Joyce's Stephen Dedalus, with whom Farrell's O'Neill/
Carr figure has much in common. A lifelong admirer of Joyce, Farrell
found in the older Irish writer early corroboration of his own thematic
concerns and challenging stylistic innovations, as in his use of dream-
montages and typographically emulated newspaper headlines. In these

novels of education, Bernard Carr learns to reject the Catholic Church, his own naive appropriation of Nietzsche, and the Communist Party, all of which he comes to find threatening to his artistic integrity. His emergence as a successful writer rounds out the Lonigan-O'Neill-Carr connected cycles. The *Carr* trilogy lacks the rootedness in place and community of the previous Chicago-based novels, but it compensates by providing a vivid rendering of the lives of New York left-wing intellectuals in the 1930s, with particular attention given to their passionate engagement with the question of the relationship between the artist and society. In addition to his large cycles and a few isolated novels, Farrell published about two hundred and fifty short stories and short novels, in which his presentation of twentieth-century life became even more inclusive. Many stories concern the protagonists of his novels (there are fifty about Danny O'Neill alone); others place new characters in familiar Chicago or New York settings, and still others are set in Europe, especially Paris. True to Farrell's realistic aesthetic, the stories are strong on character revelation and spurn machinations of plot.

Farrell's critical writings also fill several volumes. From *A Note on Literary Criticism* (1936) to *Selected Essays* (1964) and *On Irish Themes* (1982), these contain useful explanations of the relationship between his life and his work, appreciations of writers who were important to him, including Joyce, Dreiser, Chekhov, and Sherwood Anderson, and declarations of his position as a realist who writes "as part of an attempt to explore the nature of experience." In 1963 Farrell published *The Silence of History*, his sixteenth novel, and the first volume of the *Universe of Time*, his fourth fictional cycle, which in his heroic projection would have run to thirty volumes. Integrated by the central recurrent character of Eddie Ryan, another Chicago writer born like his creator in 1904, the *Universe* cycle embodies a reassessment of Farrell's life-long concern with the experience of the artist in the modern world, as well as a continuation of the "life-work" that he defined, in an introduction to the new cycle's sixth unit *Judith* (1973), as "a panoramic story of our days and years, a story which would continue through as many books as I would be able to write."

The focus of this chapter will be the eight "Washington Park" novels of Farrell's prolific and pioneering first phase. Between 1932 and 1943, he published the *Studs Lonigan* trilogy, four of the five O'Neill-O'Flaherty novels, two other Chicago-based novels (*Gas-House McGinty* and *Ellen Rogers*), and over fifty Chicago stories. *Studs Lonigan* was completed with *The Young Manhood of Studs Lonigan* (1934) and *Judgment Day* (1935), and the O'Neill series is as follows: *A World I Never Made* (1936), *No Star Is Lost* (1938), *Father and Son* (1940), *My Days of Anger* (1943), and ten years later *The Face of Time* (1953). With this body of work, Farrell almost singlehandedly brought the Irish voice into twentieth-century American fiction. These books will be used to make two points, the second of which has two parts. First, establishing the complementary connectedness of the Lonigan and O'Neill-O'Flaherty sequences will refute the most common critical misconception about Farrell's work. Second, these novels will be seen to embody Farrell's two greatest gifts to Irish-American fiction's second cycle: a criticism of life and a voice for the inarticulate. The former will be illustrated by looking at the *Studs Lonigan* trilogy and the latter by considering the O'Neill-O'Flaherty pentalogy.

No major American writer has been worse served by criticism than James T. Farrell. After the publication in 1935 of the third *Studs Lonigan* novel, Farrell labored for four decades under an unjust and unfounded accusation by influential critics who dealt with his fiction as it appeared with a party line that ran as follows: "James T. Farrell is that sad case, a one-book writer. *Studs Lonigan* is creditable fiction, albeit in the limiting and dated naturalistic mode pioneered by Theodore Dreiser. But his subsequent novels have been obsessive reworkings of the same materials, and nowhere near as good as *Studs*." The primarily New York–based writers who mouthed this line became the American critical establishment of the 1940s and 1950s, and their dismissal of Farrell was repeated in the academy by the next generation of scholar/teachers, many of whom never took the trouble to read the books in question. By the late 1970s, Farrell's last years, there were encouraging signs that the critical tide was turning. These included several honorary degrees to Farrell, his reception of the Emerson-Thoreau medal of the American Academy of Arts and Sciences, and a number of positive critical reassessments of his work.

In fact, the eight Washington Park novels comprise one coherent grand design with two contrasting movements: the downward, negative alternative embodied in Studs Lonigan, who dies pointlessly, and the upward, positive possibility embodied in Danny O'Neill, who lives to become a writer. The tragedy of the inadequate critical response to Farrell's work is that *Studs Lonigan* has been seen as the whole story, when it isn't even half of the story about Washington Park. By June 1929 Farrell had conceived the design of both series. He wrote a publisher that he was "working on two novels. One is a realistic story of a corner gang at Fifty Eighth and Prairie Avenue of this city . . . .The other novel is a tale of a boy in a Catholic high school of this city during the early part of the jazz age." After finishing *The Young Manhood of Studs Lonigan* in 1934, Farrell reported as follows to Ezra Pound: "One more Lonigan book to come, and I'm writing it, . . . and also am working on a long story of a family, Irish American, with a lot of autobiography, that extends from 1911 to 1933, and intends to shoot the works, and include a number of things I've held back in my other books. It may be anywhere from one to five volumes." Hardly stopping for breath after finishing *Studs* with *Judgment Day* in 1935, Farrell published the first O'Neill-O'Flaherty novel, *A World I Never Made*, one year later. Shortly thereafter he explained to a friend that the new series "is conceived as a complementary study to 'Studs Lonigan'. One [of] the main characters, Danny O'Neill, is planned as a character whose life experience is to be precisely the opposite of Studs." Farrell held to this conception through the writing of the remaining volumes. His Guggenheim application for support for the writing of *Father and Son* included four pages of "Differences between Danny O'Neill and Studs Lonigan," and while finishing up the third and final draft of *My Days of Anger*, Farrell wrote his publisher that "I think now, it'll come out right, and be a fitting end to the series—and a fitting companion series to *Studs Lonigan*—and that Danny and Studs will stand as I conceived them—dialectical opposites in their destinies—one goes up, the other goes down." In February 1943 he wrote Eugene O'Neill that he had just finished the final book of "the complementary series to *Studs Lonigan*."[4]

In the coherent body of fiction formed by the eight Washington Park novels, Farrell has provided the most thoroughly realized fictional embodiment of three generations of Irish-Americans—from nineteenth-century immigrant laborers to Depression-era intellectuals. Washington Park is a world in itself, with four clear reference points like the markings on a compass: the Street, the Park, the Church, the Home. This is especially true for his young protagonists, Studs Lonigan and Danny O'Neill, who seldom leave the neighborhood and for whom these perceptions of urban life are fresh and crucially formative. (As an epigraph for *Young Lonigan*, Farrell quotes Plato: "Except in the case of some rarely gifted nature there never will be a good man who has not from his childhood been used to play amid things of beauty and make of them a joy and a study.") Much more than simply a choice of locale for unsupervised leisure time, the Street and the Park emerge in Farrell's fiction as archetypal opposing options for the city child. Each represents a possible way of growing up, a style of life, and each has its own pantheon of heroes, ideal models to engage a child's imagination. In the course of the Washington Park novels, Farrell embodies this powerful opposition in the contrasting development of Studs and Danny. The Street is the destructive element, characterized by gang life with its brutalization of finer instincts by pressures to conform: to fight, drink, dissipate energy and time, all in the service of an ideal of being "tough and the real stuff." The center of street life in Washington Park is Charley Bathcellar's poolroom on Fifty-eighth Street near the El station; its heroes are the gamblers, drinkers, and loafers who congregate there. The Park, on the other hand, is the creative and liberating element, the setting for a pastoral dream of release from the disorder of the streets and the claustrophobia of apartment living. The center of park life is the athletic field, which is to the city child a kind of paradise—a lined-out, grassy place where rules are clear and enforced and success and failure unambiguous. Its heroes are sports figures, from park league stars to the Chicago White Sox, the pride of the South Side.

Danny O'Neill's most vivid childhood memory involves having watched a no-hitter pitched by Chicago's Ed Walsh in 1911. This thing of athletic beauty is his first exposure to art, and it sinks in. Danny chooses

the Park and single-mindedly resolves to become a professional baseball
player; he practices by the hour through his childhood years, mostly alone
with a rubber ball and his imagination. Baseball is at once the most beautiful sport to watch and the least team-oriented of team sports. Thus it
is not surprising that it so fascinates this young Chicago boy who is something of a lonely dreamer, with the detachment of a developing artist. It
is no more surprising that Studs Lonigan chooses the Street. A normally
inquisitive boy, he shows signs of intelligence, even imagination, in early
scenes of *Young Lonigan*. And yet he is weak-willed and easily led, and
he assumes the facile and corrupting "tough guy" values of the street-
corner society to which he is drawn after graduation from eighth grade.
He joins the Fifty-eighth Street Gang and takes his models from the poolroom and the silver-screen gangsters at the Michigan Theater. It is significant that the recurrent, ever-receding dream of Studs's short, unhappy
adulthood is of his one afternoon in the Park with Lucy Scanlan during
their eighth-grade summer. So the twig is bent for both boys, and the
opposition of Street and Park is central to Farrell's delineation of the
complex mixture of character and environment that brings Danny to his
vocation as an artist and Studs to his grave at twenty-nine. Even their
characteristic daydreams are telling. Studs walks the Street in his mind,
acting out his dream of himself as a tough guy; Danny drifts lazily across
the Park, catching imaginary fly balls for the White Sox. Several other
characters also function as opposing figures in Farrell's design. The most
important of these are the two fathers, the "successful" but ineffectual
Patrick Lonigan and the unlucky but ultimately heroic Jim O'Neill, and
the two contrasting matriarchal figures, Studs's mother Mary Lonigan
and Danny's grandmother Mary O'Flaherty.

For Farrell's Irish Catholic characters, the familiar world is an even
smaller unit than the Washington Park neighborhood. It is the parish.
Providing both continuity with Ireland and help toward adjustment in
America, as well as religion's traditional gifts of meaning and solace, the
immigrant/ethnic Catholic Church is crucial to Farrell's full evocation of
Chicago Irish life. The Washington Park novels describe this sophisticated
cultural complex in full swing, and they also illustrate the various attitudes
toward the Church among three generations of Irish Americans. For immigrants such as Tom and Mary O'Flaherty, Danny O'Neill's grandparents, Catholicism remains the tacitly accepted center of life. As he nears
death, Old Tom is genuinely comforted by conversations with the understanding Father Hunt, one of several sympathetic priests in Farrell's
novels. Mary's faith also brings her through the grief of her husband's
death and the thousand subsequent crises of her unquiet old age.

One step removed from the losses and alienation of immigration,
Farrell's second-generation-American characters are affected by their religion in many different ways. Studs's mother Mary Lonigan is a self-
righteous Catholic in the "holier than thou" mold. Lizz O'Flaherty O'Neill

comes closest to picking up her parents' values, although she exaggerates them by retreating into a concentrated piety and staking everything on the positive nature of suffering as preparation for heaven. Her fatalistic attitude clashes with her husband Jim's pragmatism, and they often fight bitterly about her incessant visits and donations to the Church, which come at the expense of personal hygiene, housekeeping, and sometimes meat for the table. Lizz walks the world in a dirty-faced daze, seeing visions of dead relatives and Satan under the bed, wishing that she had become a nun, and responding to every difficulty with blind faith in "God's will." Still, her Catholicism does sustain her through years of terrible poverty, continual pregnancies, stillbirths and infant mortality, and the death of her husband. Quite simply, Catholicism works for Lizz, and she is at once the craziest O'Flaherty and the most secure. Her sister Margaret, on the other hand, is the most insecure, troubled, and unhappy of the children. Attractive and desirous of love, money, and a "good time," Margaret is torn between two philosophies and two worlds: the puritanical Catholic morality of her training in the parish and the Jazz Age hedonism all around her in the downtown hotel where she works. An affair with a wealthy married man exacerbates her problem. Unable to resolve the contradictions in her life, she storms through a frenetic, confused young womanhood, marked by excessive drinking, paranoid delusions of persecution, and attempted suicide. The men of the second generation take religion less seriously than the women. Studs's father Patrick Lonigan and Tom's son Al O'Flaherty are unquestioning but no more than nominal Catholics, while Al's brother Ned has rejected the Church outright and substituted "New Thought," a hazy collection of self-help ideas whose main tenet is the "power of the wish," roughly translatable as "all things come to him who wishes for them."

As for the third generation, Studs Lonigan and Danny O'Neill also go different ways in their attitudes toward the religion in which they were raised and educated. For all his flirtations with street life, Studs remains a conventional Catholic, never questioning the teachings and prohibitions of the Church, and reacting typically right up to his last illness. Studs's fevered deathbed dreams reveal him as a believer in heaven and hell and the Catholic way of deciding who goes where. Moreover, he twice attempts to pull his sinking life together by joining parish groups, the young people's association at St. Patrick's Church and the Order of Christopher (modeled on the Knights of Columbus). Given his greater intelligence and the artistic bent, Danny O'Neill's reactions to the Church are understandably more complex. As a sensitive, highly imaginative child, he is terrorized by the fear of hell instilled by his family and the nuns of Crucifixion School. Danny agonizes for years under the load of guilt imposed by what he considers to have been an imperfect first confession and communion. And later he tries to force a vocation to the priesthood to please the nuns and his grandmother. And yet, there are positive aspects to Danny's exposure to Catholic culture. His seventh-grade nun is the first person to push him toward the intellectual life, and some of his priest-teachers at St. Stanislaus High School encourage him further toward learning and writing. Thus, Catholicism does provide Danny with models of educated and ideologically dedicated men and women. In addition, the Church provides other things unavailable to him elsewhere in Washington Park: a sense of order, of historical continuity, and of mystery. And it is these gifts that inspire Danny to harness his imagination with words.

So it is that, although he ultimately repudiates Catholicism, the Church and parochial schooling do have some salutary influence on Danny O'Neill's intellectual and imaginative growth. This aspect of his development combines with the efficacious faith of the immigrant O'Flahertys and Lizz O'Neill to temper the many examples of the Church's negative effects in the Washington Park novels. These include the fear and trembling of Danny's and Studs's guilt-ridden adolescences, the wilder flights of Lizz's hysterical religiosity, at its height in her performance at wakes, and the pompous and hackneyed rhetoric of Father Gilhooley's sermons at St. Patrick's. In short, Farrell's view of Catholicism is ambiguous and mixed, true to life and to his commitment to an aesthetic of realism. Though it cannot save Studs from an early death or sustain Danny into adulthood, the Church is a powerful presence throughout these novels, from Studs's graduation from St. Patrick's grammar school at the beginning of *Young Lonigan* to Mary O'Flaherty's black rosary beads at the end of both *My Days of Anger* and *The Face of Time*, marking her own death and her husband's.

After the Street, the Park, and the Church, the fourth cardinal point in the world of Washington Park is the Home, which for most residents of the neighborhood meant apartment life. Through the three main families of his eight Washington Park novels, Farrell describes an inclusive range of South Side styles of apartment living: from the struggling O'Neills to the comfortably middle-class Lonigans, with the O'Flahertys fluctuating somewhere in between. Their homes and home lives appear in meticulous, day-by-day detail, of interest to anyone who wants to know how ordinary people lived in Chicago from the 1890s to the 1930s. Jim O'Neill's slow movement toward a better life for his large family is measured in terms of the three homes they inhabit over the course of the O'Neill-O'Flaherty novels: from a cold-water tenement flat, to a freestanding cottage with ramshackle outhouse, to a comfortable apartment with indoor plumbing, gas, and electricity. Like so many Irish couples, Tom and Mary O'Flaherty begin their life in Chicago in an old immigrant neighborhood "in Blue Island Avenue," near the Chicago River. In telling their story, Farrell also documents the means by which the majority of marginally middle-class families with immigrant parents got ahead— pooling resources. Young adults lived at home until they married and were expected to contribute their earnings to the family. Thus, by the time old Tom O'Flaherty retires from his job as a teamster, his children Al, Ned, Margaret, and Louise are earning enough to maintain a decent standard of living. Extra money from Al's job as a shoe salesman allows the family to move from a crowded apartment on Twelfth Street to a "big apartment" just north of Washington Park. From this point on, the O'Flahertys qualify as what Lizz O'Neill, with mingled jealousy and derision, labels "steam-heat Irish." It is to this apartment on Indiana Avenue that five-year-old Danny O'Neill comes to live with his grandparents in 1909, because his father doesn't make enough money to support the growing O'Neill family.

Farrell's sense of the scope and the integrity of his Washington Park fiction was already clear by August 1934 when he wrote to a friend: "I hope to run to at least twenty volumes of novels and short stories attempting to describe, represent, analyze and portray connected social areas of Chicago that I have lived in, and that I have more or less assimilated. In these terms, then, the various books and stories are all panels of one work, expanding, and branching out to include more characters, and to catch something of the social processes as they come into the lives of these characters." And upon finishing *My Days of Anger* in February 1943, he told another correspondent: "I have accomplished what I set out to. Shortly after I will have reached thirty nine, I will have accomplished my two major literary objectives—not of course that I haven't more that I want to write. But this much I have done. I have now written the books I said I would write a little over ten years ago when this seemed like a wild prediction."[5]

As his early reviews of Jim Tully and Donn Byrne make clear, the young James T. Farrell noted the absence of critical realism in what little of Irish-American fiction there was available to him in the 1920s. He set out to fill this void, and his own fiction does in fact provide the first sustained critique of the social and moral failings of the Irish-American subculture. Here his 1943 essay on Chekhov is illuminating. In this piece, Farrell describes Chekhov's characters as "idle dreamers who live sunk in the commonplace; men and women who cannot react to cruelty, who cannot be free, who cannot lift themselves above the terrible plain of stagnation—people in whom human dignity is dissolving." He then quotes Gorky's statement of Chekhov's essential message: "In front of that dreary, gray crowd of helpless people there passed a great, wise, and observant man: he looked at all these dreary inhabitants of his country and, with a sad smile, with a tone of gentle but deep reproach, with anguish in his face and in his heart, . . . he said to them: 'You live badly, my friends. It is shameful to live like that'." Farrell goes on to praise Chekhov for having "raised the portrayal of banality to the level of world literature," and to explain the main motive behind that protrayal by quoting a Chekhov letter that articulates the faith of the literary realist: "The best of [writers] are realists and paint life as it is, but, through every line's being soaked in the consciousness of an object, you feel, besides life as it is, the life that ought to be, and that captivates you. . . . Man will only become better when you make him see what he is like." Farrell then reiterates by locating what he sees as Chekhov's "own doctrine: that it is sufficient for the artist to see life truly, clearly, objectively, and to mirror what he has seen." He ends the piece by repeating "the essential message of [Chekhov's] stories and his plays": "You live badly, my friends. It is shameful to live like that."[6] These are also Farrell's doctrine and message, applied throughout his fifty years of writing fiction.

Studs Lonigan has long been acknowledged as a powerful criticism of American urban life. Unfortunately, it still may need to be said that the trilogy criticizes middle-class life. The myth of Studs as a child of the slums persists among those who have heard of, but have not read, the books. What can be done in the context of this study is to examine the ethnic dimension—the ways in which the Lonigan trilogy embodies criticism of specifically Irish-American aspects of life. And in fact a central accomplishment of the trilogy is Farrell's clear-eyed critique of assumptions and consequences of Irish-American middle-class culture. He does this by scrutinizing two of this culture's most resonant symbols, familiar to us from the nineteenth-century fiction: the ideal of home ownership and the character of the matriarch as moral example. Farrell criticizes both by describing their ironic transformations. The Irish immigrant's quest for safe shelter becomes racist flight from a new, black migration to the city, and the saintly mother becomes a monster of bourgeois respectability.

Farrell's chronicle of the migratory housing patterns of the Chicago South Side Irish community is thematically central in the Lonigan trilogy. Here he criticizes the compelling Irish-American symbol of the house as measure of respectability by presenting the first detailed fictional examination of the phenomenon of "white flight" to avoid neighborhood integration. The Lonigans stand for thousands of Chicago Irish families (the O'Neills and O'Flahertys are also among them) who moved further south and eventually to the suburbs to keep ahead of the large-scale movement of black people from the rural south to Chicago after World War I. This was a part of Farrell's conception from the outset. Shortly after finishing Young Lonigan, he wrote that "a dominant theme of the sequel will be the decay of the neighborhood."[7]

As the trilogy opens, Studs's father, Patrick Lonigan, is sitting on the porch of his home in the 5700 block of Wabash Avenue on an evening in June 1916. He owns his own building in this respectable, middle-class neighborhood, and has been here since before his son's birth in 1901. He looks back with satisfaction to his childhood in poverty "around Blue Island and Archer Avenue," which suggests that, like Tom and Mary O'Flaherty, Patrick Lonigan's father settled near the Chicago River, in or near Mr. Dooley's Bridgeport, one of the first Irish working-class neighborhoods in the city. Lonigan remembers his parents as "pauperized greenhorns" from Ireland who raised a large family and never escaped the nets of poverty. His father was a laborer, driven to drink by family and money pressures. Of the Lonigan children, only Patrick has become successful. The others ran away, died young, turned to prostitution, or managed to hold only menial futureless jobs. Lonigan also recalls "those days when he was a young buck in Canaryville," the neighborhood around St. Gabriel's Church at Forty-fifth and Lowe (13-16). This suggests that, like the O'Neills and O'Flahertys, his life has also been marked by a series of moves to the south, the climax of which has been his arrival as a homeowner in Washington Park. This evening's occasion—his son Studs's graduation from eighth grade at St. Patrick's School—completes Lonigan's happiness and the picture of his situation: he is a Catholic family man and a supporter of his parish institutions, a typical middle-class Chicagoan whose success and identity are embodied in his position and property in St. Patrick's parish, Washington Park.

But Patrick Lonigan is far from secure here. Even on this happy evening, his complacent revery is interrupted by the thought that "the family would have to be moving soon. When he'd bought this building, Wabash Avenue had been a nice, decent, respectable street for a self-respecting man to live with his family. But now, well, the niggers and kikes were getting in, and they were dirty. . . . And when they got into a neighborhood property values went blooey. He'd sell and get out" (19). As the novel continues, there are further signs of unrest related to the shifting ethnic and racial makeup of Washington Park. Most graphic is the violent race riot of July 1919, during which Studs and the Fifty-eighth Street gang contribute to the chaos by roaming the border-streets between their turf and the newest black areas near Garfield Boulevard. In search of black victims to avenge the cutthroat death of a white boy (described in a famous Farrell story, "The Fastest Runner on Sixty-First Street"), they find only a single ten-year-old, whom they proceed to terrorize. Another sign of the times is the repeated bombing of the home of "the leading colored banker of Chicago," the first black in the 5900 block of South Park Avenue, and ironically an earnest, contributing Catholic parishioner.

Partly because he has worked so hard to get there, Patrick Lonigan is unwilling to leave Washington Park, despite the steady movement of blacks into the area from the north and west and the equally steady desertion of the neighborhood by his friends. In 1922 the Lonigans move to a new building on Michigan Avenue, one block east of their old home on Wabash. But after this concession, Patrick Lonigan becomes the epitome of the neighborhood die-hard, rejecting a $90,000 offer for his building, despite his daughter Fran's declarations that "the best people . . . are moving over to Hyde Park or out in South Shore," and "soon I'll be ashamed to admit I live around here" (138). In a turn of events based on Farrell's recollections of his own childhood parish of St. Anselm's, Lonigan has put his faith in Father Gilhooley's plan to build a new St. Patrick's

Church on the corner of Sixty-first and Michigan. Lonigan believes that the new church will keep the neighborhood white and double the value of his building at the same time. Two years later in 1924, Studs attends a fund-raising meeting for the new church, which is still being seen as the potential salvation of the neighborhood. The church does get built; but on Father Gilhooley's happiest day, at the first Mass in the new building, "standing in the rear of the church were four new and totally edified parishioners. Their skin was black" (320). In a few months it becomes clear to all that the new church has not stopped or even slowed the influx of blacks to the area, and many disillusioned parishioners, including the Lonigans, begin blaming Father Gilhooley. A stronger pastor, they contend, would "have organized things like vigilance committees to prevent it" (347).

Ultimately, Patrick Lonigan also gives up on his neighborhood. After reluctantly selling his building to a black man, he moves his family further south to the new neighborhood of South Shore in 1928. The scene at the old house on moving day reveals the emotional cost of such moves to people like the Lonigans, and is important to the overall design of the trilogy. From this point on, both Patrick Lonigan and his son will be displaced persons. Patrick knows immediately that he has lost his last real home; he is simply too old to make another. "You know, Bill," he confides to Studs in the empty parlor on Michigan Avenue, "your mother and I are gettin' old now, and, well, . . . this neighborhood was kind of like home. We sort of felt about it the same way I feel about Ireland, where I was born." Later on he adds that it had been his hope to "die in this parish, respected." The thought of moving to South Shore brings no comfort, for "out there there'll only be about ten buildings in our block, the rest's all prairie," and "we're not what we used to be, and it'll be lonesome there sometimes" (373-75). In his pathetic search for an explanation, Patrick Lonigan comes under the influence of the anti-Semitic radio priest "Father Moylan" (based on Father Charles Coughlin), and by the end of the trilogy he is blaming most of his troubles on "Jew real estate men" and a conspiracy of "Jew international bankers."

Moving to South Shore also contributes to the failure of Studs Lonigan to find his way in the world. Denied the sustaining context of home in a familiar neighborhood, Studs becomes even more of an aimless drifter. The move, which takes place almost exactly in the middle of the *Lonigan* trilogy, is thus a watershed event in his downward drift to death. No more at home in South Shore than his father, Studs complains that there is "no place to hang out" there. Five months after having moved away, he returns to Washington Park and finds his gang's "old corner" of Fifty-eighth and Prairie looking "like Thirty-fifth and State"; that is, like the center of the black belt. The playground, school, and church are all strange to him already, and even Washington Park itself seems alien territory: "It had used to be his park. He almost felt as if his memories were in it,

walking like ghosts" (387). Later that night, a drunken Studs goes back
to the park looking for the tree he had sat in with Lucy Scanlan twelve
years before. He can't find it and gets lost trying.

A stronger indication of Studs's displacement comes on the climactic
New Year's Eve that ends *The Young Manhood of Studs Lonigan*. The Fifty-
eighth Street Gang have a wild reunion/party—not in one of the neighborhoods where they now live, but "at a disreputable hotel on Grand
Boulevard in the black belt," in what used to be an Irish enclave. Absolved
of the civilizing pressures of community, the young men turn savage, and
the party culminates in fist fights and the vicious rape by Weary Reilley
of his date. This dark thread of violence against one's own kind in the
younger generation echoes back through earlier Irish-American fiction.
In 1895 Mr. Dooley described the mortal vendetta between thieving Jack
Carey and Officer Clancy on the streets of Bridgeport, and in 1855 Mary
Anne Sadlier told the grim story of the criminal life and violent death of
young Hugh Dillon in *The Blakes and Flanagans*. In Farrell's novel, the night
of debauched drinking results in the permanent ruin of Studs Lonigan's
health, and he ends up in "the dirty gray dawn" of January 1, 1929,
passed out beside a fireplug back at Fifty-eighth and Prairie (411). It looks
as though, in his semiconscious stupor, he has been trying to go home
again. In *Judgment Day*, set two years later, Studs is still sick. He is pallid,
weak-lunged, and subject to coughing and fainting spells and premonitions of death. Desperate for a job to support his pregnant fiancée Catherine Banahan, he foolishly sets out with the want ads under his arm on
a cold, rainy day. The job search takes him downtown, where he spends
a disheartening ten hours getting doors slammed in his face and wading
through puddles of water. He contracts a virulent pneumonia and a few
days later he dies. It is significant that this final illness overtakes him in
the alien Loop—the center of business Chicago but nobody's home.

At the end of *Judgment Day*, Patrick Lonigan also demonstrates his
displacement for a telling final time. It is the Depression year of 1931,
and along with worrying about his son's failing health, Lonigan is about
to lose his business and his house in South Shore. After closing his office,
perhaps for the last time, he embarks on a sad odyssey, literally retracing
the steps of his personal history. Driving north through the now-black
neighborhood of Washington Park, he stops to look at his old building
there and to pay a visit to St. Patrick's Church, on which he had mistakenly
placed his trust that the area would stay white. The memory of this dispossession from the home he had built here is sheer agony, especially in
the context of his present troubles, and so he leaves the area and drives
blindly, unconsciously northward again. Only when he is detained by a
stoplight at Thirty-fifth and Halsted streets, on the outskirts of Bridgeport,
does Lonigan realize, with "deep nostalgia," that he is "going back to an
old neighborhood, to look at places where he had lived and played as a

shaver" (429). As his world spins out of control, he seeks meaning in the steadying power of this most familiar place. Again, though, Lonigan is disappointed, for this visit to his childhood home brings only bitter ironies.

First, the "stockyard smell" reminds him of the poverty of his youth and "the distance he had travelled since those days." But this leads to a despairing question: "What did it mean now," when he is about to have nothing again? Immediately he comes upon a reminder of the Depression and his own lost building and business. He witnesses the eviction from their apartment of a family of six, who stand huddled by their furniture on the sidewalk. Lonigan then watches the sweep of a Communist parade down Halsted Street, and his angry response is the last irony of his visit to Bridgeport. To a policeman-acquaintance whom he spots in the crowd, Lonigan simplistically defends "God and America and the home," the very ideals that his own failure seems to have refuted, and condemns the marching "anarchistic Reds, communists, niggers, hunkies, foreigners, left-handed turkeys" (who include a brother and sister of Danny O'Neill). At the same time, he is puzzled that "even these people . . . seemed happier than he" (444). Having found no solace in his attempted return home, Lonigan turns wearily south again—toward the house in South Shore where his son lies dying. On the way he stops at a speakeasy near White City Amusement Park at Sixty-third and South Park, near the old neighborhood of his happiest years. There, he gets so drunk that he has to be driven home, after sinking so low as to scrabble for the pity of strangers by announcing to the saloon that his son is already dead. Lonigan's disillusionment is complete. All that he believed to be stable has crumbled: the economy of America and Chicago, neighborhood community life, his family, and his home. Sadly echoing the experience in Ireland of his nineteenth-century forebears, Patrick Lonigan's own imminent eviction brings the immigrant's dream of respectable home ownership full circle to nightmare.

In a supporting but crucial position, the *Lonigan* trilogy also contains the first sustained negative characterization of an Irish-American matriarch in the literature. Earlier, flawed examples discussed in chapter 5 are the mothers in John Talbot Smith's "His Honor the Mayor" (1891) and Katherine Conway's *Lalor's Maples* (1901). But the design of *Studs Lonigan* includes a thorough criticism of the traditional Irish-American conception of the idealized, saintly mother. In addition, the movement of the third volume, the ironically-titled *Judgment Day* (which begins with an epigraph from the Mass for the Dead), embodies a related achievement—the subversion of the nineteenth-century convention of the morally efficacious deathbed scene. Mrs. Mary Lonigan is a strong-willed woman who holds tenaciously to two related ideal conceptions—motherhood and respectability—both of which have become distorting obsessions. She enters

Young Lonigan as a mother on its opening page, as her son William, "on the verge of fifteen" and graduation from eighth grade, scrutinizes himself in the bathroom mirror: "He had blue eyes; his mother rightly called them baby-blue eyes." Toward the end of the first section this motif is picked up disturbingly. When Patrick Lonigan observes that Studs and Frances are "not just children anymore," Mary Lonigan snaps back, "Yes, they are. They are too. They're my children, my baby blue-eyed boy and my girl. They can't be taken from me, either." On graduation night, his mother's insistence that Studs go on to high school (he wants to work with his father) is motivated by "what the neighbors would think" if he doesn't. "It would look like they were too cheap, or else couldn't afford to send their boy to high school." The ideals of motherhood and respectability have further coalesced in Mrs. Lonigan's mind into the "dream of hope" that lights her face during Father Gilhooley's graduation speech. She wants her son to be a priest: "How would God and his poor Mother and great St. Patrick, guardian saint of the parish, feel if Studs turned a deaf ear on the sacred call?" His mother advises that Studs "should pray more, so he would know" (59-60).

The opening section of *Young Lonigan* also explains Mary Lonigan's social motive by providing examples of three stages in the Irish-American community hierarchy. These are the Lonigans, Reilleys, and Gormans, all of whom have graduating children. The Lonigans are members of the new bourgeoisie, and their transitional position helps to explain Mary's sensitivity about appearing respectable. Studs's father is a successful painting contractor and the owner of a substantial home. The Reilleys, parents of Studs's adversary, the vicious punk Weary Reilley, are at the lower end of the social scale. Closer to Ireland by virtue of their brogues, roughened by early deprivation when the husband was "a poor teamster" from "back of the yards," the Reilleys have remained coarse, uneducated, and not very well off. On the other hand, the Gormans have made it big. "Dennis P." is a pompous, dandified, but successful politician, having risen to ward committeeman, and with a judgeship on the horizon. Recalling "Dinny's" beginnings as a "starving lawyer," Patrick Lonigan ridicules his "actin' like he was highbrow, lace-curtain Irish." Gorman's clumsily pretentious wife condescends to her old friends, and their refusal of an invitation to her party infuriates Mrs. Lonigan.

After this introduction to her obsessive concerns with motherhood and respectability, Mary Lonigan becomes a seemingly minor choral figure whose occasional laments punctuate her son's dismal slide into poolroom society, bad booze, sickness, and death at twenty-nine. She reenters the foreground of the story, however, literally with a vengeance, near the end of the trilogy. The conclusion of *The Young Manhood of Studs Lonigan* is the wild New Year's Eve party, after which Studs contracts serious, persistent pneumonia. In *Judgment Day*, set two years later, he has a new girlfriend, Catherine Banahan, and another group of resolutions for the future, but his shattered health brings him down. When Catherine gets pregnant, they announce marriage plans to a "suspicious" Mary Lonigan, and Studs becomes desperate for a job. Ultimately he staggers home with a raging fever and collapses at his mother's feet, a child again in his illness, giving himself up to her care: "Mom, I'm sick," he says. "Put me to bed" (388). Mrs. Lonigan proudly quotes this line to Catherine later on, and when Studs dies, his last words are "Mother, it's getting dark" (465). As he never mentions Catherine, it appears that Mrs. Lonigan has won back her son on his deathbed. There is a disturbing regression here, and it indicates the powerful, distorting grip of the mother on her child that has persisted beneath the surface of this narrative.

The weight of his mother's dominance on Studs is registered in his fevered death fantasy, where a montage of the people who have affected his life flickers through his rapidly failing consciousness. All have advice or admonitions for Studs, and they include caricatured historical personages, familiar community and religious figures, and Studs's friends and family. His father is significantly ineffectual, "bloated to about a half ton, and wearing the uniform of a clown," and his fiancée Catherine does not appear. On the other hand, Studs's mother thoroughly dominates the dream. She is the first person to surface in her son's mind, as a "thin, distorted figure," whose "witch's face" moans out the warning that "you'll never have another mother." "I'm damn glad of that," is Studs's reply, "knowing that his words would only sink his soul more deeply in Hell." Moreover, she comes back two more times, knocking over a nun to say "No one loves you like your mother," and stepping in front of President Wilson to proclaim "in tears" that "the home is the most sacred thing on earth." These dream exchanges constitute the only place in the trilogy where Studs even dimly recognizes that mother love and the sanctity of the home have been used as weapons against him. Knowing that these apparitions are "dancing the dance of his own death," he wakes up screaming "Save me! Save me!" It is of course too late (394-96).

The importance to Farrell of the theme of crippling maternal dominance is even clearer in the original manuscript of the death fantasy sequence, which Farrell cut from fifty manuscript to three printed pages because he felt that the whole piece would distort the flow of *Judgment Day*.[8] In the long version, guilt over his sexual sins forces Studs into believing himself to be the Anti-Christ, and he decrees intercourse among all the animals of earth: "let them jazz until their sin rises to heaven in a great and powerful stink like that of the Chicago stockyards." The climax here is the appearance of Studs's mother. "Honor thy God and thy Mother!" she shouts, and Studs feels "that her long, talon-like finger would be dug into his eye." After several more injunctions, Mrs. Lonigan ultimately declares that "the home is next to heaven, your father is next

to God, and your mother is next to the Blessed Virgin Mary." Then the
fantasy sequence concludes with a piece of familiar doggerel whose acros-
tic counter-song is grimly appropriate to Mary Lonigan's role in the trilogy.

> S ing 'em, sing 'em, sing them blues, said Studs.
> M is for the million things she did for you.
> O means only that she's growing older.
> T is for the tears she shed to save you.
> H is for her heart of purest gold.
> E is for her eyes with lovelight shining
> R is right and right she'll always be.
> P ut them all together, they spell Mother
> A word that means the world to me.

This dream sequence, especially in its original form, illustrates Farrell's
importance as a literary innovator in the early 1930s. He extended his use
of surreal dream materials in *Gas-House McGinty* (1933), the novel that he
wrote and published while at work on the *Lonigan* trilogy. A factor here
was Farrell's admiration for Joyce's similar experiments in the "Circe"
chapter of *Ulysses* and in the "Work in Progress" that became *Finnegans
Wake*.

A further, climactic measure of the damage done by Mrs. Lonigan's
obsessions and dominance is her confrontation with Studs's pregnant
fiancée. This is one of the most chilling scenes in Farrell's fiction. When
Catherine comes to see the dying Studs, Mrs. Lonigan all but accuses her
outright of causing his illness. Citing their decision "to get married on
such short notice," Mrs. Lonigan declares that "my son might not have
been where he is today, only for that. He took sick after he had gone in
the rain, against my wishes, to look for a job" (402). Sensing that Catherine
is pregnant, she freezes the anxious girl with a "hard and calculating
stare," and thinks to herself, "Chippy! Whore! Street walker! She had
done it to hold him and to force him into marriage." The two women
stare at each other in an excruciating battle of wills, each knowing the
other's thoughts, neither willing to speak. The stalemate is broken only
by the arrival of a priest to give Studs the last rites of the Catholic Church.
At first, the sacrament seems to bring the women together. In their common grief, they sob "in each other's arms." Feeling that "now there was
sympathy between them" Catherine responds to Mrs. Lonigan's new encouragement of intimacy ("Now, my girl, you must not hold back anything
from me") by revealing that she is going to have a baby. But the offer of
sympathy has been a trap, which Mary Lonigan now springs: "I won't
say that you killed my son. But I will say that by making a chippy of
yourself, you have helped to ruin his chances. If you hadn't thrown yourself on him like a street-walker, he might not be on his death-bed this
very minute" (417). Taken completely by surprise, Catherine faints before

"that thin, hard, wrinkling face, calculating, intense, insane, yes, insane." This assault is so powerful because of the clarity with which Farrell has presented the motivation behind it. Mary Lonigan is faced with the imminent collapse of her central organizing ideals of motherhood and respectability: her son is dying, and her son has fathered a child out of wedlock. She feels "envy, that this girl was young, and she had known her own flesh, her own son in a way that she herself never could have known him" (402). And she feels humiliation: "It is hardly possible that you can save your name, even if my poor sick son is not called above. . . . If my son dies, I'll be ashamed at the funeral, and it will scandalize everybody" (416-17).

The scene demonstrates that, as predicted in her opening portrait, Mary Lonigan has no moral center to sustain her in her time of trouble. Sympathy, charity, and love have withered away. All that remain are the acquisitive drives to possess her children permanently and to achieve social prominence in the community. When these drives are thwarted, she strikes out viciously. She is no more a Christian than is the mother whose self-dramatizing howl of sham forgiveness for her dead, wayward daughter ends Stephen Crane's *Maggie*. To Mary Lonigan, Catholicism has become a set of forms whose main relevance is its contribution to her dream of herself as a respectable mother. A final set of ironies emphasizes her spiritual hypocrisy. One minute she is saying the rosary and thinking of "Jesus in Gethsemane, sweating blood for the sins of man." The next, she is damning Catherine as "possessed by the devil," cursed by God, and responsible for Studs's death. She also blames Studs for having "turned a deaf ear" on his vocation to the priesthood, and this line of thought leads to the final "vision" in which "she saw herself kneeling in Saint Patrick's while William celebrated his first mass. She saw herself giving a reception to friends and relatives, after his first night. Father William Lonigan smiling, meeting everyone, bestowing his blessings, she at his side, his mother. What a pride! What a blessing to her and her family!" (462). Christian motherhood is here a facade which crumbles to reveal egocentric dreams of power and pride.

In Eugene Clancy's "The Cleansing Tears," the mother dies and the son finds his soul. In *Studs Lonigan*, the son dies and the mother remains trapped in distorted self-delusion. Dozens of nineteenth-century Irish-American novels follow the convention of the climactic happy death, which heralds the beginning of eternal life for the dying soul and a rejuvenated moral life for those left behind. But in the conclusion of Farrell's *Judgment Day*, in place of the happy death, we get Studs's last delirium, a "feeble streaking of light" through his brain, "and then, nothing." And in place of spiritually edified onlookers, we get "a father sick and hurt," "an impatient nurse" who covers "the face of Studs Lonigan with a white sheet," and "a kneeling mother, sobbing and praying," though minutes earlier she has attacked the helpless, distraught girl who is carrying her son's child (465). Here are death and the death of the heart. Farrell has emphatically subverted the Christian deathbed convention.

Moreover, Studs's is the last of several such deaths, both literal and symbolic, in the three volumes. The first comes early and with premonitory force. On Studs's twenty-first birthday his Fifty-eighth Street buddy Paulie Haggerty dies of "every goddamn thing," including clap, gonorrheal rheumatism, stomach ulcers, a weakened heart, and consumption. The event prompts the first of Studs's many attempts to change his life by conventional religious means. He goes to confession, having been disturbed by thoughts of his own "waiting grave" and the potential danger of the pickup football game in which he is about to participate with the "Fifty-eighth Street Cardinals." But the game ends in a vicious brawl, several boys are hurt, and the team is banished from Washington Park by the police. These events establish a rhythm that recurs several times through the remainder of Studs's short unhappy life: examples or warnings of death, religiously implemented resolutions to reform (confession, Mass and communion, joining parish organizations), and inevitable backsliding. The effect is a blanket refutation of the morally efficacious *memento mori* tradition in nineteenth-century Irish-American literature. One such sequence at the center of the trilogy involves Studs's attendance at a parish mission. It culminates at the end of *The Young Manhood* with the symbolic death of Studs, passed out and wrapped around a fireplug on New Year's morning. At this point, he has less than two years to live. Another such sequence is at the opening of *Judgment Day*, which finds Studs and the gang, or what's left of it, on a train coming back to Chicago from the funeral in Indiana of Shrimp Haggerty, another victim of drink and dissipation. Counting up his dead friends, "Paulie and Shrimp, Arnold Sheehan, Slug Mason, Tommy Doyle, Hink Weber," makes "all the world seem to Studs like a graveyard," and the result is one more resolution to change—this time with the help of his new girlfriend Catherine. But the New Year's drunk and resultant pneumonia have weakened Studs considerably, and concrete premonitions of death in the form of recurrent illness and blackouts plague him constantly from here on out. Thus, Studs's actual death is the final step in Farrell's more pervasive accomplishment—the subversion in the trilogy of a whole range of unhealthy attitudes toward life and death that were prevalent in the Irish-American Catholic subculture. Though Farrell was probably unaware of Eugene Clancy's and Mary Anne Sadlier's work, he would not have been surprised by their fictional uses of these powerful conventions. *Studs Lonigan* constitutes a thorough criticism of distorting mythologies of character and aspiration in the culture into which its protagonist was born.

Farrell's second pioneering contribution of clarity to the fictional self-image of the American Irish is his development of a voice for the inarticulate. Many writers of the 1930s had as one of their aims speaking for the masses, but Farrell is the first American writer to grapple successfully with the Irish ethnic dimension of this challenge.[9] Beginning with Farrell's work, a central theme of Irish-American fiction is the tragic consequences of an inability to express private feeling, the heart's speech. This theme has been placed in its widest context by Gaston Bachelard, who asks: "What is the source of our first suffering? It lies in the fact that we hesitated to speak. It was born in the moment when we accumulated silent things within us."[10] The theme of tragic inarticulateness suggests a stylistic challenge, a problem of narrative voice. An author must decide how to express this theme: how can he speak for people who cannot speak for themselves? These problems of theme and style are central in immigrant/ethnic fiction generally, because much of this writing is an attempt to bridge the gap between fairly inarticulate, working-class-immigrant parents and their educated, highly literate American writer-children, whose aim it is to "speak for" their parents' generation. Hunger of Memory (1982) by Richard Rodriguez is an eloquent meditation on the ironies and frustrations of such attempts. Here, of course, the language barrier is often a pressing issue. But in this dilemma, because most came knowing English, Irish Americans are a special case, with its own set of ironies. This is because for the Irish the tragedy of private inarticulateness sometimes coexists with a marked facility for public speech, "the gift of gab," and the ironies of this seemingly paradoxical conjunction inform much Irish-American fiction.

Farrell's solution to the problem of narrative voice, of speaking for the inarticulate, is consistent with what he saw as "my constant and major aim as a writer—to write so that life may speak for itself" (Reflections 41). Through a third-person-limited point of view that shifts from character to character, he creates a kind of omniscience—but with a difference. It is an omniscience into which the consciousness of the author never intrudes. Farrell did invent a style that allows his characters to speak for themselves. It is a style of scrupulous plainness, an urban Irish-American plain style, and it is an effective mode for rendering the thoughts and speech of ordinary people for whom self-expression comes hard. Moreover, for this prodigiously gifted intellectual, encyclopedically well read and fiercely committed to the life of the mind, the forging of this style was a heroic effort of will. Through this plain style, Farrell bridges the gap between immigrant/ethnic family and writer-son. And he does so without a scrap of condescension. Finally, he does more. The reward for his faithful adherence to the plain style is that an authentic, minimal eloquence wells up at crucial points in his novels, notably in the solitary reveries of major characters. Truly organic, not grafted into the narrative by the author's imposed consciousness, this hard-won minimal eloquence embodies Farrell's faith in the ability of ordinary people to clarify and bless their own relatively uneventful lives, even if only in their own minds. This is his greatest gift to American fiction.

The O'Neill-O'Flaherty pentalogy provides excellent examples of the Farrell plain-style narrative voice. In the first place, these five novels constitute a great, extended achievement in thematic structure. Without impeding its realistic narrative flow, Farrell has made this 2500-page sequence a single, coherent work of art by organizing the material around two powerful themes. Two streams of experience mingle in these pages: the outer stream of social life, a chronicle of the works and days of three generations of Irish Chicagoans, and the inner stream of consciousness, the perceptions of that chronicle and of themselves in the minds of the individuals living it. Throughout the series, the same two watershed experiences recur: death and illuminating revery. Deaths in the family constitute the central events of the outer stream and emphasize the most important social theme of the series, what Farrell has called "the tragedy of the worker, the central social tragedy of our times."[11] Solitary reveries are the central events of the individual inner streams of consciousness in the series. These emphasize the most important internal, psychological theme, the inability of these people to articulate to one another their real perceptions, insights, and feelings. Clarifications of life and honest self-assessment come only in dreams and daydreams, and they are almost never shared. The theme gathers force in the three last volumes of the series, in which three major characters—Jim O'Neill, Mary O'Flaherty, and Old Tom O'Flaherty—all die without having spoken their minds to anyone. In the same volumes, Jim's son Danny O'Neill moves in the opposite direction. He comes to understand the social tragedy of his family's thwarted lives and the psychological tragedy of their failure to communicate. Also, his development suggests a third important theme of the series: with understanding comes the resolution to act; in Danny's case, to use art as a weapon against both tragedies.

The combined richness of detail and compassionate perspective in these books is due partly to the fact that they were for James T. Farrell very much a family affair. On February 2, 1934, begins the extraordinary group of letters in which, like James Joyce writing back to his Dublin relatives, Farrell asks his brothers and sisters for help on the O'Neill-O'Flaherty series. The first is to his sister Mary: "I've started the family saga, and maybe you could help me, by, without making it apparent that you're doing it, picking up whatever you can about LaSalle Street, and Mrs. Butcher, Mrs. Meyers, etc. I'd appreciate anything you can send me, and as you can get it, and so on." These letters go back and forth for the writing life of the pentalogy, and include questions and answers about street addresses and neighborhood characters, racing forms and "linguistic habits," and the mechanics of various jobs. "No details will be negligible I'm sure," Farrell writes early on, "so don't hesitate any time you feel so inclined to write more."[12]

In the first volume, with title and epigraph from A.E. Housman, Danny O'Neill is a wide-eyed, sensitive child, "A stranger and afraid, /

in a world I never made." The novel opens in August 1911 in seven-year-old Danny's mind, and finds him preoccupied immediately with death and revery. He thinks about dying and imagines what hell would be like. (It's Sunday morning and he's worried about the consequences of missing Mass.) He also thinks about his Aunt Louise, "who had gone to Heaven only a little while ago," and imagines playing Buffalo Bill and "saving her from the savage Indians who wanted to tomahawk her." He also asks his Aunt Margaret to "read me about Danny Dreamer in the funny papers," and he imagines himself as Billy Sullivan, the White Sox catcher, warming up Big Ed Walsh for a game with the Philadelphia Athletics (3-8).

Constant through *A World I Never Made*, Danny's dreaming is both isolating—he is often alone and lonely—and predictive of his artistic career. The novel ends for Danny, still seven at Christmastime, 1911, with two important, related imaginative experiences, a daydream of art and a nightmare of death. The first occurs on his way to the Loop with Aunt Margaret to see Santa Claus: "The telephone poles and buildings passed him like sixty. He saw himself as two Danny O'Neills. One of him was sitting in the elevated train that was going along, swish, zish. The other of him was outside, running, going just as fast as the train was, jumping from roof to roof" (457). This is an artist's dream of doubleness and control—to be able to step outside the self and walk easily through a recognizable world. The second experience occurs on Christmas Eve, when Danny dreams of hissing snakes and "a boy as big as Mother, with a beard like a dwarf and a black suit like the Devil," come to carry him off and kill him (494-96). The connection between these two dreams is not forged until the fourth volume, *My Days of Anger*, where the use of art to counter death becomes an article of faith at the beginning of Danny's life as a writer. Indeed, the early memory of "two deaths in the family this year" (11), Old Tom O'Flaherty of stomach cancer and twenty-one-year-old Louise of consumption, infuses *A World I Never Made*, which concludes with "our first Christmas without poor Father and Louise" (502).

Death and dreams continue to be important in the second volume, *No Star Is Lost*. (Again, the title and epigraph are from Housman.) Here the two most powerful sequences of events are Arty O'Neill's death from diphtheria (compounded by poverty) and Margaret O'Flaherty's self-destructive drinking bout of several weeks. Two-year-old Arty's death is a focal point for the theme of social tragedy in the series, which follows the O'Neill family's painful struggle toward a better life. In 1914 and 1915, the time of *No Star Is Lost*, the O'Neills are living in a small, cramped cottage at Forty-fifth and Wells, and on cold days the children "take turns sticking their feet in the oven." Jim O'Neill is working a back-breaking six-day week as a poorly paid teamster for Continental Express. After Arty gets sick, the doctor ignores several phone calls from the O'Neills, and the infant dies unattended. Nor will a priest come from St. Martha's just across the street to administer the last rites. "There's only one crime in this world, Lizz," says the heartsick Jim; "to be a poor man" (602). As Lizz is about to give birth to another child, Jim buries Arty with only his little daughter attending, and on the way back to the city from Calvary Cemetery, he sees middle-class homes and thinks, "In these homes the kids were happy and well-fed and had the care of a doctor when they were sick. And in these homes, the kids were alive" (620). That same day, the rest of the children are packed off to a public hospital (they all have diphtheria), and Lizz bears a stillborn son. An agonized Jim asks, "Do I have to bury this? Two in one day?" At the end of the novel, Jim is sitting alone in the darkened cottage, watching "the first gray streaks of dawn through the window."

The other tragic figure in *No Star Is Lost* is Danny O'Neill's tortured Aunt Margaret O'Flaherty. When her married lover breaks off their relationship, she goes on a terrifying drunk, a protracted psychological suicide attempt that nearly tears her family apart. Throughout this period, Margaret and her mother engage in verbal battles of epic proportion and harrowing fierceness, most of them observed by Danny, who turns eleven in the middle of all the trouble. Most of these firestorms blow over quickly, and they seem to leave few scars on the participants. At the end of one, Mary O'Flaherty blesses herself, rises from her knees, and walks to the kitchen, telling Margaret "calmly" that "I have to make me grandson a warm lunch for his little stomach." Indeed, these fights may even have a positive function, especially when compared to the very different belligerent tactics employed by Studs's mother in the *Lonigan* trilogy. The O'Flaherty family fights are, to an extent, cathartic. Margaret and her mother articulate and thus exorcise their worst fears and criticisms of each other: ungrateful, immoral prostitute/daughter versus overbearing, ignorant, greenhorn/mother. There is even a sense in which Mary and Margaret are enjoying themselves and their manipulation of the language. For Mary especially, language is still a living force, and she uses it with histrionic exuberance in imaginative metaphorical mixtures of scatology and imprecation, invective and abuse. Most of the time these people do not mean literally what they are shouting at one another. They use the language virtually for its own sake, and this acknowledgement of the power and pleasure of words is an Irish trait.

An adult immigrant such as Mary O'Flaherty still has this knack; a second-generation woman such as Mary Lonigan does not, and the loss can be explained in part by their relative positions in American society. For a good part of her life, the defining goal of Mary O'Flaherty has been sheer survival—raising a large family on very little money in a strange country. That of Mary Lonigan, better off and a generation further from Ireland, has been attaining middle-class respectability. Both women use words as weapons, but they use them differently. The ebullience, the joy

of flailing away with the language, has disappeared in the second generation, dismissed by lace-curtain aspirants as ungenteel and vulgar. The
ideal of respectability dictates control over the emotions: no more shouting
in the home, no more keening at wakes. The aim for Mary Lonigan, as
for Mary O'Flaherty, remains dominance in the family, but control is
gained now by withholding emotion, rather than by expressing it. Words
are used as stilettos rather than clubs. Mary O'Flaherty is a more attractive
character because she is more straightforward. It's the difference between
honest, if violent, assertiveness and duplicitious calculation of effect. In
addition, the transition to a pettier goal—from survival to respectability—
also makes Mary Lonigan's urge for dominance seem less attractive than
Mary O'Flaherty's. Although the matriarchal role is inherited from the
immigrant generation, the ends of power seem less justifiable.

Despite these mitigating considerations, however, Mary O'Flaherty's
sharp tongue has its negative aspect. On occasion the fighting does make
things worse, and real pain is inflicted. In addition, and regrettably, invective seems the only form of communication where vestiges of eloquence remain in this family, and this irony is a part of their larger tragedy.
The O'Flahertys can articulate their anger, but not their love. When a
briefly sober Margaret comes begging forgiveness, her mother refuses
to listen: "Tell your sorrow to Satan and the tinkers" (374). This rebuff
sends Margaret off again, and she ultimately reels home comatose, incon-
tinent, and hounded with delirium tremens so horrifying that she tries
suicide by turning on the gas. Vividly described in the novel, Margaret's
Bosch-like delirium features snakes and devils, waiters pouring gin from
phallic-shaped bottles, hideous animals, mud, slime, and excrement. This
nightmare vision is her only contribution to the pentalogy's catalog of
dreams. In My Days of Anger Margaret reaches the age of forty, chastened
and defeated, locked into a boring daily round and convinced that she
has been cheated out of her chance at life.

Farrell's most effective technique for revealing these characters, all of
whom have such trouble expressing their deepest affections and motives
aloud, is a kind of daydream-soliloquy. In No Star Is Lost, Mary O'Flaherty
has a fine long chat out in Calvary Cemetery with her husband Tom, who
has been dead five years. Recalling Ireland, the Mullingar Fair where they
met, their first hard years in America, and the death of their first son,
Mary realizes that this grave site is "the only plot of ground that they had
ever owned in America." Suddenly Old Tom seems to be standing there
with her, "a small old man in a white nightgown, with a slightly drooping
gray mustache," and Mary begins to complain about Margaret's drinking
and running around: "She's a child of Satan himself, she is." She goes
on to admit what she would never say to a living soul. She is sad because
"I'll never be seein' the old country and me people again." Finally she
reverts to her everyday self by administering a typical scolding to poor
Tom, for whom even the grave is no protection. Having been annoyed

several times by Lizz O'Neill's reports that her dead father has been speaking to her, Mary sets her husband straight one more time: "And Tom, don't you be going and giving all these visions to me daughter, Lizz, that she does tell me about. If you have messages, you give them to me. It's me that should get them, and not her. . . . I'm a hard woman when I'm crossed, Tom, a hard woman, and I'll make you toe the mark, dead or alive" (135-43).

Following its introduction in the first two novels of the pentalogy, Farrell's presentation of failed communication through the conjunction of revery and death expands in the three later novels. There he sets it beside the major contrasting theme of Danny's growth toward articulation through art. In *Father and Son*, the keystone third volume, Jim and Danny O'Neill are living only a block apart: Jim with Lizz and their other children in their best apartment ever, at Fifty-eighth and Calumet, and Danny with his grandmother at 5816 South Park Avenue. Here Danny gropes toward maturity. He goes through St. Stanislaus High School, graduating in 1923, and begins to take prelegal courses at the night school of St. Vincent's College in the Loop. Finally, he enrolls at the University of Chicago, just across Washington Park but an intellectual world away from South Park Avenue, where he is encouraged to write in an advanced composition course. These steps parallel Farrell's own attendance at St. Cyril's (later renamed Mt. Carmel) High School at Sixty-fourth and Dante Avenue, the night school at De Paul University, and the University of Chicago. During these years, Danny also holds down his first full-time jobs at the Express Company where his father worked and as a gas station attendant. And most important for his growth, he experiences the deaths of his father in 1923 and his grandmother Mary O'Flaherty in 1927.

Although the O'Neills seem finally to be out of the woods, thanks to Jim's promotion and their new apartment, their luck does not hold. In a matter of months, three crippling strokes, the legacy of his years of bone-wearying labor, render Jim O'Neill unemployed and helpless. As presented in this central novel, Jim's life and death embody both the social "tragedy of the worker" and the psychological tragedy of failed communication. Farrell's epigraphs succinctly gloss what will be the major concerns of *Father and Son*. Jim O'Neill's tragedy is set beside that of Tolstoy's hapless burgher: "Ivan Ilych's life had been most simple and most ordinary and therefore most terrible." Danny's growth toward an artist's understanding is compared to Baudelaire's: "—Ah! Seigneur! donnez moi la force et le courage de contempler mon coeur et mon corps sans dégoût"! ("Ah, Lord! Give me the strength and the courage to contemplate my heart and my body without disgust!")

Jim O'Neill is a decent working man of ordinary capabilities who fights tough odds to make a better life for his family. But he also has a violent side. As a younger man in the earlier volumes of the series, he occasionally gets drunk and fights in bars, and he has even hit his wife,

Lizz, once breaking her jaw. In *Father and Son*, though, Jim is older, wiser, and better off—until he is struck down. And yet, in a way Jim comes into his own at this point. In *Father and Son*, he faces uselessness, boredom, and death with dignity and courage. All through his life, from brawling youth to fleeting comfort to final wasting illness, Jim has been crippled by the inability to speak his mind. And the killing frustration that is the consequence of his tragic inarticulateness both makes him violent as a young man and dogs him to his dying day. In the middle of *Father and Son*, Jim attends Anna McCormack's wake and is deeply frustrated by his inability to communicate with her grieving husband: "Aware of how deeply he sympathized with Old Mike, he couldn't think of anything worth saying that would express his feelings. When you most wanted to tell another man something, you were least able to do so" (308). All through the series, and especially as he feels death approaching, Jim struggles to express himself to his family. His great frustration is Danny, whom he sees turning into a "dude" and forgetting that he comes "from poor people." One of Jim's greatest sorrows comes from sensing that, after the strokes have rendered him shambling and helpless, Danny is ashamed to walk down the street with him. Jim blames the O'Flahertys in part, but also himself, for having lost his son to his wife's family. Father and son try unsuccessfully to talk throughout this novel, but their only close moment comes when Jim asks Danny to recite Polonius's speech to Laertes. Shakespeare's words briefly bridge the gap between them, as Jim declares, "I'm your father, and I couldn't give you any better advice" (485).

Shakespeare, in fact, is Jim's companion and consolation. After his first stroke, he often sits up late alone, reading *Julius Caesar* and *Hamlet*, and struggling to understand his life and approaching death. The sincerity and depth of his solitary questioning make him one of the most memorable characters in Farrell's fiction. Jim's thoughts range widely. He meditates on the mystery of having children, and on the teachings of his Church: "He liked to think that Christ was born in a poor man's home, and never in His life was He rich. . . . A lot of people ought never to forget that" (290). Feeling that "there wasn't a great deal of justice in the world," he tries anyway to tell his children to live right, all the time asking, "would doing right get them anywhere?" (288). Regretting "the confident days of his youth," he sees that young men "like that kid Studs Lonigan" still have the same careless attitude, and watching children at play in the street "gave you the feeling that it was all so sad because they, too, were going to lose that innocence of theirs" (357). More and more, Jim feels "a lonely prisoner in life . . . and the captive of death." Frightened by a new sense of the passage of time, he is "tempted many times these days to get drunk," but realizes that "he couldn't gamble with his health and his blood pressure now, because there was too much dependent on him, his kids, his wife. If he collapsed, they would be sunk in poverty and have no one. No, he had to fight this out with himself" (357-58). When the last stroke sends him permanently home from work, he knows he will never get better and feels "that others didn't understand life and that he did. *Vanity, all is vanity*" (403).

Jim's last weeks are filled with petty indignities. Another of his children, the third, is sent away to the O'Flahertys. Lizz suggests that he put himself in a public hospital. His son Bill takes over as head of the house, and contradicts him on a point of discipline regarding the younger children. He is shamed by a Christmas basket from a Protestant charity which the family is unable to refuse. He has to make an X to get money at the bank, and he loses a five-dollar bill in the street. People on the El think he's drunk, kids mock and mimic his limp, and an apartment-house janitor chases him away as a loiterer. But worse than any of these is the fact that he has no one to talk to. All of his thinking is done in silent revery by the parlor window. He is unable to share his struggle for meaning with another living soul. Jim's last day, like Ivan Ilych's, is "most simple and most ordinary and therefore most terrible." At lunch, Lizz is full of Mrs. Muldoon's wake, where she stayed all night "because my heart bled with pity for her." When two of his children start arguing over the last bran muffin, Jim lashes out at the whole family: "You don't care about anyone else. You don't care about anything but gorging yourselves. All of you. What if your father is sick? What if your brothers work and put the bread in your mouths, none of you care." Pointing an accusing finger at Lizz ("It's your doing"), Jim leaves the room to lie down, "too tired even to be angry at what had happened" (592). These bitter words are his last. He lapses into coma and dies the next afternoon without regaining consciousness.

Father and Son also records Danny O'Neill's frustrated first attempts to articulate his thoughts. He fails with his father, of course, but also with his peers, most of whom continue to regard him as an oddball, a "goof." Danny is unable to tell a girl who is going to a different high school that he will miss her: "He couldn't say the words" (125). Nor is he able to talk honestly to himself, failing three times to start a diary of his "real feelings." There are, however, hopeful tendencies. With an O'Flaherty family fight raging around him, Danny is able to finish a story that he knows is good enough for the high school literary magazine. Printed in *Father and Son*, this is the same story, almost to the letter, that James Farrell wrote for his high school magazine in 1922.[13] "The Fruits of Sacrifice" is a romantic tale of a priest's martyrdom in Elizabethan Ireland. Its authenticity makes the story one of the few concrete links between the young Farrell's emerging literary consciousness and the rhetoric and mythologies of nineteenth-century Irish-American culture. Betrayed by an informer while saying an illegal Easter Mass in the open air, the priest, himself a convert, is murdered by British troops, "and the rock, which served as an altar, was bathed in the blood of a new martyr, Father Anthony." The troop commander turns out to be the priest's father, who then also becomes a Catholic and is condemned to death. "Two weeks later, after receiving the last rites of the Church, he went to meet his son, to whose sacrifices and prayers he undoubtedly owed the grace of his conversion and happy death" (188-90). Mary Anne Sadlier or Peter McCorry could easily have written this, and Farrell's appropriation here of his own adolescent contribution to the deathbed convention of Irish Catholic romantic/sentimental fiction makes a significant point. This is a genre of literature-as-propaganda to which, as a mature writer, he will not contribute.

Also, Danny's reaction to his father's death is a climactic encouraging sign. At first he is troubled because "he felt empty more than he felt anything." And yet he does recognize immediately two facts that restate the novel's main themes of social and psychological tragedy. First, he sees that "there was something tragic about his father. He told himself that his father was a man who'd never had a chance. His father had been a strong man, and a proud man, and he had seen that pride broken." Second, he sees that "he had never really known his father, and his father had never really known him" (601, 599). These ending revelations mark the beginning of Danny's coming of age, which is completed in the fourth novel, *My Days of Anger*. Having crossed Washington Park to attend the University of Chicago, he is at once stimulated by new friends and the world of ideas. He writes his first honest diary entries and goes on to produce a torrent of fiction in an advanced composition course. He loses his faith, at first in a dream, and wakes up a nonbeliever, "free of lies" (215). Other liberating rejections follow: of his pseudo-Nietzschean friend Ed Lanson, of the university, and of Chicago itself. At the same time, and gradually through the novel, Danny's "days of anger" (again the phrase is from Baudelaire) and confusion slowly evolve toward understanding of his family. In this process, his grandmother's death in the spring of 1927 is the crucial event.

Mary O'Flaherty's death, like that of Jim O'Neill, also embodies a statement of the tragedy of failed communication. Throughout the series, Mary has been a classic immigrant matriarch, holding her family together by sheer force of will. She often describes herself as "a hard woman from a hard country." But the other side of the coin is that the hard years have left her unable to express love and sympathy to those in the family who are most in need: Margaret in her emotional crises, Lizz swamped by the demands of her own large family, and Old Tom on his deathbed. Nor has she shared her own fears and sorrows with anyone. As she approaches death in *My Days of Anger*—she is just back from the hospital with a broken hip, thinner than ever, and eighty-six years old—a last extended daydream-soliloquy (all of chapter 26, pages 362-73) provides a summation of her character and concerns. As memories of Ireland and her parents' generation flood back, she admits the pain of emigration that she has kept to herself for sixty years. "And sure," she says to herself, "wouldn't

I be giving me right arm to be seeing the steeple of Athlone in the sun-shine, ah, but it was beautiful and wasn't it tall? Indeed, it was." Of course she was afraid, "all alone, and the boat going out of Queenstown harbor, and sure didn't I get down on me knees and pray to me God." Of course she was hurt by American mockery of her accent and her innocence: "So they think I'm a greenhorn, do they? I'll greenhorn them. Greenhorn them, I will." Of course she was saddened and frustrated by the news of her mother's death, "and there I was in Green Bay, Wisconsin, not knowing if me father had the money to give her a decent burial," and by the death of her own first child: "we christened him, the little angel, and he died, and what Christian name did we give him? And here I am forgetting the name of me own son, John. . . . and his headstone is sink-ing into the ground."

There is a refrain running through Mary's mind in this lovely, lyrical chapter—the one word, "Soon." She knows her death is near: "I do see the old men with death in their eyes. Nobody fools me. I won't be long here." She can see the circle of her life closing: "The strength is gone out of me bones. Here I am, and they take care of me just like I took care of them, and they carry me around like a baby." In a typical paradox, Mary now reveals that she has been kept going all these years by both love and love of a fight. "Last Sunday at dinner," she happily recalls, "I put me two cents in to keep them fighting away. And then I told me grandson, I told him, Son, I'm only fooling, and sure it's the fun of it I like. So I kept them at it for all they were worth." At the same time, she acknowl-edges her love and compassion for her family: for her husband: "Me poor Tom, your Mary that could run swift as the wind and sang you the songs that day of the Mullingar Fair is coming to you," for "me beautiful virgin daughter Louise . . . out with Tom in Calvary Cemetery," for "me poor son Al, carrying those heavy grips to pay all the bills," for "Lizz, me darling Lizz, the poor woman with all of those children, and one coming after the other," and even for Margaret, "wearing her hands to the bone caring for me and bathing and washing me, and cooking and caring for me and emptying me pots, the poor girl." And she also declares what Danny O'Neill has meant to her: "Me grandson, he's me son. Doesn't he call me Mother? Sure, if I didn't have him, wouldn't I lay down in the night and wouldn't I not wake up in the morning? What's kept me alive, with me family raised all these years, but me grandson?" "I'm no scholar but I met the scholars," says Mary, and she is proud of her grandson's chosen vocation: "and sure it's the poet and scholar he'll be, and don't I know that they'll be saying what a fine man he is, and it's poems he'll write." In the middle of this chapter, Mary is carried to the bathroom by Danny, who then returns to his typewriter and the book, his first novel, on which he is working. Here the point of view shifts for the only time in the chapter, and the focus on Mary's consciousness is interrupted briefly by the thoughts of her grandson: "He wanted to finish this book before she died. If he did and it were published, he'd dedicate it to her. But she couldn't read. . . . What was she thinking of by the window? What went on in her mind?" Imagining answers to these questions will be Danny O'Neill's and James T. Farrell's lifework.

Danny learns several important lessons from his grandmother's death a few days later. He is struck immediately by the incalculable value of time: "This life which he had been so spendthrift of, how precious it was." His youthful rebellion, especially against the Church, is tempered by understanding that "the sorrows of death remained, remained in the hearts of the living. . . . He understood now why people did what he could not do, what he could never do—pray" (392-93). Another sign here is that, on the morning of his grandmother's death, Danny kneels down, blesses himself, and pretends to pray with his family. This negates his earlier contention among his university friends that he agrees with Stephen Dedalus' refusing to pray at his dying mother's bedside in *Ulysses*: "What has kindness got to do with conviction?" says Danny. "I won't bend my knees" (377). Even his belief that "it was unmanly to cry," gives way to the release of real emotion, and he sobs and calls out his grandmother's name.

Danny's part in the O'Neill-O'Flaherty series leads ultimately to the summer day in 1927, a month after his grandmother's death, on which he prepares to leave Chicago for New York and a new life as a writer. Walking home down Fifty-eighth Street from the El, perhaps for the last time, he feels the weight of Washington Park as "a world in itself . . . a world in which another Danny O'Neill had lived." Feeling that he has "finally taken off a way of life, . . . as if it were a worn-out suit of clothes," Danny now has confidence in the "weapons" of his writer's trade: "now he was leaving and he was fully armed." In this, he echoes Stephen Dedalus, leaving Dublin for Paris in 1902 with his own "weapons" of "silence, exile, and cunning." Danny now also has a mature understanding of his position as an artist in relation to his family: "His people had not been fulfilled. He had not understood them all these years. He would do no penance now for these; he would do something surpassing penance. There was a loyalty to the dead, a loyalty beyond penance and regret. He would do battle so that others did not remain unfulfilled as he and his family had been" (401-02). The last pages of *My Days of Anger* are a kind of litany to this place and this family, for the weight of both is embedded in Danny's consciousness, even as he leaves them behind. From the street, he turns to "the stones, the buildings" of the old neighborhood. He enters "the alley that he had known since he was a boy," pushes open "the broken backyard gate," and climbs the stairs into the O'Flaherty kitchen. Looking into his grandmother's room, he sees, along with her clothes still hanging in the closet, pictures of Christ and the Sacred Heart, a crucifix, a holy-water fount, and rosary beads—the symbols of her life-long Catholicism, which he has also left behind, but which he no longer scorns. Then Danny walks to the parlor in the front of the apartment to sit "brooding over his plans," and his mind here at the end of the novel comes to rest where his dreams have always been centered: "He listened to the summer wind in the trees across the street in Washington Park" (402).

The idea of Mary O'Flaherty's last revery was in Farrell's mind as early as January 1938, when he asked the Guggenheim Foundation to support a research trip to Ireland, "concerned with the historic backgrounds of my characters, especially with those of Mrs. O'Flaherty who is an Irish immigrant in America. In future volumes of this series, as she ages, her memories of Ireland will become more important to her. In a future volume when she is over eighty and crippled, she will sit by her radiator through long winter days, often quiet, rethinking of her girlhood, falling asleep and dreaming of her Ireland." Farrell made the trip to Ireland in July and August of 1938. Five years later, he wrote to a friend announcing the completion of *My Days of Anger* and this phase of his writing life, these "years of driving work, years of eight to fourteen hour days concentrating on these connected books." In this letter he points with particular pride to the "long chapter, in Anglo-Irish, when Grandmother O'Flaherty sits by the window in a wheel chair, hip broken, slowly fading out of this life: it is a long revery, more or less Joycean, in which past and present jumble, time loses significance, she dreams and she awakes, and her life flows in jumbled time through her mind. . . . If I can bring it off, and I feel confident, it is quite a *tour de force*, and something fresh—the fading consciousness of an old woman, further, an old Irish immigrant woman, illiterate, who came out to America, raised her family here, seen them grow up, and sits doing this while her grandson sits preparing to write, even about her own life."[14]

Ten years later in 1953, Farrell published the fifth and last O'Neill-O'Flaherty novel. Although it was not a part of the original plan, *The Face of Time* is the perfect coda for the series. Opening in the summer of 1909, this book brings the design full circle to the deaths of Old Tom O'Flaherty and his daughter Louise, the memory of which hangs over the first volume, *A World I Never Made*. Also, in its rendering of Tom and Mary O'Flaherty's memories of Ireland and their early years in America, the novel returns to the very beginning of this family's story. The result is one of the finest American novels to deal with the felt experience of immigration. In addition, the theme of failed communication gets a final statement here, in the characterization of Old Tom, who lives out a restless retirement, alternately bored and harassed, and dies of a painful stomach cancer. Feeling useless and used up, Tom submits quietly to his wife's nagging, admitting only to himself that "he loved his Mary but he didn't love her tongue" (14). It is clear here that coming out to America has affected the O'Flahertys differently. Tom seems not to have recovered from the early humiliations, while Mary has emerged stronger, though not always in attractive ways. In fact, her dominance has turned Tom into the forgotten man of the family. Five-year-old Danny O'Neill wakes up one night frightened to find that his grandmother has gone out and left him alone in the apartment, and when she returns and reminds him that "your grandfather was here," Danny thinks, "He hadn't thought of calling Father. Why hadn't he thought of Father?" (134). And after Tom has been taken to the hospital, Mary remarks that "Ah, Pa was no trouble. You'd hardly know he was in the house" (318).

At the end of the novel, the inability to communicate becomes pervasive. On the day of his hospitalization, Tom's voice fails and he is unable to say goodbye to Danny. Her voice "breaking," Mary tells her family to "let me be," and that night they eat dinner "in silence" (312-16). The old man doesn't live on for long in the hospital, and in a last daydream-soliloquy, he reveals all the sad secrets that he has never spoken aloud. He has never felt at home in America, he is puzzled and embittered at having worked so hard and ended up with so little, and he wishes he could die in Ireland. Here is some of his moving revery:

> He'd wanted to tell Mary that he was afraid of America, afraid of it here in America, and, sure, if he told her that, what kind of a man would she be thinking him to be? Ah, she was a woman with nary a fear in her, not Mary. It was a source of wonderment to him that she had nary a fear in her heart, and the two of them, greenhorns if you like it, greenhorns in America in Brooklyn, New York, and Green Bay, Wisconsin, and Chicago. The strange people he'd seen and they were Americans and not his own people. Sure, wasn't he afraid to ask them how to find a street in Brooklyn? But not Mary, never her. Never in his life had he seen so many people as when he came out here to America, and that had been a cause for wonderment to him, where they had all come from. Hadn't he always been asking himself that question? . . . Sure, when he first came to America, he would look at the people in New York and Brooklyn, New York with wonder in his eyes because they were Americans and he was in America. And not a soul on this earth knew how he was always wanting to go back and wishing he had never come out, and himself driving the horse and wagon and not knowing the names of the streets and wanting to ask this man and that for directions and not always asking because of his brogue and his not wanting it thought he was a greenhorn, and getting lost and not knowing where he was and wanting to go home to Ireland. [334-35]

The Face of Time closes with three final echoes of its major theme. During his family's last visit to his bedside, Tom can hear Mary and Margaret discussing his imminent death, but he is unable to speak. When the hospital calls with the news of Tom's death, Mary leaves the family and shuts herself away in her bedroom, to grieve and pray alone. Standing before his grandfather's casket in the parlor, six-year-old Danny thinks, "There was Father. He couldn't talk. He was Father all right, and he wasn't Father." Then the novel and the series end with a dying fall of incoherent sound, as Danny hears "whispering voices in the dining room, the low agonized sobs of his Aunt Margaret, and then the noise of a streetcar going by on Indiana Avenue" (366).

Through these five novels, a few large themes build to powerful, cumulative statement. Of central importance in that process are the clarifying but unshared reveries and unprotesting deaths of Jim O'Neill, Mary O'Flaherty, and Tom O'Flaherty, which Farrell presents through the austere, unforced medium of his Irish-American plain style. Danny O'Neill's opposing movement in the direction of art provides effective counterpoint, but does not mitigate the force of the presentation of his family's tragedies. In fact, Danny's isolated battling toward significant speech serves, by its uniqueness, rather to underscore the problems—some internal, some imposed from without—of the culture in which he grows up. Moving, in *The Face of Time*, toward the end of her own short, lonely life, Louise O'Flaherty asks the largest question: "And was this the end of love, one going, dying, the way her father was dying? Must you, in the end, always be alone?" (321).

Throughout his prolific writing life, Farrell spoke eloquently of the purposes of his art. In his last novel published in his lifetime, *The Death of Nora Ryan* (1978), middle-aged writer Eddie Ryan realizes, while awaiting his mother's death in 1946, that some day he will turn the experience into art: "What was happening now, this present, would be the past and would be in his memory. The experience would have crystallized in his unconscious mind. . . . One morning he would wake up, sit at his desk, and start writing about it." When Nora Ryan's night nurse, Bridget Daugherty, begins to read Eddie Ryan's novel *A Son and His Father* (a significant choice), her reaction conveys Farrell's sense of an Irish-American audience: "The book was so much like life. She knew the people in this book. . . . She had known these people all of her fifty-three years. They were her own kind. She had never expected to read a book like this. She had never thought that books like this were written" (230). Elsewhere in the novel, Eddie Ryan thinks of the "simple purposes that his mother and others lived for," and wonders if her dying thoughts are of any consequence. His answer is a central tenet of Farrell's artistic faith: "Yes, it mattered. Nora Ryan's life was a world. For Nora Ryan. These thoughts brought back his most familiar and important ideas. He must one day dignify his mother's suffering in the consciousness" (321-22). From Jim O'Neill to Nora Ryan, the line of lives that have been so dignified in Farrell's work runs straight and clear.

Fortunately, the large-scale critical reevaluation of Farrell's fiction is now well under way. Our understanding of his writing springs from the work of Edgar Branch, whose essays, books, and bibliographies have created Farrell criticism and made further work possible. Branch and other critics, among them Horace Gregory, Blanche Gelfant, Nelson Blake, Charles Walcutt, and Donald Pizer, have placed Farrell firmly in the context of American realistic fiction. William Shannon was the first to draw particular attention to Farrell's ethnic dimension. Among a younger generation of critics, Ann Douglas and Alan Wald have written of Farrell's increasing relevance as a social critic, Robert Butler has established both the philosophical underpinnings and the subtle architectonics of Farrell's fiction, and Dennis Flynn has begun to open the rich Farrell Archive at the University of Pennsylvania, a voluminous collection of letters, diaries, and manuscripts that are one of the great personal records available to us of the social and intellectual history of twentieth-century America. Much work remains to be done to elucidate the full range and accomplishment of James T. Farrell as a writer. His work and influence in short fiction need to be explored in depth. His last, unfinished sequence, *A Universe of Time*, has only just begun to be considered critically. In his later fiction he often left Chicago and the Irish to continue his explorations of time, death, and the possibilities in modern life for self-knowledge, growth, and creativity. His first posthumously published work is *Sam Holman* (1983), a novel of New York intellectual life in the 1930s, and there are many more books in manuscript that need to be brought out into the light.[15]

Farrell was first and foremost an American realist: scrupulously honest, immune to sentimentality, and, in the earlier novels especially, pioneering in his commitment to giving serious literary consideration to the common life in an urban, ethnic community. His great strengths as a novelist are his development of convincing characters, the firm placement of these characters in a detailed, realistic setting, and the ability to conceive and carry through monumental fictional cycles. In addition, he brings to American ethnic fiction a sustained criticism of life and a new voice for the previously inarticulate. In their struggles, silences, and unshared epiphanies, their alienation and loneliness and endurance, Farrell's Irish continue to express essential realities of American immigrant and ethnic experience. In this endeavor, his fullest and most compassionate creation is Chicago's Irish South Side, which emerges in his fiction as a realized world, as whole and coherent as Joyce's Dublin and Faulkner's Yoknapatawpha County. He has done for twentieth-century Irish America what William Carleton did for nineteenth-century Ireland. As William Shannon declared in 1963, "No writer is more central to the history of the American Irish than James T. Farrell. . . . Time has transfigured him, and contemporaries have surrendered him to neglect, but he lives imperishably in his art. His portrayal of a vital part of the Irish experience endures."

NINE

Regional Realists of
the Thirties and Forties

When asked in 1979 by the *New York Times Book Review*, "What book made you decide to become a writer and why?" Norman Mailer answered as follows: "I read *Studs Lonigan* in my freshman year at Harvard and it changed my life. Literature through high school had been works by Sir Walter Scott, Thomas Hardy, Rafael Sabatini (*Captain Blood*) and Jeffrey Farnol (*The Amateur Gentleman*). Now, I realized that you could write books about people who were something like the people you had grown up with. I couldn't get over the discovery. I wanted to write. When I think of how bad I might have been at other occupations, I bless the memory of James T. Farrell." (Farrell had died four months earlier.) As a teenager in Irish Brooklyn during World War II, Pete Hamill felt a similar shock of recognition in *Studs Lonigan*: "I found myself abruptly and suddenly in the world outside my door and seeing it for the first time. . . . [Farrell] taught me and other city writers to look with pity and terror and compassion at the people we knew and at ourselves, to give value to the casualties of the urban wars, to speak in some way for those who have no voices" (132). Farrell has meant something like this to many writers over the years, including from his own time and place, Nelson Algren, Meyer Levin, and Richard Wright, and later writers as diverse as Tom Wolfe, Kurt Vonnegut, Jr., William Kennedy, and Bette Howland.

Certainly, Farrell's influence on Irish-American writing was immediate, pervasive, and telling. The Great Depression probably delayed the progress of Irish Americans into the literary life, but a large number of autobiographical first novels by Irish Americans appeared in the late 1930s and the 1940s, enough to constitute a legitimate new literary generation, the first since the later nineteenth century. The example of Farrell's fiction and the guidance provided by his literary criticism were crucially inspiring to their authors, who came from all over the United States. These were the regional realists, competent if unspectacular writers who used native materials to tell their own stories of earlier twentieth-century Irish ethnic experience. For the most part, their novels were single shots building toward a volley, but the best served as models for the following generations of even more numerous Irish-American writers, with whom this book will end. Farrell created a context for them, and they created a context for Edwin O'Connor, Elizabeth Cullinan, William Kennedy, and others.

It will be the burden of these last two chapters to establish that the tradition of Irish ethnic fiction continues in America right down to the present.[1]

In some ways the thirties and forties were vintage years for Irish-American culture. Farrell's great novels continued to appear throughout the period, from *Young Lonigan* in 1932 to *The Face of Time* in 1953. In addition to the direct influence of his fiction and criticism, aspiring writers had also the notable examples of F. Scott Fitzgerald and John O'Hara, novelists of Irish background who had emerged as major literary figures, albeit without concentrating on the ethnic dimension. Moreover, Eugene O'Neill, already acknowledged as America's greatest dramatist, received the Nobel Prize for Literature in 1936. Like his Irish predecessor William Butler Yeats, who had won the Nobel in 1923, O'Neill used the award as a spur to the courageous extension of his powers. In 1939 he finished *The Iceman Cometh* and in 1940 he wrote out his "tale of old sorrow, written in tears and blood," *Long Day's Journey into Night*, the wrenching family chronicle that remains the single greatest American play. And he went on in 1941 to fill out the characterization of his brother Jamie in *A Moon for the Misbegotten*. In American film there were also Irish-American accomplishments. James Cagney came into his own in *Public Enemy* (1931), and before the decade ended John Ford had won two awards for direction from the Motion Picture Academy.

An important early novel of regional realism was Joseph Dineen's *Ward Eight* (1936), the prototype for the latter-day novel of Irish-American political life. Because John T. McIntyre and his nineteenth-century forebears in the genre had been forgotten, Dineen can be said to have reinvented the type made famous twenty-years later by Edwin O'Connor's *The Last Hurrah*. Indeed, the story-line is the same: an old-fashioned boss, part rogue, part Robin Hood, runs a machine that, despite its success, dies with its leader at the end, a casualty of changing times. Furthermore, as O'Connor's hero Frank Skeffington owes much to James Michael Curley, Dineen's Hughie Donnelly is based on the career of Martin Lomasney, the real-life boss of Boston's Eighth Ward in the years encompassed by the novel, 1890 to the late 1920s.

But Dineen is more of a reporter than a novelist—he worked for the Boston *Globe*—and he is much better at observing and describing the workings of Irish-American political and social institutions than he is at creating plausible characters. James T. Farrell's incisive review of *Ward Eight* went beyond the novel at hand to locate the limitations of most works of Irish-American regional realism. Although they contain "a great deal of information" and illustrate "the ability to tell a story," these novels fail to "embody a way of seeing life that is fresh, that is individualized and that establishes implicitly and explicitly a novelist's own view of life." Furthermore, Farrell continues, Dineen relies on stock, "familiar notions of the Irish" and "picturesqueness [which] is frequently a kind of unconscious dodge on the part of a novelist who has not been able to establish his own level of perceptions, and to interpret and represent life from that level."

And yet, there is much here on which later writers including Edwin O'Connor could build. With more detail than anyone since Mr. Dooley, Dineen describes the operations of an urban ward machine and an Irish neighborhood social structure. Both are seen through the eyes of one immigrant family—the O'Flahertys. On the day he lands in Boston, Dennis O'Flaherty is led to Hughie Donnelly's office and gets a tenement flat, a job in the Sewer Department, a place in Hughie's "Doomsday Book," and these instructions: "Ye'll keep in touch wid me because there's certain things I'll be after askin ye to do, and ye'll have to do them" (4). Dennis and his wife Nora go on to raise a family that includes a politician (their first-born, "Big Tim"), a priest, a gambler, and a flapper (Mary, who runs off and marries a Protestant).

The novel further explains Hughie's political wisdom in realizing the potential power of the "second army of occupation," the Italians, whose padrone Tony DiPisa becomes Hughie's first non-Irish lieutenant. Similarly, Hughie handles a challenge from within by patiently watching the rise and insurgency of college-educated "Big Tim" O'Flaherty, who is ultimately reined in to be his son and heir as Hughie "arranges" Tim's election as District Attorney. Finally, just before his death, Hughie predicts astutely that "my little kingdom will break up like the harbor ice at ebb tide." Boss of the ward for fifty years, he has been the bridge between the first waves of frightened, unsophisticated immigrants and the more secure American-born ethnics like his successor Big Tim. An enlightened ruler, he has provided services and sympathy in exchange for votes and power in the grand old style. But his power will die with him. As he tells Big Tim, "Ye'll always be a boy to the old-timers. They'll vote for ye, but they won't vote for somebody else when you tell 'em to" (308-09).

Ward Eight also delineates the great movement toward lace-curtain respectability in Irish-American society between the nineties and the twenties. Dineen catalogues the furnishings of the symbolic "front parlor": "an upright piano, an 'art-square' carpet of Chinese design manufactured on Canal Street a stone's throw away, a parlor stove like an upright cylinder with royal studded crown, . . . an upholstered easy-chair, a sofa and rocker" (77). And he registers the later addition of a gramophone, "its huge horn resembling a mysterious bud that had violently burst into flower," as well as the ultimate transition in the twenties when "an automobile now replaced the piano as the gauge of one's social position. The larger the car the more successful and important the owner" (252).

And yet, despite the wealth of detail, the characters never really breathe. Neither Hughie's nor Big Tim's motives and thinking are fully or plausibly presented. At the end, Big Tim decides to walk away from

Hughie's mantle of power by becoming honest both politically and personally. He vows on the last page to "throw away the old system and build a new one, an honest one." He will begin by "bringing the organization down upon his head immediately" (329) by marrying his true love—a divorced Protestant woman. This grand stroke gets the novel finished, but is never sufficiently explained, and it is emblematic of Dineen's limitations. Otherwise, though, *Ward Eight* is an insightful set of observations of twenty-five crucial years of Irish-American political and social life, a pioneering book for Boston in particular and urban Irish literature more generally.

In *Such Is the Kingdom* (1940), Thomas Sugrue describes one year (1909) in the life of the "high" Irish of Kelly Hill in a Connecticut factory town near New Haven. The novel mostly registers the perceptions of six-year-old Jamie O'Mahaney, who observes with innocent wonder his three-generation extended family. The O'Mahaneys are solidly middle-class Irish who live "on the hill and walk a half a mile to the shop so the children can grow up decently, with some fresh air and no coalyards and railroad tracks." Presented as responsible, hard-working, and family-centered, they provide no surprises and little self-examination. The other local characters are fairly stereotypical as well: the kindly saloonkeeper; the intelligent priest with quietly ironic perspective, a sensitive doctor who drinks to ease his pain, a few brawling ne'er-do-wells. The texture of everyday life in another Irish-American corner is here, but nothing much happens. Even the occasional references to Yankee-Irish conflict are mild ripples in a placid pool. The climactic events are Grandfather O'Mahaney's death and wake, Jamie's near-fatal illness and miraculous recovery on Christmas morning, and the boy's first communion the following spring. But even at the end there is little psychological development and less revelation of growth or change.

Another autobiographical first novel, *Holding Up the Hills* (1941) by Leo R. Ward describes Irish-American life in rural Iowa from the 1890s to the 1930s. Its subtitle, "The Biography of a Neighborhood," suggests Ward's contention that Irish ethnic community solidarity was not limited to the cities, but his argument pushes him into what becomes a sentimental picture of Edenic pastures of plenty peopled by open-handed Irish farm folk. The picture recalls Mary Anne Sadlier's 1862 propaganda novel of Irish rural colonization in Iowa, *Con O'Regan; or, Emigrant Life in the New World*. *Holding Up the Hills* does contain some notable character sketches, including the matriarch, Mary Ann Cawley, born in Canada like many of the Iowa Irish, the posthumous daughter of a man who died "on the fever ship before they ever reached the shore," and who had thirteen children of her own, eight of whom lived to adulthood. And again, there is the saving grace of detail. Ward quotes passages of remembered speech and letters to evoke purposefully "how the Irish, left largely to themselves, speak after three generations in Iowa" (18). He also notes some telling indications of the differences in world view between the old country and the new, even in a rural setting. Wakes have been transformed from "mild carousals" with a "jigger-boss," or bartender, in charge, to "deeply religious" occasions controlled by those best suited to "lead the beads" (79-80). And he describes the shift in perspective from a communitarian to a business ethic, from belief among the farmers that "we were laboring for the growth of our own families and neighbors" to a sense that "life is big business, that one labors for money, . . . even on the farm" (108). The novel ends on a note of new crisis, as the dust storms of the early 1930s have swept away the established way of life in this community, leaving a painful, unresolved challenge for the new generation: "The hope is taken away from us now. That is the tragic condition: insurance companies holding our property! How then on earth are we to reach again, in any form whatever, a community comparable to our old one?" (202).

In *John Fury: a Novel in Four Parts* (1946), Jack Dunphy returns to the Irish South Philadelphia setting of John T. McIntyre's *The Ragged Edge* of 1902. The forty-four years between the two is another measure of the hiatus between the two cycles of Irish-American fiction. Dunphy's first novel, this is the story of immigrant coal-wagon driver John Fury, a silent, bewildered giant of a man, who is driven to drink and sudden death by forces beyond his control or understanding. The love of his life, his wife Mamie, dies, leaving John with two daughters to raise. Five years later he marries the servant-girl Bridget, a shrewd, nagging woman who sees the marriage as a business merger that will deliver her from domestic service to a home of her own. Domestic griefs come thick and fast to the ill-prepared John Fury. The son born to him and Bridget turns against his father, the two daughters both make bad marriages, and Bridget, in league with her unmarried brother, continues to hound her husband. In the end, although he is only fifty-four, John loses his job as a teamster because "it's trucks now. Trucks everywhere. Pretty soon we won't have a horse around" (262). In a fit of impotent rage, John tries to break into his own house, which has been locked against him. After smashing windows with an iron pipe, he falls over the front-porch railing, hits his head, and dies. Throughout the novel, John Fury's only self-expression comes from violence. In an early scene, he reacts to the confusion of emotions surrounding the birth of his first child by lashing out at a fellow-worker in a violent fight. Another example of working-class-Irish emotional inarticulateness, John never outgrows his "days of anger." Among the most powerful scenes are the poignantly hopeful first communion day of John's son, the counterpointing scenes of domestic violence where John lashes out at his own family, and the pathetic death of the protagonist on the novel's final page.

The book is a series of brief, impressionistic sketches, more like bare-bones prose poems then conventional paragraphs and chapters. Again,

Farrell's review extends his clarifying critique of Irish-American fiction of the 1940s: "In intention, it is the tragic story of a simple man who understands neither the social forces which contribute to his downfall, nor his own psychological motivations, which frustrate him and turn him into a non-communicative man who cannot express himself, and who can do little to win the love which he needs." However, Farrell notes the lack of sufficient social detail from John Fury's "working life" to fill out the tragedy of "the poor Irish workman, a man whose livelihood depends on his strength and health," and the lack of sufficient psychological detail to explain his fatal flaw as a "dour, silent, locked-up man." "Having stripped his story so bare," says Farrell, "the book lacks range and scope." Certainly, Farrell's own O'Neill-O'Flaherty series presented Jack Dunphy with a model of the extended analysis of character and situation lacking in *John Fury*. In a heartening late reclamation during the past decade, Dunphy has returned to his own early Irish-American experience to write two accomplished novels of the Philadelphia of his youth, *First Wine* (1982) and *The Murderous McLaughlins* (1988). The latter is discussed in chapter 10.

In *Moon Gaffney* (1947) Harry Sylvester brings in a report from the Irish middle class in Brooklyn in the 1930s. More of a polemic against Tammany politics and conservative Catholicism than a balanced work of the imagination, the novel traces the coming of age of Aloysius "Moon" Gaffney, the son of a New York City deputy fire commissioner and admired member of the Irish community who lives comfortably in a two-story brownstone apartment in Brooklyn. A non-practicing lawyer and errand boy in Al Smith's mayoral entourage, Moon is destined to rise in Tammany politics simply by hanging around and implementing the prevalent Hall policies of busting unions as Communist/Jewish fronts and bolstering the conservative Catholic hierarchy of the New York diocese. However, he begins associating with a group of young radical Catholics in the theologically liberal and socially responsible *Catholic Worker* crowd, and the result is a complete reversal of his ideology and ambitions. In the end, Moon embarks on a career as a union lawyer, thereby bringing down on himself the wrath of the Church and the regular New York Democratic party who dismiss him as another "Commie" and "Jew-lover."

There is some description of New York lace-curtain-Irish life, but the characters, including Moon, are little more than mouthpieces for Sylvester's harsh critique of the Tammany politicians and the Catholic clergy, especially the latter. For example, Father O'Driscoll deliberately misinforms young engaged girls about the "rhythm method" of birth control to make sure they get pregnant. Also, several times the priests and their middle-class, Notre Dame-educated parishioners (Sylvester was a 1930 graduate) express explicitly anti-Semitic and anti-black feelings, while continuing to see themselves as model Christians. One character rails against Irish Catholic Jansenism as having "bitched up the Church's teach-

ing so that the average Catholic thinks sex is filthy and hates or is suspicious of anyone not a Catholic. Why doesn't the hierarchy do something
about it instead of sitting around on their tails and telling each other what
a great race the Irish are? I'm half Irish and I hate the way they've bitched
up the Church, perverting her doctrines and twisting her teachings and
then patting themselves on the back. I hate their insane pride of race and
of religion and their incredible fatuousness" (262-63). Because of such
outbursts and the corroborating characterizations of priests and parishioners, *Moon Gaffney* created quite a stir in the late 1940s in Irish Catholic
circles.

Much more angrily anti-clerical than anything in Farrell, *Moon Gaffney*
nonetheless owes a good deal to Studs Lonigan and Danny O'Neill. Fueled
by unresolved frustration, Harry Sylvester gives a polemical rendering of
aspects of Irish America which Farrell had been exploring in a more balanced way for fifteen years previously. In an essay on "Problems of the
Catholic Writer," Sylvester admitted to being "by nature more polemicist
than novelist" (109). He also acknowledged his admiration for Farrell in
a 1947 review of Farrell's essays on *Literature and Morality*. In asserting
Farrell's importance as "critic and reformer of the contemporary scene,"
Sylvester calls Farrell's ideas "more basic than those which contemporary
Catholicism and Christianity now stress," a great irony given Farrell's personal renunciation of Catholicism. Moreover, a "second irony is that in
his close analysis of what is or is not right—regardless of popular no-
menclature—he ranks with the best theologians," men such as "Suarez,
Newman, Bossuet." This high praise marks a strong intellectual kinship
between these two writers. "Here is an honest man," concludes Sylvester,
"and one who writes with both clarity and power, literary virtues not
common in his time" (26-27).

Mary Deasy's *The Hour of Spring* (1948) is a Midwest family chronicle
that traces three generations of the Joyce family from 1870, when old Matt
Joyce comes to America from County Kerry with his nephew Timothy,
to 1928, when Timothy's death marks the breaking of the last living link
with the old country. The story of the Joyce family's settlement and progress into the American middle class in Coroli, Ohio, is narrated by Bridget
Joyce, old Matt's grand-daughter, who puzzles out the memories of three
aging family members while awaiting the birth of her own first child in
California. The first of several Deasy novels of Midwest Irish-American
life, *The Hour of Spring* is the closest to the author's own family experience
in Cincinnati.[2] Reminiscent of Farrell's portraits of children of immigrants
such as Margaret O'Flaherty and Lizz O'Neill, Deasy renders the bewilderment of the second-generation Joyces, caught between the Old World
and the New, and variously crippled in the working out of their American
destinies in politics, acting, the business world, and an often tempestuous
family life. As one of them puts it, "It's my generation that's betwixt and
between, that's lost the old values and the old loyalties without being

able to lose the remembrance of them too. We're your lost generation, if you like—the half-satisfied, the drifters, the rebels, torn between the old narrow loyalties and the new life inside us" (71).

The Parish and the Hill (1948) by Mary Doyle Curran contains one of the clearest embodiments of the difference between shanty and lace-curtain Irish and the problems of transition from one to the other. The tensions are embodied in the novel's narrator, Mary O'Connor, the youngest child and only daughter, who finds herself caught between her vibrant, activist shanty-Irish mother and her "strange, saturnine" lace-curtain father. As a young girl, Mary recalls literally "standing in a doorway with my father pulling me one way and my mother the other. Full of pain and panic, I wondered why neither would cross the threshold. With the clear logic of a child, I realized that I could not go both ways" (95). Identifying strongly with her mother and her maternal grandfather, Mary describes a childhood and early adolescence marred by tearing conflicts within her immediate and extended family. This autobiographical family history from the perspective of a sensitive, intelligent child is set in the Holyoke, Massachusetts of Mary Doyle Curran's own childhood. The novel distinguishes clearly between the shanties and tenements of "Irish parish," the home of Mary's mother's family, the O'Sullivans, and the lace-curtain pretensions of "Money Hole Hill," to which Mary's father, James O'Connor, brings his protesting wife and family. Mame O'Sullivan O'Connor is a fully realized, positive characterization of the Irish-American matriarch. She is sharp-tongued, passionately religious, loving to her children, loyal to her husband, hospitable to her seven rowdy brothers—an earthy, intense, and complicated woman. Her husband is dour, judgmental, narrow, conservative. A solitary, shadowy figure, he easily gives up the joys and supports of community life, for which he has little use to begin with, in order to live on the seedy "Irish" outskirts of the old Yankee bastion, "the Hill." The other strong character, and a great influence on young Mary, is her grandfather O'Sullivan, a gentle, saintly old man, still honored in the Irish community though entering his second childhood. A living link to Ireland and the immigrant past, termed by his grand-daughter "the refuge then, the symbol now, of my existence" (20), old John O'Sullivan brings the authority of his experience to his definition of the difference between the Irish Parish of his youth, "more like the old country than Boston just a hundred miles away," and "the Hill with its pot of gold and Irishman fighting Irishman to get at it" (48-49). And his is also a vivid sense of the contrasting cultures: "A dog howling on the Hill is only the howl of a dog—in the Parish it is an omen."

Set mostly in the 1920s, the novel ends with the onset of the Depression. The mills close and the O'Connor family ends up on relief. The final blow is a forced move back "to the fringes of the Parish," where young Mary finds that "there was no return to what had been," because "we had lived on the Hill." Having come full circle, she has a last, sad dream of her brother playing on his violin a slow air of "lamentation of the dead for the living" (220-21). *The Parish and the Hill* is a solid evocation of a family of New England Irish in the throes of a cultural transition in which everyone loses more than they gain.[3] Very well reviewed when it appeared, the novel was hailed in the New York *Times* as "a bold book" that "has prepared the way for the ultimate in Irish-American novels— the one about Boston" (McGrory 21).

Yet another country heard from is the Irish South Bronx of Howard Breslin's *Let Go of Yesterday* (1950), which traces the Callan family from the Armistice of 1918 to Pearl Harbor Day, 1941. This is a nostalgic and sentimental book, presenting one loving family as they move a bit too placidly through the years, and yet, the novel does contain a good deal of interesting detail about three generations of the New York Irish, beginning with the narrator's immigrant grandparents: "When Mary O'Gormley married big Michael Callan she took to his home a hope chest full of linen, eight lace curtains, an autographed copy of Thomas Moore's poetry, and her sister Eliza" (33). Along the way, Breslin defines a crucial character type: "An Irish matriarch with a touch of soft brogue on her tongue, and a core of steel. The last of an old tough breed that is dying out. Patient sufferers of their husbands; despots ever, but fierce defenders of their children. More Puritan than the Puritans, more pious than the Popes, less charitable than Cromwell, but strong and proud, drivers of themselves as well as their families" (32). Also convincing is the depiction of the conversion to Irish nationalism of second-generation Irish at the time of the Easter Rising in 1916. Young Daniel Callan "who had thought Aunt Eliza's stories a bore by the time he was ten" is surprised to find himself "shaken so deeply by the results of Easter Week . . . .The volleys of the firing squads in Dublin Castle had brought out a latent Irishness that he had not suspected. It had caught him unawares and toppled him" (61-62). In such passages, even the least successful of these regional novels help to fill in the record of early twentieth-century Irish-American life.

A number of other writers also contributed to the burst of Irish-American fictional activity in the 1940s. The best known of these, because of their successful theatrical and movie versions, were Ruth McKenney and Betty Smith. McKenney's autobiographical *New Yorker* stories contain light satire of Irish-American middle-class life. Collected as the best-selling *My Sister Eileen* (1938) and *The McKenneys Carry On* (1940), these stories were then turned into an award-winning Broadway play and a popular 1942 movie. Not herself Irish, though her step-father was, Smith provides a memorable, nostalgic evocation of the Irish Williamsburg neighborhood in *A Tree Grows in Brooklyn* (1947) and two later novels.[4] And there were many others as well. Roger B. Dooley wrote a series of novels tracing several Irish generations in Buffalo, New York, beginning with *Less Than the Angels* (1946) and *Days Beyond Recall* (1949). After producing a number of novels with Irish and continental settings, Irish-born Kathleen Coyle used an American setting in *Immortal Ease* (1939), which describes the turbulent life of an Irish writer who marries in New York and summers in Maine. Ellin MacKay Berlin wrote of the transition from New York tenements to Southampton country clubs in *Lace Curtain* (1948). Another contemporary novel of the New York Irish nouveau upper-class is Frank Leslie's autobiographical *There's a Spot in My Heart* of 1947. In *Mooney* (1950), William Brown Meloney chronicles the life of an undertaker in New York's Dutchess County. Margaret Marchand's *Pilgrims on the Earth* (1940) describes Irish life and labor agitation in a steel town near Pittsburgh. Doran Hurley wrote *Monsignor* (1936) and *The Old Parish* (1938) about the "Yankee Irish" interaction with French and Portuguese Catholics in a southern New England milltown modeled on Fall River, Massachusetts. The first of Joseph Dever's three novels of Boston Irish life, *No Lasting Home* appeared in 1947. Clyde F. Murphy's *The Glittering Hill* (1944) describes the Irish community in Butte, Montana, during the mining boom of the 1890s. And so it went. There were enough of these novels for a reviewer in 1948 to remark on what had become "a long line of fictional inquiries into the sea-change suffered by the Irish character" (McGrory 21).

Finally, there were four writers in particular who brought exemplary sophistication and craftsmanship to Irish-American materials in this period of regional realism: Charles B. Driscoll, J.F. Powers, Edward McSorley, and Brendan Gill. First came *Kansas Irish* (1943), the memorable story of author Driscoll's own family. While contributing to the 1940s Irish fictional context, the book is really an early model for the significant subgenre of late-twentieth-century Irish-American autobiography which includes Mary McCarthy's *Memories of a Catholic Girlhood* (1957), Frank Conroy's *Stop-Time* (1967), William Gibson's *A Mass for the Dead* (1968), Francis Hackett's *American Rainbow* (1971), Maureen Howard's *Facts of Life* (1978), and John Gregory Dunne's *Harp* (1989).

Kansas Irish is the story of "Big Flurry" (Florence) Driscoll a West Cork fisherman born in 1836 who comes to America in his late twenties, marries a woman half his age in 1867, and goes on to have seven children while turning himself by fierce labor into a prairie farmer in Kansas. A hard, angry man with the strength and temperament of a bull, Big Flurry dominates his family and the book. He has talents for punishing labor, parsimony, and holding a grudge. He never forgives his long-suffering wife for forcing him to buy a half-pound of tea on their wedding day, thus establishing what he imagines as a life-long habit of plotting to spend his money. But Charles Driscoll tempers his characterization of his difficult father with compassion for Big Flurry's two persistent afflictions. Like many Farrell characters, notably Old Tom and Mary O'Flaherty, Big Flurry is a type of the permanently alienated and emotionally impoverished immigrant. After thirty years in Kansas, he realizes "that he would always be an alien. . . . Who gave a God-damn whether a job-boom was fore or aft, in this prairie country? Which of his children could respect his ability to reef a mainsail in a sleet storm? Yet, he seemed to try to say, these are the items I have to offer, and there are no takers. Let me go back where these things are current coin" (274-75). And when at the end of the book his wife and children raise $2,000 to send him back to Ireland to live, he goes. Alone. Moreover, in occasional poignant scenes—for example, when his young son dies of pneumonia and the ministrations of a quack doctor—Big Flurry reveals himself to be one more emotionally handicapped Irishman who feels affection but cannot express it. Driscoll is ultimately compassionate in his last summation of his father: "I did get the feeling that the Old Man was lonely. He had made one great venture in life, a break from his native soil, for freedom. He had not found freedom, but frustration and sorrow."

Flurry's wife, Ellen Brown Driscoll, is also well drawn. Born in Ohio of a family from Cork, fourteen years younger than her husband, Ellen is the quiet, religious center of the family. She is not a sentimentalized martyr, but a woman of strength who stands up to local merchants, raises up an engaging, individualistic group of children who love her dearly, and seriously threatens her increasingly intransigent husband with divorce. Another memorable figure is Ellen's spinster sister Fannie, a generous servant girl, guilelessly admiring of her wealthy employers, fiercely superstitious and religious. During tornadoes, she showers the family with holy water to keep them safe. Another strength of the book is Driscoll's detailed descriptions of farm life—of how things worked and how they were made, from tilling the soil by hand behind a four-horse team, to handling cows, to outlasting violent prairie storms. *Kansas Irish* is clear, thorough, workmanlike, real. There is no more complete picture of late-nineteenth-century Irish immigrants to the American plains. It is unfortunate for Irish-American literature that Charles B. Driscoll otherwise occupied himself by writing stories of piracy and buried treasure, among them *Doubloons*, *Treasure Abroad*, and *Driscoll's Book of Pirates*.

In the title story of his first collection, *Prince of Darkness and Other Stories* (1947), J.F. Powers has his not-quite-failed priest/protagonist Father Burner deplore a Book-of-the-Month Club selection: "He wished the Club would wake up and select some dandies, as they had in the past. He thought of *Studs Lonigan*—there was a book, the best thing since the Bible." This wry acknowledgement of Farrell is one of few explicit references to things Irish in Powers's small, beautifully crafted body of fiction. His great gift to American letters has been the presentation of the Catholic clergy as fully realized human beings, and his commitment to the scrupulously realistic rendering of the lives and environments of ordinary priests and nuns has been no less pioneering than Farrell's commitment to urban Irish-American experience. Because he is much more concerned with Catholic than Irish experience, Powers's fiction will not be treated here in detail. And yet, he needs to be counted as a writer of Irish background who since the mid-1940s has been producing realistic fiction with stylistic grace and satiric power that has provided a healthy model for other and younger writers, Irish-American and otherwise.

The great subject of Powers's fiction is the difficult, jarring relationship between flesh and spirit, the World and the Church. To it, he brings an essentially Horatian satiric vision that is biting without bitterness. In his first novel, *Morte d'Urban* (1962), Powers rings marvelous changes on the ancient debate through his extended characterization of Father Urban Roche, a worldly, entrepreneurial priest who has a Pauline conversion to spirituality after being struck down by a golf ball on a retreat-house course. The publication of his long-awaited second novel, *Wheat That Springeth Green* (1988), about Father Joe Hackett's battle for "the separation of Church and Dreck" (316) reveals that Powers's portraits of clerical life are as clear and sharp as ever.

One early story can serve as a brief example of his major theme. "The Forks" succinctly embodies the debate in the American Catholic Church between social conservatives and social-action liberals. Here, the issue is joined between older, complacent Monsignor Sweeney, a "bricks-and-mortar, builder-priest," and his idealistic young curate Father Eudex, who reads the *Catholic Worker*. The Monsignor is exasperated by his curate's ignorance and unconcern about the trappings of priestly propriety—from automobiles to clothes to the correct use of "the forks" at table. The story ends with an impending serious break between the two priests, as Father Eudex flushes down the toilet a "donation" from a local company known for exploiting its workers. This is a gem of a story, detailed in its rendering of rectory life, perfectly pitched in tone. The importance of Powers as a model can be seen by comparing "The Forks" (or "The Lord's Day" or "Prince of Darkness") with the strident polemics against priestly hypocrisy in Harry Sylvester's *Moon Gaffney*, published in the same year, 1947. The fiction of J.F. Powers rejuvenates the tradition of Irish-American satire, the roots of which are back in the pre-Famine generations. And there is one more thing for which we have Powers to thank. His fiction provided an immediate antidote to the flood of movie sentimentality about Irish priests that had crested with the release of Bing Crosby's *Going My Way* in 1944 and *The Bells of St. Mary's* in 1945.[5]

A third exemplary regional realist of the 1940s was Edward McSorley, whose first novel, *Our Own Kind* (1946) was "good enough" in the judgment of one reviewer "to make a reader forget that we have already had so many novels about Irish-American metropolitan life" (Broderick 194). The setting is Providence, Rhode Island, in 1916, and McSorley tells the story of an illiterate immigrant foundry-worker, Ned McDermott, and his orphaned grandson Willie. This novel is extremely well crafted, with a closeness of texture and telling focus on the things of this world, starting from the objects observed by Willie on his grandparents' dresser on the opening page: last year's palm fronds, rosary beads, a host of mass cards for deaths and ordinations, a weathered black clay pipe. There are memorably authentic characterizations of the working-class people of Southern New England whose world this is, "Irish, all Irish," as Ned McDermott tells his grandson on the Providence-to-Boston train, "from Mansfield, Norwood right in to Boston and out again to Cambridge, every stick and stone of it" (288). *Our Own Kind* is a series of telling vignettes from the boy Willie's adolescence, and the tragic climax is the death of Willie's protector and encourager, old Ned, who has channeled his own American dream into his grandson, with charity and with no trace of bitterness about his own lack of opportunities.

McSorley presents their relationship lovingly and without sentimentality. Ashamed of his illiteracy, Old Ned "reads" the Sunday funnies to his grandson, filling them with "wondrous accounts about great and gay and witty Irishmen who were always getting the best of it," and the two stand often before the picture on the wall of Robert Emmet, "their refuge, their well of courage," while Ned recites their hero's speech from the dock and "the boy watched every word of the printing, now that he was learning to read in school" (8). By the time Willie realizes that his grandfather cannot read, he is fully committed to Ned's dream of education as the boy's deliverance from "pounding sand in a foundry like the rest of us" to a career as "a lawyer or a doctor or something of the kind." Ned has other valuable lessons as well. When Willie joins his schoolmates in tormenting an old Jewish man on the street, his grandfather recalls anti-Catholic feeling in his youth and before, including the burning of the Charlestown convent, and asks "And what is it, our turn now to be savages? Is it our turn to? God damn it, Willie, is that what's come of all the schools and the teaching? Sure we might have let the Yankees burn them down long ago and be done with it, if that all's to come out of it!" (66).

McSorley also gives us the most vivid rendering since Mr. Dooley and early Farrell of the old ethnic parish life. A highlight here is his rendering of Willie's fascinated attendance at the parish St. Patrick's Day play, a morality tale of Irish nationalism put on by the parishioners of St. Malachi's. In it, the landlord evicts his tenants, arrests the hero as a rebel, and offers the heroine an impossible choice: unless she marries the landlord, her true love will die on the gallows. In the end, a revolution breaks out, the landlord is defeated, and the lovers are reunited—all to the strains of Thomas Davis's "The West's Asleep." This vignette is another example, like Danny O'Neill's high-school story in Farrell's *Father and Son*, of nineteenth-century Irish culture still alive in twentieth-century America. Young Willie is fired with enthusiasm about his first play: "It was the most beautiful thing he had ever seen in his life, more wonderful than a solemn high mass!" (166). And he runs home to pour out the tale to his grandfather, who responds by packing the whole family off to the evening performance. Willie also learns Irish history from old Ned, who scorns Daniel O'Connell as a wealthy man who "owned half of Kerry" and "was always for palavering with them," while exalting his much-loved Robert Emmet: "They can talk and talk, but it's the sword will have the loudest voice in the end" (183). Willie is thus prepared to side with the rebels and his grandfather against the local priests when the exciting news comes in of the Easter Rising in Dublin in April 1916: "Street by street, building by building, the bitter losing fight was fought every night from every newspaper they could get" (84). And Willie sits absorbed while his grandfather defends the rebels in hot debate with tears rising in his eyes.

In counterpoint against Old Ned's fosterage of Willie are the roles played by the two women of this house, Ned's wife Nell and her unmarried sister Nora who lives with them. Strong-willed, sharp-tongued matriarchal figures, these two carp at and criticize the boy, seeing in him his mother, whom they had never liked or welcomed into their family. Nell spends an irascible life of duty-bound unremitting household labor punctuated by devotions to the rosary, gossip, and abstinence from drink. A cotton-mill spinner, Nora had wanted desperately to marry Ned herself, and she storms through the novel permanently soured, mean, and jealous. She plays the same role as the bachelor brother in Dunphy's *John Fury*—the troublemaker who lives out a bitter life causing distress for the married couple who have taken her in. It is a considerable part of the tragedy of Old Ned's death that Willie is left to defend himself against Nell and Nora unaided. Other well-drawn characters include Ned's two surviving sons, the compassionate labor-organizer Pat, who dies from a brutal police beating after a Socialist meeting, and the coldly cautious Chris, a bookkeeper and pillar of the Catholic men's sodality, and his mother's coddled favorite. It is Chris who informs the heartbroken Willie on the day of his grandfather's funeral that he will have to leave school and go to work. There are also two supportive, understanding young priests, the McCaffrey brothers, pragmatic Father Jim and intellectual Father Joe (a professor at the Catholic University), both of whom help Willie to grow up.

Ned's death and Willie's lonely last resolve are among the most moving passages in Irish-American fiction. Devastated by his son Pat's death, Ned contracts pneumonia and sinks rapidly. As he lies dying, he expresses his pained sense that his work with his grandson will remain unfinished. In a revery reminiscent of Mr. Dooley's eloquent canal-digging analogy for the course of a life, Ned speaks in the language of his own life's labor: "God help me the job is only half done, only started. It's only the pattern is put into the flask and the sand pounded around it, the iron's not poured into it. The wind's on the cupola and the first heat's ready. I can hear it roaring in my ears. I can see that iron streaming out. . . . I'm—I'm standing, Tim, with the empty ladle in my hands, the job only half done" (274). And on the novel's last page, Willie looks at his grandfather's "battered and sandy" work-hat hung on its nail on the kitchen door and realizes that, although he is alone and beset by his unfriendly relatives, "the trellis of dreams, more than dreams, of faith and hope his grandfather had built for him was there for him to cling to and climb," and "clinging and climbing, he would never have to know the bitterness, either, of having to say good-by to him" (304).

There are numbers of other well-drawn characters and scenes, all contributing to the action's curve of Willie McDermott's coming of age in a fully realized ethnic community poised between the Old and New World and the old and new centuries. In Irish Providence, the Easter Rising is as much a watershed as World War I, and McSorley gives us this transitional world whole, through his keen, compassionate renderings of ordinary Irish Americans in their homes, churches, schools, and factories. *Our Own Kind* marks an advance toward the considerable achievements of the slightly younger writers just ahead.[6]

A fourth culminating work of regional realism is Brendan Gill's fine first novel of 1950, *The Trouble of One House*. In this beautifully crafted book major concerns of earlier Irish-American fiction are freshly examined in a new context. Houses and mothers, real, surrogate, superseded, and manqués, are the subject matter of Gill's novel. On the opening page Elizabeth Rowan dies at age thirty-eight of cancer, and what follows is a retrospective view of her influence on the people who have loved her. The setting is an unnamed Eastern city—most likely Gill's native Hartford—on a blistering June 21 in the early 1920s. Elizabeth has an extraordinary capacity to love and an accompanying lack of fear about the risks of loving. The certainty with which she has lived is partially explained by her social and economic position. Unlike the Lonigans and Lalors of earlier works with similar concerns, the Rowans are securely lodged in the upper middle class. Although still recognizable as Irish Americans, they are a long way from the uncertainties of the immigrant generations. Elizabeth enjoys the luxury of being able to give of herself—to her husband and children, her relatives, and the "twenty men and women" who consider her their "dearest friend." She is not, however, a saint. Elizabeth holds power and knows it, although hers, because love is its fulcrum, is a more attractive variety than Mary Lalor's or Mary Lonigan's. From her secure position as loving mother, she dominates nearly everyone she meets—even including the doctor, nurse, and priest who attend upon her fatal illness. She is also willful, and thus more believable, in her insistence that she be nursed by the woman she knows to have been her husband's mistress. In addition, her gift for loving has borne some bitter fruit: in her envious sister Margaret Delaney, in her mother-in-law Mrs. Rowan, and in her husband Dr. Thomas Rowan.[7]

Over the course of their marriage, Thomas has come to see his wife's remarkable ability to love as essentially threatening, and his sense of the danger takes the form of a metaphor in which Elizabeth becomes a house:

He would grow angry thinking of how her love had found room for all of them. They were like guests in some great house that had nobody knew how many rooms and passages: the sun blazed on the windows, the wind shook the walls, the snow buried the roofs, rain streamed down the spouts, but the house stood firm with the guests gathered on the wide hearth inside, warm and well fed. The only drawback was there was no leaving that house—the end of the longest passage was never an end but only another turning, no doors led out away from all that love. No one could ever hope to be abandoned there. [76]

Reminiscent of Gaston Bachelard's concepts, this identification of Elizabeth Rowan and her house is sustained throughout the novel. In its dual opposing aspects of smothering and nurturing, it embodies the ambivalent view of motherhood that runs through Irish-American fiction. Elizabeth's death makes her the absent center of the novel, and *The Trouble of One House* is largely a study of four women who live on: Elizabeth's friend Norah Martin, the nurse Catherine Gately, Dr. Rowan's mother, and Elizabeth's sister Margaret Delaney. All are defined in terms of their relationships to Elizabeth Rowan, to the role of mother that only she plays successfully, and to the houses in which they live.

Norah Martin and Catherine Gately are unmarried and live alone. Out of fear of the risks of commitment, both are trying to remain as unconnected as possible to the rest of the world. However, they keep themselves aloof in different ways. Norah Martin, Elizabeth's old schoolfriend, is conventionally retiring. Having nursed her father through a long last illness, she is left without experience of the world, permanently threatened and unable to take up a life of her own. Thomas Rowan's former lover and an excellent nurse, Catherine Gately wears a mask of competence and apathy, and lets no one see behind it. While having affairs with Rowan and others, she gives only her body, and considers herself "a convenience . . . a receptacle." In addition, she keeps her own emotions at a distance. She goes nightly to the movies alone, and during the day shuts off her mind by spinning back the plots. Catherine's and Norah's houses underscore their situations. Norah's static existence is reflected in her continuing to live on alone in her family's house amid memories which effectively protect her from the present and future. It is a place for the dead, not the living, with its overgrown garden, broken sundial, and cemetery gates, "taken . . . from the family plot when the cemetery committee voted to do away with all those private furnishings that made a plot a sort of outdoor living room" (239). Catherine lives in the decaying mansion (turned rooming house) of an old-line Yankee spinster in a single bare, white room that stands for the way she wants to keep herself. But the exaggerated sterility of the bleak decor carries the implication of possible release. The room protests too much. This clean, well-lighted place is the fiercely willed attempt to keep out the darkness of emotion of one who can feel, but chooses not to. The one sign of hope is the faint echo of Joyce's Molly Bloom in the sound of the bed's "brass finials jingling, jingling" (178).

We first meet Dr. Rowan's mother when her daughter, Pauline Welles, brings her the news of Elizabeth's death. Her upstairs apartment allows Mrs. Rowan to express the characteristics that link her with Mary Lalor in Katherine Conway's novel—dominance and acquisitiveness: the former in her refusal of a telephone which forces her daughter into the inconvenient role of message-carrier, and the latter in her "delight in her possession of every inch of [the house], from the crown of the brick chimney tilting up through the dusky attic to the shallow cellar, with its smell of apples and knobbed cobblestone floor" (110). Upon her arrival with the Welleses at Elizabeth's house after her daughter-in-law's death, Mrs. Rowan immediately attempts a takeover. She calls for Elizabeth's sister, Margaret Delaney, whom she recognizes as her primary challenger for control of her son's house, and Margaret's first words, "Everything is settled," open a pitched battle between them that continues into the scene at the dinner table that follows.

Like Mrs. Rowan, Margaret Delaney is driven by the urge to dominate in the role of mother, but while Mrs. Rowan has been superseded in that role, Margaret never got the chance to play it. The first child and prettier than her sister, Margaret feels cheated by life. Elizabeth married Tom Rowan, a handsome doctor and the most eligible man in town. Margaret married dumpy, phlegmatic John Delaney, the undertaker. Elizabeth got a rambling, elm-shaded house and made it her own. Like Mrs. Rowan, Margaret lives in half of a nondescript two-family house that in no way expresses her identity. Elizabeth has three children. Margaret has her black automobile, John's clumsy attempt to compensate for their child-bearing deficiencies. Described as a substitute house, this automobile has "watered silk shades at every window," "tapering cut-glass vases" filled with flowers, and such an "air of being just about to receive visitors" that Elizabeth suggests that her sister "ought to entertain the sodality in it" (8-9). And yet, as Margaret reminds her husband in a bitter exchange near the end of the novel, "It isn't a good enough trick, the trick doesn't work. It doesn't sound right—it doesn't cry, it doesn't wake up at night, it doesn't make enough trouble. You weren't as clever as you thought" (302).

Margaret charges through the novel, seething with frustrated anger that finds release only in her cutting tongue. The urge to control has been channeled into a formidable gift for verbal intimidation veiled in politeness that recalls Farrell's Mary Lonigan. The Rowans' house embodies all that Margaret has missed in life, and she has only to walk through the door to be at her worst. It would be too harsh to say that Margaret welcomes Elizabeth's death, but something close to exhilaration infuses her immediate, unsolicited assumption of "the arrangements." Quickly, she telephones news of the death to Norah Martin and Pauline Welles, parcels out the younger children for the night (Ellen to herself, Michael to Norah Martin), and begins to supervise her husband's men in setting up for the wake. At the same time, she extracts condolences from everyone in sight with an obvious appropriation to herself of the importance of this death. Margaret's paroxysm of controlling behavior is stifled by her collision with Dr. Rowan's mother, but their battle is over almost before it begins. At the supper table, Dr. Rowan surprises everyone by simply and curtly sending them all away—his mother, the Delaneys, the Welleses. "All this is between Elizabeth and the children and me," he declares. "All we want is for the rest of you to go away" (219). After a self-pitying speech from his mother and a merciless tirade from his sister-in-law, Thomas Rowan and his children are finally left alone.

The catalyst for the driving out of Margaret and Mrs. Rowan has been Elizabeth's startling deathbed letter to Thomas. Acknowledging that she is being "self-indulgent and self-pitying and all the other self-things that sick people are supposed to be," Elizabeth comes fully alive as a character in this last, pathetic attempt to control her family's lives. She is not a saint, but a real, frightened woman facing an unfair early death. Moreover, the letter contains the explicit admonition that will change the direction of the novel: "Be sure to hold this house, oh, like a fort against the rest of the family; let it belong to no one but you and the children" (205). Thomas acts on this immediately, descending to the dining room, clearing the house of his relatives, and setting off to reclaim his son from Norah Martin. Thus, the novel's closing action is set in motion. Shortly thereafter, the oppressive heat, a motif throughout, breaks violently with a thunderstorm that sweeps the story to its conclusion.

There is appropriate parallelism in the later chapters. All of the women are last seen in their own houses and beds, and their ending thoughts both reveal character and point toward future conduct. Norah Martin and Catherine Gately, the fugitives from life, end up in their beds, their lives aimed in opposite directions. Left alone by the departure of little Michael with his father, Norah sinks back on "her high, old-fashioned bed—her father's bed, the bed she had been born in," and touches herself in a parody of sexuality that resolves into fatalistic certainty about her future: "She knew that she would live to be very old, as old as her father, and that her body would stay soft here, hard here, year after year, decade after decade; but it would not matter" (266). On the other hand, there is hope for change in the last view of Catherine Gately—in her bed with a new lover. Admitting to herself that "trying so hard not to feel anything" has been wrong, Catherine ends by saying, "Oh, maybe I will try to love you a little. Maybe I will try. And maybe you could love me, too, a little. Only a little, a little. And then more. And then more. And then more" (276).

Old Mrs. Rowan and Margaret Delaney are also last seen in their beds in the dark. Having been sent away by Thomas, their attempted appropriations of his house and life thwarted, these two seem destined to be consumed by their own bitterness. When the heat of the day finally breaks with a violent thunderstorm, Mrs. Rowan is saying the rosary by her parlor window. Knowing that the lights will go out and she must find candles, she rises with difficulty, "weaker now than she had ever been," because "she had spent her strength in those moments of triumph over Pauline and Margaret." Dropping the rosary, she sets in motion a series of small mistakes that build toward her defeat at her own hands. She reaches the kitchen just as the lights go out, and the knob of the drawer holding candles and matches comes off in her hand. Moving then toward the stove, she feels her glasses brushed from her face by the "finger" of a wooden towel rack. Dropping to the floor, she kneels on her glasses, crushing them. Then she smells gas—and thinks that she must have turned it on when letting go of the stove. Her house-memory fails her as "she could not remember which way [the stove knobs] faced when she turned them off." Groping her way to the bedroom, she rings the bell rigged between the two houses that will summon Pauline, and realizes suddenly that "it can't ring, the power is off. It hasn't rung. It won't ring" (289). Then she lie back, screaming, on her bed in the dark. Mrs. Rowan has broken too many taboos, and her own household gods have turned against her. A member of the immigrant generation and akin to Mary Lalor and Mary Lonigan, she is a terrifying figure—at first in her pride and presumption, and ultimately in her impotent fury turning to elemental fear. She has been the least Christian of women.

The Delaneys are also at home when the rain begins. When the lights go out, Margaret turns, cold and shaking, to John, and tries to unburden herself of her fears. She confesses that "I think I'm going to die," that "even today" she has "been trying to hurt" Elizabeth, and that she needs her husband to stay with her now. But John Delaney has finally had enough. In a burst of honest judging, he rejects her latest deceptions one by one. "It's been a wonderful day for you all round, a gala day," he says, "but this is the most fun of all, isn't it? Confessing what a naughty girl you are." He exposes her fear of death as merely another attempt to catch up with Elizabeth, who "is still one jump ahead of you." Although he then threatens to leave the room, John does not do so. Because Margaret refuses to answer, his courage fails, and the novel leaves them facing each other in the dark: "He would be able to stand anything but her silence. In spite of everything, he wanted her to have the last word" (304). Still, something has happened here. In rising from her bed, John steps on Margaret's ivory manicure box and breaks it; thus emphasizing the fact that, in exposing his wife's motives, he has departed from the silent acquiescence that has defined his role in their relationship. More than a box has been broken.

Returning with Michael from Norah Martin's, Thomas Rowan is at last alone in the house with his children. There he experiences the series of revelations with which the novel closes. First, in trying to put the now sleeping Michael properly to bed, Thomas realizes how little he knows about his children and how to raise them. Then he sees with genuine humility that "he would fail the children again and again, as he had already failed them downstairs, as Elizabeth had known he would fail them" (313). Similarly, in viewing his wife's body, Thomas finally begins to see the woman who was his wife. Once again he uses the metaphor of the house—not, as before, to express his feeling of being trapped, but with the positive, nurturing connotation that signals a change of heart: "She was that Elizabeth to whom everyone had always turned for strength and comfort, the dearest friend of each of twenty men and women, their center, the house in which they lived" (292).

In a repetition of the pattern that informs the novel's lesser resolutions, Thomas Rowan also ends up in a bedroom in the dark. When the lights go out, he feels his way from Michael's room to Elizabeth's room, in search of matches and candles. Still a stranger here, he knocks something from the bedside table which smashes on the floor. Lighting a match, he sees "pieces of glass, a bent cheap frame," and picks up a shapshot of the children. This accident echoes the smashing in their darkened houses of Mrs. Rowan's glasses and Margaret's manicure box. But the echo is there for contrast. Not sparing a moment's thought for Elizabeth, the matriarchs manquées had set out to take over her house and her role. Resoundingly thwarted, their dreams of dominance turn to bitterness, and each is left alone and cut off: Margaret frozen in stunned silence, Mrs. Rowan screaming to the wind. For Thomas Rowan, on the other hand, there is hope. Although no one involved here, not even Margaret Delaney, has had further to come than this proud, cold man, the novel's last lines suggest that Elizabeth's faith in her husband has a chance of being realized. It looks as though he is learning to love: "It was just a picture of three children on a beach. But they were his children; he was theirs. From now on, he was theirs forever. He dropped the snapshot back onto the table and sat down in the chair beyond the bed. It was getting cool in the room. The storm was passing. Soon the lights would be going on again. He would sit there awhile, then he would go down and join Elizabeth" (314).

There are hardly any references to being Irish in this novel. Nevertheless, *The Trouble of One House* is a central example of the persistence of an Irish voice in American fiction. The novel explores heart-mysteries of Irish-American family life the roots of which are in nineteenth-century fiction and cultural memory. By reintroducing the dominant mother and her fortress-house into a novel of securely assimilated, upper-middle-class Irish Americans, Brendan Gill sends these recurrent major themes with a new spin into the second half of the twentieth century.

"These Traits Endure": The Irish Voice in Recent American Fiction

When asked about his Irishness in 1985, novelist William Kennedy spoke clearly:

> I believe that I can't be anything other than Irish American. I know there's a division here, and a good many Irish Americans believe they are merely American. They've lost touch with anything that smacks of Irishness as we used to know it. That's all right. But I think if they set out to discover themselves, to wonder about why they are what they are, then they'll run into a psychological inheritance that's even more than psychological. That may also be genetic, or biopsycho-genetic, who the hell knows what you call it? But there's just something in us that survives and that's the result of being Irish, whether from North or South, whether Catholic or Protestant, some element of life, of consciousness, that is different from being Hispanic, or Oriental, or WASP. These traits endure. I'm just exploring what's survived in my time and place. [Quinn 78]

To be sure, Irish-American life has changed in many ways since World War II. After 1945, the G.I. Bill of Rights provided higher education and a leg up to solid middle-class status for thousands of Irish Americans, many of whom then moved from the old city neighborhoods out to the suburbs. John F. Kennedy's election to the presidency in 1960 was a dramatic and valid symbol of Irish-American post-war accomplishment. The economic evidence is solid, but it remains much harder to measure the degree to which latter-day Irish Americans remain significantly "Irish." There have been a number of developments, both negative and positive. Fortified by an even more stringent act in 1965, the immigration restriction laws have continued to keep the number of legal Irish immigrants very low. On the other hand, a new problem of the late 1980s has been a flood of well-educated but illegal Irish young people in flight from the severe economic troubles at home. In another area entirely, the late 1960s saw the beginning of a resurgence of Irish-American ethnic self-awareness. There were two proximate causes: the explosion into violence of the Catholic civil rights movement in Northern Ireland, which trained the world's attention on Belfast and Derry, and a burgeoning interest in ethnicity in both universities and the wider culture among American descendants of European immigrants. Some of this enthusiasm was temporary, but there have also been tangible results in the form of university Irish Studies programs, revived social and cultural organizations, and reputable programs of instruction in the Irish language, dancing, and music. Certainly, the numbers are there; in the 1980 census over 40 million Americans claimed some Irish ancestry.[1]

Finally, as marshaled in this chapter, the literary evidence is positive as well. William Kennedy is far from alone in feeling and articulating in American fiction traits and stories that are still recognizable as Irish. James T. Farrell and the regional realists created a solid base of Irish-American fiction in its second cycle, and since 1950 a host of writers have built upon it. Late in life, William Dean Howells explained his life work as a novelist by declaring, "I was always, as I still am, trying to fashion a piece of literature out of the life next at hand" (Updike 88). For numbers of American writers of Irish background, that "life" continues to have an ethnic dimension, and their fashionings continue to stimulate and clarify. The Irishness that persists in recent fiction remains relevant in our increasingly pluralistic culture. The reward of reading these novels is not filiopietistic self-regard, but illumination of still pressing issues in American life.[2]

The present chapter attempts two things: the preliminary organization of this large body of fiction to establish basic patterns in the hope of provoking others to explore further, and the making of thematic connections all the way back to the eighteenth century to establish continuity— to heal the two cycles of Irish-American fiction into one tradition. Useful perhaps in thinking about the recent fiction is a four-part classification: past lives, public lives, private lives, and stylized lives. For each, there will be a catalog of novels and a focus on one representative writer. Past lives are historical novels, and the centering figure is Thomas Flanagan. Public lives are novels of the outer world of work, and the centering figure is Edwin O'Connor. Private lives are domestic novels of family life, and the centering figure is Elizabeth Cullinan. Stylized lives are novels more or less in the modernist mode, in which style is a major component, and the centering figure is William Kennedy.

Past lives are those chronicled in historical fiction, which has been a flourishing, popular genre all the way back to the beginning. The first Irish-American novel, *The Irish Emigrant* by An Hibernian of 1817, was after all a historical tale of the 1798 rising in County Antrim. The colorful, tragic history of Irish nationalism is the subject of most such books, and their relationship to the development of Irish-American fictional self-consciousness is in the peripheral area of the fostering of images and myths of the old country. The results are often not self-images but dream-images of an idealized pastoral landscape peopled with stereotyped characters engaged in Manichaean struggles. As has been noted, most Irish-American historical novels use ready-made formulas which have provided the grist for popular, melodramatic, sentimental fiction about heroic patriots, perfidious informers, sadistic oppressors, and failed rebellions. After *The Irish Emigrant* came James McHenry's pioneering Ulster-set novels of the 1820s, Mary Anne Sadlier's dozen or so historical novels of the 1850s and 1860s, and the individual contributions of many others through the rest of the century, including Peter McCorry, David Power Conyngham, Mary L. Meany, and Alice Nolan.

The genre has remained alive for the simple reason that it makes use of sure-fire formulas for selling books, and in the past twenty years there has been an impressive resurgence of American interest in historical fiction about Ireland. Spearheading this was the popularity of American editions of Irish historical novels, notably Walter Macken's trilogy (*Seek the Fair Land*, 1959, *The Silent People*, 1962, and *The Scorching Wind*, 1964), James Plunkett's *Strumpet City* (1969), and Eilis Dillon's *Across the Bitter Sea* (1973) and *Blood Relations* (1977). Augmenting this infusion of fiction from Ireland was the extraordinary two-year bestsellerdom of Leon Uris's novel of turn-of-the-century Irish nationalism, *Trinity* (1976), a lively, boiling, escapist book. In his study of Irish historical fiction, James Cahalan has summarized the many faults: "In its foggy use of language, its simplistic, romanticized presentation of history, and its confusion about what to do with real historical characters, *Trinity* seems to be not an evolved twentieth-century historical novel at all, but a return to nineteenth-century romance" (196). Also extremely popular in America as a novel and a television movie was a kind of Irish-Australian *Trinity*, Colleen McCullough's generational saga, *The Thorn Birds* (1977). At the least, all such books have helped to sustain a context of cultural recognition of historical fiction about Ireland and Irish immigrants.

Numbers of Irish-American writers have continued to write historical novels. Typical, and better than most, is Joan Bagnel's *Gone the Rainbow, Gone the Dove* (1973), which details the heroic adventures and star-crossed loves of a young County Waterford IRA man from the Easter Rising to the Black and Tans. A more recent large-scale popular novel of the same period is James Carroll's *Supply of Heroes* (1986). In an earlier book, *Mortal Friends* (1978), Carroll also used a familiar device of Irish-American historical fiction, the narrative on two continents. The "Hibernian" author of *The Irish Emigrant* started all this by packing his hero off to Virginia. Carroll taps two reservoirs of popular lore by inventing an IRA hero on-the-run who flees Ireland during the Troubles of the early 1920s only to end up as an aide to Boston's Mayor James Michael Curley. James F. Murphy varies this formula by setting his novel of the Famine generation, *They Were Dreamers* (1983) in Ireland and Prince Edward Island. Finally, two among the many historical novels with exclusively American locales are Ramona Stewart's *Casey* (1968), a detailed picture of the Irish in Boss Tweed's New York in the 1860s and 1870s, and Carol O'Brien Blum's *Anne's Head* (1982), about the St. Louis Irish around the time of the World's Fair of 1904.

Irish historical fiction has had one exemplary American practitioner in our time. Thomas Flanagan stands head and shoulders above all the others mentioned here. A literary historian who has steeped himself in the Irish nineteenth century, Flanagan has become a late-blooming novelist of dazzling skills. He has turned the matter of Ireland into high art with two dense, deeply considered, scrupulously authentic novels rooted in the history of Irish nationalism. In *The Year of the French* (1979), about the 1798 rebellion in County Mayo, and *The Tenants of Time* (1988), which spans the thirty years from the Fenian rising of 1867 to the fall of Charles Stewart Parnell, Flanagan uses gracefully incorporated scholarship, narrating voices of startling verisimilitude, and a fluid, quite beautiful style to shatter the mold of historical formula fiction. These novels combine scene, situation, and character to form stories that are powerfully compelling without sacrificing realistic complexity. Flanagan fulfills the musing of one of his characters in *The Tenants of Time*: "But if, indeed, one could take a moment of history, a week, a month, and know it fully, perfectly, turn it in one's fingers until all the lights had played upon its surfaces . . . " (85). His method is an intricate mosaic of multiple narrators, a brilliant weave back and forth over the ground of events that effectively precludes the melodrama and stereotyping of so much fiction on similar subjects.

Furthermore, the moments that Flanagan has chosen are crucial and defining for Ireland. He has chronicled the dissolution of the two worlds that made up pre-modern Irish society. In *The Year of the French*, the old Gaelic, Catholic cultural order dies. The Gaelic poet Owen MacCarthy feels this as he rides in an open wagon "trussed up like [a] turkey" on his way to be hung for his part in the rebellion: "An image filled MacCarthy's mind: General Trench's army carried northwards into Mayo a great handsome clock, the wood of its casing shining and polished, its delicate strong springs ticking off the final hours of his world" (428). On his way to this tragic dying fall, Flanagan has provided among other things one of the most vivid pictures since William Carleton himself of life in the cabins of the Gaelic peasantry. And in *The Tenants of Time* it is the Anglo-Irish, Protestant Ascendancy that comes to its end, finished off by the Land War of the 1880s. As the landlord and belted earl Tom Forrester puts it, "It's all fading, our Ireland is, like these flowers; but everyone can see the flowers. Every fool. . . . There has been a revolution here, and we are all of us too blind to see it. The winners have fallen out amongst themselves, daggers drawn, a civil war. That happens more often than not, by my reading of history. But that doesn't help us" (685). Both of these novels are blessedly free of green-tinged idealizations of "the Cause" and romantic heroes defying death with laughing courage. Instead, there is a sense of the reality of a revolution—how it emerges from the thoughts turning slowly to action of ordinary, limited people, the small farmers and fishermen of Killala, County Mayo, in 1798 and the shop assistants and schoolmasters of Kilpeder, County Cork, in 1867.

The Tenants of Time also has one area of specific American relevance. Not since Mr. Dooley's comic sketches of the Fenian invasion of Canada and the bumbling Clan na Gael in the 1890s has there been so realistic a picture of nineteenth-century Irish-American nationalism. Flanagan presents the dark side, through strong, authentic images of the threadbare, bankrupt movement and its few fanatic hearts. Here is aged John O'Mahony, "Commanding General" of the Fenians, living out his last lonely years "in wretched rooms, dark and airless" in New York, recalling with cynicism the political uses of dead patriots: "I helped to bundle up the gin-soaked bones of Terence Bellew MacManus, and ship them off to Dublin. All the way from San Francisco. He was a useless sort of fellow in life, poor Terence; amiable but useless. But in death, by God, he put his shoulder to the wheel" (330). Or Gerald Millen, Clan na Gael councilor and informer to the British, sending a "team of five" off to wreak havoc by dynamite in London, then sitting down to write his monthly letter to "Robert Anderson, Office of Irish Affairs, Scotland Yard" (574). Or Ned Nolan, a Civil War veteran and Fenian commander at Kilpeder, hardened past reason by brutal incarceration in Portland Prison, traveling to Chicago to carry out the cold-blooded execution of a suspected traitor to the cause.

Romantic Ireland as rendered in most Irish-American historical fiction is emphatically dead and gone from these beautifully wrought novels that combine panoramic breadth of vision and close, vivid detail. *The Year of the French* and *The Tenants of Time* answer with authority and eloquence Mr. Dooley's complaint that most "histhry" is "a post-mortem examination. It tells ye what a counthry died iv. But I'd like to know what it lived iv." Thomas Flanagan's novels give us both.[3]

Public lives—novels largely concerned with Irish-American experience on the job and outside the home, novels about priests, politicians, businessmen, policemen and firemen, and other civil servants—appeared often in the nineteenth century. Worldly, especially political, behavior is the main concern of much pre-Famine satire, including the stories of "Father Quipes," "Paddy O'Flarrity," and John M. Moore's *Tom Stapleton*. Late in the century, when numbers of Irish Americans began to hold powerful positions, job-centered characterizations appear in novels by Hugh Quigley, William McDermott, John T. McIntyre, and others, and in many of Finley Peter Dunne's Mr. Dooley pieces. Later still, they figure less emphatically in James T. Farrell's fiction, in which the major concern is family life. But they continue to appear in works of other writers of the 1930s and 1940s, including the political novels of Joseph Dineen and Harry Sylvester, and the polished, insightful fiction about priests of J.F. Powers. This examination of latter-day Irish-American fiction about public lives will begin rather than end with its centering, representative figure, because he appeared so early. From the mid-1950s, Edwin O'Connor was writing accomplished fiction about politicians and priests that expanded the genre, pushed it into a spotlight, and provided influential precedents for younger writers.

Born in 1918, Edwin O'Connor was the son of a doctor from Woonsocket, Rhode Island. Educated at Catholic schools and Notre Dame, he became in turn a radio announcer, a Coast Guardsman in World War II, and a journalist, before committing himself to a writing career around 1950. O'Connor died suddenly of a cerebral hemorrhage in 1968, four months before his fiftieth birthday. He had published five novels of increasing complexity and depth in which he explored from a number of perspectives the major Irish-American concerns of politics, religion, and family. When he died, O'Connor left fragments of two novels about his own boyhood in Rhode Island and an Irish Catholic cardinal about to celebrate his golden jubilee as a priest. He was also planning a novel about Irish immigrants to Boston. He had confided to a friend: "I would like to do for the Irish in America what Faulkner did for the South," and he was well on his way.[4] An important, and very Irish, thread through O'Connor's body of work is a fascination with the spoken word, with talk. He renders speech both public and private with the warmth and wit of genuine affection. His first novel, *The Oracle* (1951) is about a hypocritical radio news commentator whose life unravels in a week of seamy revelations. Christopher Usher has no substance beyond the smooth, cant-filled broadcasting voice in which he delivers facile optimism and reactionary politics. This one-dimensional satiric portrait does not develop beyond the opening presentation: "He was uncomfortable, but he was not unhappy, for he was talking" (1). However, the novel does introduce O'Connor's preoccupation with the often humorous disparity between public speech and private ends.

O'Connor's most famous engagement with these matters is of course *The Last Hurrah* (1956), his second book and the most popular Irish-American novel since *Studs Lonigan*. This story of the last campaign of an old style Irish politician brought a phrase and a phenomenon into the American cultural idiom. Modeled to an extent on real Boston politicians such as James Michael Curley and John "Honey Fitz" Fitzgerald, O'Connor's Frank Skeffington is a memorable character who summarizes the successes and failings of the old urban politics. He combines personal charm and humane responsiveness to the problems of individuals with a quid-pro-quo mentality unencumbered by scruples and flavored with a dash of spite. Skeffington's defeat in the mayoral race by a "good government" candidate who is a cardboard media creation (complete with a rented Irish setter for television advertising) is inevitable. As John Kelleher pointed out in reviewing it for the New York *Times*, *The Last Hurrah* leaves "no doubts about what Skeffington cost the city or the Irish. . . . The tragedy is collective, the failure of the Irish as a whole to have the courage of their own qualities and to make better use of them." And yet, as Kelleher also remarks, the novel works because O'Connor was "completely at ease about being an Irish American," and was thus able to write "probably the funniest American novel in a decade." With his characteristic acumen, James T. Farrell recognized O'Connor's "keen insight into both politics and human nature—especially Irish human nature," and his review levied high praise: "He writes with truth, objectivity and very clear eyes: at the same time, his characterizations are saturated with warmth."

Not surprisingly, both the humor and the warmth of *The Last Hurrah* come mostly through talk. O'Connor creates this world through public speech at wakes, on the stump, at news conferences, and at official political functions, and through private speech that takes the form of Skeffington's nostalgic reminiscences to his nephew, the novel's narrator. There is even a classic deathbed climax, as the mayor expires surrounded by his loyal followers. But here too there is a healthy injection of humor, as Skeffington refutes the suggestion that, given the chance, he would live his life "very, very differently" with a last defiant roar: "The hell I would!" (This was the favorite part of James Michael Curley, who appropriated it in spirit for the title of his own autobiography, *I'd Do It Again*.)

O'Connor's relaxed and balanced rendering differentiates *The Last Hurrah* from most of its predecessors in Irish-American political fiction. Joseph Dineen in *Ward Eight*, John T. McIntyre in *The Ragged Edge*, and nineteenth-century novelists such as William McDermott, Maurice Francis Egan, and Mary Anne Sadlier all kept a stern, moralizing distance from their ward-boss protagonists. Precedent for O'Connor's affectionate, humorous presentation comes only in Dunne's "Mr. Dooley" sketches and the pre-Famine satire of "Paddy O'Flarrity" and John McDermott Moore. In another essay on O'Connor, John Kelleher also explains the immediate popularity of *The Last Hurrah* among Irish-American readers: "the public humorlessness that settled down over the American Irish about the turn of the century when the Irish societies drove the Irish comedians off the stage had silently lifted. The Irish could laugh at themselves again" ("O'Connor" 50). In addition, the 1958 film version was a sort of last hurrah for its Irish-American star, Spencer Tracy, and director, John Ford.

The windfall profits from *The Last Hurrah* made O'Connor for the first time financially secure, and in the comfortable following years he wrote his best book, *The Edge of Sadness* (1961), and two other novels. *I Was Dancing* (1964) is a satiric comedy of old age chronicling the struggles of "Waltzing Daniel" Considine, an aging ex-vaudevillian, to keep from being sent by his son to a retirement home. Written first as a play, this novel depends crucially on talk, much of it in monologue by Daniel, and some in archetypal father-son debate. There are stage-Irish echoes in the old routines and stories from Daniel's career, and more serious voices as this family tangle resolves itself, not without pain to all concerned.

Two years later, O'Connor published his last novel, *All in the Family* (1966), the story of the political rise and moral fall of the Kinsellas, second and third-generation "Ivy League" Irish Bostonians. Like the real-life Kennedys, though not specifically modeled on them, the Kinsella clan is led by a ruthless, hard-driving son of immigrants who imposes rigid demands for achievement on his three sons. James Kinsella, the eldest, becomes a suavely successful, media-conscious priest. His brother Charles turns into an unscrupulous politician motivated by sheer blind ambition. Elected governor, he aspires toward the presidency. The third son Philip keeps his head and signals his moral superiority by complaining about his brother's shady dealings as governor in a letter-to-the-editor signed "Edmund Burke." In a startlingly harsh denouement, Charles discredits Philip by having him committed to a mental institution with the help of a corrupt judge. The clear-eyed witness to the moral collapse of this family is the novel's narrator, cousin Jack Kinsella, whose growth toward maturity and a healed marriage is a counterpointing thematic thread. *All in the Family* is a solid, tough-minded novel that deserves to be better known.

The book is also remarkable for its presentation of the gulf between latter-day Irish America and the old country. The Kinsellas' summer in isolated, baronial splendor at a castle in Connemara, totally cut off from the realities of Irish life and culture. The only locals around are servants who keep their respectful distance, and an ancient ruin on the grounds has become a playhouse for the Kinsella children. This clear, ironic disparity recalls earlier collisions between the two cultures in nineteenth-century novels by Mrs. Sadlier, John Talbot Smith (*The Art of Disappearing*) and others, and it also points ahead to more recent treatments of disillusioning return in, for example, Jimmy Breslin's *World without End, Amen* (1973) and Elizabeth Cullinan's *A Change of Scene* (1982). A particularly rude awakening comes in the Breslin novel, when the New York cop protagonist finds in his parents' native Ulster that his Catholic relatives live on the dole like the American blacks for whom he has only contempt.

O'Connor's *The Edge of Sadness* (1961) is his most complex, subtle, and searching novel, the story of one man's relationship to his Irish background, the Catholic Church (in which he is a priest), his fellow man, and his God. It is, as John Kelleher has said, "the record of a subconscious search for essentials and of the repeated, astonished discovery that these are not at all what or where one had always taken for granted." The result is "the discovery of the ubiquity of grace in small and unprepossessing packets. And thus a justification of faith" ("O'Connor," 51). O'Connor engages these themes by means of a quiet, meditative monologue spoken by the first-person narrator, Father Hugh Kennedy.

Once again, talk itself is of paramount concern. In the ways that Hugh Kennedy both embodies and comments upon the art of conversation, his voice constitutes an expansion of the formal possibilities of Irish-American fiction. The novel opens with a seemingly digressive anecdote from Hugh's seminary days in which he recalls his spiritual advisor, "a marvelously serene old man with the face of a happy rabbit and almost no voice at all." While assuring the "overscrupulous" seminarian that not wanting to get up in the morning is nothing to worry about spiritually, the old priest launches into a digressive anecdote of his own. Unfortunately, Hugh doesn't hear it, for the old priest's voice, "as it had a habit of doing, faded off entirely, and he, poor simple kindly old man, all unconscious of this, kept on talking for some time, smiling all the while, his lips moving rhythmically, his long old hands feathering the air, presumably pointing up inaudible anecdotes" (5). How better to open a novel in which a major theme is the decline of a way of talking that is also a way of life, than by providing an inaudible digression within a digression and then, as Hugh does, apologizing because "all of [this] has nothing whatever to do with the problems of the Carmodys," the ostensible subject of his narrative. In fact, the novel's first words are these: "This story at no point becomes my own." This opening line turns Hugh Kennedy's actually central part of the story into a digression as well. And this too is fitting, for the novel thus embodies in its very form the importance of digression, of conversation for its own sake as basic human and humanizing activity.

Father Hugh Kennedy is a fifty-five-year-old reformed alcoholic and, in his own bemused designation, a "friend of the family" to the more colorful Carmodys, a wealthy clan from the old Irish neighborhood of his youth. The action of the novel begins with a surprising telephone invitation to the eighty-first birthday party of old Charlie Carmody, a meanspirited, miserly patriarch with a fortune based in real estate speculation and tenement rentals. Exiled since his alcoholic breakdown to Old St. Paul's, a crumbling inner-city parish of Hispanic, Portuguese, Syrian, Chinese, and Italian immigrants, Hugh returns to his old neighborhood with some trepidation. At the party, surrounded by Irish-American septuagenarian conversation, he feels a wave of nostalgia sweep over him, and realizes that "it was the same talk with which I had grown up, the talk which belonged, really, to another era, and which now must have been close to disappearing, the talk of old men and old women for whom the simple business of talking had always been the one great recreation. And so the result was the long, winding, old-fashioned parade of extraordinary reminiscence and anecdote, and parochial prejudice and crotchety improbable behavior" (69-70). The present round of conversation includes a kind memory of Hugh's dead father: "A lovely man. With the pipe and the smile. And never too busy for the nice long chat" (54). The climax is Old Charlie's annual birthday address, a tour-de-force of arrogance and self-pity that recalls Gabriel Conroy's milder speech in Joyce's "The Dead".

Hugh finds these dying generations at their song "all rather wonderful," but his childhood friend, Charlie's son Father John Carmody, is merely exasperated: "It's not conversation. It's not anything. Just a suffocating cloud of words that keeps on growing and growing and coming and coming. Like a fog." To this intense, solitary, intellectual priest, the old talk is pointless, "in the first place because no one is talking *to* anyone. They're just *talking*. And secondly, because in all rational talk, no matter how much you digress, you usually come back to the main road once in a while. But in my father's house no one comes back to the main road for the simple reason that there *is* no main road. Everybody there deals exclusively in detours." Furthermore, "they fool you by beginning what they have to say with something that sounds simple and sensible. . . . And then just as you think that maybe this time there just might be a possibility of some sort of logical progression you suddenly find yourself trapped in the middle of some lunatic story about a man named Danny McGee who always slept in a maple tree or Little Philsy Kerrigan who once saved up a trunkful of doughnuts. And there you are" (96).

Hugh falls silent at this point, but it's clear that he doesn't agree with his friend, and the narrative then winds along subtly to the reasons why he laments the passing of the old talk. Back in his room at the rectory after the party, Hugh finds himself slipping into another seeming digression. Instead of mulling over the afternoon at the Carmodys' as he had planned, he starts thinking about the deathbed scenes that he has witnessed as a priest over the years. "In these moments," Hugh recalls, "one hears extraordinary things, strange irrelevancies which would seem to have nothing to do with the solemn fact that death is on the doorstep and pushing hard." Sometimes, "I find myself listening to words that seem to come driving out of this dying man. He *has* to tell me this story. And what is the story? It can be the oddest and most unimportant fragment from the man's past, fetched up to the surface for some unfathomable reason to completely engulf the final, fading attention." Hugh recalls that "at such a moment a man told me, in tones of the greatest urgency, of a Laurel and Hardy movie he had once seen: fat Oliver once again discomfited by thin Stan." Another man told him that "once, years ago in Hong Kong, he had had a dozen suits made for him. They had been cheap, but all had been short in the arm. And an old woman whom I had thought dead suddenly popped her eyes open and said loudly, 'Listen to me, Father: *listen to me!*' Then with great logic and lucidity, and for perhaps two minutes, she told me of the occasion on which she had shaken Al Smith's hand in 1928." Hugh finds a clue to these stories in "the loneliness of these people. Some of them who have drifted into a place like this, after having lived God knows where and how, have been locked up so tight within themselves and their unhappy lives for so long that for years they haven't talked—I mean, *really* talked—to another soul." So now, at the hour of death, "they may want, more than anything else, just to talk to tell someone of something, anything." Or, it may simply be that among the chronically ill, those who have lived "close to death for a long time, who have faced it obliquely every day, there is developed an instinct for postponement, like that of a child who every night delays the hour of his bedtime by standing in the center of the living room and saying desper-

ately to his parents, 'Wait, wait, wait, I want to *tell* you something!' "
(108-10).

The Edge of Sadness also contains a center-stage deathbed scene. Old
Charlie Carmody suffers a heart attack and summons Hugh to administer
a peculiar absolution. For once brutally honest about his own shortcomings, Charlie admits that he has no friends and then demands to know
whether Hugh's father had liked him. Although his father had called
Charlie "as fine a man as ever robbed the helpless" (127), Hugh does not
hesitate to tell what he considers a necessary lie. Perhaps fortified by the
delusion of one respected man's approval, Charlie recovers and resumes
being as mean as ever. As we have seen, the deathbed scene is a major
concern in Irish-American culture and literature. Here, as in *The Last Hurrah*, O'Connor contributes to the twentieth-century critique of the nineteenth-century idealizing convention.

After old Charlie's birthday dinner, Hugh reluctantly begins "to go
back, once again, over all those years . . . which I can look back on with
no pride but only the deepest shame, those years which nevertheless
turned and shaped and fixed my life as no other years have done" (117-
18). As Hugh has promised to tell the story of the Carmodys, his narrative
from this point exemplifies the old Irish-American digressive talk. But,
as he has shown by the examples of his own dying parishioners, what
appears as digression to the impatient listener can be of crucial importance
to the speaker. Indulging the "instinct for postponement" is a way of
articulating and clarifying one's own life. Attention needs to be paid to
such stories. (O'Connor's next novel, *I Was Dancing*, is a book-length
embodiment of the instinct.) Hugh Kennedy's story is one of growth from
being an enthusiastic young "cheerleader in a roman collar," through a
dark night of the soul involving alcoholism after the painful cancer death
of his beloved father, to a desert rest cure and return to moribund Old
St. Paul's. In the end, it is his renewed contact with the Carmodys that
leads Hugh to realize just how much he has learned about himself, other
people, and his priestly vocation. Upon understanding the "edge of sadness" in the outwardly successful lives of the Carmody family, Hugh is
able to express this novel's philosophic center. He becomes truly enlightened about the "shattering duality" of human nature:

> I mean the fundamental schism that Newman referred to when he spoke of
> man being forever involved in the consequences of some "terrible, aboriginal
> calamity"; every day in every man there is this warfare of the parts. And
> while this results in meanness and bitterness and savagery enough, God
> knows, and while only a fool can look around him and smile serenely in
> unwatered optimism, nevertheless the wonder of it all is to me the frequency
> with which kindness, the essential goodness of man does break through, and
> as one who has received his full measure of that goodness, I can say that for
> me, at least, it is in the long succession of these small redemptive instants,

just as much as in the magnificence of heroes, that the meaning and glory of man is revealed. [253]

In addition, Father John Carmody's harsh criticism of Hugh's complacent isolation from his flock at Old St. Paul's leads to a final revelation. Hugh turns down a "promotion" to the still-flourishing Irish parish of his youth, for "suddenly it seemed to me that something might be ahead which grew out of the past, yes, but was totally different, with its own labors and rewards, that it might be deeper and fuller and more meaningful than anything in the past, and that as a priest in Old St. Paul's, . . . I might, through the parish and its people, find my way not again to the simple engagement of the heart and affections, but to the Richness, the Mercy, the immeasurable Love of God" (458). As the novel ends, Hugh Kennedy goes off alone to continue his monologue. However, we are now able to see that it has really been a dialogue all along: "And then I left the office and the rectory, and went over into the church to say my prayers."

Along the way to the authentic, hard-won revelations of this finely crafted novel, O'Connor also provides several of his characteristic brief, telling sketches of latter-day Irish Americans. As on the larger canvas of James T. Farrell's body of work, three generations appear vividly: the colorful old people from whom Hugh hears "eloquent recollections of the vital, parochial, picturesque and vanished world in which [old Charlie] and my father had been young" (227); the respectably middle-class and variously disappointed Carmody children, all of whom have been driven with some reluctance into conventional roles—the priesthood, a loveless marriage, housekeeper for old Charlie, ne'er-do-well huckster; and a third generation whose worldly self-assurance prompts Hugh to mark "the sheer speed of the polishing process: that two generations, plus the money, plus the schooling (which was not only better but of an entirely different kind), plus the new and now permissible associations, had ground down all the bumps and smoothed off all the edges" (45). That the process has not been all to the good is clear from Hugh's encounter with old Charlie's grandson Ted, a budding politician who asks Hugh if he can pass the collection basket at Old St. Paul's to further his career. Ted's total inability to understand Hugh's refusal to desecrate the Mass ("It's a prayer, after all; you can't use it for anything else"), shows Hugh that "this boy was separated, not only from Charlie and his world, but from me and mine, by a distance incalculably vast" (392). We are back once again in the world of *Paddy O'Flarrity* (1834), "Who, from a Shoeblack, has by Perseverence and Good Conduct Arrived to a Member of Congress."

The Edge of Sadness also contains indications of another, related distance (further explored in *All in the Family*), that between the old country and the new. The entrance hall of old Charlie's imposing house is graced with a large and "pointless" bust of Daniel O'Connell which is there simply because "somebody gave it to him" (323, 39). Moreover, at one point Hugh recalls a childhood treasure hunt for which he drew the map "on a piece of splotchy, time-discolored paper torn from an unread book someone had given my father long ago—I can even remember its name: *Traits and Stories of the Irish Peasantry*: a clue perhaps, to its remaining unread" (243). O'Connor here serves notice that twentieth-century Irish-American traits make stories quite different from those told by nineteenth-century Ireland's great fictional chronicler, William Carleton. *The Edge of Sadness* is, after all, a novel about story-telling which declares the importance of anecdotal conversation and celebrates the Irish-American gift of gab. It is also elegiac in registering the decline of the old talk. And yet, Hugh Kennedy, not himself a talented talker, does manage to tell his own story in a compelling and meaningful way. He talks to God and the reader, and the result is revelation. Hugh has to tell his story in order to see it clearly for himself, and in this way the novel embodies its major premise—that articulation brings saving grace.

Edwin O'Connor's fiction brings new inflections to the Irish voice in America. His five novels make advances in style and theme that form a bridge from Farrell and the regional realists to Irish-American writers of the 1970s and 1980s. Stylistically, he has a fine command of traditional narrative techniques and a good ear for the rhythms of the talk that he so loved. He also brings back into the tradition the blessed relief of humor missing virtually since Mr. Dooley's day at the turn of the century. In addition, the subtly reflexive nature of the narrative in his finest novel, *The Edge of Sadness*, represents a further stylistic advance upon which others could build. As to subject matter, O'Connor is the pioneering novelist of twentieth-century Irish-American middle-class life. He sustains the focus achieved in the single shot of Gill's *The Trouble of One House* over an impressive though tragically shortened career. Primarily a novelist of public and non-domestic lives, he writes of educated, relatively successful, most often respectable second and third-generation Irish-American businessmen, politicians, doctors, priests—his own kind, as Farrell's working-class teamsters were his. Thus, O'Connor advanced the second cycle of Irish-American fiction significantly. By his craftsmanship and thematic concerns, and also by his popularity, he cleared the way for further explorations of Irish ethnic life by another generation, the writers of our time.

One of the most versatile novelists of the public lives of Irish Americans has been Thomas J. Fleming. In three political novels about the Irish of his native Jersey City, he has charted the transfer of power from the old bossism to a new, liberal but still pragmatic Irish leadership. The thirty-year reign of Boss Dave Shea comes to an end with a 1951 election in *All Good Men* (1961), and Jake O'Connor, the son of a Shea lieutenant, leads the reformist opposition in *King of the Hill* (1965). In *Rulers of the City* (1977), O'Connor as mayor faces two crises, municipal turmoil resulting from the mandate to integrate schools by forced bussing, and a private impasse with his old-moneyed, Protestant wife. He resolves both with a climactic St. Patrick's Day speech which reminds his Irish constituents of their own history of oppression and proves his courage to his wife. There have continued to be many Irish-American political novels. *The Governor* (1970) by Edward R.F. Sheehan is a lively, informed, and ultimately pessimistic novel about a dual in Massachusetts around 1960 between the new "clean" politics, represented by young Governor Emmett Shannon, and the old, embodied in the career of Construction Commissioner Francis X. Cassidy, who helped Shannon get elected. James D. Horan's *The Right Image* (1967), the narrator of which has the unlikely name of Finn McCool, describes the power lust of a New York Irish family for the presidency. Jack Flannery's *Kell* (1977) details the working methods of a political dirty-tricks expert in Massachusetts, a practical soldier of fortune at the service of the highest bidder during the school-bussing crisis of the middle 1970s. And Wilfrid Sheed's *People Will Always Be Kind* (1973) describes the career of enigmatic Senator Brian Casey, who drives toward the presidency out of a New York Irish background marked by recovery from adolescent polio.

Clerical novels also continue to appear, though not to improve upon the pioneering mid-century fiction of J.F. Powers and Edwin O'Connor. Powers, of course, has continued to write about priests in his wonderful stories, collected most recently in *Look How the Fish Live* (1975), and in his second novel, *Wheat That Springeth Green* (1988). The best-known Irish-American novelist of the priesthood in our time has been Andrew M. Greeley, a diocesan priest from Chicago who was already respected as a pioneering sociologist of religion and ethnicity and a popular pastoral theologian before the publication in 1981 of his novel *The Cardinal Sins*. This smash bestseller about two Chicago priests who grow up in the forties into divergent roles in the changing Catholic Church began Father Greeley's continuing fictional chronicle of the lives and times of Irish Catholic Chicagoans. Because he acknowledges the sexual experience of his characters, Greeley's work as a "priest-novelist" has been the subject of intense media attention, but the blitz of notoriety surrounding *The Cardinal Sins* obscures the fact that Greeley has created a grounded, realistic picture of growing up in Irish Chicago, attending a diocesan seminary, and emerging into the young curate's insular world of the neighborhood parish.

In his subsequent novels, Greeley has continued to produce inside narratives of the clergy. In addition, he has gone on to depict many other aspects of Chicago Irish life, past and present. For example, *Patience of a Saint* (1987) contains a vivid account of the violent Republic Steel strike of 1937. And Greeley breaks fresh ground for ethnic fiction in depicting the lives both public and private of upper-middle-class Irish Americans, those who have become considerable secular accomplishers in business, the law, journalism, medicine, and the arts. These include board-of-trade financiers in *Ascent into Hell* (1983), an art-gallery entrepreneur and a psychiatrist in *Angels of September* (1986), and a Pulitzer-prize-winning columnist in *Patience of a Saint*. Greeley's protagonists have certain things in common. They tend to be conscious of their ethnicity; the cultures of Ireland and Irish America are shaping influences in their lives. Second, they come from and are aware of the importance in their lives of real Chicago neighborhoods. Unlike fellow Chicagoan Farrell's Washington Park, these tend to be solidly middle-class places such as Austin on the West Side, Beverly on the far South Side, and the affluent summer colony at Grand Beach, Michigan. Third, these characters perceive religion as an active force, literal as well as symbolic, in their lives.

In fact, in their insistence on life's religious import and their avowed moral purposes, Greeley's novels recall the work of his nineteenth-century priest-novelist forerunners, Fathers John Roddan, John Boyce, William McDermott, and John Talbot Smith. And especially in the combination of popularity with the general reading public and relative unpopularity with Catholic critics and the Church hierarchy, Greeley recalls Father Hugh Quigley, whose 1853 bestseller *The Cross and the Shamrock* earned him a transfer from Troy, New York, to a remote mission station at La Crosse, Wisconsin. Greeley has also inherited Farrell's gift for creating large, connected fictional cycles. Having completed a *Passover Trilogy*, he has since embarked upon a multi-volume chronicle of Chicago life over the past forty years, *Time Between the Stars*, the fourth and fifth stars of the Chicago flag, that is. Andrew Greeley's is a strong voice with plenty left to say.[5]

There are other novels of the clergy as well. Thomas J. Fleming's *The Good Shepherd* (1974) is an understanding portrait of an Irish-American cardinal who dies trying unsuccessfully to reconcile the older, conservative and younger, liberal factions in his archdiocese. In novels including *The Priest* (1973) and *Gate of Heaven* (1975), Ralph McInerny chronicles the difficult lives of Midwestern priests in post-Vatican II America, many of them from Irish backgrounds marked by consensus views on morality and social issues. Francis Phelan's *Four Ways of Computing Midnight* (1985) details the wrestlings with the religious life of an Irish boy from Pittsburgh who finds then loses his calling to the priesthood in a series of lucid, lyrically rendered experiences over some thirty years. A popular novel and subsequent film is John Gregory Dunne's *True Confessions* (1977), in which a Los Angeles monsignor faces a worldly dilemma when his dealings with a shady contractor stall his appointment as bishop. The crisis is forced by the monsignor's brother, who takes the equally familiar Irish-American public role of a police detective.

Of course, the annals of American detective and mystery writing have been studded with Irish names—from Harvey J. O'Higgins to Mickey Spillane. This lucrative, popular genre falls largely outside this investigation because of its concern rather with formulaic plot, action, and resolution than with ethnic self-definition. However, there are more serious writers at work here as well. Cops and robbers have been the province of George V. Higgins since his first, memorable portraits of the latter in *The Friends of Eddie Coyle* (1972). In just about yearly novelistic chronicles of low lives on both sides of the law, Higgins displays his great gift for rendering the sound of the speaking voice. Small-time Irish hoods have also been portrayed winningly in Vincent Patrick's witty novels, *The Pope of Greenwich Village* (1979) and *Family Business* (1985). A bravura example of the type is John Gregory Dunne's *Dutch Shea, Jr.* (1982), a teeming, chaotic, black-comic narrative of the life and work of a criminal lawyer who takes on more and more bizarre clients in the months after his adopted daughter is killed by a misplaced IRA bomb.

New York cops are the protagonists of novels by Jimmy Breslin and Joe Flaherty which also have significant domestic concerns. Flaherty's last novel *Tin Wife* (1983; he died of cancer at age forty-seven) is a sensitive book about the New York police and the Brooklyn Irish. Eddie Sullivan is a thoughtful cop whose change from idealist to near-racist comes convincingly from his experience of life-and-death combat on the city streets. His impatience with the formulas for urban reform of middle-class liberals who have moved to the suburbs recalls Mr. Dooley's suspicion of Chicago "ray-formers" in the 1890s. In addition, the scenes where Eddie and his "tin" (for a cop's badge) wife Sissy meet, marry, and raise their children demonstrate the persistence of a spirit of place that echoes Farrell's 58th Street and Mr. Dooley's Bridgeport. And in her fight to pull off "an out-and-out scam" against the Department to vindicate her family after her husband's death, Sissy Sullivan emerges as a street-wise character with memorable strength. Jimmy Breslin's *World Without End, Amen* (1973) is about a tormented New York cop whose parents came over from Ulster and whose father has escaped his family by recrossing the ocean to tend bar in Derry. The New York scenes, including Dermot Davey's frustrated homelife in Queens, are convincing, but sending him to Ireland in search of his roots damages the novel's authenticity. Breslin has since come into his own as a novelist, however, and his *Table Money* (1986) is a book of sustained realistic power. Set in Queens in the early 1970s, this story of the struggle with alcoholism of Vietnam hero and tunnel-digging "sand-hog" Owney Morrison solidly evokes a dangerous trade and its accompanying after-work barroom culture. And Owney's wife Dolores is another complementary figure of convincing courage and strength of will. A recent, effective book about finding a larger world beyond the ethnic family and neighborhood is Pete Hamill's *Loving Women: A Novel of the Fifties* (1989). A virtual sequel to Hamill's lyrical short novel *The Gift* (1973), this book takes eighteen-year-old Navy enlistee Michael Devlin from working-class Brooklyn to a Florida naval base in 1953. Hamill renders powerfully the boy's several initiations—to serious art and progressive jazz, to sex and love, and to racist violence in the South before civil rights. The novel is framed by the steady perspective of the middle-aged Michael returning to Florida in the wake of his third failed marriage. He finds no easy answers in either part of his life, but there is clear seeing in both directions.

Fictional treatments of the Irish in other familiar civil-service jobs have also continued to appear. A compelling novel set in the urban public schools is Alan Dennis Burke's *Fire Watch* (1980), about a hard-nosed security officer in a city and situation based on Boston during the first year of court-ordered desegregation. Peter Lyons's cynicism about his impossible job is both unattractive and undeniably authentic. Similar in its harsh honesty is Tom Molloy's first novel, *The Green Line* (1982), about the struggle for sanity of Liam Fergus, a Vietnam veteran turned cynical, angry social worker in Boston's black Roxbury neighborhood. Following his successful nonfiction *Report from Engine Co. 82* (1972), Dennis Smith has written novels about New York Irish firemen who face the daily risks of firefighting and political infighting, including *The Final Fire* (1975) and *Glitter and Ash* (1980). Smith, like Breslin, has become increasingly adept at depicting Irish-American private lives as well. In *Steely Blue* (1984), a foundering marriage and drink bring Robert "Steely Blue" Byrnes nearly to the end of his rope, and he emerges as a believable man in trouble. The best of the contemporary portraits of Irish-American working men recall the beginnings of an urban, ethnic literature of the common man in the sketches of Finley Peter Dunne. Like Dunne's Chicago firemen Clancy and Shea, Eddie Sullivan, Owney Morrison, and Steely Blue Byrnes ply their dangerous trades while plagued with the demons of self-destructive hubris.

The central position of domestic life in recent Irish-American fiction is easy enough to understand. Ethnic identity is first of all a family affair; it grows from customs and attitudes, stated and unstated, that are grounded in family life. Thus, fiction about homes and families is a major part of the Irish-American literary tradition all the way back to the start, including key representative figures all along the way: in the 1830s and forties, Charles James Cannon, the first important Irish-American Catholic novelist, in the 1850s and sixties, Mary Anne Sadlier, the central writer of the Famine generation, and toward the end of the century Katherine Conway and Maurice Francis Egan. Of course, James T. Farrell's great achievement of the 1930s and forties is in this area, as is that of the best regional realists such as McSorley, Curran, and Gill who provided a new surge of Irish ethnic fiction in the late 1940s. Numbers of novels describing identifiably Irish-American private lives have continued to appear, and these give the strongest evidence that there continue to be such lives, despite the sea-change for some of higher education, affluence, and suburbanization.[6] Many of these novels are on the light side, featuring easily skewered stereotypical targets from the world of the ethnic neighborhood and parochial school, and some find their way onto the stage in dramatic versions that recall *A Tree Grows in Brooklyn* and *My Sister Eileen*. Such are novels by Robert Byrne (*Once a Catholic*, 1970), John R. Powers (*The Last Catholic in America*, 1973, *Do Black Patent Leather Shoes Really Reflect Up?*, 1975), and Caryl Rivers (*Virgins*, 1984). However, many other books contain serious analyses of major themes. Notable here is the old claustrophobic nexus of mother and house, piety and respectability—the isolated and isolating Irish-American domestic tangle that echoes in the tradition back through the novels of Gill, Farrell, Conway, and Sadlier, and in which a major component is the dutiful self-immolation of children on behalf of their parents. Often the more recent novels contain a new dimension, the movement outward, beyond constriction to openness and freedom. This movement appears with pioneering force in Farrell's Danny O'Neill novels, where it functions in complementary opposition to Studs Lonigan's return home to die. The refutation of the pervasive cultural idealization of the saintly matriarch as distorted and dangerous is a significant accomplishment of latter-day Irish-American fiction. Elizabeth Cullinan's *House of Gold* (1970), discussed in detail further on, is a classic example of this theme.[7]

Some latter-day domestic novels seem to have been fueled by personal rage and bitterness at the perceived excesses, distortions, and injustices of Irish-American Catholic family life. For example, in Mary Gordon's *Final Payments* (1978), the movement is from a caricatured constriction to an exaggerated escape into the open air. The protagonist is the daughter of a widowed college professor, rendered an invalid by a series of strokes. Electing to nurse her father at home, Isabel Moore has been a virtual prisoner in her own house in Queens for eleven years, until her father's death releases her. The situation is made even more extreme by the further dimension of sexual guilt. Professor Moore's first stroke came just after he discovered nineteen-year-old Isabel in bed with his prize student. The governing perception of the neighborhood and main characters is similarly loaded. Isabel is trapped in a ghetto that is little more than a collection of stereotypes. Her father is an intolerant Catholic conservative who makes William F. Buckley, Jr. look like Dorothy Day: "In history, his sympathies were with the Royalists in the French Revolution, the South in the Civil War, the Russian czar, the Spanish fascists" (4). The Moores' former housekeeper Margaret Casey is a hateful, whining spinster who uses her self-indulgent piousness as a club. Professor Moore's best friend is a mawkish, alcoholic priest who retards Isabel's growth with his childish appeals that she return to normal. As for the Queens neighborhood, Isabel describes it as full of "working-class Irish who are always defending something, probably something indefensible—the virginity of Mary, the C.I.A.—which is why their parties always end in fights" (15). There is no scrap of community here—only embarrassing nets to be escaped. And escape Isabel does—to ill-considered sex, a reactionary self-immolation as Margaret Casey's servant, and a final movement up and out toward a new life.

Gordon's skewed perspective is even more pronounced in *The Other Side* (1989), her novel of the MacNamara family's cheerless odyssey in Ireland and America. Using the familiar organizing convention of the matriarch's death to bring four generations together in one house, Gordon here tells a story of near unremitting bleakness. Again, there are stereotyping generalities about working-class Irish Catholics. For example, the narrator describes the late 1950s as "the age when students were polite, the students of working-class parents who worshipped teachers as the incarnation of the intellectual life they despised and feared" (50), and charismatic Catholics are dismissed as people who "feel moved to stand and cry out 'Praise the Lord' as if they had just been given the good news of their salvation from a wild-eyed preacher holding in his hands his oversized and rusty hat" (183). But now Gordon's antipathy extends also to the Irish in Ireland. After visiting his grandparents' homeland, Dan MacNamara delivers an appalling judgment: "But for him, the country was a sign: they could never be happy, any of them, coming from people like the Irish. Unhappiness was bred into the bone, a message in the blood, a code of weakness. The sickle-cell anemia of the Irish: they had to thwart joy in their lives. You saw it everywhere in Irish history; they wouldn't allow themselves to prosper. They didn't believe in prosperity" (160). Unfortunately, nothing in this mean-spirited book (nor in Gordon's interviews since its publication) suggests that we are meant to see this wholesale indictment of a people as anything other than a realistic assessment.

Similarly distorted is James T. Maher's *The Distant Music of Summer* (1979), the protagonist of which is a twelve-year-old boy growing up in an Irish and Polish suburb of Cleveland during the Depression. Only his admirable, intelligent mother, a lawyer and community leader, saves Richard Mulcahy from a succession of sadistic teaching nuns, prurient priests, bullying alcoholic drifters, and fanatically pious neighbors. The popular radio music of the thirties, through which Richard and his sister escape from their harsh environment, rings more truly than the cast of monstrous characters. Also slanted toward the negative is Tish O'Dowd Ezekial's *Floaters* (1984), about the small-town Michigan childhood in the fifties of an Irish Catholic girl who is plagued by bleak memories of masochistic nuns, an obese, unsympathetic mother, and a troublesome, alcoholic brother who dies, leaving her bereft. The protagonist gets even with these ghostly "floaters" from her past by converting to Judaism.

On the other hand, many writers in our time have provided evenhanded renderings of Irish-American family life. One such excellent novel is *The Murderous McLaughlins* (1988) by Jack Dunphy. The epigraph from W.B. Yeats strikes the dominant note of reclaiming the past positively: "Cast your mind on other days / That we in coming days may be / Still the indomitable Irishry." Published forty-two years after Dunphy's first novel, *John Fury*, this lovely story of an eight-year-old boy and his immigrant grandmother Mary Ellen McLaughlin also takes place in Philadelphia in the 1920s. The boy's father has left home when his children came down with scarlet fever and moved back in with the "murderous McLaughlins," Mary Ellen and her husband and their other two troublesome sons, ladies' man Tom, who sings himself to sleep with Irish songs, and ill-tempered Chauncey, a bartender who spends a fair amount of time in jail. On a "mission" to get his father to come home, the boy also moves in with the McLaughlins, and becomes his grandmother's last hope for achievement in the family. Like Farrell's Danny O'Neill, the boy is encouraged by his grandmother and an elementary-school nun to consider becoming a writer.

But this is really Mary Ellen's story, the lean yet lyrical narrative of her spirited attempts at shaping the obdurate family clay. She teaches her grandson many valuable lessons over the course of his several months visit, which is punctuated by Chauncey's misfortunes, an excursion to the "shuttered wilderness" of Atlantic City in winter, and a freighter voyage back to Galway. Throughout, Mary Ellen McLaughlin is a matriarchal presence in the Irish-American tradition—iron-willed yet vulnerable, the intelligent, compassionate center of this odd, independent family. "You're not the woman I married," shouts her husband. "Of course I'm not," she shouts back. "Did you expect me to stand still as all of you have? To have learned nothing? To have seen nothing? No—when I crossed the Atlantic—" (49).

As he listens to his uncle singing "Danny Boy" in his bed, the sensitive boy narrator learns also about being Irish: "Why were we sorry for ourselves but sorrier for others? That was Irish. That is why Tom cried when he promised to drive me home 'when summer's in the meadow,' and why we were all thoughtful now listening to him sing it. Because he was really singing of the future without Chauncey, his responsibility, his little brother, his wayward little brother. Though when we met we might joke about it like everything else, in the dark we were Irish" (201). *The Murderous McLaughlins* contains several of these lyrical epiphanies, and it ends with a memorable last expression of Mary Ellen's legacy to her grandson. Dunphy conveys a sense of the immigrant experience not as exile and alienation, but as challenge and transformation into confident assumption of identity. The summer after returning home with his father, the boy hears that his grandmother has died. "The silver cord had broken," as he slips out of bed before dawn and goes over to the neighborhood swimming pool, "where I waited until the sun rose. When the swimmies opened I swam in the blue water as if it was the sea, or Galway Bay. For she had taught me to love many waters, and to feel at home everywhere, the world being her country, as it is mine" (234).

Another balanced engagement with Irish ethnicity is Edward Hannibal's *Chocolate Days, Popsicle Weeks* (1970), which takes John "Fitzie" Fitzpatrick from working-class Somerville, Massachusetts through a Jesuit education at Boston College (class of 1958) to a successful career as a New York advertising man. At the end, Fitzie is plagued by many unresolved conflicts about his background and emergence as a "success," and his mother's death leads to a set of revelations about his identity and values that recall those achieved by Danny O'Neill after his grandmother's death in Farrell's *My Days of Anger*. Fitzie had hated as well as loved his parents "generally for being who they were and for being what they had been forced to be," working-class Irish apartment dwellers. But at his mother's wake he realizes that they had lived so much inside their narrow world that they had never even understood their own isolation. And this realization drives away the hate, leaving only love, "because now he knew what to love them for. For never hurting him. For never stopping him. For letting him go. And now for telling him that they still weren't stopping him. That was love and what else do you want" (359). There is release here, and yet the flood of memories about Somerville that also comes to Fitzie now is affectionate and stabilizing. Perhaps because he has not been stopped from leaving, he will carry something of this place and his people with him from here on out.

A Good Confession (1975) by Elizabeth Savage is a quiet, retrospective novel that describes convincingly an Irish-American upbringing in a Massachusetts South Shore town. In 1928 ten-year-old Meg O'Shaughnessy comes East from California after her mother's death to be raised by her maternal grandparents, Kate (née Clancy) and her husband "Big Jim", who had come "up from the State of Maine in 1895 to work on the horsecars" (19). Both are strong, sensible people and Meg's memories of childhood and adolescence in the Irish pocket of an old Yankee town demonstrate with the clear light of a realistic narrative that hers was a good time and place to grow up. Meg confides in her grandmother, and Kate's reaction to her grand-daughter's sexual initiation (on the night of the 1938 hurricane) is notably sane and supportive. Kate explains about "men," determines that Meg is not pregnant, and then says, "Then that's all right, . . . Just make a good confession" (138). From her Irish Catholic upbringing, Meg receives a sense of the sacred in life, the rightness of ritual, and the necessity of taking responsibility for one's actions. She applies these convincingly in the course of the novel when faced with a marital crisis and her grandfather's death in 1948. What she has to say about home wakes can stand for the many quiet epiphanies in this finely wrought novel: "There has been a good deal of nonsense spoken about wakes. A wake is but three candles at the coffin's head and the neighbors coming in until you are a little used to what has happened. A wake is paying mind" (207-08).

Another novel about a strong, supportive family is Arthur Cavanaugh's *Leaving Home* (1970), a loving portrait of the Brooklyn Irish from the Depression to the fifties. A much less loving book about the same place is Joe Flaherty's *Fogarty & Co.* (1973) which depicts the three-day pilgrimage through the streets of his native Flatbush of Shamus Fogarty, caught between his ghetto upbringing and success as an avant-garde artist in Manhattan. Suspicious of both worlds, Fogarty resolves ultimately to shoulder his responsibilities as a father while remaining aloof from the conventional values of Irish Catholic working-class Brooklyn. But his compromise comes partly from the steadying power of the old town, especially as felt on a trip to Coney Island with his son.

Quite a number of recent domestic novels have Boston-area settings. Gerald Flaherty's stories of Mission Hill and environs in *Filthy the Man* (1985) are crisp evocations of working-class-Irish family and neighborhood life. Julian Moynahan's *Where the Land and Water Meet* (1979) is a tender, funny, backward look at growing up Irish in North Cambridge, Tip O'Neill's home turf, in the late 1930s. Felix "Lefty" Murray is a bright, musical, winningly hapless Cambridge High and Latin School teenager. His alcoholic father has recently died, his strong-willed mother sells encyclopedias door-to-door, and Lefty runs through a number of part-time jobs including a memorable stint as handyman/waiter at a sleazy summer hotel at Nantasket Beach. The novel solidly evokes lower-middle-class New England Irish life with such details as Harvard students heating and tossing pennies from their dormitory windows to burn the fingers of the Cambridge kids below. Another novel of North Cambridge, this time set in the late 1960s, is Elaine Ford's *The Playhouse* (1980), in which young Maureen Mullen comes of age in Porter Square through an affair with a dying man, a marriage in the old neighborhood, and an ending adjustment to the possibilities of life. Much further afield are two solid first novels that describe tangled and painful Irish-American mother-daughter relationships. Susanna Moore's *My Old Sweetheart* (1982) is about the drug-addicted mother and anxious, stifled daughter of a Philadelphia Irish family transplanted to Hawaii in the 1950s, and Diana O'Hehir's *I Wish This War Were Over* (1984) describes a young girl's journey from California to Washington in 1944 with her irresponsible, alcoholic mother. Both novelists render the movement from familial bondage to self-definition with understanding and compassion.

There has continued to be a small, legal immigration from Ireland, augmented recently by the increasing illegal immigration of educated young people, and the children of Irish immigrants continue to be the protagonists of a number of domestic novels in which old themes recur. Lack of emotional articulation within families split by the gulf of immigration is important in three that come to mind. In Pete Hamill's *The Gift*

(1973), about a breakthrough to communication of a Brooklyn adolescent and his Belfast-born father in the streets and saloons of Brooklyn at Christmastime 1952, the narrator's picture of his father is typical: "But I loved the way he talked and the way he stood on a corner with a fedora and raincoat on Sunday mornings, the face shiny, the hair slick under the hat, an Irish dude waiting for the bars to open, and I loved the way he once hit a guy with a ball-bat because he had insulted my mother. I just never knew if he loved me back" (46). In Bill Griffith's *Time for Frankie Coolin* (1982) about the family and legal troubles of a Chicago building-trades hustler who is the son of a fugitive from the Irish Troubles of the 1920s, the protagonist realizes before it is too late that his difficulties with his children are related to his own father's frustrated reticence. And a particularly evocative and balanced depiction of an American child of immigrants is in the early short fiction of Philip F. O'Connor. "The Gift Bearer" and "My Imaginary Father" are solid renderings of a San Francisco boy's dawning understanding of his Irish-born parents and uncle. The boy emerges from his family's alcoholic, mildly crazy hard times with a measured admiration for his father's rage at the death of the American dream, as embodied in the exclusivity of old-line Californians and the policy of Japanese internment during World War II. In his later fiction, O'Connor has moved away from explicitly ethnic materials, but he has retained what he calls "a way of looking. . . . Call it personality or style. It wasn't what my parents or relatives said so much as the way they said it that I seem to remember. Not so much what they did but how they did it." Like William Kennedy, O'Connor goes on to assert the persistence of ethnicity in his mind and art:

> I guess I now believe that the Irish—if I can generalize from those I knew—eat, drink, love, fear, sing, and get angry in a very special way. I suppose people of other backgrounds do too. But what I know, what is part of me, inescapable, is this that I call the Irish way. It feeds my vision and conjures for me dreams I would not have had without this Irish heritage. I feel it in my bones and know very little about it in my head. . . . What I know, even when I'm working on a story with nary an Irishman in it, is still working in me. The one last thing I have to say is: it has a lot to do with the liberty of the imagination. I don't know what that means but it feels very true. [113]

Elizabeth Cullinan is one of the most accomplished of contemporary American writers. A native of New York and graduate of city Catholic schools, she began writing fiction while working as a secretary at the *New Yorker*, where most of the stories in her first collection, *The Time of Adam* (1971) appeared. Early and late, her work is remarkable for its combination of precise craftsmanship and authenticity to felt experience. Her clear renderings of the complexity and fragility of relationships bring the fresh air of considered moral perspective to Irish-American life. In her more recent fiction, Cullinan has explored the lives of female protagonists from

Irish backgrounds on their own in the wider world. These include, in her second collection *Yellow Roses* (1977), three sketches from the life of Louise Gallagher, happy in her work and tolerably at ease as an unmarried woman in Manhattan. Cullinan also examines incisively the clash of values, attitudes, and expectations experienced by Irish Americans living in Ireland in the story "A Good Loser" (1977) and in her second novel, *A Change of Scene* (1982). In the novel, New Yorker Ann Clarke, a half-hearted student at Trinity College, experiences a number of relationships that clarify her alien status in Dublin. In the story, she returns ten years later to register subtle changes in herself and her Irish friends. As often in Cullinan's work, revelation comes here through an evocative spirit of place, or rather places—Ann's seedy but comfortable Dublin apartment of ten years before, the grotesque summer rental of her return visit, and the tenuously cozy home, a "shaky fortress," of her now-married old friend Stephen.[8]

Cullinan's first novel, *House of Gold* (1970) exemplifies contemporary Irish-American domestic fiction at its best. The private lives scrutinized here echo and elucidate major concerns of the culture, for the novel contains a definitive portrait of a formidable Irish-American matriarch who has forged a life of piety and respectability and centered it in the fiercely cherished house from which she has vowed never to move. The action takes place on the two days of her death and wake and she is never conscious during the telling, but Mrs. Julia Devlin is thoroughly alive in the conversations and thoughts of her children and their families, twelve voices in all, woven into a brilliantly controlled omniscient narrative. This technique, the archetypal house, and the matriarch's death recall Brendan Gill's *The Trouble of One House*, published twenty years earlier, but the Devlins are an anxious, insecure lower-middle-class family of immigrants and their children, closer in spirit to Farrell's Lonigans and Katherine Conway's Lalors than to the comfortable, confident Dr. and Mrs. Thomas Rowan. Mrs. Devlin imposes a rule of duty, controls her family by withholding love, and dominates her children into sharing her distorted vision of the world. And yet, she is not a caricature, but a fully realized human being whose plausible neuroses evoke sympathy and understanding, not ridicule and bitterness. The result is one of the most disturbing and salutary fictional examinations of Irish-American domestic life.

Mrs. Devlin speaks for herself in her handwritten autobiography, "The Story of a Mother," found on the day of her death by her daughter-in-law, Claire. Placed at the center of *House of Gold*, this document is a tragicomic tour de force by Cullinan. In nineteen pages she sketches the mind and motivation on which the novel rests, and in words that we do not doubt are Mrs. Devlin's. Her background, birth, childhood, and adolescence take up two paragraphs. The brevity is for avoidance of pain, for this is an immigrant narrative with more than its share of loneliness. Born in England of Irish parents, Mrs. Devlin was taken from them to New

York at age three by her mother's brother and his wife, who adopted her to relieve the burden of too many children. "Shortly after I left," she writes, "both my Parents and my eldest brother were stricken in an Epidemic of the Flu and lost their lives. . . . Never did I see any of my Family again." (Mrs. Devlin capitalizes certain nouns for emphasis, conscious or unconscious.) The uncle, who "fairly idolized" her, died when Mrs. Devlin was ten, and she was raised by her austere and snobbish aunt: "Life for me after that was very lonely." Of her marriage of fifty-odd years, there are very few references: "Without love of a Mother or Father or Family my life was starved so at 17 I married my first beau Francis Devlin. He was in the Building business at the time but in 2 years he became a Fireman and made that his Career until he retired at age 60" (151). Mrs. Devlin resents having been brought down from her aunt's "grand home" to the firehouse. Thus, her husband remains a shadowy figure, without substance in "The Story" or influence in the family, and when she begins to count off the children, Mrs. Devlin gives the impression that she raised them alone. Nor is there mention of the golden wedding anniversary that most of the other voices recall in the course of the novel, and even Mr. Devlin's death goes unrecorded by his wife. It is almost as though the man never existed.

When the children take over "The Story," we find that the first two (Francis and Michael) died young, the next four (Vincent, Julia, Catherine, and Phillip) all became priests and nuns, and the last three (Elizabeth, Justin, and Tom) went in various secular directions. At the beginning of this section, we begin to doubt Mrs. Devlin's version of her life. Francis, the firstborn, "was one of the most beautiful children on earth," and when he died, "Grown men I'd never seen or heard of before wept over his coffin. One in particular took my son in his arms, crying, I was out of a job and he gave me money to feed my wife and children and found me work. God, why did you take him!" (151, 153). Reminiscent of Mrs. Sadlier and the Famine generation, these passages describe a life that has been idealized into tract-novel sentimentality. Mrs. Devlin next describes the religious vocations of her four middle children. In each case she is careful to explain that entering the religious life was entirely the child's idea, opposed by her until the sincerity of the vocation shone through to convince her. And in the descriptions of how she finally gave in, the focus is always on her own loss, on the noble sacrifice of her children to God. However, the truth is closer to the situation of Studs Lonigan's mother, for ten-year-old Frank Devlin recalls how his grandmother "always wanted everybody to be a priest or a nun" (120).

Of her three youngest and non-clerical children, Mrs. Devlin admits to a preference for Tom, the baby and "pet." The Devlin secular accomplisher, Tom graduated from "a very fine Jesuit College," and fought in "the thick of the Battles and won many service ribbons and medals for Valor" during the Second World War. Subsequently, his mother declares, "he was selected to remain in the Regular Army and is now a Major" (163). The other two, Elizabeth, the last daughter, and Justin, the family ne'er do well, get short shrift. After listing Elizabeth's musical accomplishments—"keeping perfect time" at age six months, a piano scholarship at eleven—Mrs. Devlin says that at fifteen, "this lovely daughter was beseiged by people wanting her to give them Lessons on the Piano. At this time my Husband was thinking about his Retirement and so it was decided that Elizabeth would begin her musical Career which she did and had a very nice clientele up to the time she got married" (162). On that subtly disapproving note, Elizabeth's small part in "The Story" ends. As for Justin, it is clear that he never had much of a chance. What is not clear until the end of the novel is that his failure will be his salvation. "Before his birth there was little hope of Mother or child coming through the ordeal safely." At two, he fell into a coma from which, his mother is convinced, only "a Miracle" brought on by her prayers saved him. She dismisses Justin by explaining that he quit high school because "he was anxious to start a Career for himself," and that now he is "a success . . . in the Restaurant Business" (164). On the morning of his mother's death, Justin weaves tipsily home from his job as an all-night bartender near Times Square.

After her children, Mrs. Devlin describes her house, the acquisition of which was the high point in her life. In fact, the house gets more space in "The Story" than any of the children. Her dream of "living in the country" finally came true, and she recalls the day the family moved into the new house in loving detail, "as though it were only yesterday." This train of thought also brings evidence of insecurity. Four times in the two pages describing the house Mrs. Devlin declares that she will never leave it alive. And an authentic revelation comes at the end of the section, when she recognizes for a moment the force and motivation of her attachment to the house: "This was because of a threat or whatever you care to call it made by my aunt on the day I got married. You will be glad to come to my back door begging for help, etc. Francis will never be able to give you the life you are used to, etc. His work is unsteady, etc. You will be eating snowballs for dinner" (166).

Tom Devlin's wife Claire quickly skims the rest of "The Story," about Mrs. Devlin's trip to the Philippines, finding it "as dull as a routine travelogue." Ironically, this concluding section begins with Mrs. Devlin's assurance that "the story of my Travels . . . will seem more like a Fairy Tale than True Life," but Claire realizes that "it was the other part of the story, the family part, that read like the fairy tale—the clear lines and brilliant colors of the surfaces; tragedy and triumph and nothing in between, nothing but the bold sweep of events past all that was day to day or moment to moment, past boredom, irritation, triviality, past doubt and disorder and the effort to understand" (169). She is right of course. "The Story of a Mother" is as far from realism as nineteenth-century Irish-American didactic, propaganda fiction. Furthermore, Claire sees that "The Story" is not the work of a naive innocent. What radiates from Mrs. Devlin's narrative is egotism, self-righteousness, and an effort of will frightening in its intensity. Claire ends her meditation by asking the question that this novel was written to answer: what price have her children had to pay for this woman's life-long willed simplification of reality into illusion? "She'd made those dreams come so marvelously true, the dreams of the lonely child, and she'd made them, the children, part of her dreams, part of the fairy tale. But the proof of a fairy tale was in the ending—happily ever after" (169).

Because she is an in-law, Claire can afford to be detached and judgmental, where the Devlin children are too close to their mother and have too much to lose. In this novel the only critical perspectives are provided by the outsiders—Claire, Elizabeth's husband Edwin Carroll, and the four grandchildren, Winnie and Julie Carroll and Frank and Vinnie Devlin. The Carroll girls were released by their parents' having moved from the Devlin attic to their own apartment, although Winnie still recalls how "long ago, being sent to the first floor at night on an errand had been a terrifying ordeal, and some residue of terror still seemed to cling to the objects in the room" (143-44). Even further removed from the attitude of reverence toward their grandmother's house are Tom's children, Frank and Vinnie, who solve a problem of urgency by urinating in the privet hedge beside the front door. On the other hand, Mrs. Devlin's children have thoroughly internalized their mother's vision of herself as a saintly paragon and of her house as a house of gold. All are incapable of criticizing Mrs. Devlin for having dominated their lives or of seeing the house for what it is—a cramped and shabby place, far too close to the railroad tracks. All believe in the idealization of House and Mother that Mrs. Devlin has bequeathed them, and in bearing witness to her dream, all reveal themselves as blinded by it. Furthermore, only the outsiders have measured realistically the ill effects of Mrs. Devlin's dominance on her children. Unable to understand "why none of her family had challenged her view of how things ought to be" (63), Edwin Carroll sees the distortion and isolation imposed by his mother-in-law's view of the world, and Claire sees that none of the children, not even her husband Tom, has escaped her mother-in-law's influence: "With all his drive and determination—he'd only traded one closed society for another, this house for the service" (180).

The ultimate revelation of the novel, underlined in its title, comes to Claire, when she contemplates the "solid gold-leaf tea and coffee service," a garish artifact left over from the Devlins' fiftieth wedding anniversary, at which time the whole house had been fitted out with touches of gold. Where, Claire asks herself, would such things not have seemed "grotesque and ridiculously out of place?" "At Buckingham Palace, maybe," or on the altar of a Catholic Church: "ciborium, chalice, patten, monstrance—

the sacraments given artful shapes, intricate designs." But here in the Devlin house, she realizes, "it was the other way around."

> Simple domestic objects, a cup, a saucer, a teapot, became vaguely sacramental, symbolic. Of what? No, not of what. Of whom? Of her, Mrs. Devlin. There was a line in the Litany of the Blessed Virgin—Claire smiled to herself at the thought of it. Literally, figuratively, ironically, every way and any way that one phrase fit. Where did it come in again? What was the part leading up to it? . . . Mystical Rose. Something. Something. Tower of Something— Tower of David. That was how it went. . . . Mystical Rose. Tower of David. Tower of Ivory. House of Gold. [212]

Against the power of Mrs. Devlin's self-sustaining gold-leaf dream of herself as a kind of Virgin Queen, Cullinan has placed in realistic counterpoint one recurrent brute fact of life in this house, a fact so insistent that even the Devlins cannot ignore it: the trains. Because railroad tracks run right behind the backyard, the sound of passing trains assaults the house several times a day. The first train in the novel breaks the spell cast by Father Phil's administration to his mother of the sacrament of extreme unction, and periodically through the long course of the day the sounds of other trains break violently into the house, shattering nerves and conversations. In a brutal irony, Mrs. Devlin dies as a freight train is passing, and, as effectively as in the conclusion of *Studs Lonigan*, the noise undercuts the conventional deathbed tableau of the family gathered for the last farewell.

As for Mrs. Devlin's children, none of their lives has been spectacularly spoiled, but the negative effects of their mother's dream of life are everywhere in evidence. Father Phil, the two nuns, and Major Tom have found "vocations" that allowed them to transfer outside the home the enforced regimen and devotion to duty ("the Devlin standard," Tom calls it) on which they were raised. At the least, they are safe where they are. It is rather through the characterizations of Elizabeth and Justin that the novel's most serious questioning of the quality of these Irish-American lives takes place. Not having availed themselves of the sanctioned escape routes provided by adherence to an authority (religious or military) similar to their mother's, these two have remained at home. Justin is still there on the day of his mother's death; Elizabeth and her family have been out in an apartment for only two years.

Elizabeth suffers most during the two days that elapse in the novel. At the beginning, she wakes up on a daybed, oppressed by "the house around her, all the rooms, all the years she'd spent in those rooms" (7). Two things torment her: her having moved with her own family into an apartment, and her mother's last question to her, "Elizabeth, have I ever kept you back?" To which she has answered, after a second's hesitation, "Never!" All through her mother's dying day, Elizabeth rehashes the circumstances of her departure from the house, trying to exorcise the guilt she feels. At the same time, she prays for a chance to give a different answer to her mother's question. Now, it seems pretty clear that Elizabeth has been "held back." Having married a man without money, she was forced to bring him into the house and add to her already backbreaking Devlin duties (teaching piano and running the house) the job of making her own new home—in the attic. On these grounds it seems plausible that what Elizabeth wants now is the chance to give an honest answer, to give her mother a share of the blame for the sense of incompleteness they both feel. When her mother dies, Elizabeth, thoroughly shaken, unburdens herself of the answer she was not able to give, to the first confessional voice that presents itself, that of her mother's doctor, Harold Hyland. What she tells him provides the biggest surprise of the novel. Instead of conveying the truth of her situation in the Devlin household, she tells the doctor what "should have been said, the answer she knew she ought to have made": "I'm sorry I left her. . . . I'm sorry I ever moved" (278). Elizabeth's remorse at not having had the opportunity to tell a more ringing falsehood stands here for the family's lifetime of renunciations and delusions. Having expected a dose of honesty, we are struck by how trapped and crippled she seems as the circle of duty and guilt closes around her.

This novel illustrates once again that ethnic family life could be constricting as well as supportive. In the ambivalent metaphors of Gill's Dr. Thomas Rowan, the house could become both a shelter and a prison. In the controlled climate of her familiar four walls, surrounded by supporting artifacts, Mrs. Devlin's power grew gigantically, and she and her family became isolated, as Edwin Carroll puts it, in their "pride and ignorance," each feeding the other: "The one thing kept them from taking into account any set of standards but those they'd laid down for themselves, and at the same time it brought on the other thing, made them ignorant. And in their ignorance, they leaned harder than ever on their pride—a vicious circle if ever there was one" (237-38). To the degree that a family continues to feel more threatened than secure, the house remains an isolated and isolating world of its own. Insecurity breeds continued isolation. And this was Mrs. Devlin's position: balanced precariously on the lower edge of the middle class, with her aunt's prediction of snowballs for dinner and the noise of passing trains ringing in her ears. Only inside her house of gold was her dream of the world protected from the light of day.

Justin Devlin is different, however. Never having succeeded at anything, he has less to lose than his siblings. On the day of his mother's death, he gets up with a hangover, stumbles through the late afternoon in everyone's way, and spoils the family's already jittery supper with a tasteless, off-color joke. And yet, because he has rushed from the dining room disgraced once again before the family, it is Justin who discovers that their mother is within minutes of dying. Only his call allows them to witness her death. Cullinan does this to point out that Justin and Mrs.

Devlin are kindred spirits. He is closer to her than any of the others, because they are mirror images of the same paradox: he is an outsider in his own house, and she is an outsider who founded a home without ever finding one. What Mrs. Devlin created through force of will was not a real home, but an illusion of home. By locking herself into the role of aloof, queenly ruler demanded by that illusion, she forfeited her chance to have the real thing. Like the rest of the Devlins, Justin was born into this dream, but unlike his siblings, he has become a non-believer. He has even dared to criticize the house to his mother's face. " 'Why waste money on this place,' he'd ask, knowing how the question hurt, how much the house meant to her" (30). and he realizes after her death that "it had been her house," not his, and that now "he had no place in her house or anywhere else." There is relief as well as sadness in his reaction: "Something was missing—the opposition, the other side. There would never again be another side. There was only his side now" (298-99).

Despite his ineffectual clumsiness, Justin is the best equipped Devlin for the motherless world that the family is about to enter. He has perspective on himself and on Mrs. Devlin's dream. He has not inherited his mother's harsh legacy to the other children of the "Devlin standard"—duty enforced by guilt enforced by a sense of their uniqueness. His failures have saved him from remorse. In addition, he is good-natured, easy-going, and likable—the most human of the Devlins. It is fitting that Justin's is the last voice heard in the novel. In the closing scene at Mrs. Devlin's wake, he appears as significantly more perceptive than his brothers and sisters. From outside the door he hears the rest of the family at prayer, and with the keen ear we have come to expect only of Edwin and Claire, he picks up a telling note of contentious disunity: "above all you could hear Elizabeth's and Mother Helen Marie's voices competing for the lead, each trying to set the pace" (328). No other Devlin could have allowed himself to make this observation.

In "The Story of a Mother," Mrs. Devlin remembered that because Justin's dangerous birth took place for safety's sake in a hospital, he was teased by a brother as "the only one to be born in exile" (150). And even more appropriate is the fact that Justin shares his name with his mother's birthplace, also in exile, "the parish of Saint Justin's, outside Liverpool." As the only Devlin with neither vocation nor family to turn to, Justin is back where his mother started—but with a sixty-year chasm of difference. Mrs. Devlin was an exile who had somewhere to go (America, marriage, and motherhood) and something to prove to herself and her aunt (the immigrant's passionately imagined dream of success). Through this fine, sad novel she emerges as a latter-day Mary Lalor or Mary Lonigan, dominating her children into sharing her distorted vision of the world and holding for dear life to the house that embodies her tenuous respectability. Her son Justin is less tenaciously directed, much more of a lost soul, but better off. He may have no place to go, but at least he is free to go.

The dominant mode of Irish-American fiction has been realism. But there is also a well-established Irish-American tradition (and of course an Irish one as well) of producing determinedly stylized novels—books that are acts of authorial imperialism, in which style is a willed, obtrusive element of meaning. This is a part of what came to be known as modernism, and James Joyce is one of its revered fathers, preceded in Ireland by some of William Carleton's flights and followed by the likes of Flann O'Brien and Samuel Beckett. Insistently stylized Irish-American fiction is marked by linguistic exuberance, virtuoso rhetorical flights, and narrative experimentation, most often in the service of a comic/satiric vision. In Irish America, such fiction has strong roots in the nineteenth-century, where a number of writers play fast, loose, and flamboyantly with words and conventions, both for sheer fun and to illustrate the difficulty of pouring meaning into such rigid little molds. Notable here are many wild and witty Mr. Dooley columns in the 1890s and the vein of pre-Famine satire of the 1830s and early forties, with its playful, parodic critique of fictional types. It is not surprising that this vein has surfaced again since the 1940s, what with the G.I. Bill of Rights, the movement of so many Irish Americans into the middle class, and the consequent opportunities to fulfill the aspiration to write. And no more surprising is the continuance of this vein on into our silver age, where writing programs abound and technically skillful writers proliferate.

The practice of stylized fiction has always been a risky, double-edged business. It cleaves into two strains—one dark and one light. In the dark strain, style often conveys lack of control. On the edge of hysteria, narrative voices flirt with dissolution into madness or nonsense. In the light strain, the opposite is true. Authorial imposition exerts control. The insistently stylized voice shapes unwieldly, intransigent materials and, in the best work, blesses them. It comes down to attitude and temperament. Faced with the welter of experience, the dark stylist rages at the impossibility of encompassing it; while the light stylist celebrates diversity.

The dark strain appears in the service of black (or gallows) humor and satire, in novels where linguistic exuberance is a manic, antic, and ultimately destructive force. Such fiction brings in reports from the hysterical outposts of reason, at the risk of slipping over the edge into nihilism and despair. And sometimes the aim is linguistic subversion, the language used against itself to ridicule or declare the impossibility of meaningful discourse. In Irish-American fiction, familiar accompanying elements are the distortions of drink and mental illness. The light strain appears in the service of fruitful iconoclasm and growth, in novels where linguistic exuberance is a comic, vital, and ultimately creative force. In such fiction language is stretched but celebrated, more out of love and wonder at the possibilities of words and voices than from a sense of their limits and deceptions. Here impatience with narrative conventions is part and parcel of healthy contempt for strictures on behavior that stifle the soul groping toward change for the better.[9]

J.P. Donleavy pioneered the re-emergence of stylized/satiric, exuberantly rhetorical Irish-American fiction. Emphatically in the dark vein, *The Ginger Man* of 1955 helped establish the term "black humor," and it defines the Irish-American contribution here. Blarney and slapstick, lyricism and charm masking boozy, manipulative cruelty—these characterize Donleavy's protagonist Sebastian Balfe Dangerfield, a World War II veteran on the G.I. Bill at Trinity College, Dublin. And at their center, as V.S. Naipaul has said, "only the void; and nothing will lead to nothing. . . . In Sebastian we recognize only a barely suppressed hysteria." The context here, also relevant for more recent fiction, is an Irish American's disillusioning return to the old sod. Donleavy eventually wrote his way out of Dangerfield's blind alleys, but some of his successors in this vein were not so lucky.

In more recent Irish-American fiction, the two strains are particularly clear in Tom McHale and Maureen Howard, writers whose work suggests two sides of a single coin. Both have created stylized, satiric portraits of Irish-American family life in which aspects of that life are criticized sharply. Furthermore, as in other Irish-American novels, particularly realistic/domestic novels, the aspects are familiar—unnatural, exaggerated closeness, isolation, "pride and ignorance" (as in Cullinan's *House of Gold*), armor-plated piousness, respectability, and institutionalized guilt. "After such knowledge, what forgiveness?" In McHale's novels, there is none— only bizarre, bloody resolutions in murder and suicide. In Howard's novels, there is painful but affirmative release into possibility.

Tom McHale's first two novels, *Principato* (1970) and *Farragan's Retreat* (1971), are his most coherent and stable works, probably because they were rooted in the 1960s ethnic Philadelphia that he knew so well. Both contain excoriating, slapstick portraits of middle-class Irish and Italian Catholics whose far from ordinary lives as mobsters, hucksters, and fanatics become downright bizarre, violent, and sadistic. In the second and more Irish of the two, the Farragans are a Philadelphia trucking-company family who are caricatures of Irish-American domestic life and social and religious conservatism in the Vietnam era. They include a flag-waving, bloodthirsty super-patriot, a racist who practices shooting at targets resembling black males, a sexual puritan who turns holy pictures to the wall while making love, and a simpleton whose way into the priesthood was bought by family money. Some of this is effective though strident satire, but less entertaining is the family edict that a Farragan father execute his son for fleeing to Canada to avoid the draft, and not funny at all is the bloody denouement in which all the senior Farragans end up dead. Cut off from his home turf, McHale's four subsequent novels were increasingly strained and at sea. In *Alinsky's Diamond* (1974) an Irish-American expatriate joins a prostitute, pimp, and abortionist in following an eccentric priest from France to Israel on an improbable quest involving several murders. In *School Spirit* (1976) a prep-school football coach avenges the death twenty years earlier of a pupil by tracking down those responsible, three of his former players, and punishing them with floggings and worse. In *The Lady from Boston* (1978) and *Dear Friends* (1982) the setting becomes New England and the protagonists are White Anglo-Saxon Protestants who are drawn into escalating violence. McHale's last three novels end, respectively, in a coerced suicide, the murder of a man who has vowed to kill himself, and a double suicide. Consistent through the lifework of this troubled man who took his own life at age forty in 1982 are suicidal violence, blackly savage satire in the service of an absurdist world view, and the intense, manic, stylized narrative voice.

Two other writers form with McHale a grim triumvirate. These also mined the vein of wild linguistic exuberance to dark, entropic extremes. First, John Kennedy Toole's *A Confederacy of Dunces* (1980) was published eleven years after his suicide in 1969. In it, the dialogue is hilarious but hollow, and the situations are ultimately pointless, vaudevillian satire, under the sign of the rotting plywood Celtic cross (marking a dog's grave) in the New Orleans front yard of wildly bombastic, wholly ineffectual talker Ignatius J. Reilly. Second, there is no more shattering evocation of alcoholic degeneration than in the two stories, "O'Phelan's Daemonium" and "O'Phelan Drinking," of John F. Murray, who died tragically shortly after their publication in 1977. A final example of destructive, manic monologue is Mark Costello's *The Murphy Stories* (1973), a collection that traces the breakdown of a Midwest Irish-American marriage through craziness, drink, and sometimes violence. Irreverent, allusive, and relentlessly self-lacerating, these stories are driven by the author's love of language and the protagonist's hatred of self that comes close to despair.[10]

On the other hand, there is no stronger example of the positive side of contemporary Irish-American stylized fiction than the work of Maureen Howard. After dismissing her first book, *Not a Word about Nightingales* (1960) as "a mannered academic novel, actually a parody of that genre and so at a further remove from life" (*Facts* 80), Howard got down to business in her second, *Bridgeport Bus* (1965). Here she explores the thematic roots of her own Irish Catholic upbringing in Bridgeport, Connecticut, while stylistically bursting out to what from now on becomes her method—a mélange of styles and forms that expresses her impatience with conventional narrative modes. But Howard's frustrations are diametrically opposed to those of the dark stylists such as McHale and Murray. Hers is an argument from plenitude, not emptiness. Her fits and starts, flourishes and flights declare that experience is too tricky and fascinating, too full, for straightforward narrative. Life means too much, not too little, to be rendered in logical, linear form.

In *Bridgeport Bus* the organizing structure is the struggle of the protagonist to define and free herself through writing, from the novel's open-ing line on a pad of yellow paper ("First I will write:") through to its final line scribbled as she is carted off to deliver her baby ("it was no great sin to be, at last, alone"). Mary Agnes Keely is a thirty-five-year-old spinster trapped by her devouring mother and a dead-end job in Irish Catholic Bridgeport in the forties. She chronicles her wrenching, painful escape to the dangers and possibilities of life on her own in New York City in a free-wheeling variety of literary ways: journal entries, first and third person short stories, mock parables and fables ("The Wise Virgin," "The Foolish Virgin," "How the Sky Fell In on Chicken Little"), a one-act bur-lesque play starring all of the important people in Mary Agnes's life, dead or alive, and an extended wild pastiche of hillbilly dialect. These are all devices that further Mary Agnes's desperate need to understand and clarify her life by talking, desperate because the familiar theme of failed communication surfaces early and runs through this novel. Mary Agnes and her mother exist in their house "without words for each other" (39), Mrs. Keely's last words on her hospital deathbed are choked off by a glass of water administered by her daughter, and at the very end, Mary Agnes has won through to the writer's ambition (so central to James T. Farrell) of speaking for those who cannot speak for themselves. In the Good Shep-herd Home she talks avidly to other unwed pregnant women, "to try to get hold of their dreamlike existence, their inarticulate sojourn in a world they do not find fantastic" (303).

Mary Agnes Keely's journey from constriction to openness culminates in her triumphant unwed motherhood, and Howard defines this positive movement against the disastrous stories of two other women in the novel, Mary Agnes's doomed cousin Sherry, whose valiant pioneering escape from "the dodging Protestant affectations of the cut-glass Irish" to a career as a Broadway showgirl ends in suicide, and her New York roommate Lydia Savaard, a Vassar girl from Cleveland who ends up living a con-trolled, bloodless existence, nursing her violently mad Princeton blue-blood husband in a cottage on her mother-in-law's Long Island estate. In *Bridgeport Bus*, Howard's technical virtuosity and openness is both a figure for her protagonist's release into possibility and the memorable formal articulation of that release.

In three subsequent novels and an autobiographical volume, Howard has continued to chronicle the movement toward understanding and pos-sibility of Irish-American woman protagonists, and her books continue to exemplify the strengths of the adventurous, exuberant light stylist. In *Before My Time* (1974) Howard charts Laura Quinn's difficult growth through a combination of conventional exposition, four complete "Moral Tales," and a last "Scenario" of seventeen short vignettes. As powerful as any of the novels and equally open and stylized, is Howard's 1978 non-fiction narrative *Facts of Life*, a significant document in Irish-American cultural self-definition. In *Grace Abounding* (1982), about the middle years of Connecticut widow Maude Dowd, Howard's novelistic vision expands further into sexual fantasy, and in *Expensive Habits* (1986), about a successful novelist dying of heart disease at forty-five, she creates sharply comic satiric portraits of New York literati. In both later novels Howard continues to strain at the boundaries of conventional narrative by means of abrupt shifts of tense and point of view and brief, epigrammatic shards. She continues to be a challenging, richly rewarding writer, one committed, as she has said, to "density, not volume. The large, realistic, telling-it-all novel is not of interest to me. I like to leave something to the imagination" (*PW* 7).

A recent, lively first novel that reinforces Howard's heartening example is Ellen Currie's *Available Light* (1986), the story of a rocky but promising romance between a gambling saxophonist and Kitty O'Carolan, a New York fashion stylist and God-awful poet who narrates most of the tale in an ebullient, shifting, highly-charged monologue. There are occasional bizarre and surreal flights, but a memorable stabilizing character is Kitty's mother, "Our Lady of the Perpetual Cardigan, . . . forty years out of the slums of Belfast, pink and white and tough as a boot" (14). Again, as in so many recent Irish-American novels (by Cullinan, Dunphy, and other realists as well as by Howard and other experimental writers), the movement here is from constriction to openness, out into the "available light" of unenhanced, natural photography. When told late in the book to mind her own business, Kitty takes the words literally and with the force of a sudden revelation: "It doesn't matter to anyone, really matter to anyone, what I do. How fine a feeling. I have not had it before. I will mind my own business, my own, my business, full of ambiguities and dangers, *mine*" (213).

Perhaps the greatest of contemporary Irish-American stylists is William Kennedy. Born in 1928, he has made most of his living as a journalist while turning himself by dint of steady labor into a writer of fiction. His first novel, *The Ink Truck* (1969) appeared when he was over forty, and the books that followed had more than their share of rejections. However, in more recent times solid publishing (including paperback) contracts, a MacArthur Foundation "genius grant," and work in the movies have changed his situation dramatically. Kennedy's extraordinary fiction now has a considerable audience, and he is famous in a literary way, with a secure reputation resting on his "Albany cycle" of novels. Three of these, *Legs* (1975), *Billy Phelan's Greatest Game* (1978), and *Ironweed* (1983), share a setting, New York's down-at-heels capital city, a time frame, roughly 1925 to 1938, and a vivid cast of characters both dead and alive, bums and bootlickers and honest working men, journalists, politicians, gamblers, and gangsters. A fourth, *Quinn's Book* (1988) is both a culmination and a new departure. Set in the middle of the nineteenth century, it involves ancestors of characters from the other novels and many crucial, shaping events of Irish-American history.[11]

The Albany novels are strange, fascinating books, combining unillusioned realism in the Irish-American tradition of James T. Farrell, blasé flights into the fantastic as in the "magic realism" of South Americans such as Gabriel Garcia Marquez, and passages of compassionate lyricism, prose poetry, really, reminiscent of the fictions of William Goyen or Faulkner. Kennedy is also a prime example of a contemporary Irish-American light stylist, one who argues from plenitude and complexity toward affirmation. His body of work is well glossed by his epigraph to *Ironweed* from Dante's *Purgatorio*: "To course o'er better waters now hoists sail the little bark of my wit, leaving behind her a sea so cruel."

The first three Albany novels constitute a legitimate trilogy because of the effect of focusing in and down that reading them in sequence provides. *Legs* is a fictionalizing of the life of a real and famous person: the notorious underworld figure, Jack "Legs" Diamond, "not merely the dude of all gangsters, the most active brain in the New York underworld, but . . . one of the truly new American Irishmen of his day; Horatio Alger out of Finn McCool and Jesse James, shaping the dream that you could grow up in America and shoot your way to glory and riches" (13). The story of Legs takes in the six years, from 1925 to 1931, of his friendship with Albany lawyer Marcus Gorman, who narrates the events. The accent is on the last three years, during which Gorman works for Legs and ending with Diamond's shooting death in Albany, but there are flashbacks all the way to Legs's late-nineteenth-century childhood in the Philadelphia Irish ghetto. *Billy Phelan's Greatest Game*, describes one week in late October, 1938, in the lives of small-time hustler Billy Phelan and journalist Martin Daugherty (the narrator here) who find themselves mixed up in the kidnapping of the son of Albany's most powerful political boss. Finally, *Ironweed* details two days, October 31 and November 1, 1938, in the life of Billy's father Francis Phelan, an alcoholic derelict and seemingly the least consequential of men. Here the narrative is omniscient and much more lyrical, and it includes the final acts and thoughts of three other homeless hoboes whose deaths punctuate the book with resonant emotional impact.

What the main characters in these three novels have in common is integrity, of sorts, and a resolute refusal of illusion or self-delusion. By far the worst is Legs Diamond, an underworld potentate and cold-blooded murderer. And yet, in the eyes of Marcus Gorman, he emerges as a true and admirable paradox: "He was a liar, of course, a perjurer, all of that, but he was also a venal man of integrity, for he never ceased to renew his vulnerability to punishment, death, and damnation. It is one thing to be corrupt. It is another to behave in a psychologically responsible way toward your own evil" (118). A self-consciously mythic figure, Jack Diamond (born John T. Nolan) has a lot in common with Jay Gatsby (born Jimmy Gatz), who also emerged from his own Platonic conception of himself. Marcus Gorman contrasts Legs to "lesser latter-day figures such as Richard Nixon, who left significant history in his wake, but no legend;

whose corruption, overwhelmingly venal and invariably hypocritical, lacked the admirably white core fantasy that can give evil a mythical dimension" (216).

As for Billy Phelan, he seems to his observing narrator Martin Daugherty, "more specific than most men," in fact, "fully defined at thirty-one" (2). He refuses to join either side in the deadly kidnap game that turns the Albany underworld inside out, although the cost is ostracism from his joy and livelihood—immersion in the city's hustling night scene. Martin calls him "a generalist, a man in need of the sweetness of miscellany" (6). Martin also considers Billy "a strong man, indifferent to luck, a gamester who accepted the rules and played by them, but who also played above them, . . . a healthy man without need for artifice or mysticism," and (another paradox) "a serious fellow who put play in its proper place: an adjunct to breathing and eating" (200). And when an inadvertent tip from Billy brings the kidnapping to a happy ending, Martin credits him with unconscious, intuitive knowledge "touched with magic," and calls him "not only the true hero of this whole sordid business, but . . . an ontological hero as well" (272). To be sure, this is a heavy load of meaning for the life of a small-time bowling, cards, and pool hustler to carry, but again, as with the story of Legs Diamond, Kennedy is convincing.

Finally, comes the least and greatest of the trilogy's protagonists. At age fifty-eight Francis Phelan is an alcoholic vagrant, the murderer of three men with a share of responsibility in several other deaths, and a twenty-year deserter of his wife and children. And yet Kennedy creates him as a plausibly heroic figure holding to an austere set of values ("IRONWEED; The name refers to the toughness of the stem"), in words that come seemingly from Francis's own inarticulate soul:

> He believed he was a creature of unknown and unknowable qualities, a man in whom there would never be an equanimity of both impulsive and premeditated action. Yet after every admission that he was a lost and distorted soul, Francis asserted his own private wisdom and purpose: he had fled the folks because he was too profane a being to live among them; he had humbled himself willfully through the years to counter a fearful pride in his own ability to manufacture the glory from which grace would flow. What he was was, yes, a warrior, protecting a belief that no man could ever articulate, especially himself; but somehow it involved protecting saints from sinners, protecting the living from the dead. And a warrior, he was certain, was not a victim. Never a victim. [216]

The two days and nights of *Ironweed*, Halloween and All Saints' Day of the year 1938, are eventful for Francis. He gets sober and gets drunk, he eases the last hours of two dying hobo-companions, he finds the body of Helen, his on-the-bum girlfriend of a decade, he kills a man, and he comes home to his wife and family for dinner for the first time since 1916.

In addition, through the course of these forty-eight hours, Francis meets and converses with all of the important ghosts of his past—from his parents, to companions of his youth, to those in whose violent deaths he has been implicated. Is this delirium tremens or is it "really" happening? The quality of the writing makes the question irrelevant. It is simply one more of Kennedy's successful paradoxes that this least deluded of men has plausible encounters with the dead. Here Kennedy echoes modern Irish literature, where such encounters are commonplace; for example, the phantasmagorical "Circe" chapter of Joyce's *Ulysses*, or his wonderful ghost story, "The Dead," or Máirtín Ó Cadhain's Gaelic masterpiece *Cré na Cille* (*The Churchyard*), a novel consisting of the graveyard conversation of corpses. Moreover, the Halloween time frame of *Ironweed* actually joins two Irish feasts associated with commerce between the living and the dead, the Celtic Samhain as well as the Christian All Hallows. Closer to home, *Ironweed* also contains commentary on the key Irish-American concerns of pious respectability and matriarchal dominance. Francis Phelan and his hobo girlfriend Helen are kindred spirits in that both have fled domestic conventionality, in part because of bitter memories of their own repressive upbringings at the hands of joyless, controlling mothers. In fact, Kennedy wrote an early, unpublished novel in which this theme is central. As he explains in an interview: "And this Catholic puritanism, this kind of matriarchal possessiveness wouldn't let the children out, wouldn't let them become what they were capable of becoming" (Bonetti 77).

In *Ironweed*, Kennedy also faces the challenge, met so well by James T. Farrell, of how to render the thoughts of inarticulate people. Like many Irish-American characters, Francis Phelan has a flair for public speaking. In telling baseball stories, he has "a gift of gab that could mesmerize a quintet of bums around a fire under a bridge" (73-74). However, he cannot articulate his own heart's private speech. He is unable to express his love or his pride, his rage against fate and injustice or the marrow-deep guilt that defines him. Instead, his "traitorous" hands speak with an "evil autonomy." A former professional baseball player, Francis uses his athletic talent as a violent substitute for articulation of his quarrels with the world. He has killed three men, all in grim parody of his baseball skills. He kills a union-busting scab by throwing a baseball-sized stone with awesome force and accuracy, a fellow bum who has attacked him by swinging him by the legs so that his head smashes against a concrete wall, and the man who has just delivered a death-blow to Francis's friend Rudy by breaking his back with one crack of a baseball bat. Nor can Francis speak his mind in situations calling for the expression of love. He is virtually tongue-tied during the afternoon and evening of his return after twenty years' absence to his family's home.

Kennedy solves the problem very differently from Farrell. Instead of Farrell's scrupulous plainness and minimal eloquence, his rigorous refusal of authorial intrusion, Kennedy steps into his narrative to create *written* effects that call attention to themselves because they are beyond the ken of the novel's characters, effects attributable directly to the consciousness of a narrative voice above and beyond the action—an intrusive omniscient narrator. There is eloquence in *Ironweed*, and it blesses characters, situations, events from which it is much harder to extract human dignity and elicit compassion than in Farrell's novels; that is, the lives and deaths of people on the teetering edge of humanity—the destitute, squalid drifters of Albany in the Depression. Kennedy manages to bless these unpromising materials by authorial intrusion, and his methods are lyricism and metaphor. Throughout the novel he creates lovely, lyrical sentence rhythms, both in passages of description and in renderings of his characters' unarticulated thoughts. In addition, such passages are occasionally graced with metaphors beyond the possibility of a character to conceive, or at least to bring through into speech. Here is Kennedy's description of Francis finding sleep out in the open in sub-freezing weather, late on the first of the two nights of *Ironweed*:

> The new and frigid air of November lay on Francis like a blanket of glass. Its weight rendered him motionless and brought peace to his body, and the stillness brought a cessation of anguish to his brain. In a dream he was only just beginning to enter, horns and mountains rose up out of the earth, the horns—ethereal, trumpets—sounding with a virtuosity equal to the perilousness of the crags and cornices of the mountainous pathways. Francis recognized the song the trumpets played and he floated with its melody. Then, yielding not without trepidation to its coded urgency, he ascended bodily into the exalted reaches of the world where the song had been composed so long ago. And he slept. [90]

As in the eloquent passage where Francis sees himself as a warrior, "not a victim," these are Kennedy's words, rhythms, and metaphors. The author has stepped in to explain and bless his character. Along with considerable talent, such bold intrusion reveals a high level of confidence about the medium of fiction. Already apparent in his determinedly experimental first novel, *The Ink Truck*, this confidence has to do with Kennedy's position as a third-generation ethnic writer, a conscious literary inheritor of earlier twentieth-century Irish Americans, notably Farrell and Edwin O'Connor, but also, perhaps, Jim Tully, whose novels of hoboes and drifters published in the 1920s provide a precedent for *Ironweed*. In addition, the work of Kennedy and other contemporary stylists bears a strong family resemblance to a number of writers on the other side of the cultural divide of the 1910s and 1920s. Finley Peter Dunne and pre-Famine satirists such as John McDermott Moore, Thomas C. Mack, and "Paddy O'Flarrity" were no strangers to linguistic exuberance and confident, playful risk-taking with narrative conventions.

William Kennedy's clear Irish-American forerunners have also helped release him to look further afield for literary models such as Garcia Marquez. Because certain trails had been blazed in his own ethnic neighborhood, Kennedy has been free to strike out on his own. He explains his course as follows: "I liked Farrell's *Studs Lonigan* but I never wanted to write like that—the naturalism of the city. I was too interested in the dream element in life, the surreal." (Actually, there is a fair amount of this in Farrell: from Studs Lonigan's dying fantasies, to the protagonist's extended dream in *Gas-House McGinty*, to Mary O'Flaherty's graveyard conversations with her dead husband in *No Star Is Lost*.) And again, "I always thought Edwin O'Connor's *The Last Hurrah* was a marvelous book. I fell off the chair reading those great lines about the Curley days and I could see he understood the tension between the Church and politics extremely well. But I also felt he was leaving out things either to be polite to the Church or to Irish society, or perhaps out of squeamishness. I felt at times that he didn't reflect Irish-American life as I knew it. I felt I had to bring in the cat-houses and the gambling and the violence, for if you left those out you had only a part of Albany. . . . I felt that way of life had to be penetrated at the level of harsh reality—its wit, anger, sexuality, deviousness. It also needed to have the surreal dimension that goes with any society in which religion plays such a dominant role" (Quinn 72).

The point is that Kennedy emerged from a solid literary context. Farrell made himself and his style entirely out of his own working-class and lower-middle-class experience and literary insight. O'Connor was the most talented novelist of the Irish-American bourgeoisie to come along, and he made his considerable mark by using traditional narrative modes. If he also ended up being something of a "lace-curtain" writer, that's at least in part because he too was plowing new ground. Thus, Kennedy charts his course by the lights of his predecessors, an advantage neither of them had. He wanted to be surreal in a way that Farrell was not, he wanted to be realistic in a way that O'Connor was not, and he wanted to explore different dimensions of Irish-American life. And so we have the Albany novels, which mix hard, gritty realism with a surreal lyricism of great beauty in the depiction of, among other things, an Irish-American underclass of ruthless criminals, gamblers, and homeless bums, the lowest of the low. Certainly, Kennedy has his own full sense of his inheritance, and his own hard road has given him a special appreciation for Farrell's example: "But you think of Farrell. He never quit. It's an admirable thing, because he was getting pleasure out of what he was doing. If there are enough people who understand that, if there are other writers getting some pleasure out of reading your twenty-eighth novel, then maybe that's enough" (Quinn 68). Kennedy also pays his respects at the opening of *Ironweed*, when Francis Phelan, rolling through St. Agnes Cemetery on the back of a truck toward a day's work of digging, begins reading the names on the stones: "FARRELL, said one roadside gravestone. KENNEDY, said another" (2).

Shortly after the publication of *Ironweed*, Kennedy rejected the idea of someday setting a novel in Ireland: "For me, it's a question of imagination. I don't feel I own those Irish places, but I do own Albany. It's mine. Nineteenth-century Albany is mine as well. It's a different time and in many ways a different place from what it is now, but I feel confident I can reach it" (Quinn 78). *Quinn's Book* (1988) does just that, and the result is a tour de force of historical fiction driven by a visionary imagination. In this fascinating novel Kennedy has created an expanded panorama of nineteenth-century American life involving a large cast of exotic characters and a spectacular sequence of events, both historical and passing strange. The historical side is revisionist, dark and violent. Kennedy provides a meditative recreation of significant events and situations of New York and national life from 1849 to 1864. These include immigrant displacement and exploitation, life and death in the cholera-ridden Irish ghetto, black slavery and the underground railroad, labor agitation and mob uprisings, and the archetypal carnage of the Civil War. Countering the deadly realities of public history is the bizarre but life-affirming private history of the recently orphaned Daniel Quinn and his friends. (In one of several links with the previous Albany books, this Daniel Quinn is the great-grandfather of Francis Phelan's ten-year-old grandson Danny Quinn in *Ironweed*.) Kennedy starts the personal narrative off with a bang, as the drowned erotic dancer Magdalena Colón (born Mary Coan in Ireland) is resurrected by the necrophiliac embrace of John the Brawn McGee, a riverboat captain and fourteen-year-old Daniel's boss. The novel contains a fair amount of spirit-rapping, mysterious disappearance, and unworldly coincidence in the vein of magic realism, much of it surrounding Daniel Quinn's quest for union with Magdalena's willful, enigmatic niece, "the wondrous" Maud Fallon, who unlocks for Quinn a view of life as "a great canvas of the imagination, large enough to suggest the true magnitude of the unknown. What he saw on the canvas was a boundless freedom to do and to think and to feel all things offered to the living" (218).

"Maud, I speak to you now of the Irish," says Daniel Quinn, "the famine Irish, . . . villains in this city. It wasn't this way for the Irish when I was little, but now they are viewed not only as carriers of the cholera plague but as a plague themselves, such is their number: several thousand setting up life here in only a few years, living in hovels, in shanties, ten families in a small house, some unable to speak anything but the Irish tongue, their wretchedness so fierce and relentless that not only does the city shun them but the constabulary and the posses meet them at the docks and on the turnpikes to herd them together in encampments on the city's great western plain" (111). Thus begins Kennedy's reimagining of the Famine generation of Irish immigrants. Quinn isolates one family, the Ryans, as "paradigms of helpless, guiltless suffering" (134). Driven by eviction to live in "a ditch near Cashel," the Ryans emigrate to a one-room cabin in the Albany Irish ghetto where Quinn learns the meaning of the phrase "dirt poor": "to live day and night inhaling the odor of raw earth." The father's foundry job ends with his violent death in a labor agitation incited by the controlling plutocracy, pitting native American against Irish immigrant workers. And a lasting image of this generation is Quinn's observation of a trainload of immigrants hounded out of Albany and heading west. One of them begins a song in Gaelic: "The train whistle interrupted the sound of the song but not the singer, and as the cars moved out, his voice reached us in fragments, audible between the whistle blasts, a fervent melody struggling to be heard. And then it was gone" (139). It is this scene that forces Quinn to understand his own essential differentness from the Famine immigrants. In a revelation similar to that of *Ironweed's* Francis Phelan, Quinn boards his own train, "knowing, with every willful step, that I had once and for all obliterated the image of myself as helpless, hapless orphan, tossed off a canalboat like so much offal. Nor was I a greenhorn victim, not anymore" (139-40).

Quinn's Book also contains Kennedy's meditations on other aspects of mid-nineteenth-century Irish-American life. Notable here is the Irish con-tribution to the Civil War, in which, "using a steady supply of replace-ments off the boat, the [Irish] brigade recapitulated the fate of ancient Celtic warriors: they went forth to battle but they always fell" (217). The anachronistic echo of Shaemus O'Sheel rings more truly than that turn-of-the-century Celtic idealist would have wished, and Quinn's authori-tative observation as a correspondent of the appalling blood sacrifice of the Irish and others is powerfully rendered. Returning from "the mud-holes of hell" to an Albany bazaar in which patriotism and war are being glorified ("Such lovely revolutions. Such a grand Civil War. We must not forget how they are done"), Quinn gives the fashionable crowd a lesson in "reality" by describing the slaughter at Round Top and Cold Harbor: "A pile of dead people, that's the reality I'm talking about. The bigger the pile, the bigger the reality" (222). Such instruction is in the tradition of Mr. Dooley's mordant Civil War pieces such as "The Blue and the Gray," in which a veteran asks an armchair patriot, "Did ye iver have to wipe ye'er most intimate frinds off ye'er clothes, whin ye wint home at night?" (29). Far from uplifted by the experience, Quinn leaves the war emptied of all conviction save "a kind of fatal quizzicality" (227). As it happens, Quinn also observes one of the low points of Irish-American history, the New York City Draft Riots of 1863. The passage of a conscription law from which anyone able to pay $300 was exempt drove mobs of angry Irish into a week of violence against blacks. Although his Albany friend the freed black man and underground-railroad conductor Joshua is killed, Quinn still understands "the crystalline injustice" of the law "to the poor

Irishman . . . , mired in generational denial and humiliation as he was, and for whom free Negroes meant a swarm of competitors for the already insufficient jobs at the bottom of the world" (275).

"A brute of a kind" but "a presence to be understood" (241), John the Brawn McGee stands for a type of the mid-century Irish, a man who by dint of sheer physical strength mixed with a natural acuity fights his way up from the life-draining exploitation of pick-and-shovel labor. Quinn's first boss and both a nemesis and a model, John the Brawn is by turns a riverboat captain, professional boxer, saloonkeeper, political enforcer for the Democrats, gambling-house operator, and manager of the first Saratoga race track. He makes his reputation and his fortune "polarized as the heroic Irish champion of the United States" with a bare-knuckle victory over "Arthur (Yankee) Barker, the pride of native Americans" (241). Kennedy provides an exuberant journalistic account of the bout, which takes place on a summer afternoon in 1854, a banner year for American nativists and their Know-Nothing Party. (This is the time chronicled in Charles James Cannon's *Bickerton; or, The Immigrant's Daughter* of 1855.) Indeed, nativist animosity toward the immigrants is a major thread throughout *Quinn's Book*. The Albany and Saratoga white Protestant establishment sneers not only at the likes of John the Brawn, but also at the somewhat more respectable Irish career choices of Daniel Quinn as a journalist and his true love Maud Fallon who follows her flamboyant aunt Magdalena into the theater. (The protagonists of Kennedy's four Albany novels explore a range of typical Irish-American jobs: bootlegger, gambler, baseball player, writer.) Furthermore, Quinn helps to expose "The Society," a secret conspiracy of old-line Dutch and Yankee families, whose machinations against upstart newcomers range from poisonous newspaper letters penned by "Purity Knickerbocker" to beatings, torture, and murder.

Quinn's Book may seem at first to differ from Kennedy's earlier novels in that incident rather than character revelation drives this narrative. However, there is a unifying principle (and principal)—the consciousness of Daniel Quinn, whose book this most certainly is. This is the picaresque tale of an orphan boy cast out on the wide world alone to find his way. He meets, loses, regains, and wins his great love, the mysterious Maud, and the quest unfolds in language that recalls the flowery, exuberant rhetoric of such tales. Thus, both plot and style recall nineteenth-century popular fiction, from Dickens and Harriet Beecher Stowe to Irish-Americans such as Charles Cannon, Hugh Quigley, Peter McCorry, and Mary Anne Sadlier. Not surprisingly, the orphan Daniel Quinn has a good deal in common with Sadlier's Willy Burke ("The Irish Orphan in America"). And yet, Kennedy's narrative never relaxes into flaccid pastiche. *Quinn's Book* rings freshly because it is the book of a gifted writer who is in love with words—their variousness, power, and capacity to comfort, dazzle, and terrify. Discovering this love turns out to be the substance of Daniel

Quinn's progress to epiphany as well. While finding Maud, he also finds his true vocation. Like Farrell's Danny O'Neill and Joyce's Stephen Dedalus, the calling is art, not religion, and with the same fierce commitment. Quinn learns to oppose suffering and injustice by observing and chronicling them. While facing up to genuine mystery, he learns to reject idealizing, romantic delusions that can send people off to their deaths. In short, he learns his trade. *Quinn's Book* is a writer's book, from the thrill of wonder and control that the young boy feels in writing his first sentence, to a journalistic career that culminates in fame as a war correspondent, to the ultimate breakthrough into the heady, open air of fiction.

Along the way, there are several links between Quinn's vocation and his Irish heritage. At a critical point in his relationship with Maud, Quinn recites from "I Shall not Die," a seventeenth-century Gaelic poem which he knows as "the old Irish poem of warning" (201). Further on, Kennedy includes a parody of the language of Irish legends as "Quinn, that formidable folklorist" proceeds toward his fated reconciliation with Maud, declaring that "It is a man's duty to sing" (228-29). Through the course of the novel, Quinn puzzles over the one great, enigmatic sign of his emergence as a writer, an ancient Celtic bronze disk found in the false bottom of a buried bird cage. His only inheritance from his dead parents, the disk has a design of interwoven spirals (illustrated on the novel's title page) that becomes a protean, trompe l'oeil face: "Now it was a screaming mouth with vicious eyes, now a comic puppy with bulbous nose and tiny mouth" (73). The disk speaks to Quinn of love and violence and makes of him "a man compelled to fuse disparate elements of this life, however improbable the joining" (130). Early on, Quinn perceives dimly that not to pursue the disk's call for "linkage" and the somehow related quest for Maud would be to "fall into desuetude, like the lives of so many men of my father's generation, men who moved through their days sustained only by fragments of failed dreams, and who grew either indolent in despair or bellicose in resentment at such a condition" (130). Ultimately, Quinn comes to see the disk as his protection against the forces of darkness "like a monstrance, like a shield" (198), and in its design of "willful ambiguity by the Celtic artist" he is able to read "the wisdom of multiple meanings" (239). This message reinforces the counsel of Quinn's journalistic mentor, Will Canaday of the Albany *Chronicle*: "Move toward the verification of freedom, and avoid gratuitous absolutes" (135). The disk also declares that Quinn's gift with words is an Irish gift.

Quinn's Book ends appropriately with a last twist of the Irish-American deathbed convention, already spectacularly inverted in the necrophiliac opening scene. Sensing the imminence of her second and permanent demise, Magdalena Colón throws a party/wake for herself, advertising the event with a handbill ("Notice of Proximate Death"). She orders her maid to remove her undergarments, apply makeup, and dress her in emeralds, silver slippers, and a loose-fitting blouse. The mourners arrive "in great droves" to be wined, dined, and entertained by a magic show and Jim Fisk's German band. As he is about to consummate at last his own fifteen-year love affair with Maud Fallon, Quinn catches a glimpse of Magdalena being carried to the lake shore in the arms of John the Brawn for a final midnight tryst.

Daniel Quinn's turn from journalism to art near the end of his book is an epiphany: "I knew that what was wrong with my life and work was that I was so busy accumulating and organizing facts and experience that I had failed to perceive that only in the contemplation of mystery was revelation possible; only in confronting the incomprehensible and arcane could there be any synthesis" (265-66). And his decision "to move beyond facts to a grander sphere" has the force of an artistic credo: "Mine was clearly a life fulfilled by language. . . . By devising a set of images that did not rot on me overnight, I might confront what was worth confronting, with no expectation of solving the mysteries, but content merely to stare at them until. . . . if I used the words well, the harmony that lurked beneath all contraries and cacophonies must be revealed. This was an act of faith, not reason." He then sets out, "with the courage false or real that comes with an acute onset of hubris, [to] create a world before which I could kneel with awe and reverence as I waited to be carried off into flights of tragic laughter" (280-81). What Quinn believes, Kennedy achieves. Through the transforming power of his imagination, the novelist turns the typical nineteenth-century, Famine-generation plot line into a quest for meaning through art, one that on some level surely stands for his own career. At the same time, the sheer joy in using words that Quinn discovers is here embodied in Kennedy's style, in the newly minted nineteenth-century cadences and flourishes that somehow manage to express an authentic awakening to the power of love and art.

The best gloss for the achievement of William Kennedy's fiction is the passage in Seamus Heaney's "Station Island" where the ghost of James Joyce advises the fasted pilgrim "to write / for the joy of it. Cultivate a work-lust / that imagines its haven like your hand at night / dreaming the sun in the sunspot of a breast." Secure in his Irish-American literary heritage, Kennedy has been free to follow Joyce's further advice:

> Keep at a tangent.
> When they make the circle wide, it's time to swim
> out on your own and fill the element
> with signatures on your own frequency,
> echo soundings, searches, probes, allurements,
>
> elver-gleams in the dark of the whole sea.

And yet, in *Quinn's Book* especially, with its ebullient rhetorical envelope, its engaging bits of disparate parody, and its cavalier mixtures of person, tense, and point of view, one picks up echoes of the voice with which this study began, that of the "Vehicle General of News, and Grand Spouter of Politics," Lawrence Sweeney, "He who was wont to raise the gen'ral Smile, / And for whole Days a World of Cares beguile." These traits endure.

ELEVEN

Liberating Doubleness
in the Nineties

Irish-American literature is alive and it is well. While mass emigration from Ireland is borne back ceaselessly into the past, creative writing of depth and quality identifiable as Irish-American continues to appear. A valid opening question is why, against demographic odds, does such a body of work still exist? The beginnings of an answer come from an Irish ethnic outpost the very remoteness of which brings legitimacy to the analysis. In a seminal essay, "Imagination's Home," Australian poet Vincent Buckley, the grandson of Irish immigrants, coined the phrase "source-country," by which he means the genius loci of "a knowledge which goes very deep into the psyche, and . . . has an almost superstitious integrity. The country is a source in the sense that the psyche grows from and in it, and remains profoundly attuned to it." Such a place, "already potential to poetry," provides an artist with images, history, language, manners, myths, ways of perceiving, and ways of communicating. As "most of these things could not be brought to Australia," Buckley continues, "what remained was the ache of their absence." He finds this sense of loss in the founding generation of Irish-Australian writers—notably novelist Joseph Furphy and poet Christopher Brennan. But he also includes himself, declaring that, "after repeated stays there, I experience Ireland as a source-country in a way in which I experience no other place." Though he was born and raised in Melbourne, "for feelings of source, Ireland is primary, and Australia secondary." Given this displacement, Buckley asks, "Where's home then?" His answer is that wherever he physically lives, for Vincent Buckley as writer, Ireland is "imagination's home" (24).

This artist's self-conscious identification is only one part of the story. Buckley goes on to cite his father, the son of Irish immigrants:

> Irish to the marrow-bone, he professed non-Irishness; he resisted all talk of being "Irish." . . . He retained (or was told) not one single anecdote to do with Ireland. However, he was full of tales, yarns, jokes, near-legends, nicknames, all voiced in a vivacious on-going Irish fashion; of songs, emotional attitudes and gestures, a desire for musical instruments, an instinct or respect for poetry. All of these were Australian in content, Irish in mode (a judgement my father would not have understood or acknowledged). The source had been rejected as rejecting. It was like disowning the memory of

a cruel mother. . . . He was Australian, and that was that. Yet some of the most chilling sentences I have ever heard about death or mortality were spoken by him, in an Irish mode adopted so naturally you'd have thought he brooded on nothing else. (24-25)

Thus, for Buckley's father, Ireland—although by turns resisted and unconscious—was inescapably a source-country in terms of "mode," by which I take him to mean "style" in the deepest sense—style as understood, say, by W.B. Yeats, who equated it with "personality" (his father John Butler Yeats's term and obsession) and "character."[1]

For the purposes of this discussion, it is useful to differentiate the two ways in which Vincent Buckley tells us that a source-country can be imagination's home for an artist (or for anyone) living elsewhere: thematically by virtue of certain explicit images, places, names, historical events, legends, folklore, patterns and customs both familial and cultural; and stylistically by virtue of an implicit "mode," which he identifies as habits of perception, language retained or remembered, "an accent, a pace, a pitch, a rhythm of speech." Both concepts can help us understand the staying power of Irish-American fiction in our time.

A first example of the persistence of Ireland as thematic source-country for Irish-American writing into the 1990s is *A Country Divorce* (1992) by Ann T. Jones, the daughter of Irish immigrants to Boston. Though she had never been to Ireland until this book was substantially completed, the countryside around Westport, County Mayo, in the 1930s is assuredly for Jones imagination's home. The novel's premise is true to the conditions of Irish Catholic rural culture from after the Famine to De Valera's intensely conservative Free State. Stymied in the marriage market by his old father's reluctance to relinquish proprietorship of their sixteen-acre farm, Morgan Riley gets at age forty-three what looks like a last, miraculous opportunity to avoid the loneliness of pastoral bachelorhood on Ireland's unforgiving west coast. A friend arranges Morgan's marriage to Minnie Maughan, a vivacious twenty-year-old from a less substantial farm ten miles away, whose family hopes to rise by the match. But Minnie brings an unwanted secret dowry—she is pregnant by her young lover, Mattie O'Malley, an impetuous, passionate boy from a goodhearted but profligate family in her home place. A murderous retributive act by Mattie causes Minnie's lie to be exposed, and Morgan resolves to seek a "country divorce," a de facto accommodation sure to be traumatic and permanently frustrating for all concerned. The resolution of *A Country Divorce* is both dramatic and persuasively heartfelt, and Jones's evocation of place, custom, speech, and character in the Ireland of the 1930s rings true—the coastal farms, roads, and hamlets, directly under the wet, misty western weather; detailed cottage, pub, and church interiors; habitual farm labor and the customary events of matchmaking, marriage, wedding feast, and funeral; the conversations of the heedless young lovers, the cautious and kindly Rileys, the dimly aspiring Maughans, and the hard-luck, irresponsible O'Malleys.

Naturally, Ireland and the Irish-American past are most directly drawn upon as thematic source-countries in historical fiction, and there have been several developments in this genre during the past decade. Thomas Flanagan has completed his trilogy of complex fictional meditations on the collision of nationalism and ordinary lives in Ireland with *The End of the Hunt* (1994), a novel of the Irish Revolution and the Civil War of 1916-1923. This monumental, culminating volume does not disappoint. Again, Flanagan's hallmark is scrupulous attention to historical and cultural detail and received wisdom on the personalities of real people (Winston Churchill, Michael Collins, et al), and he is no less plausible in his projection of the impact on vividly created fictional main characters of calamitous events—the Easter Rising, the Black and Tan incursions, the logistics of guerrilla warfare as waged from rural West Cork to the streets of Dublin, and the signing of the controversial Treaty calling for partition of Northern Ireland. The fictional focus on a love affair between a member of the Galway Catholic gentry and Michael Collins's chief aide allows Flanagan entry to a range of venues and emotions extant during those confusing, dangerous times.

For nineteenth-century Irish America, we now have as well the achievement in historical fiction of Peter Quinn, whose *Banished Children of Eve* (1994) recreates Irish New York in the season of the Draft Riots of 1863. The novel provides complex, clarifying insight into several interlacing urban worlds: New York's criminal underbelly as experienced by street hustler Jimmy Dunne, domestic service through immigrant maid Margaret O'Driscoll, the music-hall scene of minstrel Jack Mulcahey, the theatrical world of mulatto actress "Eliza," who stars in *Uncle Tom's Cabin*, political business as usual at Tammany Hall, and prototypical gang life among the "Plug Uglies" and "Dead Rabbits." We also are privy to the roles in the larger, catastrophic events of Civil War America of several historical figures, notably ruined songwriter Stephen Foster, Union general George McClellan, and Catholic archbishop "Dagger John" Hughes. Quinn's book is full to bursting with information and insight.

A first example of the persistence of Ireland as stylistic, or modal, source-country for an American writer is Thomas McGonigle's *Going to Patchogue* (1992), the extended stream-of-consciousness narration of "Tom McGonigle's" journey from his Lower East Side apartment to his hometown of Patchogue, Long Island, and back. This one-day pilgrimage frames a richly layered meditation, encrusted with memories and might-have-beens, the scope of which is the narrator's life to date and his wanderings through the world—Dublin, Sofia, Istanbul, Helsinki, and Venice. The novel is a collage of conversations, recollections, Suffolk County folktales, newspaper clippings, town-meeting minutes, photographs, Long Island Railroad timetables, and handwritten notes. The challenge throughout is "how to hold all of these items in my hands" (34), and the aim is description, definition, understanding, both personal and cultural. Nearing age forty and considering suicide, the narrator seeks directing self-knowledge. As the child of a family that made the typical move of the late 1940s and 1950s from Brooklyn out to "the Island," he diagnoses suburbia as a failed Promised Land—a judgment convincingly embodied in the voices of the Patchogue bar regulars, whose anti-Semitic, anti-intellectual, and anti-African-American vitriol reveals white flight as the prime motive for their migration out of the city.

The harshness of the narrator's confrontation with his communal and personal demons is redeemed by two elements: the Rabelaisian comic vision informing the novel and the bold intelligence of the voice that drives the narrative. This flawed pilgrim soul is neither mad nor alcoholic. Nor is he a straw character created to ridicule or apologize for Irishness. "Tom McGonigle" has a relentless, questioning consciousness, courageously persistent in the hard work of psychological and cultural critique. Throughout his difficult journey, the narrator scrutinizes the ghosts that continue to haunt him: his mother, father, first love, high school friends, fellow townspeople, and most of all, himself. He is the novelist uncomfortably aware of his lack of adherence to conventions: "Here we are pages later and not a single character has made the scene; there has been no conflict laid into the story, there is no motor installed in the locomotive of plot, no sex to grease the wheels of the pages. Still sitting" (30). He is the failed, bewildered lover of his high school sweetheart, Melinda: "Each person is given one love story. Usually it doesn't coincide with another love story" (194). He is the restless but reluctant traveler in search of meanings from Patchogue to the world and back, who comes to realize that "I don't have to travel to Patchogue to be there. I am always in Patchogue" (42), and who decides to keep on living with the inconclusive nature of his findings so far: "I am not ready, please, just yet. I have places to go. I must be getting myself to Patchogue" (57).

McGonigle's ending is plausibly anti-climactic: "It is all so painful. To have gone away and not stayed. To have failed, again. . . . to have brought nothing back from this journey, not even the ash of some exotic adventure." And yet, "Tom" has come through psychologically intact: "Myself has come back. I am in the City. I have gone to Patchogue. I have been in Patchogue. I have come back from Patchogue" (212). Moreover, he has delivered salutary indictments of the persistent xenophobia and complacency of his own and the world's suburban subcultures, as, for example, in a late image of tourists, "drift[ing] to Venice for a final appearance before heading back to their empty northern hovels, their American suburbs, hurrying in fact because the new season is already underway on the television, brunch is being missed and hey, what about the World Series?" (209). *Going to Patchogue* provides a compelling figure for American as well as Irish-American migratory rootlessness. At the realistic conclusion of this often surreal narrative, two mysteries remain intact: the imaginative and meditative variousness of an individual consciousness, and the dark swervings of communal thought into prejudice and hatred. Throughout, McGonigle grounds his enterprise powerfully with a voice of moral outrage that holds together modal features that might otherwise pull apart. These include a headlong, breathless narrative push, rhetorical and linguistic exuberance, a swirling mélange of detail both real and surreal, and the shrill, edgy, blackly humorous wit that holds despair at bay. This is the lineage of Sterne and Swift, of Edgeworth and Carleton, of Joyce, Beckett, and Flann O'Brien, and of their American cousins as traced throughout this study and discussed in chapter 10 as stylized fiction, both dark and light.

Another painful chronicle of migration from Brooklyn (East New York) to Long Island (Mineola) occurs in two novels by Michael Stephens, *Season at Coole* (1972) and *The Brooklyn Book of the Dead* (1994).[2] His is a harsh, wild voice, closer than McGonigle's to the dark stylist's near-hysterical pessimism found in Donleavy and McHale. Indeed, the first novel has an epigraph from Beckett: "All is not then yet quite irrevocably lost." Still, like McGonigle, Stephens uses his intense, bleak, half-crazed, yet vibrant narrative voice to articulate a trenchant critique of the American dream of insulated, suburban family life. His evidence that all ethnic Americans do not flourish in the suburbs is the deeply troubled Coole family—unbalanced, alcoholic, violent, unregenerate, and profoundly displaced: "these folk were from the ghetto slums, the Coole tribe, but they didn't have their ghetto no more, they had to make a private shitheap within the heart of a suburban area, working as antibodies to the cancer around them, though the community thought them the malignancy, the old man got a new citation from the town government once a month, rundown house, improper shingles on roof, broken windows, . . . they needed a subway, the Cooles, a place to hang out, scribbling their graffiti on the walls, instead they did it on the walls of their castle, their Alamo" (*Season* 161-62). Through its long, rambling lament, the first novel establishes this proposition. The second supports it more coherently by focusing on one action—the return of the sixteen Coole children to East New York, "that mythical land between Bushwick and Bed-Stuy, between hell and Brownsville" (11) where the patriarch Leland Coole's will dictates that he must be waked and buried. All variously crippled and comically presented, the Cooles prove that respectability is not for everyone. They include a proudly alcoholic cabdriver, a homeless man living in an abandoned bus, the girlfriend of a Mafia hitman, and a criminal in the Witness Protection Program. Stephens walks a thin line on which gallows humor just manages to counter howling despair. What keeps the balance is his genuine yet grimly unsentimental affection for urban, ethnic life. Back for her father's funeral from a Florida "planned community," eldest daughter Samantha realizes that in all the years of her adulthood, whenever she crossed a bridge from Manhattan, "she knew she was home again, back in Brooklyn, and a combination of thrill and chill, fear and tear, woe and begone, clutched at her consciousness, forcing her to acknowledge this place, even when she didn't want to recognize it at all" (121). Stephens and McGonigle provide the strongest categorical rejections of the desirability of Irish middle-class assimilation as a truth universally acknowledged since Farrell's *Studs Lonigan* in 1935. Theirs is a disturbing and important piece of the post-World War II suburban story.

Further and outstanding examples of the persistence of Irish style in American fiction are the novels of the 1990s by two great practitioners, William Kennedy and Maureen Howard. Through 1998, Kennedy has published two additional volumes in his fictional cycle, superfluous but welcome proof that his Albany is as rich a source as Farrell's Chicago or Faulkner's Mississippi, and that he continues to carry around in his head a whole Irish-American world—from the Famine immigration up through the 1950s—vivid, coherent, and available for imaginative appropriation. *Very Old Bones* (1992) continues more explicitly the engagement with the mysteries and challenges of art in *Quinn's Book*, this time by focusing on painter Peter Phelan and his illegitimate son, the writer/editor Orson Purcell. Here Kennedy spools backwards in time from Saturday, July 26, 1958, the date of a crucial Phelan family gathering at which Peter reads his will and articulates his wishes. Other key events are the death of wandering soul Francis Phelan in 1943, fittingly on a baseball diamond coaching third, and a harrowing saga from the 1880s involving the immigrant generation of Phelan ancestors. Over the years, Peter Phelan has created two masterful series of paintings, one inspired by his hobo brother Francis ("The Itinerant Series"), and the other by a strange ancestral tale ("The Malachi Suite"). The narrator and this novel's version of the truth-seeking younger relative, Orson Purcell opens the series out beyond Albany through his army hitch in Germany with the occupying forces after World War II and his subsequent floundering into alcoholic madness in New York City. His goal and accomplishment is to find a measure of personal peace by rummaging through the "very old bones" of Phelan history.

In *The Flaming Corsage* (1996), the time frame is 1884-1912, and the pivotal events are the disastrous Delavan House hotel fire of 1894 and

the scandalous "Love Nest Killings" of 1908. Here Kennedy brings to
the fore playwright and immigrant's son Edward Daugherty and his
enigmatic, doomed wife, Katrina Taylor, an Albany Anglo-Dutch aristocrat. Both Edward and Katrina have played important though minor roles
in earlier novels of the cycle. Stylistically, Kennedy extends himself to
create a variety of effects: chapter headings and set pieces from period
tableau/melodrama, scenes from Edward's plays, Katrina's lyrical interior monologues soaked in *fin de siècle* death-fixed rumination, and
memorable realistic evocations, including the last rites and death of immigrant patriarch Emmett Daugherty, complete with candlesticks, crucifix, holy water, chrism, a lemon, a spoon, a piece of cotton, bread, salt,
and a growler of ale. And so the crazy salad and rich horn of plenty that
is the Albany cycle continues to grow.

Maureen Howard remains a classic light stylist, ever impatient with
traditional storytelling conventions, continually pursuing new directions
that both expose and celebrate the qualities of the narrative art. *Natural
History* (1992) is a dazzling, full realization of Howard's trademark and
identifiably Irish-American literary concerns with the presence of the
past, the spirit of urban place, and Joycean technical wizardry, all in the
service of emotional truth. The genius loci is her native Bridgeport, Connecticut, from the 1940s through the 1980s, and the novel charts the engagement with local history and personal memory of James and
Catherine Bray, the children of a Bridgeport police detective and a
wealthy cement-maker's daughter. (Their models to some extent are
Howard's own parents, who were so memorably evoked in her classic
memoir, *Facts of Life*.) An unsettling murder case in 1943 (a young soldier, Eddie Litwak, shot by a parvenu socialite in her kitchen) disturbs
the calm of James's and Catherine's childhood, and their father's equivocal relationship with the accused woman challenges the two as adults
forty years later, when James has become a successful movie actor and
Catherine an artistic wool-dyer and weaver.

Howard's craft-involved restlessness has never been more in evidence. *Natural History* opens with the "bird's-eye view" of a map maker:
"Lay on the page a neat grid of neighborhoods, the quirky cross-cuts of
routes that followed secondary streams or an Indian footpath, what was
decreed by nature or habit and is long forgotten, long a dead end or
confusing turn in the city—the lost logic of a marsh or a stubborn farmer's
lawsuit that will not let you pass" (1). Framed by chapters of "Natural
History" (parts I and II), the heart of the novel is eight "Museum Pieces."
Four of these are conventional narratives focused on one character: the
progress from obsession to health of the murdered soldier's brother ("The
Witness"), who for a time plotted the death of Billy Bray for having let
the guilty woman go free; James's perspective on his sister's suicide attempt during their young adulthood ("Sister Brown"); the immigrant's

mild success story of "The Music Man," Geraldo De Martino, James's clarinet teacher and the carrier of European artistic standards to the hinterlands; and a traumatic childhood revelation to Catherine that, though quite possibly mistaken, haunts her troubled adulthood ("The Spinster's Tale"). The other four are technically adventurous. They include a stage-directed "Closet Drama," in which James Bray's later life as an indolent Southern Californian is detailed; "The Lives of the Saints," containing memories of Catherine's adolescent Catholic romance with the saints and a recollection of James's surprisingly moving pilgrimage to Croagh Patrick, County Mayo, while shooting a B movie about the Irish Revolution; and a marvelously complex set of cuts between past and present, fantasy and reality, in mimicry of "Screenplays," which brings James back to California after visiting Bridgeport to explore his idea of making a movie about the Litwak murder, starring himself as his father.

The longest and most experimental of these is "Double Entry," an eighty-page section in which two different texts run simultaneously on facing pages. On the right is a narrative of Bridgeport in the novel's present time of the mid-1980s during James's assessment of his hometown's cinematic possibilities. On the left is a collection of drawings, photographs, newspaper clippings, restaurant menus, doodles, journal entries, and scraps of narrative by Howard and her characters. On one page, for example, we read about or see Bucky Fuller's Dymaxion car, Francis Bacon's 1623 plan for a museum of science and invention, the Smithsonian bust of P.T. Barnum, the U.S. Route I-95 signs on either end of Bridgeport, James Bray jogging through the crumbling city in quest of his movie, and Walter Benjamin on the angel of history: "The storm from Paradise drives him irresistibly into the future to which his back is turned, while the pile of debris before him grows toward the sky. That which we call progress is this storm" (256). To render "the quality of an album" is Howard's aim here, as she explains in an interview: "In effect, what I wanted to do by making it was to show it to the reader. And that's quite an intimate act—to say, 'Come, look over my shoulder and turn the pages with me'" ("Salvaging" 46). The "Double Entry" closes with fitting—and fittingly contrived—symmetry. The right-hand narrative ends first, with James's rejection of the movie idea ("What's the point, darlin'? I can't work his magic. . . . Besides, Billy was short and fat"), followed by five blank, ripped out pages (recalling Howard's Irish forerunner Laurence Sterne), which balance out the novel's pagination, "as if to insist that the beautiful system must hold." The left-hand album ends with James's memory of a visit to his dying father in the hospital, when, unable to enter the sickroom, he hears from the corridor "Billy's gasping *Arraugh, Arraugh* from the Irish bog, far beyond the pale of Bridgeport" (295-99).

Howard's desire in this section and in *Natural History* as a whole is

the creation of as full a picture as possible, historical and personal at
once, of the connectedness over time of a city and its people, of Bridgeport and this novel's characters and author. She begins in the post-De-
pression and postwar moment when American cities seemed to work as
never before or since, especially for the children and grandchildren of
immigrants: "Once in a pleasant land. Don't expect the baggage of kingdoms—milkmaids, cobblers, wise old women with legendary goats or
hens. Once, 1945, in a pleasant land, a favored city, the people worked
and though they made little of it, played. Work was their glory, a gratification that went beyond the weekly pay envelopes, their hours punched
into a time clock so their labor could be reckoned to the nickel, the dime."
Here is the archetypal city lovingly recalled and evoked as a place where
"a stranger getting off the train, finding his way through heavenly streaks
of sun cast from high windows of the station, passing the earthbound
lunch counter and homey newsstand, that stranger breathing the almost
country air would be quickened, feel life's hustle, walking the two blocks
to Main Street," a place where one would feel "as though he stood inside a big body with miraculous energy or a cathedral busy with birds,
music, masses, vendors, stone-cutters and carvers at dizzying heights,"
and where one "would sense at once the spiritual story here as well as
the commercial." "Castles there are none," the narrating voice continues, but "row upon row of houses, double-deckers—dark green, gray
and brown—set close, families stacked beside, atop one another on solid
wood floors. Thick plaster, modern cross ventilation. Parlors face the
street; kitchens the backyard. Clothes dry in the sun." As well, there are
"Porches, porches rubber stamped," and "Churches—steeple, steeple,
gilt dome, green dome, steeple, steeple" (349–50).

Natural History is not, however, a backward-looking book. The valedictory love in this urban, postwar passage is everywhere extended by
Howard's testaments of faith that, on into Bridgeport's blighted 1980s,
the heart survives. People remain curious, resilient, and resourceful, and
they keep demanding and making sense of the world. We realize this
ultimately in the novel's close, when we follow Catherine Bray and her
niece (now a Yale undergraduate) around the P.T. Barnum Museum,
where "all that stuff"—"etched Arabian brass, Macedonian cannonball,
giant's ring, chunks of Westminster Abbey, a stuffed parrot, . . . Zuni
pot, Dervish sword, the lantern from the old North Church hung out to
save America"—"is all curious and entertaining," and from it Catherine
emerges "enriched with the stuff of the world" (389–90). Once again, we
have the argument from plenitude.

For Howard and her characters, a significant part of that richness
remains tied to ethnicity and the creative potential of doubleness—including her own Irishness. She says as much, with characteristic punch

(and corroboration of Vincent Buckley's concept of source-country), in her foreword to a 1997 anthology of Irish-American fiction: "I am an old party, the Irish kid with a mouth on her, from a mostly Irish parish where we combined the Puritan past with mockery of our cut-glass station. Like many women who are included in *Cabbage and Bones*, I have had to reach back to Ireland, to the strong pull of that legendary soil, rocky and generative" (xiv). Early in the novel, as she follows the war in Europe on newspaper maps, Nell Bray sets up her own double vision: "Over there—Europe. The Other Side, her family had always called it. The Other Side, too distant for names. Simple, successful people putting Ireland well behind them, they traced a limited geography of work, church, home" (42). Nell's is the typical distancing experience of a child of immigrants, and yet ethnicity persists into the third generation of this family, for Catherine and James come to understand their parents by means of established Irish-American icons. For her niece's benefit, Catherine provides "sepia tinted views of Nell and Billy," who "come on as dear, infuriating Irish Ma and Pa routine, Maggie and Jiggs" (135); and James sees his father looking like "a stout fellow, a boxer with fancy footwork, those lithographs of Irish immigrants putting up their dukes" (113), and also as the real-life counterpart of all those Irish-American cops and crooks of the *film-noir* 1940s who become the would-be actor's first inspiration. (In the novel's positive resolution, James takes over his father's voice and demeanor in a popular television police series.)

In support of the context of ethnic doubleness, Howard's packed, brilliant book has a concluding grace note in its return "by a commodius vicus of recirculation" (as in Joyce's *Finnegans Wake*, with which it has a good deal in common) to another bird's-eye view of Bridgeport, this one lifted from "the earliest known map of the town," circa 1688, drawn by "the cartographer whom we know to be Braddock Mead, an Irishman, though we cannot know why he used the alias John Greer—what manner of pirate, artist, fraud." And Howard notices last how Bridgeport's spirit of place is rendered visible and human in this map's ornamental frame, a stylistic flourish by an earlier Irish-American that can stand as well for her own artistry in this novel: "Yet you can do no better than the Irishman's cartouche, beautifully drawn, in which corn is offered in trade to us by an allegorical Indian, for it was one hell of a bargain, this rich and generous place" (391).

Since the achievement of *Natural History*, Howard has continued to create unconventional narratives with Irish-American thematic echoes. *A Lover's Almanac* (1998) combines a pair of Manhattan love stories and interpolated musings on the nature of literary and scientific creativity, all contained in a literal almanac (modeled on *The Old Farmer's*) for the first three months of the year 2000. The young lovers are Louise Moffett,

a newly successful painter from a farm in Wisconsin, and underachiev-
ing computer graphics whiz Artie Freeman, conceived during the
Woodstock summer of love and born to Fiona O'Connor, a free spirit
who never revealed the father's name. Orphaned as a boy, Artie is raised
by his grandfather Cyril O'Connor, the "shanty Irish" son of a cleaning
lady and "a patrolman in Hell's Kitchen" who had fled Dublin's 1916
Rising (46, 47). On scholarship at Georgetown, Cyril's first love had been
the study of history. He was researching New York's Civil War draft riots when he met Mae Boyle, his wife-to-be, at a dance. Her lace-curtain-
Irish, financier father set up his new son-in-law on Wall Street, and Cyril's
life went on smoothly from there. In this *Lover's Almanac*, thus, Ireland
remains for Howard significantly a source-country. In the present of the
year 2000, Cyril is a reclusive widower in his late seventies, holed up in
his Fifth-Avenue apartment reading the history books he never got to,
until he is sprung loose by a late-blooming romance with a woman he
had known fifty years before—Sylvie Neisswonger, an Austrian Catholic refugee from Hitler. The vacillating love stories of Louise and Artie,
Cyril and Sylvie, play out in a typically vibrant Howard narrative, in-
tertwined with notes and scraps that highlight the creative lives of many
and various people, among them Franklin, Jefferson, Edison, and Virginia Woolf, William James, Haydn, and Emily Dickinson.

   In addition, there are two memories, italicized because they are autobiographical, of Howard's own awakening to the power and possibility of art: "*1946. The sluggish winter of my thirteenth year,*" it is a Saturday
afternoon "*in the empty house at early dusk*" when she turns on the radio
and hears "*a terrific last act of story quickly told by a man with a slippery
smooth voice, a tale of Rhine-maidens and a dwarf and a hero, of a magic ring
and potions,*" followed by the thing itself—Wagner at the Metropolitan
Opera (113, 115). And again, she recovers a complex memory of adolescent literary enlightenment in Bridgeport, leading from Edgar Rice to
William Burroughs, by way of Twain, Hawthorne, and Cather, where
the avid young reader finds "*sentences, whole paragraphs . . . which I knew
to be grand, la vrai chose, even when I did not understand the jokes, the
parables, the writers' passion for words or their passions*" (224). Just here,
three-fourths of the way through her eighth book, we can mark the start
of a remarkable writing life—that of Maureen Kearns Howard, an American original with Irish connections.

   Two significant shifts in the Irish ethnic literary territory over the
decade of the 1990s should be noted here as well. The first is the coming
of age of Irish-American poetry. For most of its two centuries' existence,
the corpus of poetry engaged with the Irish immigrant/ethnic experience has been cursed with the twin afflictions of nostalgia for the old

country and polemic about Irish nationalism. There has been in recent years a great sea change here, however—the product of the increased opportunity to pursue the muse that comes with long established middle-class status, and of a rediscovery of connectedness to the old country by Americans of Irish background who are now much more comfortable than formerly with whatever Irishness persists for them. Like Eavan Boland's nineteenth-century emigrants, these are people who still have "all the old songs. And nothing to lose."[3] The new poetic enterprise has also been reinforced by the accelerating cultural interaction between America and Ireland over the past twenty years or so. Writers now cross oceans and boundaries at will. Accomplished American poets who have been discovering viable Irish inflections include Maura Stanton, Michael Heffernan, Brendan Galvin, R.T. Smith, Nuala Archer, Tess Gallagher, Michael Lally, John Norton, and Terence Winch.[4] Conversely, among the native Irish voices enriching the American poetic landscape are those of Eamonn Wall, Sara Berkeley, Gerard Donovan, Michael Coady, Greg Delanty, James Liddy, Eamon Grennan, and the polyphonic Paul Muldoon. Their chief role model has probably been John Montague, whose writing about his own complex relationship with America began in Iowa City and Berkeley in the late 1950s.[5]

The recently augmented literary enterprise of looking at America through Irish eyes also extends, naturally enough, to fiction, where the great father figure has been Brian Moore, who, through a writing life in Belfast, Canada, New York, and California, has given us a generation's worth of wonderfully varied novels of transoceanic relevance.[6] Talented younger Irish writers following Moore's example include Jennifer C Cornell, Margaret Dolan, Aidan Hynes, Michael Collins, and Helena Mulkerns.[7] One exciting writer from this generation is Colum McCann. His first novel, *Songdogs* (1995), alternates between a difficult father-son reunion on a river in their native Mayo and the double record of the father's nomadic existence as a photographer—wartime Spain in the 1930s, Mexico in the 1940s, San Francisco, Wyoming, and the Bronx in the 1950s and early 1960s, an odyssey that the son retraces in the late 1980s. Much is attempted here, including imagined set pieces on the literary West during the Beat years and New York ethnic life in the Kennedy era. Indeed, McCann takes a forty-year swatch and the entire American continent as his province! Throughout, there are numbers of memorable images and scenes, and youthful audacity is mitigated by a fine, lyrical prose. McCann's second novel is similarly risky and ambitious. *This Side of Brightness* (1998) connects the experience of New York immigrant sandhogs in a 1916 dig with a cadre of homeless tunnel dwellers in 1991. The link is the focus on the long life into the 1990s of one of the diggers, an African American, and his Irish-American wife. McCann here takes a

plausible crack at the large contemporary American themes of racial accommodation and utterly abandoned homelessness. His is a new voice
to be reckoned with.[8]

Memoirs and autobiographies now also proliferate on both sides of
the ocean. The most visible of these in recent years has been the amazingly successful *Angela's Ashes: A Memoir* (1996) by Frank McCourt, the
bulk of which is a bleak record of a poverty-stricken youth in Limerick
in the 1930s and 1940s. There has been no more thorough prose presentation of urban misery since James T. Farrell's *No Star Is Lost* (1938). The
saving grace of McCourt's book is the narrative voice, which captures
the practical, comic, survivor's perspective of a child. The opening evocation of ethnic Brooklyn during the Depression adds considerably to
our understanding of an earlier, harsher Irish America. Other contemporary contributors in this genre include Eamonn Wall, Michael Lally,
Mary Gordon, Joan Mathieu, Maureen Waters, and Pete Hamill.[9]

Many of the writers just discussed are part of a second territorial
shift—the coming to America of the "New Irish," recent immigrants of
the 1980s and 1990s, both legal and illegal, and most of them very well
educated. The exuberance of this cultural migration is captured in the
pages of the New York journal *Here's Me Bus!*, which began publication
in the spring of 1995. Eamonn Wall, himself a contributor in both poetry
and prose, describes "this potpourri of alienation and excitement" as
"an important development in Irish writing. A generation of exiles, ex-
patriates, commuters is writing its own story as it goes along—a quilt,
or tapestry, or documentary is being created minute by minute" (11, 14).
Thus, we are blessed with something rich and strange—new creative
perspectives from Irish-Americans and Irish in America, from "returned
Yanks" (sometimes from a century or more away) and contemporary
"nomads," in Eamonn Wall's phrase. Neither group is ashamed of the
state they're in or the states they straddle. A keynote rendering of the
attitude abroad in both countries now is former President of Ireland Mary
Robinson's exhortation before the Houses of the Oireachtas to "cherish
the Irish diaspora." In that address of February 2, 1995, President
Robinson asserted that "it seems to me an added richness of our heritage that Irishness is not simply territorial," and that "after all, emigration is not just a chronicle of sorrow and regret. It is also a powerful
story of contribution and adaptation. In fact, I have become more convinced each year that this great narrative of dispossession and belonging, which so often had its origins in sorrow and leave-taking, has
become—with a certain amount of historic irony—one of the treasures
of our society. If that is so then our relation with the diaspora beyond
our shores is one which can instruct our society in the values of diversity, tolerance, and fair-mindedness" (2).

At this point, it must be emphasized that ties to Ireland explain only partially the persistence of Irish-American literary self-consciousness in our time. The availability of Ireland as source-country, along with the proximity of the old country through air travel, and the stimulation provided by the new Irish nomads in American cities simply reinforce the decisive fact that there continues to *be* an Irish-American experience, a living culture on which writers feel compelled to draw. In this context, I want to reintroduce and rename a central idea of this study. In his memoir *The Village of Longing*, Irish writer George O'Brien recalls what the emigrant County Waterford villagers back on holiday from England meant to his "seven going on twelve" year-old self: "And as for those gin-swilling, vowel-devouring peacocks in their British chain-store plumage, they became my archetypes of doubleness, embodiments of home's foreignness and the allure of the far away, specialists in longing and in longing mollifed. Welcome aliens. Metropolitans. Brothers to whom in doubleness I felt my own life obscurely but enlargingly twinned" (59). I call this "ethnicity as liberating doubleness," a view of ethnic otherness not as destructive self-estrangement but as creative expansion of possibility. This constructive, functional way of looking at one's ethnic world has been traced in these pages all the way back to the pre-Famine satirists. Thematically, I have previously described it as a movement from constriction to openness. In chapter 10, this progression was observed to have occurred between the earlier and later fiction of a number of Irish-American writers who began in the 1960s and early 1970s, among them Maureen Howard, Jimmy Breslin, Joe Flaherty, Pete Hamill, Dennis Smith, and Ellen Currie. Invariably, their later work presents a more positive evocation of the spirit of place, a deeper sense of the value of ethnic doubleness, and protagonists who find their voices, articulate their troubles, and move toward the light of resolution and change for the better. In matters of style, I have described the same propensity as a freedom to use language experimentally, creatively, in flights and gripes of tours de force, as in the novels of Kennedy, Howard, and McGonigle. As was suggested elsewhere, a good bridging figure for this quality is Finley Peter Dunne's unabashed appropriation, when he invented "Mr. Dooley" in the 1890s, of the brogue as a medium both for realistic rendering of the common life of working-class Irish Americans and for inspired riffs of linguistic fancy.

The short fiction of Elizabeth Cullinan is exemplary and paradigmatic of what I see as the decisive movement of Irish-American writing over the past quarter century toward a view of ethnicity as liberating doubleness. At the end of *House of Gold* (1970), her benchmark critique of destructive aspects of Irish-American life, there is only minimal hope— in the persons of the ne'er-do-well son, whose failure has absolved him of the weight of family responsibility, and the two teenaged granddaughters, whose skeptical perspective bodes well for their generation. However, in her more recent fiction, the Cullinan narrative voice has become that of one of those skeptical granddaughters grown into a reasonably assured and independent adulthood. It is a voice of clarity and perspective, balanced between then and now, the ethnic and the worldly, and better able to judge self and others because of the double vision.

Cullinan's stories follow a pattern of incisively observed encounters and emotional consequences that build in seemingly casual movement to climactic generalizations so appropriate and valid as to be immediately recognizable as wisdom. In "Life After Death," a series of minor events punctuate in desultory fashion a day in the life of a young New Yorker. These include picking up a check at the Catholic college where she works part-time in admissions, attending evening Mass at a city Dominican church, and passing one of President Kennedy's sisters on Lexington Avenue. This conjunction somehow causes the narrator to reflect: "There's no such thing as the whole truth with respect to the living, which is why history appeals to me. I like the finality. . . . The reasons I love Mass are somewhat the same. During those twenty or so minutes, I feel my own past to be not quite coherent but capable of eventually proving to be that. And if my life, like every other, contains elements of the outrageous, that ceremony of death and transfiguration is a means of reckoning with the outrageousness, as work and study are means of reckoning with time" (*Roses*, 178). In "The Perfect Crime," the memory of a little boy who has died of cancer and the physical resemblance between the natural gas delivery man and Picasso lead a woman "fatally attracted to the random" to "the signature of the master," a sense of life's underlying mystery: "Resemblances, contrasts, contradictions, coincidence, anomaly, incongruity, ambiguity—the spirit that moves the world has these wonderful resources with which to confound us. We live at the mercy of that spirit, and the spirit lets us live, by and large, in ignorance" (*Roses*, 119, 143). In "The Sum and Substance," surgery prompts a young woman to understand the body's primacy. She sees—and feels—that "the body took the blows. Nothing was lost on it. Blows to flesh and bone, to the senses, the faculties—the body took them and felt them more deeply than mind or spirit possibly could. Cuts, bruises, infection, disease, shock, sorrow—the body grasped them all at once and forever. The body had its own insight, its own learning" (*Roses*, 38).

A defining piece for the central concept of liberating doubleness is Cullinan's story "Commuting," in which the narrator travels from a life in Manhattan to a university job in her old neighborhood in the Bronx. The result is a model of chosen migration and a metaphor for ethnic consciousness in our time. Released from her teaching stint in the music department of an unnamed college (probably Fordham), the narrator "sailed back through the campus and out the main gate, into a daunting scene of urban decay—though I remember those surroundings as comfortable, middle class New York." This first contrast sets others in motion. The "blue jeans and t-shirts" of the street crowd remind her that "when I was in school we wore real uniforms—navy serge jumpers and boleros over tan shirts," and that hers were "my sisters' castoffs, which came to me already worn at the elbow, . . . also too big at the waist." A "plainly dressed" mother and child, "the mother in a shapeless green pants suit, the little girl in a white blouse with a gray skirt that was too long," remind the narrator of her own relationship with her mother: "like that mother and child we were each other's world, and our world was under a constant threat. It came to me then with a shock—she'd disguised the hard fact that now struck me as obvious—we were poor."

She runs an urban gauntlet of propositions for sex and stolen goods to the express bus stop for Manhattan, and measures the past against the present all the way: "My grandmother boasted of having grown up near the Boulevard, and when I was young its solid brick and Art Deco style still stood for a certain fashionable respectability. Now the street is choked with derelict buildings, desperate lives." One "point of stability," the Boulevard Grand Hotel, reminds her of her sister's wedding reception there, the scene of a tenuous reconciliation in her parents' troubled marriage. Once on the bus, the narrator experiences the familiar journey, moving "over the Harlem River Bridge and onto upper Fifth Avenue," but then the complex spirit of place again triggers comparison, this time among three different groups of migrants in the same place—nineteenth-century burghers, turn-of-the-century Irish immigrants, and contemporary African Americans. After a few blocks, with night falling, "the streets began to throb with the menace and exuberance that the very name Harlem brings to mind. What was it like at the turn of the century when my father was born there? He himself tells a tenement idyll of hardship and happiness that, passing through Harlem, I found it easy to picture. Some of the houses are as beautiful as any on the east side of New York, the proportions as noble, the facades as full of ornamental masonry." She has a quick imaginative flash: "I felt as if I might walk into some splendid, wrecked brownstone and find my father with his parents and his brothers and sisters, having their supper or sitting together by lamplight in some small room." Here the richness of context does not lead to nostalgia, but instead to deeper understanding: "Surely something was wrong even then. Only deep-seatedness would explain the persistence of his need to ruin himself and us, his readiness to punish and be punished over and over. 'Be careful!' I wanted to warn that phantom family. 'Watch what you do and say! My life is in your hands!'"

The bus comes down Fifth Avenue, "where for several blocks, shabby public housing still alternated with beautiful broken buildings; then at Central Park the city made its fresh start." Past Mt. Sinai Hospital and the Metropolitan Museum, "I began collecting my things; the next stop was mine." And the story ends with its vital revelation: "Riding that last half-mile, my head swam with relief, my heart sang—they do every week, as this realization comes over me: I've reenacted, in spirit, the journey that has given my life its substance and shape, color and brightness. I've escaped!" (35).

This gem of a story embodies the theme of ethnicity as liberating doubleness. Its complex idea of "commuting" expands from the particular New York connotation of movement between the outer boroughs and Manhattan. Sometimes, to be sure, that movement is depicted as oscillation between the solid yet parochial ethnic neighborhood and the promise-filled center of "the city," and in a sense, this does describe an aspect of the pattern of immigration from rural Europe to urban America, from outlying farm to inner city, from constricting provincial community to the freedom of an individual's urban life. However, this stark dichotomy is unfairly slanted and simplistic when used by critics who judge ethnic consciousness as necessarily narrow and unsophisticated. And this is not what many writers on into the 1990s are saying. Their work tells us instead that the doubleness of ethnic consciousness is enriching and clarifying, that the debate cannot really be resolved, and that a refusal to decide between the poles of ethnic community and cosmopolitan individuality can mark the beginning of a fruitful, compound life. The middle, straddling position, having something to compare everything with—therein lies a valuable source of energy and insight. The ethnic person has come from some place—a different culture with its own world view and mores—that still provides meaningful background. And that place has not been repudiated, has not been thrown out. It's around a corner in the old neighborhood. It's in church, where the symbolic power of religious experience that so impresses children is sometimes still there for adults, only with more meaning added to the mystery. It's in connections established with the old country through music, literature, dance, language study, and travel back.

For this message of liberating doubleness, Cullinan's central metaphor is beautifully appropriate. In contemporary parlance, commuting means literally going back and forth daily between two parts of a life, and it is of course central to the experience of many city dwellers, ethnic and otherwise. Cullinan's story acknowledges this, while reversing the usual rhythm of urban American transit in that her narrator travels from a life in the city to a job in the old neighborhood. However, her main point here is the transforming power of comparative contexts, for she is also calling up the original, Latinate meanings of the word "commute":

"To give (one thing) in exchange for another, to change (*for* or *into*); to give and take (things) reciprocally, to exchange."[10] Everything that the narrator sees while "commuting" she sees twice, and thus more clearly—as the Irish girl from the Bronx that she was, and the New Yorker that she is now. "I've escaped!"—the story's last words—express the relief of someone who has moved successfully to a larger world. But the penultimate sentence is equally important: "I've reenacted, in spirit, the journey that has given my life its substance and shape, color and brightness." This is not a repudiation of the ethnic world, but an expression of the potential, dynamic worth of interchange between two worlds. Thus, "commuting" is a figure for the persistence and value of ethnicity in America.

As both George O'Brien's glimpse of Irish migrants to England and Vincent Buckley's Australian observations suggest, a good way to define and understand the "enduring traits" of Irish-American fiction discussed throughout this study is to look through the lenses of different Irish immigrant destinations. I believe that such comparative analysis will be the most fruitful direction for the study of the Irish diaspora from here on out.[11] The Antipodean Irish and their extensive literature provide especially valuable contrast to the Irish / American literary / cultural interaction. The key historical difference, writes Oliver MacDonagh, "is that the Irish were a founding people in Australia and maintained their position in the new society, more or less, for almost a century and a half," whereas in America "the Catholic Irish at least entered a firmly stratified society, an already elaborated class structure and an established economy," and "were doomed to slotting into the bottom layers, or even layer, of the hierarchy of occupations" ("Australia" 133-34). Not surprisingly, in Irish-Australian writing the sense of ethnicity as liberating doubleness is consistently observable all along the way—from the crucial Irish contribution at the beginning of Australian literature in the 1890s, to the earliest fictional masterworks, Joseph Furphy's *Such Is Life* (1903) and Henry Handel Richardson's *The Fortunes of Richard Mahony* (1917-29), and on to the depth and assurance of later writers, such as Australians Thomas Keneally and Peter Carey and New Zealanders Dan Davin and Maurice Duggan.[12]

Here it must be said that there has not been nearly enough critical attention paid to the remarkably vibrant, various, and still burgeoning literature of Irish America. I believe that this surprising neglect has palpable historical and cultural roots. There have been in American literary history three windows of heightened tolerance for narratives featuring ethnic and working-class characters. In the 1890s, the golden age of urban journalism fostered interest in "slum stories" and explorations of "How the Other Half Lives" (sociologist Jacob Riis's title). Reporters

covered zealously the collision of burgeoning immigration and the severe national depression of 1893-97, and many turned their journalism
into ethnic fiction of urban local color and social critique.[13] In the 1930s,
economics was again the catalyst for literary production, as the Great
Depression spurred an American socialist/communist movement that
in turn encouraged the rise of "proletarian" writers, many from immigrant and ethnic backgrounds, who began telling their stories and finding their audience in this political context.[14] In the 1980s, a third window
of tolerance opened for ethnic and working-class narratives (not always
the same thing, of course), this time through the academy. By then, the
proliferation of American paperback publishing houses and institutions
of higher learning had combined to make literary study and the shaping
of course syllabi big business. Ethnic narratives began to be noticed again
through support for the concept of "multiculturalism," and working-
class narrative was newly sanctioned through praise of what was known
for a time as "minimalism."

Irish-American writing has not been well served by either of these
trends. Multiculturalism has come to be identified with the literature of
higher-profile, more recently or still disadvantaged minority groups:
African Americans, Hispanics, Asian Americans, and American Indians.
By such political criteria, the older, now more successful European ethnic groups, including the Irish, have tended to be ignored. But certainly
Irish America belongs in any ethnically grounded canon. The U.S. census of 1890 counted a high-water mark of nearly two million American
citizens of Irish birth, and well over forty million Americans now claim
some Irish ancestry. When the influx of tens of thousands of "new Irish"
immigrants in the 1980s and 1990s are added in, it is clear that the Irish
still have much to tell us about the American experience of doubleness.

Furthermore, the Irish also continue to extend in important ways
the chronicle of working-class American life. Many essays that have
praised contemporary minimalist chroniclers of that life, such as Ann
Beattie, Barry Hannah, Frederick Busch, and Bobbie Ann Mason, share a
pattern that helps by negative example to locate the contribution by Irish-
Americans.[15] Often reviewers find two ways to sanction narratives of
ordinary, limited lives. First, such narratives are praised if they are rendered with a sort of calculated restraint that is interpreted as craftsmanship. The words "austerity" and "dispassion" are casually invoked, and
sometimes even the "scrupulous meanness" of Joyce's *Dubliners* is cited,
though with little sense of the possible indicting irony of "meanness."
Second, these fictions are praised if they contain bits of odd, dark, even
grotesque behavior. Reviewers pick up on details which they find mysterious, sinister, and often comic, and they react with laughter that comes
more from assumed superiority than complicity. I believe that both criteria often mask condescension toward the lives being chronicled, cer-

tainly on the part of the critics, as the term "minimalism" itself suggests, and sometimes on the part of the writers. Stylistic cold reserve makes the medicine go down more easily; it helps the reader to read (and maybe the writer to write) about ordinary and limited characters. Similarly, grotesque quirks of behavior serve to distance the reader and the writer from a character, thus providing relief from the discomfort of possible identification. In contrast, a great strength of contemporary Irish-American fiction is the avoidance of both of the palliatives, stylistic and thematic, that pervade minimalist fiction, much of it produced by writers from outside the cultures they describe. Many writers discussed in this chapter continue to give us true inside narratives of ordinary lives unmarked by exaggerated and thus mitigating grotesquerie. In addition, they range widely in matters of style—sometimes authentically austere, harking back to James T. Farrell's plain style, and sometimes as lovely and lyrical as early Scott Fitzgerald.[16]

The good news over the decade of the 1990s includes the increased availability of Irish-American texts, the lifeblood of continuing study. For the nineteenth century, there is now an expanded second edition of *The Exiles of Erin: Nineteenth-Century Irish-American Fiction* (Charles Fanning, editor, 1997).[17] For the twentieth century, the pioneering Casey and Rhodes anthology of *Modern Irish-American Fiction* has been augmented by two collections: Patricia Monaghan, editor, *The Next Parish Over: A Collection of Irish-American Writing* (Minneapolis: New Rivers Press, 1993), and Caledonia Kearns, editor, *Cabbage and Bones: Fiction by Irish-American Women* (New York: Owl Books of Henry Holt, 1997).[18] For the accessibility of James T. Farrell's work the news is especially positive. The 1990s have seen new editions of *A Note on Literary Criticism* (1992), *Studs Lonigan: A Trilogy* (1993), *My Baseball Diary* (1998), and *Chicago Stories of James T. Farrell* (1998).

The rest of this chapter will provide a survey of the Irish-American mainstream of realist fiction in the 1990s. The ongoing body of work that is the matter of Irish America has four notable elements. The first of these is continuing consideration of the Catholic faith. Indeed, a significant contribution of this fictional corpus is the inclusion of religion as a still compelling and consequential part of American life.[19] There seems to be little engagement with the spiritual elsewhere in contemporary fiction. Second, and equally important, domestic fiction continues to be a significant strength of Irish-American writing. Willa Cather's assessment of Katherine Mansfield's New Zealand stories also describes the achievement of many Irish-Americans:

I doubt whether any contemporary writer has made one feel more keenly the many kinds of personal relations which exist in an everyday "happy family" who are merely going on living their daily lives, with no crises or shocks or bewildering complications to try them. Yet every individual in that house-hold (even the children) is clinging passionately to his individual soul, is in terror of losing it in the general family flavour. As in most families, the mere struggle to have anything of one's own, to be one's self at all, creates an element of strain which keeps everybody almost at the breaking-point. . . .

Katherine Mansfield's peculiar gift lay in her interpretation of these secret accords and antipathies which lie hidden under our everyday behaviour, and which more than any outward events make our lives happy or unhappy. (877-78)

Many younger Irish-American writers—first or second novelists whose books have appeared in the later 1980s and the 1990s—also carry on with the thematic focus on everyday life in families. Third, much of this fiction published over the past decade illustrates the phenomenon of ethnicity as liberating doubleness. The younger writers, many of them first-generation college graduates, have learned from the previous generation the value of their sort of experience—often centered in middle-class suburbia and focused on childhood in the 1960s—and ethnicity is part of it. Helping to bring this experience into American literature—this expansion of boundaries, this awakening—is one of the most valuable accomplishments of contemporary Irish-American writers. Fourth, a substantial number of the newer voices are those of women. Fifteen of the twenty-four stories in Caledonia Kearns's anthology of fiction by Irish-American women, *Cabbage and Bones*, were written since 1990. Notable here are recent works involving characters and situations from earlier periods, indicative of an increased imaginative awareness of immigrant/ethnic history, among them stories by Alice Fulton set in 1919, Kathleen Ford in 1903, and Helena Mulkerns in 1846. In addition, the seven connected stories of Maura Stanton's *The Country I Come From* (1988) trace an Irish Catholic coming of age in the upper Midwest with a poet's eye for imagery and ear for rhythms. Eileen FitzGerald's collection, *You're So Beautiful* (1996), contains carefully detailed renderings of relationship in middle-class suburban lives. Ellen Currie's stories, collected as *Moses Supposes* (1994), illustrate the range of her astute, comic vision of domestic life from the cradle to old age. The reach and range of the newer fiction is further evident, to add male voices, in Edward J. Delaney's stories, which mark the still solid connectedness of Ireland and Irish Boston in the 1950s, and in Terence Winch's collection, *Contenders* (1989), which is full of subtle, defining ethnic traces in post-Vietnam New York City.[20]

Let me end this survey and this chapter by looking in some detail at eight of the newer contributors to Irish-American fiction: Michael Downing, Tom Grimes, Thomas Mallon, Anna Quindlen, Thomas E. Kennedy, Eileen Myles, Kristina McGrath, and Alice McDermott.

A fascinating younger writer from an Irish background in Western Massachusetts is Michael Downing, whose first three novels have set impressively complex problems. *A Narrow Time* (1987) is told in the first person by a New England woman who finds herself nearly swamped by a residual legacy of unearned guilt that comes flooding home with the disappearance of her youngest child. In part, the Irish-American dimension of this gripping story is Downing's engagement with the disjunction between illusion and reality about mothers. *Mother of God* (1990) extends his exploration of motherhood and pathology with its portrait of a Pittsfield, Massachusetts, family dominated by a woman of surpassing self-delusion and selfishness. In *Perfect Agreement* (1997), Downing creates an ingenious narrative that alternates between protagonist Mark Sternum's dilemmas as a professor of basic writing skills hounded by "political correctness" in present-day Boston and his imagining of life in the nineteenth-century Shaker communities of Kentucky, Massachusetts, and Maine. Mark's serious interest in the Shakers springs from his photographer-father's obsessive chronicling of their dying culture, a life-work that led the elder Sternum to desert his large Irish Catholic family in Pittsfield. In addition, each chapter ends with a paragraph of really quite useful instruction in grammar or spelling that also manages to develop the novel's themes and characters. Downing writes beautifully and with widening philosophic engagement.

A Stone of the Heart (1990) is the first novel by Tom Grimes, born in New York City in 1954 and raised in Queens. The opening line sets the time and the crucial events, both familial and cultural: "The day my father was arrested, Roger Maris hit his sixty-first home run" (1). The narrator is the fourteen-year-old son of a disintegrating Irish and Italian family in Queens. Michael McManus's father is a petty conman with alcoholic tendencies, stuck mostly through his own fault in a dead-end clerical job. Like James Joyce's Farrington in "Counterparts," he takes it all out on his family. The situation is made bleaker by the fact that younger son Rudy seldom speaks and may be autistic. Although Grimes's title is from Yeats's poem "Easter 1916," the situation echoes Farrell's O'Neill-O'Flaherty novels, with the parents' tension, a sensitive son's love of baseball, and even the father's job working at a freight-forwarding company. Young Michael's weapons are humor, exile (to the movies and the television screen), and baseball, which provides the metaphor and means for the limited reconciliation that he achieves at novel's end. While at the Yankees game preceding the one in which Maris breaks the record (Roger goes 0 for 4), Michael communicates with his brother and gently crazy grandfather and experiences what "began to feel like a clamorous peace" (121). "Please, don't blame us," says Michael's mother, and the boy's real victory lies in his not doing so. When his father is shamefully arrested on their doorstep and when Maris breaks Ruth's record, Michael rejects "the idea of constants" and sees clearly that "the best I felt we could hope for in a world in which the illusion of order is untenable is someone who is willing to assume responsibility for us, and a capacity for forgiveness beyond our largest hopes" (129-30). Grimes's writing is spare, restrained. The affirmation here is in his having brought to these ordinary, even threadbare materials the shaping gift of narrative art.

Thomas Mallon's *Aurora 7* (1991) is set one year later than Grimes's novel and also is keyed to a historical event—Scott Carpenter's orbiting of the earth on May 24, 1962. Here the setting is middle-class Westchester, and the protagonist is eleven-year-old Gregory Noonan, son of a World War II veteran and mid-level advertising sales executive, and grandson of Noonans from Hell's Kitchen. Recently and inexplicably estranged from his father, Gregory sleepwalks through the day of Carpenter's Aurora mission, skipping school after lunch, taking a train to Grand Central Station, and narrowly missing being hit by a speeding taxi. Ultimately, he is reunited with his distraught father in the crowded terminal. The progress through this day of large and small events is also tracked in several other lives. These include Gregory's parents, his teacher, the cab driver who nearly hits the boy, a young priest having doubts about celibacy, and a smug, egocentric novelist (seemingly modeled on Mary McCarthy) who steps off the curb to pull Gregory from the taxi's path. The mixing of events and fates here is deftly accomplished. Mallon's voice is precise yet engaged, at once lightly ironic and sympathetic, and this novel achieves a genuine sense of mystery. The Noonans and others in it take their Catholicism seriously. Gregory is nearing confirmation, and one theme throughout is the disjunction between the Baltimore Catechism and lived experience. This is, of course, familiar territory in Irish-American fiction, but Mallon's treatment is fresh and impressively thoughtful. *Aurora 7* describes a pilgrimage. At the end, "whatever [Gregory had] had to do, he'd done, and he'd come through" (235), and this novel earns its concluding, open-ended and provocative meditation on free will and mercy and God's plan on earth.

Set in the early 1960s, Anna Quindlen's first novel, *Object Lessons* (1991), is an adolescent coming-of-age story which also explores the misalliance that lies beneath the smooth surface of suburban life for returning GIs and first-time home owners, many of them newly middle class. John Scanlan is an intimidating figure out of the old Irish urban neighborhood life who has made millions in religious artifacts, from communion wafers to vestments, and who now concentrates on exerting control over his children's lives. The novel's main events are the many awakenings over the course of one summer that come to John's thirteen-year-old granddaughter, Maggie. Quindlen introduces a suburban variation on the ethnic theme of the passing of the old ways with the death of the patriarch, and a crucial set of events for all concerned is the last illness, death, wake, and funeral of John Scanlan. Throughout, the local colors of both Westchester and the Bronx are credibly painted, and the Scanlans learn and grow from their various "object lessons." Particularly heartening, and a resonant sign of the emergence of strong, new Irish-American narrative voices, is the revelation that comes to Maggie on the last page. Recalling her walk down the aisle as her cousin's maid of honor the day before, Maggie realizes that "she had heard another voice, telling her to lift her chin, to keep her shoulders square, to walk slowly. And suddenly it had come to her, as she was dancing with her father, the stars of darkness exploding inside her closed lids, that the voice she was hearing was her own, for the first time in her life" (262). Quindlen's second novel, *One True Thing* (1994), focuses intensively on the domestic by exploring the growth of a daughter's sense of the profound challenges of "home-making" over the course of her mother's terminal illness.

In its focus on house and home, the weight of family history, and the difficulties of communicating emotion, Thomas E. Kennedy's *Crossing Borders* (1990) is also squarely in the mainstream of Irish-American fiction, and it, too, is a novel of breakthrough into enlightenment and healthy change. Jack Sugrue is forty, working in a dead-end public relations job, and trapped in a marriage that is coming apart. The novel is framed by the house in the suburbs, which Sugrue is allowing to fall down around him: "On the driveway and terrace, unswept drifts of cut grass decomposed and sprouted spontaneously as new grass, rooted in its own decay. Inside, leaking faucets wore green splotches into the scarred porcelain" (3). At the conclusion, however, the house has become the transfigured home ground where Sugrue will make his stand for his family and his life: "He looked around the once grand, decrepit living room, at the knotty pine ceiling, at the gummy spider webs in the corners of the moldings, the dust clumps, the blisters of peeling paint, and as the snores rose up from the base of his throat, he heard himself murmur, *Lord, I love the beauty of thy house, the place where thy glory dwells*" (206).

This is a New York commuting story of coming in from Bayside through "the shabby landscape of north Queens' shops, garages, restaurants, delis, taco stands, burger stands, dunkin' doughnuts stands," and over the 59th Street Bridge into Manhattan and work and renewed promise. The bridge is one of many borders that the protagonist crosses in this novel that is, like Mallon's *Aurora 7*, a pilgrimage with an authentic spiritual dimension. To escape the decay and stasis of his present life, Sugrue must break several taboos. He begins by grimly drinking to excess almost every night, and then starts an affair with a fellow worker that is marked by sexual abandon and roughness approaching violence. Meanwhile, Sugrue's wife has become increasingly exasperated by his lack of connection with their family world. The pragmatic daughter of a financially successful German-American father, she sees Sugrue's downward slide as emphatically ethnic: "She had seen the crummy little house they lived in. Typical Irish. All those kids in a crummy little house that was falling apart. They didn't even *see* the flaws, the dirt, the mismatched furniture. (Never marry an Irishman, Angela.)" (46). On the other hand, Sugrue remembers his parents with compassion and gratitude for their gift of self-sacrificing stability: "All those years of thirst, drinking tap water for the passion. They had been loyal to their fate. And it had been important to him and to his brothers, he knew that. The glue of their rituals, their self-control. He knew them. They were there. Always" (135). Throughout his indulgent excesses, Sugrue keeps returning to the example of his father as "a grown man who knelt beside his bed each night and bowed his face into his palms" with "the certainty of a man who has God, a certainty that had warmed Sugrue's childhood, had blessed his eyes, each time they looked into the eyes of his father" (199-200). At wit's end, Sugrue finds himself "seeking prayers" in an old grade-school book, and the prayer he finds asks for a voice: "Teach me to pronounce the judgements of thy mouth" (144).

Ultimately, Jack Sugrue does break the silence. In the novel's climactic scene, discovered in adultery, he is faced at the breakfast table with his wife's decision to take the children away to her parents' house. He shatters a final taboo, crosses the last, crucial border, by standing up and shouting: "He took a decision. They must see this. They must know. That it was not for lack of love or of passion or for fear of pain. He slammed the flat of his hand down onto the table. The cups jumped in their saucers. And he bellowed out: '*I do not want this to happen to us!*'" Moreover, in finding his voice, Sugrue's mind "flashed with thoughts of his own father and mother, the stillness in which they had lived, survived, the stand-off they had survived, dead now, gone, all of them, as his lungs heaved for air and his heart banged against the wall of his chest" (190). Thomas Kennedy's is an honest, liberating voice grounded in understanding of his culture's limitations and strengths.[21]

Another arresting new voice is that of Eileen Myles, whose *Chelsea Girls* (1994) is a series of narrative pieces alternating between adulthood as a poet and critic in Manhattan's East Village and early life in the Irish working-class Boston area (Arlington, Cambridge, Somerville) in the 1950s and 1960s. Myles's straight-on, laconic reporting style provides a steady purchase for the intensely emotional, autobiographical depiction of a parochial-school childhood marked by the suffering and death of an alcoholic father: "We always thought it was because we had been born. It was our fault. There's a picture of me and Terry in those Pilgrim stocks—you know, heads and wrists poking through holes. It was some day we went to Plymouth or Salem. My father's standing behind us. We're laughing, he looks worse, a prisoner. All the pictures look like that after a point" (213). All this is followed by a gritty, urban coming of age with automobile-backseat drinking, drugs, sexual initiations, and cultural clashes in the nexus of Harvard Square in the 1960s. From St. Agnes School, with its innocuous "punish tasks"—"Eileen Myles, 500 times, I will not talk in the corridors" (23), and quiet family vacations in Marshfield, where "there was a window over the sink and it would take me hours to do dishes, doing them perfectly, looking at the old stone church just beyond our yard" (195), Eileen moves on to "The Surf" ballroom at Nantasket Beach, stoned-out college summers on Cape Cod, clerking at Filene's Basement, to Woodstock and back, and, eventually, away to a wild life in New York City as a writer, journalist, hipster, lesbian, and sometimes out-of-control drug-taker and alcoholic. Hers is a tough, credible voice, and its strength grants moving emphasis to the infrequent admissions of vulnerability and pain, as in her definition of dread: "It's the opposite of religion. Sex without the trembling, it's just dirty, something fierce keeps coming closer, you can almost smell it and it's the monster of your childhood the thing you dreamt about" (240); or her acknowledging of the vital importance of the narrative impulse: "I always think it's such a secret story, this one, I just need to tell this story for me or else I will burst. It's lonely to be alive and never know the whole story. Everyone must walk with that thought. I would like to tell everything once, just my part, because this is my life, not yours" (258).

Kristina McGrath's *House Work* (1994) is a family story of the children of immigrants, Anna and Guy Hallissey, set in working-class Pittsburgh from the 1940s to the 1960s. Told by their youngest child, Louise, born in 1950, the novel documents the young adulthood of urban ethnic Americans who were raised during the Depression, poor people for whom making do is an article of faith, and for whom homemaking is the revered, defining experience. It is McGrath's achievement to have conveyed the centrality of home for this generation through a style of dramatic lyricism that itself affirms the moral seriousness of "house work."

For Anna Hallissey, the daughter of a German immigrant tailor, home is the saving, organizing heart of life: "Things would work out because she was in love with the everlasting furniture, with the restfulness of plates stacked in painted cupboards, with the raising of husbands and children all the way down the alley, because she knew she was a part of something that keeps so many alive" (8-9). A caring, intelligent woman, Anna pours her faith into the patterns and duties of the quotidian: "and this was daily life: around it with a rag, picking up after it, rowing with the oar of it to the Mother of God"; "Housework had a rhythm like prayer" (8, 20). But here faith is not enough, for McGrath unfolds Anna's dawning realization that her husband is ill, that "there was something wrong. There had been all along" (37). A diagnosed schizophrenic, Guy Hallissey feels increasingly trapped by the responsibilities of fathering three children. He is threatened by the same homely facts that sustain his wife: "He was frightened by his own furniture. He swore it moved of its own accord. For years now, he wanted a new bureau because of shadows the old one made on summer evenings. He knew what lay low to the floor, what slid along the woodwork. And this was daily life, a skirmish in the corner, a triptych of something plain, how a single fry pan would be three, how a bureau would multiply and tiptoe across the room" (42).

Guy recalls his own ethnicity only as it contributes to his affliction: "This yard was pig-shit Irish, something that his own drunken fool of a father would have let slip, tossed off to a gamble with the weather" (28). He remembers his father as "a gambler, a good-for-nothing, swinging in and out the door on a wave of whiskey," pausing to ridicule his boy: "You're too pretty and too skinny to ever come of use, his father said that to him often enough. Having too many losses to keep to himself, he bet his son would lose" (51). Guy is pained also by remembering his mother, "a large woman with thick, soft arms, she lugged pails on Sundays and he hated that. . . . She spent most of her life on assembly lines, at sinks or stoves, with a regular waste of time for a husband, and he hated all that, too" (47). When Guy's own aberrant behavior accelerates to a frenetic mix of drinking, paranoia, and running around, Anna has the courage to move out with her children and go back to work, though in doing so she transgresses contemporary Catholic and working-class-family mores. Guy bumps along on his own, living in a third-floor furnished room in another Pittsburgh neighborhood. A fitful, ghostly presence to his children, he dies on the street of a stroke at age forty-eight in December 1968.

For her whole family's sake, Louise "Lulie" Hallissey puzzles out this story, stitching together her own earliest recollections of "Life Before with Tumbledown Dad" (one chapter title), the chaotic middle years of family breakdown, and the aftermath of her parents' separate lives. *House Work* is in the Irish-American tradition of house-centered fiction: "Memory was the work of the house," Lulie declares. Forgiveness for both parents and a steadied sense of self are the healing work of this beautiful book. "In the future, our vertigo ended," she concludes, "and a ground came under our feet. Story was a form of gravity" (188).

In bemused defense against Marxist critics, James Joyce once said that no one in any of his books was worth more than a thousand pounds. Alice McDermott could say that too. Her primary creative work to date has been the imaginative reconstruction of the lives of lower-middle-class New Yorkers, mostly the children and grandchildren of immigrants, who came out of World War II into the possibilities opened by the GI Bill of Rights. McDermott truly has a historical imagination, fully engaged with New York City and environs from the 1940s through the 1970s. And the characters in her books are those who never quite achieved the dreams whose vividness and openness defined their generation. These are people who have had to settle for less, for the various, mostly quite ordinary reasons that constitute plot in a McDermott novel.

A sure evocation of middle-class Long Island in the early 1960s is *That Night* (1987), the story of Rick and Sheryl, high school sweethearts whose parents separate them abruptly when Sheryl becomes pregnant.[22] The narrator is a young woman who recalls her childhood observation of "that night" when the bonds of a tenuous suburban community break down as Rick and his "hood" friends enter Sheryl's house by force to try to rescue her. The neighborhood men beat them back in a shocking eruption of violence. (Sheryl has already been sent to an aunt in Ohio.) "That night" focuses for the narrator the "vague and persistent notion, a premonition or memory of possible if not impending doom," that she sees behind the facade of those "bedroom communities, incubators, where the neat patterns of the streets, the fenced and leveled yards, the stop signs and traffic lights and soothing repetition of similar homes all helped to convey a sense of order and security and snug predictability" (107). Here the fathers all have "iron crosses and silver swastikas, tarnished medals marked with bright red guns" in their attics, and most families have grandparents "who remained in embattled city apartments or dilapidated houses buzzed by highways" (163, 164). These are the same streets of lost communal place walked by Thomas McGonigle and Michael Stephens. McDermott's is a quieter but no less authoritative step.

McDermott's next novel, *At Weddings and Wakes* (1992), is much more explicitly ethnic in focus, involving the four daughters of Irish immigrants who met on the boat coming over to America. The heart of these lives and of the novel itself is the top-floor Brooklyn apartment, weighted down with family history, where three of the "Towne girls" still live with "Momma," their mother's sister, who married their father after their mother's death. The salient events in the present are the courtship and marriage of middle-aged May Towne, a former nun, and her sudden death four days after the wedding. But the past is never far from consciousness, and family happenings all the way back to immigration come up again and again. Memory is the coin of this six-room realm, and the narrative is a subtle stitching of past and present, seen mostly through the eyes of the three children of Lucy Dailey, the third Towne daughter. There is a hushed timelessness about this novel. The external world makes few impressions upon the Townes, for whom emotional life within the family is paramount. Cather on Mansfield is a useful commentary on McDermott's work, for virtually the only "outward event" in *At Weddings and Wakes* is John F. Kennedy's assassination, as reported on the cover of *Life* magazine. (Kennedy is linked to Ireland's Charles Stewart Parnell in a heated discussion at May's wedding reception: "Women were the trouble with all of them" [201].)

The novel opens with an extended description of the trip between the Daileys' Long Island home and Lucy's old neighborhood in Brooklyn. The journey, "twice a week in every week of summer," begins at the Daileys' front door—"the white, eight-panel door that served as backdrop for every Easter, First Holy Communion, confirmation, and graduation photo in the family album"—and ends in front of the bakery on the old Brooklyn street with the dispensation of just-bought bread ("the kind of bread," declares Lucy to her children, "that Christ ate at the Last Supper"), after which "her pace slowed just that much to tell them that she was home after all and as happy—she allowed them to walk a few paces ahead of her—as she'd ever be" (3, 14). Marked by scrupulous, loving detail and framed by Christian symbols, this odyssey by way of two busses and two subway lines is an opening antiphon to the variety and richness of the urban everyday.

As in *That Night*, McDermott brings a discriminating, yet deferential eye to the presentation of character and motive in ordinary life. A prime example of this is Momma's austere crankiness and the fatalism that prompts her to say of her husband, "The only thing I ever held against him was that he made me believe the worst was over" (151). These are traced to, and understood in terms of, her experience of arrival in this country just weeks before her sister died, leaving a newborn baby and three older girls under six, for whom Momma had shouldered immediate responsibility: "She had a sense—she would have it all her life—that she'd been left off in these rooms as abruptly as the darkness at her window fell away from the light" (138). Moreover, Momma's ingrained contrariness ("this need to disagree, to raise her voice in utter disagreement, came on her like hunger") is explained as her husband came to understand it: "he had discovered it too, had discovered in himself her own need to object, to stand stubbornly against something. He had discovered in a life so easily shifted, battered, turned about, this overwhelming need to be, in impersonal argument if nothing else, immovable" (144). Here McDermott gets just right the emotional fulcrum on which this family balances. Another sympathetic justification of motive is the presentation of the bond between "May's mailman" Fred and his widowed mother, a strong woman whose life of unremitting labor as a housekeeper has sustained them both. Fred's slightly embarrassed sense of himself as "a bachelor son, an Irish mother's loyal boy" (130) completes the picture of a thoughtful, sensitive man. There are no caricatures here, but solid, realized characterizations. The writing is reminiscent of James T. Farrell's fiction about Irish-American working-class life, in particular his five O'Neill-O'Flaherty novels, and of Farrell's epigraph from Spinoza: "Not to weep, not to laugh, but to understand."

The final chapter of *At Weddings and Wakes* describes the beginning of the Daileys' summer vacation on the day after May and Fred's wedding. Poised just before the news of May's death, which is about to be delivered as the novel ends, are climactic revelations. Lucy Dailey realizes why her husband gets them a different cottage every summer: "The family had no history here, no memory of another time—no walls marked off with the children's heights, no windowsills or countertops to remind her of how much they had grown." Coming from a home where family history is all but encompassing, Lucy suddenly appreciates her husband's gift: "It was as if he stopped time for them two weeks out of every year, cut them off from both the past and the future so that they had only this present in a brand new place. . . . When the past and the future grew still enough to let you notice it. He did that for her. This man she'd married." Lucy's husband has insights of his own about the Townes. Realizing that "he was suited to his wife's family, although they often wore him thin," he thinks first, "perhaps it was the challenge to distract them from their mournfulness and anger"; but he moves on to a further reflection that constitutes a major revelation of this novel: "But there was something they gave him, too, with all their ghosts, something he couldn't deny: they provided his ordinary day, his daily routine of office, home, cocktails, dinner, homework, baths, and twenty minutes of the evening news, with an undercurrent—it was like the low music that now played on the kitchen radio—that served as some constant acknowledgment of the lives of the dead" (206-7, 211). Mr. Dailey is in the tradition of William Kennedy's Francis Phelan in *Ironweed* and Joyce's Gabriel Conroy in "The Dead," characters who come to understand the presentness of the past, and whose capacity for mercy expands with that knowledge.

Charming Billy (1998) is McDermott's most explicitly Irish book, including even a trip to Ireland, where the title character takes "the pledge" against drinking and confronts the lie that has shaped his life for thirty years. In this novel, McDermott creates the connected lives of Billy and Dennis Lynch, two cousins who emerge from the war in Europe to "steady jobs at Con Ed" (73). The defining events here are all Billy's: an experience of first love in Eastern Long Island in July 1945, a revelation in Ireland in the summer of 1975, and his own funeral in Queens in April

1983. To Dennis falls the unglamourous role of loyal, saving friend, though, paradoxically, it is his well-meant lie—that Billy's Irish sweetheart has died rather than married in Ireland with the money he sent her—that starts the trouble that becomes Billy's life. McDermott's gift for authoritative cultural summary is in Dennis's sense of the largeness of that lie: "It was an audacious, outlandish thing he was doing, and he knew the workaday world, the world without illusion (except Church-sanctioned) or nonsense (except alcohol-bred) that was the world of Irish Catholic Queens New York, didn't much abide audacious or outlandish. Not for long anyway" (38-39). Similarly, McDermott also provides the precise human generalizing that is the hallmark of Elizabeth Cullinan, her fellow worker in the New York/Long Island vineyards; for example: "In the arc of an unremarkable life, a life whose triumphs are small and personal, whose trials are ordinary enough, as tempered in their pain as in their resolution of pain, the claim of exclusivity in love requires both a certain kind of courage and a good dose of delusion" (241).

There are many Irish "types" portrayed here, but McDermott lifts them from the dismissive realm of stereotype to full, human individuality. There is Dan Lynch, the mildly cranky bachelor cousin, aggressively informed but boring, having spent far too much time talking to himself in the "dim" apartment that he shares only with "his own mother's" claw-footed furniture and "neat stacks" of magazines and books, "from the Queensborough Public Library mostly. Winston Churchill and the Desert Fox, the War in the Pacific, D-Day, Guadalcanal, the *Enola Gay*, F.D.R., and Truman" (203). There is Daniel Lynch, Dennis's father, the New World–bridging sponsor of "a tenement's worth of Irish immigrants," a newlywed at forty-four, and "a streetcar conductor so full of blarney and wild verse" (as Dennis himself tells it), "of Tennyson and the Bard and Gilbert and Sullivan, that he'd had to import every brother and sister, cousin uncle niece and nephew from the other side simply to have enough ears in which to deposit it all" (45). There is the priest-friend of the family, who comes forward to console Billy's widow Maeve, "confidently, like an expert, a pro, like a slugger going to the plate or a surgeon to the operating table, a renowned attorney rising for his closing arguments. . . . He was like a physician carrying reports to a waiting family, suddenly more expert than any of them about the dying man. More expert, everything in the priest's gracious manner seemed to say, because only he understood that death was nothing that it seemed to be, to us, tonight" (176-77).

And there is "charming Billy" himself, much and convincingly loved, especially for his compelling drive to communicate, to keep in touch, through long, handwritten letters, notes scribbled on napkins and place mats, and, latterly, through urgent, incoherent late-night phone calls. Billy's eyes "held a tremendous offer of affection, a tremendous willingness to find whomever he was talking to bright and witty and better than most" (78). But the same man, as we hear at his funeral, "had, at some point, ripped apart, plowed through, as alcoholics tend to do, the great, deep, tightly woven fabric of affection that was some part of the emotional life, the life of love, of everyone in the room" (6).

To be sure, these portraits have their tempering humor and irony. Yet a desire for understanding that can bring sympathy drives the narrating voice, which is that of Dennis Lynch's daughter, a representative of the younger generation who makes it her business to figure out what happened and why. As always in McDermott's fiction, two elements tip the balance to the positive: her beautifully crafted prose style and her attention to the composition of place—from a Bronx bar and grill, site of the opening funeral lunch, to the modest East Hampton cottage, locus for key events, the interior of which we see with sparkling clarity at novel's end. McDermott celebrates ordinary life by rendering its artifacts in lyrical prose and precise detail that shines with the Duns-Scotian *haecceitas* ("thisness") of Gerard Manley Hopkins.

The greatness of this novel is in McDermott's direct yet compassionate exploration of two crucial, vexed, and all too often satirically addressed Irish-American issues: sincerely held Roman Catholic faith and the curse of alcohol abuse. The moving center of the book is the long meditation in which drinking and religion come together. One can easily imagine the ways—with anger, bitterness, corrosive satire—with which this conjunction could have been treated. But here is McDermott's narrator:

> It was just Billy's way: this need to keep in touch, to keep talking, to be called by name when he entered the crowded barroom, slapped on the back, Glad to see you, have a seat. The drink a warmth across the cheeks, a watery veil that only brought into relief the gleam on the bar, the light in the mirror, the sparkle of a bottle, silver-topped, amber-filled . . . A world where love (more difficult still) could be spoken of by a hand on the shoulder, a fresh drink placed on the bar, Good to see you, through welling tears, real ones now, Ah, Billy, it's always good to see you. Dark, sparkling, sprinkled with moments when the sound and smell and sight of the place, the taste at the back of his throat, transported him, however briefly, to a summer night long ago when he was young and life was all promise and she was there to turn to, to drink in, this was also the world where his faith met him, became actual, no longer as mere promise or possibility but as inevitable and true. . . . Heaven was there, utterly necessary, utterly sensible, the only possible reconciliation of the way he must live day by day and the certainty he'd felt that life meant something greater. (215-16)

In the middle of this passage, Dennis's daughter declares that "Drunk, when Billy turned his eyes to heaven, heaven was there," a statement harshly judgmental in isolation, but as a part of this reflection, both clear-eyed and merciful at once. Not that there is anything sentimental here. McDermott's treatment of Billy's drinking—how it starts, continues, is and is not tolerated—is laced with chilling anecdotes of abasement and self-inflicted pain, and Billy dies after having been found comatose on a street in Flushing. Indeed, the rendering of his alcoholic history recalls the restrained yet piercing sorrow of Eileen Myles's "My Father's Alco-holism" in *Chelsea Girls* and the definitive horrors of John F. Murray's portraits of "O'Phelan Drinking" and "O'Phelan's Daemonium." Fol-lowing Farrell and his Spinoza epigraph, *Charming Billy* is a novel that enjoins us not to pity or mock, but to understand.

In addition, McDermott's rendering of alcoholism is linked with that other central Irish-American theme—difficulty in articulating the heart's speech, the potentially disastrous split between private and public ut-terance. Billy's insistent epistolary urge—we first see him directly in a restaurant, dashing off a note while simultaneously charming the next table of strangers—coexists with his ardent conversational wrestling—spurred mostly by drink—with the mysteries of love and death, inexpli-cable suffering, and faith itself. Moreover, McDermott continues this thematic line on into the next generation as well, for Dennis's daughter witnesses and shares the trepidation that accompanies sober attempts to confront the deepest, most personal human questions. Naturally, Billy's funeral provokes such a moment. Dennis declares, "the problem is, it's hard to be a liar and a believer yourself, at the same time. I didn't see it until your mother died, and it gave me some trouble then. I don't know if you remember"; and his daughter responds, "I lowered my head. I remembered. And my father pushed himself away from the server, where he'd been leaning. Too much said" (42). Near the end of the same day, a similar cautious dance toward meaning takes place between Den-nis and his cousin Dan Lynch, who edges into dangerous conversational waters ("It's just that on a day like this, . . . You want to make some sense of it all") by apologizing: "Not to make too much of such things" (203-4).

Ultimately, this inquiry becomes part of a third central Irish-Ameri-can theme addressed in *Charming Billy*. This is, in fact, the concern that underlies the entire present study of 250 years of Irish-American voices: the nature, power, and efficacy of narrative. This basic concern is subtly struck in McDermott's opening pages, when a number of voices at the funeral lunch begin providing pieces of "the story of [Billy's] life, or the story they would begin to re-create for him this afternoon" (5). The novel that follows is the remarkable textual weave of a life unremarkable save for one early love and one early lie: "Telling the story, my father easily slipped from past to present: Billy was, Billy is, Billy drank, Billy drinks.

Billy sets his heart on something" (30). Near the end, Dennis and Dan Lynch sit in Dan's apartment, "concentrating on conjuring something that they both understood would be fleeting, momentary, something that would be glimpsed only briefly if they managed to glimpse it at all. A way to make sense. Or else a way to tell the story that would make them believe it was sensible" (222). And finally, McDermott gives us a closing detail: the changing of the name of the East Hampton Catholic Church to Most Holy Trinity, "no longer St. Philomena's—the poor woman having been tossed out of the canon of saints in the mid-sixties because some doubt had arisen about whether or not she had actually lived." This apparent aside leads to a last, emphatic affirmation of the wonder and the necessity of storytelling: "As if, in that wide-ranging anthology of stories that was the lives of the saints—that was, as well, my father's faith and Billy's and some part of my own—what was actual, as opposed to what was imagined, as opposed to what was believed, made, when you got right down to it, any difference at all" (280).

Notes

Introduction

1. For a classic definition of the stage Irishman, see M. Bourgeois 109-10. The stage Irishman on the British stage is treated in George C. Duggan, *The Stage Irishman* (London: Longmans, Green, 1937). Pioneering work on Irish-American drama appears in R. Dorson, "Mose" and C. Wittke, "Immigrant Theme." An indispensable survey of scholarship on ethnic drama is Joyce Flynn, "Melting Plots: Patterns of Racial and Ethnic Amalgamation in American Drama Before Eugene O'Neill," *American Quarterly* 38: 3 (1986): 417-38. Knowledge about Irish-American drama will be greatly increased with the publication of Joyce Flynn's forthcoming study, *Ethnicity after Sea-Change: The Irish Tradition in American Drama.* There is of course a considerable critical literature on Eugene O'Neill. For his Irish dimension, see especially John Henry Raleigh, "O'Neill's *Long Day's Journey into Night* and New England Irish Catholicism," *Partisan Review* 26: 4 (Fall 1959): 573-92; Raleigh, *The Plays of Eugene O'Neill* (Carbondale: Southern Illinois Univ. Press, 1965); and Harry Cronin, *Eugene O'Neill: Irish and American, A Study in Cultural Context* (New York: Arno Press, 1976).

2. This work continues, most notably in the pages of *MELUS*, the journal of the Society for the Study of the Multi-Ethnic Literature of the United States. Studies of the literature of individual ethnic groups include the following. A seminal piece on Dylan Thomas as a Welsh poet is John Wain, "Druid of Her Broken Body," *Dylan Thomas: New Critical Essays,* ed. Walford Davies (London: J.M. Dent, 1972): 1-20. Francis Russell Hart, *The Scottish Novel, from Smollett to Spark* (Cambridge: Harvard Univ. Press, 1978). Allen Guttmann, *The Jewish Writer in America: Assimilation and the Crisis of Identity* (New York: Oxford Univ. Press, 1971). Dorothy B. Skardal, *The Divided Heart: Scandinavian Immigrant Experience through Literary Sources* (Lincoln: Univ. of Nebraska Press, 1974). Rose Basile Green, *The Italian-American Novel: A Document of the Interaction of Two Cultures* (Rutherford, N.J.: Fairleigh Dickinson Univ. Press, 1974). Antonia Castaneda Shular et al., *Chicano Literature, Text and Context* (Englewood Cliffs, N.J.: Prentice-Hall, 1972). Elaine H. Kim, *Asian American Literature* (Philadelphia: Temple Univ. Press, 1982). Houston A. Baker, Jr., ed. *Three American Literatures* (New York: Modern Language Association, 1982). Robert J. DiPietro and Edward Ifkovic, eds., *Ethnic Perspectives in American Literature* (New York: Modern Language Association, 1983). Needless to say, the burgeoning critical literature in African-American studies is also of great value in the study of other minority cultures.

Early attempts to survey and compare many ethnic literatures include the following. Carter Davidson, "The Immigrant Strain in Contemporary American Literature," *English Journal* 25 (Dec. 1936): 862-68. Howard Mumford Jones, "American Literature and the Melting Pot," *Sewanee Review* 26 (April 1941): 329-46. Carl Wittke, "Melting-Pot Literature," *College English* 7 (Jan. 1946): 189-97. Daniel Aaron, "The Hyphenate Writer and American Letters," *Smith Alumnae Quarterly* (July 1964): 213-17. More recent comparative work includes Jules Chametsky, *Our Decentralized Literature, Cultural Mediations in Selected Jewish and Southern Writers* (Amherst: Univ. of Massachusetts Press, 1986), Werner Sollors, *Beyond Ethnicity: Consent and Descent in American Culture* (New York: Oxford University Press, 1986), Mary V. Dearborn, *Pocahontas's Daughters: Gender and Ethnicity in American Culture* (New York: Oxford Univ. Press, 1985), and William Boelhower, *Through a Glass Darkly: Ethnic Semiosis in American Literature* (New York: Oxford Univ. Press, 1987).

1. Backgrounds and a Habit of Satire

1. M.J. O'Brien 64. "Elegy on the Much Lamented Death," etc. presents Sweeney as a high-living ladies' man, for after his death "The Black-Eyed Virgins, Ladies of the Green, With streaming Eyes and sable Weeds are Seen."

2. The first U.S. Census (1790) recorded 44,000 Americans of Irish birth, but recent analyses suggest that this figure is much too low. The figures and accompanying historical summaries used in this chapter are based on the following sources: Doyle, *Ireland, Irishmen and Revolutionary America*; Griffin, *The Irish in America*; MacDonagh, "The Irish Famine Emigration"; Blessing, "Irish" entry, *Harvard Encyclopedia*; Jones, "Scotch-Irish" entry, *Harvard Encyclopedia*. The number of eighteenth-century Irish immigrants is still in question. In his recent exhaustive study *Emigrants and Exiles*, Kerby A. Miller says that "at best, we can guess that perhaps 50-100,000 left Ireland in the 1600s, and 250-400,000 from 1700 to 1776" (137).

3. Other early examples are George Pepper, *History of Ireland*, which was serialized in 1829 in the New York *Irish Shield* and published in 1835, and W.C. Taylor and William Sampson, *History of Ireland* (1833). On Pepper, a fiery character who also edited Catholic newspapers and published poems and plays, see Foik 44-6 and Francis R. Walsh, "The Boston *Pilot*."

4. For example, *Forensic Eloquence, Sketches of Trials in Ireland for High Treason* (1804).

5. On Burk, MacNeven, Emmet, and especially Reynolds see Twomey, "Jacobins and Jeffersonians," a valuable study of this entire generation of Irish, English, Scots, and Welsh "Jacobin" immigrants to America. On Burk and Branagan, see Joyce Flynn, "A Republic for All." On O'Connor, see Foik 12-21 and Potter 182-83.

6. F.I. Carpenter; J. Wain 21-44.

7. *Massachusetts Magazine* 1 (Dec. 1789): 758; 2 (Jan. 1790): 185. "A Fragment of Irish History," *Massachusetts Magazine* 2 (Jan.-April 1790). "Knuck Fierra," "King Finvar's Castle," "Old Raths," *Atheneum* 2: 2nd series (15 Nov. 1824): 164-66. *Atkinson's Casket* no. 5 (May 1830): 214-16. G. Pepper, "Naisi" and "O'Cahan."

8. In an earlier collection, *Tales of the Fireside* (1827), the Lady of Boston included two stories set in Ireland, both about love affairs involving Church of Ireland (Episcopal) ministers. "The Miniature Picture," set in the 1770s in Enniskillen, County Fermanagh, describes the romance between the local vicar's daughter and her father's curate, and "Rose Bradshaw, or the Curate of St. Mark's" is the story of the heroine's disastrous first marriage to a blarneying philanderer who had "visited the far-famed kissing stone," from whom she is rescued by the Reverend Mr. Bradshaw. These stories illustrate the lady's acquaintance with yet another dimension of Irish life. She may well have been an immigrant from Ulster.

9. Brown, "Irish Layman" 59-77.

10. David H. Greene (1976) has used some of this publication evidence to conclude that "a cultural gap existed between Irish novelists for upper-class native Americans and Irish novelists for Irish immigrants." He contrasts the publication of Edgeworth, Lover, and Lever by the prestigious firms of Little, Brown and Harper with the publication of Carleton, the Banims, and Griffin, "Catholics and thus identified with the Irish masses," by the smaller, "Catholic" houses of Collier, Sadlier, and Kenedy. "All one has to do," says Greene, "is compare the splendid forty-volume edition of Lever with the three-volume edition of Carleton's novels and tales, which was crudely illustrated and printed in double columns on newsprint, published by Collier in 1882, to learn something about the sociology of literary taste and the publishing industry in nineteenth-century America." By the last third of the century such a gap had certainly opened. However, in the years before the Famine all the Irish writers, Catholic as well as Protestant, were well and widely published, and, presumably, widely read.

11. These newspapers and the earliest dates when Irish fiction appeared in my brief survey are as follows: *Truth-Teller* (New York, 6 Oct. 1827); *Pilot* (Boston, April 1838); *Northwestern Chronicle* (St. Paul, Minn., May 1869); *Catholic Advocate* (Louisville, Kentucky, 1 Nov.

Catholic Advocate (Louisville, Kentucky, 1 Nov. 1894); *Western Watchman* (St. Louis, Dec. 1872); *Morning Star* (New Orleans, April 1868), *Monitor* (San Francisco, 1907); *American Celt* (Boston, 7 Sept. 1850), *American Celt* (Buffalo, 24 Dec. 1852); *American Celt* (New York, June 1870).

12. The *Dollar Magazine* published several Carleton stories in 1841 and 1842, and W.H. Maxwell's *Hector O'Halloran* was serialized in *Brother Jonathan* in 1842. A sketch on "Irish Humor" by Samuel Lover appeared in the *New Yorker* 3 (17 June 1837), 200.

13. See Mercier, Krause (who cites Boucicault, Synge, Yeats, Shaw, O'Casey, Beckett, and Behan), and M. Waters (who cites Beckett, Kavanagh, O'Casey, and Behan).

14. "Patrick O'Flagharty" and "The Irishman's Epistle" are quoted in B. Granger 224, 156-57. In his seminal essay, "The American Image of Ireland," O.D. Edwards uses this material to ask "whether the acceptance of the stage Irishman as a vehicle for Revolutionary propaganda set in motion the curious and long-standing American tradition of appealing to class prejudice in political humor" (203).

15. The "Curious Letter" was supposedly reprinted "From a Late Irish Paper" by the *Gazette*'s John Fenno, a leading anti-Irish journalist in Philadelphia. The author of *My Pocket Book* has been tentatively identified as Edward Dubois.

16. Brown, "Irish Layman" 57-59.

17. A later example of mock-heroic doggerel is the anonymous, fifty-page poem, *The Irish-Office-Hunter-Oniad: A Heroic Epic*, by "Blarney O'Democrat" (New York: no publisher listed, 1838). A rendering of a political rally in New York's Sixth Ward, the poem pillories "the present headlong system of office-hunting" by Irish immigrants who would rather hold office than work. The author points to intolerable slum conditions ignored by political hacks, and admits that most Irish citizens oppose the grafters.

18. On mainstream Federalist satire see L. Kerber.

19. The only copy extant is in the Library of Congress. Thirty of the book's thirty-two pages survive, and it has been attributed to a John McFarland. An excerpt from *Father Quipes* appears in Fanning, ed., *The Exiles of Erin* 25-33.

20. All of these prejudices appear fully formed as early as Elizabethan travelers' accounts of visits to Ireland. See David B. Quinn, *The Elizabethans and the Irish* (Ithaca: Cornell University Press, 1966).

21. *A Narrative of the Life of David Crockett of the State of Tennessee* (1834). An excerpt from *Paddy O'Flarrity* appears in Fanning, ed., *The Exiles of Erin* 34-48.

22. Another indication that the author is Irish is his reluctance to parody the brogue, which only appears briefly in two digressive anecdotes about recently arrived immigrants. On the other hand, the book contains a long passage of Southern black dialect.

23. The most famous of the "convent revelations" was the *Awful Disclosures of Maria Monk* (1836). For a detailed examination of the Charlestown convent burning in the Irish context see Potter 286-310. An excerpt from *Six Months in a House of Correction* appears in Fanning, ed., *The Exiles of Erin* 49-60.

24. On Beecher, see Potter 295. On Burchard, see Whitney R. Cross, *The Burned-Over District* (Ithaca: Cornell University Press, 1950), 188-89; and William G. McLoughlin, *Modern Revivalism* (New York: Ronald Press, 1959), 133-34. Antimasonry was an evangelical Protestant movement founded in the late 1820s in reaction against Masonic secrecy and economic dominance in the "Burned-Over District" of Western New York. *Six Months* contains several satiric references to the Antimasons, including mention of the "Morgan affair," in which a defecting Mason had disappeared in 1826, and was probably murdered by his former lodge mates. *Six Months* 59-60, 186; Cross 114-25.

25. Only a few issues of his newspapers survive. The *Irishman and Foreigners' Advocate* was a daily in 1835, and its prospectus declares that "the object of this paper shall be to protect the interest of Irishmen, and foreigners of all countries and denominations" (15 July 1835). The *European* was a weekly paper which contained news of Ireland, an "Emigrants' Guide" column, "Literary Notices," poetry, and fiction. Moore's poem "The Poet's Grave" (*Lord Nial* 268) suggests that nationalist activities prompted his departure from Ireland.

26. The serial of *Tom Stapleton* ran in *Brother Jonathan* from 1 Jan. through 14 May 1842.

The London edition, published by "J. Lofts" is undated. An excerpt from *Tom Stapleton* appears in Fanning, ed., *The Exiles of Erin* 61-77.

27. In their seamy, waterfront hangout, the city's dock loafers teach Tom to distinguish between friends ("insiders" or "go-downs") and enemies ("ticklers" or "flunkies"). Moore's interest in language and dialect also appears in his essay defining and rendering the speech of "A Dublin Jackeen."

2. The Profession of Novelist:
James McHenry and Charles Cannon

1. Irish parliamentarians often cited the American precedent in the years before the 1798 rebellion. Henry Grattan called America "the only refuge of the liberties of mankind," and declared that "the American war was the Irish harvest." See O.D. Edwards, "The Impact of the American Revolution on Ireland."

2. For example, Charles Tucker observed: "The Irish character presents in almost every thing a strong contrast to that which I have just placed before you—as ardent and impassioned as the others are cold and phlegmatic—as imaginative as the others are dull, they run into the most violent extremes." *In the Valley of the Shenandoah* (New York: Charles Wiley, 1824): 55.

3. McHenry's first books were *The Bard of Erin* (1808), a collection of seventeen poems, and *Patrick, A Poetical Tale* (1810), a narrative poem in heroic couplets about the Irish rebellion of 1798. See R. Blanc, Chapter I.

4. McHenry's own name does not appear in his novels. Of the four definitely attributable to him, the first is signed "Solomon Secondsight," and the others, "By the Author of The Wilderness." An excerpt from *The Wilderness* appears in Fanning, ed., *The Exiles of Erin* 78-89.

5. New York *Mirror* 2 Aug. 1823, quoted in Blanc 49. The piece on "Irish-American Literature" also ridiculed McHenry's poetry. It seems to have been a rejoinder to McHenry's scathing assessment in another periodical of N.P. Willis and William Cullen Bryant as poor imitators of the English Lake Poets (Blanc 100-105).

6. This campaign is recreated in gripping fashion in Flanagan's *The Year of the French* (1979). For the historical background, see Pakenham 171-72, 219-25; and R.B. McDowell, *Ireland in the Age of Imperialism and Revolution, 1760-1801* (Oxford: Clarendon Press, 1979): 542 ff.

7. McHenry may have known about the last great traditional harp competition, which had been sponsored by the Gaelic enthusiasts of Presbyterian Belfast in 1792. Ten of the old guard showed up, including the blind, ninety-seven-year-old Denis Hempson from Derry (Flanagan, *Irish Novelists* 112).

8. McHenry explained in a preface that he wanted to write "a narrative poem on some great event in the history of man." As most of the best topics had already been taken, he chose "the fortunes and catastrophe of the antediluvian world." Blanc 54-59, 111.

9. T.F. Meehan 413, W. Thorp 55-56. Cannon's first verse collection was *Poems by a Proser* (New York: W.T. Janvier, 1831), and his last was *Poems, Dramatic and Miscellaneous* (New York: Edward Dunigan, 1851). Dunigan published his *Practical Spelling Book* in 1852 and *Lessons for Young Learners* (Catholic Education Series, no. 1) in 1853. *The Oath of Office* was published in 1854 (New York: W. Taylor) and Cannon's plays were collected as *Dramas* (New York: Edward Dunigan) in 1857.

10. This is the only one of Cannon's books to bear his name in full on the title page. For the others he used his initials or the notation, "By the Author of" a previous book.

11. This is one of several Cannon novels discussed in W. Thorp, "Catholic Novelists in Defense of Their Faith, 1829-1865," an excellent study of the Catholic aspect of several novelists whose Irish dimension is the concern of the present study.

12. An excerpt from *Bickerton* appears in Fanning, ed. *The Exiles of Erin* 128-35.

13. The Bapst affair also appears as a central event in the first novel, *The House of Yorke*

(New York: Catholic Publication Society, 1872), of Mary Agnes Tincker, an Ellsworth native and Catholic convert.

14. At least one influential critic acknowledged Cannon's contribution. J.V. Huntington, himself a Catholic novelist of some repute, called *Bickerton* "a most favorable sign of improvement which is taking place in our literature. . . . We know of no Catholic story by an American author that shows more skill and tact in the use of the difficult instrument of our language." He pointed to "its very quiet but keen-edged satire" as its "chief merit," and in a reference to Cannon's preface, Huntington concluded that the novel "depicts the Protestant, or rather the Know-Nothing element of American life, as it is, leaving us only to regret that so masterly a sketch had not been filled up." St. Louis *Leader* 13 Oct. 1855. The best of the Catholic-tract novelists, Huntington (1815-1862) wrote five popular novels. See W. Thorp 70-86.

3. The Famine Generation:
Practical Fiction for Immigrants

1. On the Famine and its aftermath in Ireland see O. MacDonagh; R.D. Edwards and T. Williams, eds., *The Great Famine*; C. Woodham-Smith; F. Lyons.

2. On the American experience of the Famine immigrants see K. Miller, *Emigrants and Exiles* 280-344; L. McCaffrey, *Irish Diaspora* 59-69; P. Blessing, "Irish" entry; O. MacDonagh; Handlin; Higham; Potter; Shannon; Wittke, *Irish in America*; D. Ward; O.D. Edwards, "American Image." For the situation of women see H. Diner; Carol Groneman, "Working Class Immigrant Women in Mid-Nineteenth-Century New York, The Irish Woman's Experience," *Journal of Urban History* 4: 3 (May 1978): 255-73.

3. Blessing, "Irish" entry 529; W. Thorp 54-55. The Sadlier Company still publishes Catholic school textbooks. Edward Dunigan was publishing Christian Brothers readers with an obvious Irish slant by 1855. *Moore's Melodies* appeared in 1852, *Songs of Our Land* in "185-." A third, undated collection, *The Irish Comic Songster*, seems contemporary with the other two. All are in Harvard's Widener Library.

4. Sadlier's *The Red Hand of Ulster* appeared in the *Pilot* from January 1 through March 9, 1850, and *Willy Burke*, from June 15 through August 17. Later in the year, another, anonymous, story of the trials of an immigrant boy in Boston appeared: *Michael Murphy, A Tale of Real Life*, from October 12 through October 26, 1850. Other newspapers that published Irish-American fiction and the earliest years of such publication in my sampling are as follows: The *American Celt*, Boston and Buffalo (1850-53), the *Catholic Advocate*, Louisville, Kentucky (1869-70), the *Leader*, St. Louis (1855-56), the *Morning Star*, New Orleans (1868-71), the *Northwestern Chronicle*, St. Paul, Minn. (1867-69), the *Irish News*, New York (1856-61), the *Emerald*, New York (1868-70), the *Irish World*, New York (1870-75). For information about the Irish-American press in these years, see P. Foik; W. Joyce; R. Hueston; F. Walsh, "The Boston *Pilot*" and "Who Spoke for Boston's Irish?".

5. "Why the Little Frenchman Wears His Hand in a Sling," in *The Complete Tales and Poems of Edgar Allan Poe* (New York: The Modern Library, 1938): 517-21. This sketch was probably written before 1842. *The American Notebooks*, vol. 18, *The Writings of Nathaniel Hawthorne* (Boston: Houghton, Mifflin, 1900), 53. A.L. Williams, "The Irishman in American Humor" 188-94. Williams's diligent combing of the works of "Petroleum V. Nasby," "Orpheus C. Kerr," George Horatio Derby and their ilk turned up little of consequence. *Walden, or Life in the Woods* (1854. New York: The Heritage Press, 1939): 50, 211, 264-65. Also, chapter 1 of Thoreau's *Cape Cod* contains a vivid description of the wreck of the brig St. John from Galway, laden with immigrants, several of whom drowned. Stephen Bolger (93-95) suggests that Melville's sketch of the hermit "Oberlus" in *The Encantadas* (1854) is based on accounts of an Irish exile who lived on the islands in the early years of the century.

6. For useful surveys of the nativist fiction, see A. Siegel; S. Bolger.

7. Duganne's ghost story is "The Spirit of the Ford," published in M.M. Ballou, *Albert Simmons*, by Lt. Murray (pseud.) (Boston: F. Gleason, 1849): 58-64. Reprinted from a Boston

magazine, it first appeared before 1849. *The Two Clerks* also contains an impassioned plea for Irish freedom. Duganne (1823-1884) was born in Boston. In his last years, he seems to have swung back the other way, as a regular contributor to the New York *Irish World*. *Dictionary of American Biography* 5: 492-93.

8. On Mrs. Dorsey see W. Thorp 86-98. She and the other early Catholic writers are also discussed in the early chapters of J. White, *Era of Good Intentions*.

9. These few facts about McCorry's life appear on the catalog card for his novel *The Lost Rosary* in the Library of Congress. The title page of *Mount Benedict* declares him to be the author of a fourth novel, *The Lighthouse of the Lagan*, presumably set in his native Ulster.

10. Conyngham also wrote Civil War history, including *Sherman's March through the South* and *The Irish Brigade and Its Campaigns*. He died in 1883. S. Brown 69-70.

11. All published serially in the New York *Irish American* between May and August, 1850, Halpine's novels were *Sir Dudlley's Heir; or, A Glance at the Early Life of Mary Doyle, the Wexford Heroine; Lord Edward's Guard; or, the Foster Brothers of Kildare;* and *The Willows of the Golden Vale, A Page from Ireland's Martyrology*. See W. Hanchett 25-26. The new histories were *The Irish Confederates and the Rebellion of 1798* (New York: Harper, 1851) by Henry Martyn Field, who had known the '98 exiles William MacNeven, Thomas Addis Emmet, and William Sampson in New York, and *The Irish Abroad and at Home; at the Court and in Camp* (New York: Appleton, 1856) by Andrew O'Reilly.

12. Born at Dunkineely, County Donegal in 1852, Cassidy came to America in about 1869 and became a journalist. *Glenveigh* was serialized in the Boston *Pilot*. S. Brown 60. Several novels are also set further back in the past, including one by Conyngham, *Sarsfield; or, The Last Great Struggle for Ireland* (1871), and another of Halpine's potboilers, *The Shamrock in Italy; or, Mountcashel's Brigade* (New York *Irish American* 2 May 1857 ff.). These were prevalent in the Irish-American press, where novels such as *Kate Kearney; or, The Ballad Siege of Limerick* (New York *Irish American*, Dec. 1857-Jan. 1858) appeared often as serials.

13. Scanlan's poems include "Address to the Fenians" and "The Fenian Men," and in his preface he hopes to fan "the flame [of] hatred to England." My thanks to John Corrigan for showing me this book. Another fictional response to Fenianism is John Hamilton, *The Three Fenian Brothers* (New York: Macmillan, 1866), and there was also a piece of instant canonization, *Fenian Heroes and Martyrs* (Boston: P. Donahoe, 1868), by John Savage. On the Fenians see L. O'Broin, *Fenian Fever*, and on Irish-American nationalism in general, see T. Brown, "Origins" and *Irish-American Nationalism*.

14. An excerpt from *The Lost Rosary* appears in Fanning, ed., *The Exiles of Erin* 153-59.

15. K. Miller, with Bolling and Doyle, "Emigrants and Exiles" 97-125. A dissertation that contrasts American and Irish world views at length is J. Ibson.

16. J. Dolan 211-18. See also Jay P. Dolan, *Catholic Revivalism, The American Experience 1830-1900* (Notre Dame: Univ. of Notre Dame Press, 1978).

17. An excerpt from *Annie Reilly* appears in Fanning, ed., *The Exiles of Erin* 160-74.

18. *Us Here* (New York *Irish American* 24 Jan.-25 April 1857). Halpine's other novel was *Bartle Byrne; A Biography* (New York *Irish American* 8 Nov. 1856-17 Jan. 1857).

19. Wittke 143-47, and J. Maguire 545-624, which includes interviews with veterans. There have been many filiopietistic books detailing the contributions of the Irish on both sides of the conflict.

20. This story is cited in H. Smith, "Stereotype" 100-102.

21. "The Pope's Johnny Sullivan," *The Old Parish* 17-34. My thanks to Philip Silvia for showing me Hurley's novels. See also John F. Finerty, *The Churchyard Oath* (Chicago *Citizen* 2 March-4 May, 1901), and James Riley, *Christy of Rathglin* (1907).

22. See W. Hanchett, passim; H. Smith, "Stereotype" 135-42.

23. An excerpt from *The Life and Adventures of Private Miles O'Reilly* appears in Fanning, ed., *The Exiles of Erin* 144-52.

24. See F. Wolle, *Fitz-James O'Brien*, and "Fitz-James O'Brien in Ireland and England, 1828-1851," *American Literature* 14 (Nov. 1942): 234-49.

25. Also educated at Trinity College, Le Fanu (1814-1873) was proprietor of the *Dublin*

University Magazine and the author, between 1845 and 1873, of twelve popular novels that were full of occult goings-on.

26. On O'Brien's life, see T.D. O'Brien, "Dillon O'Brien." My thanks to Jim Rogers of St. Paul for showing me this essay.

27. Obituary, Boston *Pilot* 11 Dec. 1858. G. Potter 221-22; W. Thorp 44-48; D. Merwick 20-40. Roddan's editorial series "The Irishman in America," which ran in the *Pilot* during April and May of 1850, was an early example of solid guidance for the Famine immigrants.

28. On the Boston Catholic intellectuals and Brownson see D. Merwick 15-16, 46-47; T. McAvoy 29-30; G. Potter 554-55; J. Dolan 295-97.

29. An excerpt from *John O'Brien* appears in Fanning, ed., *The Exiles of Erin* 97-108.

30. W. Thorp 38-44; D. Merwick 40-59.

31. According to Merwick, this character was both autobiographical and based on an Irish priest whom Boyce admired, Reverend Daniel Murray, "a man who was educated at Salamanca, served admirably as president of Maynooth, became coadjutor bishop of Dublin from 1809 to 1823, and finally was appointed archbishop of Dublin while Boyce would have been at Maynooth" (43).

32. W. Thorp 39. This dramatization was by James Pilgrim, who wrote two other Irish plays, *Robert Emmet* and *Ireland and America*. *Godey's Lady's Book* 37 (Dec. 1848): 690; 38 (April 1849): 297. *Nation* 1: 3 (11 Nov. 1848): 1.

33. An excerpt from *Mary Lee* appears in Fanning, ed., *The Exiles of Erin* 136-43.

34. The letters of Major Jack Downing began appearing in the Portland (Maine) *Courier* in 1829. See Kenneth S. Lynn, ed., *The Comic Tradition in America* (Garden City, New York: Doubleday, 1958): 81-93.

4. Mrs. Sadlier and Father Quigley

1. Anna Theresa Sadlier (1854-1932) wrote children's books and historical romances set in Viking Scotland, Medieval Europe, Moorish Spain, and revolutionary America. On Mary Anne Sadlier's life, see T. Brown, "Sadlier"; W. Thorp 98-110; The *New Catholic Encyclopedia* (1967) 12: 844-45. An insightful treatment of her fiction appears in H. Smith, "Stereotype" 116-28.

2. *D. and J. Sadlier and Co.'s Catalogue of Valuable Books* (9), appended to the first edition of *New Lights; or, Life in Galway* (1853).

3. An excerpt from *The Blakes and Flanagans* appears in Fanning, ed., *The Exiles of Erin* 109-20.

4. L. McCaffrey, *Irish Diaspora* 91-92; J. Dolan 262-70.

5. On the Buffalo Convention, see C. Wittke, *Irish in America* 67-74. Bishop John Hughes of New York, who opposed McGee on principle as a dangerous radical, helped to defeat the resettlement movement. A similar plan in the 1870s was more successful. Incorporated in 1879, the Irish Catholic Colonization Society founded settlements in Minnesota, Iowa, and Nebraska.

6. The dates of the serializations of *The Blakes and Flanagans* and *Con O'Regan* are uncertain because so much of the run of McGee's *American Celt* has been lost.

7. "Biographical Sketch of the Author" by "W.M.", in Quigley, *Irish Race in California* iii-x. See also S. Brown 257-58; W. Thorp 48-54.

8. An excerpt from *The Cross and the Shamrock* appears in Fanning, ed., *The Exiles of Erin* 121-27.

9. In the form of "Pastorini's Prophecy" this prediction was much on Irish minds in the early nineteenth century, when it was often linked with Daniel O'Connell and the year 1825. W.B. Yeats uses the tradition in his poem of 1899, "The Valley of the Black Pig." See Maureen Murphy, "Carleton and Columcille," *Carleton Newsletter* 2 (4 Jan. 1971): 19-22.

10. Father John Murphy and Father Philip Roche, both country curates, became convinced of the rightness of the rebel cause and served as exhorting leaders with significant influence in the fighting in Wexford. T. Pakenham 147-48, 154-55, 190, 194.

11. On journalistic caricatures of the Irish, see L. Curtis. Very useful for teaching is *The Distorted Image*, a slide collection of nineteenth-century ethnic caricatures from the popular press. Prepared by John J. and Selma Appel, the collection is available from the Anti-Defamation League of B'nai Brith (New York). Also see John J. Appel, "From Shanties to Lace Curtains: The Irish Image in *Puck*, 1876-1910," *Comparative Studies in Society and History* 13 (Oct. 1971): 365-75.

5. Respectability and Realism: Ambivalent Fictions

1. An excerpt from *Lalor's Maples* appears in Fanning, ed., *The Exiles of Erin* 241-50. Conway's poems were collected as *A Dream of Lilies* (1893).

2. For corroboration and clarification of the transitional nature of this generation, see T. Meagher, ed., *From Paddy to Studs*, which examines the Irish in Lowell and Worcester (Mass.), Philadelphia, Chicago, St. Louis, and San Francisco.

3. Donna Merwick's reading of the influential *Sacred Heart Review* provides more evidence of the development of an Irish-American matriarchy. She finds that "with no real familial role for the father and a recognition [by the priests] of their own ineffectualness, there remained no alternative but to rely on the mother. . . . she was expected to manage the home and save the faith" (133-37). See also Janet A. Nolan, *Ourselves Alone: Women's Emigration from Ireland, 1885-1920* (Lexington: Univ. Press of Kentucky, 1989).

4. The sixteenth edition (New York: P.J. Kenedy) appeared in 1883. An 1879 advertisement declared that O'Reilly's works had sold "upwards of 100,000 volumes" in the past two years. Another popular guidebook was Sister Mary Frances, the Nun of Kenmare, *Advice to Irish Girls in America* (New York: J.A. McGee, 1872).

5. J. White 214-312; A. Baumgartner 36-64. See also Thomas F. Meehan, "The Catholic Press," in *Catholic Builders of the Nation* 4 (1923): 219-34. William L. Lucey, "Catholic Magazines: 1865-1880," *Records of the American Catholic Historical Society of Philadelphia* 43 (1952): 21-36; "Catholic Magazines: 1880-1890," ibid.: 85-109; "Catholic Magazines, 1890-1893," ibid.: 133-56; "Catholic Magazines, 1894-1900," ibid.: 197-223.

6. For the facts of O'Reilly's life, the best source is still the first: James Jeffrey Roche, *The Life of John Boyle O'Reilly* (1891). The most perceptive short essay on O'Reilly's career and import is T. Brown, "The Irish Layman" 77-97. See also A. Mann 27-44; S. O'Connell, "Boggy Ways."

7. My research has turned up about sixty Irish-American works of fiction published in the 1880s and almost exactly twice that number in the 1890s.

8. John Talbot Smith, "The Literature of Dirt, Doubt, and Despair" (1903). See also the essays of William McDermott (pseud. Walter Lecky) in *Down at Caxton's* (1895) and *Impressions and Opinions* (1898).

9. "A Philistine's Views," New York *Herald* 24 March 1889: 22. Boston *Pilot* (editorials) 26 June 1886; 28 Dec. 1889.

10. Collected in Roche's biography, O'Reilly's poems appeared separately as follows: *Songs from the Southern Seas* (1873), *Songs, Legends, and Ballads* (1878), *The Statues in the Block* (1881), and *In Bohemia* (1885).

11. A provocative presentation of O'Reilly's ambivalence is that of J. Ibson, who argues that his internal divisions drove him to self-hatred and virtual suicide.

12. See A. Mann 44-51, and R. Lane, "James Jeffrey Roche and the Boston *Pilot*," *New England Quarterly* 33 (Summer 1960): 341-63. Roche's poetry appeared as *Songs and Satires* (Boston: Ticknor, 1887), *Ballads of Blue Water* (Boston: Houghton, Mifflin, 1895), and *The V-a-s-e and other Bric-a-Brac* (Boston: Badger, 1900).

13. L. Guiney, "Patrick R. Guiney" 72. *Letters* 1: 66. See also Henry G. Fairbanks, *Louise Imogen Guiney* (New York: Twayne Publications, 1973); Alice Brown, *Louise Imogen Guiney, A Study* (New York: Macmillan, 1921); *Dictionary of American Biography* 8: 43-44.

14. MacKenzie (1809-1880) was a Limerick native who had a journalistic career in London and New York. Another early collection was *Emerald Gems. A Chaplet of Irish Fireside*

Tales, Historic, Domestic, and Legendary (Boston: Thomas B. Noonan, 1879), which aimed to "recall pleasant memories for Irish natives, and help instill into the hearts of their children, born on American soil, a love for the country of their ancestors."

15. P. Marcus 231-32, 257. Curtin's other two books were *Hero-Tales of Ireland* (1894), and *Tales of the Fairies and of the Ghost World* (1895). See Maureen Murphy, "Jeremiah Curtin: An American Pioneer in Irish Folklore," *Eire-Ireland* 13:2 (1978): 93-103.

16. Yeats's essays are collected as *Letters to the New Island* (1970). Alfred Williams claims that his 1881 anthology is the first to provide "a connected series of Irish poetry from the earliest period, and in all forms of expression, from the bardic ode to the drawing room song." He hopes to show American readers that Irish poetry is "original, strongly marked, and indigenous" (v-vi). Further attesting to the general interest, a series on ancient Irish culture by Charles de Kay ran in the *Century Magazine* in 1889 and 1890, as follows: "Pagan Ireland," *Century* 15 (Jan. 1889): 368-79; "Fairies and Druids of Ireland," *Century* 15 (Feb. 1889): 590-99; "Christian Ireland," *Century* 15 (March 1889): 675-85; "The Monasteries of Ireland," *Century* 16 (May 1889): 113-22; "Early Heroes of Ireland," *Century* 16 (June 1889): 198-209; "Woman in Early Ireland," *Century* 16 (July 1889): 433-42; "Irish Kings and Brehons," *Century* 17 (June 1890): 294-304.

17. Born James Shields in New York, O'Sheel (1886-1954) gaelicized his name in 1910. He went on to become a major figure in the Friends of Irish Freedom supporting the Irish Revolution of 1916-21. My thanks to the poet's son Patrick O'Sheel for information about him. On Celticism as a literary principle in Ireland, see Wayne E. Hall, *Shadowy Heroes, Irish Literature of the 1890s* (Syracuse: Syracuse Univ. Press, 1980): 37-63.

18. Agnes B. McGuire, "Catholic Women Writers," *Catholic Builders of the Nation* (Boston: Continental Press, 1923) 4: 188.

19. *Letters* 1: 95-96, 65.

20. Other "Celtic" texts are Barry O'Connor, *Turf-Fire Stories and Fairy Tales of Ireland* (New York: P.J. Kenedy, 1890) and the early American books of Seumas McManus, whose romantic history, *The Story of the Irish Race* (1921) is probably on more Irish-American shelves than any other title. McManus published *In Chimney Corners, Merry Tales of Irish Folklore* and *Through the Turf Smoke* in 1899 (New York: McClure). Also, in 1903 Hermione Templeton Kavanagh published her tales of a Tipperary man among the fairies, *Darby O'Gill and the Good People* (New York: McClure).

21. Alternatively, one can look into John Boyle O'Reilly, ed., *The Poetry and Song of Ireland* (1887). One volume deserves special mention as a perfect embodiment of the urge toward respectable assimilation. James Riley's *Songs of Two Peoples* (Boston: Estes and Lauriat, 1898) contains both "Songs of New England" (poems about rural Yankee life: "Thanksgiving at Aunt Sally's," "Fresh Hayin'," "Marion Harbor") and "Ireland and Her People" (picturesque poems of an idealized old country, some of them in dialect: "The House Beyant the Hill," "Morning at Killarney").

22. Other "respectable" Catholic-tract novels include these: Mary Elizabeth Carey, *Alice O'Connor's Surrender* (Boston: Angel Guardian Press, 1897). Eleanor Cecilia Donnelly, *Storm Bound, A Romance of Shell Beach* (Philadelphia: H.L. Kilner, 1898). Joseph Gordon Donnelly, *Jesus Delaney. A Novel* (New York: Macmillan, 1899). Mrs. Junius McGehee, *Glen Mary: A Catholic Novel* (Baltimore: John Murphy, 1887). Mary Frances Cusack (The Nun of Kenmare), *From Killarney to New York; or, How Thade Became a Banker* (New York: D. O'Loughlin, 1877).

23. Others of the nationalist type include these: John Finerty, *The Churchyard Oath: An Irish Story of Landlord Tyranny and Peasant Vengeance* (serialized in Finerty's Chicago nationalist newspaper, the *Citizen* 2 March-4 May 1901). N.J. Dunn, *The Vultures of Erin: A Tale of the Penal Laws* (New York: P.J. Kenedy, 1884). Emily Fox, *Rose O'Connor; A Story of the Day*, by Toler King, pseud. (Chicago: Chicago Legal News Co., 1880).

24. Other genteel novels of manners include these: Augustus J. Thébaud, *Louisa Kirkbride, A Tale of New York* (New York: Kenedy, 1878). Emily Fox, *Off the Rocks. A Novel*, by Toler King, pseud. (Chicago: Sumner, 1882). Mary G. Mahony, *Marmaduke Denver and Oth-*

er Stories (San Francisco: Women's Cooperative Printing Office, 1887). Emma Kelley, *Megda*, by "Forget Me Not," pseud. (Boston: James Earle, 1891). Harriet (O'Brien) Lewis, *Lady Kildare, or Love's Rival Claimants* (New York: Street & Smith, 1889). Emma Mary Connelly, *Tilting at Windmills: A Story of the Blue Grass Country* (Boston: D. Lothrop Co., 1888). Thomas Russell Sullivan, *Ars et Vita and Other Stories* (New York: Scribner, 1898).

25. E.J. Kahn, Jr., *The Merry Partners: The Age and Stage of Harrigan and Hart* (New York: Harper & Row, 1955). See also Joyce Flynn, *Ethnicity after Sea-Change: The Irish Tradition in American Drama* (forthcoming). Born in New York City's Seventh Ward, Edward Harrigan (1844-1911) became an actor at age 22, and began his fruitful association with Tony Hart around 1870.

26. A perceptive summary of mainstream American literary perspectives on the Irish, with special attention to Twain, Crane, Frederic, and Dreiser, is chapter 3 (170-246) of H. Smith, "Stereotype." A useful collection of references to the Irish in non-Irish American humor is in A. Williams. Invaluable for understanding the emergence of urban immigrant fiction in these years are three books which focus on Jewish-American literature: Allen Guttmann, *The Jewish Writer in America* (1971), David M. Fine, *The City, the Immigrant and American Fiction* (1977), and Jules Chametsky, *From the Ghetto: The Fiction of Abraham Cahan* (1977).

27. Sarah Orne Jewett, "Between Mass and Vespers," and "A Little Captive Maid," in *A Native of Winby and Other Tales* (Boston and New York: Houghton, Mifflin and Company, 1893); "The Luck of the Bogans," *Scribner's Magazine* 5 (Jan. 1889): 100-12; "Where's Nora," *Scribner's Magazine* 24 (Dec. 1898): 739-55. See the introduction by John Henry Raleigh to the 1960 reprint of *Theron Ware* (New York: Holt, Rinehart, and Winston). As a London correspondent for the New York *Times* in the late 1880s, Frederic became friendly with the Irish Party leaders, including Parnell. He also wrote a series of perceptive analyses of Irish politics for the *Fortnightly Review* in the early nineties. See Stanton Garner, "Some Notes on Harold Frederic in Ireland," *American Literature* 39: 1 (March 1967): 60-74.

28. These include Lelia Hardin Bugg, author of a fascinating fictionalized etiquette manual for middle-class Catholics, *The People of Our Parish* (1900; New York: Arno Press, 1978). Bugg also wrote a short story which contains a rare picture of a clash between Irish Catholics and nativists in a small Arkansas village in the early 1880s. "Westgate's Past" is in *The Prodigal's Daughter and Other Tales* (New York: Benziger Bros., 1898). For comprehensive surveys of Catholic fiction in this period, see P. Messbarger, J. White.

29. "Slob Murphy" appears in Fanning, ed., *The Exiles of Erin* 207-22. Sullivan's second collection of stories, *So the World Goes* (1898) was more essay than fiction and more explicit in its proselytizing for relief of the sufferings of the laboring poor. During and after World War I, he was an associate of Samuel Gompers and an official in the American Federation of Labor.

30. "The Stepmother" appears in Fanning, ed., *The Exiles of Erin* 231-40.

31. Cleary's Nebraska fiction is collected with a biographical essay in *The Nebraska of Kate McPhelim Cleary* (1958). The other stories mentioned are "How Jimmy Ran Away," "Jim Peterson's Pension," and "An Ornament to Society." A fuller discussion of Kate Cleary appears in Charles Fanning, "The Literary Dimension," in L. McCaffrey, et al, *The Irish in Chicago* 112-20.

32. Kelly's other two collections are *Wards of Liberty* (1907) and *Little Aliens* (1910). See *Dictionary of American Biography* 10: 310, and D. Fine 68-70.

33. At least two other novels about the Molly Maguires appeared around this time, both even more romanticized than McMahon's: R.F. Bishop, *Camerton Slope: A Story of Mining Life* (Cincinnati: Cranston & Curts; New York: Hunt & Eaton, 1893), and James M. Martin, *Which Way, Sirs, the Better? A Story of Our Toilers* (Boston: Arena Publishing Co., 1895). The definitive history of the society is Wayne G. Broehl, Jr., *The Molly Maguires* (New York: Chelsea House/Vintage, 1964).

34. O'Higgins's "The Exiles" (1906) appears in Fanning, ed., *The Exiles of Erin* 251-59.

Other relevant O'Higgins stories are "Larkin," *McClure's* 23 (July 1904): 253-61; and "An Appeal to the Past," *Century* 72 (Oct. 1906): 885-90. See *Dictionary of American Biography* 14: 5-6.

35. See these for starters. Anne O'Hagan Shinn, "The Abdication of Mrs. Dogherty," *Munsey's* 33 (May 1905): 249-52; and "Margaret McDonough's Restaurant," *Munsey's* 31 (Sept. 1904): 861-64. Owen Frawley Kildare, "Yuletide Down in Mulberry," *Outlook* 78 (24 Dec. 1904): 1022-25. Patrick Casey, "The Gay Cat," *Saturday Evening Post* 186 (4 April 1914): 10+. Amanda Matthews, "A Child-Idyl of Donegal," *Atlantic* 112 (Dec. 1913): 732-36; and "The Emigration of Mary Anne," *Atlantic* 113 (Jan. 1914): 96-101.

36. H. Quigley, *The Irish Race in California* 457-58. S. Brown 147-48. The Matthews and Jessop play, *A Gold Mine* was a hit in New York. Two of the stage-Irish musicals were *Shamus O'Brien* (London and New York: Boosey & Co., 1896), based on a poem by Sheridan Le Fanu, and *My Lady Molly* (London and Boston: Keith, Prowse & Co., 1902).

37. "The Rise and Fall of the 'Irish Aigle' " appears in Fanning, ed., *The Exiles of Erin* 191-206.

38. Boston *Pilot* 29 Dec. 1888. In his long story "The Emergency Men" (1896) Jessop presents boycotting Land Leaguers as brutal murderers. Two other writers around this time produced Irish-American fiction from the perspective of the Protestant Ascendancy. See Maude Radford Warren, "The Wearin' o' the Green," *Saturday Evening Post* 177 (24 Sept. 1904): 8+; "The Match-maker," *Saturday Evening Post* 179 (11 May 1907): 179+; "The Master-Weaver," *Atlantic* 103 (Jan. 1909): 65-72. See also John Henry Finlay, *The Orangeman* (Cincinnati: Mountford, 1915), which describes the sufferings of an oppressed group of Protestants at the hands of bloodthirsty Catholic Ribbonmen in County Monaghan in 1821.

39. Neil Schmitz, "Introduction" to Keenan's *The Money Makers* (1969).

40. Boston *Pilot* 20 March 1886. An excerpt from *The Aliens* appears in Fanning, ed., *The Exiles of Erin* 181-90.

41. P. Messbarger 89-90. For McDermott's best criticism, see "Literature and Our Catholic Poor," in *Down at Caxton's* (1895): 185-205; and "The Priest in Fiction," in *Impressions and Opinions* (1898). His judicious critique of Maurice Francis Egan is cited in chapter 6.

42. The chapter of *Père Monnier's Ward* containing this depiction appears in Fanning, ed., *The Exiles of Erin* 223-30.

43. An interesting wild Irish refutation of that distinction is John C. Linehan, *The Irish Scots and the "Scotch-Irish"* (Concord, N.H.: American Irish Historical Society, 1902). The largely Scotch-Irish Orange Order, founded in America in 1867, was closely linked with the American Protective Association. See M. Jones, "Scotch-Irish" 906.

44. "Living Catholic Authors," *Catholic World*, 64 (December 1896): 419-20; *New Catholic Encyclopedia* 13: 304; P. Messbarger 88, 150-51.

45. *A Woman of Culture* was serialized in the *Catholic World* in 1880, then published as a book in 1891. A popular success, it had three editions, the latest in 1901. Mentioning Toronto specifically, Kerby Miller documents the warm reception given in the late nineteenth century to Irish immigrants to eastern Canada who were members of the Orange Order (*Emigrants* 378).

46. See George Moore, "Homesickness," "Julia Cahill's Curse," "The Wedding Feast," "The Exile," in *The Untilled Field* (1903; New York: Books for Libraries Press, 1970); Shan Bullock, *Dan the Dollar* (1905); Seumas O'Kelly, "Both Sides of the Pond," in *Waysiders* (1917), and *Wet Clay* (1922).

6. Mr. Egan and Mr. Dooley

1. Egan, *Recollections* 17-40. C. Fanning, *Finley Peter Dunne and Mr. Dooley* 4-5. See also E. Ellis 3-15.

2. Egan, *Recollections* 17-40, *Confessions of a Book Lover* 10-36.

3. Egan, *Recollections* 17-40, 371-74, 97, 144.

4. Egan, *Confessions of a Book Lover* 175-76, *The Ghost in Hamlet* 286-87, "Irish Novels," in J. McCarthy ed., *Irish Literature* V: vii-xvii.

5. There are enough echoes of *John Longworthy* in Stephen Crane's *Maggie: A Girl of the Streets* (1893) to suggest borrowing by Crane. In both novels the focus is on one tenement house as a microcosm of the slum environment, and both describe the miracle of unspoiled children emerging like flowers from pernicious conditions.

6. Egan's poetry is predictably romantic, effete, conventionally rimey, and metronomically rhythmic. It is full of hazy mythology and moral uplift and the Irish poems feature large doses of shamrocks and sentiment. See *Songs and Sonnets* (1885). His juvenile fiction includes *Jack Chumleigh at Boarding-School* (1899).

7. Other moralistic tales of mixed marriage and related perils of life among the Protestants are "Philista," "A Descendant of the Puritans," "A Measureless Ill," and "Among the Olive Branches," in *The Life Around Us* (1885), and "A Question of Divorce" in *Short Stories* (1900).

8. "Carmel," *The Life Around Us* 391-93. A similar story in the same collection is "A Tragi-Comedy," in which the Irish mother only grudgingly forgives her son for rejecting the priesthood and marrying: "Sure, it was right to wish the best for Bernard, but if he's got the second-best, let's be thankful. His wife's a good Catholic, anyhow" (30).

9. Quoted in Seamus Heaney, "The Sense of Place," in *Preoccupations, Selected Prose 1968-1978* (New York: Farrar, Straus, Giroux, 1980): 139.

10. See Fanning, *Finley Peter Dunne and Mr. Dooley* (1978) and Fanning, ed., *Mr. Dooley and the Chicago Irish: The Autobiography of a Nineteenth-Century Ethnic Group* (1987). Unless otherwise noted, all of the Dooley quotations in this chapter appear in this 1987 anthology and are cited parenthetically in the text.

11. These include books discussed in chapter 5 by Drexel Biddle, Harriete Keyser, Alvan Sanborn, and others. When Dunne was a young reporter, the Chicago anti-immigration periodical *America* published a series of ten "Intercepted Letters" to Ireland in an offensive brogue, presenting the urban Irishman as a drunken, dishonest political hack (26 May-11 August 1888).

12. Several of these dialect series were collected into books: *Widow Magoogin* (New York: Dillingham, 1900), *The Gowanusians: Humorous Sketches of Every-Day Life among Plain People* (New York: Edmunds Pub. Co., 1894), *Mickey Finn Idylls* (New York: Doubleday & McClure, 1899), and *Mickey Finn's New Irish Yarns* (New York: Doubleday & McClure, 1902). Officer Casey appeared in the *Times-Herald* from April 14 through August 4, 1895, and was revived in the Chicago *Evening Post* in January 1906.

13. A piece clarifying Dunne's gift for dialect transcription is Clyde Thogmartin, "Mr. Dooley's Brogue: The Literary Dialect of Finley Peter Dunne," *Visible Language* 16: 2 (1982): 184-98.

14. Howells, "Certain of the Chicago School of Fiction," *North American Review* 176 (May 1903): 734-46. Dreiser, *The Letters of Theodore Dreiser*, Robert H. Elias, ed. (Philadelphia: University of Pennsylvania Press, 1959) 3: 949.

15. At one point in Part I of *Finnegans Wake*, Joyce promises to do violence to English in the service, or perhaps in memory, of Irish: " . . . if reams stood to reason and his lankalivline lasted he would wipe ally english spooker, multaphoniaksically spuking, off the face of the erse" (New York: Viking Press, 1939): 178. See also William Carleton, *Traits and Stories of the Irish Peasantry* (1830, 1833) and *The Black Prophet* (1847), and Flann O'Brien, *At Swim-Two-Birds* (1939), *The Hard Life* (1961), *The Dalkey Archive* (1964), *The Third Policeman* (1967), and *The Best of Myles* (1968).

7. A Generation Lost

1. Useful models include Nina Baym, *Woman's Fiction, A Guide to Novels by and about Women in America, 1820-1870* (Ithaca and London: Cornell Univ. Press, 1978); Ann Douglas,

The Feminization of American Culture (New York: Alfred A. Knopf, 1977); Jane Tompkins, *Sensational Designs: The Cultural Work of American Fiction 1790-1860* (New York: Oxford Univ. Press, 1985); Cathy N. Davidson, *Revolution and the Word: The Rise of the Novel in America* (New York: Oxford Univ. Press, 1987).

2. See William M. Halsey, *The Survival of American Innocence: Catholicism in an Era of Disillusionment 1920-1940* (Notre Dame: Univ. of Notre Dame Press, 1980): 99-123.

3. For complete bibliographies of both, see Daniel J. Casey and Robert E. Rhodes, eds., *Irish-American Fiction, Essays in Criticism* (1979). This pioneering and indispensable guide to Irish-American fiction focuses on the twentieth century in eleven essays and a 170-page bibliography of fifty-two writers.

4. Norris died in 1966. See her autobiography, *Family Gathering* (Garden City, N.Y.: Doubleday, 1959). The two San Francisco Irish stories were collected in *Poor Dear Margaret Kirby* (1913). "What Happened to Alanna" appeared first in *Atlantic* 106 (Sept. 1910): 418-28.

5. See Laughlin's autobiography, *Traveling Through Life* (Boston and New York: Houghton, Mifflin Co., 1934). A fuller treatment of Laughlin appears in Charles Fanning, "The Literary Dimension," in L. McCaffrey et al, *The Irish in Chicago* 116-20.

6. Similarly, in *The People of Our Parish* (1900), Lelia Hardin Bugg deplores the Irish wake with its party atmosphere and all-night drinking. Her argument is both class-conscious and assimilationist. Such wakes are lower-class affairs, taking place in "gaslit flats in a bustling American city," says Bugg. Although the house may be crowded, no rosary gets said, and the custom "calls up a thatched cottage on a desolate moor" rather than a respectable American setting.

7. On McIntyre, see Stanley J. Kunitz and Howard Haycraft, *Twentieth-Century World Authors* (New York: Wilson Co., 1942): 877-78.

8. "The Wake" appears in *Stories without Women* (1915). See Thurston Macauley, *Donn Byrne, Bard of Armagh* (New York and London: Century Co., 1929): 61, 164-66.

9. See William V. Shannon, *The American Irish* 233-49. Robert E. Rhodes, "F. Scott Fitzgerald: 'All My Fathers,' " in Casey and Rhodes, *Irish-American Fiction* 29-52. Thomas Flanagan, "John O'Hara," *Recorder* I: 1 (Winter 1985), 51-64.

10. Wilson, "F. Scott Fitzgerald," *The Shores of Light* (New York: Farrar, Straus and Young, 1952): 27-35. Cowley, "Breakdown," *New Republic* 79 (6 June 1934): 105-06. Cowley, *The Literary Situation* (New York: Viking Press, 1958): 153.

11. Wilson, "The Boys in the Back Room," *Classics and Commercials* (New York: Farrar, Straus, Giroux, 1950): 23-24. Flanagan, "O'Hara" 62-63.

12. Flanagan says that "a discussion of the Irish-American as writer might well begin with this exchange of letters" ("O'Hara" 52). He quotes most of both letters, but see Matthew J. Bruccoli, ed., *Selected Letters of John O'Hara* (New York: Random House, 1978): 75.

13. "The Cleansing Tears," *Harper's* 130 (Feb. 1915): 414-24. I have found no biographical information about Clancy. He also published two essays and four other stories, one of which traces another New York Irish boy who grows up in "sterile, unsympathetic soil." See "The One Great Thing," *Harper's* 128 (March 1914): 626-32.

14. A biographical sketch of Tully is Sara Haardt, "Jim Tully," *American Mercury* 14 (May 1928): 82-90. See also Tully, "To Those Who Read," an introduction to *Blood on the Moon* (1931): 9-12. Reviews quoted are as follows: Rupert Hughes, "An American Inferno," *New York Times* 26 Feb. 1922: 11+. George Jean Nathan, "Tully at His Best," *New York Herald Tribune* 14 Aug. 1927: 6: 3. H.L. Mencken, quoted on fly leaf of *Shanty Irish* (1928). James T. Farrell, "Shanty Irish," University of Chicago *Daily Maroon* 1 March 1929: 3.

8. James T. Farrell and Irish-American Fiction

1. "Beginnings," handwritten ms., 1961, Box 494, James T. Farrell Archives, University of Pennsylvania. L. to Ezra Pound, 17 Feb. 1932. (All letters cited in this chapter are in the Farrell Archives.) "The World I Grew Up In," *Commonweal* 83 (25 Feb. 1966): 606. "Our

Own Weren't All Handy Andys," handwritten ms., undated, Box 200. "My Irish Forbears," handwritten ms., undated, Box 398. "The Story of the Irish in America," Baltimore *Sun* 15 April 1979.

2. "Irish American experience. Public letter. 1965," handwritten ms., Box 580. L. to J.D. Adams, 25 Aug. 1945, quoted in Branch, *James T. Farrell* 16.

3. In a letter to Dunne's biographer Elmer Ellis, Farrell had these insights into Mr. Dooley's creator: "There were divisions in the man, his ambition to be a newspaper executive, and also the division in which, on the one hand, he defended the Catholic Church, and, on the other hand, he was not a practicing Catholic. It seems to me that it is perhaps the case that for a man to be a humorist, there must be divisions of this sort in his own nature. If a man is not divided within himself, if he does not have his own contradictions, it is unlikely that he can see the contradictions which exist outside of himself in the world at large. . . . Mr. Dooley was not only the creation: he was also the expression of all that was in Finley Peter Dunne's nature, a rich and intelligent nature, and at the same time, a nature which seems to me to have been tinged somehow with a puritanical tone, and with a dour, sad streak." 30 Nov. 1950. My thanks to Dennis Flynn for showing me this letter.

4. Letters to Clifton Fadiman, 24 June 1929; to Ezra Pound, 14 Feb. 1934; to Ernest W. Burgess, 9 Jan. 1937; to Guggenheim Foundation, 4 Jan. 1939; to James Henle, 12 Feb. 1943; to Eugene O'Neill, 18 Feb. 1943.

5. Letters to Jack Kunitz, 7 Aug. 1934; to James J. Geller, 16 Feb. 1943.

6. "On the Letters of Anton Chekhov," *University Review* 9 (Spring 1943): 167-73. Collected in *The League of Frightened Philistines* 60-71.

7. L. to Frederick Thrasher, 15 March 1932.

8. In an epilogue written for the new edition of *Studs Lonigan* published by Vanguard in 1978, Farrell said that "In revealing Studs's life day by day, I realized that his life itself was not so unusual; that the most unusual thing about him was his early death." Accordingly, "It was my plan to devote almost the whole of the third volume to the dying consciousness of Studs Lonigan. The setting would be the Day of Judgment as forecast in the Bible." Instead of this sustained surrealism, however, the facts of life for Studs and his family in the early years of the Depression demanded inclusion, and "The book seemed to write itself" in the same realistic terms as the first two volumes. When he finally reached Studs on his deathbed, Farrell concluded that the extended death-fantasy sequence "seemed an unnecessary tour de force," and so he cut most of it out. Badly damaged in a 1946 fire, the remains of the manuscript are reprinted at the end of the new Vanguard edition, pp. 469-86.

9. These "plebeian realists" of the early 1930s, their moment in American literary history, and Farrell's differences from the rest are discussed incisively in Murray Kempton, *Part of Our Time, Some Ruins and Monuments of the Thirties* (New York: Simon and Schuster, 1955): 126-49. The others include Richard Wright, Nelson Algren, Henry Roth, Edward Dahlberg, and Jack Conroy. A more recent revision of Farrell's narrow placement as a writer of the thirties is "James T. Farrell and the 1930s" by Donald Pizer, who credits Farrell's use of epiphany and development of stream-of-consciousness writing by "indirect discourse," and connects him with Joyce and Sherwood Anderson. This essay appears in Ralph F. Bogardus and Fred Hobson, eds., *Literature at the Barricades, The American Writer in the 1930s* (University: Univ. of Alabama Press, 1982): 69-81.

10. The Bachelard passage has been a touchstone for Irish poet Seamus Heaney, to whom I owe its discovery.

11. "Introduction," *Father and Son* (Cleveland: World Publishing Co., 1947): xi.

12. Letters to Mary Farrell, 2 Feb. 1934; 6 March 1934; 21 March 1935; 12 April 1935; 26 Aug. 1935; 12 July 1937.

13. "The Fruit of Sacrifice," St. Cyril *Oriflamme*, June 1922: 35-37. This was actually Farrell's second story for the *Oriflamme*. In the first, "Danny's Uncle," published in February 1921 (7-8), a young boy knocks the silk hat from the head of a man who turns out to be his rich uncle. The boy's name is Danny O'Neil. Both are in Box 52, Farrell Archives.

14. Letters to Guggenheim Foundation, 23 Jan. 1938; to Jim Putnam, 18 Feb. 1943.

15. See Edgar M. Branch, *James T. Farrell* (New York: Twayne Publishers, 1971), and *A Bibliography of James T. Farrell's Writings 1921-1957* (Philadelphia: Univ. of Pennsylvania Press, 1959). Branch has published bibliographical supplements as follows. "A Supplement to the Bibliography of James T. Farrell's Writings," *American Book Collector* 11 (Summer 1961): 42-48. "Bibliography of James T. Farrell: A Supplement," *American Book Collector* 17 (May 1967): 9-19. "Bibliography of James T. Farrell: January 1967-August 1970," *American Book Collector* 21 (March-April 1971): 13-18. "Bibliography of James T. Farrell, September 1970-February 1975," *American Book Collector* 26: iii: 17-22. "Bibliography of James T. Farrell's Writings: Supplement Five, 1975-1981," *Bulletin of Bibliography* 39: 4 (Dec. 1982): 201 + .

After Branch, other significant earlier criticism of Farrell's work includes the following. Horace Gregory, "James T. Farrell: Beyond the Provinces of Art," *New World Writing: Fifth Mentor Selection* (New York: New American Library, 1954): 52-64. Blanche Gelfant, *The American City Novel* (Norman: Univ. of Oklahoma Press, 1954): 175-227. Charles C. Walcutt, *American Literary Naturalism, A Divided Stream* (Minneapolis: Univ. of Minnesota Press, 1956): 240-57. Nelson M. Blake, *Novelists' America, Fiction as History, 1910-1940* (Syracuse: Syracuse Univ. Press, 1969): 195-225.

William V. Shannon began the consideration of Farrell's ethnic dimension with a section in *The American Irish*: 249-58. Solid material on the Irishness of the Lonigan and O'Neill books appears in H. Smith, "Stereotype" 247-387. Portions of the present chapter have appeared in somewhat different form in Charles Fanning, "The Literary Dimension," in McCaffrey et al, *The Irish in Chicago* 120-44; "Death and Revery in Farrell's O'Neill-O'Flaherty Novels," *MELUS* 13: 1 and 2 (Spring-Summer 1986): 97-114; and "James T. Farrell and Washington Park" (written with Ellen Skerrett), *Chicago History* 7 (Summer 1979): 80-91.

More recent criticism of many aspects of Farrell's work includes the following. Jack Salzman and Dennis Flynn, eds., "Essays on James T. Farrell," *Twentieth Century Literature* 22: 1 (Feb. 1976). Leonard Kriegel, "Homage to Mr. Farrell," *Nation* 223 (16 Oct. 1976): 373-75. Ann Douglas, "*Studs Lonigan* and the Failure of History in Mass Society: A Study in Claustrophobia," *American Quarterly* 26 (Winter 1977): 487-505. Alan M. Wald, *James T. Farrell: The Revolutionary Socialist Years* (New York: New York Univ. Press, 1978). Robert James Butler, "Christian and Pragmatic Visions of Time in the Lonigan Trilogy," *Thought* 55 (Dec. 1980): 461-75; "The Christian Roots of Farrell's O'Neill and Carr Novels," *Renascence* 34 (1982): 81-97; "Parks, Parties, and Pragmatism: Time and Setting in James T. Farrell's Major Novels," *Essays in Literature* 10 (Fall 1983): 241-54; "Scenic Structure in Farrell's *Studs Lonigan*," *Essays in Literature* 14 (Spring 1987): 93-103. Bette Howland, "James T. Farrell's Studs Lonigan," *Literary Review* 27 (Fall 1983): 22-5.

The first fruits of work in the Farrell Archives comes in James T. Farrell, *On Irish Themes*, ed. Dennis Flynn (1982). Flynn's work-in-progress is an edition of Farrell's selected letters and diary notes which will open up the possibilities of the collection for other scholars to follow. Other new directions in Farrell criticism have been taken in Irene Morris Reiter, "A Study of James T. Farrell's Short Stories and Their Relation to His Longer Fiction," Ph.D. dissertation, University of Pennsylvania, 1964; Celeste Loughman, " 'Old Now, and Good to Her': J.T. Farrell's Last Novels," *Eire-Ireland* 20: 3 (Fall 1985): 43-55; and Shaun O'Connell, "His Kind: James T. Farrell's Last Word on the Irish," *Recorder* 1: 1 (Winter 1985): 41-50.

9. Regional Realists of the Thirties and Forties

1. The best introductory sampling of many of the writers discussed in this and the following chapter is the fine anthology of twentieth-century Irish-American fiction, *Modern Irish-American Fiction: A Reader*, ed. Daniel J. Casey and Robert E. Rhodes (Syracuse: Syracuse University Press, 1989). The best introduction to the criticism is in the essays and 160-page bibliography in Casey and Rhodes, ed., *Irish-American Fiction: Essays in Criticism* (New York: AMS Press, 1979).

2. Among Deasy's other novels are *Cannon Hill* (1949), *Ella Gunning* (1950), *Devil's Bridge* (1952), and *The Corioli Affair* (1954), all published by Little, Brown and Company in Boston.

3. *The Parish and the Hill* is now available in a paperback edition (New York: Feminist Press, 1986), with a valuable afterword by Anne Halley.

4. Ruth McKenney also wrote a realistic novel of labor agitation in Akron, Ohio (*Industrial Valley*, 1938) and a novel about her forceful, socialist/Irish nationalist grandfather (*The Loud Red Patrick*, 1947). Betty Smith's other novels about the Brooklyn Irish are *Tomorrow Will Be Better* (1948) and *Maggie-Now* (1958).

5. J.F. Powers's other short-fiction collections are *The Presence of Grace* (1956) and *Look How the Fish Live* (1975). A useful bibliography of criticism of Powers's work appears in Casey and Rhodes, *Irish-American Fiction*, 330-35.

6. Edward McSorley made his living as a journalist and sometime screenwriter. He wrote two other novels, *The Young McDermott* (1949), a sequel to *Our Own Kind*, which takes Willie McDermott into young manhood as a reporter, and *Kitty, I Hardly Knew You* (1959), a love story of two Irish immigrants to New York in the early 1920s.

7. Brendan Gill's other fiction includes a novel, *The Day the Money Stopped* (1957) and a collection of stories, *Ways of Loving* (1974). A more detailed analysis of *The Trouble of One House* appears in Charles Fanning, "The Woman of the House: Aspects of Irish-American Fiction," *Recorder* 1: 1 (Winter 1985), 89-101. Gill's stories are discussed in Nona Balakian, *Critical Encounters* (New York: Bobbs-Merrill, 1978), 149-52.

10. "These Traits Endure":
The Irish Voice in Recent American Fiction

1. Recent meditations on the existence, persistence, decline, and/or resurgence of Irish-American ethnicity include the following: Lawrence J. McCaffrey, *The Irish Diaspora in America*, especially the final chapter; and McCaffrey, "The Recent Irish Diaspora in America," in Cuddy, ed., *Contemporary American Immigration*; Andrew M. Greeley, *That Most Distressful Nation: The Taming of the American Irish* (Chicago: Quadrangle Books, 1972); and Greeley, *The Irish Americans, The Rise to Money and Power* (New York: Harper and Row, 1981); William V. Shannon, "The Lasting Hurrah," New York *Times Magazine* 14 March 1976: 11 + ; Morton D. Winsberg, "The Suburbanization of the Irish in Boston, Chicago and New York," *Eire-Ireland* 21: 3 (Fall 1986): 90-104.

2. Useful, perceptive studies of recent Irish-American fiction include the following. Joseph Browne, "The Greening of America: Irish-American Writers," *Journal of Ethnic Studies* 2: 1 (Winter 1975): 71-76; Daniel J. Casey, "Echoes from the Next Parish: An Introduction to Irish-American Fiction," *An Gael* (Spring 1984): 2-6; Casey, "Irish Americana, The History and the Literature," *National Hibernian Digest*, July/August 1979 through March/April 1980; James Liddy, "The Double Vision of Irish-American Fiction," *Eire-Ireland* 19: 4 (Winter 1984): 6-15; Shaun O'Connell, "Boggy Ways: Notes on Irish-American Culture," *Massachusetts Review* XXVI: 2-3 (Summer-Autumn 1985): 379-400; Francis Walsh, "Lace Curtain Literature: Changing Perceptions of Irish American Success," *Journal of American Culture* 2 (Spring 1979): 139-45.

3. See Benedict Kiely, "Thomas Flanagan: The Lessons of History," *Hollins Critic* 18: 3 (Oct. 1981); Shaun O'Connell, "History as Fiction: The Novels of Tom Flanagan," *MELUS*, "Irish-American Issue," forthcoming; Jennifer Clarke, "Q & A with Tom Flanagan," *Irish Literary Supplement* 7: 1 (Spring 1988): 26-27.

4. A collection with useful introductions is Arthur Schlesinger, Jr., ed., *The Best and the Last of Edwin O'Connor* (Boston: Little, Brown and Company, 1970). The only full-length study to date is Hugh Rank, *Edwin O'Connor* (New York: Twayne Publishers, 1974). More recent essays are David Dillon, "Priests and Politicians: The Fiction of Edwin O'Connor," in Casey and Rhodes, *Irish-American Fiction* 73-85; and Richard A. Betts, "The 'Blackness of Life': The Function of Edwin O'Connor's Comedy," *MELUS* 8 (Spring 1981): 15-26.

5. See "True Confessions, an Interview with Father Andrew Greeley," *Irish America* 2: 6 (June 1986): 30-37; and Ingrid H. Shafer, *Eros and the Womanliness of God: Andrew Greeley's Romances of Renewal* (Chicago: Loyola University Press, 1986). The *Passover Trilogy* includes *Thy Brother's Wife* (1982), *Ascent into Hell* (1983), and *Lord of the Dance* (1984). *Time Between the Stars* includes *Virgin and Martyr* (1985), *Angels of September* (1986), *Patience of a Saint* (1987), and *Rite of Spring* (1987). All of these novels were published by Warner Books, New York.

6. Recent studies of Irish-American families in therapy corroborate the fictional evidence that the old ways persist. Characteristics noted include female dominance in family life, inability to express emotions, embrace of guilt and acceptance of suffering as one's lot in life, and high incidence of alcoholism. See Monica McGoldrick and John K. Pearce, "Family Therapy with Irish-Americans," *Family Process* 20 (1981): 223-41; and McGoldrick, "Irish Families," in McGoldrick and Pearce, *Ethnicity and Family Therapy* (New York: Guilford Press, 1982): 310-38.

7. There is evidence of the persistence of a crippling maternal dominance in Irish literature as well. The biting portrayals of Irish farmer Paddy Maguire and his bullying mother in Patrick Kavanagh's long poem *The Great Hunger* (1942) stand as archetypal, and latter-day echoes occur in powerful stories by William Trevor ("Death in Jerusalem," *New Yorker* 20 March 1978) and Edna O'Brien ("A Rose in the Heart," *New Yorker* 1 May 1978; and "Far Away in Australia," *New Yorker* 25 December 1978).

8. Insightful treatments of Cullinan's work are Maureen Murphy, "Elizabeth Cullinan: Yellow and Gold," in Casey and Rhodes, *Irish-American Fiction*, 139-52; and Eileen Kennedy, "Bequeathing Tokens: Elizabeth Cullinan's Irish-Americans," *Eire-Ireland* 16: 4 (Winter 1981): 94-102. My reading of *House of Gold* has appeared in somewhat different form in Charles Fanning, "Elizabeth Cullinan's House of Gold: Culmination of an Irish American Dream," *MELUS* 7: 4 (Winter 1980): 31-48.

9. There is a mix of light and dark motives in Joyce's *Finnegan's Wake,* where at one point the narrator declares, " . . . if reams stood to reason and his lankalivline lasted he would wipe alley english spooker, multaphoniaksically spuking, off the face of the erse" (1939; New York: Viking Press, 1958): 178.

10. In sharp contrast to the flood of manic talk in McHale, Toole, Murray, and Costello, is the rendering of madness and its family consequences in Frank Conroy's story "Midair" (1985), in which middle-aged Sean Kennedy traces his adult instability back to a terrifying childhood afternoon, since blocked from his memory, when his insane father held him suspended out a fifth-floor window. The crystalline clarity and perfect pitch of the writing here amount to a kind of super-realism, to use the analogy with painting, and the emotional intensity generated is breathtaking.

11. In addition to the interviews quoted in the text, useful pieces about William Kennedy's fiction include George W. Hunt, "William Kennedy's Albany Trilogy," *America* 150: 19 (May 19, 1984): 373-75; and Margaret Croydon, "The Sudden Fame of William Kennedy," *New York Times Magazine* 26 August 1984: 32-3+.

11. Liberating Doubleness in the Nineties

1. Richard Ellmann declares that from the 1890s, Yeats "considered [style] to be the element which in literature corresponded to the moral element in life; that is, by its emphases it determined delicate gradations of value and was a direct indication of the writer's personality. For style was a question of the vigour with which positions were taken and of the honesty with which qualifications were made; it had to do with the degree of emotion to be expressed, and with the degree of contemporaneity in the expression. How a man decided when he faced the alternatives of being affirmative, negative, skeptical, or mealy-mouthed, modern or archaistic, cautious or brazen, affected his choice of words, his clarity or obscurity in setting forth his themes, his sentence structure. . . . The quest

for style was therefore a primary interest of Yeats because it was also a quest for his own character, freed from the accidents of every day." *The Identity of Yeats* (New York: Oxford Univ. Press, 1954): 116-17.

2. Stephens has published a dozen books of prose, poetry, and drama, including a collection of stimulating essays, *Green Dreams: Essays under the Influence of the Irish* (Athens, Ga.: Univ. of Georgia Press, 1994). McGonigle has one earlier and truly international novel, set in Bulgaria, *The Corpse Dream of N. Petkov* (Normal, Ill.: Dalkey Archive Press, 1987).

3. Eavan Boland, "The Emigrant Irish," in *The Journey and Other Poems* (New York: Carcanet Press, 1987): 54. The songs have improved immeasurably as well. See (and hear) the lyrics of Terence Winch on the albums of the group Celtic Thunder: *Celtic Thunder* (GLCD 1029, Green Linnet Recording Co., 1981), *The Light of Other Days* (CSIF 1086, Green Linnet Recording Co., 1988), and *Hard New York Days* (KM 9503, Kells Music, 1995).

4. A useful anthology is David Lampe, ed., *The Legend of Being Irish: A Collection of Irish-American Poetry* (Fredonia, N.Y.: White Pine Press, 1989). See also the poems in the issue of "Irish and Irish-American Writing," *Crab Orchard Review* 1: 2 (Spring/Summer 1996).

5. Montague's American poems and prose have been collected as *Born in Brooklyn: John Montague's America*, ed. David Lampe (Fredonia, N.Y.: White Pine Press, 1991).

6. Among Brian Moore's many novels, some with central Irish/American concerns are *An Answer from Limbo* (1962), *Fergus* (1970), *The Great Victorian Collection* (1975), *The Mangan Inheritance* (1979), and *Cold Heaven* (1983).

7. See Dermot Bolger, ed., *Ireland in Exile: Irish Writers Abroad* (Dublin: New Island Books, 1993), for stories with American settings by Aidan Hynes, Eamonn Wall, and Helena Mulkerns. See also Jennifer C Cornell, *Departures* (Pittsburgh: Univ. of Pittsburgh Press, 1995).

8. McCann has also published a collection of stories, *Fishing the Sloe-Black River* (Dublin: Phoenix House, 1994).

9. See Eamonn Wall, "The English Language Belongs to Us: Notes of an Immigrant from Ireland," *Forkroads* 1: 4 (Summer 1996): 66-75; Michael Lally, "Lally's Alley," *Forkroads* 1: 3 (Spring 1996): 13-22; Mary Gordon, *The Shadow Man* (New York: Random House, 1996); Joan Mathieu, *Zulu: An Irish Journey* (New York: Farrar, Straus, Giroux, 1998); Maureen Waters, "Excerpts from *Crossing Highbridge*," *Crab Orchard Review* 1: 2 (Spring/Summer 1996): 205-17; Pete Hamill, *A Drinking Life: A Memoir* (Boston: Little, Brown, 1994).

10. *Oxford English Dictionary*, 2nd ed. (Oxford: Clarendon Press, 1989): 3: 583-84.

11. A natural place to begin is Donald H. Akenson, *The Irish Diaspora: A Primer* (Toronto: P.D. Meany, 1996). The most studied group to date is the Irish in Australia. See Colm Kiernan, ed., *Australia and Ireland, 1788-1988: Bicentenary Essays* (Dublin: Gill and Macmillan, 1986); Robert Hughes, *The Fatal Shore* (New York: Knopf, 1987); Patrick O'Farrell, *The Irish in Australia* (Kensington: New South Wales Univ. Press, 1987); Patrick O'Farrell, *Vanished Kingdoms: Irish in Australia and New Zealand* (Kensington: New South Wales Univ. Press, 1990); David Fitzpatrick, *Oceans of Consolation: Personal Accounts of Irish Migration to Australia* (Ithaca: Cornell Univ. Press, 1994).

12. For an introduction to Irish Antipodean writing, see the literary essays by Denis O'Hearn, Vincent Buckley, Colm Kiernan, and Anna Rutherford in Colm Kiernan, ed., *Australia and Ireland, 1788-1988*. See also Richard Corballis, "'It's a Long, Long Way to Tipperary, But My Heart's Right There': Irish Elements in New Zealand Literature, 1890-1990," *Anglistentag 1990, Marburg: Proceedings* (Tubingen: Niemeyer, 1991): 398-412. Contributors to the burst of Australian literary activity in the 1890s included poets and journalists Christopher Brennan, Victor Daley, John Farrell, Bernard O'Dowd, John O'Hara, and Roderick Quinn. Among subsequent writers who have described Australian Irish life are Eleanor Dark, Ruth Park, Gavin Casey, Xavier Herbert, Frank Hardy, Barry Oakley, Desmond O'Grady, Laurie Clancy, Vincent Buckley, D'Arcy Niland, Gerald Murnane,

Barbara Hanrahan, and David Ireland. New Zealand Irish perspectives appear in works by Thomas Bracken, Jessie Mackay, Eileen Duggan, Helen Wilson, David Ballantyne, Bill Pearson, Ian Cross, John Bentley, and Michael Morrissey.

13. Though the ethnic dimension is still under-represented, there has been much instructive newer scholarship on American literary realism. See Walter Benn Michaels, *The Gold Standard and the Logic of Naturalism* (Berkeley: Univ. of California Press, 1987); Michael Denning, *Mechanic Accents: Dime Novels and Working-Class Culture in America* (London and New York: Verso, 1987); Amy Kaplan, *The Social Construction of American Realism* (Chicago: Univ. of Chicago Press, 1988); Miles Orvell, *The Real Thing: Imitation and Authenticity in American Culture, 1880-1940* (Chapel Hill: Univ. of North Carolina Press, 1989); Michael Davitt Bell, *The Problem of American Realism* (Chicago: Univ. of Chicago Press, 1993); and David E. Shi, *Facing Facts: Realism in American Thought and Culture, 1850-1920* (New York: Oxford Univ. Press, 1995). A very useful collection of primary sources is Donald Pizer, ed., *Documents of American Realism and Naturalism* (Carbondale: Southern Illinois Univ. Press, 1998).

14. For Eastern, New York-based 1930s radical literature, see Alan Wald, *James T. Farrell: The Revolutionary Socialist Years* (New York: New York Univ. Press, 1978); Alan Wald, *The New York Intellectuals* (Chapel Hill: Univ. of North Carolina Press, 1987); and Alan Wald, *Writing from the Left* (London and New York: Verso, 1994). For the Midwest, see Douglas Wixson, *Worker-Writer in America: Jack Conroy and the Tradition of Midwestern Literary Radicalism, 1898-1990* (Urbana: Univ. of Illinois Press, 1994). See also James F. Murphy, *The Proletarian Moment* (Urbana: Univ. of Illinois Press, 1991); and Barbara Foley, *Radical Representations: Politics and Form in U.S. Proletarian Fiction, 1929-1941* (Durham, N.C.: Duke Univ. Press, 1993).

15. Kim Herzinger's working definition of "minimalism" runs in part as follows: "Minimalist fiction is a) formally spare, terse, trim; b) tonally cool, detached, noncommittal; 'flat,' affectless, recalcitrant, deadpan, laconic; c) oblique and elliptical; d) relatively plotless; e) concerned with surface detail, particularly with recognizable brand names. . . . [its] 'subject matter' is a) ordinary, mundane; b) domestic, local; c) regional; d) generational; e) blue-collar/working-class or white/yuppie" ("Minimalism as a Postmodernism: Some Introductory Notes," *New Orleans Review* 16: 3 [1989], 73).

16. Of the small body of useful criticism, see, for example, the special issue of *MELUS* [*Multi-Ethnic Literature of the United States*] collecting criticism of "Irish-American Literature": 13: 1 (Spring 1993). Also, fruitful attention has been paid to Irish-American texts in Shaun O'Connell, "Irish America's Red Brick City: Edwin O'Connor's Boston," in *Imagining Boston* (Boston: Beacon Press, 1990): 108-40; William Keough, "X Rays of Irish America: Edwin O'Connor, Mary Gordon, and William Kennedy," in *Memory, Narrative, and Identity: New Essays in Ethnic American Literatures*, eds. Amritjit Singh et al (Boston: Northeastern Univ. Press, 1994): 145-63; Ron Ebest, "The Irish Catholic Schooling of James T. Farrell, 1914-23," *Éire-Ireland* 30: 4 (Winter 1996): 18-32; Eamonn Wall, "The English Language Belongs to Us: Notes of an Immigrant from Ireland," *Forkroads* 1: 4 (Summer 1996): 66-75; Patricia J. Fanning, "'Maybe They'd Call the Doctor': Illness Behavior in the Novels of James T. Farrell," *New Hibernia Review* 1: 4 (Winter 1997): 81-92. Also, a portion of the present material appeared in a different form in Charles Fanning, "The Heart's Speech No Longer Stifled: New York Irish Writing Since the 1960s," in *The New York Irish*, eds. Ronald H. Bayor and Timothy J. Meagher (Baltimore: Johns Hopkins Univ. Press, 1996): 508-31. That material is republished here with the kind permission of the Johns Hopkins University Press.

Among Irish-American writers, only William Kennedy has received critical attention commensurate with his talent and productivity. Kennedy's work has been the subject of many essays and several books, including Edward C. Reilly, *William Kennedy* (Boston: Twayne, 1991); J.K. Van Dover, *Understanding William Kennedy* (Columbia: Univ. of South Carolina Press, 1991); Benedict Giamo, *The Homeless of Ironweed: Blossoms on the*

Crag (Iowa City: Univ. of Iowa Press, 1996); and Neila C. Seshachari, ed., *Conversations with William Kennedy* (Jackson: Univ. Press of Mississippi, 1997).

The good work in Irish-American history continues to proliferate. Since 1990, many essays and books have appeared. Important comprehensive studies, to which those interested should refer for specialized bibliographies, include Patrick J. Blessing, *The Irish in America: A Guide to the Literature and the Manuscript Collections* (Washington, D.C.: Catholic Univ. of America Press, 1992); Lawrence J. McCaffrey, *Textures of Irish America* (Syracuse, N.Y.: Syracuse Univ. Press, 1992); Lawrence J. McCaffrey, *The Irish Catholic Diaspora in America* (Washington, D.C.: Catholic Univ. of America Press, 1997); and Bayor and Meagher, *The New York Irish* (1996).

17. The new edition (Chester Springs, Penn.: Dufour Editions, 1997) includes excerpts from T.C. Mack, *The Priest's Turf-Cutting Day* (1841), and John Talbot Smith, *The Art of Disappearing* (1899), as well as an expansion from nine to twenty-two of Finley Peter Dunne's "Mr. Dooley" pieces. An illuminating collection of outside views of the nineteenth-century Irish in America is Jack Morgan and Louis A. Renza, eds., *The Irish Stories of Sarah Orne Jewett* (Carbondale: Southern Illinois Univ. Press, 1996).

18. See also the special issue of *Crab Orchard Review* collecting new "Irish and Irish-American Writing," including poetry, fiction, and memoir: 1: 2 (Spring/Summer 1996).

19. For a number of Catholic stories with an Irish dimension, see two useful anthologies: Amber Coverdale Sumrall and Patrice Vecchione, eds., *Catholic Girls* (New York: Plume/Penguin, 1992), and Sumrall and Vecchione, eds., *Bless Me, Father: Stories of Catholic Childhood* (New York: Plume/Penguin, 1994).

20. For Delaney, see "The Drowning," *The Atlantic Monthly* 273: 3 (March 1994): 72-84, and "A Visit to My Uncle," *Crab Orchard Review* 1: 2 (Spring/Summer 1996): 57-69. For Winch, see also the poems of *Irish Musicians/American Friends* (Minneapolis: Coffee House Press, 1985), which more directly evoke the Irish Bronx, especially the dimension of traditional music.

21. Kennedy's other fiction includes *A Weather of the Eye, A Short Novel* (Prairie Village, Kans.: Potpourri Publications, 1996); *Unreal City, Stories* (La Grande, Oreg.: Woodcraft of Oregon, 1996); *Drive, Dive, Dance & Fight* (Kansas City, Mo.: BkMk Press, 1997); and *The Book of Angels, A Novel* (La Grande, Oreg.: Woodcraft of Oregon, 1996).

22. *That Night* is McDermott's second novel. Her first, *The Bigamist's Daughter* (New York: Random House, 1982) describes a love affair between an editor for a vanity press and one of her novelist-clients. I would say that it stands in the same relation to her developing oeuvre as does Maureen Howard's first novel, *Not a Word about Nightingales*, to her career; that is, it is a well-written exercise lacking the ground sense that appears immediately thereafter, and on which she continues to build.

Works Cited

Bachelard, Gaston. *The Poetics of Space.* Trans. Maria Jolas. Boston: Beacon Press, 1969.

Bagnel, Joan. *Gone the Rainbow, Gone the Dove.* New York: Trident Press, 1973.

Baumgartner, A.W. *Catholic Journalism, A Study of Its Development in the United States.* New York: Columbia Univ. Press, 1931.

Bayor, Ronald H., and Timothy J. Meagher, eds. *The New York Irish.* Baltimore: Johns Hopkins Univ. Press, 1996.

Beer, Thomas. *The Mauve Decade.* 1926. New York: Vintage Books, 1960.

Berger, John. *And our faces, my heart, brief as photos.* New York: Pantheon Books, 1984.

Berlin, Ellin MacKay. *Lace Curtain.* Garden City: Doubleday, 1948.

Biddle, Drexel. *Shantytown Sketches.* Philadelphia: Drexel Biddle, 1897.

Blanc, Robert E. *James McHenry (1785-1845), Playwright and Novelist.* Philadelphia: Univ. of Pennsylvania Press, 1939.

Blessing, Patrick J. "Irish" entry. *Harvard Encyclopedia of American Ethnic Groups.* Ed. Stephan Thernstrom. Cambridge: Harvard Univ. Press, 1980. 524-45.

Blum, Carol O'Brien. *Anne's Head.* New York: Dial Press, 1982.

Bocock, John Paul. "The Irish Conquest of Our Cities." *Forum* 17 (April 1894): 186-95.

Bolger, Stephen G. *The Irish Character in American Fiction, 1830-1860.* New York: Arno Press, 1976.

Bonetti, Kay. "An Interview with William Kennedy." *Missouri Review* 8: 2 (1985): 71-86.

Bourgeois, Maurice. *John M. Synge and the Irish Theatre.* London: Constable, 1913.

Boyce, John. *Mary Lee; or, The Yankee in Ireland.* Boston: Patrick Donahoe, 1860.

———. *The Spaewife; or, The Queen's Secret. A Story of the Reign of Elizabeth.* Baltimore: John Murphy, 1853.

———. *Shandy McGuire; or Tricks upon Travellers. Being a Story of the North of Ireland.* New York: Edward Dunigan and Brother, 1848.

Branch, Edgar M. *A Bibliography of James T. Farrell's Writings 1921-1957.* Philadelphia: Univ. of Pennsylvania Press, 1959.

———. *James T. Farrell.* New York: Twayne Publishers, 1971.

Brennan, John. *Erin Mor: The Story of Irish Republicanism.* San Francisco: P.M. Diers, 1892.

Breslin, Howard. *Let Go of Yesterday.* New York: McGraw, 1950.

Breslin, Jimmy. *Table Money.* New York: Ticknor and Fields, 1986.

———. *World Without End, Amen.* New York: Viking, 1973.

Broderick, John. [Review of E. McSorley, *Our Own Kind*.] *Commonweal* 44 (7 June 1946): 194.

Brown, Stephen J. *Ireland in Fiction*. 1919. New York: Burt Franklin, 1970.

Brown, Thomas N. *Irish-American Nationalism, 1870-1890*. Philadelphia: Lippincott, 1966.

———. "The Irish Layman." In *A History of Irish Catholicism: The United States of America*. Dublin: Gill and MacMillan, 1970. 45-100.

———. "Mary Anne Madden Sadlier." In *Notable American Women 1607-1950*. Ed. Edward T. James. Cambridge: Harvard Univ. Press, 1971. 3: 219-20.

———. "The Origins and Character of Irish-American Nationalism." *Review of Politics* 18 (July 1956): 327-58.

Brownson, Orestes. [Review of Boyce, *Mary Lee*.] *Brownson's Quarterly Review*, Third Series I (Jan. 1860): 118-30.

———. [Review of Boyce, *Shandy McGuire*.] *BQR*, n. s. 3: 3 (Jan. 1849): 58-90.

———. [Review of Boyce, *The Spaewife*.] *BQR*, Third Series 1 (April 1853): 279-80.

———. [Review of Cannon, *Mora Carmody*.] *BQR* 11 (Jan. 1845): 134-36.

———. [Review of Cannon, poems and plays.] *BQR*, New York Series II (Oct. 1857): 503-07.

———. [Review of Cannon, *Tighe Lyfford*.] *BQR*, New York Series IV (July 1859): 410-11.

———. "The Irish in America." *BQR*, Third Series III (Oct. 1855): 538-47.

———. [Review of Quigley, *The Cross and The Shamrock*.] *BQR*, n. s. II (April 1854): 269-70.

———. [Review of Quigley, *Prophet of the Ruined Abbey*.] *BQR*, n. s. III (Jan. 1855): 143-44.

———. [Review of Roddan, *John O'Brien*.] *BQR* V (Jan. 1851): 120-24.

———. [Review of Sadlier, *Blakes and Flanagans*.] *BQR*, n. s. I (April 1856): 195-212.

———. [Review of Sadlier, *New Lights*.] *BQR*, n. s. I (July 1853): 400-407.

———. [Review of Sadlier, *Old and New*.] *BQR*, Third New York Series IV (Jan. 1863): 77-80.

———. [Review of Sadlier, *Red Hand of Ulster*.] *BQR* IV (Oct. 1850): 542-44.

———. [Review of Sadlier, *Willy Burke*.] *BQR* IV (Oct. 1850): 537-38.

Buckley, Vincent. "Imagination's Home." *Quadrant* 140 (March 1979): 24-29.

Bugg, Lelia Hardin. *The People of Our Parish: Being Chronicle and Comment of Katherine Fitzgerald, Pew-holder in the Church of St. Paul the Apostle*. Boston: Merlier, Callanan, and Co., 1900. New York: Arno Press, 1978.

———. "Westgate's Past." In *The Prodigal's Daughter and Other Tales*. New York: Benziger Bros., 1898.

Burk, John Daly. *History of the Late War in Ireland*. Philadelphia: F. and R. Bailey, 1799.

Burke, Alan Dennis. *Fire Watch*. Boston: Atlantic-Little, Brown, 1980.

Byrne, Donn. *Blind Raftery and His Wife, Hilaria*. New York: Century Co., 1924.

———. *The Stranger's Banquet*. New York: Harper and Bros., 1919.

———. "The Wake." In *Stories without Women*. New York: Hearst's International Library, 1915.

Byrne, Robert. *Once a Catholic*. 1970. New York: Pinnacle Books, 1981.

Cahalan, James M. *Great Hatred, Little Room, The Irish Historical Novel.* Syracuse: Syracuse Univ. Press, 1983.

Cannon, Charles James. *Bickerton; or, The Immigrant's Daughter. A Tale.* New York: P. O'Shea, 1855.

———. *Facts, Feelings and Fancies.* New York: Bliss, Wordsworth, 1835.

———. *Father Felix: A Tale.* New York: Edward Dunigan, 1845.

———. *Harry Layden: A Tale.* New York: John A. Boyle, 1842.

———. *Mora Carmody; or, Woman's Influence.* New York: Edward Dunigan, 1844.

———. *Oran, The Outcast; or, A Season in New York.* 2 vols. New York: Peabody and Co., 1833.

———. *Poems, Dramatic and Miscellaneous.* New York: Edward Dunigan, 1851.

———. *Ravellings from the Web of Life,* by Grandfather Greenway. New York: Sadlier, 1855.

———. *Scenes and Characters from the Comedy of Life.* New York: Edward Dunigan, 1847.

———. *Tighe Lyfford, A Novel.* New York: James Miller, 1859.

Carey, Mathew. *The Plagi-Scurriliad. A Hudibrastic Poem.* Dedicated to Col. Eleazer Oswald. Philadelphia: printed and sold by the author, 16 January 1786.

———. *A Plum Pudding for Humane, Chaste, Valiant, Enlightened Peter Porcupine.* By his obliged Friend, Mathew Carey. Philadelphia: Printed for the Author, 1799.

———. *The Porcupiniad. A Hudibrastic Poem in Four Cantos.* Addressed to Mr. William Cobbett. Philadelphia: Printed for and sold by the Author, 2 March 1799 and 15 April 1799.

———. *Vindiciae Hibernicae; or, Ireland Vindicated.* Philadelphia: Carey and Lea, 1819, 2nd ed. 1823.

Caroline Tracy, The Spring Street Milliner's Apprentice, or Life in New York in 1847-8. New York: Stearns and Co., 1849.

Carpenter, Frederick I. "The Vogue of Ossian in America: A Study in Taste." *American Literature* 2 (Jan. 1931): 405-17.

Carroll, James. *Mortal Friends.* Boston: Little, Brown, 1978.

———. *Supply of Heroes.* New York: E.P. Dutton, 1986.

Casey, Daniel J. and Robert E. Rhodes, eds. *Irish-American Fiction: Essays in Criticism.* New York: AMS Press, 1979.

———. *Modern Irish-American Fiction: A Reader.* Syracuse: Syracuse Univ. Press, 1989.

Cassidy, Patrick Sarsfield. *The Borrowed Bride: A Fairy Love Legend of Donegal.* New York: Holt, 1892.

———. *Glenveigh; or, the Victims of Vengeance, A Tale of Irish Peasant Life in the Present.* Boston: P. Donahoe, 1870.

Cather, Willa. "Katherine Mansfield." In *Stories, Poems, and Other Writings,* ed. Sharon O'Brien. New York: Library of America, 1992.

Cavanaugh, Arthur. *Leaving Home.* New York: Simon and Schuster, 1970.

Chametsky, Jules. *From the Ghetto: The Fiction of Abraham Cahan.* Amherst: Univ. of Massachusetts Press, 1977.

Clancy, Eugene. "The Cleansing Tears." *Harper's Magazine* 130 (Feb. 1915): 414-24.

Cleary, Kate McPhelim. *Like a Gallant Lady.* Chicago: Way and Williams, 1897.

———. "The Mission of Kitty Malone." *McClure's* 18 (Nov. 1901): 88-96.

———. *The Nebraska of Kate McPhelim Cleary.* Ed. James Mansfield Cleary. Lake Bluff, Ill.: United Educators, Inc., 1958.

Connolly, James Brendan. *Out of Gloucester.* New York: Charles Scribner's Sons, 1902.

———. *The Seiners.* New York: Charles Scribner's Sons, 1904.

Conroy, Frank. *Midair.* New York: Dutton, 1985.

———. *Stop-Time.* New York: Viking Press, 1967.

Conway, Katherine E. *A Dream of Lilies.* Boston: J.G. Cupples Co., 1893.

———. *Lalor's Maples.* Boston: Pilot Publishing Co., 1901.

———. *The Way of the World and Other Ways: A Story of Our Set.* Boston: Pilot Publishing Co., 1900.

———. *The Woman Who Never Did Wrong and Other Stories.* Boston: T.J. Flynn, 1909.

Conway, William D. *Beauties of the Shamrock, Containing Biography, Eloquence, Essays, and Poetry.* Philadelphia: Bartholomew Graves, for William D. Conway, 1812.

Conyngham, David Power. *The O'Donnells of Glen Cottage: A Tale of the Famine Years in Ireland.* New York: Sadlier, 1874.

———. *The O'Mahony, Chief of the Comeraghs: A Tale of the Rebellion of '98.* New York and Montreal: D. and J. Sadlier and Co., 1879.

———. *Rose Parnell: The Flower of Avondale: A Tale of the Rebellion of '98.* New York: Sadlier, 1883.

———. *Sarsfield; or The Last Great Struggle for Ireland.* Boston: P. Donahoe, 1871.

Cosgrave, J. *A Genuine History of the Lives and Actions of the Most Notorious Irish Highwaymen, Tories, and Rapparies.* Wilmington, Del.: Bonsal and Niles, 1799.

Costello, Mark. *The Murphy Stories.* Urbana: Univ. of Illinois Press, 1973.

Cott, Nancy F. *The Bonds of Womanhood: "Woman's Sphere" in New England, 1780-1835.* New Haven: Yale Univ. Press, 1977.

Coyle, Kathleen. *Immortal Ease.* New York: E.P. Dutton, 1939.

Cullinan, Elizabeth. *A Change of Scene.* New York: Norton, 1982.

———. "Commuting." *Irish Literary Supplement* 2: 1 (1983): 34-35.

———. "A Good Loser." *New Yorker* (15 August 1977): 32+.

———. *House of Gold.* Boston: Houghton Mifflin, 1970.

———. *The Time of Adam.* Boston: Houghton Mifflin, 1971.

———. *Yellow Roses.* New York: Viking, 1977.

"Curious Letter." *Gazette of the United States* 4 (11 May 1793): 394.

Curran, Mary Doyle. *The Parish and the Hill.* 1948. New York: Feminist Press, 1986.

Currie, Ellen. *Available Light.* New York: Summit Books, 1986.

———. *Moses Supposes.* New York: Simon and Schuster, 1994.

Curtin, Jeremiah. *Myths and Folklore of Ireland.* London: Sampson, Low, 1890.

Curtis, L. Perry, Jr. *Apes and Angels, The Irishman in Victorian Caricature.* Washington: Smithsonian Institution Press, 1971.

Cusack, Mary Frances (The Nun of Kenmare). *From Killarney to New York; or, How Thade Became a Banker.* New York: D. O'Loughlin, 1877.

Deasy, Mary. *The Hour of Spring.* 1948. New York: Arno Press, 1976.

Dever, Joseph. *A Certain Widow.* Milwaukee: Bruce, 1951.

————. *No Lasting Home.* Milwaukee: Bruce, 1947.

Dineen, Joseph. *Ward Eight.* 1936. New York: Arno Press, 1976.

Diner, Hasia R. *Erin's Daughters in America: Irish Immigrant Women in the Nine-teenth Century.* Baltimore: Johns Hopkins Univ. Press, 1983.

Dolan, Jay P. *The American Catholic Experience.* 1985. New York: Image Books, 1987.

Donleavy, J.P. *The Ginger Man.* Paris: Olympia Press, 1955.

Donnelly, Eleanor, ed. *A Round Table of the Representative American Catholic Nov-elists.* New York: Benziger Bros., 1897.

Dooley, Roger Burke. *Days Beyond Recall.* Milwaukee: Bruce, 1949.

————. *Less than the Angels.* Milwaukee: Bruce, 1946.

Doran, James. *Zanthon: A Novel.* San Francisco: Bancroft Co., 1891.

Dorsey, Anna H. *Nora Brady's Vow and Mona the Vestal.* Philadelphia: Lippincott, 1869.

Dorson, Richard M. "Mose the Far-Famed and World-Renowned." *American Lit-erature* 15 (1943): 288-300.

Downing, Michael. *Mother of God.* New York: Simon and Schuster, 1990.

————. *A Narrow Time.* New York: Vintage Contemporaries, 1987.

————. *Perfect Agreement.* Washington, D.C.: Counterpoint, 1997.

Doyle, David N. *Ireland, Irishmen and Revolutionary America 1760-1820.* Dublin and Cork: Mercier Press, 1981.

Driscoll, Charles B. *Kansas Irish.* New York: Macmillan, 1943.

Dubois, Edward. *My Pocket Book; or Hints for "A Ryghte Merrie and Conceited" Tour, in Quarto; to be Called, "The Stranger in Ireland."* New York: Ezra Sargeant, 1807.

Dugan, James. *Doctor Dispachemquic: A Story of the Great Southern Plague of 1878.* New Orleans: Clark and Hofeline, 1879.

Duganne, Augustine J.H. *The Tenant House; or, Embers from Poverty's Hearthstone.* New York: Dewitt, 1857.

————. *The Two Clerks; or, The Orphan's Gratitude.* Boston: Brainard, 1843.

Dunne, Finley Peter. *Mr. Dooley and the Chicago Irish, The Autobiography of a Nine-teenth-Century Ethnic Group.* Ed. Charles Fanning. Washington: Catholic Univ. of America Press, 1987.

————. *Mr. Dooley in the Hearts of His Countrymen.* Boston: Small, Maynard and Co., 1899.

————. *Mr. Dooley in Peace and in War.* Boston: Small, Maynard and Co., 1898.

————. *Mr. Dooley's Philosophy.* New York: R.H. Russell, 1900.

Dunne, John Gregory. *Dutch Shea, Jr.* New York: Simon and Schuster, 1982.

————. *Harp.* New York: Simon and Schuster, 1989.

————. *True Confessions.* New York: E.P. Dutton, 1977.

Dunphy, Jack. *First Wine.* Baton Rouge: Louisiana State Univ. Press, 1982.

————. *John Fury: A Novel in Four Parts.* 1946. New York: Arno Press, 1976.

————. *The Murderous McLaughlins.* New York: McGraw Hill, 1988.

Edwards, Owen Dudley. "The American Image of Ireland: A Study of Its Early Phases." *Perspectives in American History* 4 (1970): 199-282.

————. "The Impact of the American Revolution on Ireland." In *The Impact of the American Revolution Abroad.* Washington: Library of Congress, 1976. 127-59.

Edwards, R. Dudley, and T. Desmond Williams, eds. *The Great Famine, Studies in Irish History, 1845-52.* 1956. New York: Russell and Russell, 1976.

Egan, Maurice Francis. *Confessions of a Book Lover.* New York: Doubleday, Page, 1922.

———. *The Disappearance of John Longworthy.* 1890. New York: Arno Press, 1977.

———. *The Ghost in Hamlet and Other Essays in Comparative Literature.* Chicago: A.C. McClurg, 1906.

———. "How Perseus Became a Star." In *A Round Table of the Representative American Catholic Novelists.* Ed. Eleanor Donnelly. New York: Benziger Brothers, 1897. 132-43.

———. "Irish Novels." In *Irish Literature.* Eds. Justin McCarthy et al. New York: P.F. Collier and Son, 1904. V: vii-xvii.

———. *Jack Chumleigh at Boarding-School.* Philadelphia: H.L. Kilner, 1899.

———. *The Life Around Us: A Collection of Stories.* New York: Pustet and Co., 1885.

———. *A Marriage of Reason.* Baltimore: John Murphy, 1893.

———. "The Necessity of Being Irish." *Scribner's Magazine* 56 (Nov. 1914): 647-58.

———. *Recollections of a Happy Life.* New York: George H. Doran, 1924.

———. *Short Stories.* New York: Wildermann, 1900.

———. *Songs and Sonnets.* London: Kegan Paul, Trench and Co., 1885.

———. *The Success of Patrick Desmond.* Notre Dame: Office of the Ave Maria, 1893.

———. *That Girl of Mine.* Philadelphia: Peterson, 1877.

———. *That Lover of Mine.* Philadelphia: Peterson, 1877.

———. *The Vocation of Edward Conway.* New York, Cincinnati: Benziger Brothers, 1896.

———. *The Wiles of Sexton Maginnis.* New York: The Century Company, 1909.

"Elegy on the Much Lamented Death of Lawrence Sweeny, Esq; of most facetious Memory, who departed this life at New-York, upon Tuesday April 10, 1770." New York *Gazette and Weekly Mercury* 16 April 1770. Evans 11646. [Charles Evans, *American Bibliography,* 12 vols., chronologically catalogs works printed in America 1639-1799.]

Ellis, Elmer. *Mr. Dooley's America: A Life of Finley Peter Dunne.* New York: Knopf, 1941.

Ellmann, Richard. *The Identity of Yeats.* New York: Oxford Univ. Press, 1954.

Ezekial, Tish O'Dowd. *Floaters.* New York: Atheneum, 1984.

Fanning, Charles, ed. *The Exiles of Erin: Nineteenth-Century Irish-American Fiction.* Notre Dame: Univ. of Notre Dame Press, 1987. 2nd ed. expanded (Chester Springs, Penn.: Dufour Editions, 1997).

———. *Finley Peter Dunne and Mr. Dooley: The Chicago Years.* Lexington: Univ. Press of Kentucky, 1978.

Farrell, James T. *Boarding House Blues.* New York: Paperback Library, 1961.

———. *Chicago Stories of James T. Farrell.* Ed. Charles Fanning. Urbana: Univ. of Illinois Press, 1998.

———. *The Death of Nora Ryan.* Garden City, N.Y.: Doubleday, 1978.

———. "Donn Byrne, Writer." *Saturday Review of Literature* 6 (8 Feb. 1930): 717.

———. *The Face of Time.* New York: Vanguard Press, 1953.

———. "Fastest Runner on Sixty-first Street." *Commentary* 9 (June 1950): 538-44.

———. *Father and Son*. New York: Vanguard Press, 1940.

———. *Gas-House McGinty*. New York: Vanguard Press, 1933.

———. "Hurrah! A Good Novel." [Review of E. O'Connor, *The Last Hurrah*.] New York *Post*, 5 Feb. 1956, 10M.

———. *Judith and Other Stories*. 1973. New York: Manor Books, 1978.

———. *The League of Frightened Philistines and Other Papers*. New York: Vanguard Press, 1945.

———. *Literature and Morality*. New York: Vanguard Press, 1947.

———. *My Baseball Diary*. 1957. Carbondale: Southern Illinois Univ. Press, 1998.

———. *My Days of Anger*. New York: Vanguard Press, 1943.

———. *New Year's Eve/1929*. New York: The Smith, 1967.

———. *No Star Is Lost*. New York: Vanguard Press, 1938.

———. *A Note on Literary Criticism*. 1936. New York: Columbia Univ. Press, 1992.

———. *On Irish Themes*. Ed. Dennis Flynn. Philadelphia: Univ. of Pennsylvania Press, 1982.

———. *Reflections at Fifty and Other Essays*. New York: Vanguard Press, 1954.

———. *Sam Holman*. Buffalo: Prometheus Books, 1983.

———. "Shanty Irish." [Review of Tully novel.] University of Chicago *Daily Maroon*, 1 March 1929: 3.

———. *The Short Stories of James T. Farrell*. New York: Vanguard Press, 1937.

———. *The Silence of History*. Garden City: Doubleday, 1963.

———. "The Story of a Simple Man." [Review of J. Dunphy, *John Fury*.] *Saturday Review of Literature* 29 (9 Nov. 1946): 31.

———. *Studs Lonigan: A Trilogy*. 1935. Urbana: Univ. of Illinois Press, 1993.

———. *A World I Never Made*. New York: Vanguard Press, 1936.

———. "The Wrong Side of Beacon Hill." [Review of J. Dineen, *Ward Eight*.] Brooklyn *Eagle*, 25 Oct. 1936: C17.

Fine, David. *The City, the Immigrant, and American Fiction*. Metuchen, N.J.: Scarecrow Press, 1977.

Finerty, John F. *The Churchyard Oath*. Chicago *Citizen*, 2 March-4 May 1901.

FitzGerald, Eileen. *You're So Beautiful*. New York: St. Martin's Press, 1996.

Fitzgerald, F. Scott. *The Beautiful and the Damned*. New York: Charles Scribner's Sons, 1922.

———. *The Great Gatsby*. New York: Charles Scribner's Sons, 1925.

———. *Tender Is the Night*. New York: Charles Scribner's Sons, 1934; with Author's Final Revisions, ed. Malcolm Cowley, New York: Charles Scribner's Sons, 1951.

———. *This Side of Paradise*. New York: Charles Scribner's Sons, 1920.

Fitzmaurice, John W. *The Shanty Boy: Or, Life in a Lumber Camp*. Cheboygan, Mich.: Democrat Steam Print, 1889.

Fitzsimon, E.A. *The Joint Venture: A Tale in Two Lands*. New York: James Sheehy, 1878.

Flaherty, Gerald. *Filthy the Man*. Columbia: Univ. of Missouri Press, 1985.

Flaherty, Joe. *Fogarty & Co*. New York: Coward, McCann and Geoghegan, 1973.

———. *Tin Wife*. New York: Simon and Schuster, 1983.

Flanagan, Thomas. *The End of the Hunt*. New York: Dutton, 1994.

———. *The Irish Novelists, 1800-1850*. New York: Columbia Univ. Press, 1959.

———. "John O'Hara." *Recorder* 1: 1 (Winter 1985): 51-64.

———. *The Tenants of Time.* New York: E.P. Dutton, 1988.

———. *The Year of the French.* New York: Holt, Rinehart, and Winston, 1979.

Flannery, Jack. *Kell.* Boston: Little, Brown, 1977.

Fleming, Thomas J. *All Good Men.* New York: Doubleday, 1961.

———. *The Good Shepherd.* New York: Doubleday, 1974.

———. *King of the Hill.* New York: New American Library, 1965.

———. *Rulers of the City.* Garden City: Doubleday, 1977.

Flynn, Joyce. "A Republic for All: Burk, Branagan and the Literature of Liberation." Unpublished essay, 1988.

Foik, Paul J. *Pioneer Catholic Journalism.* 1930. New York: Greenwood Press, 1969.

Ford, Elaine. *The Playhouse.* New York: McGraw-Hill, 1980.

Forensic Eloquence, Sketches of Trials in Ireland for High Treason, etc. Baltimore: G. Douglas, 1804.

"A Fragment of Irish History." *Massachusetts Magazine* 2 (January-April 1790).

Frederic, Harold. *The Damnation of Theron Ware.* New York: Stone and Kimball, 1896.

———. *The Return of the O'Mahony.* New York: Stone and Kimball, 1892.

Frothingham, Charles W. *The Convent's Doom: A Tale of Charlestown in 1834.* Boston: Graves and Weston, 1854.

Furphy, Joseph. *Such Is Life.* 1903. Sydney: Angus and Robertson, 1944.

Gallagher, James Nestor. *Timothy Winebruiser: A Narrative in Prose and Verse.* San Antonio: San Antonio Light Press, 1886.

Gibson, William. *A Mass for the Dead.* New York: Atheneum, 1968.

Gill, Brendan. *The Day the Money Stopped.* Garden City, N.Y.: Doubleday and Co., 1957.

———. *The Trouble of One House.* Garden City, N.Y.: Doubleday and Co., 1950.

———. *Ways of Loving.* New York: Harcourt, Brace, Jovanovich, 1974.

Gordon, Mary. *Final Payments.* New York: Random House, 1978.

———. *The Other Side.* New York: Viking Penguin, 1989.

Granger, Bruce L. *Political Satire in the American Revolution, 1763-1783.* Ithaca: Cornell Univ. Press, 1960.

Greeley, Andrew M. *Angels of September.* New York: Warner Books, 1986.

———. *The Cardinal Sins.* New York: Warner Books, 1981.

———. *Patience of a Saint.* New York: Warner Books, 1987.

Greeley, Robert F. *Violet, The Child of the City: A Story of New York Life.* New York: Bunce, 1854.

Greene, David. "Literary Interactions." *Irish Times* (Supplement: "The Irish-American Link"), 15 March 1976: xii.

Griffin, William D. *Ireland: A Chronology and Fact Book 6000 B.C.-1972.* Dobbs Ferry, N.Y.: Oceana Publications, 1973.

———. *The Irish in America 550-1972, A Chronology and Fact Book.* Dobbs Ferry, N.Y.: Oceana Publications, 1973.

Griffith, Bill [pseud. Bill Granger]. *Time for Frankie Coolin.* New York: Random House, 1982.

Grimes, Tom. *A Stone of the Heart.* New York: Four Walls Eight Windows, 1990.

Guiney, Louise Imogen. *Blessed Edmund Campion.* London: Macdonald and Evans, 1908.

———. *Goose-Quill Papers.* Boston: Roberts Brothers, 1885.

———. *Happy Ending.* Boston: Houghton, Mifflin, 1909.

———. "Irish." In *Patrins.* Boston: Copeland and Day, 1897. 153-65.

———. *James Clarence Mangan, His Selected Poems with a Study by the Editor.* Boston and New York: Lamson, Wolffe and Co., 1897.

———. *Letters of Louise Imogen Guiney.* Ed. Grace C. Guiney. 2 vols. New York and London: Harper and Brothers, 1926.

———. *Lovers' St. Ruth's and Three Other Tales.* Boston: Copeland and Day, 1895.

———. *"Monsieur Henri": A Footnote to French History.* New York: Harper and Brothers, 1892.

———. "Patrick R. Guiney," In *Catholic Encyclopedia* (1910) 7: 72.

———. *Robert Emmet: A Survey of His Rebellion and of His Romance.* London: David Nutt, 1904.

———. *Songs at the Start.* Boston: Cupples, Upham, 1884.

———. "Willful Sadness in Literature." In *Patrins.* Boston: Copeland and Day, 1897. 233-43.

Guttmann, Allen. *The Jewish Writer in America, Assimilation and the Crisis of Identity.* New York: Oxford Univ. Press, 1971.

Hackett, Francis. *American Rainbow.* New York: Liveright, 1971.

———. "Mr. Dooley." *New Republic* 20 (24 Sept. 1919): 235-36.

Halpine, Charles G. *Baked Meats of the Funeral.* New York: Carleton, 1866.

———. *The Life and Adventures, Songs, Services and Speeches of Private Miles O'Reilly.* New York: Carleton, 1864.

Hamill, Pete. "Farrell." *The Big Book of American Irish Culture.* Ed. Bob Callahan. New York: Viking Press, 1987. 132-34.

———. *The Gift.* 1973. New York: Ballantine Books, 1974.

———. *Loving Women, A Novel of the Fifties.* New York: Random House, 1989.

Hanchett, William. *Irish: Charles G. Halpine in Civil War America.* Syracuse: Syracuse Univ. Press, 1970.

Handlin, Oscar. *Boston's Immigrants, 1790-1880, A Study in Acculturation.* Revised and enlarged ed. New York: Atheneum, 1969.

Hannibal, Edward. *Chocolate Days, Popsicle Weeks.* Boston: Houghton, Mifflin Co., 1970.

Harrigan, Edward. *The Mulligans.* New York: Dillingham, 1901.

Haverty, P.M. *Legends and Fairy Tales of Ireland.* New York: P.M. Haverty, 1872.

Heaney, Seamus. *Station Island.* New York: Farrar, Straus, Giroux, 1985.

Here's Me Bus! New York, Spring 1995+.

"An Hibernian." *The Irish Emigrant. An Historical Tale Founded on Fact.* 2 vols. Winchester, Va.: John T. Sharrocks, 1817.

Higgins, George V. *The Friends of Eddie Coyle.* New York: Knopf, 1972.

Higham, John. *Strangers in the Land, Patterns of American Nativism, 1860-1925.* 2nd ed. New York: Atheneum, 1966.

Horan, James D. *The Right Image.* New York: Dell, 1967.

Howard, Maureen. *Before My Time.* Boston: Little, Brown, 1974.

———. *Bridgeport Bus.* New York: Harcourt, Brace, and World, 1965.

———. *Expensive Habits.* New York: Summit Books, 1986.

———. *Facts of Life.* Boston: Little, Brown, 1978.

———. "Foreword." In *Cabbage and Bones: An Anthology of Irish-American Women's Fiction.* Ed. Caledonia Kearns. New York: Holt, 1997. xi-xiv.

———. *Grace Abounding.* Boston: Little, Brown, 1982.

———. *A Lover's Almanac.* New York: Viking Penguin, 1998.

———. *Natural History.* New York: Norton, 1992.

———. "PW Interviews Maureen Howard." *Publishers Weekly* 222 (15 Oct. 1982): 6-7.

———. "Salvaging the Family Junk." *New York Times Book Review,* 18 Oct. 1992: 46.

Hueston, Robert F. *The Catholic Press and Nativism, 1840-1860.* New York: Arno Press, 1976.

Huntington, J.V. [Review of Cannon's *Bickerton.*] St. Louis *Leader,* 13 Oct. 1855.

Hurley, Doran. *Monsignor.* New York: Longmans, Green, 1936.

———. *The Old Parish.* New York: Longmans, Green, 1938.

Ibson, John Duffy. "Will the World Break Your Heart? A Historical Analysis of the Dimensions and Consequences of Irish-American Assimilation." Ph.D. diss., Brandeis Univ., 1976.

"Irish-American Literature." *New England Magazine* 2 (1832): 490-99.

"The Irishman's Epistle to the Officers and Troops at Boston." *Pennsylvania Magazine* 1 (May 1775): 232.

Jessop, George H. *Desmond O'Connor.* New York: Longmans, Green 1914.

———. "The Emergency Men." In *Stories by English Authors: Ireland.* New York: Scribner's, 1896. 23-63.

———. *Gerald Ffrench's Friends.* New York: Longmans, Green, 1889.

———. *Judge Lynch. A Romance of the California Vineyards.* Chicago, New York, and San Francisco: Belford, Clarke and Co., 1889.

———. *Where the Shamrock Grows: The Fortunes and Misfortunes of an Irish Family.* New York: Baker and Taylor Co., 1911.

Jones, Ann T. "A Boston Christmas, 1936." *Crab Orchard Review* 1: 2 (Spring/ Summer 1996): 42-56.

———. *A Country Divorce.* New York: Delphinium, 1992.

Jones, Maldwyn. "Scotch-Irish" entry. *Harvard Encyclopedia of American Ethnic Groups.* Ed. Stephan Thernstrom. Cambridge: Harvard Univ. Press, 1980. 895-908.

Joyce, Robert Dwyer. *Ballads of Irish Chivalry.* Boston: Patrick Donahoe, 1872.

———. *Blanid.* Boston: Roberts Brothers, 1879.

———. *Deirdre.* Boston: Roberts Brothers, 1876.

———. *Irish Fireside Tales.* Boston: Patrick Donahoe, 1871.

———. *Legends of the Wars in Ireland.* Boston: James Campbell, 1868.

Joyce, William L. *Editors and Ethnicity: A History of the Irish-American Press, 1848-1883.* New York: Arno Press, 1976.

Kavanagh, Hermionie Templeton. *Darby O'Gill and the Good People.* New York: McClure, Phillips, 1903.

Kearns, Caledonia, ed. *Cabbage and Bones: An Anthology of Irish-American Women's Fiction.* New York: Holt, 1997.

Keenan, Henry F. *The Aliens. A Novel.* New York: Appleton, 1886.

———. *The Iron Game: A Tale of the War.* New York: Appleton, 1891.

————. *The Money Makers: A Social Parable*. 1884. New York: Johnson Reprint Co., 1969.

Kelleher, John V. "Edwin O'Connor and the Irish-American Process." *Atlantic* 222 (July 1968): 48-52.

————. "The Hero as an Irish-American." [Review of E. O'Connor, *The Last Hurrah*.] *New York Times Book Review*. 5 Feb. 1956: 1.

————. "Irish American Literature and Why There Isn't Any." *Irish Writing* (November 1947): 71-81.

————. "Irishness in America." *Atlantic* 208 (July 1961): 38-40.

————. "A Long Way from Tipperary." *Reporter* 22 (12 May 1960): 44-6.

————. "Matthew Arnold and the Celtic Revival." *Perspectives of Criticism*. Ed. Harry Levin. Cambridge: Harvard Univ. Press, 1950. 197-221.

————. "Mr. Dooley and the Same Old World." *Atlantic* 177 (June 1946): 119-25.

Kelly, Myra. *The Golden Season*. New York: Doubleday, Page, 1909.

————. *Little Aliens*. New York: Scribner's, 1910.

————. *Little Citizens, The Humors of School Life*. New York: McClure, Phillips and Co., 1904.

————. *Rosnah*. New York: Appleton, 1908.

————. *Wards of Liberty*. New York: McClure, 1907.

Kelly, Teague M. *Mucca Scob, or Threads of Pre-Historic and Present History Concatenated*. Oakland, Calif.: Published for the author, 1885.

Kelly, William. *The Harp without the Crown; or, Mountcashel's Fair Daughter*. New York: Francis and Loutrel, 1867.

Kenedy, P.J., ed. *The Universal Irish Song Book*. New York: P.J. Kenedy, 1884.

Kennedy, Thomas E. *Crossing Borders*. Wichita, Kans.: Watermark Press, 1990.

Kennedy, William. *Billy Phelan's Greatest Game*. 1978. New York: Penguin, 1983.

————. *The Flaming Corsage*. New York: Viking, 1996.

————. *The Ink Truck*. 1969. New York: Viking, 1984.

————. *Ironweed*. New York: Viking, 1983.

————. *Legs*. 1975. New York: Penguin, 1983.

————. *Quinn's Book*. New York: Viking, 1988.

————. *Very Old Bones*. New York: Viking, 1992.

Kerber, Linda K. *Federalists in Dissent: Imagery and Ideology in Jeffersonian America*. Ithaca: Cornell Univ. Press, 1970.

Keyser, Harriet A. *Thorns in Your Sides*. New York: Putnam, 1884.

Krause, David. *The Profane Book of Irish Comedy*. Ithaca: Cornell Univ. Press, 1982.

"A Lady of Boston." *Tales of the Emerald Isle; or, Legends of Ireland*. New York: W. Borradaile, November 1828.

————. *Tales of the Fireside*. Boston: Hilliard, Gray, Little, and Wilkins, 1827.

Lane, Elinor Macartney. *Katrine*. New York: Harper, 1909.

Larkin, Emmet. "The Devotional Revolution in Ireland, 1850-1875." *American Historical Review* 77 (June 1972): 625-52.

Laughlin, Clara E. *"Just Folks."* New York: Macmillan, 1910.

Leadbeater, Mary. *Cottage Dialogues Among the Irish Peasantry*. Philadelphia: Johnson and Warner, 1811.

Leland, Thomas. *The History of Ireland from the Invasion of Henry II*. 4 vols. Philadelphia and New York: H. Gaine, R. Bell, and J. Dunlap, 1774.

Leslie, Frank. *There's a Spot in My Heart*. New York: Simon and Schuster, 1947.

The Life and Travels of Father Quipes, Otherwise Dominick O'Blarney, Written by Himself. Carlisle, Pa.: Printed for the Purchaser, 1820.

The Life of Paddy O'Flarrity, Who, from a Shoeblack, has, by Perseverence and Good Conduct arrived to a Member of Congress, interspersed with many curious anecdotes, calculated to improve as well as divert the youths of America, Written by Himself. Washington, D.C.: n.p., 1834.

Lyons, F.S.L. *Ireland Since the Famine, 1850 to the Present.* New York: Scribner's, 1971.

McAnally, D.R. *Irish Wonders.* Boston: Houghton, Mifflin, 1888.

McAvoy, Thomas T. "The Formation of the Catholic Minority in the United States, 1820-1860." *Review of Politics* 10 (1948): 13-34.

McCaffrey, Lawrence J. *The Irish Catholic Diaspora in America.* Washington: Catholic Univ. of America Press, 1997.

———. *The Irish Diaspora in America.* 1976. Washington: Catholic Univ. of America Press, 1984.

———. "The Recent Irish Diaspora in America." *Contemporary American Immigration.* Ed. Dennis L Cuddy. Boston: Twayne Pubs., 1982: 37-58.

———. *Textures of Irish America.* Syracuse: Syracuse Univ. Press, 1992.

McCaffrey, Lawrence J., et al. *The Irish in Chicago.* Urbana: Univ. of Illinois Press, 1987.

McCann, Colum. *Songdogs.* New York: Holt, 1995.

———. *This Side of Brightness.* New York: Holt, 1998.

McCarthy, Justin, et al., eds. *Irish Literature.* 10 vols. Deluxe ed. Philadelphia: John D. Morris and Company; Regular ed. New York: P.F. Collier and Son, 1904.

McCarthy, Mary. *Memories of a Catholic Girlhood.* New York: Harcourt, Brace and World, 1957.

McCorry, Peter. *The Irish Widow's Son; or, The Pikemen of '98.* Boston: Patrick Donahoe, 1869.

———. *The Lost Rosary; or, Our Irish Girls, Their Trials, Temptations, and Triumphs.* Boston: Patrick Donahoe, 1870.

———. *Mount Benedict; or, The Violated Tomb. A Tale of the Charlestown Convent.* Boston: Patrick Donahoe, 1871.

McCourt, Frank. *Angela's Ashes: A Memoir.* New York: Scribner's, 1996.

McCullough, Colleen. *The Thorn Birds.* New York: Harper, 1977.

McDermott, Alice. *At Weddings and Wakes.* New York: Farrar, Straus, Giroux, 1992.

———. *The Bigamist's Daughter.* New York: Random House, 1982.

———. *Charming Billy.* New York: Farrar, Straus, Giroux, 1998.

———. *That Night.* New York: Farrar, Straus, Giroux, 1987.

McDermott, John. *Father Jonathan; or, The Scottish Converts. A Catholic Tale.* Philadelphia: H. and C. McGrath, 1853.

McDermott, William A. [pseud. Walter Lecky.] *Down at Caxton's.* New York: Murphy, 1895.

———. *Impressions and Opinions.* Boston: Angel Guardian Press, 1898.

———. *Mr. Billy Buttons. A Novel.* New York, Cincinnati: Benziger Brothers, 1896.

———. *Père Monnier's Ward.* New York, Cincinnati: Benziger Brothers, 1898.

MacDonagh, Oliver. "Emigration from Ireland to Australia: An Overview." In

Australia and Ireland 1788-1988, Bicentenary Essays, ed. Colm Kiernan. Dublin: Gill and Macmillan, 1986: 121-37.

———. "The Irish Famine Emigration to the United States." *Perspectives in American History* 10 (1976): 357-446.

McElgun, John. *Annie Reilly; or, The Fortunes of an Irish Girl in New York.* New York: J.A. McGee, 1873.

McGee, Thomas D'Arcy. *The Catholic History of North America.* Boston: Patrick Donahoe, 1855.

———. *A History of the Irish Settlers in North America.* Boston: Office of the American Celt, 1851.

———. "Lights and Shadows of Irish Life, The Priest, The Ghost, and the Sexton." *Sargent's New Monthly Magazine* 1: 4 (April 1843): 171-74.

———. *The Poems of Thomas D'Arcy McGee.* Ed. Mrs. J. Sadlier. New York: Sadlier, 1869.

McGonigle, Thomas. *Going to Patchogue.* Elmwood Park, Ill.: Dalkey Archive Press, 1992.

McGrath, Kristina. *House Work.* Bridgehampton, N.Y.: Bridge Works, 1994.

MacGrath, Harold. *Arms and the Woman.* New York: Doubleday and McClure Co., 1899.

———. *The Luck of the Irish.* New York: Harper, 1917.

McGrory, Mary. "Like Undiluted Irish Whiskey." [Review of M. Curran, *The Parish and the Hill.*] *New York Times,* 12 Sept. 1948: 21.

McGuire, Agnes B. "Catholic Women Writers." In *Catholic Builders of the Nation.* Vol. 4. Boston: Continental Press, 1923: 184-203.

McHale, Tom. *Alinsky's Diamond.* Philadelphia: Lippincott, 1974.

———. *Dear Friends.* Garden City: Doubleday, 1982.

———. *Farragan's Retreat.* New York: Viking, 1971.

———. *The Lady from Boston.* Garden City: Doubleday, 1978.

———. *Principato.* New York: Viking, 1970.

———. *School Spirit.* Garden City: Doubleday, 1976.

McHenry, James. *The Hearts of Steel, An Irish Historical Tale of the Last Century.* Philadelphia: A.P. Poule, 1825.

———. *Meredith.* Philadelphia: n.p., 1831.

———. *O'Halloran; or The Insurgent Chief. An Irish Historical Tale of 1798.* 2 vols. Philadelphia: Carey and Lea, 1824.

———. *The Wilderness, or Braddock's Times, A Tale of the West.* 2 vols. New York: E. Bliss and E. White, 1823.

McInerny, Ralph. *Gate of Heaven.* New York: Harper and Row, 1975.

———. *The Priest.* New York: Harper and Row, 1973.

McIntyre, John T. *The Ragged Edge; a Tale of Ward Life and Politics.* New York: Phillips and Co., 1902.

———. "The Three Wise Men." *McClure's Magazine* 27 (Sept. 1906): 551-60.

Mack, Thomas C. *The Priest's Turf-Cutting Day. A Historical Romance.* New York: Printed for the Author, 1841.

McKenney, Ruth. *The McKenneys Carry On.* New York: Harcourt, Brace and Co., 1940.

———. *My Sister Eileen.* New York: Harcourt, Brace and Co., 1938.

McKenzie, Robert Shelton. *Bits of Blarney*. New York: Redfield, 1854.

McMahon, Patrick Justin. *Philip, or the Mollie's Secret. A Tale of the Coal Regions*. Philadelphia: H.L. Kilner and Co., 1891.

McManus, Seamus. *In Chimney Corners, Merry Tales of Irish Folklore*. New York: McClure, 1899.

MacNeven, William James, and Thomas Addis Emmet. *Pieces of Irish History, Illustrative of the Condition of the Catholics of Ireland, or the Origin and the Progress of the Political System of the United Irishmen; and of their Other Transactions with the Anglo-Irish Government*. New York: Bernard Bornin, 1807.

McSorley, Edward. *Kitty, I Hardly Knew You*. Garden City: Doubleday, 1959.

———. *Our Own Kind*. New York: Harper and Brothers, 1946.

———. *The Young McDermott*. New York: Harper, 1949.

Maguire, John Francis. *The Irish in America*. 1868. New York: Arno Press, 1969.

Maher, James T. *The Distant Music of Summer*. Boston: Little, Brown, 1979.

Mailer, Norman. "The Books that Made Writers." *New York Times Book Review*, 25 Nov. 1979: 7.

Mallon, Thomas. *Aurora 7*. New York: Ticknor and Fields, 1991.

Mann, Arthur. *Yankee Reformers in the Urban Age*. 1954. New York: Harper and Row, 1966.

Manners, J. Hartley. *Peg O' My Heart*. New York: Dodd, Mead and Co., 1913.

Marchand, Margaret. *Pilgrims on the Earth*. New York: Crowell, 1940.

Marcus, Philip L. *Yeats and the Beginning of the Irish Renaissance*. Ithaca: Cornell Univ. Press, 1970.

Meagher, Timothy J., ed. *From Paddy to Studs: Irish-American Communities in the Turn of the Century Era, 1880-1920*. New York: Greenwood Press, 1986.

Meany, J.L. *The Lovers, or Cupid in Ireland*. Havanna, Ill.: Democrat Power Printing House, 1891.

Meany, Mary L. *The Confessors of Connaught; or The Tenants of a Lord Bishop*. Philadelphia: Peter Cunningham, 1865.

———. *Elinor Johnston, Founded on Facts, and Maurice and Genevieve, The Orphan Twins of Beauce: Catholic Tales*. Philadelphia: Peter Cunningham, 1868.

Meehan, Thomas F. "Catholic Literary New York, 1800-1840." *Catholic Historical Review* 4 (Jan. 1919): 410-20.

Meloney, William Brown. *Mooney*. New York: Appleton-Century-Crofts, 1950.

A Memorial of John Boyle O'Reilly from the City of Boston. Boston: City Council, 1890.

Mercier, Vivian. *The Irish Comic Tradition*. New York: Oxford Univ. Press, 1969.

Merwick, Donna. *Boston Priests, 1848-1910, A Study of Social and Intellectual Change*. Cambridge: Harvard Univ. Press, 1973.

Messbarger, Paul. *Fiction with a Parochial Purpose: Social Uses of American Catholic Literature, 1884-1900*. Boston: Boston Univ. Press, 1971.

Miller, Kerby A. "Assimilation and Alienation: Irish Emigrants' Responses to Industrial America, 1871-1891." *The Irish in America: Emigration, Assimilation and Impact*. Irish Studies 4. Ed. P.J. Drudy. Cambridge: Cambridge Univ. Press, 1985. 87-112.

———. *Emigrants and Exiles. Ireland and the Irish Exodus to North America*. New York: Oxford Univ. Press, 1985.

————, with Bruce Bolling and David N. Doyle. "Emigrants and Exiles: Irish Cultures and Irish Emigration to North America, 1790-1922." *Irish Historical Studies* 22: 86 (Sept. 1980): 97-125.

Molloy, Tom. *The Green Line.* Boston: Charles River Books, 1982.

Monaghan, Patricia, ed. *The Next Parish Over: A Collection of Irish American Writing.* Minneapolis: New Rivers Press, 1993.

Moore, George. *The Untilled Field.* 1903. New York: Books for Libraries Press, 1970.

Moore, John McDermott. *The Adventures of Tom Stapleton.* New York: Wilson and Company, 1843.

————. "A Dublin Jackeen." *Dollar Magazine* 1: 8 (Aug. 1841): 228-29.

————. *Lord Nial, A Romance in Four Cantos.* New York: John Doyle, 1834.

————. "Patrick O'Flynn; or, The Man in the Moon. An Extravaganza in Two Acts." *Brother Jonathan* 2: 9 (25 June 1842): 225- 32.

————. "The Three Avengers." *Dollar Magazine* 1: 7 (July 1841): 201-5.

Moore, Susanna. *My Old Sweetheart.* New York: Houghton, Mifflin, 1982.

Moynahan, Julian. *Where the Land and Water Meet.* New York: Morrow, 1979.

Mulhern, Donald S. *Donald Stephenson's Reminiscences. A True Story.* Pittsburgh: Wm. G. Johnston and Co., 1891.

Murphy, Clyde F. *The Glittering Hill.* New York: Dutton, 1944.

Murphy, James F., Jr. *They Were Dreamers.* New York: Atheneum, 1983.

Murray, John F. "O'Phelan Drinking." *New Yorker* (3 Oct. 1977): 40+.

————. "O'Phelan's Daemonium." *New Yorker* (24 May 1976): 33+.

Myles, Eileen. *Chelsea Girls.* Santa Rosa, Calif.: Black Sparrow Press, 1994.

Naipaul, V.S. "Castles of Fear." [Review of Donleavy, *The Ginger Man.*] *Spectator* (5 July 1963): 16.

Nolan, Alice. *The Byrnes of Glengoulah: A True Tale.* N.Y.: P. O'Shea, 1870.

Nolan, Mary. *Biddy Finnegan's Botheration, or, That Romp of a Girl.* St. Louis: Ev. E. Carreras, 1884.

Norris, Kathleen. *The Callahans and the Murphys.* Garden City, N.Y.: Doubleday, Page and Co., 1924.

————. *Little Ships.* Garden City, N.Y.: Doubleday, Page and Co., 1925.

————. *Mother.* New York: Macmillan, 1911.

————. *Poor, Dear Margaret Kirby.* New York: Macmillan, 1913.

O'Brien, Dillon. *The Dalys of Dalystown.* St. Paul: Pioneer Printing Co., 1866.

————. *Dead Broke, A Western Tale.* St. Paul: Pioneer Printing Co.,1873.

————. *Frank Blake.* St. Paul: Pioneer Printing Co., 1876.

————. *Widow Melville's Boarding House.* St. Paul: Pioneer Printing Co., 1881.

O'Brien, Fitz-James. *A Gentleman from Ireland: A Comedy in Two Acts.* New York: S. French, 1858.

————. *The Poems and Stories of Fitz-James O'Brien.* Boston: James R. Osgood, 1881.

O'Brien, George. *The Village of Longing.* 1987. Belfast: Blackstaff Press, 1993.

O'Brien, Michael J. *In Old New York: The Irish Dead in Trinity and St. Paul's Churchyards.* New York: American Irish Historical Society, 1928.

O'Brien, Thomas D. "Dillon O'Brien." *Acta Et Dicta* (Catholic Historical Society of St. Paul) 6: 1 (Oct. 1933): 35-53.

O'Broin, Leon. *Fenian Fever, An Anglo-American Dilemma.* New York: New York Univ. Press, 1971.

O'Connell, Shaun. "Boggy Ways: Notes on Irish-American Culture." *Massachusetts Review* 26 (Summer-Autumn 1985): 379- 400.

O'Connor, Edwin. *All in the Family.* Boston: Little, Brown, 1966.

———. *The Best and The Last of Edwin O'Connor.* Ed. Arthur Schlesinger, Jr. Boston: Little, Brown, 1970.

———. *The Edge of Sadness.* Boston: Little, Brown, 1961.

———. *I Was Dancing.* Boston: Little, Brown, 1964.

———. *The Last Hurrah.* Boston: Little, Brown, 1956.

———. *The Oracle.* New York: Harper and Row, 1951.

O'Connor, Philip F. Introduction to "The Gift Bearer." *Ethnic American Short Stories.* Ed. Katherine D. Newman. New York: Washington Square Press, 1975. 113.

———. *Old Morals, Small Continents, Darker Times.* Iowa City: Univ. Iowa Press, 1971.

———. *Stealing Home.* New York: Knopf, 1979.

O'Faolain, Sean. *The Irish: A Character Study.* Harmondsworth, Middlesex, England: Penguin Books, 1969.

O'Hara, John. *Appointment in Samarra.* New York: Harcourt, Brace and Co., 1934.

———. *BUtterfield 8.* New York: Harcourt, Brace and Co., 1935.

———. *The Doctor's Son and Other Stories.* New York: Harcourt, Brace and Co., 1935.

O'Hehir, Diana. *I Wish This War Were Over.* New York: Atheneum, 1984.

Old Ireland's Misery at an End; or, The English Empire in the Brazils Restored. Boston: Sold at the Heart and Crown, 1752. Newport: Sold at the Town-School-House, 1752.

O'Reilly, Augustine J., ed. *Strange Memories: Death Bed Scenes, Extraordinary Conversions.* New York: Sadlier, 1880.

O'Reilly, Bernard J. *The Mirror of True Womanhood, A Book of Instruction for Women in the World.* New York: P.J. Kenedy, 1883.

O'Reilly, Gertrude M. *Just Stories.* New York: Devin-Adair, 1914.

O'Reilly, John Boyle. *The King's Men, a Tale of Tomorrow.* [With others.] New York: C. Scribner's Sons, 1884.

———. *Moondyne: A Story from the Underworld.* Boston: Pilot Publishing Company, 1879.

———, ed. *The Poetry and Song of Ireland, with Biographical Sketches of Her Poets.* New York: Gay Brothers and Co., 1887, 2nd ed., 1889.

O'Shea, James. *Felix O'Flanagan, An Irish-American.* Cork: Flynn and Co., 1902.

O'Sheel, Shaemus. "They Went Forth to Battle But They Always Fell." *Jealous of Dead Leaves.* New York: Boni and Liveright, 1928. 12.

Pakenham, Thomas. *The Year of Liberty, The Story of the Great Irish Rebellion of 1798.* Englewood Cliff, N.J.: Prentice- Hall, 1970.

Patrick, Vincent. *Family Business.* New York: Poseidon Press, 1985.

———. *The Pope of Greenwich Village.* New York: Seaview Books, 1979.

Pepper, George. *History of Ireland.* Boston: Devereux and Donahoe, 1835.

———. "Naisi and Deirdre." *Literary and Catholic Sentinel,* May-July 1835.

———. "O'Cahan of Dungiven." *Pilot*, 16 January 1836.

Phelan, Francis. *Four Ways of Computing Midnight*. New York: Atheneum, 1985.

Plowden, Francis P. *An Historical Review of the State of Ireland from the Invasion of that Country under Henry II to Its Union with Great Britain on the first of January, 1801*. 5 vols. Philadelphia: William F. McLaughlin, 1805-06.

Potter, George. *To the Golden Door, The Story of the Irish in Ireland and America*. Boston: Little, Brown, 1960.

Powers, J.F. *Look How the Fish Live*. New York: Knopf, 1975.

———. *Morte D'Urban*. Garden City: Doubleday, 1962.

———. *The Presence of Grace*. Garden City: Doubleday, 1956.

———. *Prince of Darkness and Other Stories*. Garden City: Doubleday, 1947.

———. *Wheat That Springeth Green*. New York: Knopf, 1988.

Powers, John R. *Do Black Patent Leather Shoes Really Reflect Up?* Chicago: Regnery, 1975.

———. *The Last Catholic in America*. New York: Saturday Review Press, 1973.

Quigley, Hugh. *The Cross and the Shamrock; or, How to Defend the Faith*. Boston: Patrick Donahoe, 1853. Upper Saddle River, N.J.: The Gregg Press, 1970.

———. *The Irish Race in California and on the Pacific Coast*. San Francisco: A. Roman and Co., 1878.

———. *Profit and Loss: A Story of the Life of a Genteel Irish-American, Illustrative of Godless Education*. New York: T. O'Kane, 1873.

———. *The Prophet of the Ruined Abbey; or, A Glance of the Future of Ireland*. New York: Edward Dunigan and Brother, 1855.

Quindlen, Anna. *Object Lessons*. New York: Random House, 1991.

———. *One True Thing*. New York: Random House, 1994.

Quinn, Peter. *Banished Children of Eve*. New York: Viking, 1994.

———. "William Kennedy: An Interview." *Recorder* 1: 1 (Winter 1985): 65-81.

Rhodes, Robert E. "F. Scott Fitzgerald: 'All My Fathers.'" In *Irish-American Fiction: Essays in Criticism*. Eds. Daniel J. Casey and Robert E. Rhodes. New York: AMS Press, 1979. 29-51.

Richardson, Henry Handel. *The Fortunes of Richard Mahony*. 1917-29. New York: Norton, 1930.

Riley, James. *Christy of Rathglin*. Boston: C.M. Clark, 1907.

———. *Songs of Two Peoples*. Boston: Estes and Lauriat, 1898.

Rivers, Caryl. *Virgins*. New York: St. Martin's Press, 1984.

Robinson, Mary. "Cherishing the Irish Diaspora. Address to the House of the Oireachtas by President Mary Robinson on a Matter of Public Importance. 2 February 1995."

Roche, James Jeffrey. *Her Majesty the King: A Romance of the Harem*. Boston: Badger, 1899.

———. *The Life of John Boyle O'Reilly*. New York: Cassell Publishing Co., 1891.

———. *The Story of the Filibusters*. Boston: Badger, 1901.

Roddan, John. *John O'Brien; or, The Orphan of Boston. A Tale of Real Life*. Boston: Patrick Donahoe, 1850.

Rodriguez, Richard. *Hunger of Memory: The Education of Richard Rodriguez*. Boston: David R. Godine, 1982.

Sadlier, Mary Anne (Madden). *Aunt Honor's Keepsake, A Chapter from Life*. New York: Sadlier, 1866.

——. *Bessy Conway; or, The Irish Girl in America*. New York: Sadlier, 1861.

——. *The Blakes and Flanagans, A Tale. Illustrative of Irish Life in the United States*. New York: P.J. Kenedy, 1855.

——. *The Confederate Chieftains: A Tale of the Irish Rebellion of 1641*. New York: Sadlier, 1860.

——. *Confessions of an Apostate; or, Leaves from a Troubled Life*. New York: Sadlier, 1864. New York: Arno Press, 1977.

——. *Con O'Regan; or, Emigrant Life in the New World*. New York: Sadlier, 1864.

——. *The Daughter of Tyrconnell: A Tale of the Reign of James I*. New York: Sadlier, 1863.

——. *Elinor Preston; or, Scenes at Home and Abroad*. New York: Sadlier, 1866.

——. *The Fate of Father Sheehy: A Tale of Tipperary Eighty Years Ago*. New York: Sadlier, 1863.

——. *The Heiress of Kilorgan; or, Evenings with the Old Geraldines*. New York: Sadlier, 1867.

——. *The Hermit of the Rock: A Tale of Cashel*. New York: Sadlier, 1863.

——. *Maureen Dhu, the Admiral's Daughter: A Tale of the Claddagh*. New York: Sadlier, 1870.

——. *McCarthy More; or, the Fortunes of an Irish Chief in the Reign of Queen Elizabeth*. New York: Sadlier, 1868.

——. *New Lights; or, Life in Galway, A Tale*. New York: Sadlier, 1853.

——. *The Old House by the Boyne; or, Recollections of an Irish Borough*. New York: Sadlier, 1865.

——. *Old and New; or, Taste Versus Fashion*. New York: Sadlier, 1862.

——. *The Red Hand of Ulster; or, The Fortunes of Hugh O'Neill*. Boston: Patrick Donahoe, 1850.

——. *Willy Burke; or, The Irish Orphan in America*. Boston: Patrick Donahoe, 1850.

Sanborn, Alvan F. *Meg McIntyre's Raffle, and Other Stories*. Boston: Copeland and Day, 1896.

Sargent, Lucius M. *An Irish Heart*. Boston: Danrell, 1836.

Savage, Elizabeth. *A Good Confession*. Boston: Little, Brown, 1975.

Scanlan, Anna C. *Dervorgilla; or, The Downfall of Ireland*. Milwaukee: J.H. Yewdale, 1895.

Scanlan, Michael. *Love and Land, Poems*. Chicago: The Western News Company, 1866.

Scian Dubh [pseud.]. *Ridgeway: An Historical Romance of the Fenian Invasion of Canada*. Buffalo: McCarroll and Co., 1868.

Shannon, William V. *The American Irish: A Political and Social Portrait*. 1966. Amherst: Univ. of Massachusetts Press, 1989.

Shavley, Rufus. *Solid for Mulhooly*. New York: G.W. Carleton, 1881.

Sheed, Wilfrid. *People Will Always Be Kind*. New York: Farrar, Strauss and Giroux, 1973.

Sheehan, Edward R.F. *The Governor*. New York: World Publishing Co., 1970.

Siegel, Adrienne. *The Image of the American City in Popular Literature, 1820-1870*. New York: Kennikat Press, 1981.

Sister Agnes; or, The Captive Nun, By a Clergyman's Widow. New York: Riker, Thorne, 1854.

Six Months in a Convent; or the Narrative of Rebecca Theresa Reed, Who Was Under the Influence of the Roman Catholics about Two Years, and an Inmate of the Ursuline Convent on Mount Benedict, Charlestown, Mass., Nearly Six Months, in the Years 1831-2. Boston: Russell, Odiorne and Metcalf, 1835.

Six Months in a House of Correction; or, the Narrative of Dorah Mahony. Who Was Under the Influence of the Protestants about a Year, and an Inmate of the House of Correction in Leverett St., Boston, Massachusetts, Nearly Six Months, in the Years 18—. Boston: Benjamin B. Mussey, 1835.

Smith, Betty. *Maggie-Now.* New York: Harper, 1958.

———. *Tomorrow Will Be Better.* New York: Harper, 1948.

———. *A Tree Grows in Brooklyn.* New York: Harper, 1947.

Smith, Dennis. *The Final Fire.* New York: Dutton, 1975.

———. *Glitter and Ash.* New York: E.P. Dutton, 1980.

———. *Report from Engine Co. 82.* New York: Saturday Review Press, 1972.

———. *Steely Blue.* New York: Simon and Schuster, 1984.

Smith, Herbert J., Jr. "From Stereotype to Acculturation: The Irish-American's Fictional Heritage from Brackenridge to Farrell." Ph.D. diss., Kent State University, 1980.

Smith, John Talbot. *The Art of Disappearing.* New York, Cincinnati: Benziger Brothers, 1899. New York: William H. Young, 1902.

———. *His Honor, the Mayor, and Other Tales.* New York: The Vatican Library, 1891.

———. "The Literature of Dirt, Doubt, and Despair." *American Catholic Quarterly Review* 28 (Jan. 1903): 130-41.

———. *Saranac, A Story of Lake Champlain.* New York: The Catholic Publication Society Co., 1892.

———. *Solitary Island. A Novel.* New York: P.J. Kenedy, 1888.

———. *A Woman of Culture: A Canadian Romance.* New York: William H. Young, 1891.

Stanton, Maura. *The Country I Come From.* Minneapolis: Milkweed Editions, 1988.

Stephens, Michael. *The Brooklyn Book of the Dead.* Normal, Ill.: Dalkey Archive Press, 1994.

———. *Season at Coole.* 1972. Elmwood Park, Ill.: Dalkey Archive Press, 1984.

Stewart, Ramona. *Casey.* Boston: Little, Brown, 1968.

Sugrue, Thomas. *Such Is the Kingdom.* New York: Holt, 1940.

Sullivan, James. W *So the World Goes.* Chicago: C.H. Kerr, 1898.

———. *Tenement Tales of New York.* New York: Holt, 1895.

Sweeney, Lawrence. "The Irishmen's Petition, To the Honorable C-mm-ss-n-rs of Excise & c." New York: 1769. Evans 11485.

———. "Mr. Lawrence Sweeney, Esq.; Vehicle General of News, and Grand Spouter of Politics." New York: 1769. Evans 42008.

———. "New Year's Ode for the Year 1766." New York: 1766. Evans 41663.

———. "New Year's Verses made and carried about to the Customers of the New York Gazette." New York: 1767. Evans 41767.

Sylvester, Harry. *Moon Gaffney.* 1947. New York: Arno Press, 1976.

———. "Problems of the Catholic Writer." *Atlantic* 181 (June 1948): 109-13.

———. "Righteous Anger." [Review of Farrell, *Literature and Morality.*] *New Republic* 117 (6 Oct. 1947): 26-7.

Taylor, William Cooke, and William Sampson. *History of Ireland.* New York: Harper, 1833.

Thorp, Willard R. "Catholic Novelists in Defense of Their Faith, 1829-1885." *Proceedings of the American Antiquarian Society* 78 (April 1968): 25-117.

Tincker, Agnes. *The House of Yorke.* New York: Catholic Publication Society, 1872.

Toole, John Kennedy. *A Confederacy of Dunces.* Baton Rouge: Louisiana Univ. Press, 1980.

Tully, Jim. *Beggars of Life.* Garden City, N.Y.: Garden City Publishing Co., 1924.

———. *Blood on the Moon.* New York: Coward-McCann, Inc., 1931.

———. *Circus Parade.* New York: A. and C. Boni, 1927.

———. *Emmett Lawler.* New York: Harcourt, Brace, 1922.

———. *Shadows of Men.* Garden City, N.Y.: Doubleday, Doran, 1930.

———. *Shanty Irish.* New York: A. and C. Boni, 1928.

Twomey, Richard J. "Jacobins and Jeffersonians: Anglo-American Radicalism in the United States 1790-1820." Ph.D. diss., Northern Illinois Univ., 1974.

Updike, John. "Howells as Anti-Novelist." *New Yorker* (13 July 1987): 78-88.

Uris, Leon. *Trinity.* Garden City, N.Y.: Doubleday, 1976.

Wain, John. *Professing Poetry.* New York: Viking Press, 1978.

Wall, Eamonn. "Exile, Attitude, and the Sin-É Café: Notes of the 'New Irish.'" *Eire-Ireland* 30: 4 (Winter 1996): 7-17.

Walsh, Francis R. "The Boston *Pilot:* A Newspaper for the Irish Immigrant, 1892-1908." Ph.D. diss., Boston Univ., 1968.

———. "Who Spoke for Boston's Irish? The Boston *Pilot* in the Nineteenth Century." *Journal of Ethnic Studies* 10: 3 (1982): 21- 36.

Walsh, James B., ed. *The Irish: America's Political Class.* New York: Arno Press, 1976.

Ward, David. "The Emergence of Central Immigrant Ghettoes in American Cities: 1840-1920." *Annals of the Association of American Geographers* 58: 2 (June 1968): 343-59.

Ward, Leo R. *Holding Up the Hills.* New York: Sheed and Ward, 1941.

Waters, Maureen. *The Comic Irishman.* Albany: State Univ. of New York Press, 1984.

———. "Excerpts from *Crossing Highbridge.*" *Crab Orchard Review* 1: 2 (Spring/ Summer 1996): 205-17.

Way, W. Irving. "Mr. Martin Dooley of Chicago." *Bookman* 9 (May 1899): 217.

White, James A. *The Era of Good Intentions, A Survey of American Catholics Writing Between the Years 1880-1915.* New York: Arno Press, 1978.

Williams, Alfred. "Irish Bardic Poetry." *Catholic World* 31 (Sept. 1880): 791-804.

———. "The Jacobite and Later Celtic Poetry of Ireland." *Catholic World* 33 (August 1881): 626-41.

———. "A New Irish Poet." *Catholic World* 32 (March 1881): 735-47.

———. *The Poets and Poetry of Ireland.* Boston: James R. Osgood, 1881.

Williams, Arthur L. "The Irishman in American Humor." Ph.D. diss., Cornell Univ., 1949.

Wilson, Christopher P. *The Labor of Words. Literary Professionalism in the Progressive Era.* Athens: Univ. of Georgia Press, 1985.

Winch, Terence. *Contenders.* Santa Cruz, Calif.: Story Line Press, 1989.

———. *Irish Musicians/American Friends.* Minneapolis: Coffee House Press, 1985.

Wittke, Carl. "The Immigrant Theme on the American Stage." *Mississippi Valley Historical Review* 34 (1953): 211-32.

———. *The Irish in America*. 1956. New York: Russell and Russell, 1970.

Wixson, Douglas. *Worker-Writer in America: Jack Conroy and the Tradition of Midwestern Literary Radicalism, 1898-1990*. Urbana: Univ. of Illinois Press, 1994.

Wolle, Francis J. *Fitz-James O'Brien: A Literary Bohemian of the Eighteen-fifties*. Boulder, Colo.: Univ. of Colorado Press, 1944.

Woodham-Smith, Cecil. *The Great Hunger, Ireland 1845-1849*. New York: Harper and Row, 1962.

Yeats, William Butler. *Letters to the New Island*. Ed. Horace Reynolds. Cambridge: Harvard Univ. Press, 1970.

Index